Learning and Memory

Learning and Memory
The Basis of Behavior

Stephen C. Wilhite

Widener University
Chester, Pennsylvania

David E. Payne

Monmouth College
West Long Branch, New Jersey

Allyn and Bacon

Boston   London   Toronto   Sydney   Tokyo   Singapore

Executive Editor: *Susan Badger*
Series Editorial Assistant: *Laura Lynch*
Production Administrator: *Annette Joseph*
Production Coordinator: *Susan Freese*
Editorial-Production Service: *TKM Productions*
Manufacturing Buyer: *Megan Cochran*
Cover Administrator: *Linda K. Dickinson*

Copyright © 1992 by Allyn and Bacon
A Division of Simon & Schuster
160 Gould Street
Needham Heights, Massachusetts 02194

Library of Congress Cataloging-in-Publication Data

Wilhite, Stephen C.
    Learning and memory : the basis of behavior / Stephen C. Wilhite,
David E. Payne.
      p. cm.
    Includes bibliographical references and indexes.
    ISBN 0-205-13300-2
    1. Learning, Psychology of. 2. Memory. 3. Conditioned response.
4. Cognitive learning theory. I. Payne, David E.
II. Title.
    [DNLM: 1. Behavior—physiology. 2. Conditioning (Psychology).
3. Learning—physiology. 4. Memory—physiology. BF 319 W678L]
BF318.W55   1992
153.1—dc20
DNLM/DLC   91-33243
for Library of Congress   CIP

Printed in the United States of America

10 9 8 7 6 5 4 3 2 1   97 96 95 94 93 92

To the Memory of Bonnie Clark Wilhite
and
to Anna Lorene Wilhite, Marjorie Rose Wilhite, Marilyn R. W. Poyner,
Margaret Ann Payne, Dewey Elliot Payne, and Aaron M. Payne,
whose support and encouragement made this book possible

CONTENTS

5 NATURAL TENDENCIES IN LEARNING   151

6 MULTISTORE MODELS OF MEMORY 175

7 THE REPRESENTATION OF INFORMATION IN LONG-TERM MEMORY (PART I) 217

8 THE REPRESENTATION OF INFORMATION IN LONG-TERM MEMORY (PART II) 247

PREFACE

Learning and Memory provides an introduction to the study of learning and memory through an examination of the basic learning paradigms of classical and instrumental conditioning and issues fundamental to the structure and function of memory. Although designed to be an introduction to the field, the book does not take an encyclopedic approach. Rather, the book covers in some depth a limited number of topics that we believe provide the basis for the study of more complex issues regarding learning and cognitive processes. In our attempt to provide in-depth coverage of selected issues, we have included a number of special topics, some of which are integrated into our treatment of the basic conditioning paradigms and major memory topics. For example, a treatment of social learning theory is incorporated into the chapter on instrumental conditioning in order to illustrate how traditional instrumental conditioning approaches have been modified in relation to the cognitive concept of observational learning and the distinction between learning and performance. In addition, the issue of animal memory is considered in the context of the chapters on instrumental conditioning, stimulus control, and natural tendencies (i.e., biological constraints). In other cases, entire chapters are devoted to special topics that have especially important practical or theoretical implications. The chapters on mnemonics and amnesia permit a specialized treatment of topics that are inherently interesting to most students of learning and memory and that are nicely illustrative of critical concepts and theoretical distinctions from earlier chapters.

To help integrate these segments into a coherent whole, we describe in Chapter 1 the unifying themes of associationism and cognitivism that are evident in the historical development of all the major theoretical paradigms. We then develop these themes throughout the following chapters, using them as the basis for interpreting the general significance of specific theories and issues. Further integration is achieved by putting the development of paradigms and theories into an historical context and by beginning each chapter with a vignette about common learning and memory experiences that illustrate the application of important concepts and principles to be covered in the chapter. Throughout each chapter, reference is made to the vignette in order to demonstrate the practical implications of the issues being discussed. Every chapter then closes with concluding comments that draw the chapter contents together. In the interest of organization and integration, an attempt is also made in all of the chapters focusing on human memory to relate many of the major issues to a single comprehensive model of the memory system.

This book reflects an attempt to achieve a balance between theory and empirical results. We consistently present descriptions of research findings that bear on the major theoretical positions. In some cases, we present the research findings in depth because the methodology and results have to be considered thoroughly in order to appreciate the theoretical significance of the findings. In other cases, we illustrate in detail how theoretical positions and previously reported findings influence the design of subsequent studies and how the data collected, in turn, influence the development of the theories. In some instances, we impress upon the reader the extent to which research on a particular topic reflects long-term, sometimes intense, competition between rival theoretical positions.

We have endeavored to make the book reader-friendly. A detailed outline of the topics included in each chapter is presented in the table of contents, and a list of primary and secondary topics is provided at the beginning of each chapter. These outlines provide an overview of the chapters by illustrating the relationships among the issues to be presented. We strongly encourage the use of the outlines as an organizational framework for the study of the chapter material.

Key terms are shown in boldface, and review questions follow most sections of each chapter. The questions encourage either the recall of important information or the application of important principles from the immediately preceding section of the chapter. An abundance of research suggests that such questions can be an aid to retention if they are used by the reader as a means of promoting mental review of the information. During either the first reading or the first review of the material, the reader is encouraged to try answering the questions without first referring back to the text. Once this initial attempt has been made, looking back at the text is important in order to check the accuracy of the information recalled and in order to augment one's memory for the information. In addition to providing for an initial review of the chapter material, these questions can be used again later as a means of self-testing in preparation for an examination on the material. Once the student believes that the chapter material has been mastered, the questions can be used as a short-answer test on the material. Another check of one's answers can provide additional feedback about the degree to which the information has truly been mastered.

To facilitate use of this book as a reference work, we have included a comprehensive reference list. After each source entry is a boldface list of pages on which that source is cited in the text. Consequently, readers can easily locate material pertaining to an author's treatment of a particular topic without searching through other material. Subjects are listed in a separate index.

We wish to express appreciation to students and colleagues for helpful critiques of the original versions of the chapters. We also thank the following reviewers for comments on earlier drafts of the book: Dennis Cogan, Texas Tech University; Steve R. Coleman, Cleveland State University; Leonard Green, Washington University; Kenneth Leicht, Illinois State University; Howard Reid, State University of New York, Buffalo; David Riccio, Kent State University; and Mike Scavio, California State University, Fullerton. In addition, we gratefully acknowledge Lucille D'Amato for providing assistance with word processing and the preparation of the reference list, Mike McManus for additional assistance with references, and Sue Weaver and Philip Jarowski for assistance with proofreading.

Learning and Memory

Introduction

BEGINNING CONSIDERATIONS

It is frequently observed today that the only constant in the world is change. Certainly, change is fundamental to learning and memory. The notion of learning derives from observations of enduring change in the behavior of individuals that appears to result from environmental experiences. Implicit in this definition of learning is the assumption that a change in individuals' internal representations of their experiences underlies the observable change in behavior. Thus, memory, or the ability to store and retrieve past experiences, is inextricably linked to the study of learning. This book is entitled *Learning and Memory: The Basis of Behavior* because no aspect of human or animal existence can be considered without taking into account in some way the influence of learning and memory processes.

HISTORICAL OVERVIEW

Philosophical Traditions of Rationalism and Empiricism

Epistemology, or the study of knowledge, has occupied philosophers since the time of the ancient Greeks. How do humans acquire knowledge? What are the mechanisms by which humans come to know the "truth"? In an attempt to address these questions, Greek philosophers Plato and Aristotle established two major philosophical traditions that have had a major impact on approaches to the psychology of learning.

Plato (Gulley, 1962; Hamilton & Cairns, 1961; Ross, 1951) developed an approach to epistemology that has become known as **rationalism.** Plato argued that one's sensory experiences are not reliable sources of knowledge because the physical objects that are the source of these experiences are constantly changing. Thus, knowledge is not to be had from the perception of these constantly changing physical objects and events. Rather, Plato argued, knowledge is to be had from a discovery of what he called the Forms (or Ideas). For every common class of objects to which a name is given—such as *man, woman, boat, heat,* and so on—there corresponds a Form. Perceptions of common objects then represent imperfect copies of these Forms.

To acquire true knowledge of the Forms, one must turn away somewhat from one's sensory experiences and engage in the philosophical dialectic. The **philosophical dialectic** refers to reasoned discussion and debate in which one attempts to arrive at the truth by disclosing the contradictions in an opponent's argument and overcoming them. Actually, as Leahey (1987) points out, Plato wavered somewhat throughout his life on the importance of sensory experiences to the attainment of knowledge. In his early works, Plato suggested that sensory experiences help activate innate knowledge of the Forms. He then later argued that sensory experiences have no legitimate role in the acquisition of knowledge, only to return ultimately to the position that sensory experiences may have some potential value as a stimulus for the dialectic.

Plato's student, Aristotle, on the other hand, established the approach to epistemology that is known as **empiricism.** Aristotle's approach to knowledge (Ackrill, 1980; Lloyd, 1978; McKeon, 1941; Ross, 1966) did not involve an appeal to perfect Forms. Instead, Aristotle argued, it is from an individual's sensory experiences that knowledge of categories of objects in the world is obtained. Based on a variety of experiences, the individual distills the essence of a particular class of objects through the operation of the mind. Despite the importance of mental processes to the discovery of the universal properties of objects, Aristotle contended that the universals are not an innate property of the mind, as suggested by Plato's doctrine of the Forms. Rather, the universals, as organizational principles of experience, are properties residing in the external objects themselves and revealed through the individual's sensory interactions with the external world.

☑ *In what principal ways do rationalism and empiricism differ?*

The Continuing Rationalist Tradition in Philosophy

René Descartes

In the seventeenth century, French philosopher René Descartes (e.g., Descartes, 1641/1988; see Beck, 1965; Williams, 1978) reasserted the rationalist tradition by arguing that truth is ultimately attainable only through the exercise of reason. The correct method for acquiring knowledge, he contended, is to identify, through reason, intuitively obvious truths from which one can then logically derive or deduce other truths. The most famous of Descartes' intuitively obvious truths is "I think; therefore, I am." He arrived at this truth as part of an exercise in which he set out to doubt everything until he finally arrived at something that could not be doubted. In recognizing that he could not doubt his own doubting, Descartes believed that he had established the truth of his own existence. From this most basic of truths, Descartes went on to establish the truth of the existence of God and the world.

By stressing the importance of intuitively obvious truths, Descartes helped establish a position known as **nativism.** In the tradition of Plato, Descartes argued that certain ideas are native, being inborn in the human mind. That is, certain ideas are innate and thus not the product of environmental learning experiences. The nativist position of Descartes and others after him emphasizes the influence of inborn mental processes and structures on the organization of one's sensory experiences.

Despite the preeminent importance Descartes attached to reason and innate ideas, he did not adopt Plato's extreme position on the worthlessness of sensory experience. In Descartes' system, sensory experiences provided the raw material on which reason acts. The records of sensory experience itself are of no value, but through the exercise of reason, these records can be organized in such a way as to advance the deduction of basic truths. In addition to its role as a servant of reason, sensory experience could, according to Descartes, trigger certain reactions reflexively, that is, independently of reason. Although Descartes' theory of mind placed him primarily in the rationalist tradition, his concept of reflex action ultimately gave rise to theories that were quite outside the rationalist tradition, as we will describe later.

☑ *What is nativism, and why is Descartes' nativist position considered a part of the rationalist tradition?*

Immanuel Kant

Later, in the eighteenth century, German philosopher Immanuel Kant (e.g., Kant, 1781/1965, 1783/1912; see Ameriks, 1982; Körner, 1955) attempted to reassert the notion of absolute truths in response to the claims of other empiricist philosophers whose positions will be examined shortly. Specifically, Kant argued that human perception is ordered according to certain innate properties of the mind, that the human mind, by its very nature, orders perceptual experience in certain ways. For example, according to Kant, the notion of causation is not learned as a result of sensory experience. Rather, the human mind is inherently structured so as to assume that every experienced event has a cause. Such an assumption is, according to Kant, basic to people's ability to make sense of the world around them.

Far from accepting Aristotle's contention that universal properties reside in external objects themselves, Kant contended that external objects are interpreted by the human mind and transformed into a form that can be understood and accepted by the mind. Thus, people's knowledge of the external world is not based on literal copies of objects obtained through sensory experience. Instead, it is based on *interpretations* of those objects dictated by innate properties of the mind.

☑ *What role, according to Kant, do innate properties of the mind play in the acquisition of knowledge?*

The Continuing Empiricist Tradition in Philosophy

John Locke

Coming soon after the work of Descartes in the seventeenth century was that of Englishman John Locke. Unlike Descartes, Locke had a strong empiricist orientation. According to Locke (1690/1975; Yolton, 1970), the mind has only ideas upon which to operate, and ideas come only from sensory experience. Locke went so far as to liken the mind to a blank slate (*tabula rasa*) on which experience imprints ideas. Although this appears to be an extreme empiricist position, Locke also proposed that humans possess the ability to reflect on or observe the operations of their own minds and that the operations of the mind are innate and not the result of experience. Thus, while Locke rejected the rationalist notion of innate ideas, he did not reject the rationalist argument that the manner in which the mind manipulates and operates on ideas is innate. Although Locke is usually identified strongly with the empiricist tradition, Leahey (1987) points out that Locke and Descartes differ more in emphasis than in true orientation.

☑ *Why did Locke describe the mind as a blank slate?*

David Hume

Locke, as the standard bearer of the empiricist tradition, was followed in the eighteenth century by another Englishman, David Hume. Hume (1739–1740/1886; Wright, 1980) expanded on the empiricism of Locke in such a way as to provide some of the basic underpinnings of twentieth-century psychology. In classifying the contents of the mind, Hume divided perceptions into impressions and ideas. *Impressions* correspond to direct sensations, and *ideas* are the less vivid and distinct mental copies of the impressions. Hume also distinguished between simple and complex ideas. **Simple ideas** are derived from simple impressions or sensations that cannot be analyzed into more basic components. **Complex ideas** are collections of simple ideas and thus can represent objects or situations never directly experienced. However, the simple ideas on which complex ideas are based are ultimately derived from direct sensory experience.

The extreme nature of Hume's empiricist position can be seen in his insistence that impressions, rather than ideas, are the ultimate source of knowledge. Impressions are more fundamental than ideas because they directly represent external reality and can be checked against the real external object. Ideas, on the other hand, may represent things that have no empirical reality.

In pursuing this empiricist account of mental life, Hume stressed two concepts that will figure prominently in all of the subsequent chapters of this book. The notion of association of ideas, though introduced by others previously, became central to Hume's work. Simple ideas become linked into complex ideas by means of **associations** that are irreducible into more basic processes. As the basic component of mental life, associations are formed in accordance with the laws of resemblance and contiguity. According to the law of **resemblance,** ideas corresponding to impressions that are similar become associated or linked, whereas the law of **contiguity** specifies that ideas corresponding to sensory impressions occurring contiguously or close together in time or space will become linked in the mind.

The assumption of causation is, according to Hume, based on the principle of contiguity. Experiencing two events in succession results in association of ideas in the mind, and this linkage of ideas underlies the belief that one event causes the other. Although Hume later appeared to reduce causation to the principle of contiguity, some writers (e.g., Smith, 1949; Turner, 1967) contend that Hume actually always intended causation to be considered a separate principle of association, despite its relationship to the principle of contiguity. This view of causation as merely an association, based on experience, was one of the spurs that led the rationalist Kant to claim that causation is not learned but rather is an innate property of the mind.

The other notion stressed by Hume that will figure prominently in coming chapters is that of **habit.** In explaining the process of induction, whereby a general conclusion is reached based on a number of specific experiences, Hume argued that the tendency to draw such generalizations is the product of habit. The repeated performance of actions or mental operations under particular circumstances leads to a tendency to repeat the actions or operations when similar circumstances are encountered subsequently. Such repetition of actions is automatic in that it is not the product of reason or reflection and is based on the underlying association of ideas. As Leahey (1987) has observed, Hume ultimately reduced human knowledge to mental habit.

How, according to Hume, are habits and associations of ideas involved in the acquisition of knowledge?

The British Associationists

The associationism that was a part of the empiricist approach of Hume became the central tenet of a number of British philosophers writing in the eighteenth and nineteenth centuries. Physician David Hartley (1749/1971; Stewart, 1792) is usually credited with originating the school of philosophy/psychology that has become known as **British associationism.** Whereas the concept of association of ideas was only a small component of the philosophical systems of Aristotle, Locke, and Hume, it became the hallmark of Hartley's work.

Apart from focusing attention on how associations are formed in explaining thought and behavior, Hartley's major contribution was in suggesting a possible physiological explanation of how ideas are formed and associated through the principle of contiguity. This explanation was based on the notion of vibrations in the nervous system, in contrast to the dominant view of the time that emphasized the role of "animal spirits," or special fluids that were assumed to move through tubes in the nervous system (Marx & Cronan-Hillix, 1987). Important successors to Hartley as members of the British associationist tradition were Thomas Brown, James Mill, John Stuart Mill, and Alexander Bain.

Brown (1820) furthered the associationist influence by proposing "secondary principles" of association. These principles went beyond the doctrine of contiguity to include factors such as the frequency of co-occurrence of ideas, the recency with which ideas had co-occurred, and the idea's vividness, its duration, and the number of other ideas available that had associative connections with the idea in question. As will be obvious in the following chapters, all of these secondary principles have survived as important factors in learning and memory.

The father and son team of James Mill and John Stuart Mill furthered the suggestion that even the most complex of mental activities could be explained in terms of the association of ideas. James Mill (1829/1912; Mazlish, 1975) argued that simple ideas become associated through contiguity and thus form complex ideas that are not necessarily based on direct sensory experience. In turn, once formed, complex ideas are available for association with other simple and complex ideas. In proposing this explanation, James Mill went beyond the notions of Locke and Hume by specifying one mechanism for combining of ideas.

One of John Stuart Mill's (1843/1884) revisions of his father's position was to suggest that simple ideas may be fundamentally altered when they are combined into complex ideas, so as to lose their originally distinct identities. Thus, John Stuart Mill proposed what he called a kind of "mental chemistry." Just as the elements oxygen and hydrogen, when combined to form water, no longer exhibit in an obvious fashion the properties most characteristic of each element, the simple ideas of redness, sweetness, roundness, and crispness are blended in the formation of the complex idea of apple so as to cease to be clearly distinguishable from each other. This question of the degree to which complex concepts are decomposable into more basic elementary features remains current today, as will be seen in Chapter 8 in the description of models of long-term memory.

Alexander Bain (1855, 1859) promoted associationism by systematizing the contributions of many of the philosophers already considered and by founding the first journal of psychology, *Mind*. In proposing his laws of association, Bain emphasized the principles of contiguity and similarity, but he also included the principles of **summation** and **creativity.** His principle of summation is related to the suggestion of an earlier writer, Thomas Brown, that the strength of an individual idea can be increased by the simultaneous activation of other ideas related to that idea. Bain's principle of creativity is related to Mill's suggestion that complex ideas can arise from the association of simple ideas and thus represent knowledge that is not based directly on sensory experience.

Bain also proposed the notion of **reinforcement,** a concept that will play an important role in the description of instrumental conditioning in Chapter 3. Bain's suggestion was that the strength of associations formed is based in part on the consequences that follow the experiencing of contiguous ideas. For example, he suggested that acts that lead to pleasing results tend to be repeated and retained as part of an individual's behavior, whereas acts that lead to undesirable results tend to be eliminated from an individual's behavior.

> *What major empiricist concepts did the British associationists introduce in explaining the acquisition of knowledge?*

Rationalism and Empiricism in the Psychology of Learning and Memory Today

In the chapters that follow, the continuing influence of empiricism in the study of learning and memory will be obvious. In fact, the assumption underlying virtually all of the topics discussed in the remainder of the book is that the behavior of animals and people is largely determined by their environmental sensory experiences. Although none of the psychological accounts of learning that follow address specific rationalist proposals, such as the importance of the dialectic and the exercise of reason in the attainment of knowledge, the basic tendency of most of these theorists would be to explain any influence of the dialectic and reason in terms of the environmental experiences that are involved in the dialectic and provide the basis for the operation of reason. Furthermore, as will be discussed in more detail below, the empiricist notion of association of ideas continues to be a major explanatory principle for theorists working in a variety of specific subfields within the discipline of learning and memory.

The careful reader will also be able to detect the influence of rationalism in the chapters that follow. Descartes' emphasis on the importance of organizing sensory experiences and Kant's emphasis on the interpretation of sensory experiences are reflected in many of the psychological accounts of learning and memory that follow in this book. That is, many of the explanations of learning and memory that will be described clearly reject the notion that sensory experiences are simply passively recorded in the mind as the basis for future thought and action.

In addition, the nativism common among rationalist philosophers will be evident in the accounts that follow. Suggestions that certain learning and memory phenomena are a reflection of genetically controlled processes are clearly related to the early nativist positions of Plato, Descartes, and Kant. Psychologists have become increasingly comfortable in suggesting that certain behavioral and mental tendencies are innate, because researchers continue to discover more about how genetic information is passed from one generation to another and how it influences behavior.

What general empiricist and rationalist influences can be seen today in the study of learning and memory?

Learning and Memory as Biological Adaptations

Descartes Revisited

In considering the influence of biology on the study of learning and memory, it is appropriate to return briefly to René Descartes' treatment of mind. Descartes explicitly compared humans to animals, and although he saw much in common between human and animal bodies, he proposed that the human mind is unique. Specifically, he argued that only people possess self-conscious souls.

In essence, Descartes argued that animals are purely mechanistic creatures constantly reacting to the environmental stimuli that they encounter. An animal's nervous system, he believed, moves muscles by inflating them with fluid (i.e., "animal spirits"). Environmental stimuli trigger movements in the nerves, thereby diverting fluid to move muscles in particular parts of the body. Descartes was doubtless aware of a similar hydraulic system, constructed to entertain visitors at the Royal Gardens of Versailles: Whenever someone stepped on treadles hidden in the garden path, they diverted water to flow through underground channels to special statues nearby. The statues were designed to surprise the stroller by moving in lifelike ways when the water reached them. Descartes surmised that sensory activation of an animal's nervous system is reflected back from the brain or spinal cord, to move the muscles in a similar way, hence, the use of the term *reflexive* to describe those automatic responses.

In contrast to his purely mechanical account of animal behavior, Descartes proposed for humans a **dualism** of soul and body. The body of a human, he suggested, is mechanistic in the same way that an animal's body is; that is, it reacts reflexively to environmental stimuli. However, in humans, the nonphysical soul can intervene to direct the actions of the body. It does so by diverting the flow of fluid from the brain toward the appropriate muscles through the nervous system.

Despite his recourse to dualism in the explanation of human behavior, Descartes did assign many mental functions such as memory, common sense, and imagination to the realm of the body rather than to the realm of the mind (Leahey, 1987). In so doing, he was clearly arguing that such apparently mental activities are actually mechanistic bodily reactions and subject to scientific study.

☑ *Why is it accurate to say that Descartes described memory in humans as a biological adaptation?*

Charles Darwin's Theory of Evolution

With his publication of *Origin of Species* in 1859 and *The Descent of Man* in 1871, Charles Darwin revolutionized the study of biology and the consideration of humans' place in the natural world. By suggesting that plants, animals, and humans have all evolved biologically from simple lowly forms into currently observable forms through the process of natural selection, Darwin challenged the assumption of the dualists, such as Descartes, that certain components of human functioning defy mechanistic scientific investigation. In advocating the mechanism of natural selection as the basis of his theory of evolution, Darwin argued that those species best suited to adapt to the demands of the environments in which they live are those most likely to survive and contribute to the continuation of the species through successful reproduction.

This focus on success in meeting environmental demands encouraged psychologists working at the end of the nineteenth century to promote the study of how people and animals adapt to their environment. In doing so, a number of psychologists helped establish an approach to psychology known as **functionalism.** The functionalist approach to psychology refers to a general orientation that emphasizes the role that thought and behavior play in an organism's adaptation to its environment.

One of the founders of this movement in psychology was American John Dewey, who in 1896 published a paper entitled "The Reflex Arc Concept in Psychology." In this paper, Dewey criticized attempts to describe behavior in terms of reflexes based on separate stimulus and response units. Dewey argued that analyzing behavior into a sensory component initiated by the stimulus, a central component involving the central nervous system, and a motor component involving the execution of a response does not provide an adequate basis for understanding behavior. Instead, he emphasized what he called the "total coordination" of behavior as an organism adapts to its environment. Thus, he urged that behavior be studied in relation to its function. Any attempt to break behavior into stimulus-response units is counterproductive because such labeling detracts from identifying the function of a particular aspect of behavior in attaining and maintaining a particular goal.

Another American writer and thinker, William James, was also instrumental in popularizing the functionalist approach to behavior and thinking. In his two-volume work, *The Principles of Psychology,* James (1890/1981) proposed that psychology be viewed as a part of biology and that the focus of study be the functions of the mind that have evolved as a result of their contribution to the survival of the species. For example, in his study of consciousness, James focused on the purpose that consciousness may play in the successful adaptation of human beings. This purpose of consciousness, James suggested, is to give humans the ability to choose among various options for action and thus to free them from responses based solely on habit.

Although functionalism as such will not be explicitly discussed in the remainder of this book, its central theme—that behavior and thought are fundamentally adaptive in nature— will be apparent in many of the chapters. In fact, one of the criteria on which the various approaches to learning and memory described in the book have historically been evaluated is how well they account for the development and regulation of adaptive behavior.

A final point about the influence of Darwin's theory of evolution on psychology concerns its emphasis on the *continuity of species*. In proposing the notion of the continuity of species, Darwin argued that humans evolved from the same lower forms that gave rise to nonhuman animals and that the evolution of human behavior follows the same principles as that of animals. In so doing, Darwin laid the foundations on which later psychologists would build explanations meant to apply equally to animals and humans. Furthermore, these psychologists have used the notion of continuity of species to support their claims that principles of behavior discovered from the study of animal behavior can be applied without reservation to humans. Such assumptions will be obvious in almost all of the accounts of animal studies of learning reported in this book.

▣   *How did Darwin's theory of evolution affect the functionalist approach to learning and memory and the application of learning principles derived from animal research to humans?*

The Rise of Behaviorism

Edward Thorndike

The functionalist legacy of using animals as subjects and emphasizing the adaptive nature of behavior is clearly evident in the work of American psychologist Edward Thorndike (e.g., Thorndike, 1898, 1905, 1911/1965, 1932). As a graduate student of William James at Harvard University, Thorndike was initially interested in studying the behavior of children. However, as a result of the unavailability of children for subjects in his studies, he turned to the study of animal behavior.

In contrast to earlier studies of animal behavior, including those of Darwin, which relied primarily on uncontrolled anecdotal observations and inferred interpretations of those observations, Thorndike was devoted to experimental study of his subjects. Using cats, chicks, and dogs as his subjects, Thorndike placed each subject in a "puzzle box" that could be opened by the subject's making a particular response. Making this response enabled the animal to escape from the box and gain access to food. Each subject was then placed into the box over and over again, and on each trial, Thorndike measured the latency of the escape response. That is, he measured on each trial the amount of time it took the subject to escape from the box. He found across trials that the latency of the escape response gradually decreased, providing evidence of what Thorndike called trial-and-error learning.

On the basis of these results, Thorndike proposed the **Law of Effect:** A response that, in a particular situation, produces a good effect or a satisfying state of affairs becomes associated with that situation and thus becomes more likely to recur when that situation is again encountered. In proposing this law, Thorndike helped establish an approach to the study of learning known as **instrumental conditioning,** which emphasizes the influence of a response's consequences on learning. This approach will be treated extensively in Chapter 3 of this book.

Clearly, Thorndike's work shows the influence of the British associationists in its emphasis on how associations are formed. However, rather than stressing the association of ideas in the animal's mind, Thorndike stressed the association between the situation and the animal's response. In fact, he went so far as to argue that animals are not capable of creating ideas that can be associated. He proposed that psychologists focus on the study of animals' behavior rather than the study of their minds because the study of behavior is easier to perform rigorously. He also proposed that such an approach could be extended to the study of human behavior by focusing on observable behavior as the expression of underlying mental states.

Thus, Thorndike came to propose a **stimulus-response (S-R)** approach to psychology. Observable responses (i.e., actions and other instances of behavior) become linked or associated with observable environmental stimuli (i.e., objects, events, etc.). Even complex human behavior, he reasoned, can be described as hierarchies of S-R associations. By advocating that psychologists focus their investigations on the formation of associations between observable stimuli and responses, Thorndike contributed to the establishment of a movement in psychology that became known as **behaviorism.**

✍ *How do Thorndike's Law of Effect and his emphasis on S-R associations reflect the influence of functionalism and empiricism in psychology?*

John Watson

Although Thorndike was certainly a pioneer of behaviorism, it was John Watson (e.g., Watson, 1913, 1914, 1919, 1930) who truly founded the behaviorist tradition and became its most outspoken advocate in the early part of the twentieth century. As a faculty member at Johns Hopkins University and as president of the American Psychological Association, Watson championed what he saw as the only truly scientific approach to psychology—an approach limited to the study of observable stimuli and observable responses.

Like Thorndike, Watson began his career as an animal psychologist, and, partly for this reason, he was uncomfortable with a psychology that focused on the study of mind through the method of **introspection,** whereby one reflects on and describes mental activities that underlie one's behavior. He argued that, in attempting to apply the study of mind to animals, psychologists were forced to infer mental states in the animals. Such inferences, he reasoned, must ultimately be based on the psychologists' own mental processes and could therefore hardly be accepted as valid, scientific explanations of the animals' behavior. Thus, in proposing an objective approach to psychology, Watson opted for the philosophical tradition known as **positivism.**

The positivists (e.g., Auguste Comte) were concerned with identifying nondebatable (i.e., positive) knowledge and had proposed that such knowledge comes only from objective, public observation. It was only a small step from this position to that which emphasizes the proper application of the scientific method as the source of sure knowledge. Watson maintained that the scientific method could be applied properly to the study of publicly observable behavior but that mental states could not be studied scientifically.

The functionalist tradition in psychology was evident in Watson's approach, just as it was in Thorndike's. Watson explicitly proposed that psychology should focus on the adaptive nature of behavior; and he suggested that, through a description of the S-R associations that exist for a given organism, one could gain the information necessary for predicting and controlling the behavior of the organism. In describing the establishment of S-R associations, Watson did not accept Thorndike's emphasis on the importance of the response's effect or consequences. Instead, he focused primarily on the principles of frequency and recency that had been identified earlier by the associationist philosophers as important in the establishment of associations.

In this respect, Watson was influenced mightily by the work of Russian physiologist Ivan Pavlov. Pavlov's research on the conditioning of reflexes in animals established an approach to the study of learning known as **classical conditioning,** an approach that will be considered at length in Chapter 2 of this book. Watson and his students extended Pavlov's work by applying his principles of classical conditioning to the conditioning of emotional reactions in humans, as will also be discussed in Chapter 2. Thus, with the work of Thorndike and Watson, the study of the formation of associations became a central focus of psychology. However, the focus was shifted from the study of the association of ideas to the association of observable stimuli and observable responses.

☑ *How did positivism affect Watson's approach to psychology, and how did his emphasis on S-R associations differ from that of Thorndike?*

The Cognitive Revolution

Subsequent Developments in the Behaviorist Tradition— Hull versus Tolman

Beginning in the 1920s and continuing into the early 1950s, Clark Hull (e.g., Hull, 1943, 1952) proposed and elaborated a theory of learning that was based to a large extent on the principles first expounded by Thorndike and Watson. Hull was very much an S-R behaviorist, but he was concerned with developing a grand theoretical system for explaining the behavior of organisms based on the statement of postulates and corollaries from which specific theorems could be derived through logical deduction. For example, in his 1952 book, *A Behavior System,* he proposed a postulate for the constitution of reaction potential:

> *The reaction potential ($_SE_R$) of a bit of learned behavior at any given stage of learning, where conditions are constant throughout learning and response-evocation, is determined (1) by the drive (D) operating during the learning process multiplied, (2) by the dynamism of the signaling stimulus trace (V_1), (3) by the incentive reinforcement (K), and (4) by the habit strength ($_SH_R$), i.e.,*
>
> $_SE_R = D \times V_1 \times K \times {}_SH_R.$ *(Hull, 1952, p. 7)*

He also proposed a postulate of inhibitory potential:

> A. *Whenever a reaction (R) is evoked from an organism there is left an increment of primary negative drive (I_R) which inhibits to a degree according to its magnitude the reaction potential ($_SE_R$) to that response.*
>
> B. *With the passage of time since its formation, I_R spontaneously dissipates approximately as a simple decay function of the time (t) elapsed, i.e.,*
>
> $I'_R = I_R \times 10^{-.018t}.$ *(Hull, 1952, p. 9)*

From these postulates and other considerations, he proceeded to derive the following theorem: "Tests made after the termination of simple trial-and-error learning will show a greater spontaneous increase (reminiscence) in reaction potential if the material is learned by massed trials than if it is learned by distributed trials" (Hull, 1952, p. 36).

From this theorem, a number of predictions were generated and tested. In the course of constructing this system, however, Hull went beyond simple S-R accounts of behavior in proposing a consideration of variables in addition to those of stimuli and responses. Specifically, Hull proposed a number of *organismic* variables that intervene between the stimulus variables and the response variables. For example, he proposed the organismic or intervening variable of *habit strength,* which he specified is a function of the number of learning trials in a specific stimulus situation. Habit strength, in turn, combines with other intervening variables to determine the intervening variable of *reaction potential.*

Despite this appeal to unobservable factors and their interaction in attempting to explain observed relationships between stimulus inputs and response outputs, Hull's S-R approach was intended to be a purely objective, mechanistic explanation of the formation of stimulus-response associations. That is, he believed that there is nothing unscientific about proposing such intervening variables as long as they are defined in terms of observable stimulus conditions such as number of reinforcements.

Throughout this same period, Edward Tolman (e.g., Tolman, 1932, 1959) advocated a contrasting view of behaviorism that is sometimes referred to as **purposive S-S (stimulus-stimulus) behaviorism** (Marx & Cronan-Hillix, 1987). Tolman outlined his position in 1932 in a book entitled *Purposive Behavior in Animals and Man.* In Tolman's view, the basic unit of learning is an expectation or expectancy. If two events follow one another closely in time, the first event produces an expectation of the occurrence of the second event. The strength of the expectation is a function of the number of co-occurrences of the two events. Thus, individuals learn "what will lead to what." In his later work, Tolman saw behavior as purposive in that it is produced by the desire or demand for a particular outcome. That is, a subject anticipates the consequences of its actions.

Tolman advocated a molar as opposed to a molecular analysis of behavior patterns such as that attempted by Hull. Tolman suggested that behavior be defined in terms of acts and accomplishments rather than in terms of particular specific behaviors. This approach to behaviorism was based on the notion of S_1-S_2 association through contiguity, where S_1 represents a sign stimulus and S_2 represents a consequence. On this view, S_1 arouses the belief or expectation of S_2. Whether the expectation will actually influence behavior is then dependent on the individual's motivation or demand for S_2. According to Tolman, the particular form of behavior exhibited is relatively unimportant. It is the internal mental state of the organism that determines the nature of learning. By emphasizing concepts such as expectation and purpose, Tolman clearly attempted to move behaviorism in a cognitive direction. That is, he attempted to demonstrate that one can use objective observations of behavior as the basis for drawing inferences about the mental states underlying that behavior.

Tolman was a methodological behaviorist as opposed to a theoretical behaviorist. He accepted the Watsonian behaviorists' emphasis on the importance of objective, observable events in explaining behavior, but he rejected their position that any attempt to describe unobservable mental events is inherently unscientific. In emphasizing the importance of mental representations as determinants of behavior, Tolman was one of the twentieth century's pioneers in advocating cognitive explanations of behavior.

Tolman's cognitive approach to explaining behavior can be seen even more clearly in his use of the concept of *cognitive map.* Consider the maze shown in Figure 1–1. A version of this maze was used in a number of experiments by Tolman and his associates (e.g., Tolman & Honzik, 1930a). In the early part of training, the rat was placed in the start box at the beginning of each trial, a food reward was placed in the goal box, and the rat was forced to run each path through the maze in order to familiarize it with the maze. Without any obstructions present in the runways of the maze, the rat showed a clear preference for Path 1 followed by Path 2. Tolman was interested in what the rat would do, however, when it found the preferred path blocked at different points. Tolman and his associates predicted that upon finding a block at Point 1 in the maze the rat would retreat to the choice point and choose Path 2 but that upon finding a block at Point 2 the rat would retreat to the choice point and choose Path 3, even though during training the rat showed a clear preference for Path 2 over Path 3.

This prediction was based on Tolman's assumption that the animal's behavior in this situation is not determined simply by the strength of various S-R associations formed during training, as Hull and his followers would predict. Rather, Tolman argued, the animal's behavior is being guided by a cognitive map or mental representation of the maze that the animal acquired in the course of exploring the maze. Such a map permits the animal to make whatever response is most effective in gaining access to S_2, which in this case is the food.

The degree to which behavior can be explained mechanistically in terms of S-R associations without recourse to explanations based on cognitive concepts remains an

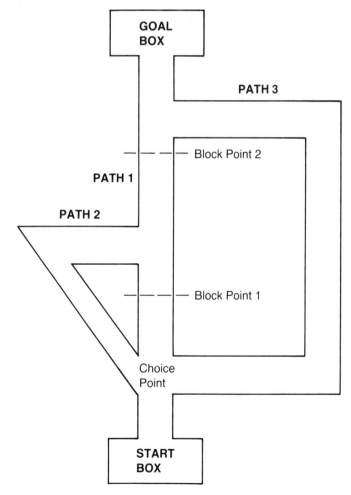

FIGURE 1–1 A version of the maze used by Tolman and associates in cognitive map experiments.

Source: Thomas Hardy Leahey, *A History of Psychology: Main Currents in Psychological Thought,* © 1987, p. 323. Reprinted by permission of Prentice Hall, Englewood Cliffs, NJ.

important issue in the field of learning and memory. The continuing nature of this debate will be emphasized in many of the following chapters. For example, in Chapter 2, the type of learning known as classical conditioning will be discussed. Traditionally, this type of conditioning has been explained mechanistically in terms of either S-R or S-S association formation. However, in response to apparent failures of traditional explanations to account for some classical conditioning phenomena, alternative cognitive explanations relying on concepts such as surprise and informativeness have been proposed. The Hull-Tolman debate is far from over.

In what fundamental ways did Hull's S-R behaviorism and Tolman's purposive S-S behaviorism differ?

The Information-Processing Approach to Human Learning

The cognitive revolt against mechanistic S-R behaviorism became increasingly obvious in the 1950s as researchers became interested in accounting for the behavior of humans in naturalistic learning situations. World War II gave impetus to the study of person-machine interactions such as those involved in flying an airplane. Researchers such as Donald Broadbent (1958) of Great Britain began to argue that traditional associative explanations of learning and memory are inadequate in accounting for various aspects of human functioning in such situations. In general, Broadbent and other early advocates of the human-information processing approach, such as George Miller (1956), endorsed Tolman's suggestion that subjects in some sense construct internal representations of the outside world as guides to behavior. However, the human information processing theorists saw Tolman's mentalistic concepts as an inadequate basis for a formal system of memory and cognition. What was needed, they suggested, was an abstract framework for describing internal events that avoided any unwarranted assumptions about the possible correspondence between internal and external behavior.

Broadbent (1958) proposed such an abstract framework in the form of his filter theory of attention. A diagram of his model is shown in Figure 1–2. In proposing this explanation of attention, Broadbent noted that humans' ability to focus attention selectively is one of those aspects of human performance for which traditional associative explanations of learning and memory provide no explanatory framework.

Broadbent's model was an attempt to account for experimental results such as those produced by Cherry (1953). In Cherry's experiment, subjects were presented with two different messages simultaneously, one to the right ear and one to the left ear. Subjects were instructed to shadow the right-ear message. This means that they were told to listen to the right ear message and repeat it aloud as it was heard while ignoring the left-ear message. The right-ear message was normal English spoken by a male voice. The left-ear message always began and ended with normal English spoken by a male voice, but the middle portion of the message on the left ear either remained the same, changed to a female voice, changed to reversed male speech, or changed to a single tone. After the shadowing task, all subjects identified the message on the rejected ear as speech, but they could not remember any portion of it or definitely classify it as English. A few subjects noticed something unusual about the reversed speech, but the change to the female voice and to the tone were almost always noted. That is, obvious physical changes were almost always noticed.

Broadbent interpreted such results as suggesting that a nonattended channel of information is in some sense blocked or filtered so as to allow for analysis of attended information. To account for such filtering, Broadbent proposed the notion of a limited-capacity processor

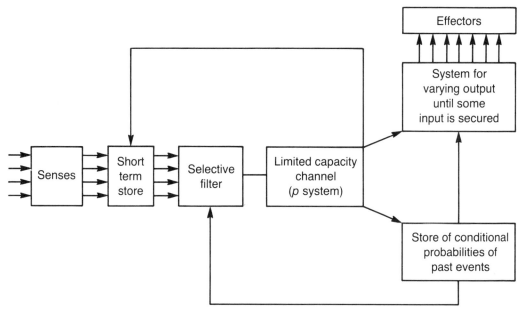

FIGURE 1–2 Broadbent's (1958) description of the human information processing system

Source: Reprinted with permission from Donald E. Broadbent, *Perception and Communication,* copyright 1958, Pergamon Press, PLC.

within the human information-processing system. This processor, he argued, can deal with only one channel of information at a time, with a channel defined in terms of the physical characteristics of the message. Thus, the selective filter is set so as to allow only one channel of information into the limited-capacity processor at a time. As required, the selective filter is reset so as to allow for the switching of attention between the various channels. The short-term store shown in Figure 1–2 was hypothesized to maintain the unanalyzed sensory signal for very brief intervals. Maintenance of information in the system was described in terms of the recirculation of information from the limited-capacity channel back to the short-term store and thus back to the limited-capacity processor.

This description of the filter theory is not intended as a comprehensive treatment of what is obviously a complex model. Rather, this description is intended to illustrate the general cognitive nature of information-processing descriptions of human functioning. Broadbent and the other information-processing theorists are clearly methodological behaviorists in the tradition of Tolman rather than mechanistic behaviorists in the tradition of Watson and Hull. The information-processing theorists clearly believe that proposed explanations of human cognitive functioning must be assessed on the basis of their adequacy in accounting for and predicting objectively observable behavior, but they also clearly reject Watson's argument that explanations in terms of unobservable mental states are not scientifically legitimate.

The information-processing theorists go beyond Tolman's mentalistic approach in their attempt to describe precisely the structure and functioning of those mental entities that must be assumed if one is to have a comprehensive explanation of how particular instances of observable behavior come about in particular stimulus situations. The information-processing theorists were aided by the advent of computer technology. Just as one can describe the flow of information through a machine in terms of temporary memory stores, permanent memory stores, coding of incoming information, programs for operating on incoming information, feedback loops that involve recycling information, and the processing capacity of the system, so too can one characterize the flow of information through the human being. By adopting such concepts, the information-processing theorists have been able to generate comprehensive cognitive explanations of learning and memory from which predictions can be rigorously derived and quantitatively tested in the manner suggested by Hull.

Examples of information-processing theories will be presented throughout this book, especially in those chapters dealing with the study of human memory. For example, in Chapter 6, Broadbent's filter theory will be discussed again as one of the original information-processing models that helped popularize the notion that memory performance can only adequately be explained by assuming the existence of several functionally distinct memory stores.

☑ *How do information-processing approaches to learning and memory represent an extension of Tolman's cognitive approach to explaining behavior?*

THEMES OF ASSOCIATIONISM AND COGNITIVISM

As the preceding sections suggest, two themes that will recur throughout this book are those of associationism and cognitivism. In every chapter in the book, the view that learning involves the establishment of associations will figure prominently. Exactly what events are being associated in the process of learning will differ from one explanation to another. For example, some will focus on the establishment of stimulus-response associations, some will emphasize the development of stimulus-stimulus associations, and others will talk about the linking of memory locations or nodes. The various approaches will also differ in the emphasis they place on the factors responsible for the formation of associations. Although virtually all of the accounts to be presented assume that temporal contiguity is a condition that facilitates association formation, some approaches will argue that reinforcement or reward is essential for links to be formed, whereas others will make no assumptions about the importance of reinforcement.

Cognitivism, as the second theme in the book, should not be seen as the direct opposite of associationism. As the brief description of cognitive approaches to learning described earlier should suggest, the formation of associations is a major component of all cognitive approaches to learning and memory. Cognitive approaches differ from traditional associative approaches such as those of the S-R behaviorists in that they argue for descriptions of learning that go beyond simple accounts of how associations are formed, to emphasize the underlying organization of mental experience. The basic position of the cognitive theorists is that association formation can only fully be understood once the mental structures and operations underlying the learning process are fully described.

Thus, some of the chapters of this book will highlight disputes between cognitive theorists and theorists who limit their explanations of learning to the description of observable stimulus conditions that promote association formation. However, it is important to remember in evaluating these disputes that the importance of association formation is not in question. What is being argued by the different approaches is the value of and need for explanations of behavior that go beyond the description of the conditions under which associations are formed.

☑ *In what ways does cognitivism differ from simple associationism?*

LEARNING AND MEMORY AS A RESEARCH SCIENCE

Why Develop Theories of Learning and Memory?

Why even ask such a question, you may wonder. Aren't theories a main focus of all scientific research? If so, then the development of theories must also be essential for the science of learning and memory.

But B. F. Skinner claimed that theories such as Hull's, Tolman's, and Broadbent's are unnecessary and may even hamper the search for facts. According to Skinner, references to mental or neural processes provide no real explanations but instead obscure important individual differences in behavior (Skinner, 1950). He argued that researchers, rather than theorizing, should merely describe what responses occur under what conditions. The best way to discover general laws, he said, is to carefully record one's observations of behavior itself—and not to speculate about processes that cannot be directly observed, as theorists do.

Most researchers, however, continue to regard theories as useful for several reasons. First, theories help researchers to focus on those variables that are most relevant to the phenomenon being studied. A **variable** is any characteristic that can vary with time or place or can differ from one learner to another (e.g., diet, temperature, age, intensity of a stimulus, duration of a response, etc.). A theory therefore increases the efficiency of research by pointing out a limited number of variables to be considered.

Second, it is generally easier to learn a theory that accounts for many facts than to learn the many facts separately. Theories are economical ways of remembering, because they use a few principles to summarize many separate observations all at once.

Third, theories may be used to predict future events on the basis of known factors. Without a theory, predictions will likely be based on the most obvious similarities among situations, not necessarily on the relevant variables.

Together with the ability to predict events may come the ability to control them, by arranging circumstances so that a particular outcome is likely. Skinner recognized the practical importance of prediction and control in scientific psychology, but he regarded formal theories as premature.

Finally, of course, theories can provide explanations that satisfy our curiosity about learning and memory. Once an event is interpreted in terms of a theory, it seems less strange and surprising. Even common-sense explanations may satisfy our curiosity in this manner, although they often fail to account for facts obtained through scientific research. For example, many people in the world still believe that the earth is flat and that the sun and moon travel over the earth. They are satisfied with this explanation because it accounts for the events that are familiar to them. We, on the other hand, know of events that cannot be interpreted via the same theory. Those additional facts have led to the development of other explanations, which we find more satisfactory. Theories of learning and memory similarly arose from curiosity about facts that are not satisfactorily explained by common sense.

Identify five benefits of theorizing about learning and memory, and indicate the harmful effect that Skinner attributed to premature theorizing.

Desirable Characteristics of Theories

Ideally, a theory should account for virtually all aspects of learning and memory, and should do so by using only a small number of principles. But no actual theory has yet achieved this ideal combination of comprehensiveness and simplicity. Theories that explain many phenomena are usually rather complex, and even the most complex theories fail to explain some important findings. A major challenge to current theorists, therefore, is to explain as many results as possible without making theories of learning and memory too complex to understand and apply.

Besides being as simple and as comprehensive as possible, good theories possess certain other characteristics, including falsifiability (Popper, 1963; Lakatos, 1970). A theory is **falsifiable** if it makes specific predictions, called **hypotheses,** so that certain kinds of contrary evidence would be enough to disconfirm the theory

It may seem strange to say that theories should be falsifiable. Instead, you might think that theories that could never be proven false would be the best theories of all. But if you find a theory that no test could possibly disconfirm, then it must surely be too vague or subjective to be taken seriously.

As a simple example, we could never really test the claim that plants are conscious. No one quite understands what causes consciousness, and there is no way to directly observe it (except in ourselves) to be sure when it exists. If someone we know has been completely paralyzed, his brain activity and other signs may help us guess whether he is conscious. But we still may never know for sure, unless he recovers enough to say so himself. It is even more difficult to evaluate claims about organisms that lack human brains. From a scientific point of view, therefore, theories of plant consciousness should be rejected because they are not falsifiable. There is no way to demonstrate compellingly that such theories are either true or false.

Why is it desirable for a theory to be falsifiable?

Scientific Progress

Thomas Kuhn (1970) has distinguished between two historical patterns of scientific activity. The first pattern, random fact finding, may be especially common in newly emerging fields of science such as psychology. Indeed, B. F. Skinner recommended random fact finding as an appropriate strategy for investigating learning and memory. In contrast, most science is characterized by a focus on a research **paradigm**—that is, on a basic set of ideas and methods shared by all researchers in that field. For example, Isaac Newton's theory of gravitation brought together many facts from physics and astronomy that had previously appeared to be in conflict. After his theory was accepted, physicists concentrated on refining and extending his general paradigm during more than a century of scientific activity.

Reprinted by permission of UFS, Inc.

Even with modifications, however, Newton's theory could not explain some later discoveries. The inadequacy of Newton's conceptualization opened the way for Albert Einstein and others to introduce a new paradigm, which may eventually be replaced by yet another one.

Despite the impermanence of scientific paradigms, researchers usually regard one paradigm as fundamentally true, at least until a better one is found. Within that accepted paradigm, individual researchers may favor one particular theory over another. But no matter how widely accepted a theory becomes, theories, like paradigms, are impermanent and cannot be proven beyond a doubt.

As mentioned before, a specific prediction that follows from a theory is called an hypothesis. For example both Newton's and Einstein's theories predict that light from a distant star will bend as it passes close to the sun, but Einstein's theory predicts twice as much deflection as Newton's does. Careful observations have shown that Einstein's hypothesis is more nearly correct, which lends support to his theory. But Newton's theory would never have been completely replaced for this reason alone. Instead, researchers would merely have searched for new factors that might be added to Newton's theory to improve its predictions. It is only when the hypothesis fails and the favored theory cannot be adequately modified that it may ultimately be rejected.

The term *paradigm* may be used not only for cosmic visions such as Newton's and Einstein's, but also for somewhat narrower formulations that provide a foundation for many theories within a discipline. Two examples of paradigms for learning and memory research are Pavlov's studies of classical conditioning (Chapter 2) and Ebbinghaus's studies of memory (Chapter 9). In both cases, subsequent research has required drastic modifications of the original theories, but many of the original methods and ideas are still regarded as basic to the study of learning and memory. In other words, although many of Ebbinghaus's and Pavlov's hypotheses were incorrect and their particular theories or original assumptions have been substantially revised, their general paradigms continue to produce successful theories. It is important to study the succession of theories, because this reveals so much about where our explanations came from, how discoveries are made, and why explanations are likely to improve in the future.

How are hypotheses used to evaluate theories, and how can a research paradigm continue to prevail despite inadequacies in the original theory?

Testing Hypotheses Scientifically

The Scientific Method

What makes a particular piece of knowledge scientific? The answer is not that it was endorsed by a famous scientist or that it was discovered in a laboratory, but rather, that it was verified using a particular method—the scientific one, of course. Although the **scientific method** is often described as consisting of several steps, its crucial feature is that detailed observations are used to systematically evaluate the truth of an hypothesis.

Apart from this one essential characteristic, applications of the scientific method may differ from instance to instance. The hypothesis, for example, may be derived from a theory or may instead arise from casual observations. Detailed observations may focus on events as they naturally occur or, alternatively, as they are generated in laboratory experiments. And statistical techniques may be used to analyze the results before reaching a conclusion, or they may not. Regardless of the particular procedures used, research is scientific if it uses planned observations to critically evaluate hypotheses.

The scientific method relies on the assumption that nature is orderly and that events can be explained through general principles. More specifically, scientific research is based on **determinism**—the belief that every event is determined by a specific cause. Scientists consequently reject capricious influences, such as free will or miracles, as explanations for their results. Instead they search for causes that can themselves be explained as the results of prior causes.

Another consequence of determinism is a reliance on replication to verify cause-and-effect explanations. **Replication** is repeated application of the scientific method to the same research problem, to make certain that the suspected cause is really responsible for the results. This search for verifiable (repeatable) effects is at the heart of the scientific endeavor.

How can you tell whether research is truly scientific?

Methodological Behaviorism

In an attempt to reduce learning and memory to its simplest cause-and-effect elements, early behaviorists emphasized reflexes and refused to speculate about mental processes that could not be observed. That radical form of behaviorism is no longer common, yet most psychologists are behaviorists in another sense: They regard observable responses as the basis for scientific research in psychology. So while much of early behaviorist theory has been rejected, the research methods of behaviorism have become part of the mainstream of psychology.

This reliance on behavior as an indicator of mental processes is known as **methodological behaviorism.** It does not disregard people's descriptions of their mental experiences, but merely treats those descriptions as verbal behavior—one of many possible indicators that something has been experienced, learned, or remembered.

Before behaviorism became an established movement, experimental psychology was dominated by the use of the **introspective method.** Introspectionists hoped that their careful observation of their own conscious experience would reveal simple laws that, they believed, govern all perceptions and feelings. But the processes of perception, learning, and memory cannot be observed directly, so there is really no alternative to relying on verbal descriptions and other observable responses. Furthermore, methodological behaviorism facilitates use of the scientific method. By insuring that researchers will record their observations in great detail and as objectively as possible, it promotes the replication of findings that is so important for evaluating theories.

What does it mean to say that most psychologists are methodological behaviorists?

Controlled Experiments

Suppose you fulfilled a research assignment by strewing your belongings across a library table, to see how long people would avoid sitting there. You then wrote a paper, complete with a description of your method and results. Would you have conducted an experiment? The answer is no, because you would not have compared the results from at least two different situations (Kantowitz & Roediger, 1984, p. 55). Until you have observed how slowly people would sit there anyway, you cannot be sure that strewing the belongings had any effect. Therefore, an **experiment** is a specific manipulation of a situation, in order to reveal changes in behavior that occur as a result of the manipulation.

The aspect of the situation that is manipulated in an experiment is called the **independent variable.** The values of the independent variable in our example are the two different conditions of the table, strewn versus bare. Independent variables studied in research on learning and memory include the duration of time allowed for studying material, the nature of the material, the delay before testing, and a host of other factors. In each case, the experimenter would have to compare at least two different values of the independent variable (e.g., long delay versus no delay) to determine whether it affects learning or memory.

The aspect of the results that is measured in an experiment is called the **dependent variable.** In our example, the dependent variable is the amount of time it takes for someone else to sit at the library table on each occasion. In other experiments, the dependent variable might be the number of words recalled from a list, the number of wrong turns made in a maze, the speed of reaction to a signal, or any other behavioral outcome. The dependent variable shows the effects of the independent variable, so you may wish to think of it as *depending* on the independent (causal) variable. Another way to remember the difference is that the values of the independent variable are chosen by the experimenter, independently of the subjects (participants) in the experiment, so only the results are dependent on the subjects.

Factors other than the independent variable may influence the dependent variable, so it is important to keep all other aspects of the situation as constant as possible while manipulating the independent variable. In our example, it would be important to make sure the library is equally full whenever observations are made, so people do not need a seat more on one occasion than another. Increased demand for seats could make it impossible for people to avoid the strewn table, even though they would like to; or people might take longer to sit at the table, not because it is strewn with belongings but merely because no one needs a seat. When other possible causes are held constant or eliminated, we say they have been *controlled*. Only a controlled experiment can show convincingly that changes in the independent variable cause changes in the dependent variable. This is true because, unless other possible causes have been controlled, there is always the potential that other, unknown factors may have caused the results.

To see whether you fully understand the concept of experimental control, note any deficiencies you can find in the following experiment. Suppose a professor wants to determine whether caffeine enhances learning, so she sends students sitting near the front of her classroom to the Student Center, with instructions to drink coffee at her expense (manipulation of the independent variable). While the coffee group is away, the remainder of the class hears a brief lecture on which they are immediately tested. The first group is dismissed, the coffee group returns, and the professor tries to repeat the lecture exactly as before. Finally, she tests the coffee group and finds its scores (dependent variable) to be higher than the first group's, just as she had expected. Should she conclude that caffeine enhances learning?

The professor has compared the results from two different situations, but unfortunately, her experiment is not well controlled. Even if one group received caffeine and the other did not (of which she has no guarantee), there are also many other differences between the groups. For example, they sat in different parts of the room, were tested after different amounts of exercise (and perhaps cream and sugar), and may have received somewhat different presentations of the material, despite the professor's efforts to repeat the lecture exactly. Not until all these differences, and several others, were eliminated would this experiment be able to reveal anything about the effects of caffeine on learning.

As you read about each experiment described in this book, identify the independent and dependent variables, and try to understand how the experimenters controlled other factors that might have influenced the results. It is a reliance on the scientific method in general, and on controlled experiments in particular, that have made these studies valuable for understanding learning and memory.

☑ *Distinguish between independent and dependent variables, and explain why it is important to control other influences in an experiment.*

PREVIEW OF FOLLOWING CHAPTERS

Learning and memory are inseparable. Unless the learner remembers something long enough to show what was learned, we cannot say that any learning occurred. And nothing can be remembered unless it was learned in the first place. Despite this interrelatedness, however, the two topics have customarily been studied by different researchers who followed different paradigms. We have followed this custom by separating our treatments of learning and memory, to some extent, in the organization of the book.

The next few chapters focus on conditioning and complex learning, making it clear how the associative and cognitive approaches have contributed to our current understanding of those areas. Chapters devoted to memory and forgetting follow, in which the contributions of the same two theoretical traditions are again apparent. The final chapters cover special topics that deserve detailed treatment apart from the overview provided in earlier sections.

In every chapter, we have anchored the information in four different ways to help you understand and remember it more effectively. First, we refer repeatedly to the associative and cognitive traditions, to show where explanations originated and how they changed as a result of new discoveries and ideas. You are already familiar with this theoretical anchor by now.

Second, we present at the beginning of each chapter an outline of the major topics to be covered. We encourage you to use each outline as an organizational framework for studying the information contained in the chapter. Each outline provides you with an overview that can help you understand how the various topics covered in the chapter are interrelated.

In addition, key terms are printed in boldface, and frequent review questions are provided throughout each chapter to emphasize major concepts. We have placed each review question immediately after the section of the chapter to which it refers in order to make it easier for you to use each question effectively as a device for reviewing key concepts and information contained in that section of the chapter. Finally, we describe actual applications and familiar examples to illustrate the practical implications of what you are learning. For example, each of the remaining chapters opens with a vignette about everyday experiences that are relevant to the topic. You may find one kind of anchor to be more useful than the others, but watch for all of them because each can be valuable for comprehending the material.

☑ *What four anchors serve as reference points for aiding comprehension throughout this book?*

CHAPTER 2

Classical Conditioning

APPLICATION: Burger Attack

Eating was the last thing on Joan's mind as she turned the television on. But when the Burger Billy advertisement appeared on the screen, she suddenly realized how hungry she was. Joan likes Burger Billy's dreamburgers so much that just the thought of them makes her mouth water. If it had not been time for her favorite game show to begin, she would have rushed out for a meal right then.

Why do Burger Billy's advertisements affect her so? Some people would attribute her reaction to an "instinctive" urge to eat. By instinctive, they mean that Joan has a natural need for nourishment, and she can't help feeling hungry when she thinks of food. But newborn babies need nourishment, too, and yet their mouths do not water when they see a dreamburger advertisement. Why this difference? The reason is primarily that newborns lack the kind of experience that makes the advertisement meaningful: They have never enjoyed the taste of a hamburger and so they don't know what a good one looks like. This example illustrates the fact that very few of our urges are completely innate; instead, the objects of our emotions and appetites depend very much on learning.

Let us dwell on this example for a moment. Although hungry newborns drool quite readily when they actually taste something palatable in their mouths, they do not drool at the mere sight of the person who feeds them. Yet after they have been fed on a number of occasions, they may begin to react to that person with virtually the same pattern of sucking and salivating that they display when they taste food itself. Thus, older infants may drool and make sucking sounds at the sight of their caregiver or their bottle, which is something they would not have done at an earlier age. They have learned what events go together.

*Advertisers routinely show their products together with people, places, and things that they believe will appeal to us. They try to devise the most humorous, or most exciting, or most soothing commercials possible, so those good feelings will become part of our memory for the products they wish to sell. In short, they expect us, like Joan and the babies, to learn from the relationships between stimuli in our personal experience—a process called **classical conditioning.***

*Salivating at the taste of food is an example of a **reflex,** which may be defined as a reliable and rapid response to a specific stimulus. Because this original reflex does not depend on conditioning through experience, it is called **unconditioned**. On the other hand, drooling at the sight of a formula bottle does depend on prior experience; consequently, it is called a **conditioned** reflex.*

For several decades, reflexes such as these were the main focus of research on classical conditioning. Ivan Pavlov was the first person to systematically investigate this form of learning, which is often called "Pavlovian conditioning" in his honor.[1] Pavlov assumed that our experiences cause new reflex connections to form in the brain, and his goal was to understand how this occurs. More recent theories of classical conditioning apply to a wide range of phenomena, including allergies, anxieties, drug addiction, and food preferences, in addition to discrete reflexes (Turkkan, 1989).

This chapter presents Pavlov's key discoveries and some of the many findings that followed from them. Although his theory of brain function is no longer considered tenable, many facts that he uncovered are still fundamental to an understanding of classical conditioning.

◪ *What kind of experience produces classical conditioning?*

HISTORICAL BACKGROUND

Cartesian Dualism

As you may recall from Chapter 1, Descartes emphasized the dualism of mind and body. A French mathematician and philosopher, he accepted the prevailing religious view that our minds are fundamentally different from our material bodies. Discoveries in physics and medicine had convinced him that human and animal bodies function according to purely mechanical processes. Nevertheless, he believed that people are unique: Unlike animals, we possess rational minds composed of a nonmaterial substance that is not amenable to scientific study.

Descartes characterized animal behavior as little more than an assortment of fixed, inborn reflexes. He believed that a stimulus such as a pin prick causes movements in our nerves, and that these movements are then reflected from the spinal cord or brain. This reflected motion ends up in our muscles, causing us to move away from the offending pin. The term *reflex* was originally intended to express this idea of reflected movement.

Descartes described nerves as if they contain long cords that can be pulled by sensory organs at one end. When the sensory cords open valves in the nervous system, fluids called "animal spirits" flow into the muscles to make them flex. Although these notions seem primitive to us today, his mechanical account of body movements was very influential in focusing attention on the reflex as an important component of behavior. It is ironic that the concept of the reflex developed by Descartes, a dualist, led eventually to Pavlov's purely deterministic theory of mental functioning.

 Twentieth-century theories of neural networks are based on our modern experience with telephone switchboards and digital computers. But Descartes was totally unfamiliar with such electrical networks; he instead based his theory on what was known about mechanics and hydraulics in his own time. Which details of his theory reflect this influence?

British Empiricism

Another important precursor of classical conditioning theory was the eighteenth-century school of philosophers known as the **British empiricists.** These thinkers revived the doctrine, first enunciated in ancient Greece, that all knowledge comes from sensory experience. According to this metaphor, the mind at birth is a *tabula rasa,* or blank tablet, on which ideas may be impressed. Locke and other British empiricists suggested that even the most complex memories and thoughts can be understood as combinations of simple ideas, and many scientists had accepted this basic notion by the nineteenth century.

Three principles that were believed to promote the association of ideas were contiguity, frequency, and recency. According to the principle of **contiguity,** experiences that are almost simultaneous (contiguous) with each other are most likely to be associated in the mind. According to the principle of **frequency,** an association becomes stronger with repetition; that is, ideas that have occurred together often are more likely to be associated than ideas which have coincided only a few times. And according to the **recency** principle, associations are strongest between ideas that have occurred together recently, and consequently have not been forgotten. Because of their keen interest in the association of ideas, later British empiricists are often called *British associationists.*

 Name and define three principles of association that are identified with British empiricism.

Darwin

There is a wide gap between Descartes' claim that human thoughts defy scientific analysis, and the empiricists' claim that our minds follow natural laws whenever we think or recall ideas. Charles Darwin's writings on evolution (e.g., 1871) helped to close this gap between reflex theory and associationism, by challenging Descartes' assumption that human intelligence is fundamentally unique.

As discussed in the previous chapter, Darwin (1809–1882) documented many similarities among living species, and argued that the mental as well as the physical characteristics of all living things evolved gradually and continuously from a shared ancestral lineage (continuity of species). From this evolutionary perspective, even the most sophisticated mental abilities of human beings are seen as natural adaptations that enhance our ability to survive and reproduce our species.

Darwin thus shared Descartes' view that animal and human bodies function in similar ways. But in treating intelligence, emotion, and behavior as biological functions, Darwin went even further: He rejected Cartesian dualism, in favor of the notion that the mind can be studied scientifically, just as the body can.

According to Descartes' theory, nonhumans are creatures of habit, whereas humans are basically rational. In what way does Darwin's thesis about the relatedness of all living things challenge both those claims?

Pavlov

Ivan Pavlov, a Russian university professor, won the 1904 Nobel Prize in Physiology and Medicine for his research on inborn reflexes. But even before he received his prize, he abandoned that line of research in order to study how reflexes can be learned. Like Darwin, he regarded learning as a biological function. Moreover, he believed he had discovered a way to study the brain processes that produce mental associations.

His earlier work was concerned with genetically inherited reflexes, particularly with the digestive secretions that occur when dogs taste food in their mouths. The research for which he won the Nobel showed how the nervous system coordinates the activities of the stomach and other organs, so that the proper kinds and amounts of digestive fluids are secreted at the right times. But he found it difficult to study these glandular responses to the stimulus of taste alone, because his dogs often responded prematurely, as soon as they *saw* or *heard* their handler bringing the food dish. Pavlov (1927/1960) realized that this anticipatory response meant the dogs had mentally associated the dish (or the handler) with the taste of food. He coined a phrase that has been translated **conditioned reflex** to refer to such learned reflexes, because they are conditional or dependent on prior experience. In contrast, an **unconditioned reflex** is any reflex that is inborn and is therefore unconditional or independent of prior experience.

Pavlov's crucial insight was the realization that simple learning could be studied scientifically, in a laboratory setting where stimulus events were carefully controlled and the results could be precisely measured. Although he eventually applied his discoveries to mental disorders and other practical problems, his immediate goal was to satisfy his curiosity: He wished to describe the complex processes of the brain that enable us to benefit from prior experience—that is, to learn.

What is the difference between conditioned and unconditioned reflexes?

EXCITATION

Excitatory Stimuli

Stimuli that elicit responses are called **excitatory.** This term distinguishes them from **neutral** stimuli, which have no effect on responding, and from **inhibitory** stimuli, which oppose the tendency to respond. Pavlov identified many determinants of excitatory conditioning in his laboratory, including some that are reminiscent of empiricist principles of association.

Acquisition

Temporal contiguity and frequency are characteristics of **acquisition procedures,** that is, procedures that are designed to establish new conditioned reflexes. The stimuli that the experimenter wants the subject to associate are typically "paired" together *closely in time* (contiguity), and this pairing must usually be *repeated several times* before learning is evident in the subject's behavior (frequency). If the two stimuli are separated by much time, or if very few pairings are given, then evidence of an association is rarely found.

Pavlov's Basic Procedure

Figure 2–1 is a schematic illustration of the sequence of events in a classical conditioning acquisition procedure. An originally neutral stimulus, called the **conditioned stimulus (CS),** is paired together with an unconditioned reflex such as the dog's salivary response to food in the mouth (Figure 2–1a). For example, the experimenter might use a bell as a neutral CS, because dogs do not usually drool when they hear bells. Each time the bell is rung, food powder is blown into the dog's mouth through one tube, and the amount of saliva is measured through another tube. Repetition of this pattern results in a conditioned reflex: The

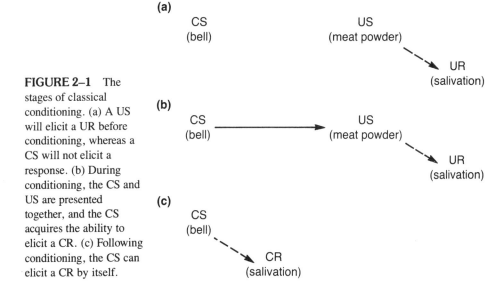

FIGURE 2–1 The stages of classical conditioning. (a) A US will elicit a UR before conditioning, whereas a CS will not elicit a response. (b) During conditioning, the CS and US are presented together, and the CS acquires the ability to elicit a CR. (c) Following conditioning, the CS can elicit a CR by itself.

subject learns to salivate to the conditioned stimulus, not just to the unconditioned stimulus of food itself (Figure 2–1b).

Salivation that occurs in response to the CS is called a **conditioned response (CR)**, but salivation that occurs in response to the **unconditioned stimulus (US)** of food in the mouth is called an **unconditioned response (UR)**. Thus the conditioned reflex and the unconditioned reflex each contain a stimulus and a response. The crucial difference is that the CR is a response to the CS, and it depends on learning; whereas the UR is a response to the US, and it does not.

The Case of Little Albert

Another illustration of classical acquisition is the case of Little Albert, an infant studied by Watson and Rayner (1920). At the age of 11 months, Little Albert feared virtually nothing except loud noises, to which he reacted by crying and falling to one side (the UR). A white rat, a rabbit, masks, and various other stimuli failed to distress him. But one day, after showing him the rat (CS), the researchers elicited Albert's unconditioned fear reaction by striking a hammer against a steel bar (loud noise US). Seven days later, after a total of seven pairings of the rat and the noise (CS - US → UR), they observed their first clear CR:

> *Rat alone [CS]. The instant the rat was shown the baby began to cry. Almost instantly he turned sharply to the left, fell over on left side, raised himself on all fours, and began to crawl away so rapidly that he was caught with difficulty before reaching the edge of the table. (Watson & Rayner, 1920, p. 5)*

Watson believed that this laboratory demonstration mimicked the way people normally learn emotional reactions to new stimuli (CSs)—namely, by experiencing the emotion repeatedly in the presence of those CSs.

Other Examples of Classical Conditioning

Thus the terms *CR, UR,* and *classical conditioning* may apply to emotions and other complex reactions, not merely to specific responses such as salivation. By now a wide variety of behaviors have been classically conditioned, including the human knee jerk (Twitmyer, 1974), Japanese quails' courting behavior (Farris, 1967), wolves' fear of sheep (Gustavson, Kelly, Sweeney, & Garcia, 1976), rabbits' eyeblinks (Schneiderman, Fuentes, & Gormezano, 1962), allergies in guinea pigs (Russell, Dark, Cummins, Ellman, Callaway, & Peeke, 1984), and many, many more. For example, Russell and colleagues exposed their subjects to a novel odor (CS) together with a substance to which guinea pigs were already allergic (US → UR). After five such pairings, presentation of the CS alone was found to raise the subjects' blood level of histamine (CR), a hormone that is an important component of the allergic reaction.

In some organisms, researchers have even pinpointed the part of the nervous system that is responsible for classical conditioning of particular responses, such as defensive gill withdrawal in the marine slug *Aplysia* (Hawkins, Abrams, Carew, & Kandel, 1983) and suppression of light-seeking behavior in the nudibranch mollusk *Hermissenda* (Farley, Richards, Ling, Liman, & Alkon, 1983). Once researchers understand the processes that underlie learning in these simpler nervous systems, it may become easier to discover the underpinnings of classical conditioning in more complex organisms, such as humans.

The Long-Lasting Effects of Classical Conditioning

No mention has yet been made of the principle of recency, which the British empiricists devised to explain forgetting. Although our main discussions of memory and forgetting are reserved for later chapters, it may be remarked that forgetting is not prominent in classical conditioning (Spear, 1978). CRs typically continue to occur to the CS unless a special procedure, such as extinction or counterconditioning, is administered in order to reduce responding (see below).

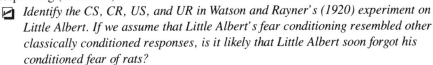 *Identify the CS, CR, US, and UR in Watson and Rayner's (1920) experiment on Little Albert. If we assume that Little Albert's fear conditioning resembled other classically conditioned responses, is it likely that Little Albert soon forgot his conditioned fear of rats?*

Generalization

After conditioning Little Albert's fear reaction to the white rat, Watson and Rayner (1920) found that Albert feared a variety of objects that were also hairy or furry. This is an example of **stimulus generalization,** which is defined as the occurrence of CRs to stimuli that generally *resemble* a previously conditioned CS. (Stimulus generalization also occurs in instrumental learning, as detailed in Chapter 4.)

Pavlov (1927/1960) witnessed the same effect when he tested his dogs with various sounds that differed from the original auditory CS. The strongest salivary responses occurred to stimuli that most closely resembled the CS, a fact that he attributed to "irradiation of energy" between parts of the brain that were activated by similar stimuli. Although Pavlov's notions of energy flow in the brain are no longer considered accurate, it is certainly true that similar stimuli usually activate areas of the brain that lie close to each other. Pavlov's basic idea, that similar stimuli produce similar patterns of brain activation, is therefore still widely accepted as an important part of the explanation of stimulus generalization.

 A digital computer will treat theatre *as a different input than* theater *(unless it is explicitly programmed to treat them the same). In contrast to the computer, people usually react similarly to both spellings of the word. On the basis of this example, do people or computers show greater stimulus generalization?*

The Importance of Timing

Strict Contiguity

Traditionally, most research on classical conditioning was concerned with the roles of contiguity, frequency of pairings, and a small number of other variables such as stimulus similarity and intensity. As noted above, research on CS similarity led to the discovery of stimulus generalization. Research on stimulus intensity revealed that moderate or intense CSs and USs are more easily conditioned than weak ones (see Gray, 1965). Both of these findings agreed very nicely with researchers' expectations that similarity and vividness would enhance conditioning. But in contrast, research on temporal contiguity led to the surprising realization that *strict* contiguity of the events is not optimal for classical conditioning after all.

If strict temporal contiguity were optimal for classical conditioning, then a CS that always starts and ends simultaneously with the US should elicit more CRs than one that is

---

separated in time from the US. In fact, however, the **simultaneous** pairings procedure is one of the *least* effective of all acquisition procedures, usually producing little if any responding to the CS.

In general, the most effective procedure for classical conditioning is a **delay** pairings procedure, in which there is a delay between the onset of the CS and the onset of the US. A crucial aspect of the delay procedure is this: Once the CS has begun, it continues until the US is presented.

Another method that commonly produces more CRs than the simultaneous procedure is the **trace** pairings procedure, in which the CS not only starts but also terminates before the onset of the US, leaving a gap in time between the two stimuli. The simultaneous, delay, and trace procedures are schematically illustrated in Figure 2–2, together with a procedure called **backward** pairings in which the CS is presented after the US.

In Figure 2–2, time proceeds from left to right. Asterisks indicate US presentations, and upward displacements of the line indicate occurrences of the CS in each of the separate procedures. The length of time measured from CS onset to US onset is called the **CS-US interval** (or interstimulus interval); its duration is traditionally designated as *positive* in the delay and trace procedures, *zero* in simultaneous procedures, and *negative* in backward procedures. Because many researchers call each occurrence of the CS a **trial,** the time between CS-US pairings is known as the **intertrial interval.**

From this figure, you can see why a strict interpretation of the contiguity principle would imply maximum conditioning in the simultaneous procedure; somewhat poorer conditioning in the delay and backward procedures, where CSs are adjacent to but not simultaneous with the US; and minimal conditioning in the trace procedure, where the CS is not even close to the US. But besides the fact that conditioning is unexpectedly weak in simultaneous procedures, and unexpectedly strong in trace procedures, another surprise is the fact that backward pairings are poor at best for excitatory conditioning. From this pattern of results, it is obvious that a strict interpretation of the contiguity principle fails to account

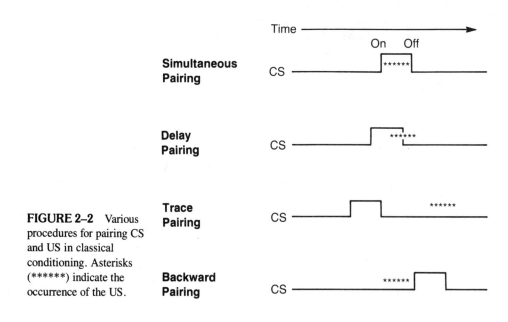

FIGURE 2–2 Various procedures for pairing CS and US in classical conditioning. Asterisks (******) indicate the occurrence of the US.

for the relative effectiveness of each procedure. A more important determinant of conditioning seems to be whether the CS comes *before* the US (as in delay and trace procedures) or not (as in simultaneous and backward procedures).

Modification of the Contiguity Principle

In most conditioning procedures, the CS and the US are presented repeatedly in cycles, so it is always possible to measure the time interval between any CS (even a backward-paired CS) and the next US. If we redefine the CS-US interval as the time from CS offset to the onset of the following US, then simultaneous and backward pairings are seen to involve the longest rather than the shortest possible intervals, and trace-paired CSs are seen to involve intervals intermediate in duration—neither as short as delay pairings nor as long as simultaneous and backward pairings. This reordering of procedures with regard to CS-US duration agrees much more closely with their relative effectiveness for excitatory conditioning, than does their ordering in terms of strict CS-US contiguity (cf. Figure 2–2).

The limited importance of strict CS-US contiguity is further demonstrated by the finding that long intertrial intervals are more effective for acquisition than short intertrial intervals (Prokasy & Whaley, 1963; Gibbon, Baldock, Locurto, Gold, & Terrace, 1977). The fact that a particular value of the CS-US interval leads to different speeds of acquisition, depending on the duration of the intertrial interval, indicates that conditioning depends on the temporal context of each pairing and not just on the pairing itself.

Acquisition thus tends to be enhanced when CSs *precede* USs rather closely, and when such pairings are separated by *long intertrial intervals*. These and other observations support the conclusion that conditioning is most rapid when the CS-US interval is brief relative to the entire time between successive US presentations (Gibbon & Balsam, 1981; Jenkins, Barnes, & Barrera, 1981). Beyond this general rule, it has been found that the optimal duration of the CS-US interval depends on a number of other factors. For instance, many skeletal motor CRs condition best when the CS-US interval is somewhat shorter than one second, whereas conditioning of visceral CRs such as heart rate is sometimes achieved only with longer intervals (e.g., VanDercar & Schneiderman, 1967). And some kinds of associations may be learned despite very long gaps in time between the CS and the US. In particular, people and some animals can acquire aversive reactions to novel tastes that are paired with sickness just once in a trace procedure, even when the CS-US interval is many minutes or hours long (e.g., Smith & Roll, 1967). Still, conditioned taste aversions are strongest when the CS-US interval is short rather than long. (Conditioned taste aversions are discussed in more detail in Chapter 5.)

Further Importance of Timing in Conditioning

There is yet a fifth procedure, not depicted in Figure 2–2, that Pavlov used to establish CRs. Called **temporal conditioning,** it is not a pairing procedure because no explicit CS is used. Instead, the US is presented alone at regular time intervals, so that time itself is the only signal associated with the US. Pavlov's dogs nevertheless learned to salivate (CR) before each food (US) presentation, thus demonstrating the effectiveness of a time interval as a CS. A similar phenomenon sometimes occurs when the CS-US interval is especially long in a delay or a trace procedure. Under those circumstances, CRs may not appear at the beginning of each CS, but may instead appear when it is almost time for the US to be presented, a phenomenon called **inhibition of delay.**

From the research summarized above, it is clear that time influences classical conditioning in many ways. The speed of acquisition depends on complex features of the temporal relationship between the CS and the US, sometimes in interaction with other variables such as the nature of the CR. Time itself can serve as a CS or as a modulator of responding to explicit CSs. Because of its ubiquity as a potential stimulus, time will be discussed again in this chapter as well as in others.

> ☑ *Events that happen only once in a great while seem to have more impact on us than events that happen all the time. How does this common observation compare to the influence of intertrial intervals on classical conditioning?*

Controlling for Nonassociative Effects

Besides establishing associations, classical conditioning procedures may also produce effects that are nonassociative in character. **Nonassociative effects** are those effects that do not depend on the temporal relationship between CS and US, but instead occur whenever the CS and/or the US have been presented, whether they were paired together or not. For example, people sometimes blink when a light or a sound (CS) is suddenly presented to them, even when they have not yet experienced pairings of that CS with a US (a puff of air to their eyes). This *false* CR, which does not depend on a specific association between the CS and the US, may merely be an exaggeration of the normal response to the CS itself, a phenomenon called *sensitization* (Grant & Norris, 1947; Groves & Thompson, 1970). Alternatively, if a recent US (air puff) has prepared the person to blink at almost any sudden stimulus, then the false CR represents a nonassociative effect called **pseudoconditioning** (Grant, 1943). In order to ensure that responding is a result of classical conditioning rather than sensitization or pseudoconditioning, researchers employ control groups (or control phases) in which the stimuli are identical to those used in conditioning but are not presented in a conditioning relationship to each other. The researchers then decide whether the paired-stimulus condition produced true conditioning, by determining whether responding to the CS in that condition exceeds responding to the CS in the control conditions.

As illustrated in Figure 2–3, repeated presentations of the CS alone have sometimes been used to control for sensitization, and repeated presentations of the US alone have been used to control for pseudoconditioning. Other common control procedures present both the CS and the US to a single control group, with the limitation that the CS and the US are not paired together in any regular way. One such procedure that has become especially popular among researchers is the **truly random control** procedure, in which the US occurs without regard to the presence of the CS (Rescorla, 1967). That is, a random CS occurs at various times, both after and before (and occasionally overlapping) the US, as shown in Figure 2–3. The advantages and disadvantages of this procedure will be discussed in relation to theoretical issues in a later section, but it may be noted here that the truly random control has become the most widely employed control procedure for assessing nonassociative effects. In general, stimuli that evoke more CRs than the random control CS are considered excitatory, whereas those that curtail CRs more than the random control CS are inhibitory.

> ☑ *Name and define two nonassociative effects that may occur during classical conditioning.*

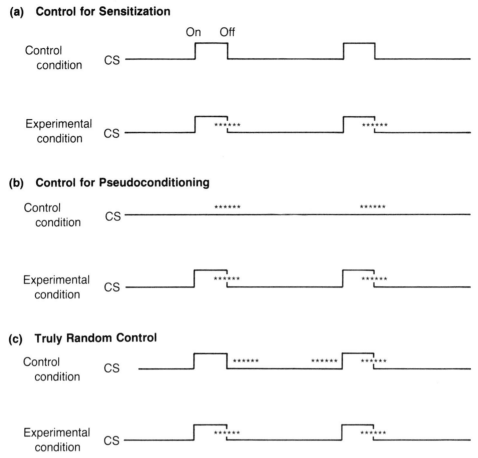

(a) Control for Sensitization

Control
condition   CS

On   Off

Experimental
condition   CS

(b) Control for Pseudoconditioning

Control
condition   CS

Experimental
condition   CS

(c) Truly Random Control

Control
condition   CS

Experimental
condition   CS

FIGURE 2–3 Control procedures for nonassociative events in classical conditioning. Asterisks (******) indicate the occurrence of the US. In each control procedure, responding to the CS in the experimental condition is compared to responding to the CS in the control condition. Greater responding in the experimental condition indicates a true associative effect resulting from the temporal relationship between CS and US, beyond any nonassociative responding exhibited by the control group. (a) Control for sensitization involves presenting the CS alone. (b) Control for pseudoconditioning involves presenting the US alone. (c) The truly random control involves presenting the stimuli without regard to the temporal relationship between US and CS.

CSs that Signal Other CSs

Higher-Order Conditioning

Pavlov believed that classical conditioning theory would ultimately provide an explanation for all learning, not just for **first-order conditioning**—that is, conditioning via pairings directly with the US. One way he expanded the scope of his theory was to investigate mediated conditioning, that is, learning that occurs when one CS is paired with another CS instead of directly with the US (cf. Rizley & Rescorla, 1972).

In one such procedure, called *higher-order conditioning,* a neutral stimulus (CS$_2$) is paired together with another stimulus (CS$_1$) that had already been made excitatory via association with food. Although CS_2 was itself never paired with food, Pavlov's dogs responded to CS_2 after it was paired with an excitatory CS_1. Pavlov interpreted the emergence of CRs to CS_2 as proof that a previously conditioned CS_1 can effectively substitute for the US in an acquisition procedure.

For example, suppose that salivation has first been conditioned to a bell CS_1, via pairings with food as the US (Figure 2–4a). The salivary response can now be conditioned to a light CS_2, by pairing it with CS_1 alone. This demonstration shows how new conditioned reflexes can be established indirectly on the basis of previously conditioned reflexes, as well as directly on the basis of the unconditioned reflex.

Sensory Preconditioning

A second procedure for achieving mediated conditioning is **sensory preconditioning.** The order of steps in sensory preconditioning is reversed from higher-order conditioning, insofar as subjects experience pairings of CS_2 and CS_1 first, before either of these stimuli has been associated with the US (Figure 2–4b). During the first phase, when CS_2 is paired with CS_1, CRs are not observed. But after subjects have supposedly learned the CS_2-CS_1 association, CS_1 is then paired with a US (such as food) in order to condition responding to it. Once responding has been conditioned to CS_1, CS_2 may be tested to determine whether it also elicits CRs by virtue of its prior association with CS_1. Responding to CS_2 during this final test phase is interpreted as evidence that the subject previously associated the CSs, while they were still neutral.

Second Signal System

Related to the idea of higher-order conditioning is Pavlov's claim that human language is a **second signal system**—that is, a system of stimuli that supplements the other (environmental and internal) signals we rely on. People who have acquired a language carry inside themselves a large number of stimuli that we call words—stimuli that can guide their own actions and those of other people.

Pavlov believed that language-based learning follows the same rules as conditioned reflexes, and that we are fundamentally similar to animals despite our unique capacity for human language. From this perspective, a word is a kind of CS that acquires its meaning

FIGURE 2–4 Procedures for conditioning one CS via another one. (a) Higher-order conditioning: CS_1 is first paired with the US and comes to elicit the conditioned response. A new stimulus, CS_2, is then paired with CS_1 and also comes to elicit the CR. (b) Sensory preconditioning: CS_2 is first paired with CS_1 without an unconditioned stimulus in the situation. CS_1 is then paired with a US and comes to elicit a CR. Subsequently, CS_2 is also found to elicit the CR, even though it was never paired with the US.

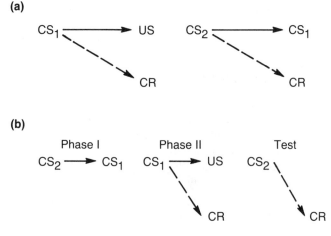

through association with things (e.g., "chair" → a real chair) or through association with other words. This analysis suggests that learning that is mediated by language may be a special instance of higher-order conditioning or sensory preconditioning or both, since we may hear a sequence of words many times before learning what the words mean (cf. sensory preconditioning) or we may learn the meaning of one word from the way it is combined with already meaningful ones (cf. higher-order conditioning).

✏️ *In an example of higher-order conditioning, Jane first learned to like (CR) British accents (CS$_1$) by hearing British performers on television (the US). She then learned to like a particular brand of blue jeans (CS$_2$) because they were advertised on television by an actress with a British accent (CS$_1$). Explain why Jane's attraction to the blue jeans is an example of higher-order rather than first-order conditioning.*

What Events Are Associated?

Theories of classical conditioning may be distinguished according to the answer they give to the question: What is learned in classical conditioning? In general, each theorist has tended to answer this question in one of two ways—either responses or stimuli. Stimulus-response (S-R) theories argue that the event that is associated with the CS is a response of one kind or another, whereas stimulus-stimulus (S-S) theories maintain that the crucial association is between the CS and another stimulus (the US or, in sensory preconditioning, another CS). Although Pavlov's theory was of the S-S variety, most North American theorists favored S-R explanations until recently, when cognitive versions of S-S theory began to gain considerable empirical support.

Traditional S-S Theory

According to Pavlov's version of S-S theory, acquisition procedures establish a connection between CS events and US events in the brain, such that activation of the CS center triggers the US center as well. This characterization of associative learning has been dubbed **stimulus substitution theory,** because it suggests that one stimulus (the CS) acquires the functions of another (the US), including the latter's ability to elicit a response. The CR is thus presumed to be virtually identical to the UR, except that it is activated indirectly by means of the CS-US association instead of directly by the US. CR-UR similarity was indeed evident in Pavlov's salivary conditioning of dogs and in Watson and Rayner's fear conditioning of Little Albert, both described earlier. An especially striking example of such similarity was observed in experiments on **autoshaping** by Jenkins and Moore (1973).

In order to autoshape a pigeon's peck response, a key (translucent disk on the chamber wall) is illuminated for several seconds before food (or water) is delivered as the US (Brown & Jenkins, 1968). As in other classical conditioning procedures, no response to the CS is required in order to obtain the US; that is, the US is always presented after the CS, regardless of what the pigeon does. Thus autoshaping is a classical acquisition procedure in which the UR is a movement of the bird's beak to consume grain or water, and the CR is a beak movement that contacts a response key (Gamzu & Williams, 1971).[2] Jenkins and Moore's pigeons learned to peck the keylight CS after a number of pairings with one (or both) of the USs, and the form of their CRs was recorded by means of high-speed photography and other methods. Photographs that were taken when the keylight signaled an impending delivery of food showed the birds pecking with open beaks, in a way that closely resembled pecking at actual grain. In contrast, photographs of pecking at signals for water showed beak movements that closely resembled drinking. This high degree of similarity between CRs and URs agrees well with the stimulus substitution account of classical conditioning.

However, some investigators have reported considerable differences between CRs and URs. For example, Timberlake and Grant (1975) used the appearance of another rat as a CS to signal the imminent delivery of food as a US. Instead of behavior resembling the UR (eating), social behavior such as sniffing and grooming was conditioned. Wasserman (1973; Wasserman, Hunter, Gutowski, & Bader, 1975) used a conventional keylight as a signal to chicks in an autoshaping procedure but, in lieu of food or water as the US, he briefly turned on a heat lamp in the cold experimental chamber immediately after the CS. Although pecking and snuggling were not part of the UR to heat, they quickly emerged as prominent aspects of the CR to the keylight. Wasserman and colleagues (1975) noted that these responses are part of the supplication behavior that chicks naturally direct toward the mother hen when they need her to brood them against the cold (cf. also Jenkins, Barrera, Ireland, & Woodside, 1978). Thus both these examples appear to lack the simple identity of CR and UR that is predicted by stimulus-substitution theory (cf. Holland, 1977).

S-R Theories

Among the alternatives to stimulus substitution theory are a variety of **stimulus-response theories,** which in one way or another focus on the conditioned response as a direct participant in the associative process. Guthrie's (1935) early S-R theory is less relevant to classical conditioning than to the history of instrumental conditioning theory, so it is sufficient here to note that he attempted to explain all conditioning on the basis of sheer temporal contiguity between stimuli and responses. That is to say, he believed that any response that accompanies a stimulus will become connected to that stimulus; hence, in his view, the CR is nothing more or less than a UR that has become connected directly to the CS because they occurred close together. This account obviously is contradicted by evidence, cited above, that the CR and the UR may differ considerably from each other.

In contrast to Guthrie's approach, some S-R theories characterize the CR as a response that somehow prepares the subject for the impending receipt of the US. For instance, Siegel (1976) has proposed a model that explains the development of tolerance to opiate drugs in terms of compensatory CRs, which serve to counteract the original pain-killing effect (UR) of those drugs. **Drug tolerance,** which is a diminished responsiveness to drugs such as morphine and heroin, develops as a consequence of repeated use of those drugs. Siegel (1976) showed that morphine loses its analgesic (pain-reducing) effects in rats after a number of administrations, but only if the rats' sensitivity to pain is tested in the *same environment* where they received the drug on previous occasions. Thus environmental (and other drug-related) stimuli function as CSs, evoking CRs that antagonize the analgesic UR and thereby produce tolerance (Eikelboom & Stewart, 1982).

This counteraction of the drug's effects helps to stabilize the internal body state, which may in general be an adaptive biological strategy. But not all CRs to drugs are compensatory. For example, the hormone insulin can depress behavior and cause convulsions (URs), and CSs that become associated with insulin do the same (Siegel, 1975). Currently there is no general rule for predicting which CRs will be compensatory and which will not. Consequently, it is difficult to accept the argument that conditioning establishes an association between the CS and CRs that serve a stabilizing function for the organism.

Other investigators have evaluated the claim of certain S-R theorists (Hull, 1943; Perkins, 1968) that CRs are responses that maximize the benefit (or minimize the damage) from the impending US. Most of these evaluations have either directly measured the adaptiveness of the CR, or altered the consequences of particular CRs in a classical conditioning procedure. If CRs are associated with the CS because they maximize benefits and minimize costs, then CRs that increase the aversiveness of a painful US or decrease the likelihood of a desirable US would not be expected to persist. In fact, however, CRs still occurred in many of these studies, even though they were clearly maladaptive in terms of their short-term consequences, as described below.

One common way of examining the issue of CR adaptiveness is by means of the **omission procedure,** in which a food or water US is withheld if a CR occurs; that is, the US is presented after the CS only if *no* CR was observed. In effect, this procedure punishes the subject for CRs, by preventing the delivery of a desirable US that would have otherwise been presented after the CS. Despite the consequent loss of valuable USs, persistent conditioned responding has been observed in many omission studies, including some on salivation in dogs (Sheffield, 1965), rearing in rats (Holland, 1979), and approach to a visual CS in pigeons (Peden, Browne, & Hearst, 1977). This persistence of CRs in the face of repeated US omission demonstrates the importance of determinants other than short-term adaptiveness of the CR. To be sure, omission-trained subjects usually do respond somewhat less than subjects whose food or water occurs independently of their CRs. But the fact that omission subjects continue to respond at all, in the face of such costs, indicates that other factors outweigh immediate response outcomes as determinants of classical conditioning.

Researchers have also evaluated the adaptiveness of inferred CRs preceding an aversive US by training rats to rate the perceived aversiveness of shocks (Miller, Greco, Vigorito, & Marlin, 1983; cf. Arabian & Desiderato, 1975). The rats in these experiments were first rewarded with water for pressing one lever after weak shocks and another lever after stronger shocks (instrumental conditioning). Later in the experiments, the subjects were required to press the levers after shocks of various intensities, with some of those shocks being preceded by CSs and some not. The rats consistently rated shocks that were signaled by a CS to be more intense than equally strong shocks that were not signaled. This fact, that CS-US trials were actually *more* aversive and not less aversive than US-only trials, suggests that CRs did not help to alleviate the painful effects of the US. (Paradoxically, the rats nevertheless preferred signaled shocks over unsignaled shocks—a finding that will be discussed in the following chapter.) Thus research employing the omission procedure and research investigating the aversiveness of signaled versus unsignaled shocks agree in their implication, that the immediate consequences of responding are not responsible for the emergence and continued occurrence of CRs.[3]

A final way in which investigators have attempted to demonstrate an essential role for the CR, as ascribed to it by S-R theories, is through devaluation of the US. **Devaluation** is a procedure for reducing the UR, for example by satiating the subject's hunger in order to eliminate the salivary response to food (US). If classical conditioning truly establishes a direct association between the CS and the CR, then altering the value of the US after conditioning should leave the CR unaffected. In fact, however, devaluing the US undermines responding that had previously been conditioned through association with that US (Holland & Straub, 1979). Similar reductions in conditioned responding have been obtained in studies of sensory preconditioning and some studies of higher-order conditioning, when the

CS that mediated the association was devalued before testing the target CS (Rizley & Rescorla, 1972; Rashotte, Griffin, & Sisk, 1977; Nairne & Rescorla, 1981). The bulk of the findings in this area therefore contradict the prediction of S-R theories, that CRs would continue to occur after devaluation. In summary, research on devaluation after conditioning, as well as on the short-term adaptiveness of CRs, has provided little support for S-R theories of classical conditioning.

New S-S Theories

In contrast to the stimulus substitution and S-R accounts of classical conditioning, **cognitive S-S theories** describe associations as involving complex expectations or memory representations (Tolman, 1932; Lashley, 1963; Kamin, 1969). CRs are generally viewed by cognitive theorists as expressions of the subject's expectations. This account of conditioned responding as an indirect expression of underlying mental representations is compatible with the varied nature of CRs mentioned above—that is, CRs sometimes resemble the UR, as in autoshaping with food and water USs; sometimes antagonize the UR, as in conditioned drug tolerance; and sometimes relate to the US in other natural ways, as in chicks snuggling a keylight that precedes heat.

Flexibility of the cognitive account regarding CRs is, however, a reflection of weakness as well as strength. Although cognitive theories are often quite precise about the presumed processes that underlie learning, they have commonly failed to provide **production rules** that specify exactly how cognitive processes might produce observable performance (Wasserman, 1981). This vagueness about the production of responses permits cognitive theories to accommodate a wide variety of findings about the form of the CR, but it also makes cognitive theories difficult to evaluate through empirical tests of predictions.

Before closing this section, let us briefly examine the rationale behind the claim that classical conditioning establishes an expectation or an association between the mental representations of stimuli. The unique advantage of this cognitive approach is well illustrated by certain studies of higher-order conditioning and sensory preconditioning, where a CS successfully mediated conditioning of particular CRs without ever evoking such CRs itself (e.g., Rashotte, Griffin, & Sisk, 1977; Holland, 1981). In one such experiment, Nairne and Rescorla (1981) first paired a tone CS_1 with a food US for hungry pigeons. According to a cognitive analysis of this procedure, the pigeons would presumably learn to expect food during CS_1 in this phase of the experiment. Although pigeons usually peck at localized *lights* associated with food (autoshaping), the tone CS_1 did not elicit pecking as a CR. Subjects then received higher-order pairings of a keylight CS_2 with the tone CS_1. Despite the fact that the tone itself did not elicit pecking as a CR, subjects learned to peck the light CS_2 that was paired with the tone.

Cognitive S-S theories focus exclusively on memories and expectations and not on behavior as such, so they have no difficulty with the fact that higher-order conditioning does not depend on responding to CS_1. From a cognitive perspective, CS_1 evokes the memory of food, thereby making that mental representation available for association with CS_2 during the second phase of the experiment. But such instances of higher-order conditioning defy explanation in terms of stimulus substitution, which maintains that CS_1 must first acquire the ability to activate the US center (and hence the response) before it can function as a substitute for the US in higher-order conditioning. The same findings challenge S-R theories by showing that conditioning can occur even though CS_2 is never followed directly by the UR.

The notion that expectations or memory representations are learned in classical conditioning has received considerable attention in recent years. A number of cognitive S-S theories have been developed, some of which will be discussed in greater detail later in this chapter.

 Use the case of Little Albert's fear conditioning (described in previous sections) to illustrate each of the three perspectives described above. In particular, identify the stimulus events (CS and US) that are supposedly associated according to stimulus substitution theory, the stimulus (CS) and response (CR) events associated according to S-R theories, and the expectation that is learned according to cognitive S-S theories.

Extinction and Counterconditioning

It was Pavlov's belief that conditioned reflexes are relatively permanent. This conclusion is supported by the fact that conditioned reflexes are fairly resistant to forgetting; that is, they may remain strong despite the passage of time. Even more compelling is the fact that responding to the CS often reemerges after treatments that were designed to eliminate it. One important treatment of this kind is the **extinction procedure,** which involves presentations of the CS alone after conditioning. For example Figure 2–5 depicts how food affected a dog that previously had been allowed to eat the food but on these four trials was only allowed to see it (Pavlov, 1927/1960). The sight of the food was thus a CS that had previously been followed by taste (US) and salivation (UR), and so a considerable amount of conditioned salivation (CR) occurred on the first extinction trial. But the dog drooled somewhat less when it saw the food 10 minutes later, and not at all when it saw the food the third time, after another 10 minutes. Because CRs appear to extinguish (burn out) when subjects are exposed to the CS without the US, both the procedure itself and the decline in responding are called *extinction.*

Notice, however, that the CS later elicited additional CRs when it was finally presented again after an especially long delay. This resurgence of responding to the CS after a period of rest without any further conditioning is called **spontaneous recovery.** A related form of recovery is **disinhibition,** which depends neither on further conditioning nor on resting, but instead occurs when a surprising sound or other stimulus is suddenly presented during the

FIGURE 2–5
Extinction of the CR with repeated presentations of the CS following conditioning. The resurgence of responding on Trial 4 following a rest period with no further conditioning illustrates the phenomenon of spontaneous recovery. (Based on data from Pavlov, 1927, p. 58.)

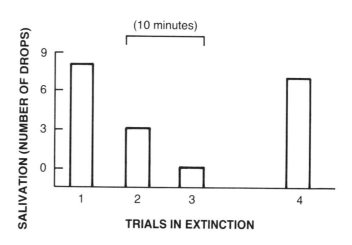

extinction procedure. Disinhibition and spontaneous recovery of the CR are two phenomena that Pavlov cited as evidence that the CS-US association continues to exist, even after conditioned responding has ceased.

Spontaneous recovery and disinhibition are also characteristic of **habituation,** which refers to a decline in a UR as a consequence of repeated elicitation by a US (Groves & Thompson, 1970). (In the literature on habituation, disinhibition is usually called dishabituation.) For example, people usually jump when a door slams in the breeze for the first time. But it this keeps happening again and again, they may get so accustomed to the sound that they hardly notice it any more. Repeated elicitation of the unconditioned startle reflex thus leads to its habituation.

Some instances of habituation share many characteristics with familiar forms of learning (Davis, 1970; Thompson & Spencer, 1966); indeed, habituation has been characterized as ''learning to ignore'' the repeated stimulus. Extinction and habituation thus have much in common. The most important difference between them is that extinction is a decline in the apparent strength of a *conditioned* reflex, when the CS is repeated in the absence of the US; whereas habituation is a decline in the strength of an *unconditioned* reflex, when a US is itself presented repeatedly. No one has to teach you to jump when a door slams—it is an unconditioned reflex, and so its decline is an example of habituation rather than extinction.

The extinction procedure is sometimes used as a therapy to alleviate maladaptive fears, called **phobias.** The irrational, exaggerated fear that constitutes a phobia may have originally been learned through classical conditioning (Watson & Rayner, 1920; Seligman, 1971; also see Chapter 5 of this text). In that case, the feared situation is essentially a CS that has already been conditioned to elicit fear as the CR. When used as a therapy, extinction is often called *flooding* or **implosive therapy.** Psychotherapists who use implosive therapy usually accompany the phobic client to the fearsome situation (the CS), giving assurances that nothing terrible will happen (no US). After experiencing the situation in this way without negative consequences, the client may become less fearful (extinction of the CR). But clients may refuse to continue such an unpleasant treatment until the CR extinguishes.

The fact that extinction is susceptible to spontaneous recovery and disinhibition convinced Pavlov that the extinction procedure creates inhibition, which prevents the occurrence of the CR but does not actually weaken the CS-US association. Most researchers now agree that extinction involves learning something new in addition to the original conditioning, rather than ''unlearning'' the original conditioning. But Pavlov's assumption that inhibition is necessarily transient and unstable has received only meager support (Rescorla, 1969; 1979).

Two other procedures for eliminating CRs are collectively termed **counterconditioning,** which involves the conditioning of a new CR that is contrary in nature to the original CR. One form of counterconditioning, **aversion therapy,** establishes negative emotional reactions in the place of positive ones. For instance, an abused drug or alcohol (CS) might be paired together with an emetic (a US that induces vomiting, the UR) in order to help someone learn to hate the abused substance (Callner, 1975). In contrast, **systematic desensitization** is often described as a form of counterconditioning that establishes positive CRs (or relaxation) in the place of negative ones, such as fear (Wolpe, 1958).

It is customary for clients undergoing systematic desensitization to construct a hierarchy of fears, or **anxiety hierarchy;** that is, a list of feared situations, ranked from the least to the most feared, that can subsequently serve as CSs in a modified version of classical conditioning. In addition to constructing the anxiety hierarchy, the client learns to relax deeply upon request (the "opposite" of fear, used instead of an actual US such as a tranquilizing drug). Once these preparations are complete, the therapist introduces the client to the least feared situation in the hierarchy, or (more commonly) just helps the client to imagine it vividly. At the same time, the client is asked to relax (cf. US → UR) in order to antagonize the fear CR and establish a new CR (relaxation) in its place. Once the client has learned to relax in response to the first CS, desensitization training proceeds with a slightly more fearsome CS. Eventually, relaxation becomes the predominant response to each of the previously feared situations (CS → new CR).

The earliest study of systematic desensitization concerned a 2-year-old boy named Peter, who feared rabbits intensely. Over a period of several weeks, Mary Cover Jones (1924) conditioned Peter's positive emotional reaction (CR) by pairing a rabbit (CS) with a US that she knew would evoke a positive emotion (candy US → positive UR). The rabbit was first shown to Peter from a distance, so the child would not become too afraid and stop eating. During subsequent sessions of desensitization, Jones "faded in" the more fearsome levels of the anxiety hierarchy by bringing the rabbit closer and closer until finally Peter touched the animal without fear (new CR to CS).

Although systematic desensitization is indisputably effective for reducing fears, at least in adults (Berman, Miller, & Massman, 1985; Graziano, DeGiovanni, & Garcia, 1979), there is some doubt whether its success is attributable to the direct conditioning of relaxation to feared stimuli (Wilson & Davison, 1971). An alternative possibility is that relaxation enhances the mental imagery commonly employed as the CS for fear, thereby facilitating extinction of the fear response (Levin & Gross, 1985).

 Most clients who receive therapy for phobias would prefer to undergo systematic desensitization rather than implosive therapy, because desensitization does not require them to confront highly feared situations at the beginning of therapy. Describe the relevant features of systematic desensitization as it is usually applied, including construction of the anxiety hierarchy, relaxation training, and progress through the hierarchy.

INHIBITION

Standard Procedures

Pavlov believed that the extinction of responding to excitatory CSs is a consequence of inhibition. This explanation of extinction continues to receive attention by researchers (e.g., Soltysik, 1985). But excitatory CSs whose CRs have been extinguished are importantly different from CSs that have become inhibitory amidst a context of continued excitatory conditioning. In the latter procedures, the US continues to be presented, but the inhibitory CS coincides with the *absence* of the US. This section will focus on one such procedure for conditioning inhibition, and on some of the ways in which conditioned inhibition differs from the outcome of other procedures such as extinction and latent inhibition.

The standard procedure for establishing conditioned inhibition involves a mixture of two kinds of trial. On what we shall call A+ trials, a single CS (designated "A") is paired with the US (indicated by the "+"). On AB– trials, the A stimulus is presented in combination with another CS (designated "B"), and this stimulus compound is *not* paired with the US (as indicated by "–"). Thus the **standard inhibitory conditioning** procedure

---

is one in which the AB combination coincides with the absence of the US, in contrast to pairings of A with the US on other trials (see Figure 2–6a). In a sense, stimulus B is analogous to the word *not* in "This restaurant will *not* be open next Thursday." Although we might otherwise expect to eat there on Thursdays, our expectation is temporarily suspended by *not*.

In one important way, however, the word *not* is *un*like most conditioned inhibitors: Only the word can be meaningfully combined with a wide variety of other stimuli (words) in order to negate various expectations. In contrast, conditioned inhibitors are US-specific; that is, they inhibit CRs solely to CSs that are associated with the same US used during inhibitory conditioning (Grossen, Kostansek, & Bolles, 1969; Weisman & Litner, 1969). For example, a CS that was conditioned to inhibit salivation on the basis of a food US would not also function as a conditioned inhibitor for fear (based on a different US). Stimuli that inhibit excitation in ways that are not specific to the US may be presumed to involve processes other than conditioned inhibition (Rescorla, 1969).

Transfer Tests of Inhibition and Latent Inhibition

Two procedures have conventionally been used for assessing the inhibitory power of CSs (Table 2–1). In a **summation test,** the suspected inhibitor is presented simultaneously with a known excitatory CS in order to determine whether the combined stimuli elicit less

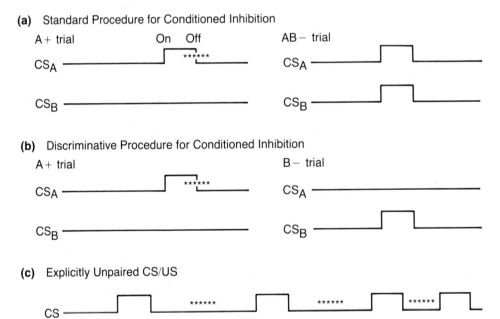

(a) Standard Procedure for Conditioned Inhibition

A+ trial   On   Off   AB− trial

CS$_A$

CS$_B$

(b) Discriminative Procedure for Conditioned Inhibition

A+ trial   B− trial

CS$_A$

CS$_B$

(c) Explicitly Unpaired CS/US

CS

FIGURE 2–6 Procedures for conditioned inhibition. Asterisks (******) indicate the presentation of the US. (a) In the standard inhibitory procedure, there are two kinds of trial: On A+ trials, the CS$_A$ is paired with the US; on AB− trials, CS$_A$ is presented in combination with CS$_B$, and this stimulus compound is not paired with the US. (b) In the discriminative procedure, there are also two kinds of trial: A+ trials are the same as in the standard procedure; on B− trials, CS$_B$ is presented alone. (c) In the explicitly unpaired CS-US procedure shown, the CS occurs in the middle of the interval between US presentations.

TABLE 2–1 Transfer Tests of Inhibition

	Phase 1	Phase 2	Phase 3
Summation Test			
Experimental Group:	Inhibitory conditioning of stimulus A	Excitatory conditioning of stimulus B	Simultaneous presentation of A and B
Control Group:		Excitatory conditioning of stimulus B	Simultaneous presentation of A and B
		In Phase 3, does A detract from responding to B in Experimental Group more than in Control Group?	
Retardation Test			
Experimental Group:	Inhibitory conditioning of stimulus A	Excitatory conditioning of stimulus A	Does Experimental Group acquire CRs slower than Control Group in Phase 2?
Control Group:		Excitatory conditioning of stimulus A	

responding than the excitatory CS does alone. Reduced responding to the excitatory CS in the presence of the suspected inhibitor is evidence of inhibition. In a **retardation test,** also called "resistance to reinforcement," the suspected inhibitory CS is paired with the US in order to determine whether excitatory conditioning is impaired; that is, whether the suspected inhibitor acquires excitation more slowly than a neutral CS that is paired with the US. The B stimulus of the standard inhibitory conditioning procedure routinely exhibits inhibitory properties in both retardation and summation tests. In other words, the effects of inhibitory conditioning *transfer* (carry over) to produce diminished responding in the summation test and impaired acquisition in the retardation test, hence the term *transfer tests.*

One difficulty that must be considered in using the summation test is the possibility of **stimulus generalization decrement,** which means simply that responding is stronger to stimuli that closely resemble the original excitatory stimulus and weaker to stimuli that resemble it less. The concern, therefore, is this: The addition of any stimulus that was not present during excitatory training makes the test situation less like the training situation, so responding may decline anyway, regardless of whether the added stimulus is truly inhibitory. This makes it difficult to tell whether reduced responding in the summation test represents actual inhibition, or whether it merely indicates that the excitatory stimulus does not seem the same any more when it is combined with the other stimulus.

The retardation test is not susceptible to stimulus generalization decrement in the same way that the summation test is, because it does not require that the target stimulus be combined with an excitatory stimulus. On the other hand, a retardation test is vulnerable to the influence of factors that would not affect a summation test. One such concern for retardation tests is latent inhibition.

In **latent inhibition,** acquisition is retarded because subjects are exposed to the CS alone before conditioning (Lubow, 1973). This retardation should not be interpreted as evidence of actual conditioned inhibition for several reasons. First, because the CS is not presented in relation to any particular US during pretraining, the effects of CS preexposure could not be US-specific, as true conditioned inhibitors are. Second, latent-inhibitory stimuli do not negate the effects of excitatory CSs in summation tests (Rescorla, 1971; Reiss & Wagner, 1972). Finally, latent inhibition training retards subsequent inhibitory as well as excitatory conditioning (Halgren, 1974). If CS-alone pretraining truly made the CS inhibitory, the subsequent inhibitory training would presumably be facilitated rather than retarded. Latent inhibition also occurs in instrumental learning, so it will be discussed again in the next chapter.

Based on the above considerations, researchers consider a combination of retardation and summation tests to be the best method for distinguishing conditioned inhibition from other phenomena, including stimulus generalization decrement and latent inhibition. CSs that have become excitatory and then have undergone extinction do not suppress responding to excitatory CSs in a summation test, nor do they acquire excitation especially slowly in a retardation test. In fact, previously conditioned and then extinguished CSs recondition *more rapidly* than novel (unfamiliar) CSs when they are subsequently paired with the US in a retardation test. Thus extinguished excitatory CSs fail to satisfy the conventional criteria for conditioned inhibition.

Invulnerability to Extinction

Once inhibition has been conditioned to B, repeated presentations of B alone (B– trials) do not serve to extinguish its inhibitory power in the same way that A– trials extinguish A's excitatory power. On the contrary, such attempts to extinguish inhibition may actually enhance the inhibition instead of weakening it (Rescorla, 1982; DeVito & Fowler, 1986). In its invulnerability to extinction, therefore, inhibitory conditioning differs notably from simple excitatory conditioning. But the conditioned inhibition of stimulus B can be eliminated by pairing it with the US, either alone or in combination with A (B+ trials or AB+ trials)—that is, by explicitly contradicting its association with "no US" (Zimmer-Hart & Rescorla, 1974; cf. Witcher & Ayres, 1984).

In a standard inhibitory procedure, a child is shown a glimpse of a funny videotape every time a yellow light (A) comes on, unless a tone (B) comes on at the same time. Assuming that the child learns to smile (CR) only when the light occurs alone, how might inhibition be exhibited in these subsequent transfer tests? (1) Summation test—the tone is sounded during a green light that has already been associated with the videotape. (2) Retardation test—the tone replaces the light as a signal that the videotape is about to be shown.

Other Inhibitory Procedures

The standard inhibitory conditioning procedure is only one of several procedures that may result in conditioned inhibition. In fact, even the trace pairings and backward pairings procedures, which were previously discussed in connection with excitatory acquisition, produce inhibitory conditioning under certain circumstances.

Discriminative Conditioning

A procedure that closely resembles standard inhibitory conditioning in some ways is the **discriminative conditioning** procedure (also called "stimulus differentiation"). As in the standard case, stimulus A occurs in a paired relationship with the US (A + trials) and B does not. In contrast to the standard inhibitory procedure, however, the B stimulus in discriminative conditioning occurs alone (B–) rather than in combination with A (see Figure 2–6b). The A stimulus nevertheless becomes excitatory while B becomes inhibitory, as in the standard procedure (e.g., Hinson & Siegel, 1986). Notice that both procedures share this feature: The inhibitory CS is a signal for the absence of the US, rather than for its presence. When the US is an aversive stimulus, the CS is sometimes called a "safety signal" because it guarantees that the US will not occur.

CS and US Explictly Unpaired

As already noted in previous sections, one important determinant of excitatory conditioning is the timing of CS presentations in relation to US presentations: Acquisition is most rapid when the CS-US interval is brief in comparison to the entire time between successive US presentations. Timing of CS presentations is also important with regard to inhibitory conditioning, insofar as CSs that occur *relatively early* in interval between USs may become inhibitory (Siegel & Domjan, 1971; Hinson & Siegel, 1980; Wagner & Larew, 1985). Just as in the case of conditioned excitation, the crucial variable is the duration of the CS-US interval *in proportion to the entire time* between successive US presentations (Kaplan, 1984). In summary, whenever the waiting time from the CS to the next US is brief in comparison to the overall wait between USs, excitatory conditioning occurs; but whenever the waiting time from CS to US is relatively long, inhibitory conditioning occurs. In the latter case, as in standard inhibitory and discriminative conditioning, the CS is more a signal for the absence of the US than for its presence.

The fact that relatively long CS-US intervals produce inhibition means that **explicitly unpaired CS/US** presentations may be an inappropriate choice, if what one needs is a "neutral" control procedure for assessing nonassociative effects (Rescorla, 1967). In the unpaired CS/US procedure, CSs are customarily presented in the middle of the interval between US presentations (see Figure 2–6c). Because this makes excitatory conditioning unlikely, researchers once assumed that the CS remains neutral in this procedure, and so could serve as a useful reference for comparison to other stimuli. But rather than providing a no-conditioning control, explicitly unpaired CSs may actually be inhibitory, and consequently may make neutral stimuli appear excitatory by comparison. For this reason, the truly random control procedure, discussed above, is sometimes preferred to control for nonassociative effects without producing either conditioned excitation or inhibition.

Opponent Process Theory of Backward-Conditioned Inhibition

Among the theories that relate to inhibitory conditioning in backward-pairing procedures is the opponent process theory of motivation (Solomon & Corbit, 1974). Opponent process theory has been used to explain a wide variety of emotional effects, including the waning of romantic love and the exhilaration that skydivers experience after they have become veteran jumpers.

According to this theory, emotional URs such as joy and fear automatically elicit compensatory processes, which become stronger and last longer after each successive elicitation (as illustrated in Figure 2–7a and b). One consequence of this model is the prediction that USs that initially are highly motivating will seem less so if we experience them often, because their "opponent" processes will become progressively stronger and cancel out the original motivation. This prediction agrees well with common experience, as when romantic passion eventually gives way to more sedate feelings in a love relationship.

Another consequence of the model is this: The removal of an accustomed US will reveal the opponent process at its full strength, as when the same ''jaded'' lovers become separated and suddenly find that they miss each other more than they could have imagined (right side of Figure 2–7b). The depression they experience at that time may be none other than the same compensatory process that subtracted from their passion while they were still together (Solomon & Corbit, 1974).

Likewise, the fear of jumping in a parachute may become weaker and weaker with each jump (just like the passion of the lovers). And after landing safely, parachutists experience the opposite of their fear—an elation and sense of power that makes parachute jumping almost addictive for some people. As in the case of the lovers, the slowly developing opponent process supposedly cancels out the original emotion and then lingers afterwards to reveal itself when the eliciting stimulus ends. This pattern of declining emotion, followed by its opposite, is the hallmark of opponent processes (Solomon & Corbit, 1974).

According to opponent process theory, CSs that follow the US in a backward pairing procedure happen to coincide with the lingering aftereffects of the opponent process. What should we expect to happen if the opponent process functions as a US that is opposite from

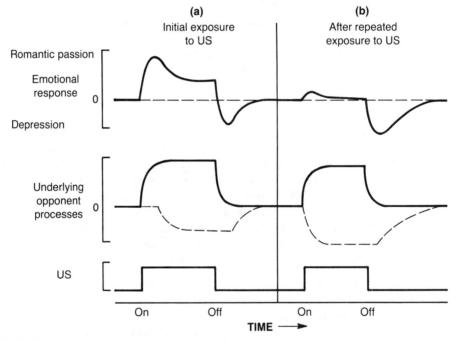

FIGURE 2–7 An opponent-process mechanism produces a change in emotional responses with repeated exposure to a US. (a) The positive emotional response is sustained during initial encounters and is followed by only weak disappointment at separation. The opponent process shown by the dashed line in the second row thus has little impact in the beginning. (b) After repeated encounters, the positive emotional response is largely cancelled by the opponent process, and separation leads to considerably more depression than after initial encounters. The opponent process is masked in the presence of the eliciting stimulus but becomes manifest after the stimulus departs.

Source: R. L. Solomon & J. D. Corbit (1974). An opponent-process theory of motivation: I. Temporal dynamics of affect. *Psychological Review, 81,* 128. Copyright 1974 by the American Psychological Association. Adapted by permission.

the nominal US? Presumably, stimuli that follow in the wake of the nominal US would acquire conditioned properties that are somehow opposite those of the US and opposite those of delay-paired CSs as well. As you might suspect, CSs that become associated with opposite USs—such as food versus shock—may function as inhibitors of responding to each other (Dickinson & Dearing, 1979). And as predicted, CSs that occur soon after the US may acquire the ability to inhibit responding to delay-paired CSs, through association with the opponent process (Schull, 1979; Shurtleff & Ayres, 1981).

> *The standard inhibitory procedure typically produces stronger conditioned inhibition than other procedures do. Examine each of the procedures to discover what is unique about the way the inhibitory CS is presented in standard inhibitory conditioning.*

Is Inhibition a "Slave" to Excitation?

Symmetry of Inhibition and Excitation

The foregoing suggestion, that inhibition and excitation may involve the conditioning of symmetrically opposite associations, forms the basis of several accounts of inhibitory conditioning (e.g., Wolpe, 1958; Konorski, 1967; Rescorla, 1967; Pearce & Hall, 1980). Essentially, this approach regards inhibitory conditioning as a kind of counterconditioning (a previously discussed method for eliminating maladaptive CRs).

The symmetrical view of inhibition and excitation is supported by evidence that some inhibitory CSs elicit overt CRs that are opposite in direction from excitatory CRs. For example, Wasserman, Franklin, and Hearst (1974) recorded approach and withdrawal behavior, which they called *sign-tracking*. They found that pigeons in a discriminative conditioning procedure approached CSs paired with food but withdrew from CSs that coincided with the absence of food, which is exactly the pattern of responses that would be expected according to the symmetrical view.

The assumption of symmetrically opposite responses to inhibitory and excitatory CSs provides a ready explanation for the results of conventional transfer tests of inhibition. In the summation test, the addition of an inhibitory stimulus presumably reduces responding to the excitatory stimulus because the inhibitory tendency competes in some way with the excitatory tendency. In the retardation test, the inhibitory stimulus already controls a tendency that is somehow the opposite of excitation, so it is reasonable to expect that it would require excessive excitatory training to overcome that tendency.

Hammond (1966) also studied the effects of discriminative CSs, but she employed the conditioned emotional response rather than sign-tracking. The **conditioned emotional response (CER)** is a disruption of ongoing behavior, that occurs during a CS that elicits fear (Estes & Skinner, 1941). Hammond first rewarded thirsty rats with drinks of water for moving a small lever that protruded into the conditioning apparatus (instrumental learning, described in the next chapter). Once all the rats had learned to press the lever at a steady rate for occasional rewards, she conditioned half of them to fear a tone CS by pairing it with a brief electric shock as the US. This experimental group also received presentations of a light CS, intermixed with the tone trials and never paired with shock. Thus the first group received discriminative classical conditioning in which fear was conditioned to the tone, but the light became an inhibitor of fear. In contrast to the discriminative conditioning group, rats in the control group received no shocks and consequently continued to be unaffected by CS presentations.

Classical Conditioning

After a few pairings of the tone with shock in the discriminative conditioning group, Hammond observed a dramatic decrease in lever pressing each time the tone was presented, so this group did indeed exhibit the CER in response to the excitatory tone CS. But each presentation of the inhibitory light CS to these subjects produced increases in lever pressing, compared to lever pressing during the intertrial interval—that is, the *opposite* of the CER. By this measure, therefore, excitatory and inhibitory CSs produced effects in opposite directions in the CER procedure, just as in sign-tracking.

Demonstrations of higher-order inhibitory conditioning (Lindberg, 1933; Rescorla, 1976) provide additional support for the idea that conditioned inhibition is symmetrically opposite to conditioned excitation. Whereas inhibition is usually conditioned by pairing a CS with the omission of (an otherwise likely) US, higher-order inhibitory conditioning involves pairing the target CS with a previously conditioned inhibitory CS. Thus the previously conditioned inhibitor substitutes for actual US omission in higher-order inhibitory conditioning, in much the same way that a previously conditioned excitor substitutes for actual US presentation in higher-order excitatory conditioning. In the case of higher-order conditioning, as well as in the case of certain overt CRs, we therefore find direct parallels between excitatory and inhibitory conditioning. This suggests that procedures that pair a CS with US omission produce effects that are symmetrically opposite the effects of excitatory procedures.

Primacy of Excitation

The symmetrical portrayal of conditioned inhibition and excitation is challenged by evidence that inhibition differs from excitation in more than just its direction. For example, if inhibitory conditioning truly resembles excitatory conditioning but with an opposite US, one would expect to observe CRs of some kind to an inhibitory CS whenever it is presented by itself. But apart from a few instances such as sign-tracking and CER, researchers have searched in vain for opponent-like CRs to the inhibitory CS itself (e.g., Rescorla & Holland, 1977). Furthermore, as mentioned in an earlier section, CSs fail to lose their inhibitory effects when they are presented alone in an extinction procedure after inhibitory conditioning (Zimmer-Hart & Rescorla, 1974). If inhibition is simply a mirroring of excitation, it should be weakened by repeated presentation of the inhibitory CS alone.

An alternative to the symmetrical approach is the possibility that inhibitors do not elicit responses directly, but instead merely modulate the effects of excitors (Konorski, 1948). In other words, like the *not* in "*not open next Thursday,*" inhibitors may cause us to cancel one plan without specifying what we must do instead. The idea that inhibition is subservient to excitation, in this and other ways, has been expressed by calling inhibition a **slave process** (Lysle & Fowler, 1985). But how can one accept this view of inhibition as a slave to excitation in light of the sign-tracking and CER experiments cited above?

With regard to Hammond's (1966) CER data, "slave" theorists would point out a fact not previously mentioned—that presentations of shock reduced lever pressing not only during the tone but also during the intertrial interval. So while the amount of lever pressing was greater during the (safe) inhibitory light than during the (somewhat feared) intertrial interval, lever pressing during the light never exceeded the original level (observed before fear conditioning began). Therefore the light may have temporarily removed the slight fear that was present during the intertrial interval, instead of eliciting another emotional CR that was the opposite of fear. Similar arguments may be made in relation to Wasserman and colleagues' (1974) study where pigeons withdrew from inhibitory CSs. It is possible that their withdrawal merely reflected a tendency to approach constant features of the experimental chamber (such as walls or overhead lights) that were associated with food slightly more than the unpaired CS. Thus it remains controversial whether inhibitory conditioning procedures truly produce a kind of counterconditioning, or whether they just cause inhibitors to modulate the expression of excitatory associations.[4]

What is meant by the statement, "Inhibitory processes are slaves to excitation"?

SIGNAL VALUE

Challenges to the Contiguity Principle

Early advocates of stimulus-stimulus and stimulus-response theories assumed that classical conditioning depends crucially on temporal contiguity. That is, they believed that the CS and the US (or the CR) will become associated if and only if they occur close together in time (e.g., Pavlov, 1927/1960; Guthrie, 1935). Pavlov was surprised to discover, for example, that presenting the CS immediately after the US (backward pairings) is not a reliable method for excitatory conditioning, even though it ensures that the CS and the US are contiguous. Nor does a simple contiguity approach appear to be consistent with the facts concerning trace pairings, in which the CS and the US are separated by a gap in time. As noted previously, trace procedures do result in conditioning—either excitatory conditioning, if the CS occurs after a relatively long intertrial interval, or inhibitory conditioning if the CS occurs after a shorter interval, as in the explicitly unpaired CS-US procedure. It is difficult to conceive of a more direct challenge to the simple contiguity view than the fact that some noncontiguous (trace) procedures produce stronger excitatory conditioning than backward and simultaneous (contiguous) pairing procedures do.

Most theorists (including Pavlov) therefore adopted the view that classical conditioning involves the aftereffects, rather than the immediate effects, of the CS in the nervous system. According to this view, when the CS precedes the US by a short time interval, the remaining "trace" of activation from the CS is contiguous with activation from the US, and conditioning occurs. But when the CS follows the US, or precedes it by too long an interval, no association is formed. This modified contiguity principle went virtually unchallenged until the 1960s (see Rescorla, 1967), when two kinds of evidence were raised against it.

Reliability of the CS

First, Egger and Miller (1962) showed that the conditioning of associations depends on the **reliability** of the CS as a predictor of the US. In their main experiment, one group of rats received a compound of tone and light CSs, paired with food as the US. One of these stimuli (CS_1) always started 0.5 second before the other one (CS_2), thus making CS_2 a redundant (less informative) signal. Notice that CS_1 was a highly reliable predictor in this group, in the sense that it was always followed by the US. Another group of rats received an almost identical conditioning procedure, except that additional presentations of CS_1 were inserted into the intertrial interval and thus not paired with the US. CS_1 was therefore an unreliable predictor in this group, in the sense that it was followed by the US about half the time only.

Egger and Miller then evaluated whether CS_1 or CS_2 was more strongly associated with food, by using each CS as a reward for lever pressing (instrumental conditioning procedure). Only in the first group, where CS_1 was a highly reliable predictor, was it clearly more effective than CS_2. This fact cannot be attributed to different numbers of CS_1-CS_2

pairings in the two groups, because all subjects received exactly 135 such pairings. Instead the difference appears to depend on the fact that the second group received additional CS_1 presentations, unaccompanied by CS_2 and food, thereby undermining the conditioning of CS_1. An analogous situation would be one in which a restaurant sometimes offers excellent specials, but the other half of the time their specials turn out to be awful. Because their advertised specials are unreliable, patrons are less likely to respond to each ad than if only the great specials were advertised.

Predictability of the US

A related challenge to the contiguity view was raised by Rescorla's (1966, 1968) demonstration that conditioning depends on the **predictability** of the US in relation to the CS. In one experiment using dogs as subjects (Rescorla, 1966), half received fear conditioning with a tone CS and an electric shock US. Shocks were thus highly predictable in this group, in the sense that they were always accompanied by the CS. The other dogs received identical training, except that additional shocks were presented in the absence of the CS (Figure 2–8). Because shocks in the second group were equally likely to occur during any portion of the intertrial interval, as well as as during the CS, this procedure exemplifies the truly random control condition that was described earlier in this chapter. Obviously, such random shocks are not predictable on the basis of the CS.

In order to determine which group of dogs feared the CS more, Rescorla measured its effects on their performance of an avoidance task (instrumental conditioning, described in the next chapter). During a prior phase of the experiment, the dogs had learned to walk back and forth to avoid shocks that were occasionally presented through different parts of the floor. Subsequent presentations of the CS caused an increase in walking, but only if the CS had been informative during classical conditioning. Dogs that had received the truly random procedure instead showed no evidence of increased fear during the CS, even though they had experienced the US in contiguity with the CS as much as the other group had. So, it was not the number of pairings that mattered, but whether the CS had provided information about the occurrence of the US: Dogs learned to fear the CS if it made the US predictable, but not otherwise.

A parallel example would be the owner of a dilapidated car, which breaks down every day it rains. If those are the only days the car breaks down, he may decide that the problem has to do with the rain. But if the car breaks down on clear days as well, he is (either rightly or wrongly) less likely to associate breakdowns with precipitation. Breakdowns in the latter case seem independent of rain, even though the two things occur together many times.

FIGURE 2–8 Procedures employed in Rescorla's (1966) demonstration of the importance of the predictability of the US in classical conditioning. Asterisks (******) indicate US presentations. In the truly random control condition, the US was equally likely during the CS and the intertrial interval. In the experimental condition, the US always occurred in conjunction with the CS.

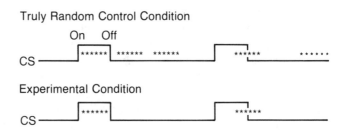

CS-US Contingency

In combination, these two experiments suggest that the signaling function of the CS is more important than the sheer number of CS-US pairings. If reliability of the CS is degraded by additional presentations of the CS alone, or if predictability of the US is degraded by additional presentations of the US alone, the association between CS and US appears to be weakened (Rescorla, 1967; but cf. Lindblom & Jenkins, 1981). Furthermore, the results of the truly random control procedure indicate that contiguous presentations of CS and US may fail to produce any evidence of conditioning, if occurrences of the US are not predictable (cf. Benedict & Ayres, 1972).

Informativeness of the CS has been defined more precisely by **contingency** theory (Rescorla, 1967; Gibbon, Berryman, & Thompson, 1974). Contingency in classical conditioning is the degree to which presentations of the US depend on presentations of the CS, a relationship that can be described mathematically. In order to achieve this precise description, contingency theory considers both the reliability of the CS and the predictability of the US. Specifically, the contingency between CS and US decreases whenever the experimenter presents fewer USs together with the CSs (unreliable CS) or more USs in their absence (unpredictable US). When the likelihood of US presentation is greater during the CS than during the intertrial interval, the CS-US contingency is a positive one that produces excitation. When US likelihood is instead greater during the intertrial interval, a negative CS-US contingency and inhibition result. Zero contingency corresponds to equal frequencies of US presentation during the CS and the intertrial interval (truly random control).

Like the development of cognitive S-S theories, mentioned earlier, this increasing emphasis on informational value represents a historic shift in thinking about associative learning. This shift does not entail the disappearance of traditional approaches because new adaptations of contiguity and S-R theories continue to sustain their viability. What is new is a broad acceptance of the cognitive approach as a valuable contributor to the enterprise of conditioning research and theory.

In what way is CS-US contingency a more complete description of the relation between stimuli, than either reliability or predictability alone?

Selective Conditioning with Compound Stimuli

Overshadowing

Although Pavlov was not aware of the CS reliability and US predictability effects described above, he did discover another circumstance in which a CS fails to be associated despite repeated pairings with a US. In overshadowing, a weak CS is presented in combination with a more intense or salient one, and this stimulus compound is paired with the US. Even though the weak CS might readily be associated if it were conditioned alone, it fails to become associated while combined with the stronger CS. Pavlov (1927/1960) called this phenomenon **overshadowing** because the stronger CS appeared to overpower the less salient one in forming an association.

One obvious possible explanation is that the learner's attention may be occupied completely by the stronger CS, so that the weak one is not noticed during conditioning. But Kamin (1969) argued against this interpretation, based on his research on overshadowing in CER procedures (conditioned emotional response, described previously). Kamin's CSs were an overhead light and *white noise,* which is a shushing sound similar to radio static or rushing water. Although his rats quickly learned to fear either CS when it was paired separately with shock, the light overshadowed the noise when the two CSs were conditioned together. In addition to this replication of Pavlov's basic finding, Kamin performed an experiment that showed that rats can indeed notice both stimuli at the same time. The additional experiment was exactly like the previous one, except that a stronger shock was used. No overshadowing occurred in the latter experiment, suggesting that the light did not divert attention from the noise after all.

As an alternative to the "occupied attention" account of overshadowing, Kamin proposed that rats in the first experiment were not surprised enough to learn about both CSs, but rats in the second experiment were. *Surprise* here refers to the amount that subjects had not yet learned about the US—an amount assumed to be greater when USs were intense than when they were moderate. A rat that has already learned to expect some pain after a light may not be surprised when a moderate shock follows the light on the next trial, but may still be surprised by an intense shock. According to Kamin, greater surprise in the latter case leads to greater learning, including learning about the noise as well as the light.

The idea that learning depends on the surprisingness of the US may also help to explain the importance of US predictability. Subjects who have learned to expect an unpredictable US at almost any time, in a truly random control procedure, are presumably not surprised by the US when it occasionally occurs in conjunction with the CS, hence their failure to associate the CS with the US. Kamin's idea also might explain why acquisition typically produces a "negatively accelerated" increase in CRs, with an initially rapid increase followed by slower and slower increases until an asymptotic level is reached (Figure 2–9; cf. Bush & Mosteller, 1955). Supposedly, the first trials are the time when expectations are weakest and surprise is greatest. Later in conditioning, when subjects largely know what to expect, surprise is smaller and consequently less is learned on each additional trial.

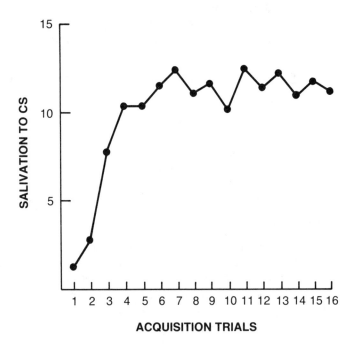

FIGURE 2–9
Negatively accelerated increase in a CR across acquisition trials. The curve depicts results from an experiment using the trace-conditioning procedure. Drops of salivation in response to the conditioned stimulus (measured before US onset) are plotted as a function of number of trials. The CR gradually increases towards an asymptotic level of about 11 or 12 drops of saliva. (After Pavlov, 1927.)

Associative Blocking

Even more renowned is Kamin's (1969) work on another phenomenon, which is closely related to overshadowing. **Associative blocking** occurs when a novel CS (which we call *B*) is combined redundantly with a CS (*A*), which has already been conditioned (via A+ trials), and this stimulus compound is then paired with the US (AB + trials; see Table 2–2). Under those circumstances, formation of an association between the redundant B and the US is retarded or prevented completely. This finding is reminiscent of overshadowing, except that associative blocking depends crucially on the prior training of A. For example, as noted earlier, the overhead light usually overshadowed white noise in Kamin's experiments when both stimuli were presented together throughout conditioning. But the reverse occurred if Kamin first conditioned fear to the noise (A), before pairing the noise-and-light compound with shock. That is, prior conditioning of the noise enabled it to block subsequent conditioning of fear to the more salient light (B).

Kamin's explanation of associative blocking is elegantly simple. Because A has already been conditioned, subjects are no longer surprised by the shock US that accompanies it. Adding a novel B to A during the second phase of the experiment does not change the fact that the subjects already expect the shock to accompany A. Consequently shocks that accompany the AB compound are not surprising, and subjects fail to learn about the redundant B. To state this more intuitively: Why should subjects learn about signals that fail to provide them with new, relevant information?

The Rescorla-Wagner Model

Kamin's theoretical language (e.g., surprise, expectation, redundancy) clearly goes beyond traditional conceptions of conditioning by describing subjects as processors of information about the environment. In fact, associative blocking and overshadowing at first appeared to defy explanation within the associative tradition. But Rescorla and Wagner (1972) soon showed that the basic aspects of both phenomena can be predicted by a mathematical formula (a model) for associations based on temporal contiguity, without any reference to cognitive processes.

The **Rescorla-Wagner model** does not describe actual responding but instead describes changes in a theoretical abstraction, "associative value" (V_X), which may be defined as the amount of conditioned strength associated with a stimulus (in this example, stimulus X). By assuming that increases in V produce more conditioned responding, Rescorla and Wagner were able to correctly predict the outcome of a variety of procedures, including associative blocking and overshadowing.

A slightly simplified version of their formula for changes in the associative value of any particular CS is

$$\Delta V_{CS} = k(\lambda - V_{total})$$

TABLE 2–2 Procedure for Producing Associative Blocking

Group	Phase I[a]	Phase II[b]	Test
Experimental	A → US	(A + B) → US	B
Control		(A + B) → US	B

[a]Thus, Phase I involves A + trials.

[b]Thus, Phase II involves AB + trials.

where λ refers to the maximum amount of conditioning that is possible with a particular US (equals zero on trials with no US); V_{total} refers to the combined associative value of CSs on a particular trial (initially zero associative value); and k is a learning rate parameter, which depends on the perceptual salience of the stimuli used as CS and US.

As forbidding as this formula may seem to some readers, it may easily be related to Kamin's surprise hypothesis: When the US is intense (i.e., a large value of λ) and little learning has previously occurred (a small value of V_{total}), then $\lambda - V_{total}$ equals a large number and much learning will occur (large ΔV_{CS}) on the current trial. But if the US is mild or conditioning is already far advanced, then $\lambda - V_{total}$ equals a small number and little learning will occur (small ΔV_{CS}). This mathematical model allows us to make more precise predictions than Kamin's verbal formulation, an advantage that has led to an astonishing array of discoveries about conditioning.

Figure 2–10a illustrates how the model explains the change in the rate of learning as conditioning proceeds. When conditioning begins, the associative value of V_{CX} is presumed to be zero, as is the value of all the stimuli in the background (represented as V_C for "value of the context"). The total, V_{total}, is therefore also zero. But when the US (value = 10) occurs at the end of the first trial, both the CS and the contextual stimuli gain in associative value, in proportion to the difference $(\lambda - V_{total}) = (10 - 0) = 10$. If we assume that the CS and the background are equally salient, with $k = .2$, then each one must increase in value by the amount $.2(10 - 0) = 2.0$. Thus the associative values of the CS and the contextual stimuli equal a total of 4.0 at the end of the first trial, as shown in the graph.

At the beginning of the next trial, if we assume that nothing else has happened in the meantime, $(\lambda - V_{total}) = (10 - 4.0) = 6.0$, which is much smaller than the time before. As a consequence, when the same US occurs at the end of the second trial, the CS and the contextual stimuli gain less in associative value. Specifically, with $k = .2$ again, each one increases this time by $.2(10 - 4.0) = 1.2$. Combined with the gains from the first trial, this results in $V_{CS} = 2.0 + 1.2 = 3.2$ (and the same thing for V_C), and $V_{total} = 6.4$. In general, with each iteration of the formula, the unused portion of the US value becomes smaller and smaller; and the increases in associative value become smaller and smaller, until there is hardly any change from one trial to the next (notice the line leveling off as it extends towards the right).

In the simplified example just shown, the Rescorla-Wagner model predicted that the associative value of the CS would grow quickly on early trials but more slowly on later trials. In a more sophisticated application to the same problem, no-CS "trials" would be interspersed between the actual conditioning trials to represent the effect of the intertrial interval, during which the background is present without the CS or US (thereby producing extinction of V_C). This would change the results as shown in Figure 2–10b, which accurately represents the fact that the CS actually retains more associative value than the context does.

Now that the basic operation of the model has been described, consider how it accounts for associative blocking. In the first phase of a blocking experiment, conditioned stimulus A is paired with shock (A+ trials) until V_A approximately equals λ, its steady level of conditioned strength. In the second phase, A is joined by B (a novel stimulus with negligible associative value, designated as AB+ trials); so V_{total} becomes $V_A + V_B = \lambda + 0 = \lambda$. This means that the combined associative value of both CSs is already at the maximum for that US. The formula therefore leads us to conclude that $(\lambda - V_{total}) = 0$, so ΔV_A and ΔV_B $= k(0) = 0$ also. That is to say, no change in associative value (no further learning) occurs

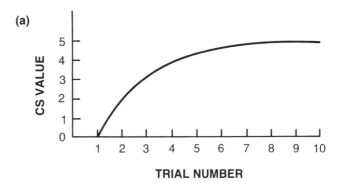

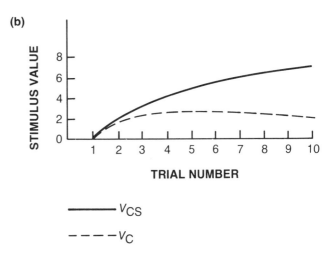

FIGURE 2–10 Growth of associative value for a CS paired with a US, as simulated by the Rescorla-Wagner model. (a) A CS is paired repeatedly with a US in the presence of contextual stimuli (associative value of the context not shown). (b) Same as (a), but with extinction of contextual stimuli during the intertrial intervals. V_{CS} = associative value of the CS; V_C = associative value of the context.

for either A or B in the compound stimulus, because A was already conditioned to the maximum value. This is indeed the blocking phenomenon.

Blocking had been discovered before Rescorla and Wagner published their model, so although the model provided a new way of understanding that phenomenon, it did not actually lead to the discovery of blocking itself. On the other hand, some things the model predicted had never been studied before. The success of a model in predicting entirely new phenomena is an extreme test of its usefulness, so let us consider some of the new predictions it made.

Whenever the combined associative value of all CSs present (V_{total}) is higher than the maximum that is conditionable by the outcome of that trial (λ), V_{CS} will be negative; that is, the CSs will *lose* some of their previously acquired associative value. In an extinction procedure, the value λ of "no US" is zero, and the model predicts that CSs presented without the US will lose their associative value—not a startling prediction. But an allied prediction is somewhat more surprising—namely, that two strongly conditioned CSs will lose associative value if presented together, *even if they are followed by the US!* This prediction, called **overexpectation,** occurs because the sum of the separately conditioned CS values is twice as large as the US can support ($V_{total} = 2\lambda$). Overexpectation was the earliest of the model's surprising predictions to be confirmed (Rescorla, 1970).

Other successes of the Rescorla-Wagner model include its analysis of several procedures for inhibitory conditioning, and its treatment of CS reliability and US predictability effects. As a final example of the way the model works, let us briefly outline its application to the explicitly unpaired CS-US procedure. This analysis is an especially interesting one because it reveals how the model explains an instance of inhibitory conditioning which, at first glance, appears to defy explanation from within the contiguity framework.

First let us review the kind of explanation suggested by contingency theory. According that approach, the explicitly unpaired procedure is likely to condition inhibition to the CS because it signals a reduced likelihood of the US; that is, the likelihood of USs is lower during the CS than during the intertrial interval (negative contingency). The CS presumably reduces subjects' expectations that the US will be presented, and consequently it should inhibit CRs.

Rescorla and Wagner (1972) provide a quite different analysis of conditioning in the explicitly unpaired CS-US procedure. Although the CS and the US are the only stimuli programmed by the experimenter in this procedure, other stimuli are constantly present in the conditioning environment. These stimuli, again designated C for context, are present when the US is delivered (equivalent to a C+ trial). Therefore, according to the contiguity principle, they should become associated with the US in an excitatory way. Mathematically, this is reflected in the development of a positive value for V_C. But intermixed with these context-conditioning trials are occasional presentations of the CS, which we may designate as stimulus A, combined with the context but not paired with the US (AC– trials). Finally, there are times when the contextual stimuli are present without A and are not paired with the US (C– trials). Although the occurrence of C+ trials produces an initial increase in V_C, this excitation tends to extinguish on AC– and C– trials.

Computer simulations of the model show that, in the long run, C retains a somewhat lower (but positive) level of associative value, which is approximately offset by a negative value of V_A, giving the AC compound a value of zero. These theoretical predictions have been confirmed: The CS in an explicitly unpaired CS-US procedure does indeed become inhibitory, and the contextual stimuli actually do become excitatory—a finding about which we will say more later. Thus the Rescorla-Wagner model demonstrates that associative theories based on temporal contiguity may still have much to teach us about classical conditioning, despite the cognitive appearance of many recent discoveries.

Successors to the Rescorla-Wagner Model

Despite its success in accommodating a number of well-known phenomena, and in predicting some others that were previously unknown, certain predictions of the Rescorla-Wagner model have been verified inconsistently or not at all (Zimmer-Hart & Rescorla, 1974; Moore & Stickney, 1985). Several derivative theories have been proposed to rectify these difficulties and to account for phenomena that the original model did not address.

One phenomenon that the Rescorla-Wagner model failed to address, and that has subsequently been addressed by all the derivative theories, is *latent inhibition* (defined previously as retardation of conditioning after exposure to the CS alone). Although Wagner and Rescorla might have accommodated the phenomenon of latent inhibition into their model by increasing its complexity, they avoided doing so because such changes would have had no obvious interpretation within the contiguity framework. Subsequently Wagner, Rescorla, and others have analyzed the successes and failures of the Rescorla-Wagner model from a cognitive perspective, resulting in varied interpretations of latent inhibition as well as of associative blocking itself.

A number of theorists have proposed that associative blocking and latent inhibition are both consequences of reduced CS processing. First, Mackintosh (1975) proposed that subjects learn to ignore stimuli that signal no change from a consequence that was already expected. For example, subjects that expect no USs in the experimental apparatus will learn to ignore CSs presented without reinforcement in a latent inhibition experiment, because those CSs signal no change in the likelihood of US presentation from that which is already expected (namely, zero). During subsequent pairings of the CS with the US, their failure to attend to the CS causes conditioning to be retarded. In associative blocking, subjects discover on the first compound-stimulus trial that the novel CS signals no change from the outcome that was already expected on the basis of the previously trained CS, and so they subsequently ignore the added CS. Thus Mackintosh's attentional theory attributes both latent inhibition and associative blocking to inattention, which results in reduced learning as well as reduced responding to a redundant CS.

More recently, Pearce and Hall (1980) proposed that subjects learn to process stimuli that are reliable predictors differently from stimuli whose outcome is uncertain. The latter stimuli are assumed to receive the kind of processing that is necessary for associative learning, whereas stimuli whose outcomes are predictable on the basis of prior learning are processed in an automatic mode, which may lead to the generation of well-learned responses but cannot engender new associations. Both the CS in the initial phase of latent conditioning experiments and the added CS in blocking experiments are stimuli whose outcomes are predictable on the basis of prior learning, so conditioning in both instances should be handicapped by this mechanism.

Each of these theories leads to unique predictions, which are now the focus of much research. Whether any one of them can be modified to accommodate all the evidence is unclear, but there is no doubt that our factual knowledge and our comprehension of the processes in classical conditioning have been bolstered by the attempt.

☑ *Most theories of associative blocking are essentially refinements of Kamin's "surprise" hypothesis. For each of the theories outlined above, identify the aspect that corresponds to the surprisingness of the US.*

The Roles of Stimulus Context

As indicated in the previous section, the Rescorla-Wagner model identifies contextual stimuli as important participants in conditioning experiments, capable of being associated with the US as if they were constantly present CSs. The fact that static contextual stimuli (e.g., the interior of the conditioning apparatus) can indeed become associated with USs has been demonstrated in many ways. For example, excitatory contextual stimuli produce many of the same effects as traditionally recognized CSs, including the evocation of CRs (e.g., Kremer, 1974; Rescorla, Durlach, & Grau, 1985) and the associative blocking of redundant CSs (e.g., Tomie, 1976).

The fact that seemingly irrelevant stimuli become associated with the US poses difficulties for some cognitive approaches to conditioning (e.g., contingency theory), which assume that only informative stimuli enter into associations. But recognition of the fact that contextual stimuli may potentially play a number of roles in conditioning has caused a dramatic increase in research on this issue.

Evidence exists of at least two functions of contextual stimuli (or "background" associations), in addition to the response-evocation and blocking effects mentioned above. First, contextual stimuli may facilitate, or set the occasion for, the retrieval and expression of other associations (Grau & Rescorla, 1984; Holland, 1985). Second, the context may generate a level of expectation or arousal that serves as a comparative baseline for the expression of excitation or inhibition (Gibbon & Balsam, 1981; Miller & Schachtman, 1985). Thus background associations may either facilitate or diminish the expression of other associations.

The roles that contextual stimuli play in classical conditioning are just now beginning to be examined in detail, but the volume of recent research in this area indicates that much is likely to be learned about these issues in the near future.

> ✏️ *Identify four of the roles that are known to be played by contextual stimuli in classical conditioning.*

CONCLUDING REMARKS: Pavlov's Legacy

Pavlov's discovery and exploration of classical conditioning followed a long history of philosophical and biological speculations about the mind. From the research he and others generated, we have now developed a wide range of approaches to the understanding of associative learning in classical conditioning procedures.

Several mathematical models of cognitive processes have been developed to account for the results of increasingly complex experiments, and investigators have begun to pay more attention to the contexts in which conditioning occurs. These increasingly sophisticated approaches have succeeded in describing and predicting, if not yet explaining, a number of basic findings concerning the roles of information as well as contiguity in conditioning.

ENDNOTES

1. Edwin B. Twitmyer reported conditioning of the human knee-jerk reflex in 1904 at a meeting of the American Psychological Association, before Pavlov's work had been published in the United States. His achievement was ignored at the time, but posthumous publication of his 1902 doctoral dissertation (Twitmyer, 1974) served as a tribute to his independent discovery of classical conditioning.

2. Gormezano and Kehoe (1975) argue that autoshaping, and certain other phenomena that are widely accepted as examples of classical conditioning, are not truly classical because they contain features that resemble operant conditioning (see Chapter 3). This argument has had little impact on most researchers because of the strong parallels that do exist between the disputed phenomena and traditional examples of classical conditioning, and because virtually all examples of classical conditioning overlap somewhat with operant conditioning, as discussed in the next chapter.

3. The omission procedure has no obvious analog in nature, so the learning processes that give rise to maladaptive responding in the laboratory may not in fact be maladaptive in a natural environment. Furthermore, as discussed in Chapter 3 with regard to preferences for signaled shock, there may be a net health benefit of concentrating the fear reaction during the CS period, even though one consequence of this concentration may be to increase the perceived intensity of the momentary, aversive US. Thus evidence cited here against S-R theories of classical conditioning does not show classical conditioning to be maladaptive in the long run, and especially not in natural settings.

4. In defense of the symmetric view, it may be mentioned that some excitatory effects appear to be invulnerable to simple extinction, in the same way that inhibition is (Rescorla, 1986). And given the current lack of production rules for predicting *either* kind of CR, excitatory or inhibitory, failures to observe inhibitory CRs may be only that—failures to observe.

CHAPTER 3

Instrumental Learning

APPLICATION: An Aspiring Actress

As she prepares to rehearse for her stage audition, Joan recalls her first attempts at acting in junior high school. Her gestures, her breathing, and her phrasing had needed so much improvement that she wondered then whether she would ever succeed. But with encouragement from her parents and others, she polished her style in front of a mirror until finally no one could deny her ability onstage.

Now Joan wonders why she waited so long to start rehearsing for tomorrow's audition. "I'm just a procrastinator," she finally admits, "and there's nothing I can do about it."

Joan is mistaken to think that nothing can be done. In this chapter and the one that follows it, you will encounter principles of instrumental learning that help to explain why a person procrastinates and how he or she might overcome that bad habit. You will also discover how persistence, motivation, and other characteristics may depend on our prior experiences with rewards.

After recounting some early developments related to the study of instrumental learning, we will take up some questions not unlike those addressed in Chapter 2. What is it, precisely, that learners learn in these conditioning procedures? How and under what circumstances is that learning expressed? Along the way to answering these questions, we will touch on various practical applications of instrumental learning.

WHAT IS INSTRUMENTAL LEARNING?

Instrumental learning is eminently practical, in the sense that it enables us to reach our goals and change our lives. Although it has much in common with classical conditioning in terms of fact as well as theory, the two kinds of learning are customarily distinguished from each other according to the goal-oriented, purposeful quality of instrumental learning, as well as its unique conditioning procedures. Thus we will avoid using the term *conditioned response* (or *CR*) to refer to all conditioned behaviors, as some authors do, and will instead reserve that term for classically conditioned responses alone.

First, consider the main differences between procedures. Unlike the signal-and-consequence (CS-US) sequence typical of classical conditioning, instrumental training procedures need not contain any explicit signals. Instead, learners may be rewarded for certain behaviors, or punished for other behaviors, whenever they occur. For example, an angler who has succeeded in catching a fish is likely to cast the fishing line again, in the hope of catching another fish. The crucial events that lead to instrumental learning in this example are the response (casting the line) and its rewarding consequences—not a signal and an outcome that occur regardless of the angler's actions. In other words, the outcome in classical conditioning procedures depends entirely on the occurrence of a prior signal (the CS), whereas the outcome in instrumental training procedures depends on the learner's own actions: Unless the angler casts the fishing line properly, there won't be any fish for dinner!

The other principal distinction between the two types of conditioning involves the apparent purposefulness of instrumental learning. We do not suppose that subjects perform a classically conditioned response (CR) because they choose to; rather, CRs are involuntary. In contrast, instrumental responses usually result either in a reward or in the avoidance of pain, which supposedly are goals that the subject wants to achieve. If Joan continues to practice after someone praises her performance, we may presume that she wants more praise (all else being equal). This apparent intentionality is one of the hallmarks of instrumental conditioning.

What two main characteristics distinguish instrumental from classical conditioning?

EARLY DEVELOPMENTS

Hedonism and Intelligence

As Chapter 1 indicated, many topics of interest to research psychologists were first addressed long ago by philosophers. Of particular relevance to instrumental learning is the belief that people are motivated by a desire to gain pleasure and avoid pain—a doctrine called *hedonism*. Like the notion of mental associations, hedonism was proposed as early as the classical age of Greece, and was then revived as a topic of philosophical debate in the eighteenth century (this time under the name *utilitarianism*).

Although the concept of hedonism was used to explain human behavior for centuries, philosophers had at the same time denied that nonhumans could anticipate and seek pleasure. But Charles Romanes, a friend of Charles Darwin's, became convinced that animals share this mental ability with humans. He sought to convince others of his conclusions in a book, *Animal Intelligence* (1882), that contained numerous anecdotal reports about the mental capabilities of animals.

Romanes believed that his anecdotes supported Darwin's theory of evolution, because they seemed to indicate a basic similarity between human and nonhuman minds. He concluded that many animals, including cats and dogs, can reason abstractly and can learn from others by imitation. His generous portrayal of animal intelligence drew much attention, including a famous response by C. Lloyd Morgan, known as ''Morgan's law of parsimony'' (or Morgan's canon): ''In no case may we interpret an action as the outcome of the exercise of a higher psychical faculty, if it can be interpreted as the outcome of the exercise of one which stands lower in the psychological scale'' (1894, p. 53). In other words, Morgan and other critics objected that Romanes was too willing to credit animals with almost human intelligence, on the basis of limited and questionable evidence. By debating this question, whether animals can intelligently choose their course of action in order to achieve future goals, Romanes and Morgan set the stage for experimental studies of instrumental learning.

Characterize the basic disagreement between Romanes and Morgan with regard to the nature of animal intelligence.

Thorndike's Connectionist Theory

Like other so-called functionalist psychologists at the end of the nineteenth century, Edward L. Thorndike was fascinated with the question of how we adjust to (or function in) our environment. Most functionalists focused on human consciousness as the main topic of investigation, but Thorndike decided to study the function of animals' actions rather than the function of consciousness. In so doing, he helped to lay the groundwork for the behaviorist movement, as we explained in Chapter 1. Thorndike and especially the behaviorists applied Morgan's canon with a vengeance, ultimately challenging the relevance of consciousness to not only animal intelligence but human intelligence as well. According to

Thorndike, learning is a matter of connecting stimuli to responses in an almost mechanical way. Consequently the name *connectionist* is typically used to identify his theory.

Learning by Trial and Error

In 1897 Thorndike constructed two dozen puzzle boxes from wooden crates, designing them so that cats and dogs could escape and get food by pulling a string or other mechanism (Figure 3–1). By observing how long it took for the same animal to escape on successive trials, Thorndike identified the basic features of instrumental learning at approximately the same time that Pavlov was first beginning to observe classical conditioning. Figure 3–2 shows a typical record of performance by one of Thorndike's cats. It is evident from the figure that

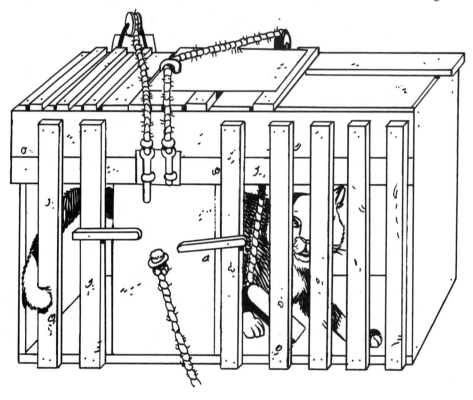

FIGURE 3–1   Thorndike's "puzzle box," designed for the study of trial-and-error learning. By pressing a lever or other mechanism, the cat could escape the box and acquire a treat.

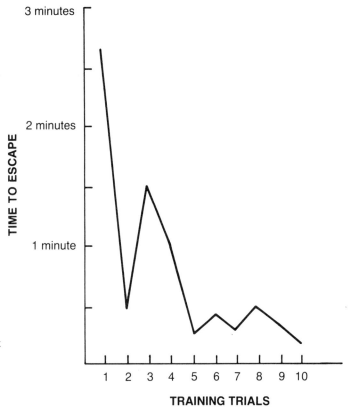

FIGURE 3–2
Acquisition of the escape habit in the puzzle box. Although the cat took almost three minutes to escape on the first trial, it routinely escaped in less than one minute after learning through trial and error.

the cat eventually needed much less time to escape the box, after it had experienced several successful escapes. This increasing efficiency is typical of instrumental learning.

Notice that instead of changing abruptly and permanently, the cat's performance improved gradually and somewhat erratically. Thorndike reported that many ineffective actions persisted for a long time, and that the animals appeared to depend on simple, haphazard *trial and error* rather than on reasoning or insight to solve the problem. These observations led Thorndike to conclude that animal learning does not involve thinking, but is an almost mechanical process of *selecting and connecting* responses to the stimuli in the problem situation. His account was, therefore, an associative one in which neural connections were emphasized, and cognitive factors such as attention and logical inference played only minor roles.

So here is how learning occurs, according to Thorndike's stimulus-response "connectionist" theory: When first placed in the puzzle box, a cat randomly engages in a variety of behaviors, most of which are completely ineffectual (vocalizing, violently rushing back and forth, clawing through the slats of the crate, etc.). When one response accidentally succeeds in freeing the cat from the box, the rewards of food and freedom automatically "stamp in" a connection between the situation (the box) and the last response that occurred there (the successful escape response). But this new response still must compete with the old tendencies, so very little improvement is apparent the next time the cat is placed in the box. Only after the correct response is stamped in again and again does it eventually

---

predominate over all other behavior in the situation, so that the cat escapes almost immediately when it is put into the box.

Two things are remarkable about Thorndike's account. First, it does not assume that the cat possesses any ideas or understanding. Thorndike's explanation deals exclusively with presumed connections in the nervous system—and in this way, it resembles Pavlov's account of classical conditioning. The second important thing to note is how closely Thorndike's theory resembles the theory of evolution by natural selection: Connections that lead to success "survive," like the fittest species in Darwin's theory, whereas unsuccessful responses gradually become extinct. Thus Thorndike sought to provide a natural (biological) explanation for behavior in much the same way that Darwin explained the origin of species. This mechanistic account, which contrasts dramatically with Romanes' explanation of animal behavior, had a profound impact on subsequent theories of learning.

▣ *What features of their behavior led Thorndike to propose that cats solve problems by accident rather than through reasoned insight?*

The Law of Effect

Because the effects (consequences) of actions determine whether they will be repeated or not, Thorndike named his discovery the **Law of Effect.** According to this law, responses that occur immediately prior to a satisfying event will be "more firmly connected with the situation, so that, when it recurs, they will be more likely to recur," but responses that "are accompanied or closely followed by discomfort to the animal will . . . have their connections with that situation weakened, so that, when it recurs, they will be less likely to occur" (1911, p. 244).

Thorndike supplemented this Law of Effect with several other laws—to explain, for example, why certain consequences are rewarding while others cause discomfort. But to his credit, he largely abandoned laws that were contradicted by evidence, such as the Law of Exercise, which claimed that mere unrewarded repetition (exercise) of a response increases future responding. Similarly, Thorndike modified the Law of Effect itself in light of facts revealed by further research.

In its original form, the Law of Effect stated that rewards increase the tendency to repeat the preceding response, whereas annoying outcomes decrease that tendency. This form of the law was called the Symmetrical Law of Effect, because it proposed that positive and negative consequences are balanced and opposite in their effects. But Thorndike's later studies convinced him that annoying stimuli do not directly weaken connections after all. Thus he abandoned the claim about discomfort, and retained only the statement about rewards (Thorndike, 1932). The remaining, simplified version was called the Truncated Law of Effect.

According to the truncated law, rewards still strengthen response connections directly, but discomfort may influence connections only indirectly, by causing behavior to become more variable. As a result of the increased variability, new responses appear that may be rewarded and may therefore replace the punished responses. But this effect of punishment is uncertain, because it depends on the new responses' being rewarded. Thorndike's analysis suggests that punishing Joan, the actress, with annoying consequences would not stop her from procrastinating unless she also is rewarded for practicing. (Other views on punishment will be discussed later in this chapter.)

As stated earlier, Thorndike's interest in animals was motivated largely by a belief that the intelligence of adult humans is based on the same fundamental processes that exist in children and in animals. This conviction was shared by most subsequent investigators, who for decades studied rats in runways and mazes, and then extrapolated their findings to people. More recently much research on instrumental learning has shifted to pigeons, and researchers have become more cognizant of differences in learning among species. But still, investigators of instrumental learning remain interested in comparing human and animal minds. Thus much of this chapter, like the previous one, describes research on nonhumans which has nevertheless influenced theories of human learning.

🔲 *Why did Thorndike eventually truncate the Law of Effect?*

ROLE OF REWARDS

Three Explanations of Reward's Effects

Reinforcement Theory

Thorndike's emphasis on rewards was embraced by many other theorists. One influential supporter, Clark L. Hull (1943), developed a complex, quasi-mathematical theory to describe how reward increases responding. According to Hull, organisms are motivated to satisfy biological needs arising from deprivation of food, water, and so on, or arising from aversive stimuli (pain). He presumed that these needs create psychological **drives** that motivate behavior, and that the reduction of those drives (by eating, drinking, escaping from pain) can strengthen stimulus-response (S-R) associations.

B. F. Skinner (1938) refused to speculate about unobservable entities such as drives and S-R associations, but he agreed that habits are strengthened by reward. Both Skinner and Hull called events that increase responding **reinforcements.** They preferred this term to *rewards,* because the latter connotes subjective experiences such as pleasure, which cannot be directly measured and which may not always accompany increased responding. Despite their many differences, therefore, Skinner's operant conditioning approach (discussed later) and Hull's drive-reduction approach are both examples of **reinforcement theory** (see Table 3–1, *reinforcement* column).

Expectancy Theory

Besides reinforcement theory, there are two other major approaches that explain the effects of rewards on learning: expectancy theory and S-R contiguity theory. Both will be presented briefly here and then discussed in more detail in later sections of this chapter.

TABLE 3–1   Three Theories of Reward

	Reinforcement	Expectancy	S-R Contiguity
Nature of the learning process:	Mechanical habit formation	Intelligent discovery	Mechanical habit formation
What is necessary for learning:	Action followed by reward	Information	Movements simultaneous with stimuli
Major theorists:	Thorndike, Hull, Skinner	Tolman	Guthrie

According to **expectancy theory** (Table 3–1, *expectancy* column), rewarding a response will cause the learner to anticipate future reward and thus be aroused and guided by that incentive (Tolman, 1932; Mackintosh & Dickinson, 1979; Colwill & Rescorla, 1988). Thus expectancy theory is akin to the common-sense notion that we perform an action because we expect it to lead to reward—not because rewards automatically strengthen habits, as reinforcement theorists maintain. Expectancies are usually conceived to be more flexible and complex than habits are, which often makes it difficult to state exactly how expectancies should affect behavior. However, some applications of expectancy theory seem quite simple and straightforward. Tinklepaugh (1928), for example, allowed monkeys to watch him while he appeared to hide pieces of banana under a box. Occasionally, however, he secretly substituted pieces of carrot or lettuce for the banana. On those occasions, the monkeys raced to the box and overturned it, but then rejected the nonpreferred vegetable and examined the box again more carefully, as if looking for the expected banana.

Whereas traditional reinforcement theory predicts that behavior will not change until after the reinforcer has occurred, expectancy theory suggests that the mere promise of reward might change behavior as a result of anticipation. Expectancy theory is thus more cognitive in its orientation, since it acknowledges that complex psychological processes mediate between the learning experience and future behavior. In fact, describing these complex processes is a major goal of such a theory.

S-R Contiguity Theory

Finally, according to **S-R contiguity theory,** rewards merely preserve S-R associations that were already established through the simultaneous occurrence of a stimulus and a response (Table 3–1, *S-R contiguity* column). As mentioned in Chapter 2, Guthrie's contiguity theory seems very simple, being built on this sole principle: ''A combination of stimuli which has accompanied a movement will on its recurrence tend to be followed by that movement'' (Guthrie, 1935, p. 26). In other words, movements automatically become associated to the stimulus situation, and the last movements that occurred in that situation will remain associated to it. From this standpoint, rewards are not important in the way claimed by either reinforcement theory or expectancy theory. Rewards do not ''stamp in'' associations as Thorndike proposed, nor do they cause the learner to anticipate rewards in the manner described by expectancy theory. The occurrence of a reward merely changes the nature of the situation, leaving the last prereward response connected to the prereward situation. Thus movements preceding reward become associated with hunger, and movements following reward become associated with satiety. So only those movements that led up to a food reward will be triggered again by future hunger.

S-R contiguity theory, which is the focus of the following section, clearly differs from both expectancy theory and common sense. But it resembles reinforcement theory in two notable ways: first in its portrayal of learning as a very mechanical and automatic process, and second in its insistence that the response must actually be performed, and be followed by reward, in order for learning to occur.

◪ *Distinguish among the three main explanations of how rewards influence behavior.*

Conditioning through S-R Contiguity

Let us now consider Guthrie's S-R contiguity theory in more detail. Guthrie himself performed little experimental research, preferring instead to devise explanations for other people's research and for his own anecdotal observations. But he did perform a classic experiment in the 1930s with a modified version of Thorndike's puzzle box, shown earlier in Figure 3–1 (Guthrie & Horton, 1946). When Guthrie's cats pushed against a pole that stood vertically in the center of the box, a mechanism opened the glass door of the box, thereby allowing the cat to escape. The same mechanism simultaneously triggered a camera to take a picture of the cat. The remarkable consistency of each cat's posture in the photographs seemed to show that individual movements became rigidly associated to the situation, being performed in much the same, stereotyped manner every time. According to Guthrie, this result did not depend on reinforcement, but merely on the fact that the situation changed as soon as the door opened. This change of stimuli supposedly left a particular set of pole-pushing movements associated with the inside of the box, so they would be triggered the next time the cat was inside the closed box.

How to Break a Habit

If our actions automatically remain associated to the situations where they occur, then unlearning those actions must depend on our substituting new ones in their place—a process that Guthrie called **associative inhibition.** Specifically he described three techniques for breaking bad habits through associative inhibition. In the *threshold* method, stimuli that would usually trigger the bad habit are presented so weakly (below the threshold) that the habitual response never occurs, and the situation consequently becomes associated with other behavior instead. In the *fatigue* method, the original habit is exhausted by means of repeated stimulus presentations until it ceases to occur, after which time other movements become associated to the same stimuli. Finally, in the *incompatible response* method, other stimuli are added to the original situation in order to evoke competing responses, which then become associated to the situation in lieu of the bad habit.

For example, one might train a horse to accept a saddle by "gentling" it with food and stroking, because calmness competes with kicking (incompatible response method); or one might gradually adapt it to the weight of the saddle by progressing slowly from light blankets on the back, to heavier blankets, and finally to the saddle (threshold method); or one might "break" the horse to the saddle by letting the horse kick until it cannot kick any more (fatigue method). Notice that all these techniques eventually manage to present the problem (the saddle) in such a way that the undesired response (kicking) is prevented from occurring.

In applying Guthrie's advice to solve practical problems, it is crucial to identify the particular stimuli and responses that comprise the bad habit. He illustrated this in the example of a 10-year-old girl who, despite her mother's scolding, routinely forgot to hang up her coat and hat when she came home (Guthrie, 1935, p. 21). The girl was clearly capable of hanging up the hat and coat, for she did so in response to her mother's complaints each time. Guthrie concluded that the girl associated the entry doorway (or separate elements of that stimulus) with dropping the clothes on the floor (or specific movements in that action). In a plan based on associative inhibition, the mother was advised to send her daughter outside again and instruct her to hang the coat and hat up as *soon as she came in.* This time the desired behavior (hanging the coat) competed with the old habit at the crucial moment; namely, when the girl took off her coat and hat *upon entering the doorway.* Under these circumstances, the daughter readily learned to hang up her hat and coat without dropping them on the floor first.

Our actress friend, Joan, can use the incompatible response technique to stop procrastinating, because she knows what stimuli govern her bad habits—She usually watches television at home in the evening when she should be rehearsing. The simplest solution would be for her to get out of the house and go someplace where there are no television sets. Alternatively, she can find another stimulus that will produce incompatible responses in the presence of her television. For example, a reminder note taped to the TV screen may push her to rehearse instead of becoming a couch potato. If she needs a more powerful stimulus to disrupt her TV watching, she can ask her friends to call in the evening and insist that she rehearse. According to Guthrie, she needs something to make her perform the actual movements of rehearsing, because whatever she actually does is what she will learn to keep doing.

> ✏ *Identify three techniques for achieving associative inhibition, and explain how they are consistent with Guthrie's characterization of the learning process.*

Critique of Guthrie's Theory

From a practical standpoint, Guthrie's advice for breaking bad habits may be useful, if only because it encourages us to observe carefully the specific aspects of each particular problem. But beyond this, his theory encounters serious difficulties. For example, Guthrie would claim that every action Joan undertakes to prepare for her auditions is a combination of tiny movements, each of which has been rigidly associated to a separate, specific stimulus. But she prepares for her auditions in many different ways, in a manner that is too flexible and too well coordinated for Guthrie's theory to explain.

This is not only true of Joan's practicing but also of human perception, language, and the execution of plans (see, respectively, Gibson, 1966; Chomsky, 1965; and Miller, Galanter, & Pribram, 1960). Rather than involving rigid associations between stimulus elements and specific movements, these processes require the integration of complex patterns of information at a speed that exceeds the brain's capacity for processing each piece of information separately (Lashley, 1951).

Furthermore, learning does not really depend on associations between specific elements of the stimulus and the response. Even the rigid behavior of the cats in Guthrie's classic experiment may have been only an artifact of his research method. The rubbing postures that appear in his photographs are typical of cats' natural social greetings; and so, rather than being conditioned through contiguity, they probably were the cats' instinctive reactions to human observers who were present during Guthrie's experiments (Moore & Stuttard, 1979).

Despite its apparent simplicity, Guthrie's S-R contiguity theory must be regarded as an ingenious but ill-fated effort to explain away the effects of reward. His attempt to characterize actions in terms of specific units of movement led to some useful techniques for changing habits, but it is not really tenable, because most actions that we learn are more flexible and more complexly coordinated than Guthrie's theory allows.

> ✏ *How highly should Guthrie's contiguity theory be regarded in terms of its adequacy to explain all the facts about learning, apart from any practical utility it may have?*

Contingencies of Reinforcement in Operant Conditioning

The Operant Response

Whereas Guthrie's contiguity theory focused on contiguity between the situation and the response, reinforcement theorists have been more interested in contiguity between the response and its reward.

Learning proceeds more rapidly if the reward occurs immediately after the response instead of after a delay (Perin, 1943). Another factor that strongly affects the rate of learning is the **reinforcement schedule,** or rule for obtaining the reinforcer. Initial learning is fastest with **continuous reinforcement,** where every instance of the response is rewarded, rather than with partial or **intermittent reinforcement,** where only some instances of the response are rewarded.

Reinforcement contingency is a broad term that refers to all the ways in which the reinforcing stimulus depends on the response. Complete specification of the reinforcement contingency therefore requires identification of not only the reinforcement schedule but also the kind of reinforcer used (e.g., food, water, opportunity to play) and its amount, as well as the amount of delay to reinforcement. Authors sometimes use the term *R-S contingency* (for *response-stimulus*) to distinguish this concept from the *CS-US contingency* of classical conditioning. Of course some events in our lives, such as the weather, are not directly contingent on our behavior. But many others are, such as getting a soft drink from a vending machine: We commonly must deposit several coins for each can or bottle (intermittent reinforcement) and then take time to open it (delay of reinforcement) before we actually get the beverage.

B. F. Skinner, the first person to systematically study contingencies of reinforcement, claimed that most actions are learned through instrumental conditioning—or **operant conditioning,** as he renamed it (Skinner, 1938). He coined this name because operant responses "operate" to change the learner's situation. For example when our friend Joan performs in the theater, she receives applause, money, and other signs of appreciation. Operant conditioning theorists would claim that Joan's acting is a complex operant behavior that was conditioned through several overlapping schedules of reinforcement.

One conclusion Skinner reached through his research was that operant conditioning exhibits several close parallels with classical conditioning, which he preferred to call *respondent conditioning.* For example, when continuous reinforcement is used to train an operant response, the speed of responding first increases rapidly and then levels off to a steady rate, much as in the acquisition of a respondent (see Figure 3–3). When responses are no longer followed by presentation of the reinforcer, operant responding extinguishes in a manner similar to classically conditioned responding (when the US ceases to be presented after the CS). And if the subject is removed from the training apparatus and later returned, the operant recovers spontaneously in a way reminiscent of spontaneous recovery in classical conditioning. By reading Pavlov's studies, Skinner gained not only an awareness of these conditioning phenomena but also a conviction that the best way to discover laws of learning is to simplify the experimental environment and record the behavior of individual organisms, as Pavlov had done.

On the other hand, Skinner believed that operants are importantly different from respondents, which occur reflexively in response to CSs and usually have little or no direct effect on the learner's situation. Whereas S-R theorists such as Thorndike and Hull considered all responses to be elicited by stimuli, Skinner characterized operants as **emitted** rather than elicited. This means that, although certain instrumental responses may occur more often in one situation than another, they are not dependent on the occurrence of particular stimuli but instead are essentially spontaneous. The assumption that responses may be emitted spontaneously, rather than elicited by stimuli, is a major difference between operant conditioning theory and other reinforcement theories.

☑ *Identify two varieties of operant reinforcement schedule.*

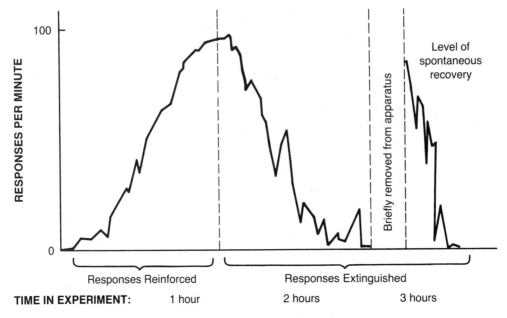

FIGURE 3–3 Acquisition, extinction, and spontaneous recovery of an operant response. As in classical conditioning, responding declines during extinction and returns after a rest period without further training.

Skinner the Inventor

Together with his descriptions of basic operant conditioning phenomena, Skinner contributed many innovations in research apparatus and techniques. Perhaps his most famous invention is the operant conditioning chamber, commonly called a **Skinner box,** which is widely used to study a variety of animal species. A subject in the Skinner box usually finds a small lever, a push button, or some other movable device mounted in one wall, with an aperture nearby for receiving food or drink as a reinforcer (Figure 3–4). Movements of the response device are recorded automatically on a computer or on electrical counters, and the presentation of reinforcers is controlled automatically as well. The exact form of the response, which Guthrie observed and photographed so carefully, does not receive much attention in studies of operant conditioning; instead, any movements that activate the device are considered equivalent to each other. This practice of defining the response in terms of its effects is called **molar,** to distinguish it from Guthrie's "molecular" emphasis on particular movement components.

Another of Skinner's inventions focused attention on the temporal patterning of responses. Instead of recording responses by marking blips (hatch marks) on a straight time line, as had previously been done, Skinner arranged a pen so it would step a small distance across the surface of a revolving cylinder whenever a response occurred (Figure 3–5). The steepness of the line drawn by such a **cumulative response recorder** directly represents the number of responses per minute, thus making it easier for researchers to notice slight changes in the rate of responding as soon as they occur. This is especially helpful when the response being studied is a so-called *free operant;* that is, a response that can be repeated freely, as often as the learner wishes. The rate of responding is not as meaningful in

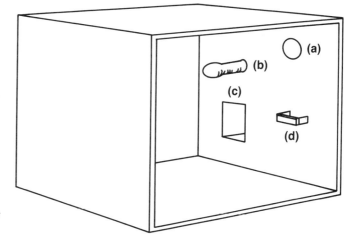

FIGURE 3–4 A Skinner box equipped for training a variety of animals: (a) a pecking key for birds, (b) a graspable lever for monkeys, (c) an aperture for dispensing reinforcement to the subject, (d) a bar lever for rodents.

situations such as Thorndike's puzzle box, where a dramatic change occurs after every instrumental response (i.e., release from the box).

Cumulative records of free operant responding, obtained under various conditions, are shown in Figure 3–6. The fact that these patterns are typical of humans, as well as many other species, is consistent with the possibility that our minds operate according to some of the same principles as nonhuman organisms. Free operant responding is affected in specific ways by tranquilizers and other chemical agents, which helps pharmaceutical companies to evaluate the potential uses of newly invented drugs. Before a new chemical compound is tested on human volunteers, its influence on rats, monkeys, or other species is carefully explored through operant conditioning procedures that have been shown to distinguish among the effects of different drugs.

Skinner has advocated that we develop a "technology of behavior" to enable us to predict and control the behavior of individual persons. Because he believes our behavior is controlled by its consequences, he sees nothing objectionable in the deliberate use of operant conditioning to achieve socially desirable ends (1953).

How did B. F. Skinner automate the process of data collection in operant conditioning experiments?

Intermittent Reinforcement Schedules

Four examples of intermittent reinforcement are represented in Figure 3–6. As the figure illustrates, Skinner observed different patterns of responding in reaction to these different schedules. First, if responding has no effect until a certain time period has elapsed, subjects learn to pause after each reinforcement before responding again. Such a **fixed interval** (FI) pattern of effort is common among students when exams are scheduled at regular intervals during a course: Most studying occurs late in each interval, close to the examination date, producing a scalloped shape on the cumulative record. The durations studied in laboratory experiments are usually considerably shorter (FI–2 minutes, FI–30 minutes) than the interval between regularly scheduled quizzes or examinations (FI–3 days, FI–6 weeks), but the scalloped pattern of responding is typical of all such intervals.

A pause is also common after reinforcement on **fixed ratio** (FR) schedules, in which a fixed number of responses is required for each reinforcement (hence a fixed ratio between

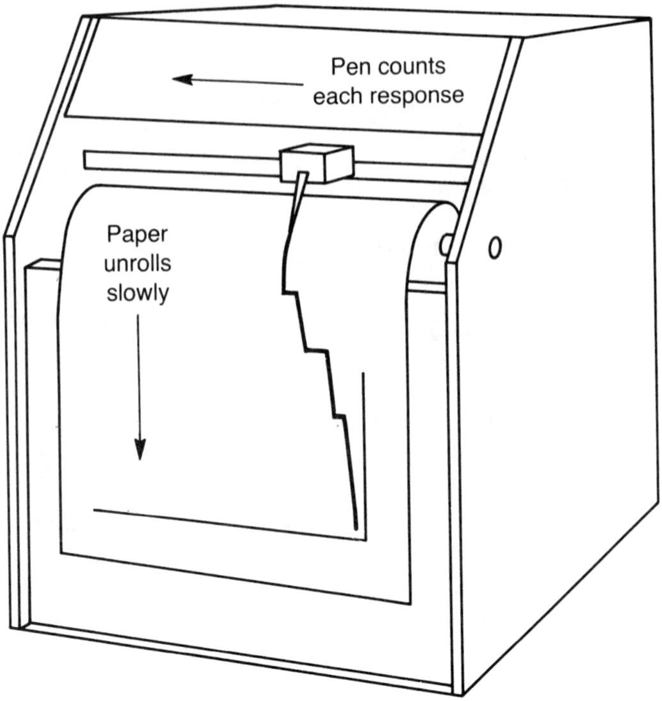

FIGURE 3–5 A cumulative response recorder, designed to display the rate of responding in the form of a cumulative record, where additional responses cause the pen to step higher on the graph. The pen has traced an acquisition curve in which responding started slowly (shallow slope where the paper hangs straight) and then became faster (steeper slope further up the tracing).

the number of responses and the number of reinforcements). For instance, tasks that are composed of a fixed number of units, such as writing several term papers of 10 pages each, may be hard to start. But once a task is finally begun, work runs along at a rather steady pace until it is completed, at which time the student typically takes another break before tackling the next paper, creating a "break and run" pattern of behavior. Pauses are usually longer when many responses (FR–2000) rather than few (FR–3) are required. Thus FI and FR schedules produce somewhat similar postreinforcement pauses, because there is a length of time after the previous reinforcement when the reinforcer is not immediately available.

In contrast, subjects seldom pause if the ratio or interval requirement changes unpredictably from trial to trial, because the reinforcer may become available at any moment. One example of such a contingency in school is the unscheduled pop quiz, which may be given (without warning) after variable periods of time. Under such a **variable interval** (VI) schedule, students never know when studying might pay off, and so they tend to keep up with assignments by studying at a constant rate. Another example involves trying to telephone a friend who makes long phone calls. If you get a busy signal, you know you must try again, but there is no way of knowing how long to wait between attempts, so you keep trying as regularly as you can.

Whenever a variable interval schedule and a fixed interval schedule both require the same average wait (e.g., FI–2 minutes and VI–2 minutes), the VI schedule produces more responding overall. This is hardly surprising when you consider that many individual intervals in the VI–2-minute schedule are actually briefer than 2 minutes, and subjects never know how long the current interval may be.

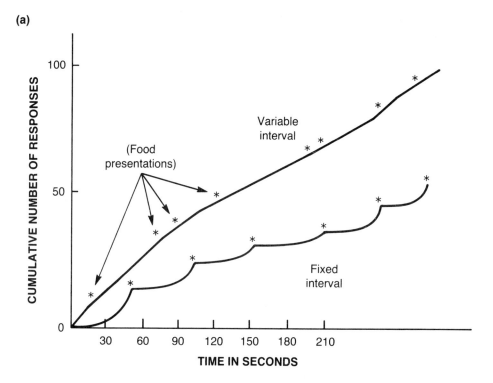

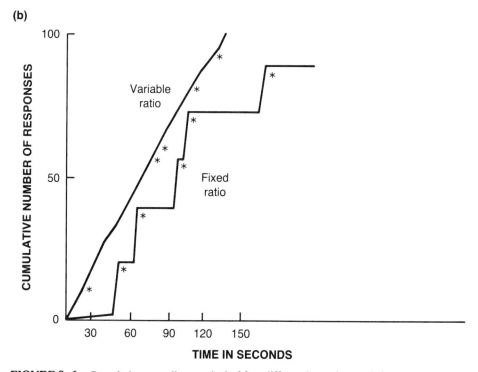

FIGURE 3–6 Cumulative recordings typical of four different intermittent reinforcement schedules: (a) variable interval and fixed interval, (b) variable ration and fixed ratio. Variable schedules produce more responding for the same number of reinforcements, partly because subjects do not pause after each reinforcement as they do in fixed schedules.

Finally, in **variable ratio** (VR) schedules, the availability of reinforcement depends on an unpredictable number of responses rather than on an unpredictable interval of time. VR responding is exemplified by a gambler who continues to hope that the next pull of the slot machine will be the one that hits the jackpot. Whereas a large number of pulls may likely win a jackpot from the slot machine, the gambler never knows how many pulls will be needed. Consequently gambling behavior is notoriously persistent, with some gamblers forgoing meals and sleep in order to keep playing. The rate of responding on a schedule such as VR–25 is generally higher than on any comparable schedule, such as on FR–25, or on a VI schedule that produced rewards coincidental with those on the VR–25 schedule. Both VI and VR schedules thus produce steady rates of responding, without the periodic post-reinforcement pauses that are typical of FI and FR schedules. And ratio schedules tend to produce more responding than interval schedules, because the rate of responding has little effect on the rate of reinforcement in interval schedules, but it directly affects reinforcement on ratio schedules.

Subjects that have been trained to respond on schedules of intermittent reinforcement continue to respond similarly during extinction, producing many more responses in extinction than subjects that were trained with continuous reinforcement alone (Jenkins & Stanley, 1950). This prolonged resistance to extinction after partial reinforcement is called the **partial reinforcement extinction** (PRE) effect. One example of persistence after partial reinforcement is the constant whining and complaining of a child whose parent finally agrees to whatever the child wants. Rather than satisfying the child for good, this intermittent reinforcement merely teaches the child that persistent complaining is eventually rewarded.

One reason for the PRE effect may be that intermittent reinforcement already involves periods when reinforcement is unavailable, and so the change to extinction is difficult to detect. In contrast, the change from continuous reinforcement to extinction is much more noticeable; hence extinction is faster after continuous reinforcement than after intermittent reinforcement (Dyal & Systma, 1976). In other words, subjects trained with intermittent reinforcement may respond more during extinction because they need more time to determine that reinforcement is no longer available. This explanation may pertain to the PRE not only in free operant procedures but also in discrete trial procedures where the response can be performed only once in a while. A response such as traversing a runway may be reinforced at the end of some trials but not others, making it difficult for subjects to detect when reinforcement has permanently ended.

But at least in discrete trial procedures, the difficulty of discriminating between extinction and intermittent reinforcement is not the only factor contributing to the PRE effect. According to Capaldi's (1967) **sequential hypothesis** of PRE, nonreward effectively becomes a signal for reward in partial reinforcement procedures, because nonreward trials are eventually followed by reward trials. Subjects trained with partial reinforcement therefore continue to respond in extinction because nonreward has become associated with reward. On the other hand, continuous reinforcement schedules produce no such association; one reward closely follows another, so nonreinforcement never becomes a signal for reinforcement. This difference should cause partially reinforced subjects to respond more persistently during extinction than other subjects do, because only the former have consistently been rewarded after periods of nonreward. Capaldi's sequential hypothesis has also been used to explain how animals remember different magnitudes of reinforcement on each trial in a series, as discussed in the following chapter.

A related explanation focuses on the feelings of frustration that accompany nonreward in partial reinforcement procedures. Frustration, like nonreward itself, is eventually followed by reward and could therefore serve as a cue for persistent responding (Amsel, 1962). Actors who have been spoiled by instant success may be very disheartened if they do not find another job immediately, whereas seasoned professionals may try harder when frustrated because they know that success can follow a series of frustrating rejections. Besides reacting differently when they do become frustrated, those who have experienced partial reinforcement may feel less frustrated: Prior experience with nonreward diminishes the amount of frustration that it causes (Brooks, 1969)

Possibly for a variety of reasons, therefore, schedules of intermittent reinforcement continue to influence responding, with each schedule producing a certain pattern of frustration and persistence during extinction.

The basic schedules of reinforcement (continuous, FI, FR, VI, and VR) may be altered or combined to produce more complicated schedules, some of which are mentioned in the following sections of this chapter. By combining schedules in various ways, we may approximate more closely the contingencies that exist in our daily lives, where we are often able to choose among several simultaneously available reinforcement schedules.

 What patterns of responding characterize the four basic schedules of intermittent reinforcement? How does intermittency of reinforcement affect responding during subsequent extinction?

Using Contingencies to Modify Your Own Behavior

The systematic application of conditioning procedures to alter people's behavior in schools, mental hospitals, or similar settings is known as **behavior modification.** When used consistently over a period of time, behavior modification is the most effective approach available for severe behavior disorders such as infantile autism, in which children may fail to develop normal language abilities and social relationships, and may also engage in compulsive rituals such as self-stimulatory rocking and hand flapping (Lovaas, 1987). This and other applications of "behavior mod" techniques (as they are sometimes called) will be described elsewhere in this chapter. Here, we need only to note that behavior modification is generally directed from one person (the teacher or therapist) toward another (the student or patient). In contrast, arranging certain outcomes in order to modify one's own behaviors is more commonly known as **contingency management.**

Reinforcers are indeed effective when self-administered, at least when a person sets his or her own performance standard (schedule of reinforcement), as shown in research by Bandura and Perloff (1967). Children in their experiment turned a wheel repeatedly to earn credit toward prizes at the end of the experiment. Those children who were allowed to decide their own performance requirements, and then reward themselves each time the requirements were met, responded as much as children who were rewarded by the experimenter under identical schedules of reinforcement.

The fact that social environment is also important in contingency management becomes evident when we consider the case of Joan, the procrastinating actress. If she surrounds herself with people who are primarily interested in theater, her rehearsals will be rewarded with more help and compliments than if she surrounds herself with television addicts. Conversely, if her best friends can think only of television, she will be rewarded for talking about television shows and personalities instead of for rehearsing. For most of us, as for

Joan, our social environment is probably as important as our physical environment in determining how we spend our time.

In a particular form of contingency management known as *contingency contracting*, you would enlist a therapist or some other trustworthy person to ensure that reinforcement occurs according to plan. By giving a friend your car keys before a party and committing her to let you drive only if you are sober, you make a contract that discourages excess drinking. Another example of contingency contracting is an agreement between parent and child, stating that the child may watch television as soon as his or her homework is finished. As is apparent from these examples, we often engage in contingency contracting on an informal basis in order to protect our long-term welfare from short-term distractions. In formal contingency contracts, or contingency management plans in general, we define complex goals clearly and measure our progress as accurately as we can. In Joan's case, she might set goals for progress toward her audition, and then reward herself (or ask someone else to reward her) for each completed step in her rehearsal plan.

☑ *What particular kind of contingency management is called* contingency contracting?

Conditioned Reinforcement

In some schedules of reinforcement, only a single kind of response is required but the subject must repeat the response a number of times. The smooth responding that results is often described as a homogeneous chain. In contrast, another kind of response chain is made up of various responses that must be executed in proper sequence before reinforcement is received (e.g., open the car door, sit in the driver's seat, insert the ignition key, etc.). Such heterogeneous chains may be quite lengthy, causing a considerable delay between the first part of the sequence and the ultimate reward. Since delaying a reward generally decreases its effectiveness, the question arises: Why do responses located early in the sequence continue to occur, even though they are far from reinforcement? After describing an associative account that is favored by reinforcement theorists, we will consider evidence suggesting that a more cognitive account is needed.

From an associative perspective, reinforcement theorists argue that events that closely precede food, drink, or some other *primary* reinforcer may acquire the capacity to serve as **conditioned reinforcers** (or *secondary reinforcers*) for earlier components of the behavior pattern. Specifically, stimuli encountered late in the sequence may become associated with the primary reinforcer and therefore serve as conditioned reinforcers for responses in the middle of the sequence; whereas stimuli encountered in the middle of the sequence may in turn serve as conditioned reinforcers for still earlier responses (Figure 3–7). In this way, conditioned reinforcers may bridge the gap between the responses at the beginning of the sequence and the primary reinforcer at the end.

For example, money appears in the middle of the sequence, "collect paycheck from payroll officer, exchange for money at bank, buy dinner at restaurant." Because of its association with the primary reinforcer "dinner," that money should serve as a powerful conditioned reinforcer. In the same way that money reinforces the act of cashing the paycheck, so too the paycheck serves as a reinforcer for visiting the payroll desk at the beginning of the sequence. Thus the first two responses in the sequence receive conditioned reinforcement by virtue of associations with dinner and other primary reinforcers that money can buy.

Expectancy theorists agree that a stimulus that marks progress toward a goal can indeed motivate and guide responding. But in keeping with the cognitive perspective, they deny that such stimuli directly reinforce responding. To determine the role played by stimuli

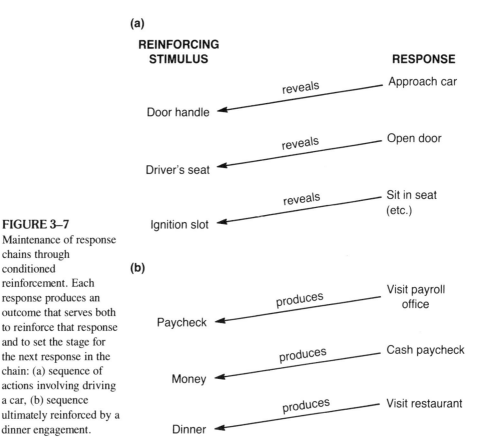

(a)

REINFORCING
STIMULUS   RESPONSE

                                    reveals   Approach car
Door handle ◄——————————

                                    reveals   Open door
Driver's seat ◄——————————

                                    reveals   Sit in seat
                                                     (etc.)
Ignition slot ◄——————————

(b)

                                    produces   Visit payroll
                                                     office
Paycheck ◄——————————

                                    produces   Cash paycheck
Money ◄——————————

                                    produces   Visit restaurant
Dinner ◄——————————

FIGURE 3–7
Maintenance of response chains through conditioned reinforcement. Each response produces an outcome that serves both to reinforce that response and to set the stage for the next response in the chain: (a) sequence of actions involving driving a car, (b) sequence ultimately reinforced by a dinner engagement.

associated with reward, Cherfas (1980) conditioned ring doves to peck two small response keys (plastic disks) embedded in the wall of a Skinner box. Pecking was rewarded according to a separate variable ratio schedule for each key, with an average of 20 responses being required on one of the keys (VR–20) compared to an average of 10 responses on the other (VR–10). The doves soon began to peck predominantly on the easier key (VR–10), at which point the experimenter terminated reinforcement on that key. This change in procedure caused the birds to eventually shift to the other key (which still provided reinforcement on a VR–20 schedule).

Under these circumstances, reinforcement theory predicts that a conditioned reinforcer such as the sound of the food dispenser should sustain responding to the first key during extinction. But Cherfas found just the opposite: The doves shifted more quickly *away* from the first key if responses continued to produce the dispenser sound during extinction. Cherfas suggests that the sound of the food dispenser interrupted the birds' pecking, causing them to reinvestigate the FR–20 key more quickly than when there was no dispenser sound during extinction. Instead of encouraging the response, as reinforcement theory predicts, events associated with primary reinforcement may deter the response if another source of reinforcement is available. In keeping with expectancy theory, conditioned reinforcers seem to alter the learner's attention or motivation, rather than automatically strengthening the tendency to respond.

Cognitive factors are also important in another way: The effectiveness of conditioned reinforcement depends on the amount of information provided by the conditioned reinforcer. In an early demonstration of this result, Egger and Miller (1962) presented both a tone and a light as signals of food delivery to hungry rats. If the onset of the tone preceded the light by 0.5 second, the tone became the more powerful conditioned reinforcer; whereas if the light preceded the tone by 0.5 second, the light became more powerful. This finding is reminiscent of the associative blocking phenomenon described in the previous chapter; namely, that subjects fail to learn about CSs that are redundant predictors of the US. Although researchers have still not agreed on a precise account of either phenomenon, Egger and Miller's results seem to implicate cognitive processes such as attention and expectation that require far more than a simple reinforcement explanation.

☑ *Characterize the difference between the views of reinforcement theorists and expectancy theorists with regard to the nature of conditioned reinforcement.*

Token Economies

When conditioned reinforcers are used explicitly as a technique for behavior modification in educational and therapeutic settings, the result is called a **token economy** (Ayllon & Azrin, 1968). Patients in mental hospitals may be rewarded systematically with tangible stimuli, such as poker chips, which serve as conditioned reinforcers for appropriate self-care or social behaviors. For example, they might receive tokens for dressing themselves or making their beds, and later exchange those tokens to obtain special privileges or sundry items. School children sometimes receive such tokens for completing assignments or sitting quietly.

Although token economies sometimes produce dramatic increases in desired behavior, critics caution that token economies may undermine other, more commonly available reinforcers such as social approval or the joy of discovery (e.g. Greene, Sternberg, & Lepper, 1976; see also the following discussion of intrinsic motivation, under the heading ''Cognitive Views of Reward''). Certainly patients for whom tokens are the only salient reward may find it difficult to adjust to life outside the institution, where rewards are often more subtle and varied than in a token economy. Token economies, therefore, should perhaps be implemented only after simpler strategies have failed, and after the transition to more normal contingencies of reinforcement has been carefully considered.

☑ *Explain how tokens are used to maintain complex sequences of behavior.*

The Structure of Operant Behavior

This section addresses the question of how operants are structured; that is, how actions are organized in relation to reinforcement. The scalloped pattern of responding on fixed interval schedules and the break-and-run pattern on fixed ratio schedules, described earlier, are recognizable structures in this sense. But the topic of structure is much broader, including also the form of the individual response and the ways in which old responses combine or change to produce new ones.

Response Shaping

In order to understand what it means to shape a response, imagine trying to teach a pigeon to bowl. This project differs in obvious ways from teaching a person: Not only would you need to use a miniature ball and bowling pins to accommodate the pigeon's limited size and strength, but you would also need different teaching methods, because the pigeon cannot understand language and cannot learn by imitating others. Of course, Thorndike's trial-and-error method of conditioning was designed to work without relying on language or imitation, but you would probably have to wait forever for a pigeon to bowl a strike by that method. Trial-and-error learning is unlikely to produce anything but frustration, unless the desired response already occurs sometimes by chance. The frequency with which a response initially occurs in the absence of reward is known as its **operant level;** thus we would say that the method of trial and error is most effective for responses that have a medium or high operant level, because this provides opportunities for reinforcement.

Skinner nevertheless succeeded in teaching pigeons to bowl, to play a simplified version of ping-pong, and to perform other behaviors that have zero operant levels, via a technique he called **shaping by successive approximations.** In order to apply this technique, one first reduces the task to easier steps and then rewards actions that resemble those steps. By gradually requiring more complete performances to earn subsequent rewards, one can shape the behavior into desired patterns. Joan's parents used a similar strategy when they praised her early attempts at acting, so she would be encouraged to try again and improve.

Specifically, the first step in training a pigeon to bowl would be to reward it each time it faces the ball (which must happen before anything else). Several reinforcements may be needed, over a span of several minutes, before the pigeon learns to turn toward the ball consistently. Once this first step has been accomplished, the trainer should no longer reward the pigeon for just facing the ball, but should instead wait until the bird actually moves its head toward the ball. By first reinforcing any movements toward the ball, and then reinforcing only those movements that place the bird's beak in contact with the ball, the trainer encourages actions that more closely approximate the ultimate response.

Each step in the shaping procedure sets the stage for responses that are even more similar to the desired response. After a bird learns to push the ball with its head, for example, some of its pushes will send the ball closer to the bowling pins just by chance. Trainers who are careful to reinforce only the best pushes will soon find the ball toppling pins fairly regularly, and will eventually be able to wait for a strike or near-strike before granting each reward. Although bowling a strike seemed a remote possibility in the beginning, now it is merely another small step beyond the previous approximation.

How may a response whose operant level is extremely low be conditioned via the technique of shaping by successive approximations?

Task Analysis and Programmed Instruction

The shaping technique has proven to be a useful behavior modification technique for a variety of therapeutic applications, such as modifying a patient's bizarre habits (Ayllon, 1963) and teaching words to speechless children (Lovaas, Berberich, Perdoff, & Schaeffer, 1966). We will now describe two derivative techniques in which the steps to be learned are defined even more specifically than in the basic shaping procedure. These techniques are task analysis and programmed instruction.

Task analysis is especially appropriate for training young children, developmentally disabled persons, and others who may have difficulty comprehending or producing a complex sequence of actions by any other means. In task analysis, the teacher analyzes the task into constituent steps and then trains those components successively, initially teaching a single step and then gradually adding steps until the entire behavior pattern has been learned.

For example, a client might learn to put on a sweatshirt by successively mastering these steps: Lay the shirt front-down on a bed, find the neck hole from the inside, insert the head through the neck hole, sit down on the bed, and finally insert the left arm and then the right arm through the appropriate sleeves. With regard to this as well as other applications, one may argue that shaping is little more than common sense: Of course it is easier to learn something after having learned simpler, related skills. But not until operant conditioners provided systematic guidelines did shaping and task analysis become widely used in institutional settings.

Programmed instruction was first developed to provide individualized instruction via school workbooks and *teaching machines,* which displayed items for learning one at a time on a revolving drum. But programmed instruction now appears most often in a newer form known as *computer assisted instruction* (often abbreviated CAI). In its simplest form, programmed instruction requires each student to answer a fixed sequence of items (for instance, filling in blanks with missing words) based on material that was read only moments before. Each response is immediately confirmed if it is correct, or corrected if it is not.

In contrast to the simple, fixed sequence that is typical of workbooks or teaching machines, many CAI programs are flexibly tailored to meet individual needs by skipping some material or branching off to include additional explanations and questions, depending on the answers that a particular student gives. But no matter whether it is presented via workbook, teaching machine, or computer, programmed instruction differs from the traditional lecture method of teaching in three ways: It requires students to respond actively to the material, it provides immediate feedback for correct and incorrect answers, and it permits each student to progress individually at his or her own pace.

It is doubtful that CAI programs or other forms of programmed instruction are available to help actresses learn their lines, but task analysis might well help novice performers who do not know where to begin planning for an audition. Task analysis might even serve well as the first item of Joan's contingency contract, to help her avoid procrastinating: After deciding what components of the final performance should be learned, and in what order, Joan might be rewarded for completing the task analysis itself. Then she might start to work on the first component of her plan, carefully note her progress, reward herself after completing that step, and so on. Ultimately, the chain of specified responses would lead to completion of the entire task.

☑ *Name and describe two practical applications of the shaping principle in which the steps are defined more specifically than in the basic shaping procedure.*

The Genesis of Responses

Our earlier discussion of shaping illustrated Skinner's view of behavioral change; namely, that reinforcement strengthens any actions that happen to precede it, including new actions that emerged randomly. According to this view, reinforcement is responsible for selecting the molar response after it has occurred, but not for generating it in the first place.

Skinner's position on the origin of responses is especially clear in his discussion of **superstition,** which he attributes to reinforcement by accident. For example, someone who wins a prize while carrying a rabbit's foot may carry the ''lucky'' charm with him forever, even though the connection was merely coincidental. Or a baseball pitcher who strikes out a series of batters may develop a ritual sequence of ''lucky'' movements (touching the cap, cocking the head, etc.) that are not really relevant to the strikeouts. Skinner (1948) showed that presenting "free" food periodically to a hungry pigeon causes the pigeon to move its head repeatedly in certain ways, or to pace around the floor—behaviors that Skinner likened to human superstitions. He argued that these actions occurred *adventitiously* (i.e., accidentally) just prior to reward, and that they were automatically strengthened by each adventitious reinforcement.

But Staddon and Simmelhag (1971) have proposed that reinforcement does much more than just preserve randomly generated responses. In their view, the periodic presentation of reinforcers calls forth specific behaviors according to natural *principles of variation*. Their detailed observations showed that extensive training with free food causes pigeons to peck the walls or floor of the Skinner box prior to food delivery, regardless of what responses were followed by reinforcement early in training. This finding is contrary to Skinner's hypothesis of adventitious reinforcement, and is supportive of Staddon and Simmelhag's claim that the origin of responses is not random, but is instead determined by such factors as the evolutionary background of the species.

Staddon and Simmelhag have identified two categories of behavior that may obey different principles of variation (Adams, 1984; Matthews, Bordi, & Depollo, 1990). **Terminal responses** are typically performed in a stereotyped manner, and are closely related to the reinforcer in terms of their timing and other characteristics (such as pecking to earn food in Figure 3–8). Well-learned operant and classically conditioned responses, including the pigeon's superstitious pecking, are examples of such terminal behaviors. **Interim activities,** in contrast, predominate during times when the recurring reinforcer is temporarily unavailable (bottom line in Figure 3–8). They include exploratory activity, polydipsia (excessive drinking after food rewards), pica (gnawing on objects other than food), and other behaviors that are not related to the reinforcer in any direct way (cf. Falk, 1971).

What are terminal responses and interim activities, and how does Staddon and Simmelhag's account of these behaviors contradict Skinner's analysis of superstition?

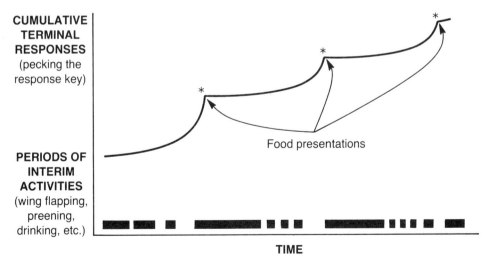

FIGURE 3–8   Time pattern of terminal and interim activities in a session of fixed-interval food reinforcement. Pecking and other food-getting behaviors predominate just before it is time for food to become available. Interim (nonfood) activities are also increased by the presence of food in the situation, but occur at times more remote from food presentation.

What Makes a Reinforcer a Reinforcer?

What characteristics must an outcome possess in order to influence behavior? This question has been debated primarily by reinforcement theorists, who have suggested a number of possible answers. The three most prominent answers focus on the reduction of drives, the optimization of arousal, and the allocation of time for performing various behaviors.

Reduction of Biologically Based Drives

One obvious influence on the effectiveness of rewards such as food, drink, or rest is the length of time we have been deprived of them. As time passes, deprivation increases the strength of an internal drive, which we may then reduce by eating, drinking, or sleeping. Some theorists, including Hull (1943), concluded that learning does not occur unless reward is associated with the satisfaction of such biologically based drives (Figure 3–9a).

(a) Drive Reduction Theory

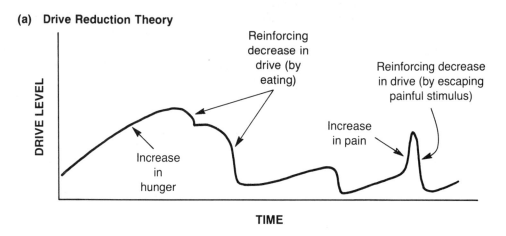

(b) Optimal Arousal Theory

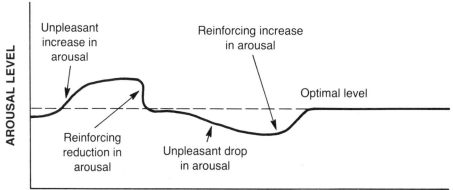

FIGURE 3–9   Two theories of reinforcement: (a) Drive reduction (eating food or escaping pain) reinforces the response that preceded it. (b) Those responses are reinforced that help to maintain arousal near an optimal level, neither too high nor too low.

Contrary to this drive-reduction theory of reinforcement, the effectiveness of rewards does not generally depend on need reduction (Eisenberger, 1972). For example, rats will learn to run down an alley for saccharin-sweetened water, even though saccharin has no nutritive value (Sheffield & Roby, 1950), and they will learn to press a response lever, even if the only consequence is to turn on a light (Kish, 1955). Monkeys will learn to push open a door in order to see another monkey or a motorized model train in a nearby cage, apparently out of sheer curiosity (Butler, 1954). These and other demonstrations of learning in the absence of an identifiable biological need have led researchers to propose alternative theories that make no mention of need-based drives.

☑ *What is drive-reduction theory, and what evidence contradicts it?*

Optimal Level of Arousal

As an alternative to Hull's drive-reduction theory, Hebb (1955) proposed that either increases or decreases in arousal may be rewarding, depending on whether the initial arousal level is too low or too high for optimal learning. According to this theory, arousal *reduction* will be rewarding if the organism is overaroused by hunger, pain, or any other condition, but stimuli that *produce* arousal will be rewarding if the organism is instead underaroused (Figure 3–9b). Like drive-reduction theory, optimal arousal theory is **homeostatic,** in the sense that it describes a mechanism for maintaining a constant (Greek ''homoio'') internal state. But while drive-reduction theory presumes a target level of zero drive, the optimal level theory presumes a target level of moderate stimulation or arousal. In other words, drive theory regards any energized state as one that organisms always try to terminate, whereas arousal theory maintains that organisms will actually seek stimulation when they are underaroused (bored, sluggish, etc.).

Arousal theory thus accounts for curiosity (e.g., monkeys watching a train) by assuming that novel stimuli raise arousal toward an optimal level. But reference to a single, overall level of arousal cannot readily explain why we try to increase certain kinds of arousal while simultaneously reducing others—such as when we attend competitive sports in search of excitement but slake our thirst during lulls in the game. That a person seeking excitement also wishes to reduce thirst is inconsistent with the idea of an optimal level. A second problem is the fact that we usually cannot measure arousal directly, which makes it difficult to confirm the role of arousal in learning. As a consequence of these uncertainties regarding arousal theory, researchers have largely turned toward a third account of reinforcement.

☑ *What is optimal arousal theory, and when does it predict that arousing stimuli will be reinforcing?*

Relative Value of Behaviors

Theories of drive reduction and optimal arousal assume that rewards are special stimuli that affect us in ways that other events cannot. In contrast, a growing number of theories characterize reinforcement as an opportunity to perform *prepotent* (preferred) responses. The basic idea is that responses that are highly preferred are reinforcing, whereas less prepotent responses are not. Thus the act of looking at a model train will serve as a reinforcer for a monkey, if the monkey chooses to watch model trains rather than perform other available activities. Likewise, parents have long known that an opportunity to play (or to watch television) is a powerful reinforcer for most children. When kids are allowed to choose what they want to do, they often engage in play, which indicates that this is a highly prepotent activity.

According to the **Premack principle** of reinforcement relativity (Premack, 1959), any behavior that the learner would freely choose to perform can serve as a reinforcing outcome for less preferred responses. From this perspective, reinforcing events are not essentially different from other events. A particular response may reinforce responses that are less prepotent than itself, but it may in turn be reinforced by responses that are more prepotent. In one study, Premack (1962) demonstrated that thirsty rats will run in a running wheel in order to obtain a drink, but once their thirst is quenched, the same rats will do the reverse (drink in order to run) because running has become more preferred. Thus a single activity (running in a running wheel, or drinking) may serve as either a reinforced response or a reinforcing response, depending on its current preferability in comparison to other activities.

Relative value is commonly assessed by measuring the relative amount of time that subjects engage in each available activity. Preferences identified in this manner have been used, for example, to reward nursery school children for sitting quietly in their classroom. When allowed to do anything they wanted, the children primarily worked jigsaw puzzles, ran and screamed, and engaged in other activities rather than sitting quietly. Permission to perform these preferred behaviors was found to be an effective reinforcer for sitting and looking at the blackboard (Homme, deBaca, Devine, Steinhorst, & Rickert, 1963). Premack's relative value principle therefore provides a useful rule of thumb for identifying effective reinforcers.

But Timberlake and Allison (1974) have pointed out that responses need not be highly preferred in order to serve as reinforcers. Even an activity that is chosen only rarely can reinforce other activities, if the learner has been prevented from performing it. For example, people may spend little time looking up at the sky, but they will work for the opportunity to do so if they have been deprived of it for a long time. And so, as an alternative to the Premack principle, Timberlake and Allison proposed the **response deprivation** hypothesis: Preventing a response increases its value and motivates the subject to seek opportunities for it. In more technical terms, subjects are considered to be deprived of activity A (such as looking at the sky) if it depends on their performing more of activity B (such as climbing a wall) than they would freely choose to do. Under these circumstances, subjects perform more B in order to engage in A, but they still do not perform A as much as they would if it were free.

Both the Premack principle and the response deprivation hypothesis agree that organisms will invest additional time and effort in one activity in order to engage in certain others. More elaborate theories have since been developed around a closely related idea—that behavior is a limited resource, which is allocated in accord with changing goals and interests (Allison, 1983; Timberlake, 1984; Collier, Johnson, Hill, & Kaufman, 1986). Heavily reliant on economic theory, this more complex approach has become known as **behavioral economics.** In contrast to earlier theories about relative value, behavioral economics deals not only with behaviors that compete for time and effort but also with complementary systems of behavior such as eating and drinking, which mutually amplify each other.

The relative value approach suggests a wide variety of reinforcing behaviors that Joan may use in her plan to overcome procrastination. Virtually anything she does, such as watching television, may be used as a reinforcer in her contingency contract. (Even her chores could serve as a reinforcer according to the deprivation hypothesis, so long as she can't stand for them to remain undone forever!) All she needs to do is refrain from watching TV until she has performed the required behavior—practicing for her audition. Promising to practice *after* TV is, of course, not the same as practicing beforehand: Once she is no longer deprived of the prepotent activity (watching TV), her motivation to practice may well disappear.

Notice that theories of relative value treat reinforcement primarily as a motivator of performance, not as a cause of learning. This emphasis is especially clear in the case of behavioral economics. Instead of answering "What are the defining characteristics of reinforcers?" it attempts to answer "How do subjects reorganize their activities in order to increase overall benefits and reduce overall costs?" This emphasis on reinforcement as a motivator of performance, rather than as a strengthener of habit, is shared with expectancy theory—the cognitive approach that is discussed in the following section. Thus one of the newest and most prominent forms of reinforcement theory, behavioral economics, represents a synthesis of the associative and cognitive perspectives.

How does the relative value approach generally differ from drive-reduction theory and optimal arousal theory with regard to the nature of reinforcement?

Cognitive Views of Reward

The traditional view of reinforcement has been seriously challenged by a number of research findings, some of which have already been described (e.g., Cherfas, 1980, on conditioned reinforcement; Staddon & Simmelhag, 1971, on superstitious behavior; and Premack, 1962, on relative value.) This section will discuss further challenges to reinforcement theory, beginning with the topic of intrinsic motivation. It will then explore the claim made by cognitive theorists that instrumental learning involves purposeful understanding rather than the automatic reinforcement of specific responses.

Intrinsic Motivation

The types of reinforcers usually mentioned by reinforcement theorists (food, money, praise, etc.) are extrinsic to the the task; that is, they are added on, instead of arising directly from the doing of the task itself. Behavior that is motivated instead by the sheer pleasure or challenge of doing it is said to be intrinsically motivated, and there is evidence that extrinsic reinforcement may undermine **intrinsic motivation.** In other words, if you are offered a reward for doing what you would have enjoyed doing anyway, it may not seem like so much fun any more.

The first experiment to clearly demonstrate this effect was conducted with nursery school children by Lepper, Greene, and Nisbett (1973). Three- to five-year-old children who enjoyed drawing with colored markers were divided into three conditions. Children in the expected-award condition were asked to draw some pictures for a person who would give them a ''Good Player Award.'' Thus they knew they would receive an extrinsic reinforcement for engaging in an activity they already liked. Kids in the unexpected-award condition also received a Good Player Award after drawing pictures but they did not know about the award until the person gave it to them. Finally, children in a no-award condition drew pictures for the person but were never offered an award.

Contrary to what you might think from common sense, children in the expected-award condition drew the worst pictures and were subsequently less likely to draw for fun than before the experiment began. Children in the unexpected-award and no-award conditions not only drew better pictures but continued to draw pictures for fun afterwards. It is as if drawing for a reward turned the drawing into work instead of play, making it a less enjoyable activity. This finding suggests that the use of grades and other extrinsic reinforcers to motivate achievement in school, for example, may tend to undermine whatever intrinsic interest school activities otherwise hold for students. But the results of the unexpected-award condition suggest that surprise rewards do not cause this problem. Therefore rewards themselves do not undermine intrinsic motivation, but the expectation of reward may indeed do so.

A similar problem arises when students expect to be evaluated on what they have learned. Grolnick and Ryan (1987) asked fifth-grade students to read some grade-level material and rate their enjoyment of it. Students who expected to be graded on their performance showed the same amount of rote learning as students who expected to just talk about it, but the grade-expectation group showed much poorer interest and conceptual learning than either the talk-expectation group or a group that was asked merely to read the material. Students who feel they must read for a test evidently concentrate on verbatim recall rather than on understanding and enjoying the material. Although this may seem more in keeping with common sense than Lepper's findings do, both sets of results lead to the same conclusion about reinforcement: Extrinsic reinforcers sometimes have effects opposite those envisioned by reinforcement theorists. Rather than increasing the tendency to repeat a behavior, the receipt of an expected reward can actually reduce the motivation for repeating that behavior on future occasions.

Lepper, Greene, and Nisbett (1973) explain their findings from a cognitive perspective. They argue that people understand themselves by examining their own actions and the circumstances in which they perform them. If the external reinforcement contingencies seem very compelling, people may attribute their behavior to those contingencies and overlook the other (intrinsic) reasons for engaging in the behavior. Although this topic requires further research, it is clear that people's expectations are a crucial factor in determining the effects of reward.

Learning as a Process of Organizing Information

In cognitive accounts of instrumental learning, reward is considered to confirm the learner's expectations or plans for reaching a goal. After understanding the situation, the learner may reach the goal in a variety of ways besides repeating the specific responses that previously led to reward. Despite his acceptance of this view, Tolman (1932) considered himself a behaviorist, because his theory was intended to explain actual behavior rather than the content of mental experience. His *purposeful behaviorism* theory therefore addressed many of the same issues raised by Thorndike, Hull, Skinner, and other behaviorists, but it approached them by considering how learners organize their behavior in relation to their purposes.

According to reinforcement theory, the presentation of a reward strengthens the tendency to repeat particular responses, especially those that immediately precede the reward. If rewards indeed exert their influence through such an automatic strengthening process, then increasing the delay between a response and its outcome should retard instrumental learning. As previously mentioned, this account is supported by the finding that learning is generally superior with immediate reinforcement rather than delayed reinforcement (Perin, 1943; Tarpy & Sawabini, 1974).

The cognitive view portrays learning quite differently, as an active organizing of information in accordance with the learner's goals. By that view, reinforcers primarily provide information that the learner can use in planning future choices. This implies that delays of reinforcement may not inevitably lead to a retardation of learning.

In accord with the cognitive view, and contrary to reinforcement theory, Buchwald (1967) proposed that learners would actually perform *better* if information about the correctness of each choice were delayed until the next time the learner faced that choice again (Figure 3–10). He reasoned that there are two ways that subjects might err after immediate feedback: They may forget the response that they made the first time, or they may forget the outcome of that choice (positive vs. negative). In contrast, by delaying feedback until the next repetition of that choice, the experimenter ensures that at least the relevant outcome is remembered. Thus the potential for mistakes should be less after delayed feedback than after immediate feedback, according to the cognitive hypothesis.

In Buchwald's experiment, college students were told to guess which number (for example, 7 vs. 9) went with each word in a list. Not surprisingly, when the list was then read a second time, subjects generally repeated their first guess more often if they were told they had been "right" rather than "wrong" the first time. But contrary to reinforcement theory, performance was better when feedback was delayed rather than immediate, presumably because there was less opportunity to forget outcomes that were announced closer to the next repetition. Evidently the outcomes did not strengthen or weaken previous responses in any direct way (as reinforcement theory claims), but instead each outcome provided information that the students used for planning their next responses.

Buchwald's comparison of different feedback conditions shows that the timing of information may affect performance in ways contrary to reinforcement theory. This finding does not negate the results of other research in which conditioning was impaired by delaying the rewards. But it does suggest that, even in those studies, the results may reflect a loss of information (i.e., forgetting) when feedback is delayed—rather than a weakened effect of reinforcement on particular responses, as claimed by reinforcement theorists.

Cognitive theorists cite a number of other phenomena as challenges to the reinforcement account of reward, especially including latent learning, place learning, and insightful problem solving.

☑ *Why did Buchwald (1967) disagree with reinforcement theorists, who claimed that delaying the outcome of a response always leads to poorer learning?*

FIGURE 3–10   Procedures used in a delayed feedback experiment by Buchwald (1967): (a) Subjects in the reinforcement procedure received immediate feedback about their guesses, which should have maximized the reinforcement effect. (b) Subjects in the cognitive procedure received feedback just before the next repetition of that stimulus, which should have maximized the information available for the next guess. Subjects in the cognitive procedure learned and remembered better.

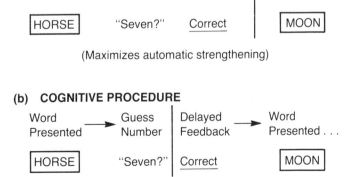

(a) REINFORCEMENT PROCEDURE

| Word Presented | → | Guess Number | → | Immediate Feedback | | Word Presented . . . |

| HORSE | | "Seven?" | | Correct | | MOON |

(Maximizes automatic strengthening)

(b) COGNITIVE PROCEDURE

| Word Presented | → | Guess Number | | Delayed Feedback | → | Word Presented . . . |

| HORSE | | "Seven?" | | Correct | | MOON |

(Maximizes accuracy of memory)

Latent Learning and Extinction

The **latent learning** experiments of Tolman and colleagues demonstrated that instrumental learning can occur without explicit rewards (see Thistlethwaite, 1951; Tolman, 1948). In the classic version of this experiment, rats were allowed to run through a maze several times over a series of days. During the first several days, rats that were rewarded with food completed the maze faster and with fewer errors (wrong turns) than rats that found the goal box empty each time. Given this fact, one might think that the unrewarded rats did not learn as much as the rats that received reward. But as the next phase of the experiment revealed, unrewarded rats had actually learned the route to the goal box just as well as the others had. This finding appears to contradict the claim that reinforcement is essential for learning.

Figure 3–11 shows the number of errors committed by three groups of rats in one of these experiments (Tolman & Honzik, 1930a). Two of the groups (Nonreward and Nonreward/Reward) received no rewards during the first 10 days of training, so they continued to make about twice as many errors as the Reward group through the eleventh day. But at the end of their run on the eleventh day, the Nonreward/Reward group found food in the goal box for the first time, and on the next day they performed as well as the group that had received reward every time. This finding surprised reinforcement theorists, who expected the Nonreward/Reward group to improve only gradually after rewards began to occur (similar to the Reward group during the first phase).

Evidently the superior maze running by the Reward group during the first phase of the experiment did not represent superior learning about the maze. Instead, the Nonreward/Reward group had learned equally much, but their knowledge remained latent until an **incentive** (food) motivated them to demonstrate what they knew. Presentation of food on the eleventh trial created a new expectancy—the goal box sometimes contained a reward. But this was just one more piece of information (albeit an important piece) in addition to everything they had already learned without reward.

The distinction between **competence** (what is learned) and **performance** (what is done) is an important one because it means that learning is not synonymous with changes in responding per se. Competence is reflected only imperfectly in actual performance, and researchers must be careful to design experiments that detect differences in competence, not differences in performance alone. This requires ingenuity, since competence cannot be observed directly but must instead be inferred from observations of performance.

Although Tolman argued that learning is possible without reward, he also acknowledged that rewards can promote learning by adding perceptual **emphasis** to relevant aspects of the situation. In other words, rewards not only motivate performance but also enhance attention to events that are related to the rewards.

Closely related to latent learning is the phenomenon of **latent extinction.** That is, showing rats that the goal box is empty is enough to discourage them from running through a maze or runway, even though they have received rewards every time they ran through it in the past. According to traditional reinforcement theory, responses that have been reinforced will remain strong until the response is repeated without reinforcement (the standard extinction procedure). Instead, research indicates that mere observation of the empty goal box is adequate to produce extinction (Moltz, 1957). Presumably the subjects still remember how to reach the goal box, but they no longer have any incentive to display that knowledge. Just like the Nonreward/Reward group in the latent learning experiment, they possess competence that their performance does not reflect.

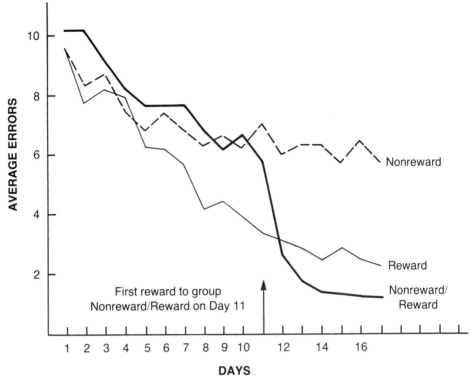

FIGURE 3–11 Results from an experiment by Tolman and Honzik (1930). After 10 trials of exploring the maze without any reward, rats in the Nonreward/Reward Group received reward in the goal box on the eleventh trial. Immediately thereafter, they matched the performance of the Reward Group, which had received reward every time.

Source: Adapted from E. C. Tolman & C. H. Honzik (1930). Introduction and removal of reward, and maze performance in rats. *University of California Publications in Psychology, 4.* © Regents of the University of California.

Some reinforcement theorists (e.g., Hull, 1952) attempted to explain latent learning by arguing that mere removal from the goal box is rewarding. This could explain why the Nonreward/Reward group improved slightly during the first phase of the experiment (Figure 3–11) and why they quickly matched the Reward group when tested with food. However, by conceding that performance is affected separately by habits (based on the sheer number of rewards) and incentives (based on the magnitude or nature of reward), these theorists moved further away from an associative framework toward acknowledging the great complexity of cognitive processes. S-R contiguity theorists were similarly forced to recognize that incentives influence performance separately from habits (Spence, 1956, pp. 133–137). We will return to the topic of learning without reward later in this chapter when we discuss learning through modeling.

☑ *How did Tolman and colleagues demonstrate that reward and nonreward both produced equal competence, even though performance was unequal under those conditions during the first phase of the latent learning experiment?*

Place Learning

Most early reinforcement theorists as well as contiguity theorists assumed that learning involves the conditioning of specific movements or specific stimulus-response associations. Tolman, in contrast, argued that subjects acquire a more comprehensive understanding of the situation, which is then used to guide responding in a flexible manner. He called the subjects' knowledge of relationships in the situation a **cognitive map,** and he generalized this concept to refer to any strategy or mental pathway for achieving any goal. After forming a cognitive map of this kind, the learner expects familiar locations or events to be related to others in consistent ways. Researchers have since discovered that certain parts of a rat's brain play a special role in forming and maintaining this kind of spatial representation (Nadel & Willner, 1980).

In one experiment designed to demonstrate reliance on cognitive maps (Tolman, Ritchie, & Kalish, 1946), rats started from either one location (Start$_1$ in Figure 3–12) or another (Start$_2$) in a cross-shaped maze, and were rewarded with food in yet another location (Food$_1$ or Food$_2$). Each rat in the Place Learning group began from both of the start boxes, on different trials, but was always rewarded for going to the same goal box (e.g., always to Food$_2$). Rats in the Response Learning group also began from both start boxes on different trials, but they were rewarded for making the same turning response every time (e.g., turn right from Start$_1$ to Food$_1$ or turn right from Start$_2$ to Food$_2$). If learning involves the automatic strengthening of movements that consistently precede reward, then learning should be fastest in the Response Learning group. On the other hand, if rats learn by relating their experiences to their map-like understanding of the environment, the consistent location of rewards in the Place Learning group should produce superior learning.

Tolman and colleagues (1946) found that Place Learning subjects learned faster than Response Learning subjects, in agreement with the cognitive map hypothesis of expectancy theory. Very similar experiments have been repeated many times by other researchers, who have observed an advantage for Place Learning under some circumstances but not all. The most sensible conclusion is that rats learn about mazes from whatever information is available, and the rate of learning depends on the salience of cues that provide that information (Tighe, 1982, pp. 156–162).

What features of maze learning demonstrate reliance on cognitive maps rather than on specific response sequences?

Insight Learning

According to traditional reinforcement theory, instrumental learning occurs only when an actual response is produced and then reinforced (or not reinforced). Such overt trial and error was the focus of Thorndike's (1911) analysis, from which he concluded that instrumental learning is naturally gradual and haphazard. But the Gestalt psychologists criticized Thorndike for using the puzzle box, claiming that its design was too artificial and obscure to allow for anything other than blind guessing (Kohler, 1925; Koffka, 1924). Learning, they contended, is often sudden and complete if the learner is given enough information to truly understand the problem.

Closely akin to this view was Tolman's (1948) analysis of *vicarious trial and error,* a period of hesitation when rats in a maze seem to be thinking about the alternative routes before choosing one to take. He observed that "smarter" rats pause to look back and forth more than rats that learn slowly, and he noted that all subjects vacillate between the alternatives more when the choice is difficult than when it is easy. These observations

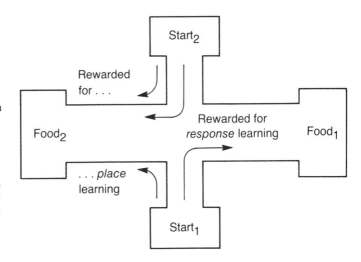

FIGURE 3–12 Maze used in Place Learning experiments by Tolman, Ritchie, and Kalish (1946). Subjects that were required to approach a constant goal location (e.g., F_2) learned faster than subjects required to turn the same way from any starting point (e.g., $S_1 \rightarrow F_1$ and $S_2 \rightarrow F_2$.

Source: Adapted from E. C. Tolman, B. F. Ritchie, & D. Kalish (1946). Studies in spatial learning. II: Place learning vs. response learning. *Journal of Experimental Psychology, 36.* In the public domain.

Labels in figure: Start₂ → Start$_2$; Rewarded for . . . ; Rewarded for *response* learning; Food$_2$; Food$_1$; . . . *place* learning; Start$_1$

suggested to Tolman that learning is enhanced if subjects vicariously "run through" their cognitive maps to discover the best route before responding.

Insight is a special kind of solution where the learner, while contemplating the familiar elements of a problem, suddenly perceives new relationships among them. In Tolman's terminology, these relationships are like a previously unexplored route to the goal through the cognitive map. Sometimes the newly perceived relationships are so surprising that the learner has an *aha* experience upon discovering them, like suddenly realizing how to solve a puzzle. Insight learning is claimed to be more thorough, more memorable, and generalizable to a wider variety of problems, than solutions learned by chance or through rote memorization.

The classic studies of insight learning were conducted with wild chimpanzees by Wolfgang Köhler (1925) while marooned in the Canary Islands during World War I. His captured chimps used boxes or sticks to reach rewards that were otherwise out of reach (Figure 3–13). In one case, his most intelligent ape, Sultan, had already learned to climb on a box to reach fruit suspended in the air. Then in another room, Sultan saw fruit suspended even higher and tried unsuccessfully to reach it with sticks. After finally throwing the sticks away and kicking the wall in apparent frustration, he sat down for a while, then scratched his head and began to stare at some nearby boxes. Suddenly he grabbed a box, dragged it and a stick toward the fruit, and climbed onto the box to successfully knock down the fruit with the stick—a combination of actions he had never seen or used before. Such sudden discoveries of new solutions through purely mental activity are the hallmark of insight learning.

Critics of this research (e.g., Epstein, Kirshnit, Lanza, & Rubin, 1984) argue that such anecdotal reports are misleading, because they ignore the preexisting skills and related experiences that subjects bring to the task. Without a detailed knowledge of the subject's history, it is difficult to know how truly novel the apparently sudden solution is. Epstein and colleagues do appear to have demonstrated a sudden and novel combination of skills in pigeons whose history of experiences is known, but it is too early to judge how closely this performance resembles the insights attributed to chimpanzees.

Clearer instances of insight have been reported by Metcalfe (1986; Metcalfe & Wiebe, 1987), who measured people's feelings of closeness to the solution, in addition to recording

FIGURE 3–13 Kohler's chimpanzees: (a) Grande creating an even more elaborate structure. (b) Grande using a stack of boxes to obtain food as Sultan watches.

Source: W. Kohler (1925). *The mentality of apes.* Andover, Eng: Routledge.

their guesses at the solution itself. She found that subjects who were most sure they were on the verge of solving certain problems were also most likely to be wrong, and that subjects who actually solved those problems correctly had no warning that they were about to do so. The suddenness of these solutions and the surprising "flash of illumination" that accompanied success is in keeping with previous anecdotal reports of insightful problem solving, including Kohler's. But Metcalfe's subjects were not engaged in an instrumental learning task, and the occurrence of insight appears to depend very much on the kind of task being performed (Metcalfe & Wiebe, 1987). It is therefore difficult to be sure how relevant her findings are for instrumental learning. More research is needed to determine whether and how insight operates in particular circumstances with various species.

How does insight learning differ from "blind" guessing?

Evaluation of Expectancy Theory

As the preceding paragraphs indicate, cognitive theorists proposed a very different interpretation of the effects of reward than had been proposed by reinforcement theorists. According to the cognitive view, reward may add perceptual emphasis and thereby focus the learner's understanding of some relationships, but reward is neither a necessary nor a sufficient cause of learning. What is both necessary and sufficient is that subjects reorganize their cognitions (perceptions, expectations) to include new information, which may or may not involve the occurrence of rewards. The result of this reorganization is a new level of competence, which is expressed in performance only under certain conditions. As an incentive for performance, reward influences the expression of competence more than it influences competence itself.

Although Gestalt and expectancy theorists demonstrated new aspects of learning that must be addressed by any comprehensive theory, their own explanations have been soundly criticized on two major points. First, many investigators have lamented the absence of clear rules for predicting observable behavior (performance) from theories of competence (e.g., Wasserman, 1981). The sharpest of these critics have charged that Tolman's expectancy theory leaves rats "buried in thought" at the junctures in a maze, knowing which way to go but having no means of acting on that knowledge (Guthrie, 1952, p. 143). But even successful reinforcement theories, including Skinner's, neglect to account for the actual form of instrumental responses. In fact, the only theories that predict specific movements are Guthrie's and closely associated S-R contiguity theories, which have been largely discredited on other grounds. This weakness of cognitive theories is therefore shared with all other viable theories of instrumental learning.

The second serious criticism of traditional cognitive theories is that they are too vague in describing competence and exactly how it changes as a result of experience. The suggestion that rats develop cognitive maps by merely wandering through a maze is far from incomplete as an explanation for place learning. For instance, what parts of the map develop before other parts, how is such a map "read," and what kinds of experience will cause rats to alter or forget parts of the map? Without a precise formulation of how maps are produced and utilized, researchers cannot be sure that maps are the best way to characterize what rats (or people) know.

Tolman himself recognized that some of these questions needed answering (Tolman, 1948, p. 193), but only much later did theorists become more precise about how learners organize and use information. Subsequent research has begun to reveal how such learning is organized, not only with regard to space (Kozlowski & Bryant, 1977; Nadel, Willner, & Kurz, 1985; Presson, DeLange, & Hazelrigg, 1989) but also with regard to time and number (Gallistel, 1990). Detailed coverage of these theoretical accounts is beyond the scope of this book, but it is generally true that they contain associative as well as cognitive features, again reflecting the trend toward synthesis we noted previously in connection with classical conditioning and instrumental reward.

What have been the two main criticisms of cognitive theories of instrumental learning, and how do such theories compare to others in those regards?

Summary

Of the three explanations for the Law of Effect, only reinforcement theory and expectancy theory are still influential, with most current theories combining aspects of both those approaches. Research on the effects of contingent rewards led to schedules of reinforcement, together with a variety of practical applications, including contingency management, token economies, task analysis, and programmed instruction. But despite these successes, reinforcement theorists have had to acknowledge the importance of nonreinforced behaviors (interim activities), the relativity of reinforcement (Premack principle), learning without reinforcement (latent learning), and the distinction between competence and performance. At the same time, cognitive theorists have had to acknowledge criticisms by reinforcement and S-R contiguity theorists concerning the need for theories to be testable.

After considering the twin topics of punishment and avoidance, we will again take up the issue of learning without reward—this time, within the context of observational learning. Like latent learning, observational learning requires that we distinguish between competence and performance in order to explain the effects of experience on later behavior.

PUNISHMENT AND AVOIDANCE

The Other Half of the Law of Effect

Earlier in this chapter, we described two different versions of Thorndike's famous law for instrumental learning. The final, Truncated Law of Effect claimed that rewards cause responding to increase, but it made no mention of ways to decrease responding. In contrast, the original Symmetrical Law of Effect had contained this additional claim: Responses that "are accompanied or closely followed by discomfort to the animal will, other things being equal, have their connections with that situation weakened, so that, when it recurs, they will be less likely to occur" (Thorndike, 1911, p. 244). Guthrie, Skinner, and Thorndike all came to agree that "discomfort" alone is not the key to weakening habits, yet recent research indicates that its effects on behavior are symmetrical to the effects of reward in many ways. This section will present some of the research relevant to this controversy and discuss the most important theories regarding learning with aversive stimuli.

The use of noxious outcomes to reduce responding is known as **punishment.** Researchers distinguish between this familiar concept and the concept of **negative reinforcement,** which applies to responses that provide *relief* from noxious outcomes. Negative reinforcement is essentially the flip side of punishment: By canceling an aversive stimulus, the negatively reinforced response improves the learner's situation from bad to neutral. This outcome encourages repetition of the response in much the same way that rewards produce **positive reinforcement** by changing a neutral situation into a pleasant one. *Reinforcement* thus refers generally to outcomes that increase the likelihood of responding. Negative reinforcement, in particular, encourages responses that help the learner either (1) **escape** from the noxious stimulus after it has begun or (2) **avoid** the noxious stimulus entirely.

As an example of the difference between punishment and negative reinforcement, consider Joan's experiences as a driver. The last time she arrived at the theater for an audition, all the nearby parking spaces were full. But the weather was good, and she had enough time to walk a few blocks, so she avoided a parking ticket by driving on to find a legal parking place. Joan's decision to avoid parking illegally would be of little interest to us, except for the fact that she had to learn her lesson the hard way: first through punishment and then through negative reinforcement. Her first year of driving had been plagued with tickets (punishment) for all kinds of violations. Because her actions produced aversive consequences, she started behaving differently. Only then did she receive negative reinforcement in the form of reduced penalties (including a good-driver insurance discount). As this example illustrates, punishment and negative reinforcement refer to opposite aspects of an aversive situation. Responses that produce aversive stimuli are punished, whereas responses that avoid or escape from aversive stimuli are negatively reinforced.

☑ *How do avoidance, escape, and punishment differ from each other, and how are they related to positive reinforcement procedures?*

Punishment

How Effective Is Punishment?

In a previous discussion of Guthrie's S-R contiguity theory, we described three methods for breaking bad habits by means of associative inhibition, wherein new movements are substituted for undesirable ones in a specific setting. According to Guthrie, punishment will not be successful unless the aversive stimulus does exactly that, by eliciting a reaction opposite from the behavior that is to be punished. Consistent with this analysis, rats that have been trained to run down an alleyway for food will run more slowly than usual if they have previously been shocked on their forepaws as they reached the food, but they will run more quickly than usual if they have previously been shocked on their hindpaws as they reached the food (Fowler & Miller, 1963). In this experiment, punishment was effective when it elicited a reaction that competed with running (namely, jumping back from the forepaws) but not when it elicited a reaction compatible with running (jumping forward from the hindpaws). In addition to this case from the laboratory, there are many practical examples where punishment is counterproductive because it actually elicits the same behavior that is being punished, such as when harsh physical punishment is used to punish bedwetting or aggressiveness, resulting in more bedwetting or aggressiveness rather than less.

Like Guthrie, B. F. Skinner was equally unimpressed with punishment, but for a different reason. He and his students performed several experiments in which rats were trained to press a lever to obtain food rewards, and lever pressing was then extinguished (reward discontinued) under different conditions. Rats that were mildly punished for pressing the lever during extinction, either by shocks (Estes, 1944) or by upward slaps of the lever against their paws (Skinner, 1938, pp. 154–159), eventually completed just as many lever presses as rats that received no punishment during extinction. This result convinced Skinner that decreased responding is merely an emotional reaction that dissipates soon after punishment is discontinued. Although the dramatic suppression of responding that sometimes occurs may mislead us into thinking that the behavior is permanently weakened, the effect is only temporary, he claimed.

Guthrie and Skinner were correct to state that punishment sometimes produces paradoxical results, and that its influence wanes if responses are no longer punished. However, this does not mean that punishment is inherently less effective than reward. Just as running could not be stopped by shocking the rats' rear paws, so also certain behaviors are difficult to condition with rewards, because the response elicited by the reward is incompatible with the required instrumental behavior. And like punishment, reward loses its effectiveness once it is no longer available; so we should perhaps not be surprised that the effects of punishment dissipate when punishment is withdrawn. The observations cited by Guthrie and Skinner therefore do not really answer the question about the effectiveness of punishment.

Administration of moderately intense punishment soon after a response is generally very effective in reducing responding (Azrin, 1956; Fraenkel, 1975). For example, Azrin (1956) rewarded pigeons with food for pecking a response key, using a variable interval 3-minute schedule of reinforcement. In addition to the food, shocks sometimes occurred during 2-minute periods when the response key was illuminated with orange light. When Azrin presented the shock without regard to the pigeons' behavior, it had relatively little effect on their pecking for food. But presenting the shock contingent on a response (punishment) caused considerable suppression of key pecking, in ways that were related to the timing of the shock presentation. If punishment was being presented according to a fixed-interval schedule, pecking was especially suppressed just before the time when punishment was due. But if punishment occurred unpredictably, according to a variable-interval schedule, responding was evenly suppressed throughout the duration of the orange light. In summary, punishment appears to be roughly comparable to reward in terms of its power to influence behavior.

▨ *Explain why Guthrie and Skinner's reservations about the effectiveness of punishment are no longer considered to prove the superiority of reward over punishment.*

Deciding Whether and How to Use Punishment

Despite the proven effectiveness of punishment, there are several reasons for preferring reward over punishment as a method of behavioral training. First, punishment must often be relatively severe in order to be effective. Mild sanctions intended as punishment may even be positively reinforcing to children, for example, if no one pays attention to them in any other way. Second, punishment itself does not specify what is to be done but only what is not to be done, so the learner may substitute another undesirable behavior for the punished one, perhaps a behavior that achieves the same outcome without a risk of being punished. It is therefore important to provide positive reinforcement for acceptable alternatives to the punished behavior rather than relying on punishment alone. Third, punishment that is severe enough to be effective often produces unfortunate side effects, such as fear of the punishing agent and avoidance of the entire situation in which punishment occurs, or aggression toward the punishing agent and others.

A less severe form of punishment that is effective in many circumstances is **time-out from positive reinforcement** (also called *reward omission, response cost,* and *negative punishment*), which involves the temporary removal of reward opportunities. Like most other instrumental conditioning procedures, time-out is exemplified by practices that are already evident in our society; for example, temporary exile and imprisonment (which obviously preclude rewards). But time-out was not widely used in therapeutic and educational settings until operant conditioning provided the theoretical basis for various techniques of behavior modification.

The therapeutic use of time-out may be illustrated by the case of an overweight schizophrenic patient who, for years, had stolen extra food from other patients and the dining room at her mental hospital (Ayllon, 1963). Coaxing and other efforts by the medical staff had failed to discourage this behavior, so a time-out procedure was established. If she approached other patients or picked up unauthorized food from the dining room counter, she was removed from the dining room and was not allowed to finish that meal. Even though the behavioral contingencies were not explained to her verbally, she quickly stopped stealing food under these conditions of time-out from food reinforcement, and her weight declined to a healthier level.

It should be noted that time-out and extinction schedules may be very frustrating to the learners, with extinction sometimes producing a temporary burst of effort to obtain the lost reinforcements (Amsel & Roussel, 1952). But this frustration is generally less disruptive than the reaction to stronger punishments would be.

Thus far we have indicated that punishment is most effective when it produces reactions opposite to the punished response; when it is strong rather than mild, although this often produces undesirable side effects; and when rewards are simultaneously used to train other behaviors as alternatives to the punished response. Like positive reinforcement, punishment must also be applied immediately and must be given every time the target behavior occurs, at least early in training, if it is to be maximally effective. Practical applications of punishment often fail because they ignore these important considerations.

Given the preceding constraints on the effective use of punishment (plus the fact that we do not enjoy being punished and do not usually enjoy seeing others punished), why do most of us rely on it in various aspects of our lives, such as child rearing, verbal disagreements, our legal system, and so on? The apparent reason is that the suppression of behavior by punishment is often more immediate and dramatic than we can achieve through extinction or through the reinforcement of alternative behaviors. This may be crucial in certain circumstances, such as when a child reaches for a hot stove or tries to run into a busy street. In their discussion of self-injurious behavior, Lovaas and Newsom (1976) argue that the limited use of punishment is the only way to stop some severely autistic children from mutilating themselves, short of tying them to their beds; and that those children's lives are improved because the procedure frees them from being bound, and thus enables them to participate in other aspects of the treatment program. Despite the moral repulsion we may feel at the thought of such measures, their careful use may prevent even greater suffering. Thus the decision to use punishment is a complex one, which reasonably depends on the likelihood of its effectiveness as well as the likelihood of undesirable side effects.

What are the main arguments against and in favor of using punishment?

Negative Reinforcement: Avoidance and Escape

Two-Factor Theory of Cued Avoidance

As you may recall from the previous chapter, Watson and Rayner (1920) trained a boy to fear a rat by associating it with a loud, scary noise. We discussed this as classical rather than instrumental conditioning, because Little Albert's response (CR, fear) did not change the situation. In other words, presentation of the rat (CS) was followed by noise (US) regardless of what Little Albert did, so his response was not an ''instrumental'' one.

But in fact, in 1920, researchers did not generally recognize classical and instrumental conditioning as two distinct kinds of learning. For example, signals that preceded painful shocks were commonly considered to be CSs, even if the subject's CR successfully prevented shock (Figure 3–14). Today we regard the latter, **cued avoidance** procedure as a form of instrumental training, because responses during the warning cue have the effect of avoiding the shock. But because cued avoidance and classical fear conditioning both involve a warning signal, many investigators assumed that cued avoidance must be virtually identical to classical conditioning.

Brogden, Lipman, and Culler (1938) explicitly compared cued avoidance versus classical fear conditioning in an experiment with guinea pigs to determine whether the added, instrumental avoidance contingency would produce more running in a running wheel than classical conditioning alone would. Shock was known to produce running as an unconditioned response (UR), and the classical conditioning group was given a pairing of cue and shock on every trial, so subjects in this group were expected to run (CR) during the cue even though their running would not avoid the shock.

The avoidance group also experienced pairings of the cue with shock, except that the cue terminated without shock whenever a running response occurred (as in Figure 3–14). According to theories of classical conditioning, these omissions of shock in the avoidance group should have extinguished some of their fear, leading to poorer conditioning. Contrary

---

to this prediction, the opportunity to avoid the shock dramatically enhanced performance in the avoidance group.

In order to explain this result, Miller (1948) and others proposed the **two-factor theory** of avoidance, which maintains that classical and instrumental conditioning both contribute to avoidance learning. According to two-factor theory, *fear does become conditioned to the warning cue,* just as it would in classical conditioning (the first factor). But once the cue has become aversive, *terminating it negatively reinforces the avoidance response via instrumental conditioning* (the other factor). For example, if a large dog attacked you every time you cut across a lawn, you might first learn to fear the lawn (or the dog)—the classical conditioning factor. In addition, you might learn to reduce your fear by avoiding the lawn entirely—the instrumental learning factor.

Notice that two-factor theory does *not* explain avoidance learning by saying that subjects avoid the shock itself (or the scary dog). Instead, what subjects learn is to escape from the conditioned aversive cue (the warning signal or the lawn). Avoidance of the shock itself is considered a beneficial result, but not an essential part of the learning process, according to two-factor theory.

Why not simply say that subjects respond because they prefer the no-shock outcome over the shock outcome? The reason is that this common-sense explanation violates three basic tenets of traditional associative theories. First, associations supposedly must involve concrete events such as stimuli and responses, not nonevents such as the cancellation of a shock that might have been presented. Therefore subjects cannot be said to learn about the cancellation per se. Second, associations supposedly depend on temporal contiguity, such as that between the instrumental running response and the end of the warning cue. Therefore subjects cannot associate responses with their ultimate effects, but can only associate them with their immediate effect on the warning signal. Third, traditional associative theories assume that responding occurs automatically as a reaction to currently present stimuli. The

(a) Before Conditioning:

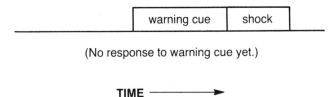

(No response to warning cue yet.)

TIME ⟶

FIGURE 3–14 Cued avoidance procedure: (a) When the subject does not respond, shock follows the warning cue as in a classical conditioning procedure. (b) When the subject does respond during the warning cue, the shock is avoided.

(b) After Conditioning:

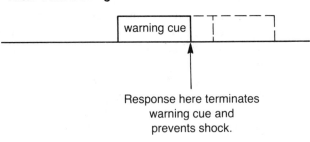

Response here terminates warning cue and prevents shock.

idea that subjects evaluate future possibilities before responding is not something that two-factor theorists would accept, although this kind of explanation is quite in keeping with a cognitive theory (soon to be discussed).

Besides explaining why cued avoidance training is effective, two-factor theory can also account for some other findings. For example, it can explain why extinction of fear to the cue causes a reduction in avoidance responding. If you prevent the avoidance response from occurring during the cue, and then omit the shock at the end, subjects experience extinction of fear because the cue is no longer followed by shock. This **response prevention** (or ''flooding'') technique results in a rapid reduction of conditioned responding, as it should if responding is motivated by classically conditioned fear (Baum, 1970).

On the other hand, avoidance persists much longer than two-factor theory would predict, in an extinction procedure where shocks are no longer presented but responding is still allowed to occur. Subjects in this simple extinction procedure may continue to respond for hundreds of trials, even though the cue is no longer paired with shock at all (Solomon, Kamin, & Wynne, 1953). In our example of the dog on the lawn, suppose the dog had moved away, but you never went close enough to find this out. In that case, you might continue to avoid the lawn indefinitely. Two-factory theory cannot explain this outcome, because the repeated presentations of the warning signal alone (the lawn without the dog) should supposedly lead to the extinction of fear (Herrnstein, 1969).

Another difficulty with two-factor theory is the frequent finding that the strength of avoidance responding is not reliably related to fear of the cue, when fear is measured by some independent method (Mineka, 1979). Yet another weakness is the fact that avoidance can still be learned even if no warning signal is used, and responses merely postpone shocks without terminating any explicit cue. The failure of two-factor theory to account for all these findings compels us to seek other explanations of avoidance learning, to which we turn next.

> *Describe the two ''factors'' identified by the two-factor theory of cued avoidance, and explain how they combine to account for cued avoidance learning.*

The Safety Hypothesis

The cued avoidance task employs discrete trials, which are identified by the presence of the warning cue. Sidman (1953) invented an alternative procedure, called **free operant avoidance,** in which no trials are used. Instead of coming at the end of a warning cue, brief shocks occur in this procedure at regular intervals (e.g., every 15 seconds) until the subject performs the required response. As soon as the subject responds, the impending shock is delayed (e.g., until 30 seconds after the response), which allows subjects to postpone the shock indefinitely if they respond often enough. The important difference between this procedure and the cued avoidance procedure is the fact that the learner in free operant avoidance cannot rely on the presence or absence of a cue to indicate whether it is safe from shock; rather, the learner's own response is the only indicator that shock has been postponed.

As was discussed in Chapter 2, events that signal the absence (or reduced likelihood) of a US can inhibit related CRs. In free operant avoidance, certain proprioceptive (body position) and kinesthetic (body movement) sensations, together with the feel of the response lever as it is pressed, signal that shock (US) will not occur soon. We might therefore expect these response sensations to become classically conditioned inhibitors of fear (CS) in the avoidance situation. The **safety hypothesis** of avoidance proposes that this conditioned reduction of fear provides reinforcement for the avoidance response. Consistent with this suggestion, avoidance is learned faster not only when the avoidance response terminates a warning signal but also when the avoidance response turns on a safety signal instead of turning off the warning signal (D'Amato, Fazzaro, & Etkin, 1968). Thus any kind of feedback that indicates safety following the avoidance response appears to enhance avoidance learning.

The safety hypothesis may explain not only why avoidance learning occurs but also why responding persists so long in the simple extinction procedure. Conditioned inhibition is generally very resistant to extinction (see Chapter 2), so we would expect responding maintained by fear inhibition to be quite persistent. This is a more adequate account of persistence in extinction than that proposed by two-factor theory, which emphasizes fear itself rather than the conditioned inhibition of fear. Thus the safety hypothesis generally agrees better with the facts of avoidance learning than two-factor theory does.

But the safety hypothesis is challenged by evidence that response feedback is not absolutely necessary for avoidance conditioning. Taub, Bacon, and Berman (1965) used surgery to deprive monkeys of all feeling from their arms, and then trained them to avoid shock even though they could not feel or see their responses; nor did the responses terminate a warning signal, as required by two-factor theory. Even in combination, therefore, two-factor theory and the safety hypothesis do not provide a complete account of avoidance learning.

The Cognitive Theory of Avoidance

The final theory we will consider here is Seligman and Johnston's (1973) **cognitive theory of avoidance,** which differs from both two-factor theory and the safety hypothesis in two important ways. First, although the cognitive theory acknowledges that fear is learned in most avoidance procedures, actual learning of the avoidance response itself is explained without reference to classically conditioned fear. Second, the theory is much more similar to Tolman's (1932) expectancy account of learning than it is to traditional reinforcement theory.

The cognitive theory assumes that fear is independent of avoidance responding, which explains why subjects can continue to avoid shock long after all signs of fear have disappeared (Kamin, Brimer, & Black, 1963). According to the theory, fear is classically conditioned through pairings of the cue with shock on the early trials, before the avoidance response is well learned. But that same fear extinguishes later, after avoidance responding has become routine. In our example of the dog on the lawn, you might not be afraid any more after you had learned a slightly different route, but you would still avoid the lawn, even though you no longer felt afraid.

Here is how the cognitive theory explains the occurrence of avoidance learning independently of fear. The learner comes to expect that shock will occur if the response is not performed, but that it will not occur if the response is performed. The stronger these expectancies are, the more likely it is that the subject will choose to perform the avoidance response. Furthermore, these expectancies are strengthened by confirmation (experiences that are consistent with them) and weakened by disconfirmation (experiences that are not consistent).

Based on the preceding assumptions, here is how the cognitive theory explains why you might continue to avoid even after the threat is gone (the dog, unknown to you, is on vacation): You know you will not be attacked if you avoid the lawn, and nothing during extinction (dog's vacation) disconfirms that expectation—that is, there still is no attack when you stay off the lawn. Nor is there any disconfirmation of the other expectation, that walking on the lawn leads to attack—because you no longer venture onto the lawn any more. So long as neither expectation is disconfirmed, the theory predicts that they will remain unchanged and you will continue to avoid the lawn. In order to change those expectations, you must receive information that disconfirms them—for example by being chased onto the lawn by a careless driver and discovering that the dog is no longer in residence. A comparable technique used in the laboratory is the response prevention procedure, which forces subjects to discover that shock no longer occurs when they fail to respond (a procedure that, you should recall, is very effective).

Although Seligman and Johnston (1973) list some findings that their theory does not explain, it clearly can account for the characteristics of avoidance learning that have concerned most researchers. It also illustrates how a theory may need to appeal to classical conditioning (of fear) as well as cognitive processes (choice based on an analysis of expectations) in order to explain the effects of an essentially instrumental procedure.

Our favorite actress, Joan, should perhaps consider using negative reinforcement if she is really serious about practicing for her audition, rather than procrastinating as she often does. One strategy that may work is for her to give a large sum of money to someone she trusts, with the understanding that she is permitted to earn it back by practicing (an example of behavioral contracting). Unless she can prove that she practiced enough, she loses $50 to her friend every day. (Did you think the friend would do all this for free?) The threat of losing all that money would hang over Joan's head each day until she practiced, at which time she would receive negative reinforcement by canceling the threat for the rest of the day. This procedure may not be as bad as it sounds: If the cognitive theory is correct, her fear of losing the money will extinguish when she becomes accustomed to earning it back. Yet she presumably will keep practicing, because the instrumental avoidance response continues independently of the fear that once accompanied it.

☑ *How does the cognitive theory of avoidance explain the persistence of responding during simple extinction, if responding does not actually inhibit fear?*

Uncontrollable and Unpredictable Events

Learned Helplessness

As we discussed in the previous section, continued responding during the standard extinction procedure may prevent learners from discovering that the risk of shock has ended (Seligman & Johnston, 1973). Expecting to be shocked unless they respond, most subjects persist for a very long time, regardless of the fact that no shocks can occur. This cognitive theory of expectancies, together with the basic facts of classical conditioning, thus successfully accounts for most of what we know about avoidance learning.

The idea that learners base their choices on expectancies also helps to explain another phenomenon in avoidance research called **learned helplessness.** This term applies to subjects who once failed in their attempts to escape an aversive experience, and who therefore will not try any more, even though an effective avoidance response becomes available to them later (Seligman & Maier, 1967). According to the cognitive account, these subjects learned to expect the same results whether they responded or not, and so they no longer respond. Even when the shock is later made avoidable, they continue not to respond and therefore never learn what would happen if they did respond. Notice that helplessness is virtually the opposite of what most subjects learn during avoidance training: Successful avoiders continue to respond, even during the simple extinction procedure, and therefore never learn what would happen if they did *not*.

If the cognitive explanation of learned helplessness is correct, subjects that are pretrained with inescapable shocks essentially learn that their responses make no difference (Seligman, 1975). But perhaps a simpler explanation can account for the effects of inescapable shock. Could it be that subjects stop trying, simply because they are exhausted from being shocked so many times?

Seligman and Maier ruled out the idea that shocks alone produce helplessness by using a **yoked control** procedure. Their subjects were dogs, half of which could escape every shock by pushing a panel with their noses. Whenever one of these "escapable shock" dogs turned off the shock for itself, it automatically did so for a dog in the inescapable shock group as well; that is, both dogs were "yoked" together in such a way that they received exactly the same number and timing of shocks. The crucial difference between the two groups of dogs, therefore, was that escapable shock dogs could control the outcome whereas inescapable shock dogs could not. Those dogs that were allowed to control shocks during pretraining learned quickly to avoid shocks later in a different setting. But their yoked companions (the inescapable shock group) did not try to avoid shocks in the new setting, even though they had received no more shocks than the first group. Their previous experience, with shocks that they could not control, prevented them from learning the avoidance response even after avoidance became possible. Thus not every shock produces learned helplessness, but rather only those shocks that the learner is unable to control.

Since Seligman and Maier's original research, criticisms and new observations have led to revisions of the theory (e.g., Abramson, Seligman, & Teasdale, 1978). In some species, inescapable shocks depress movement and may reduce sensitivity to pain, so not all of the behavioral deficit that follows inescapable shock may be attributable to cognitive factors (e.g., Drugan & Maier, 1982). And the effects of uncontrollable outcomes on human learners are not fixed, but instead depend on how those individuals interpret the situation (e.g., Dweck & Repucci, 1973). But many reliable findings are still best explained by the original hypothesis; namely, that experience with inescapable outcomes creates the expectation that actions will be ineffective.

In keeping with this cognitive account of learned helplessness, Seligman and Maier (1967) found that learners may be protected from helplessness by giving them prior experience with success. Some dogs that would later receive inescapable shocks were first trained to successfully escape shocks in a different apparatus. This *inoculation* against helplessness was then followed by the same inescapable shock pretraining and avoidance training that normally promotes learned helplessness. But these subjects, because of their prior success at escaping shock, were not debilitated by the intervening experience with inescapable shocks. During the final phase of the experiment, they learned the avoidance response as quickly as subjects that had received no shocks during pretraining. Once they had learned that responses can be effective, it was as if this expectation protected them from becoming helpless. This finding may offer new hope for warding off human depression or for alleviating it once it has occurred (Seligman, 1975).

◪ *What produces "learned helplessness" and how may it be prevented?*

Preference for Signals

A history of successful escapes from noxious stimuli can provide protection against subsequent helplessness, but so can a signal that immediately precedes or follows the uncontrollable event (Jackson & Minor, 1988). Conceivably, signals might prevent learned helplessness by reducing the perceived intensity of the shocks. But other research suggests that this is not the reason at all. Instead, signals may reduce the conditioning of stimuli in the experimental context, and thereby lower the level of chronic fear.

As Chapter 2 explained, irrelevant background stimuli that are constantly present in the experimental context may become associated with events in the experiment such as food or electric shock. But contextual conditioning may be blocked if another stimulus is reliably correlated with those events, effectively stealing the association away from the context (Durlach, 1983; but cf. Cooper, Aronson, Balsam, & Gibbon, 1990). When experiments involve shocks, contextual conditioning presumably produces chronic fear and stress. It would therefore be adaptive for subjects to seek signals that are correlated with the presence or absence of shock, and thereby reduce chronic fear and perhaps learned helplessness.

It has been repeatedly shown that animals will walk to another part of their apparatus, press a response lever, or perform other behaviors in order to receive a warning signal before shock. Some researchers have argued that the warning signal permits the animal to make postural adjustments or other responses that reduce the perceived intensity of the shock. But Miller, Greco, Vigorito, and Marlin (1983) found the opposite to be true: Instead of alleviating the pain, warning signals actually increased the judged intensity of pain.

Miller and colleagues (1983) began by training rats to rate the perceived aversiveness of shocks. The rats in this study were first trained with water as a reward for pressing one lever after weak shocks and another lever after stronger shocks. Later they were again required to press the levers to indicate intensity, but this time some shocks were preceded by warning signals and some were not. The rats consistently rated signaled shocks as being more intense than shocks that were physically equal but were not signaled. Far from alleviating the pain, therefore, signals evidently made the shock even more painful yet the animals kept choosing warning signals despite the added discomfort they felt when shocks were signaled.

One explanation for this apparent paradox is the safety hypothesis, which maintains that explicit warning signals are preferred only because they help subjects to identify safety periods when shocks will not occur. Recall that a similar hypothesis was proposed to explain the learning of avoidance responses, and that signals associated with a reduced likelihood of the US do serve as conditioned inhibitors of the CR. The safety hypothesis is also supported by studies that show that rats and other animals have fewer ulcers and other stress-related ailments after a regimen of signaled shocks than after unsignaled shocks (Seligman, 1968). These symptoms are characteristic of chronic stress, which may be prevented by limiting fear to the duration of the warning signals.

Arabian and Desiderato (1975) examined the role of safety periods by allowing rats to choose between different patterns of signals in opposite ends of a shuttlebox. Whenever one end of the box provided an explicit signal (a light) during safety periods, and no signal for shocks, the rats chose that end—even over an end in which the safety signal alternated with a warning signal for shocks. This finding clearly suggests that the warning signal itself is not the basis of the preference for signals. It also indicates that subjects were not seeking the maximum amount of information, or they would have preferred the safety signal plus a warning signal for shocks. Instead, subjects prefer environments where the threat of shock is limited to certain identifiable times. The most desirable form of information is a signal correlated with the absence of shock. However, if safety periods can only be identified by the absence of warning signals, subjects will choose to receive those signals rather than to experience chronic fear of unpredictable shock. This research thus provides yet another piece of evidence in support of the safety hypothesis.

☑ *Why might rats prefer to receive warning signals before shock, even if those signals increase the perceived intensity of the shocks?*

MODELING

A Serious Clown Story: The Modeling of Aggression

Thus far in this book, we have concentrated on learning as it occurs through direct personal experience. In classical conditioning, subjects experience a sequence of events and learn to anticipate one or more of them. In instrumental training, subjects receive punishment or reinforcement contingent on their own behavior. Even latent learning, which does not fit either of these simple schemes, involves direct experience with the layout of the maze.

Fortunately, however, direct personal experience is not the only way to learn; merely watching or hearing about the experience of others is sometimes effective also. If we could not learn indirectly from others—through personal observations, conversations, and the electronic and printed media—we would not know nearly as much as we do (Bandura, 1986).

In a now-classic study on learning by example, or **modeling** (Bandura, Ross, & Ross, 1963), preschool children learned to be aggressive by watching other people behave aggressively. Individual children watched a woman, a man, or a costumed character behave violently toward a large "Bobo doll," or toy clown. Overall, it made little difference whether the violence was enacted by an adult in person, by an adult in a realistic film, or by a costumed character in a fantasy film. Children who saw any of these examples became twice as violent as other children, when allowed to play with a similar toy clown. Many of their actions were virtually identical copies of the behaviors they had seen, such as sitting on the Bobo doll and punching it in the nose, or tossing it up while saying, "Throw him in the air." The increased level of aggression, plus its close resemblance to behavior that they had seen, indicates that the children learned aggressive behaviors through mere observation.

Further research has refined our understanding of how we learn from other people, often called **models.** For example, children are more likely to copy behaviors for which the model has received reward rather than punishment. When the model is rewarded, in a procedure called **vicarious reinforcement,** observers not only learn how to perform the actions but also learn to expect reward for performing them. This contrasts with **vicarious punishment,** where observers do not learn to expect reward for performing the modeled behavior. But they do learn and will indeed perform the behavior they saw punished, if they are offered a reward for doing so (Bandura, Grusec, & Menlove, 1966). Thus competence (knowing how to aggress) can arise through vicarious reinforcement, vicarious punishment, or modeling with no outcome, but actual performance of the learned behavior depends on the expected outcome, much as Tolman described with respect to latent learning.

Experiments using more natural settings, and more typical movie and television fare, have generally shown similar effects of filmed violence (Leyens, Camino, Parke, & Berkowitz, 1975; Huesmann, Laperspetz, & Eron, 1984; Josephson, 1987). For example, Leyens and colleagues showed either aggressive or funny movies to different groups of teenage boys in a reform school. Even though the boys' counselors were present to discourage violent behavior, both physical and verbal aggression increased after viewing the aggressive films but not the comedies.

Although increased aggressiveness is not found under all circumstances (Widom, 1989), it occurs frequently enough to warrant serious concern and further study. Parents who wish to reduce the impact of television violence on their children should explain to them how the entertainment industry achieves the appearance of violence while protecting actors from actual injury (Eron, 1982).

On the brighter side, altruistic rather than aggressive actions may be learned from models who engage in prosocial behavior (Midlarsky, Bryan, & Brickman, 1973). The examples that parents set for their children, and that television heroes set for their viewers, may therefore encourage behaviors ranging from the aggressiveness of ethnic and family violence to the altruism of community service and life-saving heroism. Parents should consequently think twice before striking their children as a punishment for fighting, since the example of their actions may speak more loudly than their words.

▱   *How do the effects of vicarious punishment differ from the effects of vicarious reinforcement? What effect do they have in common?*

Varieties of Observational Learning

If we define **observational learning** as learning through nonparticipatory observation, we find that it includes more than just modeling in humans. Researchers have reported observational learning in animals, for example, including rats (e.g. Kohn & Dennis, 1972; Del Russo, 1975), pigeons (Zentall & Hogan, 1975), and monkeys (Cook, Mineka, Wolkenstein, & Laitsch, 1985; Cook & Mineka, 1990).

Kohn and Dennis showed one group of rats some stimuli that were relevant to the task they would later learn. Other rats instead watched some previously trained animals performing the to-be-learned task. Both these groups subsequently learned faster than several control groups, when all were required to learn the same task. This finding demonstrates that learning may result from previews of the relevant stimuli, as well as from watching others perform the actual task.

Even within the realm of human modeling itself, a variety of distinctions have been made between different types of observational learning. Learning by viewing films and television, or through reading or listening to other people, is termed **symbolic modeling** because it relies on photographic or verbal symbols; unlike live or **direct modeling,** in which the model exhibits the actual behavior in person. Virtually every experiment with human subjects therefore uses modeling in the form of verbal instructions, whether or not modeling is the topic of the study.

Modeling, regardless of whether it is direct or indirect, sometimes leads to the learning of general attitudes or concepts rather than specific actions. This social transmission of concepts is termed **abstract modeling.** For example, children's expectations about their own achievement are influenced by cultural stereotypes about their gender, conveyed through such means as children's storybooks (McArthur & Eisen, 1976). Another example of abstract modeling is found in self-guidance training for impulsive children. Therapists who use this technique talk aloud while performing a task, thus showing the children how to achieve self-control through verbal self-instruction (Meichenbaum & Goodman, 1971).

Therapeutic and instructional methods such as this, which teach by demonstrating desired ways of thinking, are characterized as **cognitive modeling.**

A final example involves learning through a combination of observation and participation. Research has shown such **participatory modeling** to be extremely effective for the treatment of phobias. Bandura, Blanchard, and Ritter (1969) asked some adults who intensely feared snakes to watch through a window while a model handled a live nonpoisonous specimen. Immediately after this direct modeling phase, they were encouraged to touch the snake themselves while wearing gloves, and then they were led through increasingly daring steps until they could handle the snake confidently without gloves. Their dramatic reduction in fear exceeded that of other treatment groups, which received symbolic modeling (via film) or systematic desensitization (as described in Chapter 2). Compared to a no-treatment control group, symbolic modeling and desensitization produced significant improvement but not as much as participatory modeling.

Observational learning is quite pervasive, figuring prominently in our learning of language (Bandura, 1986, pp. 502–508), thought patterns, and emotions, as well as skilled behaviors of all kinds. The fact that it can occur without overt responding and reinforcement poses yet another challenge to the S-R contiguity and reinforcement theories, which maintain that instrumental behavior must be performed in order to be learned. The idea of learning through observation is consistent with the expectancy approach, but exactly how that learning develops and is organized has not been adequately specified by any existing theory. There thus remains room for associative theorists to assist in elaborating this largely cognitive approach.

    Give examples of the five types of modeling described in this section, as well as an example of observational learning in which no modeling occurs.

CONCLUDING REMARKS: Lack of a Unified Theory

Research on instrumental learning has led to many practical applications, some of which were presented in this chapter. Often those applications arose by accident, or as a result of theories that are so outdated (Guthrie, 1952) or so specialized (Seligman & Johnston, 1973) that they explain very few of the facts about instrumental learning. As in classical conditioning and many other areas of research, there is currently no viable, unified account for all the facts about instrumental learning.

Instead of a single adequate theory, we must again consult both the cognitive and the associative perspectives to gain a fuller understanding of learning. Each has led to important discoveries about conditioned reinforcement, avoidance, and other topics in instrumental learning. This complementarity is equally apparent in the next chapter, which investigates stimulus control and representational processes in instrumental learning.

CHAPTER 4 _____

Stimulus Control and Representation

APPLICATION: The Fruits of Understanding

Usually Joan finishes assignments on time, but unfortunately she did not do the readings before today's pop quiz in botany. She has just begun defining fruit as "the edible part of certain trees, vines, etc.," when she suddenly recalls something from her freshman biology course that makes her change her answer. "The mature ovary . . . ," she writes, and then finishes answering the question quite respectably except for misspelling angiosperm.

Our friend has luckily distinguished the common meaning of the word fruit *from its technical meaning, which includes more than just the fruits that we eat. Of course, the technical concept is not always appropriate, just as the everyday concept is out of place sometimes. Instead of responding one way all the time, Joan must judge which meaning is appropriate in each circumstance.*

The ability to discriminate between different situations is essential for intelligent behavior. Equally important, however, is the ability to recognize similarities between situations, as when Joan guessed that the definition from freshman biology would still hold up in botany class. How does Joan manage to deal with a world full of differences and similarities? How do you?

Like Joan, we need to be aware of both similarities and differences. For example, we can usually recognize a familiar face regardless of changes in facial expression, angle of view, and so forth. When we compare the face to our memory, we somehow perceive both how similar it remains and how it has changed as a result of injury, emotion, lighting, and so on. It would be easy to take these abilities for granted, except that mistakes sometimes happen. Anyone who has accidentally overlooked a friend at a party, or mistaken one person for another should realize that noticing similarities and differences is not a simple matter.

This chapter is concerned with stimulus similarity and difference as they affect instrumental learning. It is also concerned with concept formation and symbol use as they occur in related training procedures. Besides extending our understanding of instrumental learning, research in this area has led to discoveries about mental representations and memory in animals that lack human language. We will touch briefly on those discoveries as a prelude to more detailed discussions of memory in later chapters.

Explanations based on the cognitive and associative traditions appear repeatedly throughout the chapter, demonstrating again how our understanding of complex phenomena has benefitted from a diversity of theoretical approaches.

GENERALIZATION

Discriminative Stimuli

Reinforcement theorists have long disagreed concerning the role of stimuli in instrumental learning. According to S-R reinforcement theorists (Thorndike, 1911; Hull, 1943), responses become directly associated to stimuli and are then evoked by them on future occasions. In contrast, operant conditioning theorists characterize behavior as spontaneously "emitted" rather than evoked by environmental cues (Skinner, 1938).

But even Skinner recognized that operants are influenced by **discriminative stimuli** (S^Ds), which indicate the consequences of responding. For example, Joan enjoys eating oranges that have a certain color and a certain degree of firmness, but she does not enjoy oranges that are too hard and green. These S^Ds serve as cues to indicate the likely consequences of buying and eating the orange. Joan is more likely to eat oranges whose S^Ds are associated with a high quality of reinforcement (good taste).

The relationship between an S^D and a reinforced response is somewhat like the relationship between a CS and a US: The CS signals when the US is likely to occur, and the S^D signals when responses are likely to be reinforced.[1] Examples of S^Ds in everyday life include clocks, traffic signs and signals, written and spoken instructions, and whatever other stimuli guide us to perform tasks successfully. Like CSs, S^Ds tell the learner what to expect and therefore how to act. This commonality between the two types of stimuli is reflected in the use of a single term, **stimulus control,** to refer to the influence of stimuli on responding in both classical and instrumental conditioning.

As you may recall from Chapter 2, classically conditioned subjects respond not only to the stimulus that was used during original training, but also to a range of stimuli that resemble it. Such stimulus generalization is also common in instrumental learning. In both kinds of learning, generalization is adaptive for two reasons. First, even if an object stays the same from one time to the next, it is often seen from a different angle, under different illumination, and so on, so generalization helps us respond consistently to the same object despite its changing appearance. Second, generalization enables us to apply previous learning to novel situations. Instead of acting randomly, we can base our behavior on our experience in similar situations. For example, although you may never have seen this particular book before you went to buy it, you knew how to carry it to the sales counter and pay for it, thanks to generalization from items you had bought before. (By the way, do you closely inspect books that you plan to buy? If you ever find you have bought a book with many pages missing, as one of the authors recently did, you might start checking other books more carefully before you buy them—another instance of generalization.)

⬛ *What is a discriminative stimulus, and what symbol is used to represent it?*

Measuring Generalization

In order to discover the basic principles that govern stimulus generalization, researchers have conducted laboratory experiments with animals as well as people. Pigeons have excellent eyesight, and so a keylight is commonly used as the S^D when they are the subjects. The pigeon is first trained to peck the lighted response key under an intermittent schedule of reinforcement, so that responding will persist during the subsequent generalization test even if no further reinforcement is given (the PRE effect; Guttman & Kalish, 1956). During the generalization test itself, the keylight is changed to one hue (color) after another, and the bird's responses to each one are recorded. Usually the original S^D excites the most responding, and similar stimuli excite some responding but not as much. The result is a sloped **excitatory generalization gradient** with a peak at the original S^D (Figure 4–1).

As another example, imagine that someone offered you an orange which was rather red or yellow instead of orange colored. Although you might try one of these, the likelihood is not as great as if it were a truly orange-colored orange. Once reinforcement has become associated with a particular stimulus, deviations from that stimulus generally reduce responding compared to the original stimulus itself.

⬛ *What is stimulus generalization, and how is it usually measured in pigeons?*

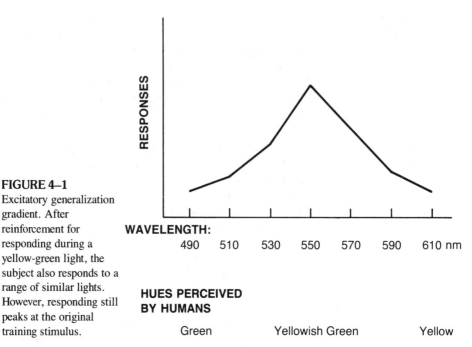

FIGURE 4–1
Excitatory generalization gradient. After reinforcement for responding during a yellow-green light, the subject also responds to a range of similar lights. However, responding still peaks at the original training stimulus.

WAVELENGTH:
490   510   530   550   570   590   610 nm

HUES PERCEIVED BY HUMANS

Green   Yellowish Green   Yellow

Theories of Generalization

Two explanations were traditionally offered to explain why subjects respond to stimuli other than the original training stimulus. According to **continuity theory,** subjects learn simultaneously about all the stimuli that are present, and then respond when stimuli resemble any from the original training situation. This assumption that learning is a simple, automatic, and nonselective process is typical of the associative tradition. **Noncontinuity theory** assumes the opposite: Subjects do not learn continuously about all aspects of their environment; they learn selectively by paying attention to some distinctions but not others. This emphasis on selective attention places noncontinuity theory in the cognitive tradition, because it suggests that complex mental processes intervene between the stimulus and the response. Let us examine how each of these theories might explain stimulus generalization.

According to continuity theory, perception is inherently variable and unfocused (Hull, 1943, pp. 188, 216). Even though the actual SD remains the same throughout training, the learner's sensations are slightly different each time; so over the course of training, responding becomes associated to a variety of stimulus experiences. The test stimuli are perceived inconsistently as well, which makes even more of them confusible with the original SD. Subjects therefore do not always exactly recognize the familiar SD, and they respond in varying degrees to other generalization test stimuli. Continuity theory thus explains generalization as a result of disorderly perceptual processes, which guarantee confusion among stimuli.

In contrast, noncontinuity theory (Lashley & Wade, 1946) assumes that perception is normally very focused and consistent, and that generalization occurs because the subject is not paying attention to the relevant aspects of the stimulus. For example, if a pigeon did not notice the hue of a keylight, we would not expect the pigeon's responding to change when the hue changed. This lack of attention would produce a flat generalization gradient (equally high responding to every hue), even though the pigeon is capable of fine stimulus discrimination among hues whenever it actually attends to them. From this perspective, therefore, the steepness of the generalization gradient for hue (or any other stimulus characteristic) is an indicator of how closely the learner is paying attention to that aspect; it is not a picture of permanent perceptual confusion, as the continuity theorists maintained.

☑ *Contrast the two traditional theories of stimulus generalization in terms of their explanations for why a pigeon might peck an orange-yellow keylight almost as much as a yellow keylight, even though rewards have been given only for pecking the yellow one.*

Subsequent research has failed to completely support either the continuity or the noncontinuity account of stimulus generalization. For example, perceptions do fluctuate somewhat from time to time, as continuity theorists claimed, but the fluctuations are not enough to account for the wide range of stimuli to which subjects often respond during generalization testing. Subjects do learn more about some aspects of a situation than others, but this does not depend on reinforcement in the way that noncontinuity theory claims. The latter point may be made clearer by two brief examples.

Noncontinuity theory incorrectly predicts that subjects will pay attention only to stimulus characteristics that have provided information about reinforcement, and not to other aspects of the stimulus (Lashley & Wade, 1946, p. 74). For example, chickens in a generalization test would be expected to disregard hue if it had never mattered before. If the whole training environment was one hue, with the S^D merely being brighter than everything else, then the subjects would be expected to attend to brightness rather than hue. In fact, however, chickens will respond more to the original hue than to others during a generalization test, even if the original hue is the only one they ever saw before (e.g., Riley & Leuin, 1971). This demonstrates that subjects pay attention to some aspects of the stimulus even if it has never provided information about reinforcement.

As another example, if subjects pay attention to only those differences that have been related to reinforcement, then a procedure that reinforces responses to green and extinguishes responses to red should increase subjects' attention only to hue. It should not refine their reactions to shape, brightness, or anything else that is the same for both SDs, and that therefore is irrelevant to reinforcement. Contrary to this prediction, discrimination training sharpens stimulus control by these irrelevant aspects as well (Switalski, Lyons, & Thomas, 1966).

Noncontinuity theory has made an important contribution to our understanding of stimulus control by suggesting testable hypotheses about attention and learning. But some degree of stimulus control occurs even without discrimination training, and discrimination training sharpens control by irrelevant as well as relevant stimulus dimensions. These findings indicate that noncontinuity theory does not adequately characterize the role of attention in stimulus generalization.

☑ *What does noncontinuity theory wrongly predict when subjects have seen only one hue before being tested for generalization?*

SIMPLE DISCRIMINATIONS

Successive Discrimination

In some discrimination procedures, such as those involving a choice between two options, the contrasting stimuli are presented simultaneously. But in **successive discrimination**

procedures, the subject must learn to respond a certain way when a particular stimulus is present but not otherwise. For example, if you want some food that is visible in a snack machine, you may insert money and obtain it. But if you see no snacks remaining, you should probably look for another machine. In other words, the visible food serves as an S^D to indicate whether responding will be reinforced. Although successive and simultaneous discriminations are similar in many ways, each type of discrimination is better suited than the other for studying particular phenomena. This section therefore focuses on successive discrimination procedures, leaving the discussion of simultaneous procedures until later.

Behavioral Contrast in Multiple Schedules

Often experimenters train subjects to learn successive discriminations by using a **multiple reinforcement schedule.** *Multiple* means that two or more independent schedules alternate with each other, signaled by a distinctive S^D (or S^Ds). In a multiple schedule for pigeons, for example, a keylight might be lit whenever a continuous reinforcement schedule is in effect but not during periods of extinction. The pigeon would eventually learn to respond only during the component signaled by the keylight S^D.

If a multiple schedule contains two or more intermittent schedules of reinforcement, subjects learn to respond in ways appropriate to each component. For instance, pecking to a yellow keylight might increase in a scalloped pattern before each reinforcement in a fixed-interval (FI) schedule, but this would quickly change to a steady, unbroken pattern of responding as soon as a blue keylight appeared as a signal for variable-ratio (VR) reinforcement.

Although the response *patterns* in multiple schedules are what one would expect from research on the basic schedules, the overall response *rates* often are not. In particular, the normal difference between response rates in the different schedules usually becomes magnified in a multiple schedule. For instance, a variable-interval 2-minute schedule (VI–2) usually produces only a moderate rate of responding. But if responding in the other component of the multiple schedule is extinguished, responding in the VI–2 component increases (Figure 4–2a). Conversely, VI–2 may produce less responding than usual if it alternates with a schedule that generates faster responding than it does (such as VR–10) (Figure 4–2b). This exaggeration of differences in response rate when one pattern of reinforcement follows another is known as **behavioral contrast.**

☑ *What is a multiple schedule of reinforcement, and how does responding on such a schedule often differ from what one would expect based on the separate schedules?*

Theories of Contrast

Some instances of behavioral contrast may be explained by the **additivity hypothesis,** which deals specifically with key pecking in multiple schedules of reinforcement. Recall that different keylights are typically used to distinguish between the components. The additivity hypothesis points out that the keylight S^D that produces faster responding also is usually correlated with an increased frequency of food (or water) presentation, almost as if it were a CS in an autoshaping procedure. This correlation may produce some classically conditioned keypecks in addition to the instrumental pecks to that S^D, thereby exaggerating the difference in responding between the components and producing behavioral contrast (Boakes, Halliday, & Poli, 1975; Schwartz, 1975).

Although the additivity hypothesis may help to explain some instances, it fails to explain contrast that occurs when rats press levers for rewards (Hinson & Staddon, 1978) or

(a) Responses per Minute

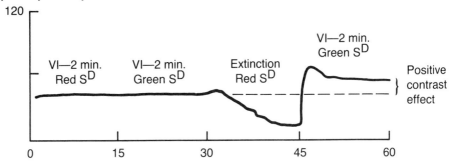

(b) Responses per Minute

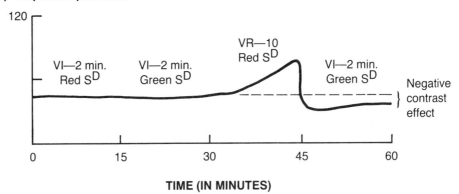

TIME (IN MINUTES)

FIGURE 4–2 Behavioral contrast occurs when subjects experience alternating schedules that control different rates of responding: (a) Extinction of responding to red produces positive contrast in the response to green. (b) Enrichment of the reinforcement opportunities in red produces negative contrast in the response to green.

when there are no S^Ds that might serve as CSs (Flaherty, 1982). One method for demonstrating behavioral contrast without S^Ds is merely to change the magnitude or quality of reward suddenly after several days of training. In a study by Crespi (1942), different groups of rats received either strong or weak reinforcement in a maze for several days and were then shifted to the opposite magnitude (Figure 4–3). Those shifted from strong to weak reinforcement ran through the maze more slowly after the shift than rats that had received the weak reinforcer from the beginning, as if those shifted from the strong reinforcement were depressed about the loss. And those shifted from weak to strong reinforcement ran more rapidly than rats that had received the strong reinforcer from the beginning, as if elated by the improvement. Thus it is not necessary to alternate schedules in synchrony with keylight S^Ds, in order to produce behavioral contrast.

The additivity hypothesis clearly cannot account for all instances of behavioral contrast. In comparison, Crespi's (1942) **elation-depression** hypothesis is much more general: Subjects who have become accustomed to small or infrequent rewards are excited by a shift to richer reward conditions, and subjects who have become accustomed to large or frequent rewards are disappointed by a decrease. This could explain not only Crespi's own findings,

---

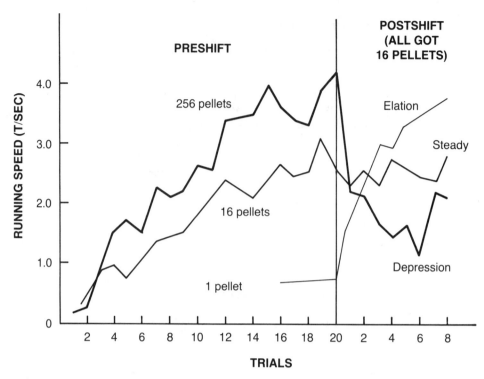

FIGURE 4–3 Contrast can occur after a single shift of reward magnitude from strong to weak or from weak to strong. In comparison to subjects who received 16 pellets throughout, subjects shifted from 256 pellets or 1 pellet showed depression or elation, respectively.

Source: Adapted from Crespi, L. P. (1942). Quantitative variation of incentive and performance in the white rat. *American Journal of Psychology, 55.* With permission of the University of Illinois Press.

but also why pecking increases (elation) in one component of a multiple schedule if the previous one contained extinction, and why it decreases (depression) in one component if the previous one contained more frequent responding and reinforcement.

Mackintosh (1974), however, casts doubt on the elation-depression account because contrast occurs much less commonly than that hypothesis predicts. Rather, he argues that contrast may result from elation or depression in some situations but may depend on other causes in other situations.

Provide two potential explanations for contrast in multiple schedules of reinforcement for keypecking. Why is the more general explanation not necessarily the correct one?

Peak Shift After Discrimination Training

When reinforcement is available during a yellow-green keylight but not during a yellow keylight, subjects learn to respond only during yellow-green. This kind of discrimination is called *intra*dimensional ("intra-" meaning "within") because the S^D's differ within a single stimulus dimension—hue. Generalization gradients measured after intradimensional training have sharper peaks than usual (less generalization), which makes sense if we assume that subjects have learned to pay closer attention to differences along the relevant dimension (Figure 4–4). Furthermore, the gradient is shifted away from the S^D for extinction, so responding is no longer maximal to yellow-green but instead peaks at green, as shown in Figure 4–4. This phenomenon, known as **peak shift,** has been a focus of much interest because it means that subjects respond more to a novel stimulus (in this example, green) than they do to the S^D for reinforcement (Hanson, 1959).

Notice also that the gradient obtained after discrimination training appears to have a "bite" missing from the right side. Two decades before this bite and the peak shift were actually observed, Spence (1937) predicted them both: He believed that inhibition, or a tendency *not* to respond, would generalize from the extinction S^D (e.g., yellow) to other stimuli (Figure 4–5). Because it is relatively close to yellow, yellow-green supposedly receives generalized inhibition, and so it no longer produces peak responding. But green, being farther from yellow, receives generalized excitation without inhibition. Therefore if excitation and inhibition add together to determine responding, we might expect green to be

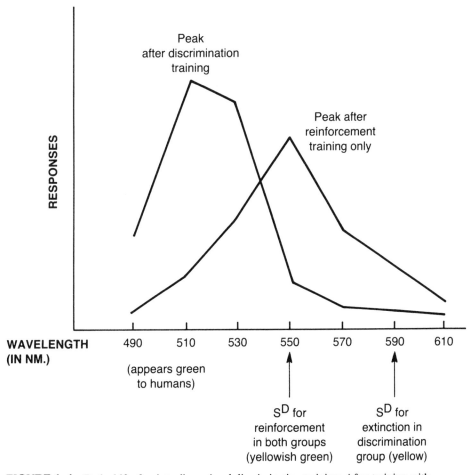

FIGURE 4–4   Peak shift after intradimensional discrimination training: After training with reinforcement during a yellow-green light and extinction during a yellow light, responding peaks to a light (green) that resembles the reinforcement S^D but is remote from the extinction S^D.

the peak of the generalization gradient. This ingenious explanation is one of the most famous in the associative tradition of learning theory.

Before concluding that Spence's (1937) explanation was correct, we need to know whether inhibition really generalizes like excitation. Unfortunately, inhibitory generalization cannot be measured separately after intradimensional training, because its effects cannot be clearly distinguished from the effects of excitation, which generalize to many of the same stimuli.

In order to measure inhibitory generalization separately, researchers may instead train subjects in **inter**dimensional ("inter" meaning "between") discrimination procedures. In interdimensional discriminations, a second S^D is created by adding an extra stimulus element to the first S^D while leaving all their other aspects identical. To record a gradient of inhibition around yellow, for instance, the experimenter might use a white + on a blank

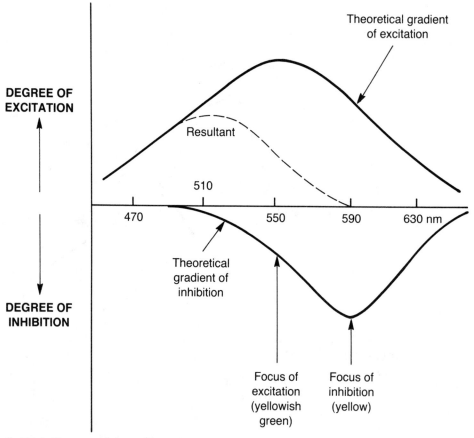

FIGURE 4–5 Additive gradients of excitation and inhibition. Generalization of inhibition from yellow may be responsible for reduced responding to yellow-green. Green, which is farther from yellow, receives less inhibition, so the peak of responding shifts to green (510) from yellowish green (550), as predicted by adding the gradients together (resultant).

Source: Adapted from Spence, K. W. (1937). The differential response in animals to stimuli varying within a single dimension. *Psychological Review, 44.* In the public domain.

background as the S^D for reinforcement, and a white + on a yellow background as the S^D for extinction (Figure 4–6). The white + would therefore be common to both stimuli, and discrimination would depend on the presence or absence of yellow. Interdimensional training does not blur the effects of excitatory and inhibitory generalization; nor does it produce a peak shift, since the S^D for reinforcement (white + in our example) is not located on the stimulus dimension being tested (hue).

The stimulus that signals extinction (white + on yellow) is often represented by the symbol S^Δ, to distinguish it from the reinforced S^D. (The symbols S + and S- are also often used, but these are potentially confusing because the + shape actually forms part of both the positive S^D and the S^Δ in our example.) In the preceding example, generalization testing would be conducted by presenting the + repeatedly in combination with various background hues. Under these circumstances, subjects usually respond least to yellow, slightly more to similar hues, and even more to dissimilar hues, yielding a U-shaped gradient like the one shown in the figure. Thus an **inhibitory generalization gradient** is approximately the mirror image of the excitatory gradient that would be obtained if yellow were the S^D for reinforcement.

Rilling (1977) summarizes additional evidence that supports Spence's (1937) explanation, except that the inhibitory S^D need not actually be inhibitory in an absolute sense in order to produce the peak shift. For example, if it is associated with intermittent reinforcement, rather than extinction, it may still produce a peak shift—so long as it controls a lower rate of responding than other stimuli do (a U-shaped gradient). Apparently, therefore, peak shift occurs when (relative) inhibition spreads unevenly to other stimuli, affecting the S^D for reinforcement but not necessarily affecting stimuli that are farther from the focus of inhibition.

 Why are interdimensional discrimination procedures useful for testing a theory about peak shift, which occurs only after intradimensional training?

Overshadowing and Blocking

The S^Δ in the preceding discussion consisted of + and yellow compounded together. The plus shape occurred alone as a signal for reinforcement, and yellow was added only during extinction; consequently, both parts of the stimulus were informative and both influenced responding at different times.

But if the parts of a compound stimulus always occur together so that they are redundant with each other, subjects may seem to learn about only one or the other part (Reynolds, 1961; Miles & Jenkins, 1973). In the experiment by Miles and Jenkins, for example, several groups of pigeons were rewarded for pecking a brightly lit response key accompanied by a tone. In other words, the S^D for reinforcement was a tone plus bright light compound stimulus in all groups (Figure 4–7).

The S^Δ was a keylight alone, which was either equally bright or dimmer than the keylight associated with reinforcement. In groups where the S^Δ was very similar to the reinforcement S^D, subjects presumably had to pay attention to the tone in order to discriminate between the two S^Ds. In other groups, however, the tone was redundant; that is, it did not add any information because the lights were already clearly discriminable.

The results depended on whether the tone was redundant or not during training. Groups tested after experience with an informative tone responded during the tone regardless of how bright the keylight was, as though they had learned only about the tone. But subjects that had been trained with a redundant tone responded primarily to bright keylights, regardless

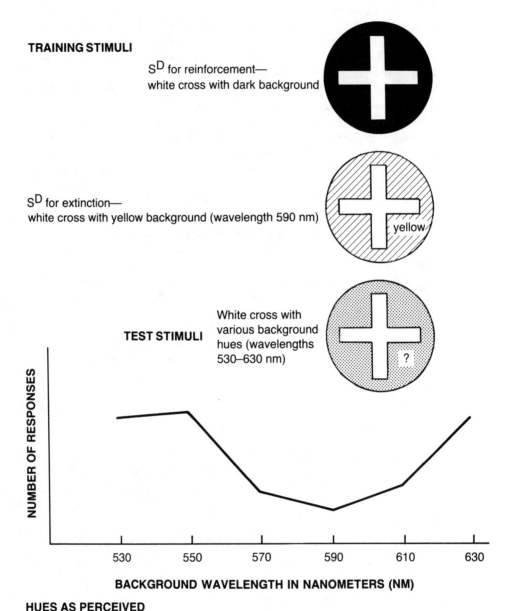

TRAINING STIMULI

S^D for reinforcement—
white cross with dark background

S^D for extinction—
white cross with yellow background (wavelength 590 nm)

yellow

TEST STIMULI White cross with
various background
hues (wavelengths
530–630 nm)

?

NUMBER OF RESPONSES

530 550 570 590 610 630

BACKGROUND WAVELENGTH IN NANOMETERS (NM)

**HUES AS PERCEIVED
BY PEOPLE:**

(green) (yellow) (orange)

FIGURE 4–6 Measurement of inhibitory generalization gradient after interdimensional discrimination training: (a) Procedure for interdimensional training; S^Ds for reinforcement and extinction share a white plus shape, but only the extinction S^D has a colored background. (b) By varying the color of the background around the color associated with extinction, researchers measure the spread of inhibition to other hues. The excitatory white shape maintains some amount of responding to all stimuli.

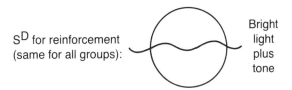

S^D for reinforcement
(same for all groups):

Bright
light
plus
tone

FIGURE 4–7 Stimuli employed by Miles and Jenkins (1973) in a study of overshadowing. When the tone was redundant with a clearly discriminable light, subjects learned less about the tone than when it was informative.

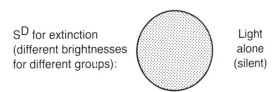

S^D for extinction
(different brightnesses
for different groups):

Light
alone
(silent)

of whether the tone was present or not. Thus the visual stimuli overpowered the tone unless it was the only clear signal for reinforcement—in which case it overpowered them instead.

This overpowering of one stimulus by another, called overshadowing, was discussed in Chapter 2 because it also occurs in classical conditioning. One possible explanation is that subjects may stop learning when they are no longer surprised by outcomes (Kamin, 1969). Subjects who learn what to expect because of the lights may learn nothing more, whereas those who continue to be confused may keep learning about the tone. This finding is paralleled by demonstrations of associative blocking in multiple schedules, where prior learning about one S^D blocks learning about an added, redundant one (e.g., Mackintosh & Honig, 1970). Thus the pattern of previous reinforcements appears to be an important determinant of what stimuli subjects learn about in instrumental as in classical conditioning.

☑ *Why did the tone strongly control responding in some of Miles and Jenkins' (1973) groups but not in others?*

Acquired Distinctiveness

Terrace (1963) reported a procedure that helps subjects to learn a successive discrimination "errorlessly"; that is, without ever responding much to the stimulus that signals nonreward. This procedure, called **fading,** requires that the reinforcement and extinction S^Ds be very different in the beginning, so that responding will not generalize from one to the other. Then the S^D for extinction is made to resemble the reinforcement S^D more and more, in such a gradual way that subjects continue to respond very differently to the two stimuli.

In Terrace's (1963) most successful fading procedure for errorless discrimination learning, pigeons were rewarded for pecking a red keylight (variable interval schedule). As soon as they learned to peck red, the key was darkened for five seconds (the S^D for nonreinforcement) and then reilluminated with red for a minute or more, then darkened for several more seconds, and so on. Darkening of the response key was soon replaced by brief presentations of a dim green keylight as the extinction S^D, which was gradually made brighter and longer in duration. Eventually the green S^D for extinction and the red S^D for reinforcement each remained bright for three minutes at a time, but subjects continued to respond only during red. In contrast subjects that received bright red and green S^Ds throughout training, or prolonged training with the red keylight before fading the green one in, made many more errors.

Several researchers have found similar fading procedures to be helpful in teaching children to discriminate among visual forms. For example, Egeland (1975) taught three groups of preschool children to discriminate between similar letters of the alphabet, such as *R* versus *P,* and *G* versus *C.* One group was taught with red highlighting on the letters' distinctive features (the right leg of *R* or the capped upright of *G*), with the highlighting being gradually faded out during training. This fading group made fewer than half as many errors as other groups and remembered significantly more than the others after a one week delay. Memory was not improved, however, in another fading group whose red cue failed to highlight the distinctive features. Thus the effectiveness of fading sometimes depends on the particular manner in which it is done.

Fading may be regarded as one technique for achieving **acquired distinctiveness** (i.e., easier discrimination learning as a result of prior training on a related discrimination). Lawrence (1952) argued that training with easily discriminable stimuli causes subjects to pay attention to the relevant dimension, and that it is then much easier to learn a more difficult discrimination involving the same stimulus dimension. Consistent with this conclusion, Marsh (1969) trained pigeons to peck a green keylight but not a yellow-green keylight. Prior training on this easy hue discrimination helped subjects learn a harder hue discrimination, more than did prior training on an easy brightness discrimination. Therefore learning an easy discrimination is not sufficient to facilitate learning a more difficult one; rather, the easy discrimination must also involve a distinction that is relevant to the difficult one.

In our earlier critique of noncontinuity theory, we argued that reinforcement does not alter attention in the simple manner proposed by that theory. But demonstrations of overshadowing, associative blocking, and acquired distinctiveness show that reinforcement is still an important factor in determining what stimuli subjects will learn about.

☑ *What distinguishes the fading procedure from other techniques for achieving acquired distinctiveness?*

Simultaneous Discrimination

In **simultaneous discrimination** procedures, two or more response options are available at the same time. Over a series of trials in a T-maze, for example (Figure 4–8), subjects may be rewarded only for turning right at the choice point. Or an experimenter could reward subjects for choosing the route marked by a checkered pattern rather than a solid pattern, regardless of whether the checkered pattern is to the left or the right. Each species learns more easily in certain situations; for example, laboratory rats tend to learn better with location cues (right vs. left) than with visual cues in the T-maze.

Because we cannot be everywhere and do everything at once, we must constantly choose what to do next. Of course, our real-life choices are usually more complicated than those in simultaneous discrimination experiments, but the phenomena we discover in simple experiments can sometimes be recognized in our daily lives as well.

Transposition of Choices

There are many ways in which we might learn to choose the stimulus associated with reward (e.g., gray rather than black). We might learn only about a positive gray stimulus (to approach it), or only about a negative black stimulus (to avoid it), or perhaps about both. Or we might learn a more general rule, such as "approach whatever stimulus is lighter in color (even if it is not precisely the same as the gray used during training)."

(a) Rewarded for Choosing the Checkered Stimulus:

FIGURE 4–8

Simultaneous discriminations: The experimenter presents a checkered pattern or a solid pattern from which subjects must choose. They may be rewarded, for example, for choosing the checkered pattern every time (left columns). Alternatively, they may be rewarded for learning the simultaneous discrimination between left and right (right columns). + indicates the choice associated with reward, – the choice associated with nonreward.

(b) Rewarded for Choosing the Stimulus on the Right:

Learning to approach gray and avoid black are examples of absolute associations, involving specific stimulus-response connections. Learning to go to the lighter of two stimuli, on the other hand, involves a relationship between stimuli more than it involves the particular stimuli themselves. According to the cognitive perspective, relational learning would permit subjects to transpose what they have learned onto new situations, in much the same way that musical arrangers transpose a melody into another key (Figure 4–9). **Transposition** preserves the relationships within a pattern, without preserving the individual identity of the parts that is so important from the associative perspective. For example, a chimpanzee that is rewarded for choosing a medium gray, rather than dark gray, might later choose light over medium gray—even though light gray has never served as an S^D before. Such a preference for more extreme choices has indeed been reported by many investigators (e.g., Spence, 1937; Kendler, 1950).

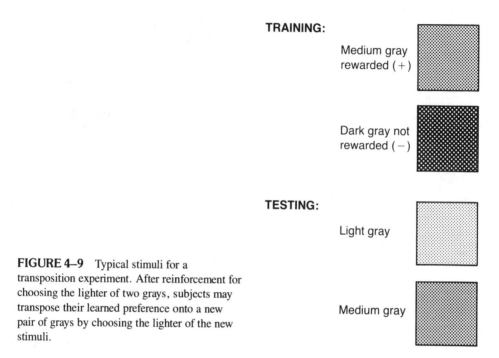

TRAINING:

Medium gray rewarded (+)

Dark gray not rewarded (−)

TESTING:

Light gray

FIGURE 4–9 Typical stimuli for a transposition experiment. After reinforcement for choosing the lighter of two grays, subjects may transpose their learned preference onto a new pair of grays by choosing the lighter of the new stimuli.

Medium gray

Although transposition in simultaneous discriminations was first thought to be explainable only in cognitive, relational terms, Spence (1937) argued that it may be explained just as well in terms of absolute associations. In fact, Spence's theory was originally developed to account for transposition rather than peak shift (even though we discussed that explanation first).

Figure 4–5 showed how Spence's theory accounts for peak shift, by assuming that inhibition generalizes unevenly from the stimulus associated with extinction. By substituting different degrees of brightness for the hues in the figure, we can see what would happen if medium gray (in the middle) was the S^D for reinforcement and dark gray (on the right) was the S^D for extinction. During the generalization test, subjects would respond most to lighter grays because they are farther from the focus of inhibition (dark gray) than the gray associated with reward is. Likewise, if the same factors determine subjects' choices in a transposition experiment, then subjects should choose lighter grays over the gray associated with reward, because they are farther from the focus of inhibition. This tendency to choose the lighter of two grays, even though the lighter one is not the S^D for reinforcement, constitutes transposition.

Researchers have tested Spence's hypothesis that generalized inhibition causes transposition as well as peak shift. If it is true, then peak shift should always occur whenever transposition does, because both are consequences of uneven inhibition. In fact, however, the inhibition that causes peak shift is not necessary for transposition. This is clear from two kinds of experiments. In the first, generalization tests revealed no peak shift even though transposition occurred in a simultaneous choice test (Marsh, 1967; Sachs, 1969). In the other kind of experiment, choices of an intermediate-sized box were reinforced while choices of larger as well as smaller boxes were extinguished. Equal inhibition from both large and small stimuli would not have shifted the peak of the generalization gradient, but chimpanzees and monkeys still transposed their preference for the intermediate size to a new set of three boxes anyway (Gonzalez, Gentry, & Bitterman, 1954; Gentry, Overall, & Brown, 1959). Evidently, transposition does not depend on uneven inhibition, and does involve relational learning after all.

The conclusion that transposition of choices occurs through relational learning, without inhibition, means that learning may differ in important ways after simultaneous versus successive discrimination training. In either case, subjects respond more to stimuli that are unlike the extinction cue than they do to the reinforcement cue itself. But this shift depends on inhibition only after successive discriminations, not after simultaneous discriminations. Transposition after simultaneous discriminations is therefore more consistent with the cognitive approach than with traditional associative theories of conditioning.

☑ *Suppose that subjects were rewarded for choosing gray rather than white, and were then tested on a choice between the orginal gray and an even darker gray. What response would represent transposition in the test?*

Learning After Shifts in Discrimination.

As we already discussed, transposition tests involve a shift in choices within a single stimulus dimension. For example, if brightness is the relevant dimension, subjects might be trained with medium versus dark gray stimuli and then tested with light vs. medium gray. Once a researcher has measured subjects' preferences between the final stimuli, the transposition experiment usually ends.

But if the researcher wants to discover how discrimination training affects later learning, rather than just later preferences, then the experiment cannot end there. Instead, the choice of one stimulus must be reinforced after the shift until it has clearly been learned. We say that this two-stage training procedure involves an ***intra*dimensional shift,** because both discriminations (before and after) are within the same stimulus dimension. For example, if subjects have learned to pay attention to brightness in the first discrimination, they generally learn another brightness discrimination faster than they otherwise would.

The hardest of all intradimensional shifts is the **reversal shift,** in which the original S^D for reinforcement becomes the S^D for extinction, and vice versa (Figure 4–10a). This kind of shift obviously involves the same stimulus dimension both before and after the shift, since the very same stimuli are used both times. But subjects must learn to choose the stimulus they previously avoided and avoid the stimulus they previously chose, which offsets the advantage of keeping the stimulus dimension the same.

Still, adults learn reversal shifts faster than they learn ***extra*dimensional shifts,** in which the stimulus dimension that was relevant in the beginning is no longer relevant after the shift (Kendler & D'Amato, 1955; Isaacs & Duncan, 1962). For example if subjects are rewarded for choosing large boxes in the first discrimination, regardless of brightness, then a shift to brightness as the basis for the second discrimination would represent an extradimensional shift (in Figure 4–10b, rewards for black boxes regardless of size). Because the size of the box is no longer relevant after the shift, strategies based on size are no better than chance responding.

The results of intradimensional and extradimensional shift experiments with adults can be explained from a cognitive perspective by arguing that subjects learn to pay attention to the relevant dimension during the first discrimination problem. As long as they continue to concentrate on that dimension, they will have greater difficulty solving problems that require attention to another dimension (extradimensional shift) than they will solving problems that

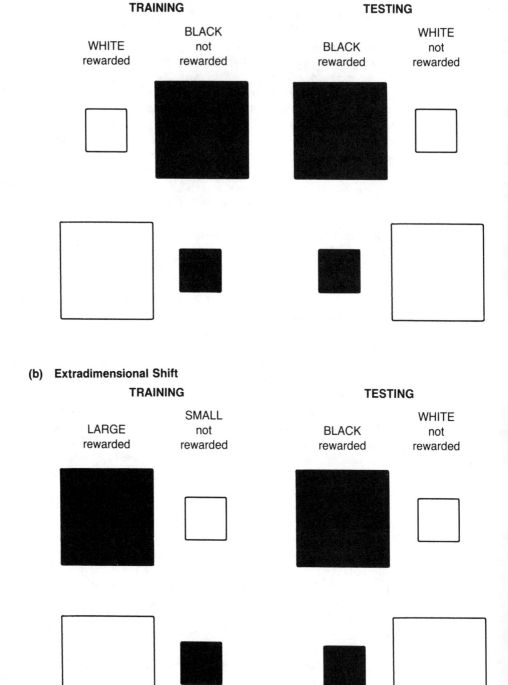

FIGURE 4–10 Discrimination shift procedures: (a) In a reversal shift, all stimuli that were associated with reward during training become associated with extinction and vice versa. (b) In an extradimensional shift, half the specific stimuli remain associated as they were in training, but the relevant dimension changes.

require attention to the same dimension (intradimensional shift). With adults, this holds true even for reversals—the most difficult kind of intradimensional shift.

But the results of research with young children cannot be similarly explained (Tighe, 1973). To begin, four-year-old children perform *better* than adults do right after an extradimensional shift; however, they do so only on half the trials. Figure 4–10b reveals why. Notice that subjects are rewarded for choosing the large black box rather than the small white one, both before and after the extradimensional shift. Apparently, young children do not usually learn general rules pertaining to large versus small boxes, or black versus white boxes; instead, they learn to choose "the large black box"—regardless of the choice required on the other kind of trial. This gives children an advantage over adults because that particular stimulus object remains correct after the extradimensional shift. In contrast, adults completely abandon their general, dimensional rule ("choose large") because it no longer works. This leaves them without a preference for any of the stimuli, until they discover a new dimensional rule ("choose black") that works.

Although children may continue to choose correctly on half the trials after an extradimensional shift, they still must learn to avoid the large white box (which was previously rewarded) and choose the small black one (previously unrewarded). Four-year-olds learn this new choice very slowly, as though it is a separate problem equivalent to a reversal shift (Tighe, Glick, & Cole, 1971). Several nonhuman species show a somewhat similar pattern of high performance on unchanged trials and low performance on changed trials (Tighe, 1973). Unlike adults, therefore, nonhumans and young children alike may learn to approach or avoid individual stimuli instead of learning general, dimensional rules (compare our later discussion of concepts).

The finding that some learners associate reward with specific objects, rather than learning to pay attention to one dimension or another, may seem at first to support the associative approach as opposed to the cognitive one. But if we consider the entire pattern of results, we see that different groups of subjects may learn very different things, even when they all perform similarly on the initial discrimination problem. The learning/performance distinction that is so important to cognitive theories must therefore be a central aspect of any successful account. Having said so, we should note that no single theory—either cognitive or associative—can yet account for all the characteristics of learning after shifts in discrimination. There is still a need for further research from both the cognitive and the associative approaches.

Explain why the concept of attention to a stimulus dimension is more useful for explaining adults' choices than it is for explaining young children's choices after extradimensional shifts.

Repeated Shifts in Discrimination: Serial Reversal and Learning Set

Reversal shifts are sometimes performed repeatedly: First the subject learns to choose consistently; then the S^Ds for reward and extinction are traded; and the process is repeated, time after time. Such **serial reversal** training results in faster and faster relearning, until finally one trial may be enough for subjects to reverse their choices completely (Dufort, Guttman, & Kimble, 1954).

A related phenomenon, **learning set,** also occurs after a series of discrimination problems. Unlike serial reversal, however, learning set does not involve just one pair of stimuli. Instead, a new pair of stimuli is presented in each problem, and one choice is reinforced until the subject learns to choose it reliably. As in serial reversal, subjects learn later discriminations faster than they learn earlier ones, and they may eventually perform almost perfectly after the first trial of each new discrimination problem.

Figure 4–11 shows some results from Harlow's (1949) classic study of learning set. His monkeys were trained in a Wisconsin General Test Apparatus (WGTA), constructed of a movable screen that hid a tray. When the screen was removed, the monkey saw two different objects on the tray, each of which covered a food cup. The cup under one object always contained a raisin or a peanut, and the monkeys learned to look first under that object. As the figure shows, performance improved only gradually from trial to trial during the first discriminations the monkeys learned. But after solving hundreds of discrimination problems, the monkeys' accuracy was nearly perfect, except for the very first trial of each discrimination (when they had to guess randomly between two new objects).

Harlow (1959) suggested that learning is slow during the early problems because of several error factors, or systematic biases, that the monkeys must overcome in the WGTA, such as a preference for one side, or a persistent preference for certain objects regardless of reward. But Harlow's hypothesis about error factors has not been supported by other

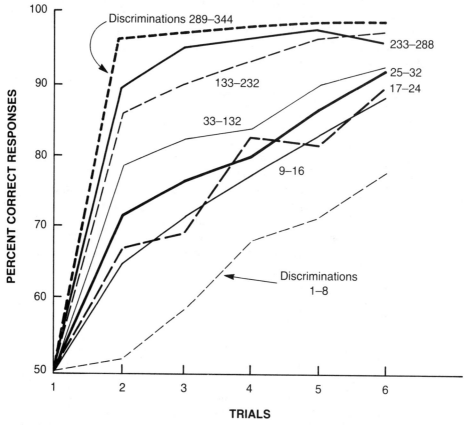

FIGURE 4–11   Results of Harlow's (1949) experiments on learning set. After monkeys had solved hundreds of discrimination problems, they developed the ability to perform almost perfectly by the second trial of each discrimination problem.

Source: Adapted from Harlow, H. F. (1949). The formation of learning sets. *Psychological Review, 56.* In the public domain.

research, which shows that learning set involves more than just simple associations and stimulus biases (Mackintosh, 1974, pp. 610–614).

As an alternative to Harlow's hypothesis, Restle (1958) has argued that learning set is a matter of learning how to learn; in particular, subjects may learn a **win-stay lose-shift** strategy that helps them solve later discrimination problems. If the first response is rewarded (win), subjects "stay" with that choice on the next trial; if not, they "shift" to the other choice. This account is more cognitive than Harlow's error factor hypothesis: Rather than assuming that nonreinforcement merely weakens response tendencies, the win-stay lose-shift hypothesis maintains that subjects expect to be rewarded for the alternate choice after nonreinforcement has occurred.

The win-stay lose-shift strategy may also be used in serial reversals, where the sudden omission of reinforcement for one choice indicates that the other choice is being reinforced again. The idea that both procedures may train the same strategy is supported by the finding that monkeys trained with a serial reversal procedure perform very well when switched to a learning set procedure (Warren, 1966). To be sure, rats and certain other animals improve substantially during serial reversals and yet do not exhibit learning set. But this may merely mean that it is too hard for them to generalize the win-stay lose-shift strategy to entirely new discriminative stimuli, as they must in order to demonstrate learning set.

✎ *Describe the development of learning set by monkeys in a WGTA, and explain why win-stay lose-shift would be a useful strategy in this situation.*

Concurrent Schedules of Reinforcement

All the simultaneous discriminations we have described thus far have involved discrete choices: Rats turned left or right at the choice point in a T-maze, monkeys chose the left object or the right object in a WGTA, and so on. But a different approach may be used when the response is a free operant, such as lever pressing or key pecking, which is not limited to one occurrence per trial. In such cases, simultaneous discriminations are often trained via a **concurrent schedule** of reinforcement, in which two (or more) schedules of reinforcement are in effect at the same time and subjects may respond freely on either schedule. When we have more than one source of reinforcement available to us at once, as we usually do in our daily lives, we must decide how much time to spend pursuing each one, and when to change from one to another. The same is true for subjects in a concurrent schedule.

In some cases, the decision is easy. For example, pigeons that can obtain food by pecking one response key 25 times (FR–25) or another response key 50 times (FR–50) respond almost entirely on the first key (Herrnstein, 1958). But if the alternatives are two variable interval schedules, subjects instead change back and forth between them because reinforcement is unpredictable and may become available on the other key at any time. In fact, pigeons responding to concurrent VI schedules sometimes switch so often that the experimenter cannot accurately measure their preference for one schedule over the other (Herrnstein, 1961). Consequently most researchers impose a **changeover delay** of reinforcement; that is, they arrange that responses that occur within a few seconds after changing over cannot be reinforced. This added cost of changing over makes subjects respond for longer periods before switching to the other option in the concurrent schedule, and therefore ensures a clearer measure of preferences.

When a changeover delay is used, responding to the different sources of reinforcement usually follows the **matching law** (Herrnstein, 1970): Namely, the percentage of responses that a subject makes to a particular option matches the percentage of reinforcements obtained from that option. For example, if 0% of all reinforcements are obtained from a particular option (extinction schedule), responding also declines to 0% for that option and switches entirely to other options (where 100% of the reinforcements are obtained). If 50% of the reinforcements are obtained from each of two options, then responding is divided 50%–50%. And if 20% of all reinforcements are from a certain option, 20% of the responses will occur there, and so on.

Because concurrent schedules provide a sensitive measure of preference, several variations have been developed. One that is especially interesting is the **concurrent chain** schedule, which commits subjects to stay with whatever option they happened to be pursuing at a crucial point in time. This may sound familiar to students who have enjoyed taking courses in many different areas, but who will soon have to concentrate on one major area in order to graduate. The more the student takes in a certain field, the more likely it is that he or she will have to commit to staying with that field of study.

The chain in such a schedule is composed of two links, one after another (Figure 4–12a). In the first or choice link, two intermittent schedules operate simultaneously, just as in a regular concurrent schedule. This is roughly analogous to a variety of course options for students who have not had to concentrate on a particular area. But at a crucial point in time (which may vary, for example, according to a VI schedule), the next response determines which option the subject will be committed to. The other option is then canceled, leaving only the chosen option available for the terminal link. This link corresponds to the situation of a student who has no more free electives available and who must concentrate exclusively on courses in one major field. Generally subjects respond more during the choice link to the option that is associated with the prefered terminal link.

Rachlin and Green (1972) used a concurrent chain procedure to study preferences for quick rather than delayed rewards. Sometimes the unwillingness to wait for reinforcement has undesirable consequences, as in the case of dieters who cannot resist snacking. Rachlin and Green showed that pigeons can be impulsive in this way, too, but they can also exhibit **self-control,** defined as the choice of larger delayed rewards over small but quick rewards.

In their basic procedure (Figure 4–12b), pigeons pecked either of two white response keys during the choice link. Pecking one of them made it change to red for the terminal link, and a peck to that red keylight produced immediate access to food. Pecking the other white keylight made it change to green for the terminal link, and a peck to that green keylight produced twice as much food as the other option did—but only after a four-second delay. Under these conditions, the pigeons showed almost no self-control and virtually never received the large reward.

However, most of the same pigeons showed almost perfect self-control when a delay was inserted between the two links. That is, instead of changing to red or green immediately after the choice link, both keylights became dark for 16 seconds before red or green appeared. So the pigeons had to wait at least 16 seconds anyway (20 seconds for the large reward), and this remoteness from the consequences made all the difference. When the rewards are both still far away, pigeons do commit themselves to wait a little longer if the longer wait will produce a larger reward.

In the same way, dieters who plan their meals in advance can stick to their diets more easily than those who wait until mealtime to decide what they will eat. Several hours beforehand, it is easy to choose the greater long-term benefits associated with sensible eating and weight loss. But once the time to eat has arrived, the immediate availability of

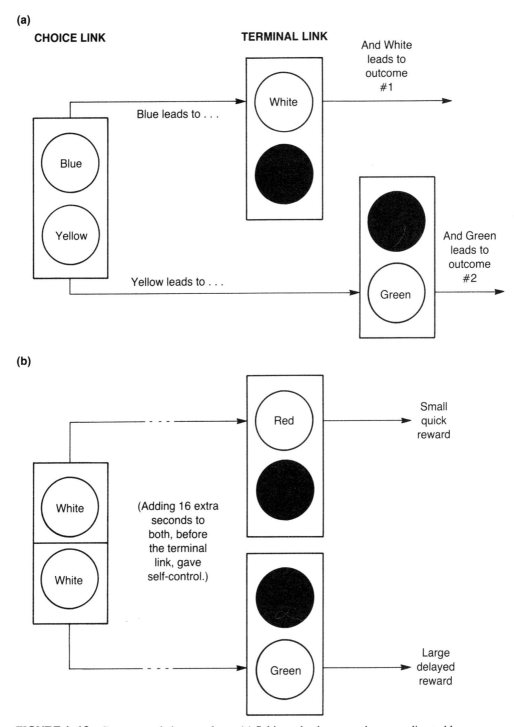

FIGURE 4–12 Concurrent chain procedures: (a) Subjects that happen to be responding to blue at a crucial point in time are restricted to white and an opportunity to earn outcome #1. Subjects instead responding to yellow are restricted to green and outcome #2. (b) In Rachlin and Green's (1972) study of self-control, preference for the quicker, small reward predominated when it was available immediately upon entering the terminal link. But preference for the slower, large reward predominated when the time for reward was lengthened by virtue of an imposed delay between links.

food may outweigh the long-term benefits of dieting. That may also be why people find it easier to resist snacking if they make the decision before the temptation is right in front of them.

Rachlin and Green's results also suggest a solution to Joan's problem with procrastination, described in the previous chapter. As you may recall, Joan is prone to watch television or do other things when she should be practicing for her stage audition. If she really wants to practice instead of watching TV, she should make a commitment well ahead of time rather than wait until it is time for the TV show to come on. That way, the desire to watch TV will not provide an immediate temptation and will not outweigh her desire for ultimate success. Of course, besides planning ahead, she should still use techniques mentioned in the previous chapter (notes taped to the TV, support from friends, contingency contracts, etc.) to support her commitment.

☑ *What does the matching law predict about responding if subjects obtain 75% of their reinforcements from one particular option in a concurrent schedule?*

CONDITIONAL DISCRIMINATIONS

Relation to Simpler Discriminations

The previous section described discrimination procedures in which each S^D was consistently associated with a particular outcome or schedule of reinforcement. In contrast, reinforcement sometimes depends on a combination of discriminative stimuli, so that learners cannot predict reinforcement from each S^D individually. These more complex arrangements are called **conditional discriminations.** For example, Joan's botany professor gives unannounced quizzes when he thinks they are warranted—but only on Fridays, when he has time to grade the answers. Knowing that it is Friday does not alone guarantee a pop quiz, nor does the fact that he is scowling. But if he scowls on Friday, look out! The combination is dangerous.

An equivalent definition of conditional discriminations is that the significance of each cue depends on the other cues. In the above example, the professor's frowns signal a quiz only if it is Friday, and the arrival of Friday signals a quiz only if the professor frowns. Each kind of cue gives significance to the other.

Given their greater complexity, it is not surprising that conditional discriminations are generally harder to learn than simple discriminations. But we do eventually learn them, as do a number of other species.

In an early forerunner of current procedures, Hunter (1913) hid food behind one of three doors and then signaled its location by briefly turning on a light above the correct door. Subjects received reward only if they chose the door that matched the location of the light. Rats, raccoons, dogs, and children all chose the correct door, so long as they were allowed to approach it soon after the light went out. Notice that Hunter's procedure did not involve a simple choice among lights; rather, it involved a choice among doors, and those doors gained meaning through combination with the corresponding lights.

In a somewhat different experiment, Weise and Bitterman (1951) installed small light bulbs at the entrances to the arms of a multiple-unit maze, and then rewarded rats for choosing the right arms when the lights were lit and the left arms when the lights were not lit, or vice versa (cf. Lashley, 1938). Figure 4–13 shows one of the units with lights lit for a right turn. Neither the left arm nor the right arm alone, nor lights on or off, was a reliable

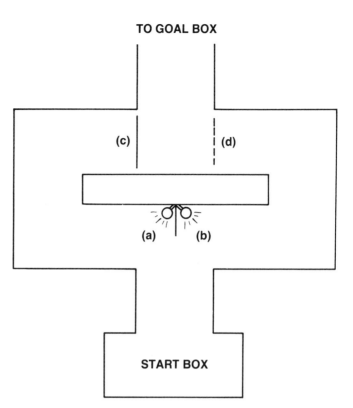

FIGURE 4–13
Apparatus used by Weise and Bitterman (1951) to study conditional discrimination in rats: (a) illuminated entrance to left arm, which is blocked at c; (b) illuminated right arm, which is open at d toward the goal box. Subjects learned to go right when both lights were lit (c blocked) and left when neither light was lit (d blocked).

cue for reinforcement; instead, subjects learned to choose the right arm with lights or the left arm without lights. Again, one kind of stimulus gave meaning to the other.

Clearly several species of animals can learn to respond according to the way stimuli are combined. This might be explained from a cognitive approach by supposing that subjects learn complex rules, such as, "If the lights are lit, choose the right arm; but if they are not, choose the left arm." But acquiring this kind of rule is not the only way that subjects might learn such a discrimination. For example, they might perceive each stimulus combination as a unique configuration, such as "right arm with lights lit," and merely associate each combination with reward or nonreward.

A great variety of conditional discrimination procedures have been devised, some of which seem quite different from others. All of them, however, require subjects to evaluate events in combination with each other. The most commonly studied of those procedures, matching to sample, will be discussed next.

◪ *Explain why Weise and Bitterman's T-maze procedure is considered to be a conditional discrimination.*

Matching to Sample

Rules for Matching

In **matching to sample** (MTS) procedures, subjects are shown a set of *comparison* stimuli and are required to choose the one that matches a prior reference cue, called the *sample* stimulus. Figure 4–14a illustrates a typical training trial for birds. The top line shows a star (the sample stimulus) on the center response key and darkness on the two side keys. The next line shows how the display would look a few moments later, after the addition of the comparison stimuli on the side keys. If the subject presses the comparison that matches the sample (the star on the right), reward follows immediately. But if the subject commits an error, a time out ensues in which the stimuli disappear and no reward is available until the next trial. MTS thus qualifies as a conditional discrimination procedure, because the

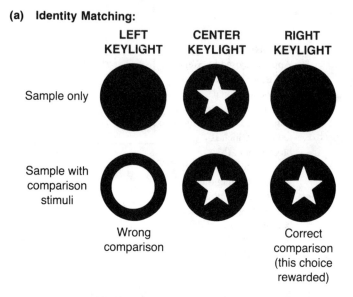

(a) Identity Matching:

| | LEFT KEYLIGHT | CENTER KEYLIGHT | RIGHT KEYLIGHT |

Sample only

Sample with comparison stimuli

Wrong comparison

Correct comparison (this choice rewarded)

(b) Delayed Symbolic Matching:

Sample only

Delay interval

Comparison stimuli

Correct comparison (this choice rewarded)

Wrong comparison

FIGURE 4–14
Matching to sample tasks: (a) identify matching, where the subject's task is to choose the (side) comparison stimulus that appears the same as the (center) sample stimulus; (b) delayed symbolic matching, where the task is to recall the sample stimulus and choose vertical stripes if the sample was a star, or horizontal stripes if the sample was a circle.

meaning (correctness) of the various comparison stimuli depends on another stimulus (the sample).

One way in which a subject might solve such a task is to learn the general rule, "Press the side stimulus that is the same as the center stimulus." Subjects who do so should then perform well on a transfer test where new stimuli are used as samples and comparisons but the general rule still applies. And in fact, children (Sidman & Tailby, 1982), chimpanzees (Oden, Thompson, & Premack, 1988), and bottlenosed dolphins (Herman, Hovancik, Gory, & Bradshaw, 1989) perform much better than chance under such circumstances, indicating that they can learn such a rule.

But whether pigeons and many other species use the general rule is a matter of dispute (Sidman, Rauzin, Lazar, Cunningham, Tailby, & Carrigan, 1982; Roitblat, 1986). Apparently some animals solve the problem by learning each stimulus combination separately. That is, they seem to learn specific associations such as "circle goes with circle" and "star goes with star," which does not help them respond correctly to new combinations such as a square matching a square. As we concluded in our earlier discussion of intradimensional and extradimensional shifts, subjects do not necessarily learn the same thing, even when they perform similarly on the initial discrimination task.

The standard version of MTS shown in Figure 4–14a is called *identity* matching, because subjects are required to choose the comparison that matches the sample stimulus identically. Identity MTS is the most straightforward version of matching to sample, but it is not the only version. In oddity MTS, for instance, subjects must choose the comparison that *differs* from the sample (choose the "odd" circle instead of the star in Figure 4–14a). Yet another version is *symbolic* MTS, in which the sample stimulus bears no obvious relationship to the comparison stimuli.

In symbolic matching, there is no general rule to be learned. Instead, the experimenter arbitrarily assigns certain comparison stimuli to serve as matches for certain samples. For example, subjects might be required to choose a vertical-stripes comparison to match the star sample, a horizontal-stripes comparison to match the circle sample, and so on. In symbolic as well as oddity MTS, therefore, matching does not imply physical similarity between the sample and the correct comparison.

The unique characteristics of these MTS procedures make each one especially useful for studying certain aspects of learning and memory. We have already described how the identity matching procedure is used to study the concept of sameness. Next we will describe a special use of symbolic matching to study memory in nonverbal species.

What general rule would enable subjects to solve any identity matching task, and how might subjects solve such a task without actually learning the general rule?

Delayed Matching and Animal Memory

Sometimes researchers present the sample stimulus only briefly, and then remove it before the comparison stimuli are presented (Figure 4–14b). In these **delayed matching to sample** (DMTS) procedures, therefore, subjects must remember information long enough to choose the correct comparison stimulus after a delay. This kind of procedure has been used extensively to investigate the memory capabilities of animals, especially pigeons and monkeys (Spear, Miller, & Jagielo, 1990).

In symbolic versions of DMTS, where the comparison stimuli differ radically from the sample stimuli, it is interesting to ask what the subjects are remembering during the delay.

Do they remember the sample itself, or do they instead remember the comparison stimulus they are supposed to choose at the end of the delay?

Figure 4–14b illustrates one trial from such a task. In this procedure, the experimenter has arbitrarily assigned a vertical-stripe stimulus as the correct choice after star-shaped samples, and a horizontal-stripe stimulus as the correct choice after circular samples. The top two lines of the figure show the star sample, followed by a delay interval in which all keys are darkened. The third line shows the subsequent presentation of the comparison stimuli, from which the subject must choose the vertical stripes to obtain reward.

Various experimental manipulations using the symbolic DMTS procedure have shown that pigeons usually remember what comparison stimulus they will have to choose after the delay, not what sample stimulus occurred before the delay (e.g. Roitblat, 1980; Santi & Roberts, 1985). However, monkeys may remember the sample stimulus instead (Worsham, 1975), and even pigeons may do so under some circumstances (Urcuoli & Zentall, 1986). Thus animals do not necessarily all remember the same information, just as they do not necessarily solve discrimination problems the same way.

☑ *In what manner do pigeons usually retain information about the correct choice during the delay in DMTS procedures?*

Sequential Responding

As our discussion of MTS procedures indicates, researchers often interpret performance on conditional discrimination tasks as evidence that subjects are using some form of rule, image, or other internal representation as a basis for responding. Other conditional discrimination procedures have similarly been used to examine complex learning and memory capabilities in a variety of species. The following is a brief sampling of procedures in which the outcome of the current response depends on the pattern of previous stimuli and responses; in other words, procedures in which subjects must produce organized sequences of behavior.

Memory in Mazes

Recall that Hunter (1913) studied animals' ability to choose the correct door, as signaled by a prior light. This is analogous to delayed matching to sample, in the sense that subjects chose among several comparison stimuli (the doors) based on a previous sample stimulus (the light). Hunter later (1920) developed another conditional discrimination procedure, this time using a maze constructed of two rectangles that were joined to make the figure-8 pattern shown in Figure 4–15. Rats, raccoons, and monkeys were rewarded for circling a certain number of times around one half of the figure-8 and then the same number of times around the other half, such as two circles to the left followed by two circles to the right. Therefore, in order to choose between the right and left arms at the end of the common path, subjects had to remember which way they had turned on previous circles. In the twice-left and twice-right example, if the previous two choices had been to the left, a turn to the right would lead eventually to reward; otherwise, a turn to the left would.

Rats learned to circle once to the right and once to the left in the figure-8 maze, which amounts to the conditional discrimination, "left after a right turn but right after a left turn."

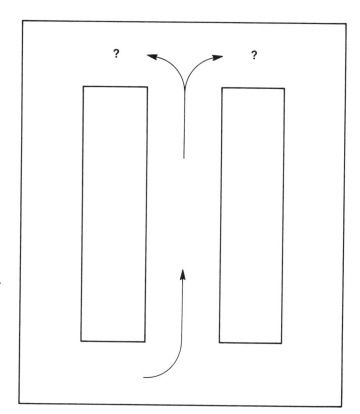

FIGURE 4–15
Hunter's (1920) temporal maze, in which the only clue to the correct choice is the subject's memory for what it did at the choice point the previous time(s). The experimenter rewarded animals for simple-, double-, and triple-alternation patterns of running to the right and the left, and found that species differed in their performance on this task.

Yet only raccoons and monkeys could learn to circle two or more times around the same half before switching to the other half. On the basis of results from the figure-8 maze, therefore, we might be tempted to conclude that rats can remember only one previous choice, not more. That conclusion would be incorrect, however. Research with a different type of maze has demonstrated that rats can remember a long list of previous choices.

The **radial arm maze** typically contains eight arms that radiate outward from a central hub, as shown in Figure 4–16. The entire maze is usually open so the rats can see the surrounding room, and is elevated a few feet above the floor so they will stay on the central platform and arms. A pellet of food is placed out of sight in a small cup at the end of each arm, and the subject is then allowed to search the arms in any order, returning to the center after each choice. After 10 daily repetitions of this training procedure, rats usually find all eight food pellets without repeating any choices (Olton & Samuelson, 1976).

The high degree of efficiency exhibited by rats in the radial arm maze does not depend on odor cues or on a fixed sequence of responses, such as continuing around the arms in a single direction. Instead, it involves remembering the arms that have already been visited (Roitblat, 1982). This memory persists for several hours if the rat is forced to wait after the fourth reward (Beatty & Shavalia, 1980), but it can also be reset for a new trial immediately after the eighth reward is found (Olton, 1978). These findings indicate that rats possess flexible memories for spatial location that enable them to choose a previously unchosen arm almost every time. This is roughly analogous to the oddity matching task, which is solved

FIGURE 4–16
Overhead view of a radial arm maze, with a central platform and eight radiating arms elevated above the floor of the laboratory.

Source: D. S. Olton & R. J. Samuelson (1976). Remembrance of places passed: Spatial memory in rats. *Journal of Experimental Psychology: Animal Behavior Processes, 2,* 98. Copyright 1976 by the American Psychological Association. Reprinted by permission.

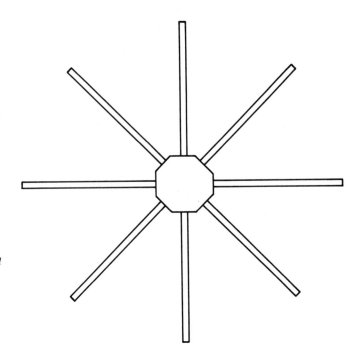

by choosing comparison stimuli (cf. arms) that are different from the sample stimuli (cf. previously chosen arms; Olton, 1978).

Superior performance in the radial arm maze may reflect a natural adaptation for food foraging (Spear, Miller, & Jagielo, 1990). In rats' natural environment, food is more likely to be found at sites that have not been recently exploited. A natural tendency of rats to investigate different locations on each trial would supposedly contribute to learning in the radial arm maze—and in Hunter's (1920) simple alternation task, where a single left choice was to be followed by a right choice, but not where the same route was to be repeated twice or more in succession. Other examples of natural tendencies that may affect learning are discussed in the next chapter.

📓 *Rats are very efficient at finding all the food in the radial arm maze. What does this tell us about the ability of rats to remember previous choices?*

Learning a Series of Choices

Rats in the radial arm maze find the rewards without learning a fixed sequence of responses. But other, more traditional mazes provide only one route to food in the goal box. Under these circumstances, rats do appear to learn the regular sequence of places where they must go, and later the fixed series of reponses they must make to get there—such as to turn left once, right twice, and then left again (Mackintosh, 1974, pp. 553–556). Early learning may focus on cues from the surroundings, but those cues become less important as the subject acquires an habitual series of responses leading to reward.

The ability to learn a fixed sequence is, of course, not limited to rats. For example, pigeons can peck a fixed sequence of colors, even when the colors are presented simultaneously on different response keys. In an experiment by Straub, Seidenberg, Bever, and Terrace (1979), pigeons received food only if they pecked four colors in a particular sequence, such as blue-green-yellow-red. Subjects could not rely on a fixed series of movements, because the location of each color changed from one trial to the next. Instead, the pigeons had to find blue and peck it, then find green and peck it, and so on. The only way they could finish the sequence was to remember what colors they had already chosen, much as rats must remember what arms they already checked in the radial arm maze.

Once pigeons have learned this task, they usually respond in the correct order to the entire array of four colors, or to any subset that contains the first or the last color in the sequence (blue-yellow, green-red, etc.). But they respond in random order if the subset does not contain one of the end colors, even if it mimics part of the training sequence exactly (green-yellow) (Straub & Terrace, 1981). This means that pigeons do not merely associate each color with the next one, pair by pair, but instead they represent the entire set of colors as an ordered list, with the end colors serving a special function. They can also organize parts of the sequence into mental subgroups, or "chunks"—a process that facilitates learning in pigeons much as it does in humans (Terrace, 1987). In short, performance on this kind of conditional discrimination task cannot be adequately explained without reference to complex cognitive processes.

◪ *What is the difference between learning a color sequence as an ordered list of stimuli (which pigeons do) and learning a color sequence as a chain of stimulus pairs (which pigeons do not)?*

Sequences of Reinforcer Magnitude

Research with mazes of various kinds, including the radial arm maze, has shown that rats excel at remembering the location of food rewards. The next research we will consider used runways to demonstrate that rats can also remember the amount and order of rewards.

In one experiment, Capaldi and Verry (1981, Experiment 3) measured the running speed of rats after extensive training with two different patterns of reward and nonreward. In one series of three trials, designated 5-0-20, the goal box at the end of the runway contained 5 food pellets on the first trial, none on the middle trial, and 20 on the third trial. In another three-trial series, designated 20-0-0, the goal box contained 20 pellets on the first trial and none thereafter. The same rats experienced both patterns each day for several weeks. By the end of the experiment, they were running much faster on the third trial of the 5-0-20 series than on the third trial of the 20-0-0 series, suggesting that they remembered the amount of reward that was customary on each one (20 vs. 0 pellets, respectively).

In Capaldi and Verry's Experiment 3, the outcome of the third trial could only be predicted from events on the first trial. A moderate (5) or large (20) reward on the first trial may therefore be considered analogous to the sample stimulus in delayed matching to sample, whereas the unrewarded middle trial is analogous to the delay interval. In other words, 5 pellets signified "respond yes on the third trial," whereas 20 pellets signified "respond no on the third trial." Of course, subjects did not choose among multiple comparison stimuli on the third trial as they would have done in an actual DMTS task. But the fact that they accurately anticipated reward or nonreward on the third trial indicates that they did remember the first-trial outcome ("sample") as well as the order of events in both series.

In another, similar experiment, rats were shown to utilize information from as many as eight trials earlier (Capaldi & Verry, 1981, Experiment 5). How can we best explain this impressive performance?

One possibility, related to Capaldi's sequential hypothesis of partial reward effects (see Chapter 3), is that each trial number becomes associated with the outcome of the next trial in that sequence (Capaldi, Nawrocki, & Verry, 1982). For example, the first trial in both the 5-0-20 and the 20-0-0 series becomes a signal for nonreward (0), so running is slow on the next trial. But the middle trial of the 5-0-20 series becomes associated with a large reward (20), so running is fast on the final trial of that particular series. In contrast to this associative account, Hulse (1978) has argued that rats learn more general rules about each serial pattern, such as whether it involves consistent decreases from one trial to the next. Domjan and Burkhard (1986) have summarized evidence favoring this cognitive account, as well as evidence favoring the associative one.

We have described a wide variety of procedures that require subjects to combine information, presented either simultaneously or sequentially, in order to obtain reward. In addition, Rescorla (1990) has argued that even simple discriminations in instrumental learning involve combinations of response information and stimulus information, such that discriminative stimuli give significance to responses in much the same way that sample stimuli give significance to comparison stimuli (cf. discussion of stimulus context in Chapter 2). The study of conditional discriminations is therefore likely to promote our understanding of the learning process in many ways, including the achievement of new syntheses between associative and cognitive approaches.

Rats trained with repeated series of reinforcers can anticipate the magnitude of reinforcement by combining information about trial number with information from previous series. How is this achieved according to Capaldi's associative theory? According to Hulse's cognitive theory?

LEARNING ABOUT CATEGORIES AND SYMBOLS

Concept Learning in People and Animals

As we noted previously, some subjects learn each choice separately in identity matching tasks. For example, they may learn that a circle goes with a circle, and a star with a star, without learning the general principle that "same goes with same." As a consequence, they do not immediately transfer what they have learned to related problems, such as matching a square to a square. Such piecemeal learning can perhaps be explained in terms of simple rules such as "peck star after star," or in terms of associations between specific stimulus combinations (such as "star with star") and reward.

In contrast, humans and some other species seem to learn a general rule that enables them to match identical sample and comparison stimuli, whether or not they have seen them before. Mastery of this general rule suggests they have learned the abstract concept of "sameness," so that any two stimuli that appear identical to each other will be recognized as having the same relation as star-with-star.

A **concept** is a generalized mental representation of a class of objects, events, or other concepts. This implies something more than mere generalization and discrimination among stimuli. For example, children may be asked to sort objects into categories according to color, without respect to size and shape. So long as they sort them properly, we may presume that the children possess concepts for red, yellow, green, and so on, regardless of whether they can name those colors or not. The fact that they treat all the red objects as equivalent, all the yellow objects as equivalent, and so on, means that the objects in each group share a common color representation. Thus even this seemingly simple behavior involves complex mental processes.

Why can't such performance be attributed to simple generalization and discrimination? One reason is that the children could sort the objects according to other features if we asked them to. By heeding color and disregarding other characteristics of the objects, they produce an arrangement that differs from others they might have produced. This degree of cognitive flexibility far exceeds the proposals made by noncontinuity theorists, whose cognitively oriented account of stimulus control was discussed earlier in this chapter. Demonstrations of conceptual behavior thus require new theories to explain how learning can relate, not merely to a stimulus or a response but to an organizational scheme.

▶ *How does behavior based on concepts differ from behavior based on simple generalization and discrimination?*

Concept Identification

In one of the first attempts to study concept learning, Hull (1920) asked college students to learn verbal responses to some of the pseudo-Chinese characters shown in Figure 4–17. He began by presenting a set of 12 characters one at at time while naming each one (using nonsense names such as *li* and *ta*). He then repeated the series until all 12 names had been learned. Next, the subject learned to associate the same 12 names to a second series of characters, then to a third series, and so on, until each of the names was associated with many different characters. What Hull did not tell his subjects was that the same 12 radicals, or distinctive components, were present in every series of 12 characters, and that each nonsense word was associated with the same radical every time.

Although they were not informed of the radicals, Hull's subjects learned each new list faster than the previous one, and they often guessed the names of new characters correctly without any prompting from him. To Hull, this indicated that associating each response to several related stimuli can automatically produce general concepts. However, his subjects may simply have generalized their responses to new stimuli without forming an organized mental representation. His conclusions, therefore, may not pertain to concepts as we have defined them. Of greater importance was his suggestion that concept learning should be studied by asking subjects to guess at instances of the concept.

Several decades after Hull's (1920) pioneering effort, research on concept learning entered a new era with the work of Bruner, Goodnow, and Austin (1956). Using artificial stimuli that varied along specific dimensions such as color, shape, and size (Figure 4–18), they designed **concept identification** (or *concept attainment*) experiments in which subjects tried to discover visual concepts through trial and error. For instance, subjects might be told *yes* whenever they picked any stimulus card that contained red squares and *no* when they picked any other type of card. In the meantime, they guessed at the solution after each choice, until they finally guessed that "red square" was the crucial combination of features defining the concept.

Research on concept identification has yielded descriptions of various strategies that subjects use for evaluating hypotheses (Levine, 1966; Bourne, 1970). For instance, a subject could first test the hypothesis that cards containing triple borders are correct, then the hunch that cards containing squares are correct, and so on, through each possible rule.

FIGURE 4-17 Pseudo-Chinese characters used by Hull (1920) to study concept learning. Subjects learned to pronounce nonsense names for all the characters in a column before learning to apply the same names for related characters in the second column, and so on. All columns contain the same 12 radicals, as illustrated at the left of each row.

Source: Hull, C. L. (1920). Quantitative aspects of the evolution of concepts. *Psychological Monographs, 28.* In the public domain.

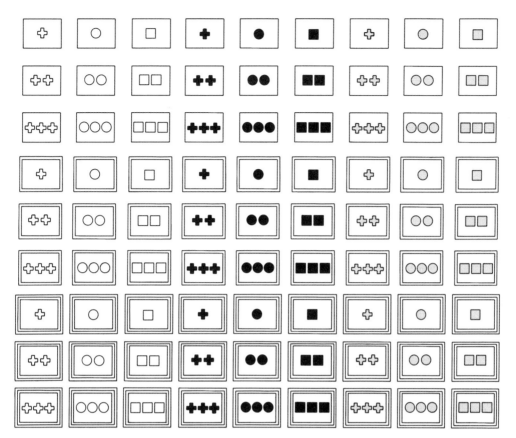

FIGURE 4–18 Concept identification materials used by Bruner, Goodnow, and Austin (1956). The cards vary with regard to color (3), form (3), number of forms (3), and number of borders (3).

Source: Bruner, J. S., Goodnow, J. J., & Austin, G. A. (1956). *A study of thinking.* New York: Wiley. Reprinted with permission of J. S. Bruner.

Unfortunately for the subject, this *conservative focusing* strategy tends to take a very long time if the rule involves more than one stimulus dimension, such as "red *and* square." Another strategy, called *global focusing,* involves keeping track of several different hypotheses at the same time. This usually eliminates the incorrect possibilities much more quickly than does conservative focusing, which tests only one at a time. But global focusing also requires a greater reliance on memory to hold and evaluate information about several hypotheses simultaneously.

People may use hypothesis-testing strategies such as these to distinguish among the categories in scientific classification systems; for example, in diagnosing psychological disorders. Scientific classification usually involves specific indicators (e.g. depersonalization, heightened arousal, loss of contact with reality) that are analogous to the features studied in concept identification experiments. However, hypothesis testing is probably not how we learn everyday concepts, such as vegetable, chair, and game, which are hard to characterize in terms of necessary and sufficient features. We must look beyond concept identification research for insights into the development of these more familiar concepts.

Natural Categories

Unlike the artificial categories in concept identification experiments, most categories we encounter in our daily lives are not well defined. It is hard to think of a single feature or even a combination of features that is shared by all vegetables but not shared with any fruits. So how do we judge whether a particular example is an instance of a vegetable?

One possible explanation, called **prototype theory,** has received considerable attention (Posner & Keele, 1968; Rosch, 1973). According to prototype theory, category membership is decided by evaluating an item's overall resemblance to the average or most typical member of the category, called the *prototype*. Items that share many features with the prototype, or have similar characteristics on many dimensions, are classified as members of the same category. No particular set of features is necessary for membership; only a certain degree of "family resemblance," like children who each share a parent's nose and hair, or eyes and hair, or nose and eyes, but not all three features or any one in particular. (Theories couched in terms of discrete features are sometimes called *feature set* models to distinguish them from prototype theories that involve continuous dimensions.)

Data consistent with prototype theory were obtained in an experiment by Franks and Bransford (1971), where subjects viewed patterns composed of geometric forms and then tried to recognize which patterns they had seen. Stimuli presented during the recognition test included training patterns they had actually seen, novel patterns that bore a family resemblance to the training patterns, and prototype patterns from which all the others had been derived through changes in one or more components (Figure 4–19). When asked to choose the original training stimuli, subjects picked patterns that closely resembled the prototypes—whether those particular patterns had been shown before or not! In fact, the patterns they were most certain they had seen were the prototypes themselves, which had never been shown. This strongly supports for prototype theory, which holds that learners abstract general concepts from instances that share a family resemblance.

Despite its success in explaining results such as these, prototype theory is challenged by evidence that learners sometimes remember specific instances, or exemplars, of a concept instead of remembering the prototype (see discussion by Glass & Holyoke, 1986, pp. 173–175). More research is needed to determine whether prototypes are indeed the basis for most decisions concerning membership in natural categories.

 How do concepts that represent natural categories differ from those acquired in traditional concept identification experiments?

Concept learning has been studied most thoroughly in humans, but it also occurs in a variety of other species. In some cases, nonhuman subjects not only acquire concepts but also express them through the use of symbols, as we will describe later. First, however, let us consider another kind of evidence that indicates a capacity for concept learning—namely, evidence that subjects can learn to discriminate category members from nonmembers and can then apply that learning correctly to new instances as well.

For example, Herrnstein and Loveland (1964) trained pigeons to peck pictorial stimuli that contained images of a person. Responses to slides of people were intermittently reinforced, while responses to other slides were not. Even though the slides contained a variety of scenes that differed in many ways, the subjects learned to categorize them properly

A Prototype Stimulus

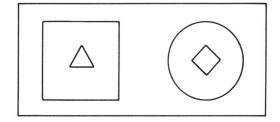

**Transformations of the Prototype
That Retain a Family Resemblance**

FIGURE 4–19   An example of a prototype stimulus and two of many stimuli derived from it by various transformations (Franks & Bransford, 1971). Subjects trained with the transformed stimuli were confident they had seen the prototypes, which were never presented during training.

Source: Adapted from Franks, J. J., & Bransford, J. D. (1971). Abstraction of visual patterns. *Journal of Experimental Psychology, 90,* 61. Copyright 1971 by the American Psychological Association. Adapted by permission.

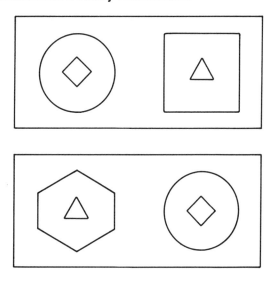

according to the presence versus absence of people. Similar results were obtained with pictures involving other categories—specifically, trees, water, and a particular person (discriminated from the absence of trees, the absence of water, and other people, respectively) (Herrnstein, Loveland, & Cable, 1976).

Subsequent research has demonstrated that pigeons can classify as many as four categories of slides at a time, including classes of artificial objects such as cars and chairs (Bhatt, Wasserman, Reynolds, & Knauss, 1988). Once they have learned such discriminations, subjects can also respond correctly to new slides. They can even learn a concept when every single slide is new to them, in a training procedure that involves a series of 2,000 nonrepeating slides (Bhatt et al., 1988). Correct categorization in this case cannot easily be dismissed as a result of learning about repeated exemplars, although generalization from previously learned exemplars cannot yet be ruled out.

Perhaps the clearest evidence of general concept learning in the pigeon comes from training with repeated reversals, where tree slides are initially positive (responding to them is reinforced) for several sessions, then negative (nontree instead) for several sessions, then positive again, and so on. Pigeons trained in this procedure eventually adjust to each reversal after just a few slides, as if all the tree slides are equivalent and need not be relearned individually (Vaughan, 1988). This ability to treat all category exemplars as though they are interchangeable is essentially what we mean by the term *concept*.

Language Learning in People and Animals

Speech, writing, and hand signs enable people to communicate in ways that are extremely flexible and complex. The natural signals of fish, birds, insects, and most mammals can convey only a limited set of messages, whereas human words can be combined and recombined to express meanings in endless variety. The capacity for symbolic language was widely believed to exist only among human beings, until Gardner and Gardner (1969) and Premack (1971) directly challenged this belief with results from their research. They found that chimpanzees can learn to label various actions and objects, and that they can use those labels to communicate with people.

Previous researchers had found it virtually impossible to teach a vocal language to chimps (Hayes & Hayes, 1952), so Premack and the Gardners trained their subjects with visual symbols instead. Rather than spoken words, Premack taught one chimpanzee (Sarah) to use colored tokens of various shapes, and the Gardners taught another chimpanzee (Washoe) to recognize and use gestures from American Sign Language, a natural language common among deaf people in North America (Figure 4–20). Success with these visual symbol systems was quite dramatic: The apes in both studies acquired vocabularies of many dozens of words, and the researchers concluded that chimpanzees *can* learn language, so long as they do not have to use their vocal apparatus for speech.

The claim that apes can talk and understand language sparked considerable controversy and additional research. The idea has great popular appeal; indeed, many pet owners are confident that animals (at least their own pets) understand human language quite well. But for reasons we will soon consider, many experts remain unconvinced that anyone other than a human being can truly understand language.

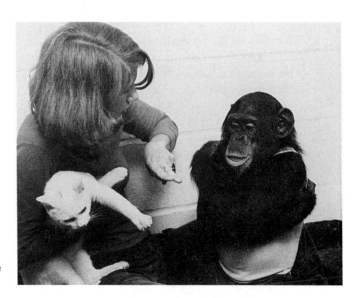

FIGURE 4–20 Nim signing ''me hug cat'' to his teacher, Susan Quimby.

Source: Terrace, H. S. (1979, November). Can an ape create a sentence? *Science, 206,* figure 1. Copyright 1979 by the American Association for the Advancement of Science.

It is important to remember that the controversy over animal language is not about whether animals can communicate, for there is no doubt that many species communicate naturally via sounds, smells, and visual and tactile stimuli (e.g., see the discussion of honeybee communication in Chapter 5). The controversy is instead about whether animals can understand and use symbols in meaningful combinations, like the words of human language. Psychologists have reasons to be skeptical about such claims, including a reason named Clever Hans.

A Horse of a Different Color: Clever Hans

At the turn of the century, a German farm horse named Hans became famous for his uncanny ability to answer questions by tapping his hoof on the ground (Figure 4–21). For example, if his owner posed a math problem to him (in German), Clever Hans would paw the ground slowly until he had counted to the correct answer; then he would stop to receive a carrot. This performance puzzled the eminent scientists and officials who came to test him, because his owner did not appear to be using any tricks to cue the correct answer. The horse even performed correctly when the owner was out of sight. However, he seemed unable to perform correctly when wearing blinders. If he could not see someone who knew the answer, he kept tapping endlessly; and this fact finally led to the discovery of his secret (Fernald, 1984).

It seems that Clever Hans knew very little about mathematics or German, but he knew all he needed to know about body language. So long as his audience leaned forward expectantly, he kept on tapping. But when the time arrived for the final tap, those who had been leaning forward straightened up. By doing so, they unintentionally provided a discriminative stimulus for Hans: All he had to do was tap until the audience unwittingly presented the S^D, and then stop tapping!

It is common for observers to credit pets and work animals with a degree of language understanding they do not possess. Like Clever Hans, many of these animals can respond appropriately to a combination of cues, including body language, tone of voice, and stock phrases. But consonant sounds are virtually impossible for most animals to recognize. As a result, many words that sound quite different to us are completely indistinguishable to them.

FIGURE 4–21 Clever Hans and his owner, Mr. van Osten.

Source: Photo from *Psychology: Science, Behavior and Life,* 2nd ed. by R. Crooks & J. Stein, copyright © 1991 by Holt, Rinehart and Winston, Inc. Reprinted by permission of the publisher.

Therefore, while pets may respond to certain familiar phrases, they cannot understand our conversations as we might like to imagine.

The story of Clever Hans is instructive for those evaluating research on ape language. To show convincingly that an animal understands language, researchers must rule out simpler explanations such as discrimination learning. If a species such as the chimpanzee is found to exhibit genuine language ability, the skeptics will have to modify their conception of human uniqueness. But if the apes' behavior can be explained in terms of simpler processes, then that is a horse of a different color.

☑ *Explain the sense in which Clever Hans was more of a mindreader than a mathematician.*

Productivity and Syntax in Human Language

After describing some of the essential characteristics of human language, we will return to consider the performance of Washoe, Sarah, and other apes trained to use visual language symbols.

One of the hallmarks of human language is that the meaning of a sentence depends on how its words are grouped together. For example, "The boy hit the ball" does not mean the same thing as "The ball hit the boy," even though both sentences contain the same words. The crucial difference between these sentences is not in the individual words themselves but in the orderly relations among the words.

The speakers of a language must therefore take patterns of word order, or *syntax,* into account. And since it would be impossible to memorize the meaning of every sentence separately, this means that each language learner must discover the general rules that govern the syntax of that language. These rules are not taught explicitly in school. Instead, we learn them naturally, by listening to other speakers during our earliest years; and although we grasp them intuitively, we may not be able to state them as rules. For instance, we could create a new sentence by substituting the word *girl* for *boy* in "The boy hit the ball." The resulting sentence would still sound perfectly grammatical, because the order of the words would still conform to the implicit rules of English. Young children already understand grammaticality in this intuitive manner, long before they learn to state the rules explicitly.

Our implicit understanding of linguistic rules allows us to create an unlimited number of grammatical sentences, many of which we have never heard before. This potential for endless variety, called **productivity,** is a second hallmark of human language.

The essentially creative character of language is already apparent in early childhood. For example, around two years of age, most children start to combine words into two- or three-word utterances, including consistent phrases such as "where sock" and "no want" that they may have never heard anyone say. By the age of three years, they have begun to integrate multiple verbal relationships into longer utterances, but these utterances still do not merely mimic adult speech (e.g. Bloom & Capatides, 1987).

☑ *Explain how an implicit understanding of syntax rules can contribute to language productivity.*

Language in Apes: Is a Swan by Any Other Name the Same?

Language-trained chimpanzees sometimes produce novel combinations of signs that are reminiscent of human phrases. The most famous instance involves Washoe, the first chimpanzee trained to use hand signs. When asked to identify a swan on the water, for which she knew no specific sign, she produced two signs: *water bird*. This spontaneous combination of signs is particularly striking because it conforms to the familiar adjective-noun sequence of English. However, as Terrace, Petitto, Sanders, and Bever (1979) pointed out, this single anecdote is not sufficient to show that there was any regularity to the order of Washoe's signs; in fact, she may have been signing *bird* in response to the swan and *water* in response to the water, simply because she was not sure which one her trainer had pointed to!

Terrace and colleagues examined films and videotapes of signing by a number of apes, including Washoe and the gorilla Koko (Patterson & Linden, 1981), and found no convincing evidence that rules of syntax were being followed by any of them. In addition, they intensively studied the performance of Terrace's own language-trained chimpanzee, Nim Chimpsky. Nim did produce certain two-sign combinations in a regular order, rather like the two-word phrases that infants create. But often the trainer had just performed the same sequence of signs, so Nim's phrases may have resulted from prompting and imitation rather than from a natural tendency to organize words into regular sequences.

Another important finding by Terrace and colleagues was that the complexity of chimpanzee utterances does not continue to increase beyond two years of age. Unlike the orderly expansion of syntax that characterizes children's language development, Nim's sign combinations did not become longer and more complex on the average. When long sequences of signs did occur, they merely involved irregular repetitions (e.g., "give orange me give eat orange me eat orange give me eat orange give me you") (Terrace et al., 1979). Results such as these led Terrace (1979) to radically revise his optimistic view regarding language in chimpanzees.

While Washoe and Nim were rewarded with praise or other reinforcements for learning individual hand signs, the chimpanzee Sarah was rewarded for learning specific sequences of tokens according to the rules of Premack's (1971) artificial language. Sarah used these tokens as if she was asking and answering questions about various objects and features of objects. For example, when she produced the sequence of symbols representing "Mary give apple Sarah," she received an apple as a reward. A related strategy for language instruction was developed by Rumbaugh his associates (Rumbaugh, 1977), whose ape subjects learned to press symbols on a computer console according to the rules of an artificial language called *Yerkish*. Chimps in both artificial language projects also showed an ability to substitute certain symbols, such as *banana* for *apple,* or *David* for *Mary,* depending on the circumstances. This ability to properly substitute one symbol for another bears at least a superficial resemblance to our earlier illustration of implicit rules in human language.

However, both teams of researchers later revised their interpretations of these results, acknowledging that many aspects of their subjects' performance are explainable in terms of discrimination learning rather than actual language understanding (Premack, 1976; Pate & Rumbaugh, 1983). For example the presence of a banana, or situational cues associated with bananas, could serve as an S^D for the response of placing the *banana* symbol into the third position in the sequence.

Although some advocates of ape language training have moderated their views, it should be remembered that subjects in these studies did learn extremely complex tasks, often involving hundreds of symbols and rules by which they were to be used. This confirms that members of these species are highly intelligent, and suggests that future research may yet provide clearer evidence of syntax rules. In addition, training techniques that were developed through this research have been found to facilitate language learning in people with verbal handicaps, such as the extremely developmentally disabled (Rock, 1979). Research is therefore continuing on this topic of vital interest for both theory and practice.

☑ *What alternative explanations have been proposed for the language-like regularities in Nim's two-sign sequences, and for Sarah's symbol substitutions?*

Concept Naming by Animals

As the preceding discussion indicates, some nonhuman species are quite impressive in their ability to use symbols as labels for actions, objects, and features of objects. Especially impressive, however, is the ability to use labels for abstract concepts such as same/different. This capacity has been demonstrated not only in primates but also in birds.

Premack (1983) has shown that chimpanzees can properly respond with the label *same* or *different* regarding a particular attribute, such as color, even when the test items have nothing in common with the items used to train the concept. For example, after training Sarah to use the "same" and "different" symbols with pairs of green and blue objects, the experimenter could test Sarah with new color combinations. In this case, subjects cannot simply be learning a response to a concrete discriminative stimulus, because it is the relation between each two stimuli that must be labeled same or different.

Even more intriguing is evidence of abstract concept labeling by an African Grey parrot named Alex (Pepperberg, 1987). Pepperberg presented Alex with two objects that resembled each other in some way and then asked "What's same?" or "What's different?," with the possible answers being color, shape, or material composition (for which Alex was trained to say "mah-mah," matter). The parrot was able to pronounce the name of the correct dimension with high accuracy, not only for both the familiar training items but also for previously untested items. However, despite this facility for verbal labeling, Alex was not reported to combine words into novel sequences. His ability to label objects and abstract concepts therefore did not involve language learning as we have defined it, in terms of rules of syntax.

☑ *In what sense do these achievements of Sarah and Alex represent abstract rather than concrete concepts?*

IS AWARENESS NECESSARY?

The Controversy

In this final section, we briefly consider whether conscious awareness is necessary for learning. The current chapter has already touched on several topics related to awareness, including attention in discrimination learning, hypothesis testing in concept identification, and verbal communication. Now let us turn to research that has investigated the role of awareness more directly, primarily by asking subjects what they consciously remember.

Attempts to measure awareness by means of self-report have produced inconsistent results, sometimes suggesting that learning can occur without awareness and sometimes suggesting that it cannot. For example, some investigators have subtly rewarded subjects for using certain words (e.g., plural nouns), either by saying "Mmm-hmm" as soon as the subject pronounced the word, or by giving the subject false positive feedback about another task he was performing. DeNike and Spielberger (1963) found that only those subjects who were able to verbalize the rule for reinforcement during a postexperiment interview, and who desired the reinforcement, showed an increase in the reinforced response. This is consistent with the hypothesis that conscious awareness is necessary for learning, since reinforcement was ineffective in subjects who could not verbalize the rule. Rosenfeld and Baer (1969, 1970), however, found that some subjects exhibit increases in reinforced responding despite their inability to verbalize the rule. Thus, verbal awareness is not consistently related to conditioning in such procedures.

Investigators have also examined a variety of other procedures in efforts to clarify this issue. Levine (1971) found that subjects who expected a position-based discrimination were unable to solve even a simple discrimination based on features instead. This suggests they may have failed to learn the simple discrimination because of their concentration on position, which prevented them from noticing the features. In contrast, Hefferline and Perera (1963) demonstrated that thumbtwitches, which are too small for the subject to notice, can be instrumentally conditioned by using an electromyograph to detect the responses. And Stadler (1989), studying the acquisition of a visual search skill, found that subjects who had learned to use sequence information could neither describe the sequence rules they were following nor verbally predict the location of the next target stimulus, even though they had been responding according to that information. This range of findings seems to indicate that learning can occur without awareness under some circumstances but not others.

A Synthesis

Some theorists (e.g., Kellogg, 1982) have proposed that stimulus familiarization, and perhaps certain other learning processes, are automatic and largely independent of awareness, whereas intentional learning involves more controlled attentional processes accompanied by conscious awareness. In the experiments cited above, for example, the learning of thumb twitches (Hefferline & Perera) and visual search sequences (Stadler) may be less amenable to attentional control, whereas complex concept identification (Levine) and the name-generation task used by DeNike and Spielberger may permit subjects to consciously examine their options before responding. This theoretical synthesis thus seems compatible with the bulk of the studies cited above.

Dichotomies between intentional and automatic processes have also been proposed with regard to memory systems, as will be discussed in later chapters. This theoretical parallel between learning and memory suggests that these twin areas of study may become even more integrated in the future, perhaps around a core of mainly associative models for some kinds of learning and memory and mainly cognitive models for others.

CONCLUDING REMARKS: Control by Stimulus Representations

This chapter illustrates how conditioning techniques, which were developed largely within the associative tradition, have been adapted to explore a wide range of cognitive processes in humans and nonhumans. Theories of perception, memory, and concept representation now seem increasingly important for understanding the behavior of many species.

As animals were shown to possess more and more complex abilities, there arose a need for a new terminology—one that would adequately express the complexity of their learning but without superimposing upon it our assumptions about human learning. That new terminology emerged slowly, eventually including such phrases as acquired distinctiveness,

---

learning set, *and* matching law. *Indicative of this change is the phrase* **stimulus-as-coded,** *which Lawrence (1963) coined to denote representations that mediate between physical stimuli and behavior. It is the stimulus-as-coded, not the ultimate response, that is the focus of interest among today's researchers.*

ENDNOTE

1. Even more similar to S^Ds are certain CSs in conditional discrimination procedures, which modulate the expectation that food or another important stimulus will follow a certain event (i.e., that the US will follow another CS, rather than that the reinforcer will follow a response as in operant conditioning) (Ross & LoLordo, 1987).

Natural Tendencies in Learning

As Joan scratched her pet's head and stroked his back, she exclaimed, "My, what a good parrot you've been today!" In reply, Bennie snuggled against her cheek and declared, "Gotta go, gotta go."

Should Joan worry that her pet parrot has other plans for the evening? Certainly not! Talking birds may sound like people but they can only mimic phrases they have heard again and again. Bernie cannot combine words in new ways to express whatever he wants. So although Joan and Bennie both learned to speak English phrases, the similarity is only superficial.

This raises an important issue: Does learning follow the same principles, regardless of who is doing the learning or what is being learned about? Or does learning differ fundamentally from one case to another, depending on the nature of the learner and the things being learned?

THE GENERAL PROCESS VIEW OF LEARNING

This chapter is devoted to a discussion of whether the principles of learning are truly universal, or whether each species has instead developed unique ways of learning certain things.

According to the **general process view,** the same set of laws applies regardless of the species and regardless of what is to be learned. Organisms may differ in terms of what stimuli they can perceive, what responses they can perform, and how fast they can learn, but they do not differ in terms of the basic principles by which they learn. This view largely dominated the psychological literature until the 1960s (cf. pronouncements by Pavlov, 1927/1960, p. 38; Skinner, 1956, p. 230; Tolman, 1938, p. 34).

A different view was held by some psychologists, whose work focused on species similarities and differences in behavior—a subfield known as **comparative psychology** (e.g., Schneirla, 1933; Bitterman, Wodinsky, & Candland, 1958). Instead of assuming that all species learn in the same manner, these pioneers were intrigued by evidence that different species faced with the same problem may solve it in different ways. But their attempts to promote an evolutionary perspective received little attention in comparison to the grand theoretical schemes of the general process theorists (Dewsbury, 1984).

Another divergent view was prevalent in **ethology,** which is the biological study of animal behavior in naturalistic settings. Ethologists commonly study instincts, or, more properly, **species-typical behaviors,** which are patterns of action that are exhibited throughout a species and that are less flexible than the behaviors studied by most psychologists of learning. The early ethologists sharply distinguished between instincts and learned behaviors, and maintained that many behaviors that psychologists attribute largely to learning (e.g., aggression) are really instinctive. Later, however, most ethologists came to believe that different species have naturally evolved distinctive ways of learning, just as they have evolved distinctive body structures in adapting to their environments (Lorenz, 1965). Thus ethology and comparative psychology each gave rise to an evolutionary perspective that opposed the general process view.

The vast majority of psychologists overlooked indications that learning may be biologically specialized, until the evidence of such specialization could no longer be ignored. By the late 1960s, the accumulated evidence from both conditioning and ethology finally compelled a fundamental reassessment of the general process framework—a reassessment that is still continuing.

▱ *Why do ethologists disagree with the general process view of learning?*

REVOLT AGAINST THE GENERAL PROCESS VIEW

The Challenge Is Given

The following three examples illustrate the breadth of the challenge posed to the general process approach. They show how learning in certain species, and with certain stimuli and responses, has seemed to violate general principles of instrumental and classical conditioning.

Instinctive Drift

After learning the techniques of instrumental conditioning in B. F. Skinner's laboratory, Keller and Marian Breland left graduate school to train animal acts for advertisements, circuses, movies, and television programs. They were largely successful with dozens of species, but occasionally their efforts ended in failure and frustration (Breland & Breland, 1961).

For example, a pig was trained to deposit large wooden ''coins'' into a giant piggy bank in order to advertise new bank facilities. Before long, the pig had learned the sequence of fetching a coin, carrying it several feet, and finally dropping it into the slot to obtain a food reward. But after a few weeks, the pig began pushing the coins around with its snout as if it were ''rooting'' for food on the ground, even though this greatly postponed the actual food reward. When the Brelands instead tried to train a raccoon to deposit coins into a box, the raccoon ended up dipping the coins in and out of the box and rubbing them together as if it were washing them in water, sometimes for minutes at a time. Increasing the animals' hunger only made these problems worse.

Because rooting and washing are what pigs and raccoons do instinctively with food before they eat it, the Brelands coined the phrase **instinctive drift** to signify that sometimes ''learned behavior drifts toward instinctive behavior.'' From these and many other examples, they concluded that species differences are important, and that all responses are not equally conditionable to all stimuli.

Conditioned Taste Aversions

Rats are notoriously difficult to poison because they sample only small amounts of anything strange—and they never eat it again if they become sick afterwards. One reason rats can avoid poison bait after just one experience is that they are biased to associate nausea with taste, much more than with other stimuli. Garcia and Koelling (1966), for example, let rats drink flavored water from spouts that were wired to produce a click and a flash of light every time they drank. While they were drinking this ''bright-noisy and tasty'' water, half the rats received poison or x-rays to make them nauseous, while the other half received electric shocks through the floor to make them afraid. So although different rats experienced different consequences, they all experienced the same bright-noisy and tasty warning stimulus (Table 5–1). Later, to determine which aspects of the warning stimulus had become

TABLE 5–1 Design of Garcia and Koelling's Bright-Noisy Tasty Water Experiment on Conditioned Taste Aversions

Training	Testing
Group X-Rayed	
flash ⎫	flash-click: drink
click ⎬ x-ray (sickness)	taste: AVOID
taste ⎭	
Group Poisoned	
flash ⎫	flash-click: drink
click ⎬ poison (sickness)	taste: AVOID
taste ⎭	
Group Shocked	
flash ⎫	flash-click: AVOID
click ⎬ shock (pain)	taste: drink
taste ⎭	

aversive, the experimenters gave each rat separate opportunities to drink water that was just bright-noisy (clicks and flashes) or just tasty. The rats that had been shocked avoided only the bright-noisy water, as though flashes and clicks were fearsome but taste was not. In contrast, the rats that had gotten sick avoided only the tasty water, as if the taste disgusted them but the sights and sounds did not. Such avoidance of flavors associated with illness is called **conditioned taste aversion.**

This pattern of results makes sense in relation to rats' natural survival. Poisonous bait is more easily identified by its taste than by its sound and appearance, so there is an obvious advantage to avoiding tastes after sickness. Predators may be heralded by their sound and appearance but not by their taste. So these biases seem to make sense from an ecological perspective; at the same time, however, they seem to refute the claim that learning follows the same principles for all perceptible stimuli.

Imprinting

In 1973, Konrad Lorenz shared the Nobel Prize in Physiology and Medicine for research on the genetic determinants of behavior. He was interested in the fact that geese, ducks, and many other birds must learn to recognize and follow the leader soon after they hatch, a phenomenon called **imprinting** (Lorenz, 1937). Although goslings would normally learn to follow their mother goose, Lorenz showed that a person or an object may substitute for her if it appears near the nest during a brief **critical period** after hatching (Figure 5–1). To the extent that imprinting can occur only during a critical period and only in certain species, it seems to contradict the general process view of learning.

Biological Preparedness

Genetic tendencies to learn certain things rather than others are often characterized as *biological constraints*. But the word *constraints* seems inadequate to describe the genetic enhancements of learning as well as the restrictions.

FIGURE 5–1 Konrad Lorenz with imprinted goslings in tow.

Source: Thomas McAvoy, *Life Magazine* © Time Warner Inc.

Somewhat more useful is the concept of **preparedness** (Seligman, 1970), which includes enhancements as well as restrictions along a dimension from *prepared* to *contraprepared* learning (Table 5–2). For example, rats are especially prepared to learn about taste as a warning for sickness, but they are contraprepared to learn about it as a warning for pain. According to this scheme, evolution has especially prepared each species to learn things crucial for its survival, but has left it less prepared to learn about arbitrary relationships such as those that Pavlov and Skinner studied, and even less prepared to learn about other relationships. The principles of classical and instrumental conditioning may therefore pertain only to *unprepared* learning, such as dogs salivating to a bell and rats pressing a lever for food—learning that is neither prepared nor contraprepared.

The notion of preparedness thus preserves a limited role for the familiar principles of learning, but suggests that many associations are virtually unlearnable (contraprepared) or are so easily learned (prepared) that the usual laws of conditioning are largely irrelevant.

TABLE 5–2 Seligman's Preparedness Continuum

Contraprepared	Unprepared	Prepared
		rats avoid taste if sickened
rats avoid taste if shocked		
		raccoons wash coins
	pigs drop coins for food	
		duck imprinting
	dogs salivate to bell	
	rats bar-press	

Some researchers have objected to this concept, arguing that it is premature to abandon the search for truly general principles. Others have objected that the one-dimensional concept of preparedness does not go far enough in recognizing the true diversity of natural learning. The rest of the chapter will further pursue this controversy.

◩ *Apply the preparedness concept to each of the phenomena described previously in this chapter.*

Rallying the Defense

According to defenders of the general process approach, at least some apparent exceptions to the familiar laws of learning are not really exceptions. Instead, they merely reflect interactions between instrumental responses on the one hand and classically conditioned responses on the other. If this is true, then some of the examples in the previous section may not contradict the principles of instrumental and classical conditioning after all.

Two examples will serve as illustrations. The first example, instinctive drift, is already familiar from the preceding section. The second example, autoshaping, was previously discussed in Chapter 2.

Instinctive Drift Revisited

As we have said, Breland and Breland (1961) rewarded pigs and raccoons with food for depositing coins in a container. According to the general process argument, the food played two roles at once. First, as an instrumental reinforcer, it increased the animals' tendency to deposit coins, just as the Brelands wanted. But the food also functioned secondarily as an unconditioned stimulus (US) in a way that the Brelands never anticipated. As a US, the food elicited the feeding response and served as a basis for classically conditioning the rooting and washing responses (CRs) to the coins. These CRs ultimately interfered with the instrumentally trained response, resulting in instinctive drift. Notice that this account relies entirely on familiar principles and denies the need for special laws about instinctive drift.

At first it may seem puzzling to regard rooting and washing of the coins as CRs. The rooting and washing were observed in an instrumental procedure, not in a classical conditioning procedure with an explicit CS-US sequence. But the coins were regularly encountered before food, almost as if they were CSs, so responses to them may indeed have been classically conditioned CRs. Furthermore, rooting on the ground and washing food are components of the natural feeding patterns for these animals. This makes it less surprising that they might also be CRs, since CRs often resemble the unconditioned response. Thus classical conditioning provides a plausible explanation for instinctive drift, albeit one that remains to be tested through research.

Autoshaping

By the 1960s, pigeons had become as popular as rats in research on instrumental learning. But instead of pressing levers as the rats did, the pigeons usually learned to peck a visual target called a keylight.

Originally researchers trained pigeons by the same method used with rats—namely, shaping by successive approximations. But in 1968 Brown and Jenkins reported that pigeons naturally peck keylights that precede food, even if no response is required. Merely illuminating the keylight as a signal before free food is sufficient to produce key pecking, and it is much easier than shaping the behavior by hand. The rapidity of learning by this **autoshaping** (self-shaping) technique suggests that pecking may be especially prepared to serve as an instrumental response when food is the reinforcer (Seligman, 1970). If so, this would violate the general process assumption that learning occurs in fundamentally the same way, regardless of what is to be learned.

Is autoshaping somehow unique? Defenders of the general process view have argued that it is not. They say that autoshaping, like instinctive drift, can largely be explained by taking classical conditioning into account. Much evidence supports this argument, and in fact most researchers now regard autoshaping as primarily an instance of classical rather than instrumental conditioning. For instance, pecks directed toward the keylight are very similar to pecks at food, just as CRs and URs are often similar to each other (Jenkins & Moore, 1973). Presenting extra food in the absence of the keylight causes responding to decrease, as usually happens in other instances of classical conditioning (Gamzu & Williams, 1973).

Furthermore, autoshaped pecking persists even in the **omission training** procedure, which prevents food from ever occurring in coincidence with key pecks. Omission training guarantees that instrumental reinforcement cannot occur even by accident, and it thereby demonstrates that instrumental conditioning is of minor importance in autoshaping.

Figure 5–2 illustrates the omission training method for autoshaping. At first the keylight (cf. CS) is followed by food (US), which elicits food pecking (UR) and conditions pecking to the key besides (CR). But unlike regular autoshaping, the omission procedure punishes CRs by omitting the food that would have followed that CS. If autoshaping were dependent on accidental instrumental reinforcement, then pigeons in the omission procedure would learn responses other than key pecking. However, subjects not only learn to peck the keylight under these circumstances but they continue responding at substantial rates (Schwartz & Williams, 1972).

So it appears that autoshaping does resemble other examples of classical conditioning in many ways, including the fact that it persists in omission training. Once considered to be an exceptional instance of instrumental conditioning, autoshaping is no longer considered instrumental, but primarily an instance of classical conditioning.

Insofar as autoshaping, instinctive drift, and other examples of classical conditioning conform to a uniform set of principles, they serve to justify our confidence in the general

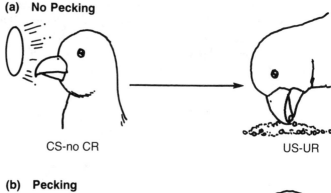

(a) No Pecking

CS-no CR   US-UR

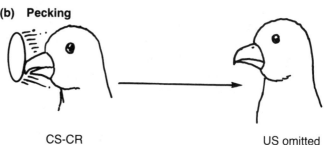

FIGURE 5–2
Omission training
procedure for
autoshaping: Food (US)
follows the keylight
signal (CS) so long as no
pecks occur. But pecks to
the keylight (CRs) cancel
food presentation.

(b) Pecking

CS-CR   US omitted

process approach. The following sections look more broadly at classical conditioning, as well as instrumental conditioning, instinct, and language, to determine whether other apparent violations can be so easily accommodated to the general process framework.

 How have general process theorists answered charges that depositing coins is contraprepared in pigs and raccoons, and that key pecking is highly prepared in pigeons, when food is the instrumental reinforcement?

BELONGINGNESS

What Exactly Is Belongingness?

The word *belongingness* has two very different meanings in psychology. Although humanists use it to denote a need for social acceptance, it has quite a different meaning with reference to learning and memory. Thorndike (1935) first used **belongingness** to mean that certain events are naturally perceived as belonging together, and are therefore more readily associated than other events. The inclusion of this term in Thorndike's associationist theory is quite surprising, because it suggests that learning does not depend entirely on contiguity and reinforcement, after all. Instead, learning also depends on the learner's perception of a meaningful relationship between events. This concept is decidedly cognitivist in character.

Ironically, Thorndike was first led to this cognitivist concept by the same puzzle box experiments that gave rise to his associationist Law of Effect (see Chapter 3). In most of those experiments, cats learned to pull a string or move a lever in order to receive a reward. But sometimes Thorndike rewarded the cats for other responses instead, such as licking or scratching themselves. Even though they often perform these responses spontaneously, it proved very difficult to make cats do them for reward. Thorndike concluded that belongingness favors the learning of manipulative responses, at least when the reward is escape from confinement.

A quite different example of belongingness involved people's memory for sequences of words they heard. In this research, Thorndike read a series of sentences aloud in the same order 10 times. For example, two of the sentences were "Norman Foster and his mother bought much. Alice Hanson and her teacher came yesterday" (Thorndike, 1932, p. 66). He then asked his subjects to recall what word had occurred next after particular words or phrases, such as after "Norman Foster and his mother" (correct answer: bought) or after "and his mother bought much" (correct answer: Alice). When the correct answer was in the same sentence as the cue words (bought), recall was relatively good. But when the answer was in the next sentence (Alice), recall was much poorer. Thorndike concluded that associations within a sentence have greater belongingness than associations across a sentence boundary.

In many cases, the concept of belongingness overlaps with the concept of biological preparedness that was introduced earlier. Learning to push and pull things, for example, is generally more adaptive for cats than learning to scratch and lick themselves when confined. In this instance, belongingness appears to coincide with biological preparedness. However, it is harder to credit biological preparedness for the bias that Thorndike observed in people's memory for words. To begin with, that bias may have arisen through experience with language customs, rather than through inherited tendencies. Furthermore, it is not clear how such a bias in word memory might aid survival and reproductive success. Thus we can speak of belongingness in some cases where biological preparedness may not be relevant.

To demonstrate belongingness, it is enough to show that the strength of learning depends on how the events are combined, rather than on the characteristics of the separate events themselves (Schwartz, 1974). For instance, Thorndike's subjects recalled some words better than others, not because the words were uniquely memorable but because they belonged in the same sentence as the cue words. And his cats learned to pull a string to escape more easily than they learned to scratch themselves to escape—not because scratching is too hard to do but because scratching naturally belongs with itching rather than with escaping from confinement.

The next sections concentrate on evidence from laboratory research in classical and instrumental conditioning. In some cases it appears that patterns of belongingness would be adaptive in a species' natural environment, in keeping with the notion of biological preparedness. In other cases preparedness seems less relevant even though belongingness is clearly apparent.

▣ *What did Thorndike mean by belongingness?*

Belongingness in Classical Conditioning

Many training procedures contain aspects of both classical and instrumental conditioning. This kind of overlap was already mentioned in connection with instinctive drift and autoshaping, and it pertains to many other procedures as well. But to the extent that some learning depends primarily on stimulus pairings (classical) and other learning depends more on the consequences of responding (instrumental), the distinction between the two types of conditioning remains useful for organizing our ideas.

This section focuses on conditioned taste aversions and fear conditioning, both of which result from unavoidable pairings of a neutral conditioned stimulus and an aversive unconditioned stimulus.

Focus on Conditioned Taste Aversions

As we indicated earlier, rats are biased to associate nausea with tastes and to associate pain with sights and sounds, rather than the opposite. Although rats sometimes acquire conditioned nausea to sights and sounds (e.g., Mitchell, Kirschbaum, & Perry, 1975), taste is much more effective in that role. Reliance on taste would presumably be adaptive for rats avoiding toxic foods in the wild, so conditioned taste aversions may reflect biological preparedness as well as mere belongingness.

Research with certain birds has uncovered a different but related pattern. Wilcoxon, Dragoin, and Kral (1971) found that, whereas rats avoid the taste of a distinctive fluid after poisoning, quail primarily avoid its color. This makes good evolutionary sense, because quail rely on sight rather than taste or smell to locate food. Chickens similarly avoid colored food or fluid after poisoning, unless the fluid dispenser limits visibility of the fluid (Gillette, Martin, & Bellingham, 1980). It should be noted that these grain-feeding birds sometimes learn aversions to tastes. But when taste and color cues are both present, the primary effect of taste is to enhance conditioning of the visual stimuli (Lett, 1980; also see Brower, 1969 [regarding blue jays] and Nicolaus, Cassel, Carlson, & Gustavson, 1983 [regarding crows]). Thus belongingness seems to be tailored to the distinct needs of each of these species, with regard to the sensory modalities they use in searching for food.

A variety of other birds and mammals, including humans, have been shown to develop conditioned taste aversions. In research by Bernstein and Webster (1980), cancer patients learned to dislike the distinctive flavor of an ice cream that was paired with nausea after chemotherapy. This occurred even though most of these patients understood that the chemotherapy rather than the ice cream was responsible for their nausea. Conditioning of this kind may help to explain the loss of appetite suffered by many chemotherapy patients. Evidently such anorexia is a side effect of our biological preparedness for taste aversions.

Several hours often pass after the ingestion of a toxic substance before any ill consequences occur. So taste aversions must be susceptible to conditioning despite this long delay, if they are to truly benefit survival. And indeed, conditioning has been reported with delays up to 24 hours between taste and illness (Etscorn & Stephens, 1973). This contrasts considerably with most other examples of conditioning, which depend on much shorter delays.

In an effort to achieve long-delay learning using a different procedure, D'Amato and colleagues studied animals' preferences for goal boxes associated with reward (D'Amato & Buckiewicz, 1980; Safarjan & D'Amato, 1981). These researchers allowed monkeys and rats to explore mazes until they reached a goal box, and then removed them from the goal box for 30 minutes before giving them rewards. Despite the 30-minute delay, subjects reliably preferred the goal box that had been followed by instrumental reinforcement. Long-delay learning thus appears not to be entirely unique to taste aversion conditioning, as researchers originally supposed. Perhaps this capacity for learning route preferences evolved separately from the capacity for learning taste aversions. Alternatively, both may involve a single, general capacity for long-delay learning that is used only under certain circumstances. Either way, the occurrence of long-delay learning in these situations but not others is difficult to reconcile with the general process approach.

In summary, different patterns of belongingness in food and drink aversions often reflect species' distinct evolved needs. Furthermore, taste aversions can be conditioned with longer delays than have been reported for other kinds of learning. These features of conditioned taste aversions are generally consistent with the notion of biological preparedness more than with the general process view. Although other instances of long-delay learning have been discovered, their rarity suggests that they are also limited to certain tasks and certain species.

How do quail differ from rats with regard to taste aversions, and how is this difference consistent with each species' survival needs?

Belongingness and Fear

Watson and Rayner (1920) conditioned fear in an infant boy by pairing an originally neutral stimulus with a loud, startling sound (see Chapter 2 regarding Little Albert). But Bregman (1934) was unable to condition fear in any of 15 infants, even though the loud, startling sound that she used made all of them cry. One possible reason for this discrepancy is that Watson and Rayner used a live rat as the neutral stimulus, whereas Bregman used inanimate objects. Perhaps infants are biologically prepared to acquire fears of only certain stimuli, and fear conditioning to other stimuli will occur much more slowly or not at all.

Phobias are exaggerated fears of specific objects or situations, often involving threats that were supposedly significant in human evolution: snakes or other animals, high places, severe weather, and so on (Zafiropoulou & McPherson, 1986). If most phobias arise through biologically prepared fear conditioning, then typical phobic stimuli should be especially effective as conditioned stimuli for fear conditioning. Consistent with this hypothesis, a heart-rate fear response in humans becomes conditioned more strongly to images of snakes and spiders than to images of flowers and mushrooms (Cook, Hodes, & Lang, 1986). All the conditioned stimuli in this experiment seem to have evoked equal interest, so stronger responding to the prepared stimuli presumably represented belongingness rather than greater attentiveness to those stimuli in general.

Belongingness is apparent in the laboratory during human fear extinction as well as acquisition. Specifically, responding that involves supposedly prepared fear (of snakes) is especially resistant to extinction (Ohman, Eriksson, & Olofsson, 1975). The special persistence of these conditioned fears does not, however, parallel clinical results with actual phobias—which all respond equally well to treatment, whether they relate to evolutionary threats or not (McNally, 1987). Thus phobias and deliberately conditioned fear both exhibit evidence of belongingness during acquisition, but only conditioned fear seems to show belongingness during extinction in humans.

LoLordo and associates have demonstrated that fear conditioning in animals can be affected by the sensory modality chosen for use as the CS. For example, rats in an experiment by Jacobs and LoLordo (1977) responded more to a tone than to a light after each stimulus had been paired with unavoidable shock. The rats had previously learned to run in a running wheel to avoid shock, so increased running during the tone was interpreted as conditioned fear. In contrast, when the light and the tone signaled safety from shock, the rats ran less than usual during the light but not during the tone. Decreased running during the light was interpreted as conditioned inhibition of fear. Thus the light was more effective as a safety signal, whereas the tone was more effective as a danger signal.

Shapiro, Jacobs, and LoLordo (1980) paired an auditory and a visual conditioned stimulus with two different unconditioned stimuli to determine how each combination would affect the behavior of pigeons. They found that a light paired with food elicits pecking reliably as a conditioned response, whereas a tone does not. When paired with shock instead, the same tone elicits head raising and side-to-side prancing, whereas the light does not. Thus little conditioning was apparent when the tone signaled food or the light signaled shock, even though the pigeons were perfectly capable of learning about both signals. (This suggests that rapid conditioning of pecking in the autoshaping procedure may involve belongingness, after all—but belongingness in classical conditioning rather than in instrumental conditioning as originally proposed by critics of the general process framework.)

The latter experiment raises an important issue that we have thus far overlooked: Our conclusions may be radically altered by changing the way that fear is measured. Do pigeons always raise their heads and prance from side to side when they are afraid, or does that form of expression depend on the presence of an auditory signal? Perhaps the pigeons learned to fear the light as much as the tone, but they did not display their fear in the same manner. More research is needed to determine whether belongingness in fear conditioning mainly affects the formation of associations, or instead affects the translation of those associations into various responses.

☑ *What neutral stimuli appear to be most effective as CSs for fear in people? in rats? in pigeons? What may account for these effects, other than faster learning of the association between the CS and the US?*

Belongingness in Instrumental Learning

Unlike classical conditioning, where stimulus pairings are crucial, the central relationships in instrumental conditioning are between the response and its reinforcer or between the response and its cue. This section explores ways in which belongingness affects learning about these instrumental relationships, beginning with negative reinforcement (avoidance).

In most studies of avoidance, the threat of painful electric shock is canceled as soon as the subject performs the required response. Is each species biologically prepared to learn only certain responses for avoiding pain and other responses for obtaining food?

Species-Specific Defense Reactions

The role that fear plays in avoidance learning is unclear (Mineka, 1979). Although subjects in such experiments often experience fear, it does not seem to be a necessary motive for avoidance responding. For example, dogs that showed fear early in avoidance training may later jump to safety without apparent emotion. This contradicts two-factor theory, which ascribes a central role to fear as the motivator of avoidance (see Chapter 3).

Even if fear is not necessary as a motivator, it may be extremely important in another way: By limiting the range of responses that can occur, fear may determine both *whether* and *how* avoidance is learned.

Bolles (1970) has argued that animals are innately equipped with certain **species-specific defense reactions** (SSDRs) to threatening situations (e.g., rats often run away or attack other animals or objects when they are afraid). Distinct types of threat situations tend to evoke different SSDRs (Fanselow & Lester, 1988). If one of the SSDRs is effective as an avoidance response, it may quickly become predominant in that situation. But if none is effective, avoidance learning will occur very slowly or not at all.

The SSDR hypothesis could explain why rats and pigeons easily learn to avoid by fleeing to a safe area, but not by pressing levers (rats) or pecking response keys (pigeons)—

responses that they readily learn if food is used as the reinforcer (D'Amato & Schiff, 1964; Macphail, 1968; Schwartz, 1973). Also consistent with the hypothesis, researchers who identified rats' and gerbils' defensive behaviors in advance found that avoidance learning is much faster when the required avoidance response is compatible with their SSDRs (Galvani, Riddell, & Foster, 1975; Grossen & Kelley, 1972).

But an experiment by Crawford and Masterson (1978) suggests that the avoidance response itself is not as important as the stimulus consequences of that response. These investigators trained five groups of rats to press a lever during an auditory warning stimulus (clicks), with each response producing a compound feedback stimulus (tone plus retraction of the lever) and handling by the experimenter—all of which should enhance acquisition (Jacobs & LoLordo, 1977; Lieberman, McIntosh, & Thomas, 1979). Still, three of the groups avoided shock much better than the others. Those three groups shared one additional advantage: They were exposed to a safe compartment soon after pressing the response lever. Interestingly, it did not matter whether these groups reached the safe compartment by running there (an SSDR) or by being carried there by the experimenter. Thus rats can readily learn to press a lever if it achieves access to a safe place. This finding raises the possibility that SSDRs are learned easily, not because they are the only responses compatible with fear but because they are the only responses that produce flight-related stimuli such as access to a safe place. Crawford and Masterson termed this explanation the **consummatory** (pronounced CONS-mah-tory) **stimulus reward** hypothesis, suggesting that rewards must somehow resemble the successful consummation of escape as it occurs in the wild.

By proposing that only certain behaviors can be readily learned as avoidance responses, Bolles' SSDR hypothesis has drawn attention to the importance of belongingness in avoidance. It appears, however, that the nature of the response itself may be less important than the stimuli that it produces. Furthermore, some species are certainly capable of more flexible avoidance learning than occurred in these studies. It seems that neither these theories nor those presented in Chapter 3 can account for the various patterns observed across different species.

Only further research can determine whether the stimulus consequences that promote avoidance learning are related to each species' evolutionary history, in keeping with the notion of biological preparedness. But it is already evident that belongingness is an important factor in avoidance learning in some species of animals.

Summarize both accounts of why SSDRs seem to be learned more easily than other avoidance responses.

Species-Specific Food-Getting Responses

In a counterpart to Bolles' SSDR hypothesis, Shettleworth (1975) has proposed that some animals are prepared to learn only certain behaviors for obtaining food. She found that activities that hungry hamsters naturally use to search for food are readily increased by food rewards, whereas nonfood-getting behaviors such as face washing and scent marking are much harder to reinforce. Attempts to reinforce the latter activities led instead to increases in rearing or digging, two food-getting behaviors that normally accompany face washing or scent marking, respectively. Thus digging, rearing, and certain other instrumental responses may naturally belong with the anticipation of food, in much the same way that SSDRs belong with pain.

Despite this demonstration of belongingness, Shettleworth (1978) rejected the conclusion that hamsters are biased to learn only certain associations. Rather, belongingness in this case is a matter of performance—the ease with which various associations can be expressed through responding. For example, Shettleworth's hamsters that were rewarded for face washing did collect their rewards faster and faster, indicating that they were forming stronger and stronger expectations of food in association with that response. So why didn't they wash their faces more to obtain more food? One reason is that the expectation of food automatically *inhibits* nonfood-getting behaviors such as face washing, often causing subjects to stop before they have performed the complete response. In contrast, digging and rearing are not inhibited by the expectation of food, so hamsters can perform them without interruption until food is obtained. Domjan's (1983) review of research on preparedness indicates that performance factors also may underlie other instances of belongingness in relation to positive reinforcement.

▨ *Why can hamsters learn to rear for food more easily than they can learn to wash their faces for food?*

Belongingness and Cue Utilization

The two previous topics concerned belongingness between responses and reinforcers. Another place where belongingness might operate is in the relationship between responses and discriminative stimuli, the cues that indicate when and what responses to perform.

Dobrzecka, Szwejkowska, and Konorski (1966) reported evidence of such a bias in dogs' discrimination learning. The dogs were first rewarded for placing their right forepaws on the feeder when they heard a rhythmical click ahead of them, and placing their left forepaws on the feeder when they heard a buzzer behind them. Eventually the dogs learned to perform flawlessly on this task, and the experimenters conducted a test to determine whether they were depending mostly on the location (front/back) or the type (click/buzz) of stimulus they heard (Table 5–3). The clicking metronome was moved to the location originally occupied by the buzzer, and vice versa, so the dogs could no longer rely on both cues in combination, but would have to choose either the old location (ahead = right paw, behind = left paw) or the old stimulus quality (click = right paw, buzz = left paw) as a basis for responding. In this experiment, where the response involved a choice between left and right paws, almost all the dogs relied on the location more than the type of sound (Figure 5–3a).

In contrast, when another group of dogs was rewarded for placing the right paw during one stimulus (click ahead) but *neither* paw during the other (buzz behind), the final results were quite different. These dogs learned this "go versus no go" discrimination as easily as

TABLE 5–3 Design of Dobrzecka, Szwegkowska, and Konorski's Experiment with Right Paw/Left Paw Discrimination (results in Figure 5-3a).

	Training (All Subjects)	Testing (All Subjects)
Click from ahead }	Right paw rewarded	Buzz from ahead
Buzz from behind }	Left paw rewarded	Click from behind

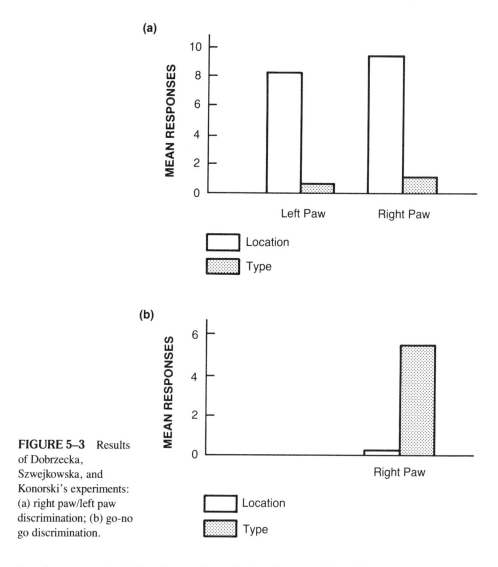

FIGURE 5–3 Results of Dobrzecka, Szwejkowska, and Konorski's experiments: (a) right paw/left paw discrimination; (b) go-no go discrimination.

the other group, but during the test they relied on the type of sound more than the location (Figure 5–3b). This finding indicates that making the front/back distinction is not generally easier than the click/buzz distinction for dogs. Instead, the front/back aspect of the cues belonged with left/right choices, whereas the click/buzz aspect belonged with go/no go choices. It is hard to explain why an organism would learn these associations more readily than the others. But we can characterize this bias as an instance of belongingness, even though we cannot yet identify its cause.

Biological preparedness was likely a factor in an experiment where hummingbirds searched for artificial nectar (Cole, Hainsworth, Kamil, Mercier, & Wolf, 1982). The experimenters first presented a sugar solution through an artificial flower, and then presented a choice between two more flowers—one located in the same place as before and one located some distance away. Only one of the latter two flowers ever contained any sugar solution, and the birds' task was to learn which one, using the location of the first flower as a cue. In particular, some birds were always rewarded for staying at the same location where the cue flower had appeared, while other birds were always rewarded for shifting to the other location.

Before discussing the results of this experiment, consider what would be predicted within the general process framework. Most theories of conditioning predict that rewards increase the tendency to repeat the rewarded response. This would mean faster learning in the "stay" group, which is rewarded for revisiting the site where the cue just provided reward. The "shift" group, on the contrary, would not receive reinforcement for revisiting the cue location and should therefore learn more slowly. In fact, however, hummingbirds begin with a tendency to shift locations, and this tendency is strengthened by reward much faster than is the tendency to stay. Similar results have been obtained with rats (Olton & Schlosberg, 1978), although the reverse is true for many species.

Cole and colleagues (1982) explain their results in the context of biological evolution by pointing out that hummingbirds feed from flowers that require a long time to replenish their nectar. A readiness to shift away from depleted flowers would be more valuable for survival in the wild than a readiness to stay. Similar considerations may apply to rats, whose food is usually scavenged over a wide area rather than found in one location. These biases toward shift rather than stay learning may therefore be instances of biological preparedness that are appropriate to certain ecological niches but not all.

✎ *Do hummingbirds learn fastest when sugar water is always in the same place the second time or never in the same place the second time? Why does this make sense for hummingbirds?*

The Adaptationist Approach

Examples of belongingness challenge the general process assumption that the principles of learning are universally applicable. In classical conditioning, the effect of a particular unconditioned stimulus (e.g., poison) may depend on how much the conditioned stimulus resembles related events in the species' natural context (tastes). In instrumental conditioning, the natural consequences of certain behaviors (SSDRs, food getting) may matter more than the experimental contingencies of reinforcement do, in determining what responses will be performed. Certainly the general principles formulated during the first half of the twentieth century are inadequate to account for these complexities.

One reason for the inadequacy of traditional theories is that psychologists remained largely ignorant of research in natural settings. A strong preference for experimental control led to the neglect of naturalistic studies and to a widespread disregard of natural problems that have shaped the evolution of behavior in each species. More recently, however, many psychologists have begun to employ more naturalistic research tactics, or at least to consider how biological evolution may have influenced the results of their conventional research. This trend is quite evident in the studies mentioned earlier in this chapter.

As we learn more about the natural behavior patterns of each species, it may become possible to relate particular instances of belongingness to more general principles of adaptation. In biology, similar adaptations inherited from a common ancestral species are termed **homologous,** whereas similarities that emerged independently in unrelated species are termed **analogous.** Analogous similarities, such as the wings of birds and butterflies, often serve similar functions even though they may differ fundamentally in both their structure and their origin. Genetically inherited biases in learning may also be classifiable as homologies or analogies, leading to the discovery of general principles like those in comparative anatomy and physiology. For example, all food aversions might share many features, but those that evolved independently in different species might also differ in predictable ways. Theoretical developments in evolutionary biology may contribute to the comparative psychology of learning in other ways, as well (Demarest, 1983).

Other instances of belongingness may instead represent learning set, acquired distinctiveness, or some other effect of earlier experience on attention, perception, or memory. Thus the identification of biases that share a common origin or function could lead to a fuller understanding of belongingness, perhaps including new, general laws to describe this widespread phenomenon.

Joint emphasis on the adaptive function of learning in both the species (phylogeny) and the individual (ontogeny) has been termed the **adaptationist approach** (e.g., Beecher, 1988). Much broader than the biological preparedness hypothesis or any existing theory of learning, it provides a framework that can include belongingness as well as the traditional laws of learning. It is therefore an extension, as well as an alternative, to the general process approach (cf. Domjan, 1983).

☑ *Contrast the general process approach and the adaptationist approach with regard to their breadth and their complexity.*

LEARNING IN NATURAL CONTEXTS

Ethology

The biological field of ethology has long been concerned with the adaptive function of behavior from an evolutionary and ecological perspective. Ethologists eschew the artificial experiments that have typified most psychological research, preferring instead to study behavior in more naturalistic settings (both in the field and in the laboratory). And they have been much more willing to include instinct and biologically prepared learning in their explanations of behavior, although their recognition of prepared learning lagged somewhat behind their recognition of instinct (Lorenz, 1965). It could even be said that they have sometimes been too eager to provide explanations in terms of special processes, rather than general principles of learning and memory.

For example, herring gulls were claimed to possess a specialized learning ability that enables them to recognize their own chicks soon after hatching. Although this would make sense from an evolutionary viewpoint, there is now some doubt whether such recognition actually occurs (see Beecher, 1988, p. 246). As another example, it was asserted that many birds innately fear the shadow of a hawk in flight. More recent research indicates that birds may be equally alarmed by any unfamiliar shadow, and that even hawk shadows are ignored after they have become familiar (see Domjan & Burkhard, 1982, pp. 44–45). In this instance, too, inheritance was given undue credit.

Although ethologists have been known to overemphasize natural specializations, just as psychologists underemphasized them, nevertheless ethologists have discovered much that is important from an adaptationist perspective. Many of their discoveries were made through naturalistic observation, and others through experiments that mimicked natural situations. Such naturalistic research, in combination with other approaches, is essential for discovering the general principles that underlie the diversity of natural behavior patterns.

Instinctive Behavior

Among the species-typical behaviors studied by ethologists are taxes (pronounced TAX-eez) and fixed action patterns. A **taxis** is a movement that is continuously oriented toward an environmental stimulus. A **fixed-action pattern** is a stereotyped sequence of movements that is exhibited throughout a species (unless limited to a certain age or sex). Both kinds of behavior resemble reflexes in the sense that they are automatic. But reflexes, such as an eyeblink to a puff of air, are simpler than fixed action patterns and lack the directedness that characterizes taxes.

A taxis and a fixed action pattern (FAP) occur together when a greylag goose retrieves an egg that has rolled from its nest (Tinbergen, 1951). These geese build nests on the ground, and it is not uncommon for eggs to roll out of the nest within reach of the parent. Rounded objects near the nest are therefore important **sign stimuli,** or stimuli that automatically release the internally fixed action pattern (also called *releasing stimuli).*

In this particular FAP, the goose extends its neck beyond the egg and uses the bottom of its bill to draw the egg slowly back into the nest. If the egg slips away, the slow neck movement often continues anyway, all the way back to the nest without the egg—hence the name *fixed action.* But usually the egg does not slip away, thanks to the presence of a taxis, which keeps the bill centered on the far side of the egg.

A more complex example of genetic constraints is provided by the female digger wasp, who must find her hidden larvae each day in order to feed them. Each larva stays in a separate hole in the ground, to which the wasp brings either one or several caterpillars daily, according to the needs of that individual larva. Surprisingly, if landmarks (such as pine cones) around the nest hole are moved during her absence, the returning wasp orients according to the overall configuration of remaining landmarks rather than to a single, simple stimulus, as shown in Figure 5–4 (Tinbergen, 1969/1951).

Perhaps the most intriguing aspect of the digger wasp's activity concerns her memory for the individual needs of her larvae. Before starting her daily hunting routine, the wasp inspects all the nest holes to determine how many caterpillars are needed for each one. Few caterpillars are needed if the larva is young or if food remains from the day before, whereas many caterpillars are needed if a larva is ready to pupate. Once these determinations have been made, the wasp kills and carries one caterpillar after another, until every nest has been provisioned in accordance with the morning inspection. Although this demonstrates an amazing ability to remember information for several hours, the wasp's memory is strangely limited: It cannot be updated to reflect new conditions encountered later in the day. For example, if a researcher provisions the nest while the wasp is hunting, this makes no difference to her. She will still drag a caterpillar into the almost full nest (using one FAP), hunt another caterpillar (using another FAP), drag it in, and so on, until she has brought the number of caterpillars indicated by the morning inspection. Or if the researcher robs several caterpillars from the nest after she inspects it, she will still deposit only one caterpillar— even though that leaves the nest practically empty. Fortunately for the wasp, landmarks and dead caterpillars rarely move.

Field experiments such as these have confirmed very clearly that species differ in how they learn and remember, at least with regard to certain tasks. Other specializations in learning and memory have been documented through research on migratory bird navigation (Emlen, 1975), bird song learning (Marler & Peters, 1981; Thorpe, 1956), flower learning in bees (Gould, 1985; Menzel, 1985), offspring recognition in cichlid fish (Tinbergen, 1969/1951), and many other phenomena. Often, as in the case of the digger wasp, there is

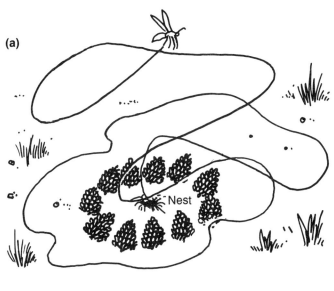

(a)

(b)

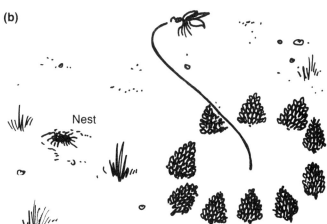

FIGURE 5–4 Homing flights of the digger wasp, *Philanthus triangulum,* after displacement of landmarks (pine cones) during her absence.

Source: Adapted from Tinbergen, N. (1969). *The study of instinct.* Oxford, England: Oxford University Press. By permission of Oxford University Press.

only a limited period when learning can best occur—although that period may span several months in some instances (e.g., song learning). This dependence on timing is also shared by imprinting, the topic to which we turn next.

🖾 *Greylag geese and digger wasps may appear quite intelligent as they tend their nests, but ethologists have shown that some aspects of their behavior are surprisingly inflexible. How does the digger wasp's reliance on memory illustrate this rigidity?*

Focus on Imprinting

Imprinting occurs in many animals, but it has been studied mostly in ducklings and chicks. Lorenz (1937) believed that moving objects serve as sign stimuli to release the fixed-action pattern of following, during a critical period soon after the birds hatch. He also believed that the sign stimuli must possess certain characteristics, and that imprinting is instantaneous and cannot be altered.

Although imprinting usually occurs soon after birth, it also can occur later and can be reversed (Gaioni, Hoffman, DePaulo, & Stratton, 1978). Thus the period of optimal sensitivity is not truly critical for imprinting, nor do imprintable stimuli share the characteristics that Lorenz expected (Hoffman & Ratner, 1973). Some authors have therefore questioned whether imprinting really differs much from ordinary learning (Hoffman & Ratner, 1973; Rajecki, 1973).

However, most criticisms of the imprinting concept are based on research from laboratory experiments that used only artificial visual stimuli. Those settings differ radically from the wild, where, for example, the hen's vocalizations can be heard by her brood even before they hatch. When researchers use more naturalistic settings for their experiments, imprinting in some species seems to occur more rapidly and be more difficult to reverse, much as Lorenz described (Colombo, 1982; Gottlieb, 1973; Hess, 1972).

Although some writers have suggested that there might be an optimal period for human bonding somehow comparable to imprinting, the evidence does not support this conclusion (Lamb, 1982). Human emotional attachments require some length of time to become firmly established, and the first few hours after birth do not matter more than all the rest. Of course, imprinting itself is not strictly confined to a critical period; however, it often occurs most readily at a certain age, whereas the evidence for such a sensitive period in human infancy is far from decisive.

In conclusion, although imprinting may depend in some ways on common processes of learning and memory, it is uncommonly sensitive to timing and certain features of its natural context. This set of characteristics is probably adaptive in these species' natural settings, where the young bird's first encounter would almost certainly be with its own mother. But if the adaptationist approach is correct, we will have to discover more about the ecology and evolution of imprinting species before we can hope to fully understand this specialized form of learning.

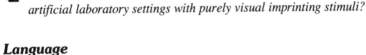 *What characteristics of imprinting are stronger in naturalistic settings, compared to artificial laboratory settings with purely visual imprinting stimuli?*

Language

The Language of Honeybees

The Nobel Prize that Konrad Lorenz received in 1973 was shared with two other ethologists: Niko Tinbergen, some of whose work was cited earlier, and Karl von Frisch, whose most outstanding discovery was the secret of communication among honeybees (von Frisch, 1967). At least since the time of Aristotle, it had been thought that bees somehow inform each other about the location of pollen. Through meticulous observation, von Frisch discovered that they communicate via a system of dance-like movements.

Von Frisch installed glass windows in a beehive so he could observe the behavior of "scout" bees bringing news of food. Once a bee located a food source, she returned to the dark interior of the hive to feed samples of the substance to other bees and then dance vigorously on the vertical honeycomb. If she had found the food within about 100 meters of the hive, she ran around and around in a small circle, both clockwise and counterclockwise, in what von Frisch called a **round dance** (Figure 5–5a). But if the food source was farther away, she danced in a figure-8 pattern called a **waggle dance,** which signifies both the direction and the distance to the food, as explained below (Figure 5–5b).

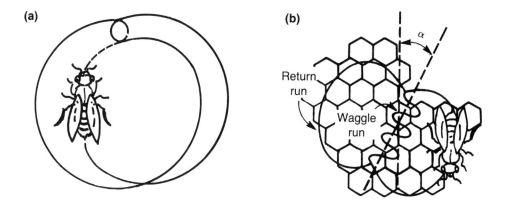

FIGURE 5–5 Dance language of the honey bee: (a) the round dance, in which the bee makes small circles to signal a nearby food source; (b) the waggle dance, in which the angle of the straight run in relation to the vertical is equal to the angle of flight to the food source in relation to the sun.

Source: Illustrations from *Biology: The science of life* by Karl von Frisch, translated by Jane M. Oppenheimer. Copyright © 1964 by Bayerischer Schullbuch-Verlag. Reprinted by permission of HarperCollins Publishers.

No less astonishing than the scout's performance was the other bees' ability to respond to it. They crowded around her, touching her with their antennae all the while. Then, following a round dance, most of the "recruits" that observed it would leave the hive and search nearby. In contrast, a waggle dance would send them flying in the general direction of the food source. This specialized form of observational learning obviously increases the efficiency of food gathering and thereby promotes survival of the honeybee colony.

The waggle dance was named for a wagging movement the bee makes where the halves of the figure-8 join together. She swings her abdomen rapidly from side to side all along this line, while simultaneously buzzing her wings. This is the part of the waggle dance that contains information about distance and direction. The slower and longer the waggling, the longer the flight will be. The more her direction slants away from straight up, the more the flight path must deviate from the sun. For example, a waggle run slanted 30 degrees to the right of vertical means that the food is 30 degrees to the right of the sun, whereas waggling straight down the wall means the food is directly opposite the sun. Although some researchers argue that this dancing is less important than odors and other cues, Gould (1975) has presented evidence that the waggle dance is of primary importance in at least some circumstances.

Complex though it is, the honeybee's dancing is inadequate to express anything other than the location of its destination. The meaning of each movement pattern is rigidly constrained by genetics in a way that human words and signs are not. Not only can we use different words to express the same idea (cf. different languages) but we can also use the same words to express different ideas ("The boy hit the ball" is not the same as "The ball hit the boy"—see the discussion of language syntax in Chapter 4). The mere fact of communication in different species is not, therefore, evidence of general processes at work. Rather, a comparison between human language and the language of the honeybees shows us just how diverse such adaptations can be.

📝 *What feature of the waggle dance indicates the direction bees should fly in relation to the sun?*

Human Language Learning

The claim that human language is unique is a very old one (e.g., Descartes, 1637/1965). But such claims are inconsistent with the general process approach, which assumes that language is based on the same processes of learning that operate in other species. Several authors have attempted to explain language acquisition in terms of conditioning theory (Skinner, 1957; Staats, 1968).

The uniqueness of human language was strongly reasserted by a linguist, Noam Chomsky (1959), who contended that speech is too rich and creative to be explained through general principles of learning. Children do not depend on imitation and conditioning, he argued, but instead are equipped from birth to use sounds and gestures in certain ways. They naturally discover and apply an amazing array of natural language "rules" in their first few years, far outdistancing the specially trained chimpanzees we discussed in Chapter 4 (Slobin, 1979). This rule-governed quality of human language is responsible for our ability to constantly create new sentences that our audience can understand, even though they have never heard those sentences before.

In support of the idea that people are biologically prepared for language, Lenneberg (1967) suggested that there is a critical period for language learning, as was claimed for imprinting in other species. In support of his suggestion, he cited evidence that it may be more difficult to learn a new language after puberty than before. However, more recent research indicates that this finding is perhaps limited to countries such as the United States, where fluency in a second language is regarded as unusual. Under different cultural expectations, adolescents and adults may learn new languages more easily than children do (Snow & Hoefnagel-Hoehle, 1978).

Studies of second-language acquisition therefore have not consistently supported Lenneberg's hypothesis regarding a critical period. Still, there are at least two good reasons not to reject Chomsky's proposal that we are biologically prepared to learn language. First, although the brain functions as a whole in performing intellectual tasks, certain areas in the left hemisphere of the brain are especially crucial for speech comprehension and production. It is difficult to imagine why these brain areas evolved, unless their linguistic functions depend on the existence of a special neural apparatus—one that only we seem to possess.

Second, human language is extremely adaptive because it enables people to accumulate knowledge across individuals and generations in a way that no other species has achieved. We do not know precisely what role verbal culture played in creating human niches around the globe, but it is hard to imagine a more useful resource for adaptive radiation than the ability to communicate about other times, places, and conditions. Any other species possessing a similar capability would presumably exhibit it naturally, and the fact that none has done so suggests that only we possess it. It should be noted that the effects of this specialization need not be limited to language alone, but may involve more fundamental thought processes as well (Fodor, 1975).

Thus it is plausible that our language ability may have evolved as a special biological adaptation. This hypothesis, of course, is not amenable to experimental test, so we may never know what evolutionary factors fostered such a unique form of communication. But if we wish to understand our uniqueness and yet our relatedness to other species, we may do well to view our language abilities within the broader context of biological preparedness.

☑ *List three arguments to support the claim that human language learning involves more than just general processes of learning common to all species.*

CONCLUDING REMARKS: The Evolutionary Perspective

Some early indictments of the general process approach, including those based on instinctive drift and imprinting, were softened somewhat when it was discovered that the results differed less from familiar conditioning than was first thought. But a host of other findings eventually made it clear that the general process view of Pavlov and Skinner is no longer tenable. In its place, the broader and more complex general framework known as the adaptationist approach still holds considerable promise.

Several examples of belongingness and species-typical learning can reasonably be attributed to biological preparedness, including conditioned taste aversions, hummingbirds shifting after reward, wasp provisioning, and honeybee recruitment. But other demonstrations of belongingness are further from a satisfactory explanation. Until more is known about their ecological role and their evolution, they will remain a challenge, not only to the general process view, but also to every other account of learning.

CHAPTER 6

Multistore Models of Memory

APPLICATION: Baking and Memorizing

Alan is baking a cake for his wife's birthday and is using one of his mother's favorite recipes. As he begins his initial preparations, he first consults the card on which the recipe is written, and with the ingredients in mind he goes to the cupboard and the refrigerator to collect the necessary items: flour, sugar, butter, vanilla flavoring, cinnamon, salt, eggs, baking soda, and oatmeal. He then consults the card again and proceeds to combine the ingredients in the order specified.

Later in the day, Alan goes to his study to begin his preparation for an anatomy examination scheduled for later in the week. He opens his notebook and proceeds to try to memorize the names of the carpal bones in the order in which they are arranged in the hand: navicular, lunate, triquetral, pisaform, greater multangular, lesser multangular, capitate, and hamate. To help him remember the order of the bones, Alan commits to memory the sentence, Never let thy pig get lost coming home, *in which the first letter of each word corresponds to the first letter of the appropriate bone in the sequence. Half an hour later, to test his memory for the names, Alan takes a picture that shows the bones of the hand, covers the labels on the picture, and proceeds to try to write the name for each carpal bone shown. He then checks his answers and retests himself two hours later as he completes his study session.*

The central question to be addressed in this chapter is whether Alan was using two distinctly different types of memory in performing the tasks described. That is, was Alan relying primarily on a short-term memory store to remember the ingredients of the cake and the order in which they are to be combined, and was he relying primarily on a long-term memory store to remember the carpal bones for the anatomy exam to be taken later?

HISTORICAL BACKGROUND

James's Primary-Secondary Memory Distinction

The distinction between two types of memory store dates back at least as far as the nineteenth century. For example, in his landmark work, *The Principles of Psychology*, originally published in 1890, William James (1890/1981) distinguished between what he called primary and secondary memory. James equated **primary memory** with consciousness. Events that have not left conscious awareness are a part of primary memory. According to James, primary memory is the memory that "makes us aware of . . . the *just* past. The objects we feel in this directly intuited past differ from properly recollected objects. An object which is recollected, in the proper sense of that term, is one which has been absent from consciousness altogether, and now revives anew" (p. 608). Primary memory "has a breadth of several seconds, a rearward and a forward end, and may be called the specious present" (p. 609). However, "properly recollected objects" are a part of **secondary memory** or memory proper. James thus defined secondary memory as "*the knowledge of an event, or fact,* of which meantime we have not been thinking, *with the additional consciousness that we have thought or experienced it before*" (p. 610).

▨ *According to James, on which type of memory would we be relying when we attend to an item, and on which type of memory would we be relying in trying to remember the name of our first-grade teacher?*

Broadbent's Filter Theory of Attention

Despite the clarity with which James articulated this distinction, the contrast between a temporary memory store and a more permanent memory store did not become a major interest of research psychologists until the 1950s when the issue of attentional processes in humans spurred the emergence of what is sometimes referred to as the **information-processing approach** to learning and memory. The information-processing approach represented a major reemergence of the mentalistic tradition in learning theories. The researchers and theorists working within this framework emphasize the importance of trying to describe explicitly the types of processes and structures that must exist in the mind in order for humans to behave as they do in certain situations.

As noted in Chapter 1, Donald Broadbent presented in 1958 a theory of attention in his book, *Perception and Communication,* that attempted to explain why it is that humans cannot process information presented simultaneously as well as they can process the same information presented successively. For example, in a series of experiments, Broadbent found that when two short lists of three digits each were read to subjects simultaneously, one list to one ear and the other list to the other ear, subjects could on average recall only four to five of the items, whereas when one list of six digits was read to both ears, most subjects could recall all of the items without error.

In proposing what has come to be called the **filter theory of attention,** Broadbent presented the description of the information-processing system shown in Figure 6–1. Basically, he argued that information arriving at the senses is maintained briefly in a short-term store and that certain information in the short-term store will be selected for analysis—that

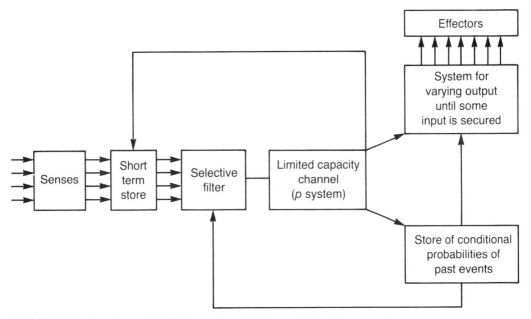

FIGURE 6–1 Broadbent's (1958) description of the human information-processing system.

Source: Reprinted with permission from Donald E. Broadbent, *Perception and Communication,* copyright 1958, Pergamon Press, PLC.

is, will be allowed to pass through a selective filter into a limited capacity channel. Once in the limited capacity channel, the input is fully perceived and is available for a variety of mental operations, including transfer to a store of past events. Although Broadbent in his original model distinguished between a short-term store, a selective filter, and a limited capacity channel, these structures obviously correspond to what James called primary memory, and Broadbent clearly differentiated between these structures and long-term memory storage. Thus, in the attempt following World War II to study processes such as attention that had not been addressed by the verbal learning tradition discussed in Chapter 9, researchers such as Broadbent began to find James's characterization of different types of memory useful.

📝 *How was the concept of primary memory elaborated in Broadbent's filter theory?*

The Brown-Peterson Distractor Task

The possible utility of distinguishing between different types of memory was also underscored by demonstrations in the late 1950s that forgetting of a very small number of items being held in memory can occur within very short intervals. In 1958, John Brown, a British researcher, published the results of a series of studies from his doctoral dissertation. These studies showed that even when the number of stimuli to be remembered by the subject is well below the memory span, forgetting occurs if the presentation of additional stimuli delays recall for several seconds.

For example, in one of Brown's studies, subjects were presented in the experimental trials with between one and four pairs of consonants to be remembered, and these required stimuli were followed by five pairs of digits. All stimuli were presented at a rate on one pair of stimuli every 0.78 second. Subjects were instructed to read aloud all of the stimuli presented and to attempt to remember the consonants. As soon as the presentation was over, subjects were asked to write the to-be-remembered consonants in the order in which they were presented. In the control trials, the digits following the consonants were omitted and the 4.7-second interval was left unfilled. Brown's results, shown in Figure 6–2, demonstrated that recall performance declined as the number of to-be-remembered consonants increased, but the decline was much more pronounced in the experimental condition in which the additional distracting digits were presented. Brown argued that this effect was due to the distracting stimuli preventing rehearsal (i.e., repetition of the to-be-remembered items).

In 1959, two American researchers, Lloyd Peterson and Margaret Peterson, published a similar study in which they varied the length of the retention interval during which distracting events were presented. In their experiment, subjects on each trial received as the to-be-remembered items a set of three consonants (a consonant trigram). The consonants were immediately followed by a three-digit number, and subjects had to count backward by three or four from this number in time to the clicking of a metronome. The length of this distracting activity of counting backward was varied from 3 to 18 seconds. A flashing light signaled the subjects to stop counting and to attempt to recall the three consonants in the order in which they were presented.

Peterson and Peterson reported the results shown in Figure 6–3. As the length of the distractor-filled retention interval increased, the frequency of correct recall declined markedly until, with the longest interval of 18 seconds, the probability of recall was near zero. Peterson and Peterson concluded that forgetting of verbal items can occur in a matter of

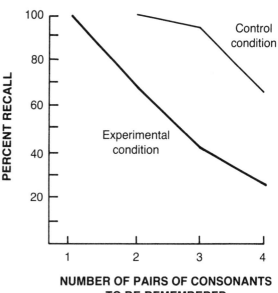

FIGURE 6–2 Recall of consonants in Brown's (1958) experiment. Forgetting was more pronounced in the *experimental condition,* in which five pairs of digits were read by subjects during the 4.7-second retention interval, than in the *control condition,* in which the retention interval was unfilled.

Source: Brown, J. (1958). Some tests of the decay theory of immediate memory. *Quarterly Journal of Experimental Psychology, 10,* 15. © The Experimental Psychology Society.

FIGURE 6–3 Recall of consonant trigrams in the Peterson and Peterson (1959) experiment as a function of the length of the distractor-filled retention interval.

Source: Peterson, L. R., & Peterson, M. J. (1959). Short-term retention of individual verbal items. *Journal of Experimental Psychology, 58,* 195. In the public domain.

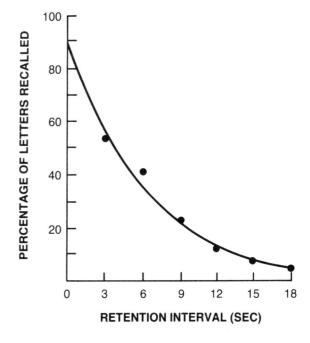

seconds when rehearsal of the items is prevented, and they argued that their results demonstrated the importance of studying systematically short-term retention and its contribution to long-term retention.

The emphasis of these two sets of researchers on the importance of short-term retention, as distinct from long-term retention, thus contributed directly to the popularization of the type of primary-secondary memory dichotomy proposed by James. As a result of their efforts, the study of short-term retention became a major research effort of the 1960s. In the subsequent research on short-term retention, the basic methodology of Brown and Peterson and Peterson was widely employed and has come to be known as the **Brown-Peterson distractor task.**

📝 *What was the basic methodology employed by Brown and Peterson and Peterson in demonstrating the phenomenon of short-term forgetting?*

The Waugh-Norman Two-Component Model of Memory

This reemergence of the primary-secondary memory distinction in the work of the information-processing theorists was made explicit in 1965 when Nancy Waugh and Donald Norman published a formal model of the memory system that directly argued for the existence of distinct primary and secondary memory stores. A representation of their proposed memory system is shown in Figure 6–4. Basically, Waugh and Norman argued that any item attended to enters primary memory, an immediate memory system of sharply limited capacity. An item already in primary memory can be displaced by a newly arriving item. If the old item is displaced, it will be permanently lost, but rehearsal of an old item maintains the item in primary memory and promotes the transfer of the item to secondary memory, a long-lasting memory system of virtually unlimited capacity.

Waugh and Norman used the phenomenon of the limited **memory span** as the starting point for their investigations. The memory span task involves determining the largest number of unrelated items that a person can recall verbatim in the order presented after just one presentation. Waugh and Norman noted that the memory span is usually found to be fewer than 10 items. They reasoned that this limitation in immediate memory is due at least in part to an inability to rehearse earlier items in the list while attempting to process and store later ones, and they set about to try to discover why unrehearsed items should be forgotten so rapidly.

The experiment they devised was designed to test whether the item is lost through **decay** (i.e., through the passage of time regardless of the events occurring as time passes) or through **interference** from other items arriving after it in memory. The procedure employed in the experiment involved presenting aurally a list of 16 digits at a rate of either 1 or 4 digits per second. The last digit in the list, the probe digit, had appeared earlier in the list and was accompanied by a tone to signal the end of the list and to indicate to the subject

FIGURE 6–4 The Waugh-Norman (1965) model of the human memory system.

Source: Waugh, N. C., & Norman, D. A. (1965). Primary memory. *Psychological Review, 72,* 93. Copyright 1965 by the American Psychological Association. Reprinted by permission.

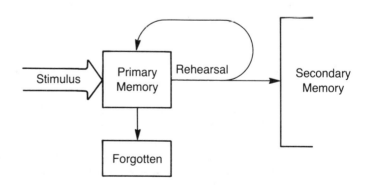

that recall of the item following the probe digit in the list was requested. On any given trial, the probe digit could have appeared initially in the list in position 3, 5, 7, 9, 10, 11, 12, 13, or 14. Thus the number of interfering items occurring between the item to be recalled and the recall cue in the form of the probe digit was varied from 12 to 1.

Waugh and Norman reported that the probability of successfully recalling the item following the probe digit in the list decreased as the number of interfering items increased. Furthermore, they found that the rate of presentation of the items did not affect significantly the pattern of results. Therefore, they concluded that forgetting from primary memory is due primarily to interference in the form of newly arriving items that prevent rehearsal of items already in the memory store; if decay were a major factor in the loss of information, they reasoned, forgetting should have been more pronounced with the slower presentation rate of one digit per second, as more time would have elapsed between the presentation of an item and its recall, than with the faster presentation rate of four digits per second.

Waugh and Norman then formulated a quantitative model of the memory system that stipulates that the probability of recalling an item is a function of the probability that the item is in primary memory, in secondary memory, or in both, and that these probabilities are determined essentially by the number of items that have intervened since the presentation of the to-be-recalled item. They then applied their model to a variety of experimental results from studies employing a variety of different memory tasks, and found that it could account for many of the findings.

Opponents of the multiple memory store approach argued that it is unparsimonious to assume the existence of more than one memory store when most variables appear to affect short-term and long-term retention similarly. In response, Waugh and Norman argued that such findings are not unexpected if one assumes that the two proposed memory systems are not mutually exclusive and that the recall of an item is dependent both on the probability that it is still in primary memory and on the probability that it has been successfully transferred to secondary memory. It should not be assumed that items recalled within a specific period of time after their occurrence are being retrieved exclusively from primary memory, whereas items recalled after that specified period of time are being retrieved exclusively from secondary memory.

Finally, they argued for the utility of the two-memory system on the basis of introspective evidence concerning the production and understanding of speech. Waugh and Norman suggest that it would be impossible to generate or understand a grammatical statement without the ability afforded by primary memory to recall verbatim the most recent items from the sentence produced or heard.

What mechanism did Waugh and Norman use to explain forgetting from primary memory?

THE ATKINSON-SHIFFRIN MODAL MODEL OF MEMORY

Original Formulation of the Model

Shortly after the publication of the Waugh and Norman model, a more detailed account of a multiple-component memory system was proposed by Richard Atkinson and Richard Shiffrin (1968, 1971). The impact of this model has been so great on memory research in the intervening years that Baddeley (1976) and others have suggested that the Atkinson-Shiffrin model has become the modal model of memory. In their model, Atkinson and

Shiffrin proposed a memory system composed of three distinct memory stores: sensory registers, short-term store (STS), and long-term store (LTS). A schematic representation of their model is shown in Figure 6–5.

The Sensory Registers

Atkinson and Shiffrin suggested that incoming information is first represented in the sensory registers where it is held for very brief intervals before it decays. Thus the sensory registers of this model correspond to what Broadbent called short-term memory in his original multistore model. In discussing the sensory registers, Atkinson and Shiffrin concentrated on the visual sensory memory as that for which the clearest research picture existed at the time, but they stressed that sensory registers must exist for all sensory modalities. Their argument for the existence of a visual sensory memory was based in large part on the pioneering work of George Sperling (1960, 1963) involving the brief presentation of visual arrays such as that shown in Figure 6–6.

Sperling (1960) reported that when subjects were asked to recall all of the letters from the array, following a presentation of the array for 50 milliseconds, subjects on average recalled between four and five of the letters. Sperling called this condition the **whole report procedure.**

However, Sperling hypothesized that more information was actually available in the subjects' sensory system immediately after the presentation of the array than was being recalled in the whole report condition. To test this possibility, Sperling introduced the **partial report procedure** in which subjects were signaled to recall only one row of the array. Following the presentation of the array, a tone of a particular pitch was sounded to indicate which row of the array should be recalled. Then, based on the subjects' average recall of the requested row, Sperling estimated the total number of array items available in the visual system at the moment recall was requested by multiplying the average recall of

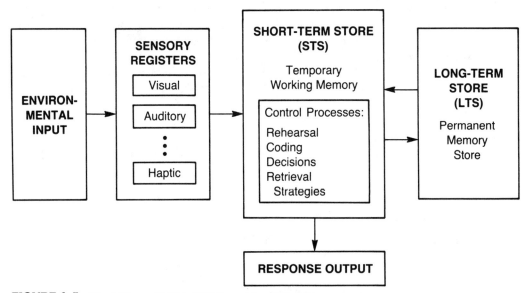

FIGURE 6–5 The Atkinson-Shiffrin (1971) modal model of memory.

Source: From "The control of short-term memory," by R. C. Atkinson & R. M. Shiffrin, *Scientific American,* 225, 82. Copyright © 1971 by Scientific American, Inc. All rights reserved.

FIGURE 6–6 An array of letters such as that used by Sperling (1960) in investigating visual sensory memory.

the single requested row by the total number of rows in the array. This estimation procedure was justified because the subjects did not know until after the presentation of the array which row they would have to recall.

Sperling found that when the array contained 9 items, as shown in Figure 6–6, subjects recalled on average 2.7 of items in the requested row in the partial report procedure. This then suggests that subjects had available in the sensory memory at the time recall was requested a total of 8.1 items (the number of items available in any one row of the array, 2.7, times the number of rows in the array, 3).

Thus, in using the partial report procedure, Sperling found that immediately following the presentation of the array, subjects had available in sensory memory a snapshot-like image of the array. However, the considerably lower estimate of the number of items available obtained with the whole report procedure suggested that the image decays rapidly. That is, the lower estimate of the number of items available obtained with the whole report procedure could be due to the decay of part of the array before the subject can scan and report all of the initially available items. To test this possibility, Sperling varied the delay between the presentation of the array and the recall signal in the partial report condition. He found that the estimate of the number of items available in sensory memory declined as the delay increased until, with a delay of about 500 milliseconds, the partial report estimate was no greater than the whole report estimate. Thus Sperling's results suggested that information in the visual sensory memory (usually referred to as the **iconic memory**) decays within a matter of several hundred milliseconds.

In the Atkinson and Shiffrin model, the maintenance of information for such brief intervals in the sensory register allows for the matching of the incoming information with its already existing representation in the long-term store. Such a matching process allows for the retrieval of features, such as the name of the incoming items, and thus makes possible the transfer of information from the sensory store to the short-term store. Thus the transfer of information from the sensory store to the short-term store is not a direct process but involves the intermediate step of first retrieving from long-term store already stored features of the incoming information that permit it to be efficiently represented in the short-term store.

 According to the Atkinson and Shiffrin model, what must occur before information can be transferred from the sensory registers to short-term store?

The Short-Term Store

Atkinson and Shiffrin argued that this component of the memory system is of pivotal importance and corresponds roughly to consciousness. Thus, the STS of the Atkinson and

---

Shiffrin model is clearly related to James's concept of primary memory. STS is the central component of the system in that it governs the flow of information in the system. In an early description of their model, Atkinson and Shiffrin (1968) proposed that information represented in STS is, like information in sensory memory, subject to loss through decay, but they argued that the decay process in STS is longer lived. They suggested that in the absence of rehearsal, information is likely to be lost from STS within 15 to 30 seconds. They based this estimate of the decay process, in part, on the results of the Peterson and Peterson (1959) distractor task study discussed previously.

As the system's working memory component, STS governs the flow of information in the system through the existence of **control processes** that determine the manner in which information in STS is manipulated. These control processes include rehearsal and coding. **Rehearsal** refers to the repetition of to-be-remembered information, and **coding** involves altering the presented information in some way so as to increase its memorability. Examples of coding include the use of imagery and organizational strategies that involve elaborating the to-be-remembered information. Given a list of words to remember, one could use the control process of imagery by creating a visual picture of the object named by each word, and one could use an organizational strategy of trying to group certain words based on their membership in a particular category such as plants, articles of furniture, and so on.

In the example given at the beginning of the chapter, Alan was, in terms of the model, using rehearsal to help him maintain the ingredients of the cake in STS, and he was using rehearsal and the coding processes of organization and elaboration to help him in the transfer of information about the bones of the hand from STS to LTS. Note that the control processes in STS are dependent on the use of information already in LTS. Rehearsal involves the use of the name of the to-be-remembered words, and, if the words are presented visually, the names of the words will have to be retrieved from LTS as part of the matching process that occurs while the words are being held in sensory memory. Likewise, the generation of images of the objects to which the words refer and the use of information about the category membership of presented words necessitates the use of information about the words that is presumably already stored in LTS, and that can also be retrieved as part of the original matching of information in sensory memory with its representation in LTS.

In their descriptions of the model, Atkinson and Shiffrin emphasized the control process of rehearsal. They argued that the process of rehearsal serves two important functions in the system. Rehearsal helps prevent the decay of information in STS, and it increases the probability that the information will be effectively transferred to LTS. In order to use rehearsal effectively, Atkinson and Shiffrin suggested that part of STS is devoted to the creation and use of a **rehearsal buffer,** or a bin that contains a limited number of slots into which items can be placed for rehearsal. In this way, the model suggests that the capacity of STS is limited, just as the Waugh and Norman model argues for capacity limitations in primary memory. Atkinson and Shiffrin proposed that measures of the memory span represent an estimate of the lower limit on the capacity to rehearse items in an ordered fashion.

The concept of a rehearsal buffer also allows for a displacement mechanism, in addition to the process of decay, by which information may be lost from STS. Once the rehearsal buffer has been filled, the addition of new items to the buffer will result in the displacement of old items from the buffer. In their 1968 paper, Atkinson and Shiffrin suggested that a displaced item is still in the component of STS not devoted to the rehearsal buffer but is then subject to rapid decay and loss from STS. Although the Atkinson and Shiffrin model, as proposed in 1968, placed its greatest emphasis on the role of decay in forgetting from STS, it did, nevertheless, provide for a displacement mechanism of forgetting similar to that proposed in the Waugh and Norman model.

In addition, in later descriptions of the model (e.g., Atkinson & Shiffrin, 1971), Atkinson and Shiffrin revised their description of the forgetting process from STS in light of findings by Reitman (1971). Using a version of the Brown-Peterson distractor task in which subjects had to remember a sequence of three words, Reitman substituted a signal-detection task for the arithmetic task in one condition of the study. In the signal-detection task, subjects had to monitor for the occurrence of a weak tone in white noise, and Reitman reported no forgetting of the to-be-remembered letters following 15 seconds of the signal-detection distractor task.

These and related findings from experiments of their own, together with the original Peterson and Peterson findings of major forgetting with the arithmetic distractor task, led Atkinson and Shiffrin to conclude that the type of distractor material presented during the retention interval will determine whether the to-be-remembered information will be lost from STS. When the distractor task involves verbal processing similar to that involved in maintaining the to-be-remembered information, as in the case of the arithmetic task, forgetting will occur. Therefore, Atkinson and Shiffrin concluded, the primary cause of forgetting from STS is interference from other similar information entering the store and not simply the passage of time, as a decay explanation of forgetting would suggest. Thus Atkinson and Shiffrin ultimately rejected a decay explanation of forgetting from STS in favor of an interference explanation that can include a displacement mechanism of the type described above. That is, displacement of earlier presented items from the rehearsal buffer by later ones could contribute to an interference process that promotes forgetting from STS.

It should be noted here that some subsequent studies have reported an apparent effect of decay on forgetting from STS. For example, in a followup study in 1974, Reitman did report findings she argued are consistent with a decay effect. In the followup study, the number of words to be remembered on each trial was five, rather than three as in the original study, with recall requested either immediately or after 15 seconds of distraction in which subjects listened for the occurrence of a weak tone. Reitman increased the number of words to be remembered in order to determine if the failure to find evidence of decay in the original study was due to a ceiling effect. That is, she suggested that with only three words to remember, decay-produced forgetting may have been occurring in the delay conditions of the original study but that enough of the memory trace remained to allow subjects to reconstruct the to-be-remembered items.

The findings of the followup study showed a 12% greater forgetting rate following the 15 seconds of tone detection than in the immediate recall condition. Thus, Reitman argued, when the distractor task is demanding enough to prevent rehearsal of the to-be-remembered items and yet does not involve verbal processing so as to minimize interference with the to-be-remembered items, a decay process may operate.

Similar conclusions can be drawn from a study by Shiffrin and Cook (1978) that involved a somewhat different procedure. In their study, subjects were given special instructions intended to minimize their tendency to rehearse the presented items. Subjects were told the study was concerned with how well people can forget presented information and with whether a tone detection task can facilitate forgetting of presented information. Each trial consisted of 40 seconds of tone detection with five consonants presented either 32.5 or 12.5 seconds before the end of the trial. Subjects were asked to repeat the consonants and then put them out of mind as they continued with the tone detection. At the end of each trial, recall of the five consonants was requested.

Shiffrin and Cook reported a forgetting rate of 20% when the consonants were presented only 12.5 seconds before the end of the trial, compared to a forgetting rate of 30% when the consonants were presented 32.5 seconds before the end of the trial. Thus the longer the consonants were held in STS in a situation in which the distractor task did not involve potentially interfering verbal processing and in which subjects' tendency to rehearse was minimized, the more likely they were to be forgotten, as a decay explanation would predict. However, in both of these studies, subjects were tested on more than one trial and there remains the possibility that some of the forgetting found may have been produced by interference from items learned on previous trials. That is, **proactive interference** may have been responsible for at least part of the effect. (See Chapter 9 for a review of the issue of proactive interference.)

At any rate, the Atkinson and Shiffrin model's shift from a decay to an interference explanation of forgetting from STS did not alter the model's emphasis on the importance of rehearsal in maintaining information in STS and promoting its transfer to LTS. In describing the transfer process, Atkinson and Shiffrin emphasized that coding processes influence what is rehearsed in STS and therefore what is transferred to LTS. Thus the selection of a particular coding strategy will have a direct bearing on the probability of successfully retrieving the target information from LTS after a delay.

For example, Alan's use of the coding mnemonic in trying to remember the bones of the hand described at the beginning of the chapter would presumably mean that, in addition to repeating the names of the bones, Alan would also repeat or rehearse the additional information provided by the sentence mnemonic. The sentence mnemonic should be transferred to LTS relatively easily because the words of the sentence are already represented in LTS and the rules of grammar, also already represented in LTS, impose restrictions on the order of the words in the sentence. Therefore, to the extent that Alan is successful in transferring the sentence, as well as the names of the bones, to LTS, he will have available at the time of the test a wider range of information in LTS that can lead him to the specific information requested by the teacher. A request to "List the bones of the hand" would have the potential of accessing an organized region of LTS that includes the "pig sentence." The sentence, in turn, could prompt retrieval of the bone names in the appropriate order.

📝 *What functions was rehearsal assumed to have in the Atkinson and Shiffrin model, and what mechanisms does the Atkinson and Shiffrin model assume may contribute to forgetting from STS?*

The Long-Term Store

The Atkinson and Shiffrin model portrays the final component of the memory system as a relatively permanent memory store of unlimited capacity. In one of the earlier descriptions of the model, Atkinson and Shiffrin (1968) suggested that loss of information from LTS could occur as a result of decay or interference. However, in their later 1971 description of the model, Atkinson and Shiffrin suggested that the primary mechanism of long-term forgetting is retrieval failure, resulting from selection of an inadequate probe for the search of LTS. The probe may be inadequate because it is not included in or related to the to-be-remembered information or because it results in the accessing of too large a region of the LTS, such that even if the target information is included in the region being searched retrieval is likely to fail.

In opting for a retrieval failure explanation of forgetting from LTS, Atkinson and Shiffrin rejected the traditional interference explanations of long-term forgetting that are described in Chapter 9. That is, they formally rejected the notion that the long-term memory trace of a particular event may be eroded by other memory traces for events occurring either before or after the target event. In arguing for a retrieval failure explanation in preference to a traditional interference explanation, Atkinson and Shiffrin cited studies in which they manipulated list length in a free recall task.

Rather than asking subjects to recall the list studied most recently, Atkinson and Shiffrin asked subjects to recall the list before the last. They used lists of 5 and 20 words in one of four combinations: 5-5, 5-20, 20-5, and 20-20, with the first number representing the length of the list being recalled and the second number representing the length of the intervening list. They reported that words in the 5-word lists were better recalled than words in the 20-word lists but that the length of the intervening list had little effect on the recall of words from the lists of either length. If interference were responsible for forgetting in this situation, Atkinson and Shiffrin contended, recall should have been lower with an intervening list of 20 items than with an intervening list of 5 items.

The retrieval failure approach can explain the superior recall of 5-word lists in terms of the recall probe being able to restrict the search of LTS to a smaller region. The retrieval failure approach can also explain the lack of an effect of the length of the intervening list by arguing that even after an intervening list of 20 items, there are still sufficient cues available to enable the subjects to gain access with reasonable efficiency to the restricted region of LTS containing the preceding list.

 In what fundamental ways does LTS differ from STS in the Atkinson and Shiffrin model?

Evidence Consistent with the Model

In popularizing the Atkinson and Shiffrin model, researchers have interpreted many findings from the study of human memory as supporting the basic tenets of the model.

Capacity Differences

Demonstrations of the limitations of the immediate memory span have been explained in terms of the capacity limitations of STS. In a typical memory span task, the subject might hear a series of digit sequences, beginning with a short sequence of only one or two digits followed by sequences of gradually increasing length. Immediately after hearing each sequence, the subject attempts to recall the items from the sequence in the order in which they were presented. The subject's memory span is then defined as the longest sequence recalled correctly before the first error occurred.

In a series of studies in 1956, George Miller confirmed earlier reports suggesting that the ability of humans to hear and reproduce in order sequences of items is limited to seven, plus or minus two, items. However, Miller demonstrated that an "item" may contain a number of nominally separate components. For example, a subject might group or "chunk" the digit sequence 177614921945 into the three units, 1776—1492—1945, and thereby increase the total number of digits that can be successfully recalled in order. On the basis of these results, Miller proposed a description of short-term memory that argued for the existence of seven slots into which incoming information can be placed for temporary storage. The similarity of this description to the rehearsal buffer of the Atkinson and Shiffrin model is obvious.

On the other hand, in tasks designed to measure retention over longer periods, and thus, in terms of the Atkinson and Shiffrin model, involving LTS to a much greater extent than does a memory span test, researchers have found results that clearly suggest that long-term memory capacity is not strictly limited. For example, Bower and Clark (1969) asked one group of subjects in their study to combine the 10 words in each of 12 presented lists into a story. Then, unexpectedly, after each of the 12 lists had been studied and tested individually, subjects were asked to attempt to recall all 120 words studied. Bower and Clark found that the subjects in the story group recalled on average 93%, or 111.6, of the words. Clearly, in situations in which subjects are free to use organizational coding strategies, such as weaving words into a story, very large numbers of items can be effectively retained for relatively long periods of time.

How are results from studies of the memory span and from studies of long-term retention of large amounts of information consistent with Atkinson and Shiffrin's distinction between STS and LTS?

Coding Differences

In describing STS coding in their 1968 paper, Atkinson and Shiffrin cited the results of a study by Conrad (1964). In his study of the memory span using consonant sequences, Conrad found that, in making errors, subjects frequently reported a consonant that *sounded* like the correct consonant (e.g., reporting P for T or V for B) even though the consonants were presented visually. On the other hand, incorrectly reporting a consonant that *looked* like the correct consonant (e.g., reporting X for K or F for T), was much less frequent. Atkinson and Shiffrin interpreted these results as suggesting that linguistic information is initially represented in STS in an acoustic or articulatory code (i.e., in terms of the sound of the name of the item or in terms of the way in which it is pronounced) rather than in a visual code (i.e., in terms of a visual image of the item).

Other results pointing to the importance of acoustic coding in the short-term memory for information were provided by Baddeley (1966b). Subjects attempted to recall sequences of five words immediately after their presentation in the order in which the words were presented. The words in each sequence were either acoustically similar (*cap, cad, can,* etc.), acoustically dissimilar (*few, hot, pen,* etc.), semantically similar (*broad, large, wide,* etc.), or semantically dissimilar (*late, safe, hot,* etc.). The results showed a large difference in the recall of acoustically similar and dissimilar words, 9.6% correct recall versus 82.1%, but the effect of semantic similarity was much smaller, with 64.7% of the semantically similar words correctly recalled versus 71.0% of the semantically dissimilar words. These results suggest that acoustic characteristics are more important than semantic characteristics in retaining items in STS.

To rule out the possibility that the apparent acoustic similarity effect was due to the greater visual and formal similarity (in terms of letters in common) of the acoustically similar words, Baddeley conducted a followup experiment. He compared the immediate recall of the following three sets of words: acoustically similar words low in visual similarity (*bought, taut, caught,* etc.), acoustically dissimilar words high in visual similarity (*rough, cough, through,* etc.), and acoustically dissimilar words low in visual similarity (*plea, friend, sleigh,* etc.). He found very little difference in the recall of the two sets of acoustically dissimilar words, suggesting that visual similarity among items being held in STS does not importantly affect retention of the items. However, the set of acoustically similar words was significantly more poorly recalled than either of the sets of acoustically dissimilar words. Thus, in showing that it is difficult to retain sequences of items that sound alike over very short retention intervals, Baddeley provided strong evidence that acoustic coding is importantly involved in the representation of information in STS.

On the other hand, other research points to the greater importance of semantic coding in LTS. In a study in 1967, Sachs tested her subjects' recognition memory for sentences presented in stories that they heard. She varied the delay between the presentation of the target sentence and the recognition test by stopping the story after either 0, 80, or 160 succeeding syllables of the story had been presented. Four types of test sentence were used. For example, in the story about Galileo used in the study, one of the target sentences was "He sent a letter about it to Galileo, the great Italian scientist." The four test sentences were:

Identical: He sent a letter about it to Galileo, the great Italian scientist.

Semantic change: Galileo, the great Italian scientist, sent him a letter about it.

Syntactic change: A letter about it was sent to Galileo, the great Italian scientist.

Formal change: He sent Galileo, the great Italian scientist, a letter about it.

Subjects were asked to indicate whether the test sentence had been presented verbatim in the story they heard. With an immediate test, Sachs found that subjects were equally good at rejecting all three types of changed sentence, suggesting that, immediately after the presentation of the sentence, subjects had available in memory a verbatim representation of the presented sentence. However, with a delay of 160 syllables, subjects failed to detect that the syntactically changed and the formally changed test sentence were different from the target sentence actually presented in the story, but they did consistently detect that the semantically changed sentence was not a part of the story. Given that the syntactically changed and formally changed test sentences retained the meaning of the target sentence, whereas the semantically changed test sentences did not, these results suggest that information may be coded in LTS primarily in terms of its meaning or semantic characteristics.

In a study of long-term retention using the same four sets of words described above (acoustically similar, acoustically dissimilar, semantically similar, and semantically dissimilar), Baddeley (1966a) also reported results suggesting that semantic coding is important in long-term memory. On each of four trials, subjects received a sequence of 10 words from one of the four sets followed by a 20-second digit span task. Then subjects were asked to recall the words in the order in which they were presented. A delayed test on all four lists was given 20 minutes after the test on the fourth list, with subjects again asked to recall the words from each list in the order in which they were presented. The results showed that the semantically similar sequences were significantly more poorly recalled than the semantically dissimilar sequences, whereas there was no significant difference in the recall of the acoustically similar and dissimilar sequences. Thus, semantic coding would appear to be more important than acoustic coding in LTS, and collectively such results on coding differences in the short-term and long-term retention of information were widely interpreted as supporting the STS/LTS dichotomy.

◪ *How have STS and LTS been distinguished on the basis of the relative importance of acoustic coding and semantic coding?*

Forgetting Rates

The observation that information appears to be lost at different rates over short and long retention intervals has also been interpreted as supporting the STS/LTS dichotomy proposed by Atkinson and Shiffrin. For example, the findings of Brown (1958) and Peterson and Peterson (1959), discussed previously, showing the loss of subspan information within seconds when rehearsal of the to-be-remembered information is prevented, contrast with findings of much lower rates of forgetting in studies of long-term retention, such as those of one of the pioneers of experimental memory research, Hermann Ebbinghaus (1885/1964).

In his studies of the serial learning of nonsense syllables (consonant-vowel-consonant, CVC, trigrams), Ebbinghaus studied forgetting over retention intervals ranging from 19 minutes to 31 days and reported that the rate of forgetting was much more pronounced at the shorter retention intervals than at the longer retention intervals, as shown in Figure 6–7. The fact that the amount forgotten declined so little as the retention interval was increased from 6 days to 31 days led Ebbinghaus to conclude that forgetting ''in the latter intervals of time is evidently so slow that it is easy to predict that a complete vanishing of the effect of the first memorisation of these series would, if they had been left to themselves, have occurred only after an indefinitely long period of time'' (p. 76). Such observations are consistent with the assumption of the existence of two distinct memory stores in which the loss of information through retrieval failure, interference, and/or decay proceeds at very different rates.

How does the forgetting rate appear to differ in STS and LTS?

The Free Recall Serial Position Effect

One of the most reliable findings in free recall studies of memory, the **serial position effect,** has been interpreted by Atkinson and Shiffrin (1971) and innumerable subsequent writers as directly consistent with the distinction between STS and LTS. In the **free recall task,** subjects are free to recall items from a presented list in any order so as to maximize recall

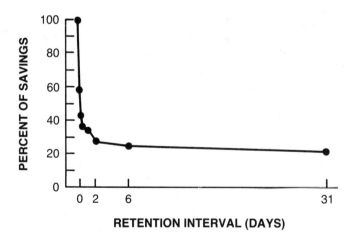

FIGURE 6–7 Forgetting as a function of retention interval, based on the research of Ebbinghaus (1885). Forgetting here is expressed as ''percent of savings,'' where:

$$\text{percent of savings} = 100 \times \frac{\text{trials to learn the list initially} - \text{trials to relearn the list}}{\text{trials to learn the list initially}}$$

Source: Hintzman, D. L. (1978). *The psychology of learning and memory.* San Francisco: W. H. Freeman and Company. Reprinted with permission.

of the list. Figure 6–8, from a study by Glanzer and Cunitz (1966), shows the typical serial position effect in which words at the beginning of the list and words at the end of the list are more likely to be recalled than are the words in the middle of the list, when recall is requested immediately after the presentation of the list. The superior recall of the beginning words is called the **primacy effect,** and the superior recall of the ending words is called the **recency effect.**

In their 1971 paper, Atkinson and Shiffrin summarized the results from a number of studies in which various manipulations were found to affect differentially the primacy and recency effects, suggesting that the recency effect reflects retrieval from STS, whereas the primacy effect reflects retrieval from LTS. For example, as shown in Figure 6–8, Glanzer and Cunitz (1966) found that following the list with a 30-second distractor task eliminated the recency effect while leaving the primacy effect unaffected. This result is consistent with the assumption that the distractor task eliminated the recency effect by causing the loss of the final list words from STS. The suggestion that the recency effect reflects recall from STS is supported, according to Atkinson and Shiffrin (1971), by the general finding that subjects tend to recall the last items from the list first when recall occurs without a delay following the presentation of the list.

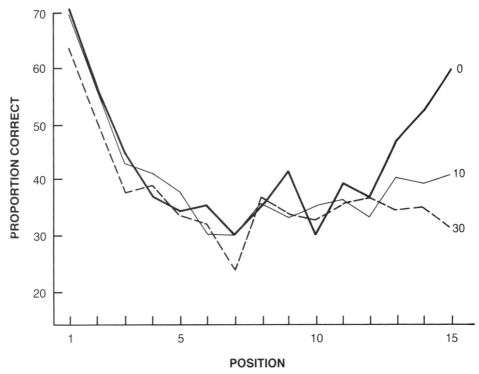

FIGURE 6–8   The free recall serial position effect. With a 0 delay between presentation of the list and recall, both the primacy effect and the recency effect are evident. Distractor-filled delays of 10 and 30 seconds eliminated the recency effect but left the primacy effect unaffected.

Source: Glanzer, M., & Cunitz, A. R. (1966). Two storage mechanisms in free recall. *Journal of Verbal Learning and Verbal Behavior, 5,* 358. Reprinted with permission.

On the other hand, Glanzer and Cunitz (1966) found that a change in presentation rate from three to six to nine seconds per word affected significantly the primacy portion and the middle portion of the free recall curve, while leaving the recency portion unaffected. As the rate of presentation was slowed, the probability of recall of items from the beginning and the middle of the list increased, consistent with the assumption that presentation rate affects the efficiency with which the items are transferred to, and thus retrieved from, LTS.

In addition, the Atkinson and Shiffrin model appears to provide a straightforward explanation of why the primacy effect occurs at all in the recall from LTS. According to the model, the first words in the list will remain in the rehearsal buffer longer than other words in the list because the buffer is empty as the learning trial begins. Only after the buffer is filled will newly arriving items begin to replace those already there. This means that the first items in the list will receive more rehearsals than later items and thus be more likely to be transferred effectively to LTS. This explanation received direct support from a study by Rundus and Atkinson (1970) in which subjects were asked to rehearse the list items aloud. Consistent with the model, the items early in the list received more rehearsals than items in the middle or at the end of the list. Thus, the model appears to provide a framework for explaining the serial position effect in terms of the effective transfer of early list items to LTS as a result of a large number of rehearsals (the primacy effect) and the immediate recall of the final list items from STS (the recency effect).

How can the Atkinson and Shiffrin model explain the free recall serial position effect?

THE LEVELS OF PROCESSING APPROACH

An Alternative Conceptualization of the Memory System

In 1972, Craik and Lockhart published a paper that directly challenged the usefulness of the multistore model of memory and proposed an alternative approach to studying memory processes. Based on their own review of the literature, Craik and Lockhart argued that support for the multistore model is far from consistent. In particular, they argued that evidence for separate short-term and long-term stores in terms of capacity differences is not convincing because of the widely different estimates of STS capacity, ranging from 2 to 20 items, that are produced when different types of to-be-remembered material are used. To take account of such differences, they suggested, necessitates an undesirably complicated revision of the original characterization of STS. To explain these differences in capacity estimates in terms of the process of chunking, one would have to admit that coding processes in STS can involve semantic analysis as well as phonemic analysis. In so doing, one admits that the distinction between short-term and long-term stores in terms of the different types of coding employed is not valid.

In addition, Craik and Lockhart charged that it is impossible to distinguish clearly between STS and LTS on the basis of how information is forgotten from the two stores. They claimed that estimates of how rapidly information is forgotten from STS have ranged from 1 to 25 seconds or more depending on the materials and procedures employed. They reasoned that only if short-term forgetting rates were invariant across different experimental paradigms would one be justified in trying to distinguish between STS and LTS on the basis of differences in forgetting rates in the two stores.

Then, having outlined these criticisms of the multistore approach, Craik and Lockhart proposed their alternative approach based on the notion that memory for information is a by-product of the perceptual analysis of the information. Craik and Lockhart argued that incoming information is subjected to a series of analyses that range from analysis of physical features of the information (e.g., lines, angles, brightness) to pattern recognition (i.e., matching the sensory information against information in memory) to the analysis of semantic features of the information (i.e., the meaning of the information). In describing this continuum of analysis, Craik and Lockhart introduced the concept of "levels," or **depth of processing,** and they defined depth in terms of the degree to which semantic processing occurs.

Furthermore, Craik and Lockhart argued that greater depth of processing is associated with better retention of the information. That is, they predicted that the greater the degree to which the semantic features of the to-be-remembered information are analyzed, the more durable the memory trace for the processed information will be. Although they admitted that it might be possible to describe these various stages of processing as constituting different memory stores, they rejected such an approach in favor of a more general approach intended to emphasize the flexibility of the encoding processes that can be performed on incoming information in response to different situational demands.

According to the levels of processing approach, what type of processing leads to good retention?

Distinction between Type I and Type II Processing

In their description of this levels of processing approach, Craik and Lockhart distinguished between what they termed Type I and Type II processing. They defined **Type I processing** as "recirculating information at one level of processing" (p. 676), and they proposed that such processing merely maintains information in consciousness without actually promoting the establishment of a permanent memory trace of the event. For this reason, Type I processing is often referred to as **maintenance rehearsal.** Alan's repeating the ingredients of the cake in order to be able to retrieve them from their respective locations in the kitchen, cited at the beginning of the chapter, is an example of Type I processing.

According to Craik and Lockhart, once attention is shifted from the information being subjected to Type I processing, the information will be lost from memory at a rate determined by the level of processing at which it was being maintained. In describing Type I processing, Craik and Lockhart did employ the concept of primary memory, as introduced by James. That is, they defined **primary memory** as the memory for information still in consciousness as a result of its being actively maintained at some given level of analysis, but they stressed that they were using the concept of primary memory in a much more restricted fashion than did other theorists such as Broadbent and Waugh and Norman.

On the other hand, Craik and Lockhart characterized **Type II processing** as processing that leads to deeper analysis, and thus improved long-term retention, of the information. Thus, Type II processing involves **elaborative rehearsal** that promotes analysis of the semantic features of the to-be-remembered information. Alan's attempt to memorize the bones of the hand for an anatomy test, also cited at the beginning of the chapter, is an example of Type II processing. The mnemonic sentence he employed was presumably analyzed at the semantic level, and the successful use of the mnemonic would necessitate a deep semantic understanding of how the sentence can be used to prompt recall of the bones.

▣ *How did Craik and Lockhart distinguish between Type I and Type II processing?*

Evidence Consistent with the Levels of Processing Approach

Although Craik and Lockhart reinterpreted a number of earlier findings in terms of their levels of processing framework, they did not present new empirical evidence in support of their alternative approach. However, in 1975, Craik and Tulving published a series of 10 experiments that were specifically designed to address various issues related to the levels of processing formulation. In a number of these experiments, they employed an **incidental learning task** in which subjects were not informed initially that their memory for the words being processed would be tested.

For example, in a typical experiment, subjects were shown a word in a tachistoscope for 200 milliseconds following a question about the word. The questions were designed to encourage processing at different levels of analysis. Some questions (the structural questions) were intended to promote a shallow level of analysis by focusing on the word's physical appearance (e.g., *Is the word in capital letters?*). Other questions (the phonemic questions) encouraged an intermediate level of processing at the phonemic level (e.g., *Does the word rhyme with CRANE?*). Two additional types of question (the category questions and the sentence questions) encouraged semantic analysis of the word (e.g., *Is the word in the category BIRD?* or *Would the word fit in the sentence: "He met a _____ in the street."?*).

Subjects were told that the experiment was designed to test perception and speed of reaction, and thus they were encouraged to respond to each presented word in the list as quickly as possible. After a series of responses to these question-word pairings, subjects were unexpectedly given a retention test on the words presented. Table 6–1 shows the results from one of the experiments in which subjects were given an unexpected recognition test on the words. As the means demonstrate, recognition performance increased with increasing depth of processing. Performance was by far poorest for those words about which a structural decision, involving the most shallow level of processing, was made. Substantially higher performance was shown for words about which phonemic decisions, involving an

TABLE 6–1 Typical Questions and Mean Recognition Performance in One of the Craik and Tulving (1975) Experiments

Level of Processing	Questions	Yes Response	Mean Proportion Recognized
Structural	Is the word in capital letters?	TABLE	.18
Phonemic	Does the word rhyme with WEIGHT?	crate	.78
Category (Semantic)	Is the word a type of fish?	SHARK	.93
Sentence (Semantic)	Would the word fit the sentence: "He met a ____ in the street"?	friend	.96

intermediate level of processing, were made. The highest levels of performance were shown for words about which semantic decisions, involving the deepest level of processing, were made.

In their original paper, Craik and Lockhart interpreted the intentional/incidental findings of researchers such as Hyde and Jenkins (1969) as being explicable in terms of the levels of processing framework. In their experiment, Hyde and Jenkins compared the free recall performance of a number of different groups of subjects. The conditions employed in their study are shown in Table 6–2. As you see, there was one group who received standard intentional free recall instructions (i.e., Study these words so as to be able to recall them later). Each of three other groups received incidental instructions that oriented the subjects to make certain judgments about each of the words presented, but at the time the words were presented the subjects did not know that their memory for the words would be tested later. The final three groups in the study received both the intentional free recall instructions and one of the three sets of incidental processing instructions.

The results of the study are also shown in Table 6–2. Clearly, the intentional learning instructions did not increase the level of performance above that shown in the incidental processing condition that required a semantic judgment about the words. These results were interpreted by Craik and Lockhart as demonstrating that the intention to learn facilitates memory performance by encouraging subjects to process the material deeply. Also, performance in an incidental learning situation that involves deep semantic analysis of the material will lead to performance that equals or exceeds that found with intentional learning instructions.

☑ *What sorts of judgments about words produced the best memory retention in the studies by Craik and Tulving and by Hyde and Jenkins?*

Elaboration of Processing—The Depth of Processing Framework Is Revised

Craik and Tulving further examined the issue of intentional versus incidental processing task in some of their experiments. In one experiment, prior to answering either a structural, phonemic, or semantic question about each word presented, subjects received intentional learning instructions. However, a levels of processing effect was still found. That is,

TABLE 6–2 Mean Number of Words Recalled in the Intentional Learning Conditions and the Incidental Learning Conditions of the Hyde and Jenkins (1969) Study

Conditions	Mean Words Recalled
Intentional Instructions	16.1
Incidental Instructions	
Pleasantness rating	16.3
E checking	9.4
Number of letters	9.9
Incidental and Recall Instructions	
Pleasantness rating	16.6
E checking	10.4
Number of letters	12.4

subjects' recall of words about which they had made semantic judgments was significantly greater than their recall of words about which they had made either phonemic or structural judgments.

Craik and Tulving interpreted this finding as being inconsistent with the original levels of processing framework. They argued that the original levels of processing approach would predict that, with intentional learning instructions, subjects would deeply analyze the words regardless of the type of processing question presented. Thus Craik and Tulving reasoned that the levels of processing approach would predict equal levels of retention across the various processing conditions in the intentional learning situation. The unanticipated finding of a levels effect under intentional learning instructions led Craik and Tulving to consider the possibility that deep semantic processing can vary in degree. In order to emphasize the proposal that processing at any given level of analysis, be it physical, phonemic, or semantic, can vary in extent or degree, Craik and Tulving suggested that the notion of depth of processing be replaced with the notion of **elaboration of processing.**

If a to-be-remembered item is thought of as a collection of physical, phonemic, and semantic features or attributes, then elaboration refers to the number of these features that are activated at the time of encoding. In Craik and Tulving's view, elaboration at either the physical, the phonemic, or the semantic level involves a **spread of encoding** to include more of the possible features than can be used to describe the to-be-remembered item. This concept of elaboration of processing, they suggested, would permit the assumption that although the intentional learning instructions encouraged the subjects to process all words at the semantic level, the semantic questions were more likely than the other types of questions to encourage elaborate semantic processing and thus improved retention of the words.

In one experiment in which subjects judged whether the presented word would fit in a sentence frame, Craik and Tulving manipulated the complexity of the sentence frame from very simple (e.g., *He dropped the _____.*) to complex (e.g., *The old man hobbled across the room and picked up the valuable _____ from the mahogany table.*) to test the effect of elaboration of encoding. For both sentence frames, the presented word was *watch*. As the examples suggest, all questions required semantic analysis of the word, but Craik and Tulving argued that the more complex questions would produce more elaborate encoding and thus better retention of the words. The results were consistent with their predictions. For both free recall and cued recall (in which the sentence frames were presented as recall cues), words about which a positive judgment was made in the context of a complex sentence frame were better recalled than words about which a positive judgment was made in the context of a simple sentence frame. However, Craik and Tulving found that complex sentence frames did not lead to higher recall for words about which a negative judgment was made.

This finding of better retention for words about which positive responses were made in the incidental semantic processing task was also reported by Craik and Tulving in a number of the other studies described in their paper. The researchers suggested that this finding is more easily explained in terms of an elaboration of encoding framework than it is in terms of a depth of processing framework. They argued that it is not "intuitively reasonable" (p. 281) to assume that positive responses lead to deeper processing, but that it is reasonable to assume that positive responses promote the integrating of the encoding question and the target word into a more richly elaborated representation of the information that will promote retention of the target word. Thus, in their treatment of elaboration, Craik and Tulving also introduced the concept of **congruity,** or **compatibility, of encoding** to argue that the more congruous the encoding question or context is with the target information, the more integrated, elaborated, and retrievable the information will be.

In their reformulation of the levels of processing approach, Craik and Tulving also explicitly rejected the notion that processing takes place in a fixed hierarchical sequence of stages, ranging from physical to semantic analysis. They noted that expectations based on the semantic analysis of earlier information may lead to a superficial structural analysis of the expected stimulus. For example, an individual who has read "The enthusiastic student eagerly raised her" may give the expected word *hand* only a very cursory structural analysis in order to confirm the expectation.

📝 *How do the concepts of elaboration of processing, spread of encoding, and congruity represent a fundamental modification of the levels of processing approach?*

PROBLEMS WITH THE LEVELS OF PROCESSING APPROACH—THE MULTISTORE MODEL REVISITED

Criticisms of the Levels of Processing Approach

Without a doubt, the levels of processing approach has had a dramatic impact on the study of memory in the past 5 years. Craik and Lockhart's (1972) and Craik and Tulving's (1975) suggestion that researchers turn their attention to the internal strategies that determine long-term memory retention struck a responsive chord in a large number of investigators, and the levels of processing approach became the dominant influence in the study of long-term retention. However, the approach has not been without its critics. In two major reviews of the approach, two prominent British researchers, Alan Baddeley (1978) and Michael Eysenck (1978), challenged many of the assumptions of the approach.

The Problem of Defining Depth

One problem with the levels of processing framework raised by both Baddeley and Eysenck is finding a way of determining depth that is independent of the subjects' level of performance and is not based simply on the investigator's intuitive judgment. Both theorists point out that there is a tendency toward circularity of explanation in the approach. This circularity results when an investigator suggests that the better memory performance resulting from the use of processing strategy *A* supports the suggestion that processing strategy *A* results in deeper processing than does processing strategy *B;* however, as Baddeley and Eysenck note, the investigator cannot then also attempt to explain the better performance using processing strategy *A* in terms of greater depth of processing. That is, the depth of processing concept becomes circular if one attempts to explain better performance in one condition in terms of greater depth of processing, and then attempts to argue for greater depth of processing in that condition based on the greater level of memory retention.

The difficulty in relying on researchers' intuitive judgments in the definition of depth, Eysenck points out, is that different researchers reach different decisions about the depth of the same type of processing. For example, some researchers have defined judging whether a word is a noun or a verb as a semantic task (Mandler & Worden, 1973), whereas others have specified it to be a nonsemantic task (Hyde & Jenkins, 1973).

Baddeley and Eysenck argue that attempts to arrive at measures of depth that are independent of memory performance have been unsuccessful. Craik and Lockhart (1972), in their original formulation of the approach, suggested that time taken to process might be used as a measure of depth, with deeper processing associated with longer processing times and better retention. However, Craik and Tulving (1975) found evidence inconsistent with this suggestion. In one of their studies summarized earlier, they found that the non-semantic task of deciding whether a word, such as *hornet* fits the pattern CVCCVC (where *C* stands for consonant and *V* stands for vowel) takes more time than the semantic task of deciding whether a hornet is an animal, but produces poorer retention of the processed word.

Furthermore, Gardiner (1974) found that the nonsemantic task of deciding whether a word contains a particular phoneme takes longer than the semantic task of deciding whether a word belongs to a particular category, but produces poorer retention of the word. Clearly, processing time is not an adequate independent measure of depth of processing, and it is far from certain that such an independent measure will be found. Wessells (1982) notes that attempts to measure depth in terms of processing resources required and subjects' subjective ratings of depth have not proven successful.

Eysenck argues that Craik and Tulving's alternative concepts of elaboration, spread of encoding, and congruity of encoding are similarly vague. For example, in describing elaboration and spread of encoding, Craik and Tulving suggest that a complex sentence frame, such as that used in one of their experiments described earlier (e.g., *The old man hobbled across the room and picked up the valuable —— from the mahogany table.*), involves the activation of more of the features of the word whose appropriateness in that particular frame is being judged than does a simple sentence frame (e.g., *He dropped the ——.*). However, Eysenck points out that the complex and simple sentence frames may also differ on a number of other dimensions, such as imagery and relevance to the presented word. Thus, at the very least, a more precise and detailed determination of what elaboration involves is needed, but, just as in the case of depth, it is far from obvious that a measure of elaboration independent of level of retention will be found.

How have investigators attempted to define depth of processing, and why, according to Baddeley and Eysenck, have these attempts been unsuccessful?

Evidence that Deep Processing Is Not Always Necessary for Successful Long-Term Retention

One of the most basic assumptions of the levels of processing approach, as was described earlier, is that deep semantic processing (Type II processing) is necessary for successful long-term retention of information. However, Baddeley cited experimental evidence that directly challenges this assumption. Kolers (1976) had subjects practice reading text that was inverted (i.e., upside down) and then retested their ability to read such text 13 to 15 months later. He found that the subjects retained much of their ability to read such text even after the year's retention interval, and that they were better at reading pages of inverted text they had read during training than they were at reading new pages of such text. These results imply that the processing of typographical information, a presumably shallow level of processing on the Craik and Lockhart continuum, promoted effective long-term retention of superficial typographical information.

In 1977, Morris, Bransford, and Franks compared the effects of a phonemic processing task and a semantic processing task on two types of recognition memory in an incidental learning situation. The phonemic processing task involved rhyme questions (e.g., —————— *rhymes with legal?*), followed by the target word, whereas the semantic processing task involved deciding whether the target word would fit in a sentence (e.g., *The —————— had a silver engine.*). One of the recognition tests required the subjects to select words on the test list that were semantically equivalent to the target words, and the other recognition test required the subjects to select words on the test list that rhymed with the target words. On the semantic recognition test, the semantic processing task led to better performance, but on the rhyming recognition test, the phonemic processing task resulted in superior performance.

Apparently deep semantic processing of information only facilitates long-term retention of semantic features of the processed information. The results of both of these experiments suggest that the effects of different levels of processing on long-term retention are dependent on the type of retention test employed. Contrary to Craik and Lockhart's original formulation, deep semantic analysis does not inevitably produce better retention than more shallow levels of analysis. Even in his own research, Craik has produced similar results that challenge this basic assumption of the levels of processing approach (see Fisher & Craik, 1977).

In addition, Eysenck suggests that there is evidence inconsistent with Craik and Tulving's alternative hypothesis that it is elaboration of encoding that promotes long-term retention. Under certain circumstances, semantic elaboration may actually hinder the retention of information. Bransford, Barclay, and Franks (1972) exposed their subjects to sentences (e.g., *Three turtles rested on a floating log, and a fish swam beneath them.*), and they found on a subsequent retention test that subjects were very likely to recognize falsely a similarly worded inference (e.g., *Three turtles rested on a floating log, and a fish swam beneath it.*). These results suggest that elaborative processing may involve processing information not actually presented and may, as a result, lower retention of the information as presented.

Further evidence that elaborative processing of material does not necessarily promote accurate retention comes from Bartlett (1932). Bartlett found that in recalling materials such as American Indian folktales, his British subjects considerably distorted the original story by, among other things, incorporating into their recalls information not contained in the original story. Bartlett's research is described in more detail in Chapter 9.

✍ *Under what conditions may phonemic processing lead to better retention than semantic processing, and why does elaborative processing sometimes not promote good verbatim retention of information?*

Maintenance Rehearsal May Promote Long-Term Retention

As described previously, Craik and Lockhart's formulation of the levels of processing framework contends that maintenance rehearsal does not facilitate the long-term retention of information. Evidence in support of this position has come from experiments such as that by Craik and Watkins (1973). In their experiment, subjects performed in an incidental learning situation in which they heard sequences of words of unknown length. They were told that their task was to listen for words beginning with a certain letter and that they would, at the end of the list, be asked to report the last word in the sequence beginning with that letter. The experimenters manipulated how far from the end of the list the last word beginning with the target letter occurred and thus manipulated the amount of time the subjects presumably had to maintain the item in primary memory (or STS) through maintenance rehearsal. They found that words that were maintained for longer intervals were not subsequently better recalled on an unexpected free recall test of all of the words presented.

However, Baddeley contends that there is also considerable evidence to challenge the assumption that maintenance rehearsal is never effective in promoting long-term retention. For example, Darley and Glass (1975) conducted an incidental learning study in which subjects were told that their primary task was to search for a particular word in each list presented. Thus subjects had to maintain the target word in STS until it was found in the list and a response was made. The researchers found that when target words occurred late in the list, and had therefore received more maintenance rehearsal, they were better recalled on a final unexpected free recall test than when they occurred early in the list.

In addition, Rundus (1980) found that when words were rehearsed as part of a distractor task for 60 seconds, their recall was improved relative to that of words rehearsed for lesser periods of time. In a similar study, Glenberg and Adams (1978) found that maintenance rehearsal of distractor words for intervals less than 60 seconds did not facilitate unexpected recall of the words but did facilitate performance on an unexpected recognition test of the words.

An obvious rejoinder that adherents to the levels of processing approach might make is that in these situations, subjects were using elaborative rehearsal (Type II processing) rather than maintenance rehearsal. However, the demands of the tasks in these studies do not appear conducive at all to elaborative rehearsal. If such a counterargument is accepted, it then becomes very difficult to predict when each type of rehearsal will be employed by subjects.

☑ *Under what conditions has maintenance rehearsal been found to promote long-term retention?*

Evidence that Processing Is Not Hierarchical

The original levels of processing formulation described the processing of information as hierarchical in nature, with physical analysis followed by phonemic analysis followed by semantic analysis. Baddeley argues strongly that such a strict hierarchy of processing stages is clearly wrong. He cites, for example, studies by Kleiman (1975) of the effects of articulatory suppression on reading as demonstrating that phonemic processing is not a preliminary shallow stage of reading that precedes deep semantic analysis. The articulatory suppression technique used involved asking subjects to repeat a sequence of random digits as they simultaneously read various materials. The procedure of repeating the digits is designed to prevent silent covert vocalization (i.e., articulation), and thus phonemic processing, of the material being read.

If phonemic processing is a necessary preliminary step in reading, then the articulatory suppression should have disrupted the subjects' ability to read. However, Kleiman found that no such disruption in terms of subjects' ability to make judgments about the meaning of words being read. He concluded that phonemic processing during reading may be a relatively late process that occurs after semantic analysis and that helps in the temporary storage of information of particular relevance to the text being read. The evidence that processing does not always proceed in the specific sequence proposed by Craik and Lockhart was so overwhelming that, in their modification of the approach, Craik and Tulving specifically rejected the original description of a fixed sequence of processing stages, as was noted earlier in the description of the elaboration of processing approach.

☑ *How do results of Kleiman's articulatory suppression study demonstrate that processing of information does not necessarily occur in the sequence of stages suggested in the original levels of processing framework?*

Baddeley's Revision of the Multistore Model: Working Memory

In criticizing the levels of processing approach, Baddeley objected to its emphasis on trying to identify general overall principles of memory. He made a strong argument in favor of a return to the examination of "specific subcomponents of human memory" (p. 148). That is, Baddeley argued for continued research within the tradition of the multistore models of memory, although at the same time he emphasized major revisions that he and his coworkers have made to the original Atkinson and Shiffrin model.

The major revision in the model suggested by Baddeley focuses on STS. Baddeley and colleagues (Baddeley, 1976, 1978, 1981, 1983, 1988; Baddeley & Hitch, 1974, 1977) have proposed that STS consists of several separate components: a central executive and at least two interrelated subsidiary systems, the articulatory rehearsal loop, and the visuo-spatial scratch-pad. The proposed system is represented in Figure 6–9. To distinguish their treatment of STS from the Atkinson and Shiffrin model and to emphasize the role that STS plays in cognitive tasks such as reading and thinking, Baddeley and colleagues have used the term **working memory** to refer to this part of the system. Baddeley argues that this multicomponent description of STS is necessitated by his findings from studies employing a **simultaneous task procedure.**

> *In what fundamental ways does Baddeley's description of working memory differ from Atkinson and Shiffrin's description of STS?*

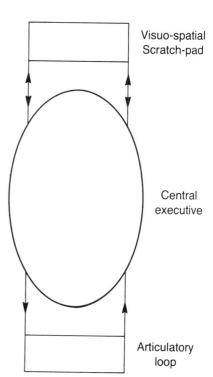

FIGURE 6–9 A simplified representation of Baddeley's (1983) working memory model.

Source: Baddeley, A. D. (1983). Working memory. *Philosophical Transactions of the Royal Society of London, B302,* 315. Reprinted with permission.

Evidence for the Articulatory Rehearsal Loop

In the original set of studies (Baddeley & Hitch, 1974), subjects were required to remember sequences of up to six digits while performing simultaneously tasks such as verbal reasoning, comprehension, and learning of verbal materials. The results showed that performance on the various tasks was not affected by a concurrent digit load of up to three. However, with sequences of six digits, performance on the all of the tasks declined significantly. This pattern can be explained, Baddeley argues, if one assumes that the short-term memory system consists in part of a **central executive** that is responsible for attending to and coordinating the processing of all incoming information, and a secondary **articulatory rehearsal loop** that functions as an auxiliary "slave" system to the central executive by storing in speech-like form material that can be recirculated without making major demands on the central executive.

Baddeley estimates that the articulatory loop can hold up to two seconds of spoken material. In the experiments just described, Baddeley suggests that the rehearsal loop was able to maintain up to three digits, leaving the central processor free for the simultaneous reasoning, comprehension, or verbal learning task. However, a digit load of greater than three exceeded the capacity of the rehearsal loop and placed additional demands on the central processor. As part of the central processor capacity was allocated to maintaining the longer digit sequences, performance on the other tasks declined.

The fact that the loop is time-based (i.e., can only handle verbalizations that can be made within a limited amount of time) is supported by findings of a word length effect in measurements of the memory span. In a typical memory span test, Baddeley argues that both the central executive and the articulatory loop of short-term memory are employed, with the loop holding a limited number of the to-be-remembered items in the appropriate order in speech-like form. If the loop is time-based, then the longer items take to be verbalized, the fewer the loop will be able to hold. Thus fewer multiple-syllable words than single-syllable words could be held in the loop, and the memory span for multiple-syllable words should be less than that for single-syllable words. This was the result reported by Baddeley, Thomson, and Buchanan (1975). However, when they prevented the use of the articulatory loop during the memory span task with the articulatory suppression procedure of requiring the subjects to count to six repeatedly, they found that the memory span was not affected by the number of syllables in the words in the list.

The time-based properties of the articulatory rehearsal loop are also supported by a study by Lorsbach and Gray (1986). They found that the memory span in a group of learning-disabled children was strongly positively correlated with the speed with which the children could name words. Similarly, in a study of serial recall in children ranging in age from 4 to 10 years, Hulme and Tordoff (1989) found that increases in recall with age were a function of increases in speech rate. The results of these studies are consistent with the assumption that increases in naming speed and speech rate result in the articulatory rehearsal loop's being able to accommodate more information.

Baddeley also argues that phonemic coding in short-term memory reflects primarily the operation of the rehearsal loop. This is demonstrated in his earlier findings (Baddeley, 1966b) that the short-term retention of phonemically similar sequences of words is poorer than the short-term retention of phonemically dissimilar sequences of words. Baddeley bases this argument in part on findings that this phonemic similarity effect in short-term memory is eliminated when the loop's contribution to short-term memory is eliminated through the use of articulatory suppression.

In the study mentioned above, Hulme and Tordoff (1989) found that the phonemic similarity effect increased with the age of the children and was related to the children's speech rate. That is, as the children's speech rate increased with age, the size of the phonemic similarity effect increased. This finding suggests that the phonemic similarity effect is due to the smaller number of phonemically similar items that can be accommodated in the rehearsal loop because of the greater amount of time required to articulate a phonemically similar sequence.

Gathercole and Baddeley (1989) have recently provided evidence in support of the view that the articulatory rehearsal loop, as a short-term phonological storage component of working memory, plays an important role in vocabulary acquisition by young children. They demonstrated that a measure of phonological memory at age 4 was a better predictor of vocabulary knowledge at age 5 than was vocabulary score at age 4.

Vallar and Baddeley (1987) investigated the comprehension difficulties of a brain-damaged woman whose reduced auditory memory span was shown to be the product of a defect of the articulatory rehearsal loop. The subject's comprehension of short sentences was intact, but her detection of anomalies in complex sentences was seriously impaired. Vallar and Baddeley therefore suggest that the articulatory rehearsal loop functions importantly in the storage of incoming strings of words when the material is so complex as to tax the immediately available resources of the central processor. Baddeley and Wilson (1988) have applied a similar interpretation to their study of a brain-damaged man with a seriously impaired memory span. They found that the man's comprehension of individual words and short sentences was intact, but his comprehension of sentences declined markedly with increases in sentence length.

The distinction between an articulatory rehearsal loop and a central executive as components of short-term or working memory has also been used by researchers in investigating the relationship between aging and memory. For example, a number of researchers (e.g., Baddeley, Logie, Bressi, Della Sala, & Spinnler, 1986; Morris & Baddeley, 1988; Morris, Gick, & Craik, 1988; and Spinnler, Della Sala, Bandera, & Baddeley, 1988) have presented evidence that they interpret as demonstrating that short-term memory deterioration in the elderly reflects impairment of central executive functioning rather than impairment of functioning of the articulatory rehearsal loop.

Other phenomena that have been interpreted in terms of the distinction between a central executive and the articulatory loop include the finding that unattended speech adversely affects immediate memory, whereas noise does not. Salame and Baddeley (1987) concluded that this finding is consistent with the claim that unattended speech, because it is phonemic in nature, disrupts the articulatory loop, whereas noise, because it is not phonemic in nature, does not. This interpretation, in turn, is consistent with Vallar and Baddeley's (1984) suggestion that auditory spoken material automatically engages the articulatory loop, whereas visually presented material engages the articulatory loop only if the central executive elects to use the control process of rehearsal to maintain the visually presented items.

Although the articulatory rehearsal loop is similar to the rehearsal buffer described by Atkinson and Shiffrin in their model, Baddeley argues that the working memory proposal clearly differs from the Atkinson and Shiffrin model. The working memory model specifies that the rehearsal loop is only a useful adjunct to the central processor and can be preempted, through articulatory suppression, for example, without severely disrupting the operation of the remainder of the short-term system. On the other hand, the Atkinson and Shiffrin model, as described earlier, treated the rehearsal loop as the central component of STS.

How does Baddeley use the concept of an articulatory rehearsal loop to explain the effects of digit load on the simultaneous performance of reasoning, comprehension, and memory tasks?

Evidence for the Visuo-Spatial Scratch-Pad

More recently, Baddeley and colleagues (Baddeley, 1981, 1983; Baddeley & Lewis, 1981; Baddeley & Lieberman, 1980) have focused on the second proposed subsidiary slave system: the visuo-spatial scratch-pad (VSSP). The argument for this second interrelated subsystem is based on results from experiments in which the simultaneous task procedure has involved a visual imagery memory task and the concurrent performance of some visuo-spatial task. Baddeley (1983) reports that the impetus for this research came from his observation, as an Englishman visiting America, that listening to a radio broadcast of a football game seemed to interfere with his ability to drive safely on an American freeway.

In creating a laboratory approximation of this real-world interference situation, the Baddeley group employed in many of its studies a visual imagery memory task first devised by Brooks (1967). This task is illustrated in Figure 6–10. In the procedure, one of the squares in the matrix is designated as the starting square, and the subject's task is to remember and repeat back a series of statements. When the statements consist of spatial material describing spatial relationships between numbers, as shown in Figure 6–10, subjects can recode the statements into a particular pathway through the matrix. However, when the statements are nonsensical, again as shown in Figure 6–10, spatial recoding is not possible. Brooks has shown that subjects can recall the statements describing spatial relationships much more easily than they can recall the nonsense statements, suggesting the spatial statements are being recoded into a spatial pattern that is then converted back into the original statements at the time of recall.

In one of their simultaneous task procedures, Baddeley and colleagues (Baddeley, Grant, Wight, & Thomson, 1975) required subjects to learn either the spatial statements or the nonsense statements at the same time that they performed (as their primary task) a tracking procedure in which they were required to try to keep a stylus in contact with a spot presented on a revolving disk. They found that the tracking task interfered with memory for the spatial statements but not for the nonsense statements. In another experiment in the same sequence, Baddeley and colleagues presented the memory test as the primary task and found that memorizing the spatial statements interfered more with the tracking task than did memorizing the nonsense statements.

These results, Baddeley argues, are consistent with the assumption that working memory contains a subsystem specialized for recirculating and maintaining visuo-spatial images. It is this subsystem that subjects employ in remembering the spatial statements in the Brooks' task, whereas some other component of working memory, probably the articulatory loop, is used in remembering the nonsense statements.

Support for the distinction between the VSSP and the articulatory rehearsal loop comes from a study by Farmer, Berman, and Fletcher (1986) in which they employed an articula-

		3	**4**
	1	**2**	**5**
		7	**6**
		8	

SPATIAL MATERIAL

In the starting square put a 1.
In the next square to the *right* put a 2.
In the next square *up* put a 3.
In the next square to the *right* put a 4.
In the next square *down* put a 5.
In the next square *down* put a 6.
In the next square to the *left* put a 7.
In the next square *down* put an 8.

NONSENSE MATERIAL

In the starting square put a 1.
In the next square to the *quick* put a 2.
In the next square to the *good* put a 3.
In the next square to the *quick* put a 4.
In the next square to the *bad* put a 5.
In the next square to the *bad* put a 6.
In the next square to the *slow* put a 7.
In the next square to the *bad* put an 8.

FIGURE 6–10   The Brooks' (1967) visual imagery memory task.

Source: Baddeley, A. D. (1983). Working memory. *Philosophical Transactions of the Royal Society of London, B302,* 319. Reprinted with permission.

tory suppression task and what they called a *spatial suppression task*. The spatial suppression task involved continuous sequential tapping of four metal plates, arranged in a square, using a metal-tipped stylus. Concurrent with the performance of one of these suppression tasks, subjects performed either a spatial reasoning task or a verbal reasoning task. The spatial reasoning task involved the visual presentation of a manikin figure, either upright or upside down, with a circle in one hand and a square in the other, and with one of the shapes appearing below the figure. The task was to indicate by pressing a response key as quickly as possible which of the manikin's hands contained the shape shown below the figure. The verbal reasoning task involved deciding as quickly as possible whether a statement correctly or incorrectly described the order of a pair of letters shown. The researchers found that the spatial suppression task disrupted concurrent performance of the spatial reasoning task but had no effect on performance of the verbal reasoning task, whereas the articulatory suppression task only interfered with the verbal reasoning task.

The usefulness of such a component of working memory can be illustrated using again the example of Alan presented at the beginning of the chapter. The VSSP could help Alan as he sets about baking the cake by enabling him to maintain a visual record of the location of various ingredients in the refrigerator and in the cupboard, while other components of working memory are involved in repeating the list of ingredients and in executing the actions necessary to retrieve the ingredients from their storage locations and to combine them in the appropriate order. The VSSP might also be involved in Alan's learning of the bones of the hand if he uses visualization of the arrangement of the bones in conjunction with the sentence mnemonic for remembering their names.

In subsequent studies, Baddeley and Lieberman (1980) produced results they interpret as showing that the system relies more on spatial coding than on purely visual representation. They found that the visual, nonspatial task of judging the brightness of a patch of light interfered less with memorizing the spatial statements in the Brooks' task than did the nonvisual, spatial task of tracking the location of a sound source while blindfolded and using a flashlight. (Feedback in the form of a change in the sound was provided whenever the flashlight was on target.) On the other hand, the nonvisual, spatial task interfered less than the visual, nonspatial task with memorizing the nonsense statements.

Additional evidence in support of the distinction between the VSSP and the central executive comes from a study by Logie, Baddeley, Mané, Donchin, and Sheptak (1989) in which they examined the effect of a number of different secondary tasks on a complex computer game, "Space Fortress." They found that different aspects of game performance were negatively affected by different secondary tasks. For example, aspects of game performance based on tracking and aiming, and thus involving visuo-spatial processing and presumably the VSSP, were affected by secondary tasks involving visuo-spatial processing and the VSSP, such as the Brooks spatial task described above. On the other hand, aspects of game performance based on the time taken to change the weapon system, and thus involving more general processing of the type assumed to be handled by the central executive, were affected by a number of secondary tasks, not just those involving visuo-spatial processing.

In an attempt to test the suggestion that the VSSP is, like the articulatory loop, an active subsystem that maintains information through recirculation or a rehearsal process, Baddeley and coworkers (Baddeley, 1983) attempted to devise a visual analog of the articulatory suppression procedure. The researchers reasoned that the maintenance of information in the VSSP may involve that part of the system that controls voluntary movement of the eyes. Therefore, a simultaneous task requiring movement of the eyes should interfere more with another task involving use of the VSSP than should a simultaneous task not requiring movement of the eyes.

This prediction was confirmed when the researchers found that the simultaneous task of tracking with the eyes a target on a computer display screen interfered with memorizing the spatial statements from the Brooks' task, whereas the simultaneous task of continuing to fixate a stationary target on the computer screen as the background moved did not interfere with memorizing the spatial statements. The tracking task involving eye movements did not interfere with memorizing the nonsense statements, which, as was noted above, presumably involves some component of working memory other than the VSSP. Thus, Baddeley (1983) concludes, the VSSP involves an active rehearsal process that is associated with the system controlling voluntary movements of the eyes.

⊿ *What types of simultaneous task were found by Baddeley and colleagues to interfere most with memory for the spatial statements in the Brooks' imagery task, and how are these results consistent with Baddeley's assumption that working memory contains a visuo-spatial scratch-pad?*

An Alternative Explanation of the Recency Effect

Another way in which the working memory model differs from the Atkinson and Shiffrin model is in its explanation of the recency effect. The working memory model rejects the Atkinson and Shiffrin model's explanation of the recency effect in terms of retrieval from the short-term store. One of the primary reasons the working memory model rejects this explanation is because of findings of long-term recency. That is, researchers such as Baddeley and Hitch (1977) have reported superior memory for the last items in a series even after delays sufficiently long to ensure that the effect could not be the result of recall from STS. In their study, Baddeley and Hitch (1977) tested the ability of rugby players to recall the teams that they had played against during the season and found that the opponent teams best recalled were, in general, those that were played most recently.

Baddeley and Hitch (1977) also demonstrated a similar long-term recency effect in a more traditional laboratory test of memory, as have other researchers (e.g., Bjork & Whitten, 1974; Dalezman, 1974; Glenberg, Bradley, Stevenson, Kraus, Tkachuk, Gretz, Fish, & Turpin, 1980; Tzeng, 1973). The working memory model also rejects an explanation of short-term recency in terms of retrieval from STS because of findings by Baddeley and Hitch (1974) that a concurrent digit span task did not disrupt the recency effect. Thus the working memory model argues that it is more parsimonious to explain both short-term and long-term recency in terms of a retrieval strategy whereby an individual uses recency cues (such as "items that occurred near the end") to prompt retrieval of information. The model explains the elimination of the recency effect in situations such as those reported by Glanzer and Cunitz (1966) by arguing that, in such situations, the distractor task is treated by the subjects as part of the to-be-learned information and thus the recency cues become associated with the distractor task rather than with the last to-be-recalled items.

▣ *How does the working memory model attempt to explain both short-term and long-term recency effects?*

Possible Future Development of the Model

Finally, it should be noted that in his more recent descriptions of the working memory system, Baddeley (1981, 1983) points out that other subsidiary slave systems, in addition to the articulatory loop and the VSSP, are likely to be identified as research by his group continues. At present, Baddeley admits that the functioning of the central executive in the working memory model is only vaguely specified. However, he argues that as more of the peripheral slave systems are identified, the number of functions assigned to the central executive will be reduced. Thus the task of describing more precisely the role of the central executive will be made easier. The working memory model will require continuing revision as more is learned about additional component systems that contribute to short-term memory.

It should be noted, however, that some researchers (e.g., Reisberg, Rappaport, & O'Shaugnessy, 1984) have suggested that the slave systems that contribute to what is collectively called short-term or working memory store are more accurately described as temporarily employed strategies than as permanently available storage components. For example, Reisberg and colleagues (1984) argue that the use of the articulatory rehearsal loop does not involve the use of a component of memory that is a permanent part of working memory. Rather, the articulatory loop is a temporary component that exists only as long as particular rehearsal strategies are being employed by the central executive. On this view, it is argued that there is no limit to the number of different slave system processes that can be employed by the central executive. There may, however, be limits to the number of these slave systems that can be used simultaneously by the central executive.

▣ *How is the working memory model's treatment of the central executive likely to change as the model is developed further?*

Broadbent's Revision of the Multistore Model: The Maltese Cross

An even more outspoken advocate of the view that a multistore model is essential to explain memory performance and to guide future research is the Englishman Donald Broadbent, whose pioneering work in the 1950s (as was described earlier in this chapter) contributed directly to the rise of the multistore approach. In 1984, Broadbent published a very important paper in which he outlined a new multistore model that differs in a number of respects from the Atkinson and Shiffrin modal model. The model, dubbed the **Maltese cross** because it represents the memory system as a cross-shaped structure with the arms of the cross pointing toward the center, is represented in Figure 6–11. The Maltese cross replaces the STS of the Atkinson and Shiffrin model with four separate components: the sensory store (not to be confused with the sensory registers of the Atkinson and Shiffrin model), the motor output store, the abstract working memory, and the processing system. Even the long-term store of the Maltese cross differs from its counterpart in the Atkinson and Shiffrin model.

How does the Maltese cross model's description of STS differ from that of the Atkinson-Shiffrin model?

The Long-Term Associative Store

The treatment of the long-term store in the Maltese cross model differs from that in the Atkinson and Shiffrin model in that Broadbent argues that much of the long-term retention of information takes place in the processing system rather than in the long-term store. Specifically, he suggests that much pattern recognition, such as being able to recognize that 2 and *two* are equivalent, is handled in the processing system (which will be discussed in detail later), whereas the Atkinson and Shiffrin model assigned pattern recognition to the long-term store. Broadbent contends that because the form of long-term storage is different in the processing system and in the long-term store, it is important to distinguish between

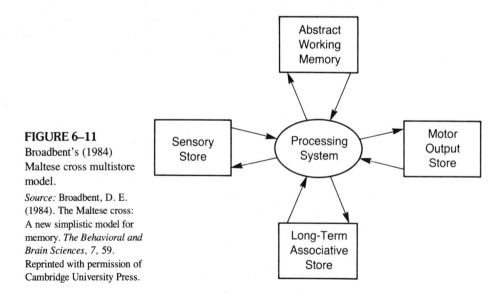

FIGURE 6–11
Broadbent's (1984) Maltese cross multistore model.

Source: Broadbent, D. E. (1984). The Maltese cross: A new simplistic model for memory. *The Behavioral and Brain Sciences, 7,* 59. Reprinted with permission of Cambridge University Press.

long-term storage in these two components of the system. For example, the processing system's long-term memory for operations such as converting the visual pattern *horse* into the sound of the name of the word is different, Broadbent suggests, from the long-term associative store's memory for the occurrence of the word *horse* in a list of to-be-remembered items.

In support of this distinction, Broadbent (1983) cites Warrington and Weiskrantz's (1974) study of amnesia. They found that certain amnesic patients, compared to normals, show grossly impaired memory for words when given a standard recall test, but that cuing recall with a fragment of the presented word results in equal performance by amnesics and normals. Broadbent interprets this evidence as supporting the distinction between long-term memory for events (represented in the long-term associative store) and long-term memory for processing operations (contained within the processing system). Broadbent argues that amnesics of the type studied by Warrington and Weiskrantz have sustained brain damage that disrupts the long-term associative store but not the processing system. A detailed description of the processing system will be presented later.

Like the Atkinson and Shiffrin model, the Maltese cross assumes that the long-term store is of relatively unlimited capacity and that, as a result, retrieval processes play a critical role in determining whether memory for events in the store will succeed. Effective retrieval cues, the model suggests, are events that are associated with the target item. Broadbent, Cooper, and Broadbent (1978) found that, under certain conditions, matrix organization and hierarchic organization are equally good in promoting long-term retrieval. Other researchers (e.g., Jones, 1976, 1978, 1979; Wilhite, 1981, 1982) reported that, in remembering an event containing elements *A* and *B,* recall of *A* given *B* is often equal to recall of *B* given *A.* Based on such findings, the Maltese cross model rejects the notion that each event or item is represented in long-term store by a single node (or memory location) that is connected by hierarchically arranged associative links to other nodes in the store.

Instead, based largely on the work of Gregory Jones (1976, 1978, 1979) and Stephen Wilhite (1981, 1982), the model suggests that the long-term store is composed of fragments, with each fragment consisting of an association between two or more items and with a given item possibly appearing in a number of different fragments. A cue thus accesses a fragment containing the cue and provides for retrieval of other associated items contained in the fragment, which in turn may be used to access other fragments.

In the case of Alan, described at the beginning of the chapter, the use of the strategy for remembering the bones of the hand would, according to the Maltese cross model, promote the formation of fragments in the long-term store that contained the mnemonic sentence and information about how it could be used in prompting recall of the bones. Then, at the time of recall, accessing these fragments should promote long-term memory performance by generating letter cues to help in accessing in order the memory fragments containing the actual names of the bones.

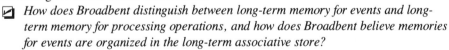 *How does Broadbent distinguish between long-term memory for events and long-term memory for processing operations, and how does Broadbent believe memories for events are organized in the long-term associative store?*

The Sensory Store

Despite the similarity in name, the sensory store of the Maltese cross is clearly different from the sensory registers of the Atkinson and Shiffrin model, and represents in Broadbent's

Maltese cross model a major component of short-term memory. Recall that Atkinson and Shiffrin based their characterization of the sensory registers in large part on Sperling's (1960) investigations of iconic memory (the sensory register for vision), and Broadbent certainly accepts the existence of such sensory registers, even though they are not explicitly represented in the Maltese cross diagram. However, he suggests that there exists a sensory store that is separate from the sensory registers (e.g., see Broadbent, Vines, & Broadbent, 1978) and that can retain "relatively raw input from the senses" (Broadbent, 1984, p. 59) for periods much longer than the few seconds or less assumed to characterize storage in the sensory registers.

Broadbent bases his argument for a longer-lived sensory store in part on findings that the recency effect (i.e., the better recall of the final items in the sequence) for acoustically presented items, even after substantial retention intervals, tends to be abolished by auditory but not by visual intervening events (e.g., see Broadbent, Vines, & Broadbent, 1978; Martin & Jones, 1979). These findings, Broadbent argues, are consistent with the suggestion that the sensory store is divided into distinct regions based on the physical characteristics of incoming information and that succeeding information belonging to the same physical class will overwrite the information already residing in that particular region of the sensory store. However, the original event will be maintained in the sensory store indefinitely as long as succeeding events do not contain any of the features of the original event.

Broadbent also argues that the sensory storage of visual information is longer lived than studies of the visual sensory register (i.e., the icon) would seem to suggest. In making this argument, Broadbent cites a study he conducted with his wife, Margaret, (Broadbent & Broadbent, 1981b) in which subjects were asked to remember visual patterns made of arbitrarily shaped lines. They found a recency effect when the to-be-remembered items appeared successively in the same location on the display surface, but the recency effect was reduced when successive items were presented in different locations on the display surface. Broadbent interprets this result as indicating that the recency effect in such a situation is dependent on later items overwriting in sensory store earlier items from the list that occurred in the same place.

On this view, the probability of successful recall of the earlier items is progressively reduced as more and more later items containing similar features occur. Such an overwriting process, as a contributor to the recency effect, implies retention of information in the sensory store for intervals considerably longer than those associated with storage in the visual sensory register. This result from the study of visual storage also indicates, Broadbent suggests, that physical features, such as location of occurrence, are also important dimensions in the division of the sensory store into different regions.

Although Broadbent and colleagues have not studied other sensory modalities, evidence from a study of memory for taste and smell by Barker and Weaver (1983) is consistent with Broadbent's suggestion that different regions of sensory store can maintain sensory information from different modalities for relatively long periods of time. Barker and Weaver report that, after an initial rapid loss of memory for the intensity of tastes and smells, the remaining memory for these sensory events remains unchanged for at least three days.

In what fundamental way is the sensory memory of the Maltese cross different from the sensory registers of the Atkinson and Shiffrin model?

The Motor Output Store

The motor output store is another of the four components proposed by Broadbent as an alternative to the STS of the Atkinson and Shiffrin model. The motor output store "contains a string of commands for a sequence of actions" (Broadbent, 1983, p. 243) that may be converted into an overt action or that may simply provide for temporary storage of the sequence. According to the model, interference with memories in a particular motor system will only be produced by operations involving the same motor system. An example is the articulation and covert internal repetition of a sequence of to-be-remembered items, as in repeating a telephone number long enough to dial it or as in Alan's repeating the ingredients of the cake until they are retrieved from their respective locations in the kitchen. Memory in these situations is not disrupted by walking across the room, dialing the telephone, or opening the refrigerator, because such actions involve motor systems different from that used in repeating the to-be-remembered items. However, memory in these situations is disrupted by having to answer a question, because such an action does involve the motor system being used to maintain the items.

Thus, in the case of articulation, the motor output store of the Maltese cross is very similar to the articulatory rehearsal loop of the working memory model. In fact, in arguing for the existence of an articulatory motor store, Broadbent cites much of the same evidence from studies of articulatory suppression (described earlier) that was used by Baddeley in proposing the articulatory rehearsal loop of the working memory model. However, the Maltese cross model clearly differs from the working memory model in that it argues for the existence of other motor output stores in addition to the articulatory store.

For example, Broadbent proposes that there may be a motor output store for hand gestures. Hulme (1979, 1981) has tested subjects' recognition memory for meaningless shapes following visual presentation alone and following visual presentation accompanied by the opportunity to trace around the shapes with the hands. He reported that the opportunity to trace the shapes improved memory for the shapes relative to the visual presentation only condition and that this benefit from tracing was eliminated by a manual interference task but not by a visual interference task. Thus, Broadbent argues, hand gestures, just like articulatory movements, may be held in temporary storage to facilitate memory performance.

Kornbrot (1989) has argued that the concept of a motor output store for hand movements, in which commands can be hierarchically organized, is useful in accounting for the performance of her subjects as they learned to translate a visually presented digit sequence into a series of keystrokes. In addition, Broadbent suggests that there is tentative evidence for the existence of a separate motor output store for spatial movements, based on the research described above by Baddeley's research group that led to the proposal of the visuo-spatial scratch-pad.

 What evidence has Broadbent cited in arguing for the existence of the motor output store, and how does the motor output store of the Maltese cross differ from the articulatory rehearsal loop of the working memory model?

The Abstract Working Memory

The third component of short-term memory proposed by the Maltese cross model is the abstract working memory, so called because it is neither sensory nor motor in nature. Again, Broadbent's proposal that such a store exists is based in large part on Baddeley and Hitch's articulatory suppression results. Recall that in those studies Baddeley and Hitch found evidence that there is a component of working memory that is not affected by articulatory suppression, word length, or phonemic similarity, and that can proceed with a reasoning task while part of the system concurrently holds two or three to-be-remembered items. In the working memory model, this component of short-term memory was called the central executive, to distinguish it from the articulatory rehearsal loop.

Broadbent attempts to differentiate the various functions assigned to the central executive in the working memory model by distinguishing between the representation of information and the processes that operate on that information. In order to do so, his Maltese cross model argues for the existence of an abstract working memory that temporarily stores or represents a limited amount of information not being held in sensory or motor store, and a separate processing system that can operate on this stored information. This processing system will be discussed shortly.

In support of his proposal for an abstract working memory, Broadbent cites studies of short-term retention in which the subject's ability to perform does not appear to be attributable to either the sensory or the motor store. For example, Broadbent and Broadbent (1981a) studied the retention of trigrams (sets of three items) presented visually, one after the other in the same location, with and without articulatory suppression. They found that, in the absence of articulatory suppression, subjects tended to recall the trigrams in an all-or-none fashion and that meaningful trigrams such as USA were better recalled than nonmeaningful trigrams. Both of these effects were also found with articulatory suppression, although the overall level of performance was reduced.

These results imply that the successively arriving letters were held somewhere temporarily until all three arrived and were combined into a group. Given that the letters were presented visually in the same location, they were not being held in sensory store because each succeeding letter presumably overwrote the preceding one. Given that the grouping effects were obtained even under conditions of articulatory suppression, the letters were not being held in the articulatory motor output store because it was presumably occupied by the articulatory suppression task. That leaves, Broadbent contends, the abstract working memory as the temporary storage location for the letters.

Broadbent and colleagues (e.g., Hayes & Broadbent, 1988) have subsequently suggested that one of the primary functions of abstract working memory is the formation of associations that can be verbally reported. On this view, two of the three available slots in abstract working memory can be used to represent the two initially unrelated items, and the third slot can be used to store the new relation or association being formed between them.

Hayes and Broadbent (1988) reported results from two experiments that they interpret as being consistent with the view that abstract working memory is importantly involved in the formation of new associations. In these studies, subjects were asked to perform either a random letter or a random digit generation procedure. This procedure requires that subjects call out either random letters or digits at a rate set by the experimenter. Hayes and Broadbent argue that, since this task requires that subjects randomize the items being produced, it involves more than just articulatory suppression. It necessitates that subjects retain information about the relationship between recently generated items and is thus likely to involve the abstract working memory.

Hayes and Broadbent found that these tasks interfered with a learning task that necessitated selective, effortful learning and reporting of new associations, and that would also rely on abstract working memory. The random generation procedures did not interfere with a learning task that involved unselective accumulation of information about the frequency of occurrence of certain events, and that therefore would presumably not tap abstract working memory.

 In what way does the abstract working memory reflect Broadbent's attempt to refine the concept of the central executive as proposed in Baddeley's working memory model, and how has Broadbent attempted to demonstrate the existence of this memory store?

The Processing System

The final component of the Maltese cross, and one that also represents a major revision of Atkinson and Shiffrin's STS, is the processing system. As Figure 6–11 shows, this component occupies the center of the cross, with the four previously discussed stores represented by the arms of the cross. The processing system occupies this position because it is responsible for the transfer of all information from one of the four stores to the other. As the arrows leading into and out of each of the four stores indicate, transfer of information can occur between any of the four stores—it is not assumed that information is transferred from one store to another in a fixed sequence of stages. Because this transfer of information between stores involves establishing a new representation in the receiving store to correspond to the already existing representation in the original store, the transfer operations involve coding the information into a form that can be accommodated by the receiving store. For example, in transferring the visual pattern 2 from sensory store to the articulatory motor output store, the processing system must convert the visual pattern into a motor program for articulating the name of that pattern (i.e., into a motor program for saying *two*).

As was mentioned earlier in discussing the long-term associative store, this type of coding by the processing system implies that there is long-term storage in the processing system of information involved in pattern recognition, but Broadbent insists that the retention of such information in the processing system is different from the representation of an event in the long-term associative store. The coding operations of the processing system may also involve combining separate codes from the various memory stores into a single code, as, for example, in combining the sight, smell, name, and place of encounter of a pig into the long-term associative fragment "I saw Suzy the pig at the state fair."

As was also noted earlier in the description of the abstract working memory, Broadbent argues that this component of the system is essential in order to differentiate between representation and processing within the system. This differentiation is necessary, he believes, in order to avoid focusing on one to the exclusion of the other, and he gives the levels of processing approach as an example of one prominent framework that has emphasized the study of processing to the point of ignoring how representation of information in memory store importantly affects memory performance.

To help illustrate how the processing system functions to interconnect the various memory stores represented in the four arms of the Maltese cross, Broadbent provides the following description:

The system being advocated can be understood by analogy with a man sitting in an office. On his left he has an "in-basket" (the sensory store). Messages arriving from the outside world can sit in this and wait to be handled until the man has a spare time period. Any later piece of paper will cover earlier ones and make them inaccessible, however. Perhaps we should allow the man several in-baskets, for papers from different sources, to preserve the analogy with separate stores of acoustic and other events.

On the man's right, he has an ''out-basket'' (the motor store) into which he puts outgoing papers when he has taken a decision. They need not go at once, and he can take them back to revise them, change their destination, and so on; but if he puts another paper on top of one that is waiting in the out-basket, the latter becomes inaccessible. Again, the man should be thought of as having several out-baskets for different destinations.

In front of him, there is a restricted space or ''desk top,'' on which he keeps the papers he is actually handling at this moment. This is the abstract nonsensory, non-motor memory; it is safe from fresh inputs or outputs, but only a limited number of separate items can be held in this way. Last, there is behind the man a ''filing cabi-net,'' in which he can place papers he wants to save. To be able to find them again, however, he needs to associate each with something he can use for retrieval; he might, for example, put each letter in a file with the name of the person who signed it. This is the associative long-term memory.

This analogy preserves a lot of the essence of the Maltese cross, but it misses one point. The actual passage of a paper through the system can be variable. It may go from in-basket to file, be retrieved weeks later when another input arrives, and be held on the desk for a few minutes. Then a consolidated reply might go into the out-put, or it could be handled straightaway, or it could go into output temporarily to clear the desk, be brought back for modification, and only then go out. What actu-ally happens is decided by the little man who is in the middle of the office analogy. (1984, p. 64)

Broadbent stresses, however, that one should not assume that the processing system (the man in the middle) is equivalent to a man with full decision-making abilities. Instead, one should think of the actions of the processing system as being governed by rules retrieved from the long-term associative store in response to input from the other three memory stores.

◪ *What major functions are performed by the processing system of the Maltese cross model?*

CONCLUDING REMARKS: The Continuing Usefulness of the Multistore Approach

Clearly, the multistore model as originally proposed by Atkinson and Shiffrin is rapidly ceasing to be the dominant framework for the investigation of memory processes. However, as the detailed descriptions of Baddeley's working memory model and Broadbent's Maltese cross model indicate, the multistore approach to the study of memory processing has not been abandoned. Of course, neither of these models is currently universally accepted by prominent memory researchers (e.g. see criticisms of the Maltese cross by Carr & Brown, 1984; Loftus, Loftus, & Hunt, 1984; Roediger, 1984b; Watkins, 1984). However, there is a growing number of researchers who do accept the position that we must now begin to consider the existence of several distinct types of short-term memory (see Carr & Brown, 1984; Crowder, 1982, 1983, 1984; Coltheart, 1983; Phillips, 1983).

In the absence of other clearly articulated models, the comprehensiveness of Broadbent's Maltese cross model is likely to make it popular in the coming years as a framework for investigations of both short-term and long-term memory. In addition, as research by Baddeley and colleagues on additional component systems of working memory continues, it may become possible to integrate the working memory model within the Maltese cross framework.

The comprehensiveness of Broadbent's model can be made obvious by again considering the example of Alan, given at the beginning of this chapter. In the case of remembering the ingredients of the cake, the model would attempt to explain Alan's performance in terms of the involvement of the sensory store, the motor output store, the abstract working memory, and the processing system. The degree to which each of these components would be involved would depend importantly on what else Alan was doing at the same time. In attempting to explain Alan's learning of the bones of the hand, the Maltese cross not only provides a framework for explaining how memory fragments can become established in the long-term associative store, as described earlier, but it also provides a framework for explaining how the information might be stored and processed in short-term memory during the establishment of those long-term associative fragments.

This attempt of the updated multistore models, such as the Maltese cross, to explain how the storage of information in the various components of the system makes possible the processing of information required by various types of cognitive task is their greatest attraction. Because they fail to describe explicitly how the storage of incoming information contributes to and interacts with the processing of the information, frameworks such as the levels and elaboration of processing approaches are clearly incomplete as comprehensive accounts of learning and memory and do not really constitute an alternative to the multistore approach.

This is not to say that these processing approaches have not made an important contribution to the field. The levels of processing approach has had the very desirable effect of redirecting research attention to the importance of internal mental processes and away from situational determinants of performance such as the nature of the material being learned, as Eysenck (1978) has noted, but it is entirely possible to incorporate the insights of the levels of processing approach into a multistore model. In fact, even in their original formulation of the levels of processing approach, Craik and Lockhart never really completely rejected the notion of multiple memory stores and found it useful to employ the concept of primary memory in describing maintenance rehearsal. Certainly the processing system of the Maltese cross represents an attempt to make explicit the role that processing plays in the learning and retention of information.

However, the Maltese cross has not yet been described in all of the detail desirable. In particular, of all of the components of the Maltese cross, the processing system is the least well specified at this point. Broadbent's man-at-his-desk analogy shows that the model assigns a multiplicity of functions to the system, but its role beyond that of translating from one code to another is only vaguely specified. In addition, there are issues of long-term storage that require further attention within the context of the Maltese cross or any other multistore model. In Chapter 7, some of these issues of long-term storage will be examined.

Furthermore, Broadbent and collaborators have already proposed modifications to the model, as described in the preceding pages. For example, FitzGerald and Broadbent (1985) have suggested that the original treatment of the motor output store may have to be modified as a result of their investigations of the effect of articulatory suppression on output interference. Specifically, they found that articulatory suppression did not reduce the order-of-report effect in which recall of items is adversely affected by the earlier output of other items.

Articulatory suppression would be expected to reduce the order-of-report effect if both involve the motor output store. Thus they propose that the motor output store may have to be replaced with a "generalized output store" and an auxiliary articulatory loop that serves as a slave system to the generalized store. In turn, they conjecture that such a generalized output store may ultimately be found to be indistinguishable from the abstract working memory of the model.

To return to the question raised at the beginning of the chapter in describing Alan's memory performance, there does indeed appear to be a great deal of experimental evidence and a number of theoretical accounts of the memory system that argue for a distinction between short-term and long-term memory. However, it has also become obvious that this distinction is too simplistic and that further distinctions between different types of short-term memory and between different types of long-term memory will be necessary as researchers attempt to account for more and more of the complexities of human memory.

Finally, it should be noted that all of the accounts of the human memory system described in this chapter represent a major reemergence of the cognitive or mentalistic tradition in the field of learning and memory. All of the models discussed in this chapter, whether they be models postulating the existence of multiple memory stores or models focusing on different types of processing, are based directly on the assumption that a comprehensive account of human learning must attempt to describe in detail the internal structures and/or processes that underlie memory performance.

CHAPTER 7

The Representation
of Information
in Long-Term Memory (Part I)

APPLICATION: Shooting Hoops and Studying

Alan leaves biology lab at 5 o'clock and walks with his friend, Stan, to the bike rack outside the science building. After discussing whether material covered in the afternoon's lab is likely to be included on the upcoming unit exam, Alan unlocks his bike and rides the three miles to his home. Alan is greeted at home by his younger brother, Joseph, who asks Alan if he would like to play basketball. For the next hour, Alan plays a fast-paced game of one-on-one before showering and settling into the study to begin his preparation for the biology exam.

During Alan's two-and-a-half hours of study before dinner, he reviews his notes for the preceding two weeks of lectures and outlines the five textbook chapters that are to be tested on the exam. To test his mastery of the material, Alan attempts to answer a list of study questions that the instructor has provided. Once he has written an answer for each of the 35 questions, he begins to check the accuracy of his responses, only to be interrupted by his father's calling him to dinner.

Clearly, Alan's before-dinner activities, both physical and mental, were based to a considerable degree on information represented in his long-term memory store. In this chapter, we shall examine the ways in which learning and memory psychologists attempt to characterize and classify long-term memory representations.

DISTINCTION BETWEEN PROCEDURAL AND DECLARATIVE KNOWLEDGE

The issue of how information is represented in long-term memory is one of major importance to theorists of human memory. A number of these theorists have proposed descriptions of long-term memory that focus on the types of information represented in long-term store and how that information is organized. In this chapter, some of the most influential characterizations of long-term store will be considered. Most of these formulations represent the cognitive approach to memory in that they include assumptions about the organization of mental events that go beyond the notion of simple associative linkages between items in memory. However, in many of these treatments the influence of associationism will also be evident. Thus, as in preceding chapters, further evidence of the almost universal appeal of certain associative notions will be encountered, underscoring again how, despite its limitations as a comprehensive explanation of mental life, associationism remains a major influence in descriptions of memory.

ACT Theory's Proposed Distinction

In 1976, John Anderson proposed a computer simulation model of cognitive processes that he dubbed ACT (for Adaptive Control of Thought). Since then, he has continued to revise and refine the framework (e.g., see Anderson 1983, 1987, 1989, 1990). Anderson sees ACT as a successor to an earlier computer simulation model, HAM (for human associative memory), that he developed in conjunction with Gordon Bower (Anderson & Bower, 1973). The model describes the cognitive system in terms of two components: **declarative knowledge,** which refers to knowing facts, and **procedural knowledge,** which involves knowing how. Declarative knowledge, it is assumed, is organized into an associative network, and procedural knowledge is represented as a production system that operates on that factual knowledge in the performance of various tasks.

For example, in unlocking his bicycle and riding it home, Alan was, in Anderson's terms, relying on both declarative knowledge and the execution of productions. Alan was relying on declarative knowledge in that the knowledge of facts, such as *I parked my bike in the rack outside the science building,* is presumably involved in performing the skill. Alan was relying on productions in that unlocking and riding a bicycle obviously involves "knowing how" in the sense of executing a series of step-by-step procedures when certain conditions are met. For example, the production for unlocking the bicycle might involve the step of turning the key to the right once the key has been fully inserted into the bike lock. Thus Anderson's model assumes the existence in long-term memory of a body of factual, or declarative, knowledge that determines when and under what conditions procedural knowledge in the form of ordered productions is exhibited.

☑ *What is the basic distinction ACT makes between declarative and procedural knowledge?*

Declarative Knowledge as a Network of Associated Propositions

In arguing that declarative knowledge is organized in an associative network, Anderson makes the further assumption that declarative knowledge is represented in the form of propositions. In the sense used by Anderson and other cognitive psychologists, a **proposition** is defined as a unit of language that expresses a relationship between two or more concepts. Alternatively, a proposition can be defined as the smallest unit of language about which it makes sense to judge true or false.

Consider the sentence *The happy boy who lives next door hit the bicycle.* This sentence can be described as consisting of three propositions: (1) the boy is happy, (2) the boy lives next door, and (3) the boy hit the bicycle. Each of these units specifies a relationship between at least two concepts, and it is possible to judge the truth of the unit, whereas it is not possible to judge the truth of a unit such as "the boy." If one assumes that this sentence is represented in memory in the form of its constituent propositions, then one can further assume that these constituent propositions are linked into a network by means of labeled associations (see Figure 7–1).

In this figure, the associative links are labeled in terms of the relationship that exists between the two linked concepts. This assumption has been justified by Anderson and Bower (1973) and others (e.g., Collins & Quillian, 1969; Collins & Loftus, 1975) on the basis of retrieval efficiency. It is argued that the labeling of associations within the memory network would speed retrieval by limiting the number of associative links leading from a concept that would have to be searched. For example, if a subject studies the to-be-remembered sentence *The boy hit the ball,* and then is prompted with the sentence frame *The _____ _____ the ball,* the memory search can be limited to those associative pathways from *ball* labeled with an "object" relationship.

However, Anderson (1975) failed to find empirical support for this assumption. He found that the speed of verifying as true or false a sentence containing a particular concept, such as *Nixon,* was affected by the total number of sentences studied in which *Nixon* appeared, regardless of the logical role of *Nixon* in the various sentences. Thus Anderson found that if subjects, for example, studied 10 sentences in which *Nixon* appeared as subject and only 1 sentence in which *Nixon* appeared as object and were then asked to decide if the

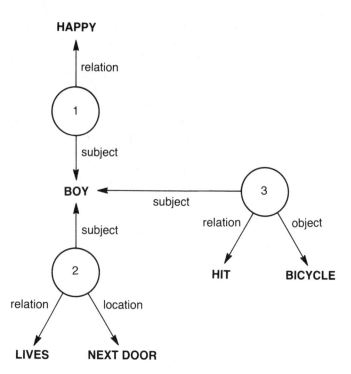

FIGURE 7–1 The sentence *The happy boy who lives next door hit the bicycle* represented as three constituent propositions linked by labeled associations.

sentence *The lawyer kicked Nixon* had been studied, they were just as slow as were subjects who had studied 10 sentences in which *Nixon* appeared as object and only one sentence in which *Nixon* appeared as subject. Thus ACT assumes that a memory search will evaluate all propositions containing a target concept regardless of the relationship the concept has to the rest of the proposition.

However, ACT still assumes that associative links are labeled and that these labels are used in evaluating possibly relevant propositions activated by the search process. That is, the associative links between concepts must be labeled if the propositional representation is to express precisely the meaning of the information being represented. If the representation of *The boy hit the bicycle,* as shown in Figure 7–1, did not indicate the relationship that existed between *hit* and *boy* and between *hit* and *bicycle,* it would not be possible upon retrieving the representation from memory to decide whether the boy hit the bicycle or the bicycle hit the boy, unless additional information regarding word order in the original sentence was represented in memory. However, it is obviously highly desirable to have an abstract representation of information that is independent of order of information. Otherwise, the basic underlying similarity of *The boy hit the bicycle* and *The bicycle was hit by the boy* would not be adequately reflected in the system.

☑ *In what form does ACT assume that declarative knowledge is represented in long-term memory?*

Procedural Knowledge as a System of Productions

Anderson (1976, 1983, 1987, 1990) defines a **production** as a rule consisting of a condition and an action. In turn, the condition consists of a goal and a set of tests for determining if the production is appropriate to the goal. If the application tests are satisfied, the action is performed. Table 7–1 contains some example productions. In the shifting gears production, the actions of depressing the clutch, moving the stick to the upper right, and releasing the clutch are only executed if the goal is to shift from first to second gear and if the car is currently in first gear, going more than 10 miles an hour, and has a clutch and a stick shift.

TABLE 7–1   Example Productions from Anderson's ACT System

Production for Shifting Gears

Production:	Changing from first to second gear in one kind of car.
IF	the car is in first gear
	and the car is going faster than 10 mph
	and there is a clutch
	and there is a stick shift,
THEN	depress the clutch
	and move the stick to the upper right
	and release the clutch.

Production for Making a Noun Plural

Production:	One way to make a noun plural.
IF	the goal is to generate a plural noun
	and the noun ends in a hard consonant,
THEN	generate the noun with an ''s'' on the end.

Production for Parsing a Sentence

Name of Production		Form of Production
NP	IF	the string is of the form *A noun*
	THEN	the meaning is an instance of *noun*
RELATIVE	IF	the string is of the form *person who verb object*
	THEN	the meaning is that *person* has the relation *verb* to *object*
MAIN	IF	the string is of the form *person verb object*
	THEN	the meaning is that *person* has the relation *verb* to *object*

Production for Inferencing

IF	person 1 is the father of person 2
	and person 2 is the father of person 3
THEN	person 1 is the grandfather of person 3.

Source: Portion reprinted by permission of the publishers from *The Architecture of Cognition* by John R. Anderson, Cambridge, MA: Harvard University Press, Copyright © 1983 by the President and Fellows of Harvard College. Portion from *Cognitive Psychology and Its Implications,* 3rd ed. By John R. Anderson. Copyright © 1980, 1985, 1990 by W. H. Freeman and Company. Reprinted with permission.

It is important to understand that in describing procedural knowledge as a collection of production systems, Anderson is not limiting his conceptualization to procedures involving physically observable actions, such as shifting gears or riding a bicycle. He includes within his conceptualization of procedural knowledge cognitive activities such as making a noun plural and parsing a sentence (i.e., analyzing the sentence into its constituent parts so as to make interpretation of its meaning possible), and drawing inferences. Productions that might be involved in these activities are also shown in Table 7–1.

The production for making a noun plural is self-explanatory. In the production for parsing a sentence, three productions are applied. The first identifies a noun phrase and assigns a meaning to it. The second identifies a relative clause embedded in the original noun phrase and assigns a meaning to the whole unit. The third identifies a complete sentence pattern consisting of the already interpreted noun phrase plus verb and object and assigns a meaning to the complete sentence. This sentence parsing example is instructive in illustrating how ACT theory stresses the organization of productions into subroutines that continually interact with each other in the execution of some procedure.

The third set of productions for inferencing would be appropriate if an individual were holding in short-term or working memory information such as *John is the father of Bill* and *Bill is the father of Steve*. The execution of the production would result in the action of recording in working memory that *John is the grandfather of Steve*. This example production shows how productions are driven by, and in turn influence the contents of, working memory.

📝 *What, according to ACT, are productions, and how are they involved in the representation of procedural knowledge?*

Distinguishing Features of Procedural and Declarative Knowledge

In justifying the distinction between procedural and declarative knowledge, Anderson argues that declarative knowledge is possessed on an all-or-none basis, whereas procedural knowledge can be possessed partially or in degrees. For example, Alan either knows or doesn't know where in a woman's body the ovum if fertilized, but Alan can possess the ability to shoot a hook shot to varying degrees. Furthermore, Anderson contends that declarative knowledge can be described verbally or expressed symbolically through language, whereas procedural knowledge often cannot be. Procedural knowledge can often only be demonstrated through the performance of specific behaviors. Alan, for example, might have great difficulty describing verbally how he executes a lay-up, whereas he might be able to demonstrate the move easily. Finally, Anderson suggests that declarative knowledge is often acquired rapidly through a single experience, whereas procedural knowledge is often acquired only gradually through repeated experience or practice in performing the skill. Alan's knowledge of where an ovum is fertilized may be acquired from a single reading of a passage in the textbook, but his knowledge of how to execute a hook shot is likely to be acquired only through repeated practice of the skill.

📝 *In what three ways do procedural and declarative knowledge differ?*

Interactions of Procedural and Declarative Knowledge

Although procedural and declarative knowledge are assumed to be distinct, ACT also assumes that there is constant interaction of procedural and declarative knowledge. The nature of this interaction is represented in Figure 7–2. The execution of productions in utilizing procedural knowledge is determined by information held in working memory, and

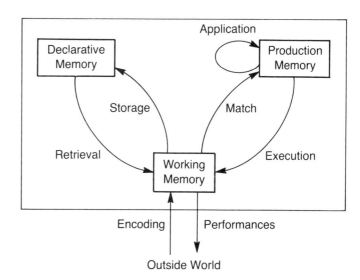

FIGURE 7–2 An illustration of the interaction of declarative and procedural knowledge in the ACT framework.

Source: Reprinted by permission of the publishers from *The Architecture of Cognition* by John R. Anderson, Cambridge, MA: Harvard University Press, Copyright © 1983 by the President and Fellows of Harvard College.

the information in working memory is provided by the long-term declarative knowledge propositional network in conjunction with sensory inputs from the outside world. That is, production systems are driven by data provided to working memory by the declarative knowledge propositional network. Such data include information about the current stimuli being encountered, past memories, current goals, and so on.

For example, Alan's execution of productions involved in riding his bicycle might be influenced by traffic patterns on the sidewalk adjacent to the bike rack and on the streets on his route, his recollection of a major construction project on one of the streets he normally travels, and his desire to be home in time to study before dinner.

Furthermore, productions are only executed if the declarative knowledge propositional network specifies through working memory that certain conditions have been met. Alan will only exert pressure on the right pedal of his bicycle through his right leg once the bicycle lock has been removed and the bicycle is oriented properly for riding to begin.

Finally, once executed, productions result in changes in working memory and in the declarative knowledge propositional network. Once an action such as removing the lock has been performed, this knowledge must be represented in Alan's system in order for relevant productions involved in riding the bike to proceed. Similarly, once Alan has arrived at a meaningful interpretation for a passage in his biology textbook through the application of relevant productions, this interpretation must be represented in Alan's declarative memory system in order for productions involved in integrating the textbook information with lecture material to proceed.

How specifically does declarative knowledge affect the execution of productions, and how does the execution of productions affect declarative knowledge?

Evidence Consistent with the Distinction

Performance of Amnesics. One body of evidence that has been cited as consistent with the distinction between procedural and declarative knowledge comes from the study of persons suffering from **anterograde amnesia.** This memory deficit is associated with brain trauma of various sorts and is characterized by difficulty in forming new long-term memo-

---

ries for events occurring *after* the brain trauma. In his description of the memory deficits of these amnesics, Baddeley (1983) cites a number of findings consistent with the assumption that procedural knowledge may be relatively intact in such individuals but that they suffer from a profound difficulty in effectively encoding new declarative knowledge.

For example, Baddeley notes that amnesics are relatively unimpaired in learning motor skills such as those involved in performing a pursuit rotor task, tracing a path through a maze, and performing a typing task. They are also unimpaired in perceptual learning tasks. For instance, they are able to detect an anomaly in a drawing faster and faster with repeated presentation of the drawing (Warrington & Weiskrantz, 1973), and they are able to assemble a jigsaw puzzle faster and faster with repeated presentations of the puzzle. However, anterograde amnesics' profound deficits in acquiring new declarative knowledge is illustrated by the fact that in all of the cases of procedural learning just noted, the amnesics reported no awareness of earlier trials as the trials on the task continued. That is, the amnesics apparently had no conscious awareness of the prior learning episodes.

Additional evidence of amnesics' deficits in acquiring new declarative knowledge will be described in Chapter 11. At present, it is sufficient to note that this pattern of deficits in anterograde amnesics is being widely interpreted as supporting the distinction between procedural and declarative knowledge.

Independent Acquisition of Procedural and Declarative Knowledge. Another line of research that has been advanced in support of the distinction between procedural and declarative knowledge involves attempts to demonstrate that procedural learning can develop in normal subjects in the absence of conscious awareness (i.e., in the absence of declarative knowledge) that the learning is occurring. Willingham, Nissen, and Bullemer (1989) had subjects perform a reaction time task that involved pressing one of four keys, arranged horizontally beneath four different locations on a video monitor. The subject's task on each trial was to press as quickly as possible the key beneath the location in which an asterisk appeared. Unbeknownst to the subjects, the location of the asterisk was varied according to a predetermined pattern that recurred every 10 trials. Thus, over the entire set of 40 trials, subjects experienced the same 10-trial sequence of asterisk locations four times in succession.

Subjects were questioned after the reaction time procedure concerning their awareness of any repeating pattern or sequence, and a number of the subjects reported no awareness whatsoever of the repeating pattern. However, when the reaction time data from these subjects who reported no conscious awareness of the repeating sequence were analyzed, Willingham and colleagues found that these subjects nevertheless showed a significant decrease in reaction time (i.e., they came to respond faster) across the four blocks of 10 trials (Figure 7–3). This decrease in reaction time cannot be attributed to subjects' simply learning about the general demands of the task because Nissen and Bullemer (1987) showed that subjects exposed to truly random asterisk placement showed a minimal reduction in reaction time across blocks of trials.

Thus some of the subjects with normal memory studied by Willingham and colleagues showed specific procedural learning in the absence of explicit declarative knowledge, just as persons with amnesia do. These results support the validity of ACT theory's distinction between procedural and declarative memory. However, the researchers note that the results are at odds with Anderson's (1987) claim that procedural knowledge is necessarily derived

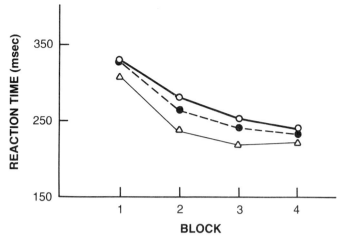

FIGURE 7–3 Reaction times of subjects to visual targets presented in different locations across blocks of trials as a function of degree of declarative knowledge possessed about the repeating sequence of target placements. (Open circles = no declarative knowledge; filled circles = some declarative knowledge; open triangles = full declarative knowledge.)

Source: Willingham, D. B., Nissen, M. J., & Bullemer, P. (1989). On the development of procedural knowledge. *Journal of Experimental Psychology: Learning, Memory, and Cognition, 15*, 1051. Copyright 1989 by the American Psychological Association. Reprinted by permission.

from preexisting declarative memory representations of the same information. It would appear that in some situations the development of procedural knowledge can precede the development of corresponding declarative knowledge.

 What evidence from the study of anterograde amnesics and the development of procedural learning in normal subjects supports the distinction between declarative and procedural knowledge?

Explicit versus Implicit Memory

The sort of evidence summarized above as supporting the distinction between declarative and procedural knowledge can also be interpreted as supporting a distinction between explicit and implicit memory (e.g., see Graf & Schacter, 1985; Johnson & Hasher, 1987; Richardson-Klavehn & Bjork, 1988; Schacter, 1987). **Explicit memory** refers to memory displayed in response to a direct test of memory that taps an individual's awareness that he or she is remembering a specific prior event. **Implicit memory,** on the other hand, refers to memory displayed in response to an indirect test of memory that does *not* tap an individual's awareness of a specific prior event but that does assess whether his or her current behavior is being influenced by some prior event.

In the case of the amnesics' performance described earlier, the measures of motor skill learning and perceptual learning were indirect tests of memory in that subjects were being tested to determine whether prior performance of the tasks influenced later performance of the tasks, regardless of the subjects' awareness of having previously performed the tasks. On the other hand, asking the amnesic subjects if they remembered having performed the task previously was a direct test of memory. Thus the performance of the amnesic subjects can be interpreted in terms of their having impaired explicit memory but intact implicit memory.

Similarly, the results from the Willingham, Nissen, and Bullemer (1989) study described in the immediately preceding section can be interpreted in terms of the subjects developing implicit memory for the repeating asterisk pattern in the absence of explicit memory for the pattern. Although the distinction between explicit and implicit memory may ultimately be found to be subtly different from the distinction between declarative and procedural memory, we shall follow the lead of Anderson (1990). We shall equate explicit memory with declarative memory, because explicit memories are those of which a person is conscious and can declare, and we shall equate implicit memory with procedural memory, because the performance underlying demonstrations of implicit memory is based on performing various kinds of procedures.

▣ *How can the distinction between explicit and implicit memory be explained in terms of the distinction between declarative and procedural knowledge?*

The Cognitive-Associative Traditions

ACT nicely illustrates the continuing the influences of the cognitive and associative traditions on the study of learning and memory processes. Principles of associationism are the basis of ACT's representation of the declarative knowledge system. However, in augmenting this characterization of declarative memory as an associative network with a description of procedural knowledge based on the concept of productions, Anderson has introduced notions that go well beyond simple associationist principles of mental life. Perhaps Anderson's demonstration that associationist notions can be integrated so effectively with more complex cognitive functions will be one of the most enduring aspects of his work.

▣ *Is ACT primarily cognitive or associationist in its focus?*

Schemas as a Component of Procedural and Declarative Knowledge

Schema Defined

Another notion concerning the representation of information in long-term memory that can be used to supplement the distinction between procedural and declarative knowledge is that of schemas. Earlier in this century, Englishman Sir Frederic Bartlett (1932) argued that information in memory is highly organized into structures called **schemas.** These knowledge structures concerning objects, events, situations, and the like in turn influence how new episodes are represented in memory by arousing expectations that influence how the new information is interpreted and incorporated into the existing schemas.

These schemas, or existing knowledge structures, thus influence what Bartlett called the "effort after meaning." That is, he argued, human learners do not passively store away the information that is presented to them. Instead, they attempt to arrive at a meaningful interpretation of the information, and this interpretation is strongly influenced by prior knowledge that is activated at the time of study. Bartlett suggested that the more successful the individual is in his or her effort after meaning, the more successful the learning will be.

Returning again to the example of Alan, Bartlett would argue that in studying for his biology exam, Alan will activate schemas relevant to the topic being studied. In studying the material on human reproduction, Alan might use previously established general schemas regarding fertilization of the ovum as a basis for interpreting and integrating in memory new information concerning the specific physiological processes that are involved in the uniting of ovum and sperm cell. Alan's schema might include the information that each ovum and sperm cell contains 23 chromosomes, and such knowledge might lead him to expect to find in the textbook material information about how the chromosomes are involved in the physiological processes that constitute fertilization.

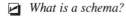 *What is a schema?*

Schemas and Comprehension of Text

Bartlett's notion of schemas was popularized in the 1970s in part by the work of Bransford and colleagues. In a landmark study, Bransford and Johnson (1972) presented subjects with the following passage and asked them to study it for a later memory test. Try this task yourself. Read the passage through once at your normal reading speed. Then put your textbook aside and write your recall of the passage. Try to make your recall as similar to the original passage as possible.

> *The procedure is actually quite simple. First you arrange items into different groups. Of course one pile may be sufficient depending on how much there is to do. If you have to go somewhere else due to lack of facilities that is the next step; otherwise, you are pretty well set. It is important not to overdo things. That is, it is better to do too few things at once than too many. In the short run this may not seem important but complications can easily arise. A mistake can be expensive as well. At first, the whole procedure will seem complicated. Soon, however, it will become just another facet of life. It is difficult to foresee any end to the necessity for this task in the immediate future, but then, one never can tell. After the procedure is completed one arranges the materials into different groups again. Then they can be put into their appropriate places. Eventually they will be used once more and the whole cycle will then have to be repeated. However, that is part of life. (Bransford & Johnson, 1972, p. 322)*

Now, if you found this passage difficult to comprehend and recall, you had the same experience as those subjects in Bransford and Johnson's experiment who heard the passage without first being given a title for the passage. However, suppose that you were told in advance of reading the passage that the topic of the passage is "washing clothes." Read the passage again now. You probably find it much more understandable.

Bransford and Johnson found that subjects who received the title before hearing the passage rated it as significantly more comprehensible and recalled significantly more of it. Subjects given the topic information *after* hearing the passage rated it as no more comprehensible and recalled no more of it than did those subjects given no topic information at all. Thus these results suggest that the activation of relevant schemas contributes importantly to the comprehension and retention of to-be-remembered information.

This line of research has been further developed by researchers such as Voss and associates, who have focused on the relationship between the reader's prior knowledge about a particular topic, such as baseball, and the ability to comprehend and recall the information. In one study, for example, Chiesi, Spilich, and Voss (1979) manipulated at input the number of context sentences preceding the baseball-related sentence that was the target of the investigation. When subjects were asked to recall target sentences that had been presented alone, subjects with low preexisting knowledge about baseball did just as well as subjects with high preexisting knowledge about baseball. However, recall of target sentences by low-knowledge subjects declined as the number of context sentences increased, whereas recall of target sentences by high-knowledge subjects increased as the number of context sentences increased.

Voss (1984) interprets these findings as showing that low-knowledge subjects were not adept at integrating the sentence sequence and thus suffered interference as a result of treating the sentences as separate pieces of information. Similarly, Wilhite (1988, 1989) has examined the effectiveness of headings in text in promoting retention of the information as a function of readers' prior knowledge about the topic. He found that only high-knowledge subjects benefited from the inclusion of headings. Wilhite suggests that readers lacking relevant prior knowledge may not be able to use headings as an integrative device with regard to the organization and retention of passage information.

☑ *How does the research of Bransford and Johnson and the research of Voss and associates support the contention that schemas are important in comprehension and memory of text?*

Structure of Schemas

Other researchers have attempted to characterize the structure of schemas in long-term memory. Rumelhart and Ortony (1977) have presented the examples of schemas for *break* and *face* shown in Figure 7–4. As these diagrams show, Rumelhart and Ortony assume that schemas are composed of a network of interrelated concepts or subschemas. Thus, in the

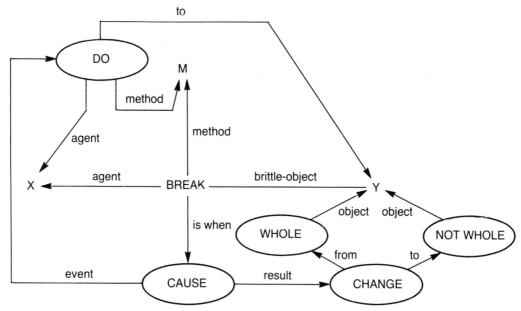

FIGURE 7–4 Representation of a schema for *break* and a partial representation of a schema for *face*.

Source: D. E. Rumelhart & A. Ortony (1977). The representation of knowledge in memory. In R. C. Anderson, R. J. Spiro, & W. E. Montague (Eds.), *Schooling and the acquisition of knowledge.* Hillsdale, NJ: Erlbaum. Reprinted with permission.

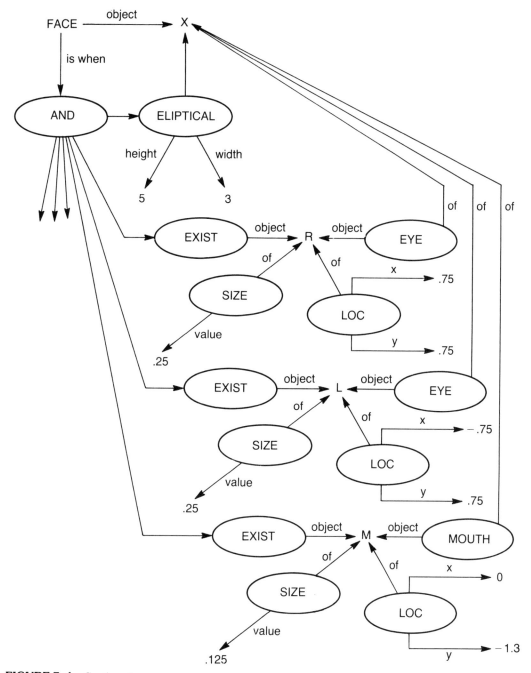

FIGURE 7–4 Continued

case of *break*, the schema includes the subschemas of *do, cause, whole, change,* and *not whole*. The schema also includes the variables *x, y,* and *M*. (A **variable** is a slot in the schema that can take on different values as a function of the situation or context in which the schema is activated.) There are, however, constraints built into the schema that limit the range of values a variable can assume. As Figure 7–4 shows, the variable *y*, as the object of the action, must have the property of being brittle, and the variable *x*, as the agent of the action, must be capable of initiating the action.

In turn, the values of *x* and *y* will influence the value assigned to *M*, the method of breaking employed. Consider the following sentences:

> David broke the glass.
> David broke the chain.

According to Rumelhart and Ortony's conceptualization, both of these sentences would result in *x* being bound to *David*, whereas *y* would be bound to *glass* in the case of the first sentence and to *chain* in the case of the second sentence. These two different bindings of *y*, in turn, suggest different interpretations of *M*, the method. In the first case, the method may be interpreted, depending on the context, as involving the act of dropping the glass; whereas, in the second case, the method my be interpreted as involving the act of pulling or yanking on the chain.

This notion that there are slots or variables in the schema can help explain how humans interpret verbal material by drawing inferences that go beyond the information actually provided. In many cases, the material encountered will activate schemas and yet fail to fill all of the slots or variables. In such situations, some of the slots may be filled with the most typical or expected value for the variable. That is, the system makes use of what is known as **default knowledge.** Consider the following passage about a construction site from a study by Johnson, Bransford, and Solomon (1973):

> *The construction worker was trying to secure the door frame. He was pounding the nail when the foreman came out to watch him and help him do the work. (p. 203)*

When given a recognition test on the passage, many subjects incorrectly indicated that the following sentence had been presented in the passage:

> *The construction worker was using a hammer to secure the door frame when the foreman came out to watch him and help him do the work.*

Such a finding can be explained by assuming that, in the absence of explicitly supplied information about the instrument being used, that slot in the *pound* schema was filled with the default value *hammer.*

✎ *What are slots or variables in a schema, and how are they related to default knowledge?*

Relationship of Schemas to Declarative and Procedural Knowledge

The example schemas for *break* and *face* discussed by Rumelhart and Ortony (1977) are obviously in some sense much more elemental or specific than schemas for washing clothes, sexual reproduction, or baseball, cited earlier in the discussion of other research focusing on the role of schemas in comprehension and memory. However, Rumelhart and Ortony are in no sense suggesting that schemas are limited to the representation of relatively simple concepts. Rather, they argue that one think of schemas in memory as being embedded within each other. Just as the representation of the *face* schema shown in Figure 7–4 shows the schemas of *eye* and *mouth* embedded within it, one could construct a representation of a *washing clothes* schema that would include within it subschemas for *sorting clothes, loading the washing machine, starting the washing machine,* and so on. Thus one can talk about schemas of varying levels of specificity.

The issue of schemas will be considered again later in Chapter 9 in conjunction with the issue of retrieval through reconstruction. At present, it is sufficient to note that the assumption of the existence of schemas is compatible with the assumption of discrete, yet interrelated, representations for declarative and procedural knowledge. In fact, Rumelhart (1980) has explicitly likened the operation of schemas to the performance of procedures, arguing that "schemata are active computational devices capable of evaluating the quality of their own fit to the available data" (p. 39). In the example above concerning the construction site passage, arriving at a meaningful interpretation of the passage presumably involved a procedure for filling the instrument slot in the *pound* schema that included a production for activating the default value *hammer.* Thus, to the extent that schemas are a psychological reality, their activation and use might also involve procedural knowledge in the form of productions.

> *How can schemas be incorporated into the distinction between declarative and procedural knowledge?*

DISTINCTION BETWEEN SEMANTIC AND EPISODIC KNOWLEDGE

If one accepts the distinction between procedural and declarative knowledge as persuasive, there are additional assumptions about the representation of information in long-term memory that can be incorporated into the procedural-declarative distinction. One of these is Tulving's (1972, 1983, 1984) suggestion that propositional declarative knowledge in long-term memory can be divided into distinct episodic and semantic systems. One means of representing this classification of long-term memory systems is shown in Figure 7–5.

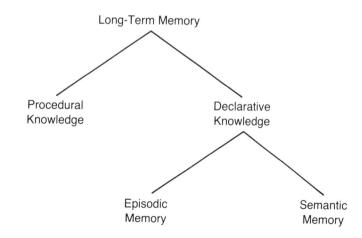

FIGURE 7–5 One possible organization of long-term memory systems.

Tulving's Rationale for the Distinction

Tulving (1972) suggests that it is useful to conceptualize **semantic memory** as "memory necessary for the use of language" (p. 386). As such, semantic memory includes memory for the meaning of words and concepts, grammatical rules governing the order of words in sentences, and so on. Thus semantic memory can be thought of as a storehouse of general world knowledge in which the information is independent of when and how it was learned. On the other hand, Tulving (1983) argues, **episodic memory** should be thought of as memory for "temporally dated episodes or events and temporal-spatial relations among them" (p. 223). That is, episodic memory is autobiographical memory that includes temporal information about past events and episodes.

Episodic memory is memory for personally experienced unique episodes. For example, an item in a to-be-remembered list could be coded in episodic memory in terms of the fact that it was presented visually and not aurally, that it occurred in List 1 rather than List 2, that it was near the beginning of the list, that recall was going to be required, and so on. Tulving argues that most memory experiments tap episodic rather than semantic memory. That is, the subject is being asked to remember that the presented information was part of a specific temporal-contextual event. In Tulving's formulation, the studying of a word in a to-be-remembered list results in the creation of a unique episodic representation of the item. Information about the word from the semantic memory store may be included in the episodic representation, but the episodic representation of the word is separate and distinct from the semantic representation. This interaction of episodic and semantic systems is illustrated in Figure 7–6.

In the case of Alan, presented at the beginning of the chapter, the operation of episodic and semantic memory systems would be initiated by different types of memory tasks. If, upon arriving at home, Alan was asked by his brother whether he picked up a videotape at the local video store, Alan's response would be based on episodic information. Likewise, if Alan received a telephone call from a classmate who asked him if he had yet studied the chapter in his biology textbook on endocrinology, in responding he would tap episodic memory for his recent study activities. On the other hand, if Alan attempted to explain to his younger brother how the type of clothes worn when cycling is related to wind resistance and speed, he would rely primarily on his semantic memory. Similarly, if Alan proceeded to explain to his classmate the distinction in biology between excitatory and inhibitory neurotransmitters, Alan would be tapping his semantic memory store.

Tulving argues that episodic information is more vulnerable to interference than semantic information because episodic memory is organized temporally, whereas semantic memory is organized conceptually. This difference in organization also has implications for retrieval of the information. According to Tulving, retrieval from episodic memory often requires conscious, deliberate effort, whereas retrieval from semantic memory tends to be automatic.

How does Tulving distinguish between semantic and episodic knowledge?

Evidence Supporting the Distinction

Dissociation Effects

In summarizing evidence consistent with this distinction, Tulving (1983, 1984) has focused on **dissociation effects** or evidence that variables affect performance on semantic and

SEMANTIC MEMORY

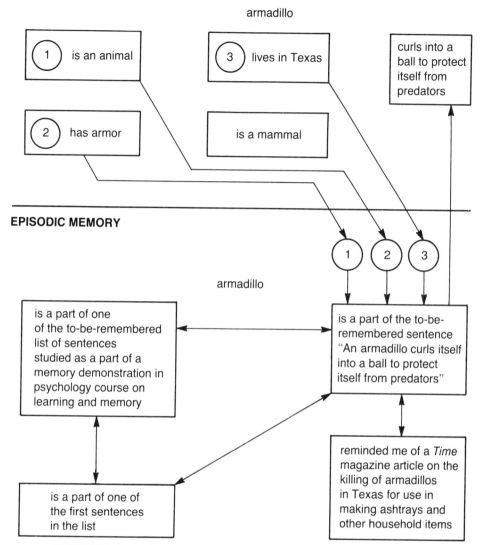

FIGURE 7–6 An illustration of the interaction of semantic and episodic memory in remembering the sentence *An armadillo curls itself into a ball to protect itself from predators.* In this illustration, semantic elements 1, 2, and 3 are assumed to be activated and included in the episodic encoding of the sentence. This illustration also assumes that the studying of the sentence results in the addition of new general information to the semantic representation of *armadillo.*

episodic tasks differently. In one two-phase experiment, Jacoby and Dallas (1981) had subjects perform a levels of processing task in the first phase of the study. For each word presented, subjects made a judgment about either its appearance (*Is the word in capital letters?*), its sound (*Does the word rhyme with DIME?*), or its meaning (*Would the word fit in the sentence "He folded his hands across his _____"?*).

In the second phase of the experiment, subjects performed either a semantic task or an episodic task on the words. The semantic task required subjects to respond as quickly as possible with the name of each word presented very briefly in a tachistoscope (a device for briefly presenting visual stimuli). Some of the words presented in this naming task were the same as the words presented in the first phase of the study. The episodic task consisted of a standard recognition test on the words presented in the first phase of the study. That is, the words presented in the first phase of the study were presented in conjunction with a number of words that had not been presented in the first phase of the study, and the subjects had to judge whether each word on the test had been presented in the first phase of the experiment.

As shown in Table 7–2, Jacoby and Dallas found that the type of processing to which the words were subjected in the first phase of the study had a large effect on performance on the episodic task in phase two but had no effect on performance on the semantic task in phase two. That is, subjects in phase two who performed the recognition test were significantly better at correctly recognizing phase one words about which they had made meaning judgments than they were at correctly recognizing phase one words about which they had made either appearance or sound judgments. However, subjects in phase two who performed the naming task did not differ in the accuracy with which they correctly named phase one words about which they had made either appearance, sound, or meaning judgments. Thus the type of judgments made about words in the first phase of the study affected performance on the following episodic task but not on the following semantic task, supporting the contention that the episodic and semantic systems are distinct.

A study by Kihlstrom (1980) involving subjects with differing degrees of hypnotizability has also been cited by Tulving as supporting the same conclusion. In this study, subjects of either very high, high, or medium to low hypnotizability learned words under hypnosis and were then given posthypnotic suggestions to forget them. In the posthypnotic period, some of the subjects were asked to perform the semantic task of free association in which one responds to presented words with the first word that comes to mind. Some of the words presented as prompts were strong associates of words studied in the first part of the study. Other subjects were asked to perform the episodic task of free recalling the words studied in phase one of the experiment.

As shown in Table 7–3, Kihlstrom found that hypnotizability of the subjects was strongly associated with performance on the episodic task but not on the semantic task. That is, the more hypnotizable the subject, the more likely the subject was to comply with the suggestion to forget and thus the lower the subject's free recall score was. However, the

TABLE 7–2 Response Probabilities from a Study by Jacoby and Dallas (1981) Showing Evidence of Dissociation Effects for Semantic and Episodic Tasks

Task	First-Phase Encoding Condition		
	Appearance	*Sound*	*Meaning*
Semantic identification	.80	.81	.82
Episodic recognition	.50	.63	.86

Source: Tulving, E. (1983). *Elements of episodic memory.* Oxford, England: Oxford University Press. By permission of Oxford University Press.

TABLE 7–3   Response Probabilities from a Study by Kihlstrom (1980) Showing Evidence of Dissociation Effects for Semantic and Episodic Tasks

Task	Hypnotizability of Subjects		
	Very High	*High*	*Medium/Low*
Semantic free association	.61	.50	.53
Episodic free recall	.01	.47	.86

Source: Tulving, E. (1983). *Elements of episodic memory.* Oxford, England: Oxford University Press. By permission of Oxford University Press.

hypnotizability of the subject was not related to the tendency of the subject to generate a word studied in phase one in response to a strong associate on the free association task in phase two.

 What sorts of dissociation effects has Tulving used in arguing for the semantic-episodic distinction?

Performance of Amnesics

Certain phenomena from the study of amnesia are also interpretable in the context of the episodic-semantic distinction (Tulving, 1983, 1984; Tulving, Schacter, McLachlan, & Moscovitch, 1988; Lewis, 1986). In a study by Warrington and Weiskrantz (1974), the performance of amnesic and control subjects was compared on a standard episodic recognition test and a semantic word-fragment completion task. In the word-fragment completion task, the subject is given a stem such as ST __ __ __ and is asked to supply the missing letters so as to make a word. The researchers found that control subjects performed significantly better than amnesics on the episodic recognition task, but the amnesics and controls did not differ significantly on the semantic word-fragment completion task. Such evidence suggests that the primary deficit of some amnesics may be limited to the episodic memory system.

 How can the performance of amnesics be explained in terms of the episodic-semantic memory distinction?

Criticisms of the Distinction

In 1984, Tulving published in the journal *Behavioral and Brain Sciences* a summary of his 1983 book, *Elements of Episodic Memory,* in which he had described in elaborated fashion his conceptualization of the episodic-semantic distinction. As is the custom with that journal, commentary on the summary was invited from other theorists and researchers. In the commentaries, one of the most common objections was that neither reasoned argument and conjecture nor available empirical evidence support the assumption that propositional declarative knowledge is organized in long-term memory into two separate and discrete systems.

Objections to the Conceptual Basis for the Distinction

A number of memory theorists (e.g., Hintzman, 1984; Kihlstrom, 1984; Klatzky, 1984; Lachman & Naus, 1984; McKoon, Ratcliff, & Dell, 1986; Roediger, 1984a) have argued

---

that the long-term declarative knowledge system is most parsimoniously described as a single system of propositions, some of which represent semantic knowledge and some of which represent episodic knowledge about personal experiences.

For example, Hintzman (1984) contends that the primary difference between the episodic and semantic systems as described by Tulving is that "episodic memory represents temporally and spatially localized events, while semantic memory represents the abstract or generic information commonly called concepts" (p. 241). However, Hintzman argues that semantic memory can be generated from episodic memory traces, thus making the assumption of the existence of separate episodic and semantic systems unnecessary. Specifically, he suggests that in responding to a semantic-memory question such as *What is an elephant?* various episodic memory traces involving *elephant* would be activated, and all would contain specific temporal and spatial information concerning a specific episode involving *elephant*. However, he postulates a model in which all such temporal and spatial information that is not common to all of the activated traces would be canceled out, leaving abstract conceptual information common to all of the activated traces as the basis for answering the question.

Furthermore, McKoon, Ratcliff, and Dell (1986) argue that the distinction between episodic and semantic knowledge based on temporal versus conceptual coding is ultimately untestable because episodic memories are, by definition, temporal. In addition, McKoon and colleagues contend, the distinction will be impossible to assess as long as it is unclear what sort of semantic information is included in the episodic trace of an event. They also argue that Tulving's suggestion that episodic memories are more subject to forgetting is difficult to test because of the difficulty in ensuring that "episodic and semantic memories are equated on dimensions such as degree of learning, difficulty of material, and so on" (p. 297). They also cite evidence from amnesic patients suggesting similar rates of forgetting for newly learned episodic and semantic information (e.g., Zola-Morgan, Cohen, & Squire, 1983; Cohen, 1984).

> *What are the major arguments used by critics in advocating that long-term memory be viewed as a single, unitary store rather than as separate semantic and episodic systems?*

Alternative Interpretations of Dissociation Effects

A number of the critics of the episodic-semantic distinction have also argued that the dissociation effects emphasized by Tulving are not convincing evidence for the existence of separate systems. Hintzman (1984) notes that evidence that one independent variable affects two tasks differently means only that the two tasks involve at least one different underlying process but that such an assumption does not justify the claim of two different memory systems. Similarly, Kihlstrom (1984), Klatzky (1984), Roediger (1984a), and Wolters (1984) argue that one can explain why certain variables affect semantic and episodic tasks differently simply by assuming that episodic and semantic memories differ in the type of information contained in the memory trace.

No assumption of separate memory systems is required to explain the dissociation effects. For example, take the Jacoby and Dallas (1981) experiment cited by Tulving and discussed above in which it was found that the level at which the words were processed in the first part of the study affected performance on the following episodic recognition task but did not affect performance on the following semantic identification task. Kihlstrom,

Klatzky, Roediger, and Wolters argue that this dissociation can be explained by assuming that the type of judgment made about each word in the first part of the experiment affected recognition-relevant episodic information but did not affect naming-relevant semantic information included in the memory representation. That is, whether one judges if the word *acrobat* is written in capital letters or not or would fit in the sentence *He undressed the* _____ may affect the episodic contextual information included in the memory representation of *acrobat,* and such information may in turn affect one's ability to recognize subsequently that *acrobat* was one of the words processed in the first part of the study. However, regardless of whether one makes the capital letter judgment or the sentence judgment, the memory representation of *acrobat* is likely to contain the semantic information necessary for naming the word. Thus semantic identification would not be affected by the type of processing to which the word was subjected in the first part of the study.

Alternative Interpretation of Amnesics' Performance

Baddeley (1984) also challenges Tulving's interpretation of amnesics' performance in terms of the episodic-semantic distinction. The Warrington and Weiskrantz (1974) findings that amnesics performed significantly more poorly than normals on an episodic recognition test but just as well as normals on a word-fragment completion task is better interpreted, Baddeley argues, in terms of the distinction between declarative and procedural knowledge. Specifically, Baddeley argues that the word-fragment completion task should not be conceptualized as a semantic memory task. Rather, the word completion task is better described as a test of procedural knowledge involved in retrieving items from the lexicon, or mental dictionary.

Thus the Warrington and Weiskrantz results are better interpreted, Baddeley claims, in terms of amnesics being impaired in their ability to encode new declarative knowledge while remaining unimpaired in the performance of tasks tapping primarily procedural knowledge, consistent with other evidence cited earlier in this chapter in the discussion of the procedural-declarative distinction. Baddeley's description of additional evidence in support of this position will be considered later in the discussion of amnesia in Chapter 11.

 How are critics' interpretations of dissociation effects different from Tulving's interpretation?

Status of the Debate

Despite these criticisms of Tulving's arguments for distinct episodic and semantic long-term memory systems, many of the critics admit that the distinction does have value in guiding and furthering investigation of how information is represented in a unitary long-term store of declarative knowledge. As Kihlstrom (1984) observes, the distinction provides "a useful means of categorizing the *kinds* [emphasis added] of information stored in memory and supplied by queries to the memory system, and the kinds of retrieval tasks to which the rememberer can be put" (p. 244).

McKoon, Ratcliff, and Dell (1986) suggest that the semantic-episodic distinction must be made more specific if it is to become a useful theoretical framework. They conclude by observing:

> *We do not think that more progress will be made toward an understanding of memory for semantic and episodic information until more theoretical work is done. The*

episodic-semantic distinction is an interesting idea that has had much heuristic value for interpreting and generating data over the past 14 years. Now it needs theoretical development. (p. 304)

In his responses to these criticisms, Tulving (1984, 1985, 1986a, 1986b) has been remarkably muted. In fact, he has accepted a number of the criticisms as valid. In doing so, in 1984 he proposed a modification of his episodic-semantic distinction in which episodic memory is viewed as a "functionally distinct system that grows out of but remains embedded in semantic memory" (p. 259). On this view, episodic memory is seen as a subsystem of semantic memory. Although Tulving contends that conceptualization may make it possible to answer some of the criticisms leveled against the distinction, such a reformulation is likely to be seen by critics as a major retreat. In fact, McKoon and colleagues (1986) have already argued that, in proposing the embeddedness concept, Tulving has moved closer to the single-store position.

The situation has been further complicated by Tulving's (1985) suggestion that semantic memory should, in turn, be viewed as a specialized subsystem within the procedural memory system. Thus, in place of the classification scheme for long-term memory shown in Figure 7–5, Tulving is now proposing a scheme of the type illustrated in Figure 7–7. Furthermore, Tulving (1985; Hayman & Tulving, 1989) has also suggested that an additional memory system, which he has dubbed the **QM system** (for Question Mark or Quasi-Memory system), may exist as a precursor to the episodic memory system. Tulving has specifically proposed the QM system in order to account for priming effects that cannot be easily interpreted in terms of either the distinction between procedural and declarative knowledge or the distinction between semantic and episodic declarative knowledge.

How has Tulving responded to criticisms of the semantic-episodic distinction?

The Principle of Encoding Specificity

Thomson and Tulving's (1970) Study of Retrieval Cue Effectiveness
Tulving's argument for the distinction between episodic and semantic memory systems arose in part out of his demonstration of an episodic memory phenomenon that he and colleagues dubbed encoding specificity. In 1970, Thomson and Tulving reported three experiments in

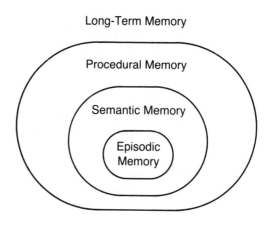

Long-Term Memory

Procedural Memory

Semantic Memory

Episodic Memory

FIGURE 7–7 Tulving's classification of long-term memory systems in which semantic memory is a specialized subsystem within procedural memory and episodic memory is a specialized subsystem within semantic memory.

which they studied the effectiveness of retrieval cues in a situation involving the learning of three lists of words. Each list consisted of 24 cue-target word pairs, such as sky-BLUE and swift-GO. Thus some of the cue words were strongly associated, on the basis of previous experience, with the paired target word, and some were not. The selection of strongly and weakly associated cues was based on responses of other subjects to the cue words on a free association test. Strongly associated cues were those that tended with a high probability to elicit the target word on a free association test, whereas weakly associated cues were those that tended to elicit the target word with only a low probability.

Following each of the first two lists, subjects were asked to recall as many of the target words as they could in response to the provided cue words. However, following the third list, some of the cue words presented on the test had not been presented during study. Of these new cue words, some were strong associates of target words from the list, and others were weak associates of target words. Thus each recall cue on the test of memory for the third list represented one of four encoding-retrieval conditions:

strong/strong → The cue provided was a strong associate of the target word and had been present during the study of the list.

strong/weak → The cue provided was a weak associate of the target word and had not been present during the study of the list; instead, at study, the target word had been paired with a strongly associated cue.

weak/weak → The cue provided was a weak associate of the target word and had been present during the study of the list.

weak/strong → The cue provided was a strong associate of the target word and had not been present during the study of the list; instead, at study, the target word had been paired with a weakly associated cue.

Thomson and Tulving were particularly interested in whether strongly associated cues would be the best retrieval prompts regardless of whether or not they had been present at the time of study. Table 7–4 shows the results from their experiment.

Clearly, the strongly associated cue was not universally a better retrieval prompt. Weakly associated cues that were present at the time of encoding were better retrieval prompts than were strongly associated cues that were not present at the time of encoding. These results led Tulving and associates to propose the original version of the **encoding specificity principle.** That principle stipulated that effective retrieval cues are those that contain information that was included in the original encoding of the item or event. That is, the relationship between the memory trace and the retrieval cue is emphasized. Remember-

TABLE 7–4 Percentage of Items Recalled in the Thomson and Tulving (1970) Study as a Function of Encoding/Retrieval Condition

	Cue Present at Encoding	
Cue Present at Retrieval	*Strong Associate*	*Weak Associate*
Strong associate	83	33
Weak associate	3.5	73

ing is based on a match between information contained in the retrieval cue and information contained in the memory trace. Thus, the effectiveness of a retrieval cue cannot be predicted in the absence of information about the conditions of encoding.

☑ *What were the most important findings of Thomson and Tulving's (1970) investigations of retrieval cue effectiveness?*

Implications of the Encoding Specificity Findings

Such a notion may seem now intuitively obvious, but at the time it was proposed, the principle challenged a number of popularly held assumptions, including what Tulving and associates called the **associative continuity assumption.** This assumption involves the notion that the strength of association between items in memory is a function of the number of times the items have been encoded together. Tulving and associates argued that the concept of strength of association is meaningless to the extent that it is based on the assumption that most items in memory have a unitary representation that is simply updated with each subsequent occurrence of the item.

Instead, Tulving and associates (e.g., Tulving & Thomson, 1971, 1973) argue, each occurrence of an item results in a unique memory representation of the item that may or may not include a lot of information about the item's past associations. The contents of the memory representation of the item will be determined by the conditions under which encoding takes place. Thus it is meaningless to talk about certain items being more memorable than others or certain study activities being more effective than others without considering the conditions under which retrieval will take place.

For example, as was discussed in Chapter 6, semantic processing of to-be-remembered information does not invariably lead to superior retention of the information. If at the time of retrieval, rhyme cues are presented to prompt memory, having processed the information semantically at encoding may produce performance inferior to that exhibited after having processed the information phonemically at encoding because the memory trace of the event will be less rich in phonemic information likely to overlap with that provided in the retrieval cue. The implications of such a view of memory for the traditional distinction between recall and recognition and for other issues associated with memory retrieval will be discussed in Chapter 9.

In his review of research generated by the encoding specificity principle, Tulving (1983, 1984) notes that experiments designed to test the principle must simultaneously manipulate conditions of encoding and retrieval in order to assess the level of performance exhibited when the retrieval environment is and is not compatible with the encoding environment. Since the proposal of the principle, a large number of such studies have been conducted, and a large percentage of these have found the expected crossover interaction in which performance is a joint function of encoding and retrieval conditions.

A particular type of encoding condition is effective only to the extent that retrieval conditions prompt the use of information likely to have been encoded. One such encoding-retrieval experiment was that of Morris, Bransford, and Franks (1977), referred to in an earlier paragraph and described in more detail in Chapter 6. When the retrieval task involved a rhyming recognition test, phonemic processing of the words at encoding resulted in superior performance. When the retrieval task involved a standard recognition test, semantic processing of the words at encoding resulted in superior performance.

☑ *How is the encoding specificity principle consistent with the episodic-semantic distinction?*

State-Dependent Memory

Investigations of other more exotic memory phenomena can be also be viewed as examples of encoding/retrieval experiments, and the results can be interpreted in terms of the encoding specificity principle. One of these phenomena is that of **state-dependent memory.** Most generally, this concept refers to findings that information learned in a particular physiological state is best recalled when one is in that same physiological state. Physiological state has been manipulated through the use of drugs, including alcohol, marijuana, amphetamines, barbiturates, and Parkinson's disease medications (e.g., Adams, Castro, & Clark, 1974; Bustamante, Jordán, Vila, González, & Insua, 1970; Goodwin, Powell, Bremer, Hoine, & Stern, 1969; Huber, Shulman, Paulson, & Shuttleworth, 1989; Petersen, 1977; Weingartner, Eich, & Allen, 1976).

In a typical study by Eich, Weingartner, Stillman, and Gillin (1975), half of the subjects studied a list of words after smoking a cigarette containing active marijuana, and half of the subjects studied the list after smoking a cigarette that contained placebo material. Then, prior to testing, half of the subjects in each of these two encoding conditions smoked a marijuana cigarette and half smoked a placebo cigarette. When the subjects were asked to free recall the words studied, the researchers found a significant interaction of encoding and retrieval condition. Those subjects in the marijuana-marijuana condition recalled significantly more words than those subjects in the marijuana-placebo condition, whereas those subjects in the placebo-placebo condition recalled more words than those subjects in the placebo-marijuana condition, although the difference was not significant.

Eich (1980) argues that such effects are directly interpretable in terms of the encoding specificity principle. If one assumes that the memory representation of an item or an event includes information about the pharmacological state of the person at the time of encoding, then the individual's pharmacological state at the time of retrieval would represent an additional source of cues. When the pharmacological cues at retrieval match those that were present at encoding, successful retrieval is enhanced.

Mood Effects.   Mood effects on memory are also interpretable as an instance of state-dependent learning. Bower (1981), for example, has manipulated the mood of subjects through the use of hypnosis. Subjects encouraged to adopt a sad mood prior to studying a list of words showed better recall of the words when they were also sad at retrieval than when they were happy at retrieval. Conversely, subjects encouraged to adopt a happy mood prior to encoding the words showed better recall of the words when they were also happy at retrieval than when they were sad at retrieval. Just as one can assume that information about a person's drug state can be included in the memory representation of an item or event, one can assume that information about a person's mood can be included in the memory representation. Thus a mood state at retrieval that matches that present at encoding will facilitate retrieval by providing additional cues for locating the target memory trace.

How can drug and mood effects on memory be viewed as examples of state-dependent memory?

Generality of the Effect.   It is important to note, however, that findings of state-dependent learning are not universal. Eich (1977, 1980) has pointed out in two large-scale surveys of research on the topic that at least half of the published studies of this issue have not found evidence of state-dependent learning. Eich's (1980) analysis of these conflicting findings have led him to propose that the state-dependent effect is only likely to be found when memory for the target information is tested in the absence of clearly identifiable and observable cues.

For example, in the Eich and colleagues' (1975) study described above, the state-dependent effect was not found when recall of the words was cued with the names of the categories to which the words in the list belonged. Likewise, in a later study also involving marijuana, Eich and Birnbaum (1982) found that matching pharmacological state at encoding and retrieval facilitated the uncued recall of category names from a to-be-remembered list containing both category names and exemplars of the categories but had no effect on the recall of category members in response to the category names. Such findings suggest that physiological cues may be relatively weak in their effects on memory compared to linguistic or conceptual information likely to be included in the memory trace of target information.

In a review of research on mood-dependent memory, Ucros (1989) also found a number of studies in which state-dependent effects were not obtained. Her analysis of the studies suggested that variables such as subjects' commitment to the experiment and the complexity of the experimental environment may influence the emergence of the state-dependent effect.

▨ *What evidence suggests that physiological cues involved in state-dependent learning may be relatively weak in their effects on memory?*

Environmental Reinstatement Effect

Also interpretable within the encoding specificity framework is the **environmental reinstatement effect.** This phenomenon refers to the finding that information learned in a particular physical environment is best remembered in that same physical environment. With regard to the example of Alan presented at the beginning of the chapter, the environmental reinstatement effect suggests that Alan's performance on his upcoming biology exam would be enhanced by his studying for the exam in the same environment in which he is to take the exam.

In an experimental test of the environmental reinstatement effect, Godden and Baddeley (1975) had scuba divers learn lists of words either under water or out of the water. Then, half of each group were asked to recall the words in the same environment in which they had studied, and half were asked to recall the words in the other environment. A significant interaction was found. Those who studied the words under water recalled significantly more words when tested under water, whereas those who studied words out of the water recalled significantly more when tested out of the water. Consistent with the encoding specificity principle, these results suggest that environmental stimuli present at the time of study can become a part of the memory trace for the material and thus acquire the power to cue retrieval of the information from memory.

▨ *How can the environmental reinstatement effect be viewed as an example of encoding specificity?*

Smith's Demonstrations of the Environmental Reinstatement Effect. In a series of experiments, Smith and colleagues (Smith, 1979, 1982, 1984, 1985, 1986; Smith, Glenberg, & Bjork, 1978) reported evidence of an environmental reinstatement effect in situations involving much less dramatic manipulations of environment. In these experiments, Smith used different rooms in university buildings as his experimental contexts. In general, Smith has found that memory for word lists is better when subjects are tested in the same room in which they studied the words.

In his experiments, Smith attempted to demonstrate that these findings are in fact a function of a match/mismatch of study and test environments and are not due to other factors. For example, to control for the effect of a general disruption between study and test, subjects in both the same- and different-context conditions have been required to move from the study environment to a waiting room before being taken to the room in which they are asked to recall the information. In addition, to control for the possibility that subjects in the different-context condition may do more poorly simply because they are unfamiliar with the test environment, Smith, in many of his experiments, familiarized subjects with the test environment prior to the test phase of the study by having them make drawings of the room.

▣ *What controls did Smith employ in his demonstrations of the environmental reinstatement effect?*

Lack of Evidence for the Environmental Reinstatement Effect.

However, the environmental reinstatement effect no longer appears to be as reliable as Smith's program of research would appear to suggest. Eich (1985) found no environmental reinstatement effect for subjects asked to generate isolated images of the to-be-remembered words, but an environmental reinstatement effect was evidenced by subjects asked to create images of the to-be-remembered words that linked each word with some physical feature of the room context. The failure to find the environmental reinstatement effect for the isolated imagery condition led Eich to suggest that the environmental reinstatement effect may be much rarer than Smith's research would indicate. Furthermore, in a series of eight experiments, one of which represented an attempt to replicate one of Smith's (1979) original experiments, Fernandez and Glenberg (1985) failed to find a consistent environmental reinstatement effect. Finally, Wilhite (1991) has found in two experiments that subjects who studied and were tested in different rooms showed significantly better memory than subjects who were tested in the same room in which they studied.

Wilhite's results are noteworthy because he employed many of the same controls used by Smith in his research and because he used prose materials as well as word lists as the to-be-remembered materials. In interpreting his results, Wilhite suggests that reinstating environmental context at the time of test may not invariably facilitate memory performance because environmental cues may be subject to overloading just as verbal cues are.

For example, it has been found that verbal cues become less and less effective as they become associated with increasing numbers of to-be-remembered items (Eich, 1985; Watkins & Watkins, 1975). Thus, Wilhite argues, under some conditions environmental cues may lose their effectiveness by becoming associated with multiple target items. As a result, the performance of same-context subjects may suffer, relative to the performance of different-context subjects, because overloaded environmental cues may interfere with alternative retrieval strategies involving cues such as the items' position in the list.

Saufley, Otaka, and Bavaresco (1985) sought evidence of the environmental reinstatement effect in a study designed to determine whether changing the classroom environment at the time of an examination alters contextual associations sufficiently to lower students' examination performance significantly. Across the seven courses, a total of 21 comparisons were made between the examination performance of those students tested in the usual lecture room and the examination performance of those students tested in a different classroom.

None of the comparisons revealed a significant difference in the performance of the same- and different-context groups, and there was no evidence of a trend favoring the same-context group. Saufley and colleagues argue that the total lack of an environmental reinstatement effect in this study was almost certainly, at least in part, a function of the degree to which learning in an academic course is decontextualized by the use of a variety of materials, such as lecture notes and textbooks, that permit study and learning outside the lecture hall.

☑ *What sorts of findings challenge the reliability of the environmental reinstatement effect?*

Further Evidence for the Environmental Reinstatement Effect.   In an investigation of how the type of encoding performed on the to-be-remembered information might influence the environmental reinstatement effect, McDaniel, Anderson, Einstein, and O'Halloran (1989) performed five experiments involving 38 separate tests of the environmental context effect. Of the 38 comparisons, only 8 showed a statistically significant environmental reinstatement effect. Thus the results of this study are, in general, consistent with the view that environmental context effects are far from overwhelming, perhaps because people's experiences have taught them that the room in which information is encoded is not a reliable cue for its recall (Wickens, 1987).

However, based on their analysis of the limited number of cases in which the reinstatement effect was found, McDaniel and colleagues argue that reliance on environmental context as a source of retrieval cues, and hence the emergence of the environmental reinstatement effect, is most likely in situations in which other potentially more useful retrieval cues are not available or are not employed. For example, they found that memory for common sentences was more affected by reinstating environmental context than was memory for bizarre sentences. McDaniel and colleagues suggest that this finding emerged because a variety of nonenvironmental cues for retrieving the bizarre sentences may be generated as a result of the more elaborate or distinctive encoding afforded the bizarre sentences (Einstein & McDaniel, 1987; Hirshman, Whelly, & Palij, 1989). This interpretation by McDaniel and colleagues is consistent with the failure to find an environmental reinstatement effect in the naturalistic classroom study by Saufley and colleagues (1985) described above. The test questions used in the college courses included in that study may have provided sufficient retrieval cues so as to make contextual associations involving the room environment relatively unimportant.

The conflicting pattern of results regarding the environmental reinstatement effect illustrates one of the weaknesses of the encoding specificity principle. It is far from obvious how one can, with any degree of certainty, predict in advance what sorts of information will be included in the memory representation of the event and will, therefore, function as effective retrieval prompts. In this regard, the research by McDaniels and colleagues represents a promising direction for future investigation of the environmental reinstatement effect. Rather than focusing on whether the environmental reinstatement effect is reliable, researchers need to try to establish the boundary conditions for the effect by investigating the conditions under which information about the physical environment tends to be included in the memory representation of items and tends to prompt memory effectively.

☑ *Under what general conditions is the environmental reinstatement effect most likely to emerge, according to McDaniel, Anderson, Einstein, and O'Halloran (1989)?*

CONCLUDING REMARKS: The Maltese Cross Model Revisited

It would be useful at this point to consider how the various issues and distinctions presented in this chapter can be related to Broadbent's Maltese cross model of memory presented in Chapter 6. The distinction between declarative and procedural knowledge is generally consistent with Broadbent's distinction between the long-term store and the processing system. Broadbent proposed the distinction between the long-term associative store and the processing system in part in order to make clear the distinction between the representation of information and the processing of information within the memory system. This same representation-processing distinction underlies Anderson's description of declarative and procedural knowledge.

Although Broadbent has not dealt with procedural knowledge in the formalized way that Anderson has, his description of the processing system is compatible with Anderson's production-based characterization of procedural knowledge. That is, it would certainly appear possible to represent the duties assigned to the processing system in the Maltese cross model as a system of productions. For example, Broadbent argues that the processing system is responsible for the transfer of information from one memory store to another and that transfer operations involve transforming the information into a form that can be handled by the receiving store. Such operations could be represented as condition-action rules of the type that constitute the production systems in Anderson's description of procedural knowledge.

The distinction between episodic and semantic memory can also potentially be integrated into the Maltese cross model's description of the long-term associative store and the processing system. For example, it would certainly be possible to argue that the long-term associative store is composed of distinct episodic and semantic components, although Broadbent has not yet done so. The important point to note here is that the Maltese cross model provides a potentially useful general framework within which a number of concepts and distinctions regarding long-term memory can be incorporated. What remains to be determined is which of the concepts and distinctions presented in this chapter will prove to be sufficiently useful to warrant inclusion in such a general model of long-term memory.

The Representation
of Information
in Long-Term Memory (Part II)

APPLICATION: More Studying and Daydreaming

Following dinner, Alan returns to his preparation for the upcoming unit exam in his biology course. As Alan reviews the various classes of vertebrates, his consideration of the distinguishing features of the bird class leads him quite involuntarily to begin mentally listing a number of specific examples of birds. Before long, Alan is thinking about ostriches, even though information about ostriches is not a part of the to-be-tested material. He is reminded of the fact that they have long thin legs, they are tall, and they can't fly. He even experiences a mental picture of an ostrich running, flapping its wings, and failing to become airborne. Thinking about long thin legs, in turn, leads Alan to begin thinking about the human female anatomy. When he finally realizes that his mind has wandered, he shifts his focus of study to the anatomy of the human heart, another topic to be covered on the test.

In this case, Alan quite deliberately creates a vivid mental picture of the heart and its surrounding structures in order to promote memory for the information. Later, when Alan reviews the heart again just before going to bed, he first generates a mental picture of the heart as a means of prompting his listing of the various to-be-remembered structures.

These mental experiences of Alan involve that component of long-term memory identified in the preceding chapter as semantic memory. They also involve the use of mental images, which a number of memory theorists believe to be another important component of long-term memory. In this chapter, we shall examine how learning and memory psychologists have attempted to describe the representation of semantic knowledge in long-term store and the role that images play in long-term memory representations.

MODELS OF SEMANTIC MEMORY

Despite the continuing debate over whether semantic and episodic knowledge should be conceptualized as separate and distinct systems within the long-term store that was described in the preceding chapter, a number of formal models of semantic memory have been proposed. These models have in common the aim of describing how decontextualized conceptual knowledge might be represented in long-term store.

Hierarchical Network Model

Collins and Quillian (1969, 1972) proposed one of the first formal models of semantic memory, based in part on the results of experiments using the *speeded verification task*. In this task, sentences tapping subjects' general knowledge (e.g., *A canary is a bird*) are presented, and the amount of time it takes subjects to respond "true" or "false" is measured. The time taken to respond to the sentences is assumed to reflect the organization or structuring of information in memory, because the organization of information will influence how quickly the relationship between concepts can be located in memory and evaluated.

In order to explain the pattern of reaction times found, Collins and Quillian proposed that concepts are arranged hierarchically and interconnected by labeled associations, as illustrated in Figure 8–1. They proposed three types of associations or links: *isa*, representing a subset relation; *has*, representing an attribute relation; and *can*, representing another

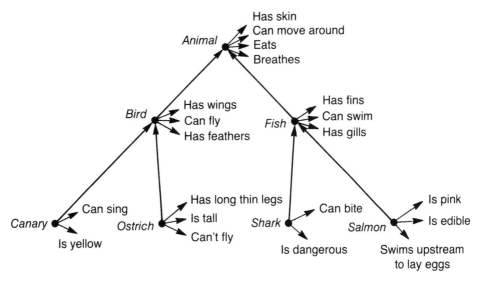

FIGURE 8–1 An example of the hierarchical organization of concepts in semantic memory proposed by Collins and Quillian (1969) in their hierarchical network model of semantic memory.

Source: Collins, A. M., & Quillian, M. R. (1969). Retrieval time from semantic memory. *Journal of Verbal Learning and Verbal Behavior, 8,* 241. Reprinted with permission.

type of attribute relation. Alan's daydreaming about ostriches can be explained within the context of the Collins and Quillian model by assuming that thinking about the concept *birds* led to the activation of the concept *ostrich* by means of an *isa* link. In turn, activating *ostrich* led to the consideration of attributes such as *has long thin legs* by means of the *has* attribute relation.

In proposing a hierarchical arrangement of concepts, Collins and Quillian incorporated into their model what is known as the **cognitive economy assumption.** This assumption stipulates that each property is stored only at the highest possible level in the hierarchy. For example, in Figure 8–1, the properties *has skin* and *eats* are represented in the hierarchy only at the level of *animal* and not at the lower levels of *bird, fish,* or *shark.* Thus responding to "true" statements in the speeded verification task is often an inferential process in that a number of associative pathways may have to be traversed in finding an associative link between the concepts.

The search process is based on the assumption that it takes a constant amount of time to move from one level to another in the hierarchy and that the verification time is therefore based on the number of associative pathways that have to be traversed in finding the link between concepts. These assumptions were supported by early experiments of Collins and Quillian showing, for example, that it took subjects longer to verify *A canary has skin* than *A canary is yellow,* and it took subjects longer to verify *A canary is an animal* than *A canary is a bird.*

▨ *What are the most important distinguishing features of the hierarchical network model of semantic memory?*

Problems with the Hierarchical Network Model

Familiarity/Relatedness Effects.   Other evidence, reported by Rips, Shoben, and Smith (1973), quickly challenged some of the assumptions of the hierarchical network model. They found, for example, that subjects are faster in verifying *A bear is an animal* than in verifying *A bear is a mammal,* despite the fact that *bear* and *mammal* are closer in the hierarchy than are *bear* and *animal.* That is, subjects are faster in responding to the more familiar concept *animal* than to the less familiar concept *mammal.* Apparently, subjects perceive *bear* and *animal* to be more closely related than *bear* and *mammal.*

Typicality Effects.   Subjects also verify a dominant or salient member of a category consistently more rapidly than they do a less salient item (Wilkins, 1971). For example, *A robin is a bird* is verified faster than *A chicken is a bird.* These findings are inconsistent with the model in that the model predicts equal verification times because the instances of a category are equidistant from the main category node or memory location (see Figure 8–1).

Associative Frequency Effects.   Similarly, Conrad (1972) has argued that the strength of preexisting associative links between items being processed in a verification task is a powerful determinant of reaction time. Take, for example, the noun-property pairs, *salmon is edible* and *salmon can move around.* In the Collins and Quillian hierarchy, *is edible* is closer to *salmon* than is *can move around.* However, research suggests that *is edible* is no more strongly associated with *salmon* than is *can move around.*

Conrad (1972) obtained what are called **production frequency measures** by asking subjects to list all of the properties associated with a concept such as *salmon* and by counting the number of subjects who produced each property (hence, the term *production frequency*). When other subjects were asked to verify the two statements, verification times did not differ. Thus Conrad (1972) has argued that the strength of the noun-property association would appear to be more important than the hierarchical distance between the concepts in determining verification times. The fact that *shark eats* is verified as rapidly as *animal eats* can be explained on the same basis. The typicality and familiarity/relatedness effects cited above can also be viewed as associative frequency effects, and all of these findings argue against the cognitive economy assumption of the hierarchical network model.

▨   *Why are findings of familiarity/relatedness effects, typicality effects, and associative frequency effects inconsistent with the hierarchical network model?*

Acquisition of General Properties.   Collins and Loftus (1975) have also argued that the manner in which the general properties of a category are acquired argues against the strong form of cognitive economy incorporated in the model. They note that the knowledge of general properties is based on specific instances involving subordinate items. Thus, during acquisition, specific properties are likely to be multiply represented. Even as properties common to most instances of a category are generalized to the category as a whole, they may, in some instances (as suggested by evidence cited above), also remain strongly associated with specific instances of the category.

Responding to False Sentences.   Evidence that certain false statements are rejected more slowly than others is also a problem for the model. For example, *A St. Bernard is a cat* is rejected relatively slowly despite the absence of hierarchical associative pathways between the units. Thus the slowness of response would appear to be a function of the semantic relatedness of the concepts. The model must be increased in complexity to cope with such negative instances.

> ✐ *How is the hierarchical network model deficient in explaining the acquisition of general properties and the response to false sentences?*

Spreading Activation Model

In order to deal with the problems associated with the hierarchical network model, Collins and Loftus (1975) proposed a revision of the model. The revised model retained the associative network but rejected the strict hierarchical structure of the original model. An illustration of the revised model's representation of semantic knowledge is shown in Figure 8–2.

Organization of Concepts

The strict hierarchical structure of the original Collins and Quillian model was replaced by a structure based on the concept of **semantic distance** (or **semantic relatedness**) in order to account for familiarity/relatedness effects. In this model, lengths of associative links are used to represent the strength of the relationship between concepts, with strength determi-

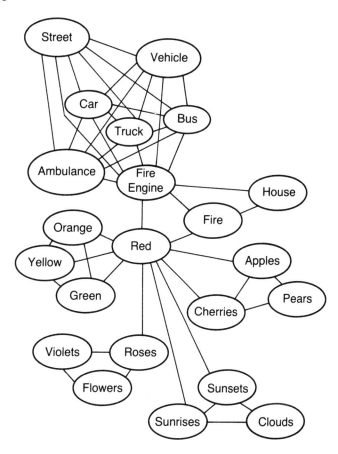

FIGURE 8–2 An example of the interrelationship of concepts in semantic memory as represented in Collins and Loftus's (1975) spreading activation model of semantic memory. In this representation, the length of the associative links between the concepts represents the strength of the relationship.

Source: Collins, A. M., & Loftus, E. F. (1975). A spreading-activation theory of semantic processing. *Psychological Review, 82,* 412. Copyright 1975 by the American Psychological Association. Reprinted by permission.

nations based on production frequency norms. Other methods for determining relatedness include rating word pairs for relatedness and rating typicality of category instances. On this model, in representing the semantic distance between *bird* and *ostrich* and between *bird* and *robin* in Alan's semantic memory store, the associative link between *bird* and *ostrich* would probably be longer.

The model's rejection of a strict hierarchical arrangement of concepts also involved a rejection of the cognitive economy assumption. The Collins and Loftus model allows for much more prestored knowledge such that less inferencing based on searches of the network is required. As an example of prestored knowledge, the model also includes the additional associative link of *isnota*. Such a link, it is argued, is needed to account for fast false responses to items such as *A bat is a bird*. The speed of the response suggests that the response is not based on the search of the network, but instead reflects direct accessing of the unit *A bat is* not *a bird*.

☑ *How does the spreading activation model differ from the hierarchical network model in its description of how information is organized in semantic memory?*

Retrieval Processes in the Spreading Activation Model

This spreading activation model of Collins and Loftus assumes a more complicated retrieval process than does the hierarchical network model. Activation of a given concept is assumed to spread to related concepts. Thus the activation of *bird* in Alan's semantic memory store spreads to related concepts such as *ostrich,* which in turn spreads to related concepts such as *has thin long legs,* which in turn spreads to *human female anatomy.* This last example of spread of activation within Alan's memory can be accounted for, in part, because the spreading activation model does not assume a strict hierarchical arrangement of concepts.

This spread of activation notion replaces the original model's simple retrieval process of moving from one node to another. As the activation spreads, its strength decreases. Thus concepts farther from the originally activated node are less likely to be activated than are closer concepts. The spread of activation is also dependent on the strength of initial activation. Greater initial activation of a concept results in greater spread of activation from that concept. The model also assumes that links between concepts differ in accessibility or strength, based, for example, on their frequency of use, and that the strength of a link determines the speed with which activation spreads.

These assumptions thus provide a basis for explaining typicality effects. *A robin is a bird* is verified faster than *A chicken is a bird* because the more frequent accessing of the *robin-bird* associative link has made that link stronger, more accessible, and more quickly traversed at the time of retrieval. In a verification situation, the system is monitoring for the intersection of activation spreading from the concepts contained in the statement, because an intersection is evidence that the activated concepts are related in some way. If an intersection of activation is detected, decision processes evaluate the total strength of the activation involved in the intersection. If the total activation exceeds a criterion or threshold value, the type of intersection found is evaluated and a response is executed.

Collins and Loftus (1975) also incorporated into the model a provision for mutually exclusive links, in accordance with suggestions by Holyoak and Glass (1975). (See Glass & Holyoak [1975] for a description of their related marker-search model of semantic memory.) Such an assumption helps explain why subjects are so fast at rejecting as false statements such as *A mallard is an eagle.* Presumably *mallard* and *eagle* share the superordinate *bird*. Thus the model assumes that when activation spreads from *mallard* and *eagle* to *bird,* the activation of links that are mutually exclusive provides strong evidence in favor of responding "false."

The model also incorporates a counterexample strategy, again based on the work of Holyoak and Glass (1975), as a source of negative evidence in evaluating statements. Subjects' very fast rejection of statements such as *All birds are canaries* can be explained by assuming that, once the superordinate relationship between *canaries* and *birds* is confirmed, an attempt is made to generate another subordinate of *birds* that is mutually exclusive from *canaries.*

✏ *How does the spreading activation model explain retrieval from semantic memory?*

Priming and Semantic Context Effects

The model provides an explanation for semantic priming effects in lexical decision tasks. A **lexical decision task** can involve a subject's deciding whether a group of letters is a word. For example, a subject might see in succession the following letter groups:

nwat
red
truck
taleb

The subject's task would be to respond to each letter group as quickly as possible with "yes" or "no," indicating that the letter group is or is not a word. If the speed with which a subject responds "yes" to *truck* in the above sequence is compared to the speed with which a subject responds "yes" to *truck* in the following sequence, a clear difference is usually found:

nwat
car
truck
taleb

The response to *truck* in the second sequence is usually faster (e.g., see Huttenlocher & Kubieck, 1983; Meyer & Schvaneveldt, 1971; Neely, 1977).

This effect whereby the processing of one word facilitates the processing of another word related to it in meaning is an example of **semantic priming.** The notion of a spread of activation to related concepts is consistent with this finding. The spread of activation from *car* to *truck* would mean that *truck* would already be somewhat "turned on." Thus when the word *truck* itself is presented, its representation in memory already stands out somewhat. Thus, the memory representation of *truck* will be accessed and matched against the incoming letter pattern faster than if *car* had not been presented previously.

Furthermore, the notion of semantic relatedness or semantic distance can account for the fact that preceding *truck* with *car* produces a larger priming effect than does preceding *truck* with *vehicle*. As represented in Figure 8–2, the length of the association between *truck* and *car* is shorter than the length of the association between *truck* and *vehicle,* meaning that there will be a greater transfer of activation between *car* and *truck.*

This basic notion of spread of activation can also help account for semantic context effects in general. *As Mary accelerated onto the freeway, the car in front of her suddenly stopped. Reflexively, Mary stepped on the _____. In the process of reading these sentences, the individual might activate her or his schema for driving, which would result in a spread of activation to concepts, such as brake,* contained within that schema. Thus the reader might only have to analyze superficially the sensory input associated with the next word in the sentence in order to confirm the expectation that *brake* did occur (Lindsay & Norman, 1977; Rumelhart & Siple, 1974).

✏️ *How can the spreading activation model account for priming and semantic context effects?*

Assessment of the Model

As was indicated in the preceding description, the model's flexible assumptions regarding both the representation and processing of information enable it to account for many of the phenomena that could not be explained easily by the original hierarchical network model. However, the model's flexibility is a weakness as well as a strength. Kintsch (1980) has essentially argued that the model is so general as to make it impossible to derive critical predictions that can be tested. In the absence of such critical tests, the adequacy of the model is difficult to assess.

Likewise, Chang (1986) has noted that while the model can explain phenomena such as typicality effects and the slowness of responding to false statements containing related concepts it does not strongly predict such effects. In addition, Johnson-Laird, Herrmann, and Chaffin (1984) have criticized the spreading activation model, as well as other models of semantic memory, for its failure to account for various important components of semantic processing. For example, the model, they claim, does not explicitly account for relationships such as synonymy and antonymy. However, Chang (1986) does emphasize the potential utility of this type of general explanatory approach in observing that the model may serve as an overall framework within which more specific models of semantic representation and processing may be incorporated.

✏️ *What are the major strengths and weaknesses of the spreading activation model?*

ACT Theory

In considering the Adaptive Control of Thought (ACT) representation of semantic memory, it must be remembered that Anderson has consistently rejected the assumption of distinct episodic and semantic long-term stores (Anderson & Bower, 1973; Anderson, 1983; Anderson, 1990). Therefore, the representation of semantic information described in the following section would also apply, according to ACT, to episodic information. As was noted in the preceding chapter in the discussion of ACT's distinction between procedural and declarative knowledge, ACT assumes that declarative knowledge is represented in the form of a network of propositions, as illustrated in Figure 7–1 for episodic declarative information. As is shown in Figure 8–3, this same sort of propositional network can be used to represent semantic information.

Critical to ACT's description of semantic memory, as it is to Collins and Loftus's model, is the concept of spread of activation. Once a unit in the propositional network is activated, the activation will spread along associative pathways to associated concepts. The concepts most affected by this spread will be those most closely linked with the original site

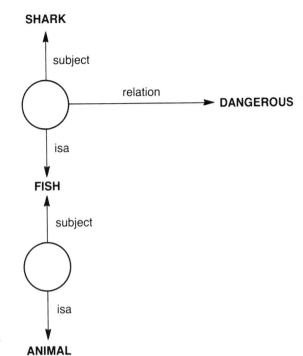

SHARK

subject

relation → **DANGEROUS**

isa

FISH

subject

isa

FIGURE 8–3 Semantic knowledge represented as a network of propositions.

ANIMAL

of activation. Thus, in these general terms, ACT's emphasis on spread of activation is almost identical to Collins and Loftus's spreading activation model.

According to ACT, how are declarative episodic and semantic information represented in long-term memory?

Spread of Activation and the Execution of Productions

ACT goes beyond the spreading activation model in attempting to describe more precisely what determines the closeness of links between concepts within the network and thus what determines the spread of activation. In his update of ACT, Anderson (1983) argues that each concept node (where node refers to a memory location) has an associated strength based primarily on its frequency of use.

ACT also assumes that the spread of activation affects the execution of productions. Recall that productions are condition-action pairs. The action is performed only when certain conditions, as represented in declarative memory, are met. A pattern matcher, consisting of a sequence of pattern tests, monitors for a match between activated nodes in declarative memory and the conditions of the production. ACT stipulates that the degree of activation of a particular pattern-matcher node is a function of the strength of that node (based on its frequency of application), the level of activation of the declarative memory structures being matched, and the degree of match between the memory structures and the conditions embodied in the pattern matcher.

As activation spreads through the declarative memory network, its spread affects the application of productions linked to particular declarative memory structures. For example, Table 8–1 shows productions that Anderson (1983) has incorporated into ACT to help explain the effects of semantic priming on lexical decision tasks. In the case of automatic lexical decisions (i.e., where subjects are judging whether sequences of letters are words but are not consciously anticipating the occurrence of a particular word), if the word to be judged (say, for example, *doctor*) has been preceded by a related word (e.g., *nurse*), the spread of activation in the declarative memory network from *nurse* to related items will speed the rate at which productions 2 and 3 can be applied. If, on the other hand, *doctor* is preceded by an unrelated word, such as *rocket,* the execution of productions 2 and 3 will be unaffected.

▶ *What major factor determines the spread of activation through ACT's propositional network, and how does the spread of activation affect the execution of productions?*

Explanation of Semantic Verification Results

Anderson has also used the notions of spread of activation and execution of productions to account for semantic verification results of the type described in the presentation of the hierarchical network model and the Collins and Loftus spreading activation model. Anderson (1983) argues that the recognition of a fact associated with a particular concept will take

TABLE 8–1 Example Productions for Performance in the Lexical Decision Task Based on Anderson's ACT System

---

1. **A word-naming production**
   P1   IF the word is spelled F-E-A-T-H-E-R
        THEN assert that the word is similar to FEATHER.

2. **Productions that perform automatic lexical decision**
   P2   IF the goal is to judge if the stimulus is spelled correctly
        and a word is similar to the stimulus
        and the stimulus mismatches the spelling of the word
        THEN say no.
   P3   IF the goal is to judge if the stimulus is spelled correctly
        and a word is similar to the stimulus
        and the stimulus does not mismatch the spelling of the word
        THEN say yes.

3. **Productions that perform deliberate lexical decision**
   P4   IF the goal is to judge if the stimulus matches an anticipated word
        and a word is anticipated
        and the stimulus does not mismatch the spelling of the word
        THEN say yes.
   P5   IF the goal is to judge if the stimulus matches an anticipated word
        and a word is anticipated
        and the stimulus mismatches the spelling of the word
        THEN change the goal to judging if the stimulus is correctly spelled.

4. **An optional production that capitalizes on nonwords similar to the anticipated word**
   P6   IF the goal is to judge if the stimulus matches an anticipated word
        and a word is anticipated
        and the stimulus is similar to the word
        and the stimulus mismatches the spelling of the word
        THEN say no.

Source: Reprinted by permission of the publishers from *The Architecture of Cognition* by John R. Anderson, Cambridge, MA: Harvard University Press, Copyright © 1983 by the President and Fellows of Harvard College.

longer the more facts there are associated with the concepts. This argument is based on the assumption that the more facts there are associated with a concept, the less activation each of the pathways leading from the concept will receive as a result of the activation of the concept itself. On this basis, ACT can explain why Collins and Quillian found that *A canary is a bird* is verified faster than *A canary is an animal.* Presumably, there are in memory more associative links leading from *animal* than from *bird,* and, as a result, the execution of the productions involved in matching the test sentence against declarative memory structures will be slower.

ACT can also explain the typicality and semantic relatedness effects that were such a problem for the hierarchical network model in terms of the strength of nodes and the resulting spread of activation. *A bear is an animal* is verified faster than *A bear is a mammal,* because the strength of the *animal* node, and thus the degree of activation of links leading from it, is greater than the strength of the *mammal* node. In this case, it has to be assumed that the greater strength of the *animal* node more than compensates for the greater number of links leading from it. Otherwise, based on the argument given for the *canary* example, one would have to predict that *A bear is a mammal* would be verified faster.

Anderson (1983, 1984) explains the slow rejection of false statements such *A St. Bernard is a cat* in terms of coincidental interconnections between the concepts. The larger the number of associative interconnections between the concepts, the longer it will take to evaluate all of the connections because of the smaller amount of activation each connection will receive. Anderson suggests a waiting model to explain the rejection of such false statements. That is, the model does not assume that all interconnections are evaluated. Rather, if the execution of productions has not resulted in verification of the statement within a particular time period, a "false" response is made.

◪ *How does ACT account for the original Collins and Quillian findings, typicality/ semantic relatedness effects, and the slow rejection of false statements?*

Assessment of the Model

Clearly, ACT provides a framework for explaining many of the effects found in research on semantic memory. Furthermore, it must be remembered that ACT is intended as a framework for cognitive processes in general and is in no way limited to the semantic memory paradigm. In fact, in the final major section of this chapter, ACT will again be discussed in conjunction with imagery effects, and it will be considered in some detail again in Chapter 9 on retrieval from long-term memory. The scope of ACT as an explanatory framework is both its strength and its weakness. Anderson's systematic program of research has shown that ACT can be adapted to account for a wide variety of cognitive activities. However, as was mentioned earlier, ACT has become increasingly complex as an explanatory framework. As a result, it is difficult to determine what sorts of findings would count as evidence against the model.

Relevant to this issue is what Smith (1978) calls the **sufficiency/transparency tradeoff.** Models such as ACT and the spreading activation model of Collins and Loftus strive for sufficiency in their explanation of semantic memory in that they incorporate more and more detailed assumptions about representation and processing of information in order to explain more and more discrete findings. The problem with this trend, Smith notes, is that the addition of details to the model makes it less transparent. That is, the proliferation of details in the model makes it harder and harder to discern the major assumptions and claims of the model. In turn, the harder it becomes to identify the major predictions of the model, the harder it becomes to know what sort of evidence will tend to disconfirm the model. Smith argues that theorists proposing complex theories of cognitive functioning have a responsibility to identify clearly the major assumptions of the model and what would constitute evidence contrary to the model.

☑ *What is the major problem with comprehensive explanations of cognitive processes such as ACT?*

Feature-Comparison Model

The Set-Theoretic Approach

The feature-comparison model of Smith and colleagues (Smith, Shoben, & Rips, 1974; Smith, 1978) represents an alternative to the network theories of semantic memory. It is an example of set-theoretic models in which concepts are represented by sets of features or attributes. (See Meyer [1970] for a description of his predicate-intersections set-theoretic model.) In the set-theoretic approach, the contents of semantic memory are the attributes of the objects represented. Concepts do not exist independent of the features of which they are composed. The representation of *bird,* for example, might include features such as *is living, can sing, can fly, has feathers,* and so on. Thus there is an emphasis on computed rather than prestored knowledge. In verifying *A robin is a bird,* for example, the model assumes that the relationship is computed at the time of verification by comparing the lists of features associated with the two concepts. Features can be viewed as component parts of an object or values on a dimension. Dimensions represented might include perceptual properties (e.g., shape, size, color), functional characteristics (e.g., mode of locomotion, eating habits), or even abstractions (e.g., honesty, beauty).

This model's emphasis on computed rather than prestored knowledge means that the feature-comparison model is less associative and more cognitive in nature than is the spreading activation model. Whereas the spreading activation model emphasizes the associative links that exist in long-term memory, the feature-comparison model emphasizes mental processes that operate on the stored representation of concepts.

Central to the model is the distinction between defining and characteristic features. **Defining features** are those central to the meaning of a concept. To be considered a member of a particular category, the object must have the defining features. All objects in a particular class share the defining features for that class. *Has feathers* and *is living,* for example, might be defining features of *bird.* **Characteristic features,** on the other hand, are attributes typical of the category but not necessary to its definition. *Can fly* and *can sing* are characteristic of *bird* in that most birds exhibit these properties, but certainly not all birds can fly or sing.

☑ *How does the set-theoretic approach to semantic memory differ from network theories, and how does the feature comparison model distinguish between defining and characteristic features?*

The Comparison Process

Based on this distinction between defining and characteristic features, the feature-comparison model postulates a two-stage process of feature comparison for the situation in which an individual is asked to verify a statement, such as *A canary is a bird.* Stage 1 involves matching all of the features, regardless of whether they are defining or characteristic, for the relevant concepts. If a large number of features match, a quick "true" response is made. If very few features match, a quick "false" response is made. Within the system, decision processes set the criteria for what constitutes high and low feature similarity. Thus the criteria can vary from situation to situation. When an intermediate number of features are shared, stage 2 of the comparison process must be executed. In stage 2, only the defining features are matched. If all defining features match, a true response is made. If any defining features do not match, a false response is made. As stage 2 requires additional comparison time, decision times will be slow when feature similarity is neither very high nor very low and stage 2 has to be executed.

☑ *How does the feature-comparison model's comparison process operate?*

Application of the Model

On the basis of this rather elegantly simple two-stage process, the model can account for typicality and familiarity/relatedness effects. According to the model, characteristic features play a crucial role in the effects. For example, consider verification of the statements *A robin is a bird* and *A chicken is a bird.* As members of the category *bird, robin* and *chicken* have the same defining features. Thus, differences in verification time must be due to differences in characteristic features. *Robin* has more features characteristic of the *bird* category and thus can be verified rapidly based on high feature similarity following the stage 1 comparison. *Chicken,* on the other hand, has fewer features characteristic of the *bird* category and thus the feature similarity found in stage 1 is less likely to exceed the criterion for making a "true" response. As a result, verification would be slowed because of the need to execute stage 2.

Smith and colleagues (1974) also argue that there is evidence from the study of linguistic hedges (e.g., *a true, technically speaking,* and *loosely speaking*) that is consistent with their model. The hedge *a true* is used when the subject noun contains both defining and characteristic features of the predicate noun, as in *A robin is a true bird. Technically speaking* is used when the subject noun contains the predicate noun's defining features but not its characteristic features, as in *Technically speaking, a chicken is a bird. Loosely speaking* is used when the subject and predicate nouns do not have matching defining features but do share a number of characteristic features, as in *Loosely speaking, a bat is a bird.* In the case of negative statements in which the subject and predicate nouns share many characteristic features but do not share defining features, *technically speaking* is used, as in *Technically speaking, a bat is not a bird.*

Smith (1978) argues that the general set-theoretic approach in which concepts are represented by sets of features or attributes also provides a framework for explaining some effects of context on word meanings. For example, Barclay, Bransford, Franks, McCarrell, and Nitsch (1974) had subjects process the word *piano* in the context of one of two sentences: *The man lifted the piano* or *The man tuned the piano.* Then, subjects received cues for recall of all of the sentences processed. Barclay and colleagues found that *heavy* was a better cue than *musical* for the first sentence, whereas the reverse was true for the second sentence. Smith suggests that the word *lifted* in the first sentence would increase the saliency of the feature *weight* in the representation of *piano* and thus the saliency of the *weight* feature in the composite semantic representation of the entire sentence. In the second sentence, the feature of *music-producing* in the representation of *piano* and in the composite representation of the sentence would be enhanced by the word *tuned.* Thus the semantic features of contextual information may influence subtly the feature representation of particular words without in any way fundamentally changing their meaning.

In another study of context effects on meaning, Anderson and Ortony (1975) found that subjects interpreted the word *container* to mean *basket* when it occurred in the sentence *The container held the apples* but interpreted it to mean *bottle* when it occurred in the sentence *The container held the cola.* In the case of the second sentence, Smith (1978) argues that characteristic features of *cola* are added to the features of *container* and result in the activation of the more specific concept *bottle.* In the case of the first sentence, Smith proposes that the function of *container* is determined by examination of its features and that features of *apples* relevant to this function are then added to the representation of *container,* resulting in the identification of the more specific concept *basket.*

☑ *What semantic memory effects are well explained by the feature-comparison model?*

Problems with the Model

Despite the model's success is accounting for many phenomena of semantic verification and natural language use, a number of criticisms have been leveled against it. One central challenge involves the issue of defining features. Various researchers (e.g., McCloskey & Glucksberg, 1978; Rosch & Mervis, 1975) now argue that natural categories, in fact, may not have defining features. That is, there may be no features that are common to all members of the category. Instead, Rosch and Mervis (1975) suggest that natural semantic categories be conceptualized as networks of overlapping attributes. The greater the extent to which a category member bears a family resemblance to other members of the category, the more prototypical it is judged to be.

When McCloskey and Glucksberg (1978) asked subjects to decide whether items belonged to particular categories, they found that subjects disagreed with each other in judging intermediate-typicality items, as in deciding, for example, whether *bookends* is part of the category *furniture,* and that subjects were inconsistent in their own judgments from one session to the next. As a result of these findings, McCloskey and Glucksberg suggest that natural categories are fuzzy sets with no clear boundaries separating members from nonmembers. Thus, to the extent that the concept of defining features is questionable, the processing details of the feature-comparison model require reexamination.

Evidence produced by Holyoak and Glass (1975) in the study of responses to false statements also presents a problem for the feature-comparison model. They found instances in which the usual familiarity/semantic relatedness effect was reversed. For example, they found that *All fruits are vegetables* was rejected more quickly than *All fruits are flowers,* and *Some chairs are tables* was rejected more quickly than *Some chairs are beds.* This finding is contrary to the feature-comparison model because the second instance in each pair would be more likely to require stage 1 processing only. This prediction follows from the stipulation that stage 1 processing terminates in a quick "false" response when the number of features in common to the two concepts is so low as to exceed the criterion for low feature similarity. For both example pairs, such low feature similarity would be more likely for the second statement.

Collins and Loftus (1975) argue, however, that this result can be explained by the spreading activation model's assumption that *fruits/vegetables* and *chairs/tables* are labeled as mutually exclusive subordinates, whereas *fruits/flowers* and *chairs/beds* are not. Discovery of such negative evidence would lead to a fast "false" response.

In an analysis of other false statements, Holyoak and Glass (1975) also found that statements such as *All animals are birds* are also rejected quickly. Again, this finding is troublesome for the feature-comparison model because the high feature similarity of *ani-*

mals and *birds* would mean that the statement could only be correctly rejected as "false" following the stage 2 comparison. Using production frequency measures, Holyoak and Glass (1975) found that the speed of rejecting such statements was better predicted by people's tendency to produce, in response to the subject noun, a concept that is a counterexample to the predicate noun (e.g., *fish*) than by people's tendency to produce the predicate noun itself. That is, they found that the semantic relatedness of the subject and predicate nouns was less important than the tendency to produce a counterexample to the predicate noun.

Collins and Loftus (1975) cite both of these findings from the research of Holyoak and Glass as evidence of the need to incorporate into models of semantic memory multiple strategies for disconfirming, such as searching for mutually exclusive links and counterexamples. The lack of alternative processing strategies, they contend, is thus one of the limitations of the feature-comparison model.

Yet another set of findings involving semantic relatedness is also problematical for the feature-comparison model. In their research, McCloskey and Glucksberg (1979) attempted to manipulate the criterion for relatedness that might be used in making a stage 1 comparison by presenting false statements in which the subject and predicate nouns were semantically related (e.g., *All birds are canaries*) interspersed in a list also containing true statements. The reasoning here is that subjects experiencing such a list would have to set a very strict criterion for feature similarity in stage 1 in order to avoid making quick erroneous responses to the false statements containing related nouns.

However, if the feature-comparison model is correct, setting such a strict criterion should mean that the usual semantic relatedness effect for true statements should be reduced, because the probability of having to execute stage 2 would be increased. That is, verifying *All robins are birds* should take just about as long as verifying *All penguins are birds* because, even in the case of the *robins* statement, the degree of feature similarity might not be sufficient to exceed the criterion for a "true" response in stage 1. Contrary to this prediction derived from the model, McCloskey and Glucksberg found that the semantic relatedness effect was even more pronounced than in a situation in which the false statements contained unrelated nouns.

In interpreting this evidence against the feature-comparison model, it should be noted that the accumulation of such evidence is to a great extent a function of the model's specificity. Unlike the spreading activation model, the feature-comparison model does clearly generate testable predictions and thus can be falsified. However, the model's specificity is also a function of its limited scope, which certainly makes it far from a comprehensive approach to describing semantic memory. As Cohen (1977) has observed, any network model can represent a variety of relationships and thus can be extended as needed, while it is not clear how set-theoretic models such as the feature-comparison model can represent relationships other than class membership and properties.

Certain aspects of the feature-comparison model may profitably be incorporated into more general network models that allow for greater flexibility in representation and processing. It is entirely possible that the analysis of concepts into component features may be important under certain conditions, but the ecological validity of any model that assumes that feature analysis of concepts is invariant must be questioned (e.g., see Kintsch, 1974). Surely concepts such as *bird* have a unitary prestored representation in the semantic system that under many conditions does not require decomposition into constituent features.

◪ *What are major weaknesses of the feature-comparison model?*

Property-Comparison Model

In conjunction with their presentation of evidence inconsistent with the feature-comparison model, McCloskey and Glucksberg (1979) proposed an alternative that has become known as the property-comparison model. In this model, McCloskey and Glucksberg subscribe to the set-theoretic approach of describing concepts as sets of properties, but they dispense with the distinction between defining and characteristic features. Each property is composed of attributes, with only typical values of each attribute stored. The model provides for a comparison process in which the subject noun is matched against the predicate noun. As the comparison of attributes proceeds, positive and negative evidence is accumulated, and the probability of the statement's truth or falsity is assessed. Once the probability exceeds some threshold value established for the task at hand, a response is made.

McCloskey and Glucksberg have demonstrated that this model can account for their finding that including in a list false statements in which the subject and predicate nouns are semantically related (e.g., *All birds are canaries*) increased the semantic relatedness effect for true statements. The model can explain this effect by assuming that there is a higher probability that a given comparison will yield positive evidence when, in fact, the statement is false in the situation in which the list contains false statements with semantically related elements. This means that each comparison for true statements that yields positive evidence will contribute less to reaching the "yes" decision threshold.

In turn, more comparisons will have to be made in evaluating true statements in order to reach the decision threshold. This increase in the number of comparisons needed will be greater for true sentences containing weakly related nouns than for true sentences containing strongly related nouns, because the proportion of comparisons that yield positive evidence is lower for true statements containing weakly related nouns. However, the model is hardly comprehensive. For example, Chang (1986) has pointed out that the model does not provide a framework for explaining the verification of single-property statements such as *A bird has skin*.

📝 *How does the property-comparison model differ from the feature-comparison model?*

Schema Theory

In his commentary on the limitations of models of semantic memory, Kintsch (1980) suggested that investigators must begin to consider units of language beyond the individual word and he proposed schema theory as a profitable framework for extending semantic memory research. Consider again the example schemas shown in Figure 7–4. The representations shown there clearly bear a resemblance to the associative network models that have been considered in the discussion of semantic memory. Recall that Rumelhart and Ortony (1977) assume that schemas are embedded within each other and thus range in specificity from the relatively elemental units shown in Figure 7–4 to very much more generalized knowledge structures such as that for *washing clothes*. Within this approach, concepts are represented in terms of the interrelationships that exist among the constituent elements of the concept (Rumelhart, 1980).

Note also that a schema approach such as that of Rumelhart and Ortony provides a mechanism for explaining context effects of the type discussed in conjunction with the feature-comparison model. The different interpretations of *broke* in the sentences *David broke the glass* and *David broke the chain* can be explained in terms of other stored information in memory concerning glasses and chains. As Kintsch (1980) observes:

> *Words obtain their meaning from the scripts, categories, and schemata in which they participate. It is the relatively stable structure of semantic memory that provides a basis for the semantics of words. These larger units ought to be the main concern of semantic memory research. (p. 617)*

It is important to recognize that the schema approach is not incompatible with some of the models of semantic memory previously discussed. The notion of schemas could certainly be incorporated into Collins and Loftus's spreading activation model. It must be remembered that the spreading activation model was proposed to account for a relatively limited body of findings from the semantic memory literature and did not describe the structure of the underlying memory representation with as much specificity as Rumelhart and Ortony have. However, the model could certainly be elaborated to include the more detailed type of propositional networks employed by Rumelhart and Ortony in representing the relationships among concepts. Most importantly, the concepts of spread of activation and schemas are perfectly compatible.

The notion of schemas can also be incorporated within ACT. Although Anderson (1983) has criticized specific schema theories for failing to distinguish between declarative and procedural knowledge, ACT's organization of concepts into networks of propositions in declarative memory is certainly consistent with the types of knowledge structures proposed by Rumelhart and Ortony. In fact, in his textbook of cognitive psychology, Anderson (1990) specifically talks about propositions being organized into schemas.

⬛ *How is the notion of schema compatible with many of the associative network models of semantic memory?*

THE ROLE OF IMAGERY

The role of imagery in the representation of information in long-term memory has been extensively debated by cognitive psychologists in the last 20 years. The crux of the debate is whether it is necessary to assume that there exist in memory imagery representations of information that are separate and distinct from propositional representations.

Facilitative Effects of Interactive Images on Memory

Although the role of images in the representation of information in long-term memory is a continuing source of debate, the facilitative effect on memory of encouraging subjects to employ visual imagery is well established. For example, in a series of experiments in 1972, Bower demonstrated the beneficial effects of imagery instructions on subjects' paired-associates (P-A) learning. You will recall that, in P-A learning, the subject has to try to recall the second member of each pair in response to the presentation of the first member of the pair.

In one experiment, Bower demonstrated that subjects receiving instructions encouraging them to image the two members of each pair interacting in some way recalled significantly more items than subjects receiving no special study instructions. In another experiment, imagery subjects also significantly outperformed a group of subjects explicitly instructed to repeat or rehearse each presented pair. This finding suggested that instructions to image do not have their effect simply by encouraging verbal processing of the items.

In a third experiment in the series, Bower investigated the influence of a simultaneous motor task on the use of imagery in learning P-As. While trying to learn a list of P-As using imagery, half of the subjects performed a visual tracking task in which they had to follow with two fingers an irregular, wavy black line being fed through a machine at a constant rate. While simultaneously trying to learn the P-As using imagery, the other half of the subjects performed a tactile tracking task in which they had to follow with two fingers a string glued to the paper in an irregular, wavy pattern. Bower reasoned that if instructions to image do indeed result in visual processing the visual tracking task should interfere more with the learning of the P-As than should the tactile tracking task. Consistent with this prediction, he found that the tactile tracking group recalled more P-As than did the visual tracking group.

Finally, Bower investigated the importance of the nature of the image formed. One group received instructions to image the members of the pair interacting, while the other group received instructions to form separate images of each member of each pair. Only the interactive imagery group outperformed the subjects from the first experiment who received no special study instructions. Clearly, these results suggest that creating interacting visual images can facilitate memory for verbal materials.

In the example of Alan, presented at the beginning of the chapter, his attempt to remember the relationships involving the heart and surrounding structures was based on the generation of interactive visual images. In Chapter 10, further evidence of the facilitative effect of imagery on memory will be presented, but first a consideration of theoretical explanations of the effect is in order.

🖉 *How did Bower's research on P-A learning point to the important role of imagery in facilitating memory for verbal materials?*

Paivio's Dual-Code Hypothesis

In order to explain the beneficial effects of imagery, Paivio (1971, 1986) has proposed the dual-code hypothesis. This explanation argues that information may be stored in long-term memory in two forms: verbal codes and image codes. The verbal code is available for any event or object that can be described. The image code is available for any event or object that can be visualized. Thus some items can be remembered through only one of the codes, whereas others can be remembered through both. For example, concrete nouns such as *houseboat* and *table* can be represented through both codes, whereas abstract nouns such as *democracy* and *truth* can be represented only through the verbal code. Thus, Alan was able to use imagery, as well as verbal representations, to represent the heart and its surrounding structures because they can be visualized, but he might have had difficulty using imagery to try to represent the biochemical process responsible for the contraction of the heart.

Information represented by two codes, Paivio argues, has a retrieval advantage. Representing information with more than one code increases the probability of locating and retrieving the information at the time of test. Multiple retrieval routes to the information are established. Thus imagery instructions of the type employed in Bower's experiments increase the probability that the information will be multiply represented in long-term memory and therefore more likely to be successfully retrieved. Central to the dual-code hypothesis, of course, is the assumption that imagery representations exist in memory that are separate and distinct from verbal (or propositional) representations.

📝 *What are the major assumptions of Paivio's dual-code hypothesis?*

Evidence that Images Are Analog Representations

In investigating the assumption that there are distinct imagery representations, researchers have attempted to demonstrate that images have *analog properties*. That is, they have attempted to demonstrate that imagery representations contain visual information that is processed in a manner similar to the processing of visual perceptual information.

Shape Comparisons

Shepard and Chipman (1970) asked subjects to judge the shape similarity of states. One group was given only the names of the states to be judged. The other group was given picture outlines of the states. The two groups were found to use similar criteria in judging the states in that they separated the states into similar groupings. Furthermore, the name-only group reported using imagery in making the judgments. These results suggest that imaging and visually perceiving (as in actually looking at the shape outlines of the states) are similar activities.

Image Scanning Effects

Image scanning effects have been interpreted as supporting the same conclusion. Kosslyn, Ball, and Reiser (1978) asked subjects to hold an image of a map in memory and to imagine a black dot moving from one location to another on the map. Subjects were instructed to push a button when the dot arrived at the second location. Kosslyn and colleagues found that time to push the button was greater when the actual distance between the locations on the map was greater. This finding suggests that spatial information in images of maps may be represented and processed much as it would be represented and processed in visually inspecting the maps.

📝 *How are the findings from the study of subjects judging the shape similarity of states and subjects scanning maps consistent with the view that imaging and visually perceiving are similar activities?*

Selective Interference Effects

Other evidence of the analog properties of images comes from studies of selective interference effects. In one such study, Brooks (1968) used a block letter such as that shown in Figure 8–4. Subjects were asked to form an image of the letter, and then while holding the image in memory, subjects had to scan the image and decide whether each corner was a part of the very top or the very bottom of the figure. Some subjects were asked to respond verbally, and others were asked to respond by pointing at Ys and Ns arranged in an irregular pattern, as shown in Figure 8–4.

Brooks found that responding visually took twice as long as responding verbally. In order to rule out the possibility that responding visually takes longer regardless of what else the subject is doing, Brooks also tested subjects in a situation in which they had to perform a verbal task and respond either verbally or visually. For that task, responding verbally took

(a)

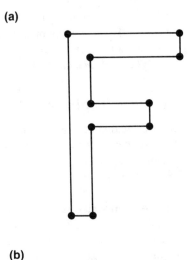

(b)

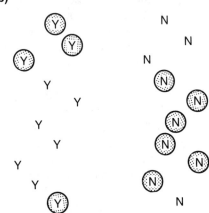

FIGURE 8–4 (a) The type of block letter shown to subjects in the image scanning study by Brooks (1968). (b) The irregular pattern of Ys and Ns to which subjects had to point in the visual response condition of the Brooks study. The shaded circles indicate the correct pattern of responses for the letter *F.*

Source: Brooks, L. R. (1968). Spatial and verbal components in the act of recall. *Canadian Journal of Psychology, 22,* 350–351. Reprinted with permission.

longer. Thus Brooks's results suggest that imaging and perceiving visually (as required in the visual-pointing task) are similar activities in that they interfere with each other.

◩ *What evidence did Brooks (1968) find that imaging interferes with visual perception?*

Mental Rotation Effects

Mental rotation effects reported by Shepard and Metzler (1971) can also be interpreted as supporting the view that imagery representations contain visual information that is processed in a manner similar to the processing of visual perceptual information. In one of their experiments, subjects were timed as they decided if a pair of drawings showed the same three-dimensional objects. Figure 8–5 shows the type of drawings used in the study. In those cases in which the drawings did depict the same object, the difference in orientation of the two drawings was varied from 0 to 180 degrees. Shepard and Metzler found that the greater the difference in orientation of the members of a pair, the longer it took subjects to respond. They interpreted these results to suggest that subjects made the shape comparisons by mentally rotating one object at a constant rate, just as one would rotate and judge an actual physical object.

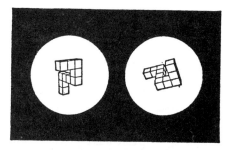

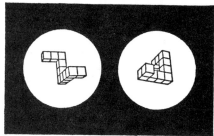

FIGURE 8–5 An example of two pairs of drawings of three-dimensional objects used in Shepard and Metzler's (1971) study of mental rotation effects. The subject's task was to decide if the left- and right-hand member of each pair depicted the same object.

Source: Shepard, R. N., & Metzler, J. (1971). Mental rotation of three-dimensional objects. *Science, 171,* 702. Copyright 1971 by the American Association for the Advancement of Science.

Image Size Effects

A final piece of evidence in support of images having analog properties comes from Kosslyn's (1975) study of image size effects. Subjects were asked to generate either a small or large image of an animal by imaging it in relation to another animal. For example, imaging *dog* in relation to *whale* should result in a relatively small image of dog, whereas imaging *dog* in relation to *wasp* would result in a relatively large image of dog. Then, subjects were asked to judge the appropriateness of various features for the animals imaged (e.g., *Is a beak an appropriate feature of a dog?*). Kosslyn found that the time to judge the appropriateness of features was greater for small images than for large images. This suggests that subjects' performance was influenced by the perceptibility of parts of the image, just as performance might be influenced by the perceptibility of parts of an actual photograph or visual scene.

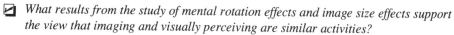 *What results from the study of mental rotation effects and image size effects support the view that imaging and visually perceiving are similar activities?*

Collectively, these results suggest that images do contain visual information that is processed in a manner similar to the perceptual processing of visual information. Although such evidence has been widely interpreted as supporting the argument for distinct imagery representations in long-term memory, this view is not universally held, as the next section will show.

The Propositional View of Pylyshyn

While admitting that images may be generated and used in performing specific tasks, Pylyshyn (1973, 1981) nevertheless argues that the basic unit of representation in long-term memory is the proposition. In Pylyshyn's view, all images are based on underlying abstract propositions.

Pylyshyn uses a number of arguments in defending this position. First, he notes that images differ from pictures and physical objects in terms of inaccuracies and forgotten "bits." If something from an image is forgotten, one does not experience a gap in the way one does if a section is torn from a photograph. Instead, the gaps are filled in. For example, if Alan was to generate an image of the area outside the biology building that included the bike area, his image might not contain all of the objects in that area. However, if the fire hydrant next to the bike rack were omitted, Alan would not experience a hole in his image at that location. Instead, the area containing the fire hydrant would be filled in.

In addition, Pylyshyn notes that whole bits tend to be forgotten and that one often knows that bits are missing. Alan is very unlikely to generate an image that contains half of the fire hydrant, but he may be aware that his filled-in image that lacks the fire hydrant is somehow incomplete. Such introspective evidence is consistent, Pylyshyn claims, with the position that an image is based on an abstract underlying propositional representation that includes information about the lost bits.

Pylyshyn also argues that the ability to generate images of events never witnessed before is evidence that the formation of images is dependent on general world knowledge represented in propositional form. Alan, for example, can create an image of an ostrich walking a tight-rope. He is able to do this because he has available general propositional knowledge about giraffes and walking a tight-rope that can be combined into a reasonable image representation.

The facilitative effects of imagery on memory are due, Pylyshyn suggests, to the elaborative propositional processing necessary for image formation. That is, the superior memory resulting from the use of imagery is not due to storing away in long-term memory visual copies of the images formed. Rather, the superior memory is the result of having elaboratively processed the underlying propositional information in order to generate the images. Generating an image of a giraffe walking a tight-rope will necessitate a more extensive consideration of the features and associations connected with *giraffe* and *walking a tight-rope* than will simply repeating the phrase *giraffe walking a tight-rope*. Generating the image will thus make the information more accessible at the time of retrieval.

Some indirect experimental evidence in support of Pylyshyn's position that visual copies of images are not stored in long-term memory comes from a study of picture memory by Nelson, Metzler, and Reed (1974). They compared memory for information contained in a simple sentence (e.g., *A smiling old man holds a little girl*) with memory for the same information presented in the form of a nondetailed drawing, a detailed drawing, and an actual photograph. The results showed the phrase to be more poorly recognized than the three types of pictorial stimuli, but recognition of the three types of pictorial stimuli did not differ. This suggests that the superior memory for pictures was not due to the storing of detailed visual copies in long-term memory. Rather, pictures of any sort result in a more elaborative propositional representation of the information. Pylyshyn makes the same argument for images.

◪ *What general arguments has Pylyshyn advanced in arguing against images as a basic form of long-term memory representation?*

Kosslyn's Updated Dual-Coding Position

In defending the dual-coding position, Kosslyn (1980) has attempted to identify more precisely the representations and processes that underlie imagery effects. He accepts

Pylyshyn's suggestion that images are sometimes constructed from underlying propositional knowledge. However, he also argues that there are nonpropositional long-term imagery representations. Furthermore, he maintains, these imagery representations have analog properties. Thus Kosslyn argues for both propositional representations and analog codes.

As analog codes, images possess **emergent properties.** That is, they possess properties not easily discerned by a consideration of propositional representations alone. For example, in judging which of two types of bird is prettier, Alan might find images useful because prettiness is an emergent property that could not be easily determined by considering only the propositional information he has stored about the two types of bird (unless, of course, Alan has made this comparison in the past and has recorded his conclusion as a proposition in memory). A series of comparisons of propositional information pertaining to color of plumage, facial features, size, and so on might not permit a quick and easy decision about a holistic property such as prettiness in the way in which a comparison of images might. Thus, in arguing that images have emergent properties Kosslyn stresses the functional role of images in cognitive processing. Not only do images permit comparison of emergent properties but they also permit such valuable cognitive operations as mental rotation and scanning.

It must be stressed here, however, that in arguing for imagery representations, Kosslyn is not suggesting that images are more or less exact mental copies of the objects or events that they represent. Rather, images are in Kosslyn's view **quasi-pictorial,** meaning that they preserve many of the analog properties of pictures but are also more abstract in nature. The most important property preserved is the spatial arrangement of the elements contained in the image. In arguing for the abstract quasi-pictorial nature of images, Kosslyn accepts Pylyshyn's observations that images differ from pictures in important ways.

With regard to the type of information represented in images, a further observation is in order here regarding Brooks's (1968) investigation of selective interference effects in the use of imagery. In addition to the experiment described earlier involving the scanning of the letter and verbal versus visual responding, Brooks also conducted a letter-scanning study in which verbal and spatial responding were compared. For the spatial responding condition, subjects had their eyes closed and scanned with their fingers a series of raised Ys and Ns arranged in the type of irregular pattern shown in Figure 8–4. Subjects were slower to respond in the spatial responding condition than in the verbal responding condition. Thus the interference found in the visual responding condition in the earlier experiment may have been spatial rather than visual in nature. Such a conclusion is consistent with the position that images are abstract spatial representations rather than mental pictures of visual scenes.

It should also be noted that Kosslyn's dual-coding position goes well beyond that of Paivio. In particular, Kosslyn's model (Kosslyn, 1980, 1987) attempts to describe in detail the structures in long-term memory that enable one to use imagery and the cognitive processes that are involved when one uses imagery. For example, Kosslyn's model (Kosslyn, 1980, 1987; Kosslyn, Reiser, Farah, & Fliegel, 1983; Kosslyn, Holtzman, Farah, & Gazzaniga, 1985) includes a description of the type of information stored in long-term memory from which an image in the **visual buffer** (or short-term store) can be generated, using what Kosslyn calls the **picture-processing module.** Such a long-term memory representation might include information about shape (such as lines and angles) in a form that is separate and distinct from the propositional representation of the image.

In addition, Kosslyn's model proposes processes that operate on the underlying image representations. For example, the "put" procedure operates on an image residing in the visual buffer by integrating into the pattern at the correct location the stored image representation of some relevant part. An example is Alan's putting a major blood vessel into an already generated image of the heart or Alan's putting additional tail feathers into an already generated image of a running ostrich. In order for the "put" procedure to operate, however, other processing procedures, the **shape-encoding** and **location-encoding processing subsystems,** must first operate to locate the relevant location within the image.

Other research generated by the model suggests that multipart images of three-dimensional objects are generated one part at a time, beginning with nearer surfaces and proceeding to more and more distant surfaces (Kosslyn, Cave, Provost, & von Gierke, 1988; Roth & Kosslyn, 1988). Thus Kosslyn's approach takes the basic dual-coding notion proposed by Paivio and attempts to construct a very specific model of how images are represented and processed within the system.

☑ *How does Kosslyn's dual-coding position differ from the propositional view of Pylyshyn and the dual-coding approach of Paivio?*

ACT Theory's Treatment of Imagery

John Anderson's position regarding imagery has undergone an interesting evolution. Earlier (e.g., Anderson & Bower, 1973; Anderson, 1976), he argued for propositional representations only. Part of his argument for this position was based on his contention that it is not possible to distinguish between imagery and propositional representations in memory (Anderson, 1976, 1978, 1979). Thus, in pursuit of parsimony, only propositional representations should be assumed.

In more recent versions of ACT (Anderson, 1983), however, Anderson argues for image representations that are separate and distinct from propositional representations. In fact, ACT now embodies three types of representation: abstract propositions, spatial images, and temporal strings (which represent the order of sets of items). Like Kosslyn, Anderson (1983) argues that images most importantly contain information about the orientation and spatial relationships of elements being represented. Thus ACT can explain Pylyshyn's (1973) observation that subjects may be able with certainty to report that the presence of a lamp in their image of a room scene and yet be unable to describe the lamp in detail. The image may represent the relative location of various objects in the room without containing detailed information about the visual properties of the objects.

Just as productions operate on propositional information represented in declarative memory in the ACT model, so too do productions operate on information contained in the image representations. For example, ACT attempts to account for the Shepard and Metzler (1971) mental rotation effects in terms of a production system that operates on the image representations of the two objects being compared.

☑ *How does ACT now deal with imagery in describing the representation of information in long-term memory?*

Imagery and the Associative-Cognitive Debate

The treatment of imagery in ACT and in Kosslyn's model is yet another example of how the study of learning and memory processes has moved away from a strict associative approach. The representation and processing of images described by the two models is not strictly associative in nature. These models are proposing that the storage and use of images involves much more than the linkage of items in memory. However, the propositional systems assumed by both models also allow for an important contribution of associationist principles. Although Kosslyn does not provide a detailed description of his propositional system, such systems by their very nature tend to be associative, as was seen in many of the descriptions of semantic memory.

◩ *How have recent explanations of imagery affected the associative-cognitive debate?*

CONCLUDING REMARKS: The Maltese Cross Model Revisited

As noted in the concluding section of the preceding chapter, it is possible to relate many of the issues raised in considering the representation of information in long-term memory to Broadbent's Maltese cross model of memory presented in Chapter 6. For example, it would certainly be possible to incorporate notions such as semantic distance, spread of activation, mutually exclusive associative links, node strength, and imagery representations into the model's treatment of the long-term associative store, even though Broadbent has not yet done so. It would even be possible to incorporate feature comparison processes, property comparison processes, and image manipulating processes and productions into the Maltese cross model's description of the processing system. Before this integration occurs, however, greater consensus is needed as to which of these various notions pertaining to semantic memory and imagery representations are empirically worthy of inclusion in such a general model of memory.

CHAPTER 9

Forgetting and the Retrieval of Information from Long-Term Memory

APPLICATION: In Search of the Answer

Alan is taking one of the three major exams of the semester in his biology course. With 20 minutes left in the class period, he has answered most of the exam questions. However, two of the short-answer questions and one of the discussion questions are giving him difficulty. In the case of one of the short-answer questions, Alan remembers reading about the concept being quizzed by the question, and he even remembers the professor discussing the concept in class. However, as he attempts to answer the question, information about related concepts studied more recently in the semester keeps coming to mind instead of the information specifically relevant to the question. In the case of the other short-answer question that is giving him difficulty, Alan has drawn a complete blank until he comes across a term in another question that suddenly leads him to the answer to the troublesome question. In trying to respond to the discussion question, Alan finds that he has only a few bits of information readily available, and he begins to cast about in his mind for any even remotely related information that he can use as the basis for his answer. Alan begins to sweat as the remaining minutes in the period tick away.

Alan's performance during the exam illustrates the potential impact of interference from other memory traces on successful retrieval, the phenomenon of retrieval failure and the importance of retrieval cues, and the process of reconstruction of memory for information, based on readily available knowledge structures. Each of these issues will be addressed in this chapter.

EBBINGHAUS AND THE VERBAL LEARNING TRADITION

Ebbinghaus's Pioneering Studies

In 1885, Hermann Ebbinghaus published a monograph entitled, in translation, *Memory: A Contribution to Experimental Psychology*. In this work, Ebbinghaus attempted to demonstrate that higher mental processes can be studied under carefully controlled conditions. This research was based on the work of the empiricist philosophers, especially the British associationists, whose major tenets were summarized in Chapter 1. Central to the associationists' view was the notion that stimuli encountered in the environment give rise to corresponding ideas in the mind. As stimuli are encountered in the same succession over and over again, the ideas become associated or linked in the mind. Thus, it was argued, ideas become associated through temporal contiguity. That is, ideas become associated simply because their corresponding stimuli are encountered contiguously over and over again. Ebbinghaus set about to test such notions of associationism by employing the scientific method.

The Ebbinghaus Experiment

In all of his investigations of memory, Ebbinghaus used only one subject—himself. As the to-be-learned materials, Ebbinghaus constructed a special pool of items, **CVC** (consonant-vowel-consonant) **trigrams** or **nonsense syllables** (e.g., XEG, KIB, BIY, QEP). In all, he generated over 2,300 of these nonsense syllables from which he could draw items for use in his experiments. Ebbinghaus generated these special stimuli in an attempt to avoid stimuli that had previously been associated in his experience. As he was studying association formation, he wanted stimuli that were not already associated in his memory.

The basic methodology of the Ebbinghaus experiment was simple. He would read aloud a list of these CVCs at a fast rate in time to a metronome. As soon as he thought he could repeat the list in its entirety without looking at the written version, he put the paper aside and presented himself with a written version of the first syllable only. If he could recall the rest of the syllables without hesitation, he considered the list learned. He then immediately recorded both the time taken to learn the list and the number of repetitions required to learn the list. By making these observations, Ebbinghaus introduced objective, quantifiable observations into the study of learning and memory. That is, Ebbinghaus demonstrated the application of the scientific method to the study of learning and memory processes. If he hesitated in his recall, he studied the list again and tested himself again until he could produce it without hesitation. Ebbinghaus's dedication to the task was truly heroic in that in the course of his investigations he probably learned many thousands of such nonsense syllable lists.

✒ *How did Ebbinghaus introduce objective, quantifiable observations into the study of learning and memory?*

Factors Investigated by Ebbinghaus

Ebbinghaus investigated a number of factors that possibly affect the learning process. One of these was list length. In investigating list length, Ebbinghaus became the first researcher to demonstrate a measure of the memory span, the maximum number of items that can be learned and repeated back in order with only one presentation of the list. Ebbinghaus found that he could learn a list of seven syllables with only one reading of the list, consistent with modern estimates of the memory span of 7 ± 2 items.

As the list was increased over and above seven syllables, Ebbinghaus found, not surprisingly, that it took him longer and longer to master the list. However, he discovered that the relationship between list length and number of trials to learn the list was not a simple one. When the list length was increased to 36 CVCs, Ebbinghaus required 55 repetitions to learn the list, not 5 repetitions as one might predict on the assumption that an additional seven items could be committed to memory on each additional trial. Thus Ebbinghaus demonstrated that the learning process is more complex than had been previously imagined but that it can, nevertheless, be described in objective, quantifiable terms.

Ebbinghaus also investigated the influence of **retention interval** on forgetting. That is, in some experiments he studied the effect of varying the amount of time between the original learning of the list and retesting himself on the list. Some of the results from these studies were reported previously in Chapter 6. These results suggested that the rate of forgetting is most pronounced over the shorter retention intervals, with the rate of forgetting declining with increasing retention intervals. Again, in demonstrating that most forgetting of information occurs within the first 48 hours after original learning (see Figure 6–7 in Chapter 6), Ebbinghaus documented through controlled experimentation a phenomenon that was not anticipated at the time of his investigations.

In his investigation of the phenomenon of **remote associations,** Ebbinghaus produced results that suggested a major modification in the principle of contiguity as proposed by the British associationists and other empiricist philosophers. In order to check for the development of associations between noncontiguous items in a sequence, Ebbinghaus employed the **method of derived lists.** For example, assume that Ebbinghaus first learned the list A, B, C, D, E, F, G, H, where the letters represent to-be-remembered CVCs. A derived list of one degree of remoteness would then be A, C, E, G, B, D, F, H, and a derived list of two degrees of remoteness would be A, D, G, G, E, G, C, F. If associations between noncontiguous items were formed during the learning of the original list (i.e., if remote associations were formed), then Ebbinghaus should have found that it took him less time to learn the derived list than it took him to learn the original list.

As Table 9–1 shows, this is what Ebbinghaus found. These results suggested that the law of contiguity does not apply in an "all-or-none" manner. Rather, the findings suggested that associations are formed not only between adjacent items, which is the conscious intent of the learner, but also between nonadjacent items without conscious deliberation of the learner. As Ebbinghaus observed:

> *As a result of the repetition of the syllable-series certain connections are established between each member and all those that follow it. . . . The strength of the connection, and therefore the amount of work which is eventually saved, is a decreasing function of the time or of the number of the intervening members which separated the syllables in question from one another in the original series. It is maximum for immediately successive members. (Ebbinghaus, 1885/1964, p. 107)*

In some experiments, Ebbinghaus also examined the effect of continuing to study the list even after he had successfully committed it to memory. That is, he examined the effect of **overlearning.** He found that overlearning did produce a memory savings. Overlearning retarded forgetting of the material. Ebbinghaus also investigated the influence of the type of material studied. He compared the learning of stanzas of Byron's *Don Juan* to the learning of lists of nonsense syllables. He found that stanzas from the poem were much easier to learn. He interpreted this finding in terms of the facilitative effects of meaning, rhythm, and rhyme on the to-be-learned information in the poem. Implicit in this conclusion that meaning facilitated memory is the assumption that meaning is based upon an item's association with other items in memory. Thus the more meaningful material is, the more one is able to rely on prior associations in remembering the material.

What were Ebbinghaus's major findings in his investigations of the influence of list length, retention interval, remote associations, overlearning, and type of material studied on the learning and memory process?

Ebbinghaus's Major Contribution

Many of the specific findings of Ebbinghaus have been replicated in the ensuing 100 years, but far more important than the specific findings just described was Ebbinghaus's success in establishing the study of memory as a scientific discipline, complete with objective, quantifiable observations. He succeeded in establishing an empirical basis for the study of associationism. His methodology of studying memory under simplified, highly controlled

TABLE 9–1 Mean Percent Savings as a Function of the Degree of Remoteness of the Derived List in Ebbinghaus's Experiments

	Degree of Remoteness of the Derived List			
	1	*2*	*3*	*4*
Percent savings	11.9	7.5	6.1	3.3

conditions and of focusing on verbatim memory of the material studied was the dominant approach through the 1960s and continues to be reflected in much of present-day research. However, even as researchers in the last 20 years have moved away from a strict reliance on verbatim measures of memory and highly simplified and artificial learning materials and situations, they have continued to employ the type of objective, quantifiable measures of learning pioneered by Ebbinghaus.

 What was Ebbinghaus's major contribution to the study of learning and memory?

Interference Theory

Ebbinghaus's study of the effect of retention interval on forgetting helped to stimulate interest in the mechanism that causes information to be forgotten. In 1932, McGeoch challenged the view that forgetting is due primarily to the decay or fading of the memory trace with disuse over time, just as a muscle will atrophy over time with lack of use. Operating within the framework of associationism and following Ebbinghaus's lead in focusing on the experimental study of rote learning under highly simplified, controlled conditions, McGeoch proposed an interference explanation as an alternative to the decay or disuse explanation of forgetting. McGeoch argued that decay appears to occur with the passage of time simply because the longer the delay, the greater the probability that interfering events will occur.

In support of this position, McGeoch cited a study by Jenkins and Dallenbach (1924) in which retention of a list of 10 nonsense syllables was assessed over retention intervals ranging from one to eight hours. Half of the subjects slept during the retention interval, and the other half remained awake. As shown in Figure 9–1, Jenkins and Dallenbach found much more forgetting in the waking condition. This is contrary to decay theory. If forgetting is due simply to the passage of time, there should have been equal rates of forgetting in the sleeping and waking conditions. The results suggest that events occurring during the retention interval are important determinants of forgetting. The finding that there was some forgetting by subjects who slept during the retention interval might suggest that decay was also contributing to forgetting, but interference theorists, such as Ekstrand (1972), argue that sleep does not produce a mental vacuum and that dreaming may produce interference in subjects who sleep during the retention interval.

How are the Jenkins and Dallenbach (1924) sleep study results relevant to the question of whether forgetting from long-term memory is primarily due to interference or decay?

The Distinction between Retroactive and Proactive Interference

McGeoch and other researchers in the first half of the twentieth century who followed the Ebbinghaus tradition of focusing on the experimental study of rote learning adopted other techniques in addition to serial learning as a means of assessing learning. Paired-associates (P-A) learning, pioneered by Calkins (1896) and Müller and Pilzecker (1900), became especially popular. As has been described previously in Chapter 6, P-A learning involves the learning of pairs of items. The left member of the pair is designated the *stimulus,* and the right member of the pair is designated the *response.* As learning progresses, the subject learns to produce the response when the stimulus is presented alone. P-A learning proved to be an especially useful technique as followers of Ebbinghaus's rote verbal learning tradition began to focus more specifically on explanations of forgetting.

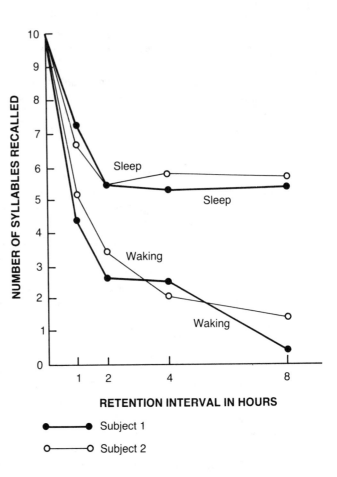

FIGURE 9–1
Performance of subjects who slept and subjects who remained awake during the retention interval in the study by Jenkins and Dallenbach (1924).

Source: Jenkins, J. G., & Dallenbach, K. M. (1924). Oblivescence during sleep and waking. *American Journal of Psychology, 35.* In the public domain.

Initially, the work of McGeoch and other interference theorists focused on the interfering effects of events occurring after the to-be-remembered episode. This type of interference has come to be known as **retroactive interference** or **inhibition** (RI). The RI paradigm is easily demonstrated for the situation involving P-A learning. As shown in Table 9–2, the procedure involves three phases. In phase 1, both the control subjects and the experimental subjects learn one list of P-As, list A-B, where A stands for the stimulus member of each pair and B stands for the response member of each pair. In phase 2, the experimental subjects learn a second list of P-As, list A-D. This means that the experimental subjects now have to learn a second list in which the stimulus terms are the same but the response terms are different. That is, they have to learn to associate each stimulus with a new response. On the other hand, the control subjects in phase 2 perform a distractor task that does not involve learning another P-A list. Finally, in phase 3, both groups of subjects are tested on list A-B, the first list learned.

Typically, the experimental group performs more poorly than the control group. Thus RI is the interference of newer learning with older learning. Events occurring *after* a particular learning episode negatively affect one's memory for that episode. Alan's problem

TABLE 9–2 Retroactive and Proactive Interference Paradigms Employing P-A Learning

	Phase 1	Phase 2	Phase 3
	Retroactive interference paradigm		
Experimental group	Study List A-B	Study List A-D	Recall List A-B
Control group	Study List A-B	Perform unrelated activity	Recall List A-B
	Proactive interference paradigm		
Experimental group	Study List A-B	Study List A-D	Recall List A-D
Control group	Perform unrelated activity	Study List A-D	Recall List A-D

in answering one of the short-answer questions because related information learned more recently during the semester keeps coming to mind can therefore be attributed to RI.

In 1957 Underwood suggested that events occurring *before* a particular learning episode can be just as important a determinant of forgetting. That is, Underwood suggested that older learning can interfere with the learning of new information. This type of interference has come to be known as **proactive interference** or **inhibition** (PI). This interference paradigm is also illustrated for P-A learning in Table 9–2. Again, the demonstration involves three phases. In phase 1, the experimental subjects learn list A-B, whereas the control subjects perform a distractor task. In phase 2, both groups of subjects learn list A-D. In phase 3, both groups of subjects are tested on list A-D. Typically, the experimental subjects perform more poorly on the test, thus demonstrating PI. Their memory for list A-D is negatively affected by the previous learning of list A-B.

Although RI and PI are presented here in the context of P-A learning, it should be noted that RI and PI effects are also reliably found using other memory procedures, such as serial recall and free recall (Underwood, 1983). This has been pointed out earlier in Chapter 6. PI has also been implicated in studies of short-term retention using the Brown-Peterson distractor task (see Chapter 6). RI and PI effects have also been found in studies employing materials other than word lists, including sentences and passages of prose (Underwood, 1983).

✒ *What is the distinction between retroactive and proactive interference?*

Explanations of RI

Response Competition. To explain RI, McGeoch (1942) proposed a response competition explanation. The learning of A-D following the learning of A-B negatively affects memory for A-B because the association of two responses with each stimulus item results, at the time of the test on A-B, in competition between each A-B and each A-D association. Subjects have difficulty deciding which of the two responses was learned first and thus is the correct response. The D responses may be particularly likely to interfere with the correct recall of B responses, because the A-D associations have been learned more recently and thus may be stronger at the time of test. Recall of B responses may be temporarily blocked by recall of D responses.

In one test of the response competition explanation of RI, Melton and Irwin (1940) had subjects in the experimental group learn two lists of P-As, and they varied the number of trials spent learning the second list (list A-D) from 5 to 40. Subjects in the control group learned only list A-B. Melton and Irwin reasoned that the more trials spent learning A-D, the greater the RI exhibited should be in the recall of A-B because the increasing strength of the A-D associations would increase the probability that they would compete with the successful recall of A-B associations.

Melton and Irwin made the further prediction that, with increasing trials on list A-D, subjects should show more and more D response intrusions in attempting to recall the first list B response items. That is, as A-D associations become stronger and stronger, they should come to compete more and more with the recall of A-B associations and result in the incorrect recall of D responses when attempting to recall B responses from the first list. In addition, if response competition alone is responsible for RI, the amount of RI exhibited should be equal to the number of D response intrusions made when tested on list A-B.

With the amount of RI defined as the amount by which the performance of control subjects exceeded that of experimental subjects in the recall of list A-B, Melton and Irwin found only partial support for their predictions (Figure 9–2). They found that RI did increase as the number of trials on list A-D increased from 0 to 20, but there was no further increase in RI as the number of list A-D trials was increased to 40. Furthermore, the number of D response intrusions in the recall of list A-B by the experimental subjects increased as the number of trials on list A-D increased from 0 to 10, but then declined as the number of trials on list A-D was increased further to 20 and 40. In addition, in all of the experimental conditions, the amount of RI exhibited exceeded the number of D response intrusions. Thus an explanation of RI solely in terms of response competition was not supported, and Melton and Irwin proposed that a second factor, unlearning, works in conjunction with response competition to produce RI.

✎ *What is response competition and why is it considered inadequate as a comprehensive explanation of RI?*

Unlearning. Unlearning as a component of RI can be related to the process of extinction in instrumental conditioning discussed previously in Chapter 3. Recall that extinction in instrumental conditioning involves the discontinuation of a reinforcer following a response, as when the delivery of food following a lever press by the rat is discontinued. Gradually, as the response continues to be exhibited without the receipt of reinforcement, the frequency of the response declines.

In the RI paradigm, when subjects set about learning list A-D following the learning of list A-B, they occasionally produce B responses. These B responses, in the context of learning list A-D, are treated as errors, and subjects are thus not rewarded for producing B responses. As a result, so the unlearning explanation suggests, A-B associations that lead to incorrect B responses during list A-D learning are gradually weakened or unlearned. (This view of extinction contrasts with explanations based on the influence of inhibition. See Chapter 2.) When subjects are subsequently tested on list A-B, RI is exhibited because, in part, of the unlearning of some of the A-B associations during the learning of list A-D. In proposing that both response competition and unlearning contribute to RI, Melton and Irwin (1940) originated what has come to be known as the **two-factor theory of forgetting.**

To try to test for the occurrence of unlearning, independent of response competition, Barnes and Underwood (1959) introduced a procedure known as **modified-modified free**

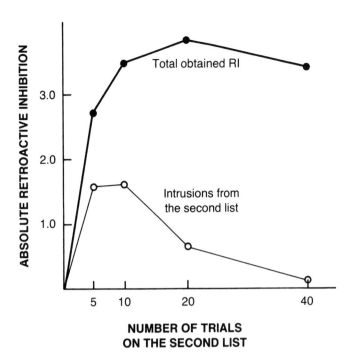

FIGURE 9–2 RI and the number of second-list intrusions as a function of the number of trials spent learning the second list (list A-D) in the study by Melton and Irwin (1940). The absolute retroactive inhibition was defined as the difference in recall of the experimental group and a control group that learned only the first list.

Source: Melton, A. W., & Irwin, J. M. (1940). The influence of degree of interpolated learning on retroactive inhibition and the overt transfer of specific responses. *American Journal of Psychology, 53,* 198. Reprinted with permission of University of Illinois Press.

recall (MMFR). In the MMFR procedure, experimental subjects learned both list A-B and list A-D. The memory test consisted of giving the subjects the A stimulus terms and asking them to recall, under unlimited time conditions, both the B and D response terms. Under these conditions, it was reasoned, response competition would be minimized, and any evidence of RI would therefore be attributable to unlearning. When list A-D was studied for 20 trials, subjects could only recall about 50% of the B responses, thus supporting the notion that the learning of A-D associations contributed to the unlearning of A-B associations.

However, verbal learning studies investigating the phenomenon of spontaneous recovery present a problem for the unlearning component of the two-factor interference theory. Recall from Chapter 3 that, once an instrumental response has undergone extinction, reexposure to the testing situation following a delay typically results in a reemergence of the response. That is, with the passage of time, the strength of the extinguished response appears to recover—hence, the term *spontaneous recovery.* If in the RI paradigm list A-B associations are unlearned and thus weakened in a manner analogous to the weakening of an instrumental response undergoing extinction, then list A-B associations should recover strength with the passage of time.

Although some investigators have reported evidence of spontaneous recovery in verbal learning studies of RI (e.g., Forrester, 1970; Shulman & Martin, 1970), such findings are rare (Keppel, 1968). Furthermore, Postman, Stark, and Fraser (1968) have noted that even in those rare situations in which spontaneous recovery in the RI verbal learning paradigm is observed, the size of the effect tends to be very small.

How is unlearning different from response competition, and why does the failure to find evidence of spontaneous recovery in the RI verbal learning paradigm represent a problem for the unlearning explanation of RI?

Response Set Suppression. The results from a P-A study by Postman and Stark (1969) were an even more direct challenge to unlearning explanation of RI than were the inconsistent findings of spontaneous recovery in studies of RI. In the Postman and Stark study, subjects learned lists A-B and A-D and then were tested on list A-B by being presented with each A stimulus term and a set of B responses from which the correct B response was to be chosen. Thus the test on list A-B involved a multiple-choice recognition test. Postman and Stark found no evidence of RI using this type of recognition test of list A-B associations. If the learning of list A-D resulted in the unlearning of some list A-B associations, then evidence of RI should have been found on the recognition test of list A-B. Such results led Postman and Stark (1969; Postman, Stark, & Fraser, 1968) to propose yet another factor that may contribute to RI. They called this factor **response-set suppression.**

The basic notion is that competition at the time of test may involve not only competition between individual stimulus-response associations but also competition between groups or sets of responses. As subjects learn list A-D, they come to suppress or temporarily inhibit the entire set of B responses learned originally by adopting a "rule" that involves evaluating whether each potential response was a member of the most recently studied list (Postman, 1969). (Note the similarity to explanations of extinction based on the concept of inhibition. See Chapter 2.)

Thus A-B associations are, according to this explanation, not unlearned or made permanently unavailable; rather, they are made temporarily inaccessible or difficult to retrieve, as a result of the subjects' focusing on the learning of list A-D. Following list A-D learning, subjects are unable to access immediately the entire set of B responses when list A-B is again tested. A particular set of responses possesses inertia, resulting in a tendency for subjects to continue to give responses from the most recently learned set (Postman & Underwood, 1973).

The introduction of this notion of response-set suppression represented a major departure from traditional interference theory and basic associationism with its emphasis on the individual association as the basis for explaining forgetting. As such, the notion further complicated interference theory and contributed to growing concern with the general usefulness of the theory. The introduction of the concept of response set suppression and its attendant assumptions that go beyond the basic tenets of associationism can also be seen as another example of the movement toward cognitivism in the explanation of basic memory phenomena.

◩ *How does response-set suppression differ from response competition, and why does the notion represent a major departure from the basic tenets of traditional interference theory?*

Cue-Dependent Forgetting. Further supporting the suggestion that second list learning does not result in the unlearning of the first list is evidence of the effectiveness of retrieval cues in reducing RI. In a study by Tulving and Psotka (1971), subjects learned six different word lists. Each list was comprised of 24 words, 4 words from each of six different semantic categories. In order to make the categorized nature of the list obvious to subjects, the four instances of each category occurred together in the list. A free recall test immediately followed three presentations of each list. Once all six lists had been studied and tested in this fashion, subjects were asked to recall all of the words from all six lists. Figure 9-3 shows the results from this overall free recall test, with the number of words recalled plotted as a function of the list in which they were learned.

RI was obvious in that the level of recall of a list was inversely related to the number of other lists studied after it. Following the overall free recall test, a cued recall test was also administered. On this test, subjects were given the names of the categories from which all of the items in the six lists were drawn. The results from this cued recall test are also shown in Figure 9–3. The RI noted in the overall free recall test was virtually eliminated. Recall from the first list studied was only very slightly less than recall from the last list studied.

These results suggest that RI is not the product of an unlearning process that makes previously learned associations permanently unavailable. Rather, succeeding learning episodes appear to make previously encoded information temporarily inaccessible. Tulving (1974, 1976, 1984) has interpreted these findings in terms of cue-dependent forgetting. That is, Tulving argues that forgetting from long-term memory is best thought of in terms of retrieval failure resulting from the lack of effective cues at the time memory is tested. In the Application presented at the beginning of the chapter, Alan's sudden discovery of cues in another exam question that led him to the answer to one of the troublesome short-answer questions illustrates this cue-dependent view of forgetting.

How do Tulving and Psotka's (1971) findings that category cues can lead to the recall of items not produced on a free recall test contradict an unlearning explanation of RI?

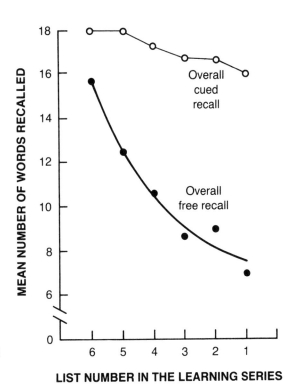

FIGURE 9–3 Free recall and cued recall results from the Tulving and Psotka (1971) study.

Source: Figure from *Cognitive Psychology* by Michael G. Wessells. Copyright © 1982 by Michael G. Wessells. Reprinted by permission of HarperCollins Publishers.

Explanations of PI

Response Competition.   Just as in the case of RI, interference found in the PI paradigm can be interpreted in terms of competition between the individual stimulus-response associations acquired in studying the two lists. Thus when tested on list A-D again after a delay following the original learning of list A-D, performance may be adversely affected by the intrusion of unwanted A-B associations. One phenomenon for which such an explanation of PI must account is the gradual development of PI with increasing delay following the learning of list A-D.

For example, Morgan and Underwood (1950) found that a minimum delay of 20 minutes following the original learning of list A-D was necessary to find evidence of PI on the subsequent test of list A-D. This gradual development of PI can in turn be explained in terms of the unlearning of A-B associations during the learning of list A-D and the subsequent spontaneous recovery of A-B associations with increasing delay. As the unlearned A-B associations recover, they come to interfere with the correct recall of A-D associations. However, the evidence challenging the phenomena of unlearning and spontaneous recovery already cited poses a problem for this aspect of a response competition explanation of PI.

A further complication for the response competition explanation of PI comes from studies employing the MMFR technique. If the technique does in fact eliminate competition between responses associated with the same stimulus by encouraging recall of both responses in the absence of time constraints, then PI should not be found using the MMFR technique. However, PI has been demonstrated with the MMFR technique (Ceraso & Henderson, 1965; Postman, Stark, & Fraser, 1968).

📓 *Why do studies of unlearning and MMFR studies of PI present problems for a response competition explanation of PI?*

List Differentiation Hypothesis.   In response to these difficulties with the response competition explanation of PI, Underwood (1969) proposed the list differentiation hypothesis. This hypothesis proposes that, at the time of the delayed test on list A-D, both A-B and A-D associations may be available but the individual has difficulty deciding which associations were acquired more recently and should thus be the basis for responding on the test. One obvious prediction of this position is that any manipulation that increases the discriminability of list A-B and list A-D should reduce the PI observed.

Consistent with this prediction, Underwood and Freund (1968) found less PI when the learning of list A-B and the learning of list A-D were separated by three days than when both lists were learned on the same day. Similarly, Underwood and Ekstrand (1966) found that when list A-B was learned over a four-day period (a condition psychologists call **distributed practice**) and list A-D was learned in a single session (a condition psychologists call **massed practice**) there was less PI than when both lists were learned under conditions of massed practice. The list differentiation explanation can account for this result by arguing that the difference in practice conditions in the first instance made the two lists more distinctive and thus less susceptible to interference.

Note, however, that just as in the case of the response-set suppression explanation of RI, the list differentiation hypothesis represents a fundamental departure from traditional interference theory and its reliance on basic principles of associationism. In introducing the concept of list discriminability, Underwood also moved away from an explanation of forgetting based solely on competition between individual stimulus-response associations.

Here again there is evidence of a trend toward a more cognitive view of forgetting as retrieval failure resulting from inadequate retrieval cues at the time of test. In the case of the list differentiation hypothesis, Underwood and colleagues have focused on the role that temporal or recency cues, among others, can play in successful retrieval.

☑ *Why does the list differentiation explanation of PI represent a fundamental departure from traditional interference theory?*

FORGETTING AS CUE-DEPENDENT RETRIEVAL FAILURE

As an alternative to traditional interference theory, the approach to forgetting as cue-dependent retrieval failure provides a general framework for interpreting a number of memory phenomena. For example, this view of forgetting is related to Watkins and Watkins' (1975) suggestion that interference effects be viewed as the product of cue overload. The **cue overload principle** argues that the effectiveness of a cue is inversely related to the number of long-term memory representations containing information that matches the cue (Stern, 1985). As the number of representations containing information that matches the cue increases, each representation will be less strongly activated by the presentation of the cue, on the assumption that a given cue will only support a certain maximum amount of activation in the long-term store. Thus both RI and PI effects can be seen as the result of overloaded retrieval cues.

This cue-overload principle is consistent with other memory findings such as the **list length effect** in free recall (Murdock, 1962). The list length effect refers to the fact that the probability of recall declines as list length increases. The cue-overload principle would argue that the cues prompting recall of list members become less and less effective as the number of to-be-remembered items associated with them increases, resulting in greater dispersion of activation at the time of retrieval.

As another example of memory phenomena that can be interpreted with the framework of cue-dependent forgetting, consider the context effects on memory that were discussed in Chapter 7 in relation to the encoding specificity principle. Recall that being in a drug state or a mood state at the time of retrieval that is different from one's state at the time of encoding adversely affects memory performance. Such a finding is interpretable in terms of the degree of difference in cues present at the time of encoding and at the time of retrieval. When one is in a different drug or mood state at the time of retrieval, there are fewer cues present that match those that were included in one's memory representation of the information, making it less likely that the information will be successfully accessed in memory.

☑ *How can the cue-overload principle and state-dependent learning effects be viewed in the context of cue-dependent forgetting?*

Organizational Factors in Memory Retrieval

This view of forgetting as cue-dependent retrieval failure is also generally consistent with approaches to memory that emphasize the importance of organizational factors in effective memory retrieval. As researchers in the 1950s and the 1960s turned to consider how organizational factors may influence the encoding and retrieval of information in long-term memory, they found interference theory and simple associationism to be inadequate as a general framework for their investigations. Instead, researchers focusing on organizational issues tended to rely on more cognitive accounts of the memory system, such as the multistore models and descriptions of long-term memory as networks of associated nodes, as the basis for interpreting their findings.

Objective Organizational Factors

Category Clustering. In 1953 Bousfield presented subjects with a list of 60 nouns belonging to four distinct semantic categories: animals, male names, professions, and vegetables. The nouns were presented in random order as subjects studied for a free recall test on the items, but in their recall of the items subjects tended to recall together items from the same semantic category. Bousfield called this tendency **category clustering.** If recall order were random, one item from a particular category should have followed another item from that same category approximately 25% of the time. Instead, Bousfield found that items from the same category followed each other in subjects' recall approximately 45% of the time. This finding demonstrated that subjects actively attempt to organize items, based on their meaning and prior associations, even when not explicitly instructed to do so.

Objective Organizational Frameworks. From Bousfield's demonstration that subjects will attempt to organize information, researchers turned to demonstrating that organizing information improves its retrieval. In 1969 Bower, Clark, Lesgold, and Winzenz presented subjects with 112 words to be remembered. The words were drawn from four main semantic categories, and within each of these main categories, the items could be further organized into a hierarchy of subcategories. The top portion of Figure 9–4 shows this hierarchical organization for the main category of minerals. One group of subjects saw the items hierarchically arranged in this fashion. The other group of subjects saw the items in a

HIERARCHICAL DISPLAY OF THE MINERALS CATEGORY

		Minerals		
	Metals		Stones	
Rare	Common	Alloys	Precious	Masonry
platinum	aluminum	bronze	sapphire	limestone
silver	copper	steel	emerald	granite
gold	lead	brass	diamond	marble
	iron		ruby	slate

RANDOM DISPLAY OF THE MINERALS CATEGORY

		Brass		
	Ruby		Gold	
Granite	Steel	Lead	Iron	Sapphire
minerals	limestone	metals	masonry	alloys
emerald	rare	precious	aluminum	diamond
copper	stones	slate	common	platinum
	silver		bronze	marble

FIGURE 9–4 Example of the hierarchical and random presentation of words from one of the four main categories in the Bower, Clark, Lesgold, and Winzenz (1969) study.

Source: Figure from *Cognitive Psychology* by Michael G. Wessells. Copyright © 1982 by Michael G. Wessells. Reprinted by permission of HarperCollins Publishers.

random arrangement, as shown in the bottom portion of Figure 9–4. Each group experienced four study-test trials. The hierarchical arrangement group showed consistently better recall of the items. On the first test, the hierarchical group recalled 73 of the 112 words, whereas the random group recalled only 20. On the fourth test, the hierarchical group recalled all 112 words, whereas the random group recalled 61.

In a followup to this study, Santa, Ruskin, Snuttjer, and Baker (1975) demonstrated the importance of organizing the material hierarchically at the time of study. Three groups of subjects were employed and studied the materials used in the Bower and colleagues' (1969) study just described. One group studied the words arranged in the meaningful hierarchical arrangement, and the other two groups studied the words in random arrangement. Following an attempt to free recall the words, recall cues were provided. For each major category, the top three levels of the hierarchy were provided spatially arranged as in Figure 9–4 as recall cues for the hierarchical group and one of the random groups. The other random group received the same words as cues but they were arranged in random order. The mean number of additional words recalled for the three groups respectively were 19.0, 10.2, and 4.8. Thus organization at the time of encoding clearly facilitates later retrieval, but an organizational structure can improve recall somewhat even when present only at the time of recall.

Other researchers have compared the effectiveness of different organizational frameworks in promoting retrieval. Broadbent, Cooper, and Broadbent (1978) compared a hierarchical and a matrix retrieval scheme in the memory of sets of words. Figure 9–5 shows the two alternative organizational schemes for the sets of words used in one of their experiments. When they compared the memory of words studied in one of the two organizational frameworks with the memory of words studied in a random arrangement, they found that both organizational schemes produced better recall than that shown with random presentation, but there was no difference in the effectiveness of the two organizational arrangements. Thus there may be no generally preferred manner of organizing information for efficient encoding and retrieval. What may be most important is that the information be organized in such a way that effective retrieval cues can be generated and used at the time of test.

What is the significance of category clustering in free recall, and why do objective organizational frameworks promote effective memory retrieval?

Subjective Organization

There is also now considerable evidence to suggest that subjects impose their own organization on to-be-remembered material that lack a clear objective organization. In a study by Tulving (1962), free recall of a list of 16 unrelated nouns was measured on 16 trials, with a different order of presentation of the nouns on each trial. Tulving found that recall order became more and more stereotyped across trials. That is, the correspondence between order of recall on successive trials increased across the trials. Because the stereotyped recall order across trials was highly idiosyncratic to individual subjects, this type of organization has been dubbed **subjective organization.**

Tulving went on in this experiment and in a subsequent one (Tulving, 1964) to demonstrate a high correlation between the degree of subjective organization displayed and amount recalled. That is, he found that both subjective organization and the number of words recalled increased across trials, as shown in Figure 9–6. Some other investigators have reported similar correlations between degree of subjective organization and recall (e.g.,

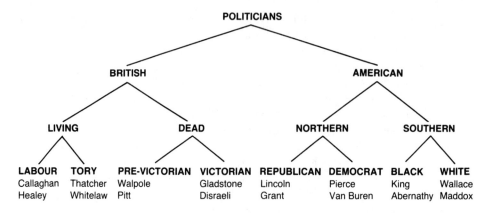

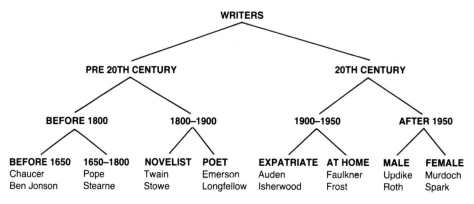

POLITICIANS

	BEFORE 1900		AFTER 1900	
	BRITISH	AMERICAN	BRITISH	AMERICAN
A–L	Gladstone Disraeli	Lincoln Grant	Callaghan Healey	King Abernathy
M–Z	Walpole Pitt	Pierce Van Buren	Thatcher Whitelaw	Wallace Maddox

WRITERS

	BEFORE 1900		AFTER 1900	
	BRITISH	AMERICAN	BRITISH	AMERICAN
A–L	Chaucer Ben Jonson	Emerson Longfellow	Auden Isherwood	Faulkner Frost
M–Z	Pope Stearne	Twain Stowe	Murdoch Spark	Updike Roth

FIGURE 9–5 Hierarchical and matrix organizational schemes for to-be-remembered items in one of the experiments by Broadbent, Cooper, and Broadbent (1978).

Source: Broadbent, D. E., Cooper, P. J., & Broadbent, M. H. P. (1978). A comparison of hierarchical and matrix retrieval schemes in recall. *Journal of Experimental Psychology: Human Learning and Memory, 4,* 494–495. Copyright 1978 by the American Psychological Association. Reprinted by permission.

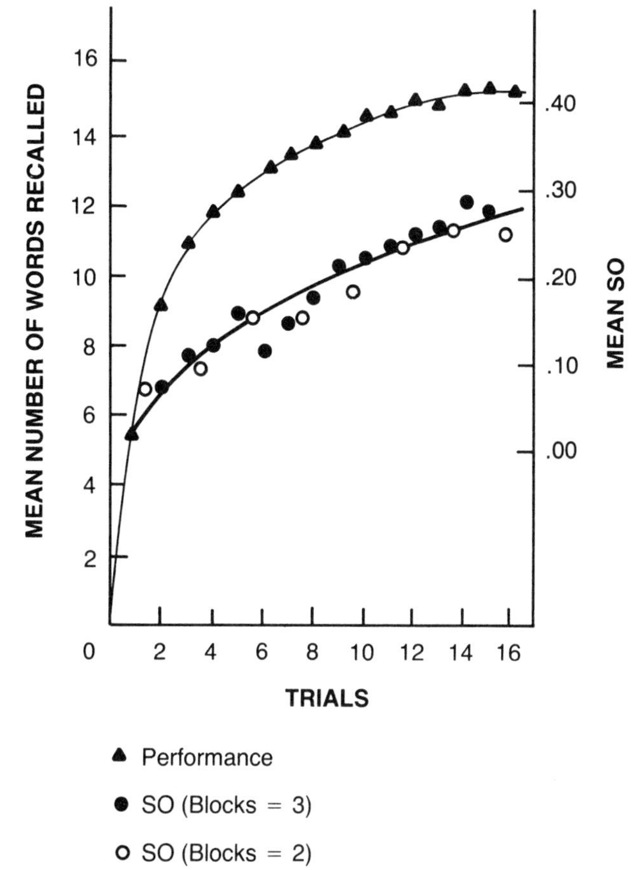

FIGURE 9–6 Mean number of words recalled and amount of subjective organization exhibited as a function of trials in the study by Tulving (1962). Subjective organization was measured over blocks of both two and three trials.

Source: Tulving, E. (1962). Subjective organization in free recall of "unrelated" words. *Psychological Review, 69,* 349. In the public domain.

▲ Performance

● SO (Blocks = 3)

○ SO (Blocks = 2)

Allen, 1968; Mayhew, 1967). Yet, other investigators (e.g., Postman, 1970; Shapiro & Bell, 1970) have failed to obtain significant correlations between degree of subjective organization and amount recalled.

In attempting to reconcile these conflicting findings, Wood (1972) endorsed Postman's (1970) suggestion that multiple associations involving individual items are established in the process of list learning and that consistency of output order at recall may, therefore, not be the best way to attempt to organize one's memory for the material. This argument is based on the assumption that, with varied presentation order from trial to trial, it can sometimes be to the subject's advantage to investigate multiple ways of organizing the list instead of deciding early to adopt a particular scheme that is then pursued consistently on succeeding trials. Furthermore, to the degree that multiple associations among items are established during learning, measures of subjective organization that rely exclusively on consistency of output order at recall are not adequate. In view of the possible inadequacy of output order consistency as a measure of subjective organization, Wood (1972) suggested that results from free-recall part-whole transfer studies are less equivocal in demonstrating the importance of subjective organization.

In a 1966 study, Tulving had two groups of subjects learn a list of 9 words over 12 trials. Next, the subjects learned a list of 18 words over 12 additional trials. For one group

---

of subjects, the second list consisted of the 9 words from the first list plus 9 new words, presented in random order. For the second group of subjects, all 18 words in the second list were new. If learning of list items consists primarily of the gradual development of associations between individual items and contextual information, such as the fact that the word is being studied as a part of a memory test, then positive transfer should have been found for those subjects who studied the second list that contained 9 old words. That is, having studied part of the 18-word list previously should have facilitated the learning of the whole list.

On the other hand, if learning is critically dependent on the development of a subjective organization, positive transfer would not necessarily be expected, because the subjective organization appropriate for the 9-word list would not necessarily be appropriate for the 18-word list. In fact, Tulving's results showed a slight negative transfer effect, as illustrated in Figure 9–7. The part-learning group outperformed the new-list group on early trials on the 18-word list, but after 7 trials the subjects who learned a completely new list surpassed the part-learning group. Tulving suggested that the subjects in the part-learning group failed

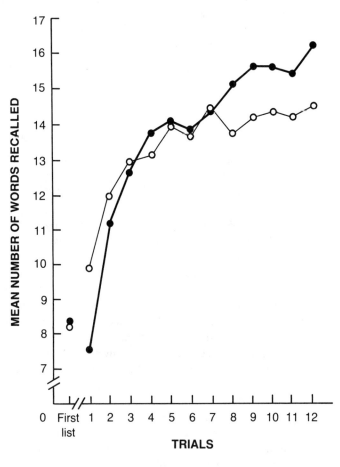

FIGURE 9–7 Mean number of second-list words recalled across trials as a function of whether subjects experienced part-whole transfer in the study by Tulving (1966). The subjects who received old plus new words experienced part-whole transfer, in that half of the words contained in the second list had comprised the first list studied.

Source: Tulving, E. (1966). Subjective organization and effects of repetition in multi-trial free-recall learning. *Journal of Verbal Learning and Verbal Behavior, 5,* 197. Reprinted with permission of Academic Press.

● All 18 "new" words

o 9 "old" plus 9 "new" words

to change previously adopted subjective organizational schemes that were not maximally effective for the expanded list.

Perhaps even less ambiguous are the results from a whole-part transfer study by Tulving and Osler (1967). In this study, two groups of subjects first learned an 18-word list and then learned a 9-word list. For the whole-part group, the second list consisted of 9 words taken from the 18-word list learned originally. For the control group, the second list consisted of 9 new words. Tulving and Osler found that the control subjects performed better on the second list than did the whole-part subjects. These results suggest that the whole-part subjects attempted to employ during the learning of the second list the organizational scheme devised during the learning of the first list and that the scheme was inappropriate with only part of the list present.

☑ *How can the results from part-whole and whole-part transfer studies of free recall be interpreted as supporting the importance of subjective organization in memory?*

Mnemonic Techniques

Many special techniques that have been devised to promote memory employ organizational processes extensively. These will be examined in detail in Chapter 10. At present, it is sufficient to note that these techniques are based on the assumption that retrieval failures can be minimized by using organizational frameworks that provide for easy access to cues with which the to-be-remembered information has been associated.

Impact of Research on Organizational Factors

The research on organizational influences summarized above represents a continuation of the Ebbinghaus tradition in that the emphasis is on objective, quantifiable measures of verbatim memory under highly controlled laboratory conditions. The Ebbinghaus tradition is also evident in the importance attached to association formation in the interpretation of these studies. However, this research also represents part of the trend over the past 30 years toward viewing the learner as an active interpreter of the material to be learned. As an active interpreter of the material to be learned, the learner, it has been increasingly assumed over this 30-year period, employs a number of mental strategies or techniques that go beyond simple, straightforward association formation. This alternative focus in the study of retrieval processes is even more evident in the description of the Bartlett tradition that follows later in the chapter.

Recognition versus Recall

The Generation-Recognition Model

Within the context of cue-dependent forgetting, it is of interest to examine briefly the traditional theoretical distinction that has been drawn between recognition and recall processes in long-term memory. This distinction is drawn most clearly in the generation-recognition model of recall (e.g., Anderson & Bower, 1972, 1974), also known as the **two-stage theory of recall.** This model suggests that learning a list of words involves learning that the words occurred in a particular context. Thus, during study, the stored representation of each word is given a list "tag" that contains the contextual information necessary for determining that the word was a part of the studied list. That is, an attempt is made to associate a list tag with the stored representation of each presented word. Recall, then, involves an initial generation phase in which access is gained to words that possibly contain the list tag. Once a candidate item is generated, it is subjected to a recognition check to determine if, in fact, the list tag is present.

On the basis of this model, recognition and recall are seen as fundamentally different memory processes. The generation-recognition model argues that recall involves a generation or retrieval process that is absent in straightforward recognition tasks. Thus recognition represents a simpler process of simply judging the familiarity of the item based on the tag information found when the memory representation of the item is accessed. On a recognition test, retrieval of an item's representation in memory through the **copy cue** (i.e., through a copy of the item itself) is guaranteed, because each item is assumed to have only one representation in memory.

Note that this assumption is inconsistent with Tulving's (1972, 1983, 1984, 1985) position, described in Chapter 7, that there exist in long-term store distinct episodic and semantic representations of an item. Tulving's **encoding specificity view** therefore assumes that recognition tests, just like recall tests, involve retrieval processes because there are multiple representations of items in the episodic memory system. Thus Tulving's encoding specificity view argues that recall and recognition differ only in the types of retrieval cues provided at the time of test.

☑ *Why does Tulving's encoding specificity view assume that recognition involves a retrieval process, yet the generation-recognition model does not?*

Recognition Failure of Recallable Words

One of the basic assumptions of the original generation-recognition model is that recallable words will always be recognized. This assumption follows from the position that in order to be recalled, words have to pass the recognition check. Therefore, no word from a studied list should be produced on a recall test that has failed to be recognized on a separately administered recognition test of the to-be-remembered items. Tulving's encoding specificity position makes no such assumption. If one assumes the existence of multiple episodic representations of an item, there exists the possibility that retrieval cues present at the time of recall may lead one to retrieve successfully the representation of an item containing the list tag but then on the recognition test have the copy cue access another representation of the item that does not include the list tag. Under such circumstances, one would recall the item and then fail to recognize it.

To test this prediction of the generation-recognition model, Tulving and associates (Tulving & Thomson, 1973; Watkins & Tulving, 1975) devised a procedure in which subjects study pairs of words (A-B), being told that B is the to-be-remembered item and that A is a cue that may help in remembering B. Subjects are then tested first for recognition of the B words and then for recall of the B words given the A words as cues. The procedure has consistently demonstrated that subjects frequently recall a number of B words that they previously failed to recognize. This phenomenon of recognition failure of recallable words appears to be very reliable (Gardiner, 1988).

☑ *Why do findings of recognition failure of recallable words contradict the generation-recognition model?*

The Modified Generation-Recognition Model

In response to such findings, the generation-recognition model has been modified (e.g., Reder, Anderson, & Bjork, 1974). The modified version of the model argues that each different semantic sense of a word has a separate representation in the memory system and the word's context at the time of study determines which of the senses will be tagged. Thus, to the extent that the demonstrations of recognition failure of recallable words by Tulving and associates involved words with multiple meanings, the modified generation-recognition model can account for the results. Words are recalled that were not recognized because on the recognition test one of the untagged senses of the words was accessed. Then, on the cued recall test, the cues led to the accessing of tagged sense of the words and thus to their recall. However, this modification of the generation-recognition model represents a fundamental change in that the model is now admitting that recognition, just like recall, does involve a retrieval process. The copy cue does not automatically provide access to the to-be-remembered item. Thus one of the major distinctions between recognition and recall proposed in the original generation-recognition model is lost.

However, Tulving and associates have not been content to try to reconcile the modified generation-recognition model with their encoding specificity position. Instead, they have proceeded to try to demonstrate that the modified generation-recognition model is also seriously flawed. In particular, they have challenged the prediction of the modified model that for words with a single meaning there should be no recognition failure of recallable words. This prediction is based on the assumption that words with a single meaning will have only one representation in memory. Therefore, if the word is recalled, its single representation is tagged and thus it will be recognized on a separate recognition test. On the other hand, Tulving and associates assume that even single-meaning words have multiple representations in episodic memory as a result of multiple past experiences with the words. Therefore, the encoding specificity position predicts there will be instances of recognition failure of recallable single-meaning words.

Using words defined by the dictionary as having only one meaning (e.g., *cactus, enzyme, leprosy*), Tulving and Watkins (1977) did indeed demonstrate recognition failure of recallable single-meaning words. In response to criticisms that some of the words used in the Tulving and Watkins may have nevertheless had multiple meanings represented in memory (e.g., Muter, 1984), Nilsson, Law, and Tulving (1988) also demonstrated recognition failure of recallable words in a study in which the to-be-remembered words were unique names of places and famous people (e.g., *Canterbury, Morocco, Albert Einstein, Alfred Nobel, George Washington*) for which multiple meanings seem unlikely. Thus, Tulving and associates appear to have successfully vanquished the generation-recognition model in both its original and modified versions. (For further elaboration of this point, see Gardiner [1988]).

 On what basis have Tulving and associates challenged the modified generation-recognition model?

Flexser-Tulving Model of the Recognition-Recall Relationship

In place of the generation-recognition model, Flexser and Tulving (1978) proposed a formal mathematical model of the relationship between recognition and recall based on the principle of encoding specificity. Successful retrieval on a test of *either* recognition or recall depends on the degree of overlap between features encoded at the time of study and features activated at the time of test. Sometimes context cues provide a better match with the features of an item encoded at study than do copy cues. In such situations, recognition failure of recallable items is observed. Thus, the encoding specificity model, unlike the generation-recognition model, assumes that recall and recognition are essentially independent (i.e., one does not depend on the other) and differ only in terms of the type of retrieval information provided at the time of test. This conceptualization of recognition and recall is thus consistent with the general view of forgetting as cue-dependent retrieval failure. Even forgetting demonstrated on a recognition test can be attributed to a failed retrieval process.

Synergistic Ecphory Model of Retrieval

The Flexser-Tulving model of the relationship between recognition and recall has in turn been modified and incorporated into Tulving's (1983, 1984) synergistic ecphory model of retrieval. In his description of episodic memory, Tulving has proposed a framework he calls the **general abstract processing system** (GAPS). Within GAPS, Tulving describes elements that are involved in the retrieval process (Figure 9–8). Central to this process is what Tulving calls **ecphory.** Ecphory refers to the process whereby information contained in a specific memory trace (referred to in Figure 9–8 as the *original engram*) is utilized to produce conscious memory for the event. Tulving describes this process of ecphory as

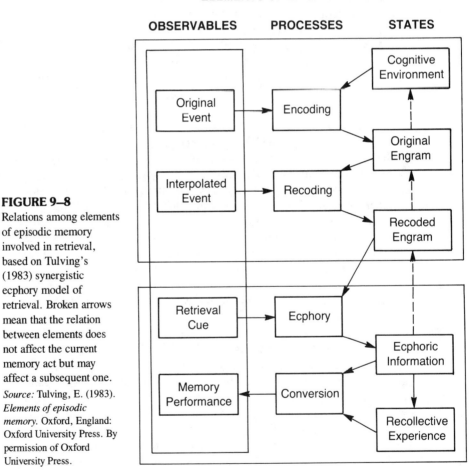

ELEMENTS OF EPISODIC MEMORY

FIGURE 9–8

Relations among elements of episodic memory involved in retrieval, based on Tulving's (1983) synergistic ecphory model of retrieval. Broken arrows mean that the relation between elements does not affect the current memory act but may affect a subsequent one.

Source: Tulving, E. (1983). *Elements of episodic memory.* Oxford, England: Oxford University Press. By permission of Oxford University Press.

constructive, or synergistic, in nature. By this he means that ecphory is a process whereby information in the activated memory trace is combined with the semantic memory information contained in the retrieval cue to produce a conscious recollection of the original item or event. That is, information available at the time of retrieval complements the information available in the activated memory trace of the event.

Alan's attempt to answer exam questions, described at the beginning of the chapter, does not, according to Tulving's ecphory model, simply involve the straightforward accessing and reporting of stored memory traces. Instead, the information contained in the exam questions themselves is integrated with the information available in memory to determine Alan's response to the questions.

Tulving notes that this view of retrieval differs from descriptions that characterize retrieval as the activation of stored associations with cues functioning solely to determine which stored associations are activated during retrieval (e.g., Anderson & Bower, 1973). On this nonecphoric view, Tulving argues, recall and recognition reflect a relatively passive process of responding based solely on the activation of stored memory traces. Such a nonecphoric, associationist view of retrieval, of course, is the basis of the generation-recognition model of recall.

The apparent triumph of the encoding specificity view over the generation-recognition model and the subsequent incorporation of the encoding specificity view into the synergistic ecphory model thus illustrate again the triumph of cognitivism over simple associationism. Tulving's work certainly reflects the continuing Ebbinghaus tradition in that he is a rigorous methodologist who has built his synergistic ecphory model of retrieval on a vast body of empirical results obtained largely from studies of verbatim memory under highly controlled laboratory conditions.

However, the ecphoric process described by Tulving clearly represents a movement toward explanations of retrieval that involve processes that go well beyond the formation and activation of associations in long-term store. In fact, the emphasis in the synergistic ecphory model on retrieval as a constructive process that utilizes information not contained within the stored memory representation of the event reflects the influence of a contrasting tradition in the study of memory, that of Sir Frederic Bartlett.

📝 *How does the synergistic ecphory model's emphasis on retrieval as a constructive process reflect the trend toward cognitive explanations of learning and memory?*

BARTLETT AND THE RECONSTRUCTIVIST TRADITION

Rejection of Ebbinghaus's Emphasis on Memory as a Passive Process

In 1932, Sir Frederic Bartlett published a book entitled *Remembering* in which he outlined an approach to the study of learning and memory that contrasts sharply with that of Ebbinghaus. In this book, Bartlett rejected the view that stimuli are simply imprinted on a person's memory, in the way that Ebbinghaus and the empiricist philosophers seemed to suggest. Rather, he argued, humans by their very nature attempt to impose meaning on the stimuli they encounter. That is, they engage in what Bartlett called an "effort after meaning." Bartlett argued that the attempt to devise completely neutral stimuli, such as Ebbinghaus's CVC trigrams, is futile because subjects will impose meaning on stimuli designed to be meaningless. Therefore, Bartlett was opposed to simplifying the learning situation in the way Ebbinghaus and his followers did. He suggested that making the learning situation highly artificial and oversimplified will lead to results that are basically useless when it comes to predicting how people remember information in real-world situations.

☑ *How does Bartlett's emphasis on "effort after meaning" represent a departure from straightforward associationism?*

The Bartlett Experiment

Bartlett conducted a series of studies that exemplify this alternative approach to memory encoding and retrieval. In Bartlett's experiments, the stimuli used were highly meaningful, complex materials. These materials included stories, other types of prose passages, pictures, and American Indian picture writing (Figure 9–9). In assessing subjects' memory for these materials, Bartlett often employed the method of repeated reproduction. With this method, materials were presented to a subject, and the subject was then asked to recall the materials on several different occasions, with delays ranging from minutes to months.

Evidence of Memory Distortions

Perhaps the most famous of the materials used in Bartlett's experiments is the American Indian folktale, "The War of the Ghosts." The original version of this tale reads as follows:

> *One night two young men from Egulac went down to the river to hunt seals, and while they were there it became foggy and calm. Then they heard war-cries, and they thought: "Maybe this is a war-party." They escaped to the shore, and hid behind a log. Now canoes came up, and they heard the noise of paddles, and saw one canoe coming up to them. There were five men in the canoe, and they said:*
>
> *"What do you think? We wish to take you along. We are going up the river to make war on the people."*
>
> *One of the young men said: "I have no arrows."*
>
> *"Arrows are in the canoe," they said.*
>
> *"I will not go along. I might be killed. My relatives do not know where I have gone. But you," he said turning to the other, "may go with them."*
>
> *So one of the young men went, but the other returned home.*
>
> *And the warriors went on up the river to a town on the other side of Kalama. The people came down to the water, and they began to fight, and many were killed. But presently the young man heard one of the warriors say: "Quick, let us go home: that Indian has been hit." Now he thought: "Oh, they are ghosts." He did not feel sick, but they said he had been shot.*
>
> *So the canoes went back to Egulac, and the young man went ashore to his house, and made a fire. And he told everybody and said: "Behold I accompanied the ghosts, and we went to fight. Many of our fellows were killed, and many of those who attacked us were killed. They said I was hit, and I did not feel sick."*
>
> *He told it all, and then he became quiet. When the sun rose he fell down. Something black came out of his mouth. He face became contorted. The people jumped up and cried.*
>
> *He was dead. (Bartlett, 1932, p. 65)*

PICTURES

PORTRAIT D'HOMME

AMERICAN INDIAN PICTURE WRITING SYMBOLS AND THEIR TRANSLATIONS

FIGURE 9–9 Examples of pictures and American Indian picture writing used as stimuli in Bartlett's (1932) studies of memory.

Source: Bartlett, F. C. (1932). *Remembering.* Cambridge, England: Cambridge University Press, pp. 180, 178, 116. Reprinted with permission.

As subjects were asked to recall the passage with increasing delays, Bartlett found that subjects increasingly distorted the story. The following is one subject's recall of the story after four months:

> *I have no idea of the title.*
>
> *There were two men in a boat, sailing towards an island. When they approached the island, some natives came running towards them, and informed them that there was fighting going on on the island, and invited them to join. One said to the other: "You had better go. I cannot very well, because I have relatives expecting me, and they will not know what has become of me. But you have no one to expect you." So one accompanied the natives, but the other returned.*
>
> *Here there is part I can't remember. What I don't know is how the man got to the fight. However, anyhow the man was in the midst of the fighting, and was wounded. The natives endeavored to persuade the man to return, but he assured them that he had not been wounded.*
>
> *I have an idea that his fighting won the admiration of the natives.*
>
> *The wounded man ultimately fell unconscious. He was taken from the fighting by the natives.*
>
> *Then, I think it is, the natives describe what happened, and they seem to have imagined seeing a ghost coming out of his mouth. Really it was a kind of materialisation of his breath. I know this phrase was not in the story, but that is the idea I have. Ultimately the man died at dawn the next day. (Bartlett, 1932, pp. 70–71)*

Here is the recall of another subject asked to reproduce the passage after a six-month delay:

> *Four men came down to the water. They were told to get into a boat and to take arms with them. They inquired "What arms?" and were answered "Arms for battle." When they came to the battle-field they heard a great noise and shouting, and a voice said: "The black man is dead." And he was brought to the place where they were, and laid on the ground. And he foamed at the mouth. (Bartlett, 1932, pp. 71–72)*

Based on an analysis of such recalls, Bartlett catalogued a number of characteristic ways in which subjects tended to distort their memory for the passage.

Omissions
Subjects tended to leave out a lot of the details, especially those that did not fit with their prior expectations. In the recalls presented above, a great many of the details from the original story were omitted, especially those relating to the supernatural.

Rationalizations
Bartlett noted that unusual or unexpected features were reinterpreted in a form more consistent with subjects' prior experience. For example, in one of the recalls presented above, "Something black came out of his mouth" became "He foamed at the mouth."

Dominant Detail

Bartlett detected a tendency for certain features to take on critical importance and become more and more dominant with successive recalls of the material. That is, certain features became the central theme around which the recall was organized, despite their not being the actual main theme of the original passage. For example, subjects tended over time to make the death scene in "The War of the Ghosts" the central theme of their recalls, even though the death scene comprises only a small part of the original story.

Transformation of Detail

Specific items in the original materials were often changed to a more familiar form. In "The War of the Ghosts," for example, *canoe* was often recalled as *boat*.

> *What sorts of memory distortions did Bartlett discover in his investigations of memory for prose material?*

Recall as a Process of Reconstruction

Such evidence, Bartlett believed, is consistent with his position that information is not passively stored away in memory. Rather, the gist of the message is extracted, resulting in a loss of elements of the original. Extracting the gist of the original results in distortion. The more complex the material, the more obvious the distortion becomes as an attempt is made to relate the new material to information already in memory.

As you will recall from Chapter 7, it was in this context that Bartlett introduced the concept of **schema.** It was Bartlett's contention that information already in memory is highly organized into memory structures, or schemas. In attempting to remember material such as "The War of the Ghosts," individuals rely on a number of different schemas, a number of different organized networks of knowledge based on past experience. For example, in interpreting the story, subjects might rely on their schemas for Indians, ghosts, wars, fighting, and so on. The activation of schemas, Bartlett suggested, results in expectations that may influence the bits of the story to which subjects are particularly likely to attend and thus influence the bits of the story most likely to be remembered. However, these expectations can lead to unintentional distortion of the material when it is inconsistent with expectations and can lead to very accurate recall when the material is compatible with expectations.

Bartlett believed that schemas influence the "effort after meaning." The more successful the effort, the greater the learning will be. Bartlett stressed what has come to be known as the **reconstructive (or constructive) view** of memory. This view suggests that information is seldom remembered exactly as it was presented. Frequently at the time memory retrieval is required, individuals only have readily accessible in memory fragments of the to-be-remembered information. Recall, according to the reconstructivist view, then becomes a process of using general knowledge and expectations to combine remembered fragments into a coherent reproduction of the gist of the original. It is just such a process of reconstruction that Alan is attempting in his response to the difficult discussion question in the Application at the beginning of the chapter.

> *What role do schemas play in Bartlett's characterization of memory reconstruction?*

Bartlett's Major Contribution

Bartlett, unlike Ebbinghaus, was not a great methodologist. He did not precisely measure or quantify the amount recalled by his subjects or the number of distortions exhibited. Instead, he relied on rather subjective, imprecise prose interpretations of his findings. Such a reliance on nonobjective accounts would be unacceptable today. However, the notion of schema and the emphasis on the learner as an active encoder who interprets rather than records the stimulus is one of the dominant themes in the learning literature today.

☑ *What is Bartlett's major contribution to present-day investigations of learning and memory?*

Schema Theory's Relationship to Retrieval from Long-Term Memory

Schemas as Comprehension and Memory Facilitators

In Chapter 7, Bransford and Johnson's (1972) landmark study employing the "Doing the Laundry" passage was presented in support of Bartlett's contention that the activation of relevant schemas contributes importantly to the comprehension and retention of to-be-remembered information. In a later study, Bransford and Johnson (1973) found additional results consistent with this position. In this study, one group of subjects read the following passage:

> **Watching a Peace March from the 40th Floor**
> *The view was breathtaking. From the window one could see the crowd below. Everything looked extremely small from such a distance, but the colorful costumes could still be seen. Everyone seemed to be moving in one direction in an orderly fashion and there seemed to be little children as well as adults. The landing was gentle, and luckily the atmosphere was such that no special suits had to be worn. At first there was a great deal of activity. Later, when the speeches started, the crowd quieted down. The man with the television camera took many shots of the setting and the crowd. Everyone was very friendly and seemed glad when the music started.*
> *(Bransford & Johnson, 1973, p. 412)*

A second group of subjects read the same passage but with the title "A Space Trip to an Inhabited Planet." Of particular interest to Bransford and Johnson was subjects' recall of the target sentence *The landing was gentle, and luckily the atmosphere was such that no special suits had to be worn.* On a free recall test, only 18% of the subjects who read the passage with the "Peace March" title recalled the target sentence, whereas 53% of the subjects who read the passage with the "Space Trip" title recalled the target sentence. When recall of the target sentence was cued with the sentence frame *The landing _____ and luckily the atmosphere _____* , the pattern of results was the same: 29% recall by the "Peach March" group and 82% by the "Space Trip" group. The large difference in recall in the two title conditions can be attributed to how well the target sentence fits into the preexisting memory structure activated by the title of the passage. In the "Peace March" condition, the target sentence cannot readily be linked to old information in memory relating to the topic of marches. Such results are consistent with Bartlett's position that what is remembered is the product of both the actual input and the prior knowledge structures that are activated at the time of processing.

Brewer and Treyens (1981) have also demonstrated that schemas can play a role in people's memory for places. They had subjects wait in the office shown in Figure 9–10 for 35 seconds without telling them that their memory for the room would later be tested. When subjects were subsequently asked to recall everything in the office, they did very well in recalling objects that are likely to part of one's office schema. For example, 29 of the 30 subjects recalled that the office contained a desk, a chair, and walls. However, there was also a tendency to recall schema-consistent objects that were not actually in the office they were asked to recall. Of the 30 subjects, 9 incorrectly recalled that the office contained books. There was also a tendency not to recall objects that were actually present in the office but are not part of most people's office schema. Only 1 subject remembered the picnic basket, and only 8 subjects remembered the skull.

Closely related to such research are investigations demonstrating the importance of the reader's or listener's perspective to what is remembered. In 1977 Pichert and Anderson had two groups of subjects read the same passage describing two boys and the house in which they were playing. One group read the passage after being asked to adopt the perspective of a potential home buyer. The other group read the passage after being asked to adopt the perspective of a burglar. The results demonstrated that subjects' recall was strongly affected by the perspective they adopted when reading the material.

For example, subjects who read with the perspective of a burglar were much more likely to recall that there was a color television set in the house, whereas subjects who read with the perspective of a home buyer were much more likely to recall that there was a leak in the roof of the house. Furthermore, when subjects were asked after completing their recall attempt to adopt the other perspective, they succeeded in recalling additional information consistent with the new perspective. This finding suggests, in accordance with Bartlett's

FIGURE 9–10 The office that subjects were asked to recall in the Brewer and Treyens (1981) study of schemas for places.

Source: Brewer, W. F., & Treyens, J. C. (1981). Role of schemata in memory for places. *Cognitive Psychology, 13,* 211. Reprinted with permission of Academic Press.

view, that subjects may have available at the time of test information in memory that is not actually recalled because it is not consistent with the schema that subjects are using to guide their reconstruction of the original information.

Stereotypes can also be seen as examples of schemas that can affect subjects' reconstruction of their memory for a person or event. Snyder and Uranowitz (1978) had subjects read a narrative about events in the life of Betty K. The narrative included facts about Betty's social life, such as "Although she never had a steady boyfriend in high school, she did go out on dates." After reading the narrative, subjects were given additional information about Betty to lead them to stereotype her. One group was told that Betty later adopted a lesbian lifestyle. The other group was told that Betty later married and became a housewife.

When recall was requested, the "lesbian lifestyle" group showed greater recall of the fact "she never had a steady boyfriend" than they did of the fact "she did go out on dates." The "married/housewife" group showed the opposite pattern. One possible interpretation of these results is that subjects used their *lesbian* and *housewife* schemas at the time of recall to guide their reconstruction of their memory for the narrative. Memory of other people appears to be susceptible to reconstruction based on subsequently acquired information.

☑ *How can passage titles, instructions to adopt a particular perspective in reading information, and stereotyping be related to the issue of schema activation and memory?*

Schemas and the Inferencing Process

In the preceding chapter, the possibility that schemas can lead to memory distortion by encouraging one to encode and subsequently retrieve information beyond that actually given was discussed. Further evidence of such a process comes from a study by Sulin and Dooling (1974). Half of the subjects in the study read the following passage:

> **Carol Harris's Need for Professional Help**
> *Carol Harris was a problem child from birth. She was wild, stubborn, and violent. By the time Carol turned eight, she was still unmanageable. Her parents were very concerned about her mental health. There was no good institution for her problem in their state. Her parents finally decided to take some action. They hired a private teacher for Carol. (Sulin & Dooling, 1974, p. 256)*

The other half of the subjects read the passage with the name "Helen Keller" substituted for "Carol Harris." A recognition test followed the reading of the passage. For each sentence presented on the test, subjects had to judge whether it was one presented in the passage. On a delayed test one week later, 50% of those in the "Helen Keller" group incorrectly indicated that the test sentence *She was deaf, dumb, and blind* was in the passage read, whereas only 5% of those in the "Carol Harris" group incorrectly indicated that this test sentence was in the passage read. This finding is interesting in relation to the distinction between semantic and episodic knowledge discussed in Chapter 7.

The type of memory distortion found in the Sulin and Dooling study and in the Johnson, Bransford, and Solomon (1973) study summarized in the preceding chapter is different from the distortions Bartlett identified as being the product of an attempt to incorporate into existing schemas new information that is inconsistent with the schemas. In fact, the findings from the Sulin and Dooling study suggest that successful integration of new episodic information into existing schemas can lead to errors on verbatim tests of episodic memory when the test includes distractors that are part of the semantic memory schema activated by the to-be-remembered information. To the degree that establishing an episodic memory trace of to-be-remembered information involves incorporating information from relevant schemas in semantic memory, subjects may subsequently be unable to distinguish between that information acquired as part of the most recent learning episode and that provided by the semantic memory schema.

☑ *How does schema-based inferencing sometimes lead to memory errors?*

Distortions Based on Reconstruction

The extent to which reconstruction and memory distortion, as opposed to the straightforward retrieval of an available memory trace, occurs at the time of memory retrieval has been investigated by Spiro (1977, 1980a, 1980b). Spiro set about to investigate the hypothesis that distortions are particularly likely to occur when presented information violates the subject's expectations.

In one of his studies, subjects read a story about an engaged couple, Bob and Margie. At the time they read the story, subjects in the incidental learning group were simply told that they would be asked later about their reactions to the story. They were not told to expect a memory test on the passage. The subjects read that Bob and Margie were happily planning their marriage but that Bob had a problem he was reluctant to discuss: he did not want children. Finally, he shared his feelings with Margie. In one version of the passage used, subjects read that Margie was horrified because she wanted to be a mother and that a fight followed. Eight minutes after reading the passage, subjects were given by the experimenter additional information about Bob and Margie that was either confirmatory with regard to the expectations the passage had created in the readers (e.g., Bob and Margie broke off their engagement) or contradictory with regard to their expectations about Bob and Margie's relationship (e.g., Bob and Margie did get married and are living together happily).

It was Spiro's prediction that the contradictory information would lead subjects to develop new expectations that would in turn lead them to systematically distort their memory for the passage. For example, in recalling the passage, subjects might systematically reduce the severity of the initial disagreement or incorporate into their memory events to resolve the conflict. After a delay of two days, three weeks, or six weeks, subjects were unexpectedly asked to reproduce the original story. As predicted, subjects in the contradictory condition distorted the story more frequently and in a systematic fashion, particularly following the longer delays of three and six weeks. Examples of the systematic distortions produced by subjects in the contradictory condition were:

1. *They separated but realized after discussing the matter that their love mattered more.*
2. *They underwent counseling to correct the major discrepancy.*
3. *They discussed it and decided they could agree on a compromise: adoption.*
4. *She was only a little upset at the disagreement. (Spiro, 1980a, p. 91)*

In addition to asking for recall of the passage, Spiro also asked subjects to rate such sentence recalled as to how confident they were that the meaning of the sentence was explicitly expressed somewhere in the story. Spiro found that with three-week and six-week delays, subjects were more confident that their distortions were part of the story than they were that correctly recalled elements were part of the story. Clearly, confidence in one's memory is no guarantee of accuracy.

However, Spiro had another group in his experiment in which subjects were told prior to reading the story that they would be asked to recall it. Subjects in this group made very few errors or systematic distortions. Furthermore, subjects in the contradictory condition made no more errors than subjects in the confirmatory condition. Thus the instructions given to subjects are powerful determinants of encoding and retrieval processes. Spiro concluded that distortions are more likely to occur when: (1) the subject is not oriented to encode the exact wording (i.e., when the subject is not expecting a verbatim memory test), (2) the remembered fragments of information conflict with present expectations, and (3) very few details are actually available in memory, as, for example, when recall is requested after a delay.

It is certainly the case that even in a natural environment outside the memory laboratory individuals do sometimes show verbatim memory for material with little or no evidence of an attempt at reconstruction. Rubin (1977) assessed college students' memory for material learned outside the laboratory. The material subjects were asked to recall included passages from the 23rd Psalm, the Gettysburg Address, the Preamble to the Constitution, Hamlet's soliloquy, and the "Star Spangled Banner." Rubin found that subjects showed all-or-none verbatim recall for the portions of the materials that were remembered. This tendency of subjects either to remember portions of the materials word-for-word or not at all may reflect a societal convention that emphasizes the verbatim memory of these materials.

What remains unclear, however, is the extent to which people outside the memory laboratory routinely demonstrate reconstruction as opposed to what Bahrick (1984) calls **replication,** or recall that closely matches the to-be-remembered information. Bahrick has pointed out that people routinely show replicative memory for overlearned information, such as one's own name or the name of close family members, the meanings of common words, routine facts (e.g., who was the first President of the United States), and other information that comprises much of one's general knowledge. Neisser (1984), on the other hand, argues that replicative memory is the exception rather than the rule and that memory for events from one's life is routinely influenced heavily by schemas.

Interestingly, the examples of replicative memory given by Bahrick and the materials used by Rubin in demonstrating long-term verbatim memory involve what Tulving (1983, 1984, 1985) would call procedural or semantic memory, whereas Neisser's argument for the importance of reconstructive memory is based largely on examples of episodic memory. Thus Tulving's classification of memories as procedural, semantic, and episodic may also be important in helping frame research on the conditions under which memory is likely to be reconstructive versus replicative.

What factors influence the tendency of individuals to show reconstruction versus replication in their memory for information?

Eyewitness Memory as Reconstruction
Evidence of the Unreliability of Eyewitness Accounts. There is now a considerable body of research that suggests that eyewitness accounts of events are unreliable, perhaps because they are often a reconstruction of the event rather than the recall of a specific, readily available memory trace (e.g., Loftus, 1977; Loftus, 1979a, 1979b; Loftus & Greene, 1980; Loftus & Loftus, 1980).

In 1974 Loftus and Palmer had subjects watch a film of an automobile accident. Subsequently, subjects were questioned about the speed of the cars involved in the accident. One group of subjects was asked: "About how fast were the cars going when they *smashed* into each other?'' The other group of subjects was asked: ''About how fast were the cars going when they *hit* each other?'' The subjects who received the ''smashed'' question gave significantly higher estimates of speed. Furthermore, the subjects who received the ''smashed'' question were significantly more likely to report seeing broken glass as a result of the accident than were the subjects who received the ''hit'' question, when, in fact, no broken glass was shown in the film. Similarly, Loftus (1975, Experiment 3) asked subjects after viewing a film, ''How fast was the white sports car going when it passed the barn while traveling along the country road?'' when in fact no barn was shown. She found that the misleading question increased the likelihood that subjects subsequently reported seeing a barn.

These results appear to show that questions or other subsequently encountered information can guide one's reconstruction of an event. Such evidence strongly suggests that leading questions during a criminal investigation or a trial are very undesirable and that their use should continue to be discouraged. Such evidence is particularly noteworthy, given that victims of a traumatic episode are particularly likely to have trouble retrieving information about the episode and may, therefore, be particularly prone to memory reconstruction under the influence of questioning. These results do not, however, address the issue of whether subsequently encountered information produces permanent distortion of the actual memory trace for the event.

What effect, based on the research of Loftus and her colleagues, are leading questions likely to have on eyewitness accounts of an event?

Evidence that Misleading Information Distorts the Stored Memory Representation of the Event. To address this question, Loftus and colleagues (Loftus, Miller, & Burns, 1978) extended the research on eyewitness memory by presenting a series of slides that showed an automobile-pedestrian accident. The critical slide showed a traffic sign at the intersection where the accident occurred. Half of the subjects saw a slide that included a stop sign, and the other half of the subjects saw a slide that included a yield sign. In a subsequent series of questions, one half of the subjects of each group received a question that stated that there was a stop sign at the intersection, and the other half of the subjects received a question that stated that there was a yield sign at the intersection. Thus half of the subjects received information in the question that was misleading with respect to the event actually witnessed, and half of the subjects received information in the critical question that was consistent with respect to the event actually witnessed.

In the memory test in one of these experiments, subjects were shown, after a 20-minute delay, 15 pairs of slides and had to select from each pair the one they had been shown earlier. One of the pairs of slides showed the stop sign and the yield sign. Loftus and colleagues found that 75% of the subjects who received the consistent question chose the slide actually seen, whereas only 41% of the subjects who received the misleading question chose the slide actually seen. Given that 50% correct responding in such a situation would be expected on the basis of chance alone, the results showed that subjects receiving the consistent information performed significantly above chance and the subjects receiving the misleading information performed significantly below chance.

However, there remains the possibility that subjects who received information in a question that conflicted with the information originally encoded detected the discrepancy but simply decided to be cooperative by assuming that the information contained in the question must be correct. When subjects were questioned extensively following their participation in another of the experiments, only 12% indicated that they had detected the discrepancy. That still leaves the possibility that the results were due to the subjects' failure to encode the sign information originally. If this were true, then the results would say nothing about the distortion of memory by subsequently encountered misleading information. Rather, the results would simply be a product of memory for the information encountered in the questioning period.

Loftus and colleagues then conducted another study in which subjects were asked after viewing the slides to fill in a diagram of the accident scene. Some 45% of the subjects included the correct sign in their drawing of the scene. On the basis of the results of this series of experiments, Loftus and colleagues concluded that subsequent misleading information is integrated into the witness's memory of the event and in the process fundamentally alters the original memory.

☑ *On what basis do Loftus and associates conclude that misleading information alters the stored memory representation of an event?*

A Challenge to the View that Misleading Information Alters the Original Memory Representation of the Event. The conclusion that misleading information actually alters the original memory trace has been strongly challenged by McCloskey, Zaragoza, and their colleagues (McCloskey & Zaragoza, 1985a, 1985b; Zaragoza, McCloskey, & Jamis, 1987; Zaragoza & Koshmider, 1989). McCloskey and Zaragoza have challenged the conclusions of Loftus and colleagues on both methodological and logical grounds. At the heart of their argument is the contention that the poorer memory performance by the misled subjects in the Loftus and colleagues' studies is the product of a response bias inherent in the recognition test procedure used, and that a more appropriate test of memory reveals that misleading postevent information does not affect the actual memory trace for the original event.

In criticizing the recognition test procedure used, McCloskey and Zaragoza contend that poorer performance by misled subjects would be expected even if misleading information has no effect on memory for the original event. To make their point, McCloskey and Zaragoza (1985a) compare hypothetical situations involving misled subjects, as in the Loftus and colleagues' study described above, and control subjects, who view the original event but receive no subsequent information about the critical detail.

Assume that the study involves 100 control subjects and 100 misled subjects. Furthermore, assume that 60 control subjects and 60 misled subjects at the time of test do not remember the sign. A portion of the 60 control subjects who do not remember the sign will guess, based on the two alternatives presented. Given that they have received no postevent information about the sign, it can be assumed on the basis of chance that half of them (i.e., 30) will guess correctly. Thus the number of control subjects who respond correctly will be 40 (those who remembered the sign shown in the original slide sequence) plus 30 (those who guessed correctly), for a total of 70.

However, it cannot be assumed that all 60 misled subjects who do not remember the sign at the time of test will simply guess. Some of these 60 misled subjects will remember at the time of test the information that they received *after* viewing the event and will therefore respond on the basis of the remembered misleading information. If, for example, 20 of the misled subjects who do not remember the sign presented in the original slide sequence do however remember the sign mentioned in the subsequent question, then only 40 of the 60 misled subjects who do not remember the original sign will guess at the time of test. Thus the number of misled subjects who will answer correctly is 40 (those who remember the sign shown in the original slide sequence) plus 20 (50% of the 40 misled subjects who remember neither the sign shown in the original slide sequence nor the sign mentioned in the subsequent misleading question), for a total of 60. In this example, the performance of control subjects exceeds that of misled subjects by 10.

This disadvantage for misled subjects would be even more pronounced if their performance were compared with subjects who received subsequent information that was consistent with the original event, as in the Loftus and colleagues' (1978) study described earlier. Assume that 60 of 100 subjects who received consistent postevent information do not remember the sign shown in the original slide sequence. Some portion of these 60 subjects will remember the sign information presented in the subsequent question and will thus respond correctly. If this number is assumed to be 10, then the number of subjects in the consistent postevent information condition who respond correctly will be 40 (those who remember the sign from the original slide sequence) plus 10 (those who remember the sign information presented in the question) plus 25 (50% of the 50 subjects who remember neither the sign from the original slide sequence nor the sign mentioned in the subsequent question and who must therefore guess), for a total of 75.

Therefore, in these hypothetical examples, the performance level would be 60, 70, and 75 for the misled, control, and consistent conditions, respectively. The critical point in this demonstration is that, even if one assumes that misleading information has no effect on the subjects' ability to remember what they saw originally, performance in the misled condition using this type of recognition procedure must, on the basis of logic alone, be worse than in the control and consistent conditions.

McCloskey and Zaragoza (1985a), therefore, proposed an alternative recognition procedure that avoids the type of response bias just illustrated. In the original recognition procedure used by Loftus and colleagues, subjects have to choose between the sign presented in the original slide sequence and the sign mentioned in the misleading question. In McCloskey and Zaragoza's modified recognition procedure, subjects choose between the sign presented in the original slide sequence and a new sign not mentioned in the misleading question.

To see how this removes the response bias, consider again a hypothetical situation involving 100 control subjects, who receive no relevant postevent information, and 100 misled subjects. Making the same assumptions as in the preceding illustration, 70 of the control subjects would ultimately respond correctly. With the modified test procedure, however, different results will obtain for the misled subjects. Given that the misleading sign is not presented as one of the two response choices using the modified test procedure, *all* of the misled subjects who do not remember the sign shown in the original slides must guess which of the two signs presented on the test is correct. That is, misled subjects who do not remember the original sign but who do remember the sign mentioned in the subsequent question must guess when presented on the test with two signs that do not match the sign mentioned in the subsequent question, just as the misled subjects who remember neither the original sign nor the sign mentioned in the subsequent question must guess.

If, as above, it is assumed that 60 of the misled subjects do not remember the sign shown in the original slide sequence, then the number of misled subjects who will ultimately respond correctly is 40 (those who remember the sign shown in the original slide sequence) plus 30 (the number of those subjects who do not remember the sign but would be expected to guess correctly) for a total of 70.

McCloskey and Zaragoza thus predicted that, if misleading postevent information does not in fact affect the original memory for an event, then control subjects and misled subjects should show equal levels of performance using the modified recognition test procedure. In six experiments (McCloskey & Zaragoza, 1985a), this prediction was consistently confirmed. In two subsequent experiments, Zaragoza, McCloskey, and Jamis (1987) further evaluated the hypothesis that misleading postevent information impairs memory for the original event. They used a procedure in which subjects' memory for details shown in the slides was tested by using a cued recall procedure that prevented subjects in the misled condition from giving the misleading information as a response. As with the modified recognition test procedure, they found no difference in the level of performance shown by control and misled subjects.

On the basis of the results of these two series of experiments, Zaragoza and Koshmider (1989) conclude that misleading postevent information neither causes the original information to be lost from memory nor makes the original information inaccessible. Rather, they argue, gaps exist in people's memory for witnessed events that have nothing to with the presentation of misleading postevent information, and people simply sometimes use the misleading information to fill these memory gaps.

🖉 *On the basis of what sorts of experimental results does the McCloskey and Zaragoza group conclude that misleading information does not alter the memory representation of the original event?*

An Alternative Explanation of Why Misleading Information Contributes to Inaccurate Memory for Witnessed Events. It is important to note here that McCloskey, Zaragoza, and their colleagues are not disputing the fact that eyewitness accounts are often inaccurate, and that, if given the opportunity, subjects exposed to misleading postevent information will often incorrectly report the misinformation on subsequent tests of memory for the event. What they are disputing is the assumption that such inaccuracy is the result of the misinformation acting to cause the original information to be forgotten or made inaccessible.

Using the misleading postevent information paradigm, Zaragoza and Koshmider tested to see if subjects who believed the misinformation to be accurate would also come to believe that the misleading information was a part of the original event. They found that, even with a 24-hour delay, subjects were quite good at remembering that the accepted misinformation was acquired during exposure to the postevent information and not during the witnessing of the original event. This finding suggests that even when individuals accept postevent information as part of their memory for the event, they do not make it part of a single underlying memory representation of the event. That is, an individual's report of an event may involve an integration of old and new information that are separately represented in memory.

With regard to eyewitness testimony, Zaragoza and Koshmider note that these findings suggest that explicitly cautioning witnesses not to report information they do not specifically remember seeing may help them avoid reporting misleading postevent information. Nevertheless, they found that between 15 and 16% of the control subjects in their two experiments reported seeing the misleading detail. Although subjects who have been exposed to postevent information may be good at discriminating between the information actually witnessed and the information acquired after the event, even subjects who have not been exposed to misleading postevent information tend to show a relatively high rate of errors in remembering witnessed events.

Collectively, findings that misleading postevent information leads to distorted accounts of a witnessed event are consistent with Tulving's synergistic ecphory model of retrieval, discussed earlier in this chapter. McCloskey and Zaragoza's view that misleading postevent information is used by subjects to fill gaps in their memory for a witnessed event coincides with Tulving's view that retrieval is a constructive process. The reported memory of an event is, according to the synergistic ecphory model, the product of combining information from the actual memory trace for the event with other relevant information available at the time of retrieval. When this other relevant information is misleading, a distorted eyewitness account can result.

☑ *How do the views of the Loftus group and the McCloskey and Zaragoza group differ with regard to the effect of misleading information on memory for a witnessed event?*

CONCLUDING REMARKS: Further Evidence of the Cognitive Trend

Two great traditions in the study of forgetting and retrieval from long-term memory were described in this chapter. As the pioneer in subjecting the philosophical tenets of associationism to rigorously controlled empirical test, Ebbinghaus helped establish an approach to the study of memory and forgetting that culminated in interference theory and its attempt to explain all forgetting in terms of competition between, and unlearning of, stimulus-response associations. As the originator of the view that memory not be viewed as passively stored associations, Bartlett established a cognitive framework within which schema theory has emerged as a basis for explaining and interpreting instances of reconstructive memory.

Forgetting as cue-dependent retrieval was presented as an alternative to interference theory and as a general framework within which cognitive processes that go beyond simple association formation, such as those involved in organizing and interpreting to-be-remembered information, could be incorporated. The potential usefulness of this cue-dependent forgetting approach was also illustrated in the consideration of the distinction between recognition and recall processes in long-term memory and Tulving's synergistic ecphory model of retrieval. Tulving's model of retrieval reflects the influence of the Ebbinghaus tradition in that it is built on results of verbatim tests of memory conducted under highly controlled laboratory conditions. But it also reflects the influence of the Bartlett tradition in that it assumes conscious recollection of an episode involves a reconstruction of the event that includes information from sources in addition to the available memory trace itself.

One daunting task that still awaits memory theorists is that of incorporating general approaches to forgetting and retrieval into a comprehensive account of the memory system, such as that provided by the Maltese cross multistore model. For example, it would be useful to have an account of how Tulving's ecphory retrieval process could be explained in terms of the operation of components of the Maltese cross model, such as the long-term associative store and the processing system. Successful integration of explanations of forgetting and retrieval into the Maltese cross model would lend support to the usefulness of both the retrieval explanation and the Maltese cross model.

CHAPTER 10

Mnemonics

APPLICATION: A Mental Walk

Alan has been asked by his mother to pick up 10 items at the grocery store on his way home from the campus. He could of course simply take the slip of paper on which his mother has written the items to ensure that he doesn't forget them, but Alan wants to practice a new memory technique he has recently learned about in one of his psychology classes. As a part of the technique, Alan has established in memory a particular route through his house. As he takes this mental walk, he begins in his upstairs bedroom and proceeds along the upstairs hallway, down the stairs, and into the living room. He continues his walk across the living room, through the dining room, and into the kitchen. He proceeds across the kitchen and through the door into the garage and exits from the garage through the side door that faces the house next door.

As he sits at the kitchen table and looks at the slip of paper listing the items, Alan attempts to apply this new memory technique by taking this mental walk through the house, distributing the items at various locations along the route. As he begins the mental walk in his bedroom, he creates an image of apples overflowing the wastebasket that is just inside the bedroom door. As he proceeds along the upstairs hallway, he creates an image of a gigantic box of laundry detergent hanging from the wall, dumping powder on the hallway table. As he begins down the stairs, he generates an image of onions hanging from the handrail, and so on until he has mentally distributed all of the items on his mother's list. Once at the grocery store, Alan plans to mentally retrace his route in order to find at the various locations along the route the items he is supposed to buy. As we shall see later in the chapter, Alan is attempting to employ a mnemonic technique with a history that can be traced to the ancient Greeks.

The word mnemonics *comes from mnemosyne, the Greek word for memory. Mnemosyne, in ancient Greek mythology, was the daughter of Uranus and Gaea and was the mother by Zeus of the nine Muses (Yates, 1966). Today, mnemonics refers to special methods or techniques that are designed to ensure the retention of material that would otherwise be forgotten. These techniques are related to the issue of the role of prior knowledge in memory (discussed in previous chapters) in that they often involve the use of highly overlearned material as a foundation for the retention of the new information.*

In this chapter, we shall consider a number of mnemonic techniques, some primarily verbal in nature, some based on visual imagery, and some composites of verbal and imagery processing. Attention will be given to the relevance of these techniques to theoretical issues raised in earlier chapters. The chapter concludes with a final word on the themes of associationism and cognitivism.

VERBAL MNEMONICS

Reduction and Elaboration Coding

Many verbal mnemonic techniques involve either reduction or elaboration coding. **Reduction coding** involves transforming presented information into a smaller more manageable amount. An example is the use of the acronym *ROYGBIV* as an aid to the memory for the order in which the colors of the spectrum appear. The major problem with the use of reduction codes is the tendency to reduce the original information to the extent that it cannot be reconstructed from the code that is left. The importance of the reconstruction process is evident from Miller's (1956) study of subjects' memory for sequences of binary digits (0s and 1s). He found that he could substantially increase subjects' memory span for binary sequences by teaching subjects to recode the binary digits as decimal digits. For example, given the sequence

111000101100

subjects were taught to group the digits into sets of three and then translate the three-digit binary sequence to a decimal equivalent, using the following conversion code:

$000 \rightarrow 0$ $100 \rightarrow 4$
$001 \rightarrow 1$ $101 \rightarrow 5$
$010 \rightarrow 2$ $110 \rightarrow 6$
$011 \rightarrow 3$ $111 \rightarrow 7$

The to-be-remembered binary sequence is thus recoded as 7054. In this way, the load on immediate memory is reduced from 12 items to 4 items. However, the successful use of the technique requires that one remember the translation operations for converting the decimal digits back to binary digits at the time of recall. For efficient use of such a strategy, the translation process must be well established and readily accessible in long-term store.

The reduction coding in the Miller study involved a type of reduction coding commonly called *chunking*, whereby individual items are grouped into a single unit through the imposition of a meaningful interpretation on the group. In the Miller study, each group of three binary digits was reinterpreted as a single decimal digit. Similarly, subjects can improve their memory for the letter sequence *IBMUSSRFBICIAFCCFDA* by chunking the letters into meaningful units: *IBM   USSR   FBI   CIA   FCC   FDA*. The usefulness of the technique will obviously be limited by the extent to which the to-be-remembered items lend themselves readily to chunking into meaningful units.

Elaboration coding, on the other hand, involves adding information beyond that actually required in order to improve the memorability of the material. Using the statement *Richard of York gains battles in vain* as a means of retaining memory for the order of the colors in the visible spectrum is an example of elaboration coding. In this example, the first letter of each word corresponds to the first letter of the appropriate color name. The usefulness of such a technique presumably derives from the relative ease with which a meaningful statement can be encoded and retrieved from long-term store compared to a fixed sequence of seven color names. However, in addition to remembering the statement, one has to remember what one is supposed to do with the information provided by the statement in order to retrieve successfully the to-be-remembered information. In general, elaboration coding provides for a more flexible means of dealing with information. Most of the specific mnemonic techniques to be considered in the remainder of the chapter rely primarily on elaboration coding.

Ericsson, Chase, and Faloon (1980) present the interesting case of an undergraduate, to whom they refer as S.F., whose development of an exceptional digit span with extensive practice shows the influence of both reduction and elaboration coding. S.F. practiced a memory span task for three to five hours a week for one and a half years and gradually increased his digit span from 7 to 80. Based on verbal descriptions of his strategies that he gave to the researchers, it appears that S.F. decided it was important to chunk the digits into sets of three and four. However, given that most three- and four-digit sequences do not match already established meaningful units in semantic memory, S.F. developed the strategy of elaborating each digit group into a meaningful unit. S.F. was an avid runner and so interpreted many of the digit groupings as running times: 3492 became *three minutes and 49 point 2 seconds, near world-record mile time*. Other groupings he interpreted as ages: 893 became *89 point 3, very old man*. As the number of digits in the sequence became longer and longer with training, S.F. also began to group the recoded three- and four-digit units into higher-order groupings. For example, he used 11 different major categories of races, ranging from marathon to the half-mile, with several subcategories within each of the major categories. Such an extensive classification system enabled him to categorize 62% of the digit groupings formed as running times.

☑ *What is the basic distinction between reduction and elaboration coding, and how are both based on information already established in long-term memory?*

Rhyme

Rhyme is an important component of verbal mnemonics in that it can help to impose structure on to-be-retained information. For example, the date of Columbus's discovery of America is made more memorable by the rhyme, *In fourteen hundred and ninety-two, Columbus sailed the ocean blue*. Memory for the number of days in each month is encouraged by teachers with the use of the rhyme that begins *Thirty days hath September. . . .* Rhyme presumably helps with memory retrieval by reducing the number of candidate items that can fit at a particular point in a rhyming sequence.

In the Columbus rhyme, if one remembers *Columbus sailed the ocean blue,* then the possible dates of his sailing are restricted to those that would rhyme with *ocean blue*. Associated with rhyme is the factor of rhythm, or the regular recurring sequence of stressed and unstressed elements in speech. In the number-of-days-in-the-month rhyme, rhythm as well as rhyme helps with the process of memory retrieval. To produce the line that follows *Thirty days hath September,* one has be generate months whose names match the number of syllables and the stress pattern found in that first line of the rhyme.

Obviously, one of the greatest limitations on the use of the rhyme mnemonic is the difficulty of fitting the target information into an appropriate rhyming pattern. The tendency of subjects to rely on the type of acoustical coding of information that underlies the use of the rhyme mnemonic is also evident in findings that subjects given randomized word lists will sometimes cluster in their recall words that rhyme when other organizational schemes are not immediately obvious (e.g., Bousfield & Wicklund, 1969; Fagan, 1969).

☑ *Why is rhyme helpful in the encoding and retrieval of information?*

Natural Language Mediation

With **natural language mediation,** a meaningless input is converted into a meaningful form, thereby enabling the person to establish associations with other meaningful units in memory. The result is a richer set of potential retrieval pathways. The unfamiliar term is coded in terms of its resemblance to meaningful units already established in long-term store. For example, in remembering nonsense syllables, subjects frequently employ the strategy of converting the nonsense syllables into meaningful units. The pair *ter-dut* might become *tear-duct,* or the pair *bah-tel* might become *bath-towel.* The pair *jkl-thor* might become *jackal-tamer,* or the pair *dnv-qsn* might become *Denver-quicksand.* What is being suggested here is that subjects sometimes convert nonsense material into "word-plus-transformation" for memory storage and then decode the stored representation at the time of retrieval (Bower & Hilgard, 1981). It has been shown that natural language mediation can provide for efficient encoding and retrieval. Montague, Adams, and Kiess (1966) demonstrated that the probability of recall of nonsense material was enhanced if subjects could remember the mediator.

Prytulak (1971) demonstrated that nonsense syllables differ in the ease with which they can be converted into words, and that such a measure of convertibility correlates very highly with the successful recall of the nonsense syllables. In fact, it became apparent very early to followers of the Ebbinghaus verbal learning tradition that nonsense syllables were not meaningless. Glaze (1928) devised a measure of the meaningfulness of nonsense syllables that involved determining the percentage of subjects who could produce an association to the syllable within a certain period of time. This, of course, was a point made by Bartlett in his attack on the use of artificial materials such as nonsense syllables. Bartlett argued that it is virtually impossible to prevent people from converting nonsense material to meaningful form as they engage in the "effort after meaning."

Natural language mediation is now championed in books devoted to memory improvement. For example, in their very popular book, *The Memory Book,* Lorayne and Lucas (1974) describe at length the technique of "substitute words." This technique involves converting abstract material into "something—anything—that sounds like, or reminds you of, the abstract material and *can be pictured* [Lorayne and Lucas's emphasis] in your mind" (Lorayne & Lucas, 1974, p. 37). In illustrating this technique, Lorayne and Lucas do not limit its applicability to nonsense material. For example, in trying to remember the state name *Minnesota,* one might image a *mini soda* that could then be associated with other to-be-remembered names.

The issue of the importance of imagery in Lorayne and Lucas's description of this and other mnemonic techniques will be discussed later in the chapter. The important point here is that Lorayne and Lucas are advocating the application of a natural language mediation technique to verbal units that are already meaningful in and of themselves. In the context of meaningful verbal units, this natural language mediation approach is more generally referred to as semantic elaboration.

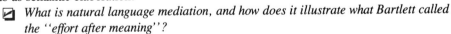 *What is natural language mediation, and how does it illustrate what Bartlett called the "effort after meaning"?*

Semantic Elaboration

Semantic elaboration is related to natural language mediation in that it typically involves converting pairs of words into sentences or lists of words into stories. The apparent usefulness of this technique was demonstrated by Bower and Winzenz (1970) in a study involving three groups of subjects who learned a list of 30 P-As. One group was told to rehearse the items, a second group was told to form an interacting image for each pair of words (e.g., for the pair *giraffe-dress,* one might image a giraffe wearing a dress), and the third group was told to combine each pair of words into a sentence. The results showed 87% recall by the imagery group, 77% recall by the sentence group, and only 37% recall by the rehearsal group.

Similarly, Bower and Clark (1969) had two groups of subjects study 12 lists of 10 nouns each. One group of subjects was given standard instructions to study and learn the words. The other group of subjects was encouraged to combine the words into sentences so as to form a story. After the presentation of all 12 lists, subjects were asked for serial recall of the 120 words. The results are shown in Figure 10–1. The researchers reported 93% overall recall by the story group, compared to only 13% recall by the standard study instructions group.

The importance of weaving the generated sentences into a story was demonstrated by Belleza, Richards, and Geiselman (1976). In their study, one group was asked to use each word in a sentence, but no instructions were given to combine the sentences into a story. The other group was asked to combine generated sentences into a story. Recall by the story group was significantly greater than recall by the individual-sentences group.

☑ *What specific verbal mnemonic techniques are examples of semantic elaboration?*

Depth/Elaboration of Processing and Distinctiveness

These findings relating to verbal mnemonics are, in general, compatible with the **levels/elaboration of processing approach** to memory described in Chapter 6. Recall that this approach argues that the more deeply or elaboratively information is processed, the better its long-term retention will be. On this view, elaboration involves a spread of encoding to include more of the possible features that can be used to describe the to-be-remembered information. Elaboration of encoding, in turn, can be described as involving two highly interrelated components, within-item and between-item elaboration. **Within-item elaboration** refers to the extent to which the features or attributes of an item are activated and

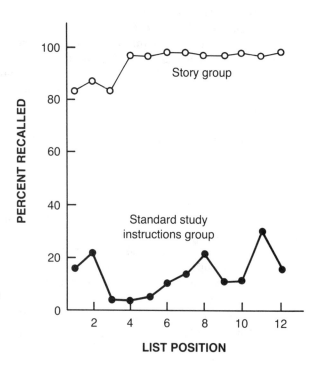

FIGURE 10–1 Percentage of words recalled from each list by subjects asked to link the words into a story and by subjects asked simply to study and learn the words in the study by Bower and Clark (1969).

Source: From Bower, G. H., and Clark, M. C. (1969). Narrative stories as mediators for serial learning. *Psychonomic Science, 14,* 181. Reprinted by permission of Psychonomic Society, Inc.

analyzed at the time of encoding, whereas **between-item elaboration** refers to the extent to which items are related to other items in memory.

These components are interrelated in that processing focused on between-item elaboration will inevitably result in a more extensive analysis of the features comprising the memory representation of a target item. Conversely, processing focused on within-item elaboration will inevitably result in the activation of features that themselves have distinct representations in the memory system. Within-item elaboration can result in between-item elaboration, but the spread of activation may to be to items other than those being presented as a part of the memory task. For example, if in elaborately processing the word *hermit*, one activates the feature *reclusive,* there may be a spread of activation to *reclusive* and other related items in memory, even though *reclusive* may not be one of the items presented as part of the memory task. Nevertheless, this spread of activation may help with the eventual retrieval of the target item in that it increases the number of retrieval pathways or cues by which the item can be accessed at the time memory is tested.

These components of elaboration are in turn related to the concept of memory distinctiveness. The more elaborately an item is processed, the more distinctive its resulting memory representation should be. That is, the more component features of an item and the more of an item's associations with other items that are activated, the easier it should be to discriminate that item at the time of retrieval from other items in memory. This view of elaboration helps explain why semantic processing often leads to better retention than does physical or phonemic processing, as predicted by the original levels of processing framework (Craik & Tulving, 1975) and as discussed previously in Chapter 6.

On this view, it is often easier to establish a distinctive representation of an item based on semantic analysis than on physical or phonemic analysis because words in memory share such a small number of physical and phonemic features, whereas the variation in semantic features and in the associations between words based on meaning is much greater. That is, with semantic processing it is often easier to establish cues that will be much more restricted in their activation of stored memory traces than is the case with physical and phonemic processing.

The importance of distinctiveness to the levels of processing effect was demonstrated by Moscovitch and Craik (1976) in an experiment in which they manipulated the number of different semantic judgment questions used to induce semantic processing by subjects experiencing an incidental learning paradigm. The procedure was very similar to that used by Craik and Tulving (1975) in their series of experiments described in Chapter 6. Subjects saw a series of questions, each followed by a very brief presentation of a word.

Question	**Word**
Rhyme question:	
Does it rhyme with *boat* ?	*coat*
Category question	
Is it in the category "animals"?	*frog*

Subjects were told that their task was to respond to the question as quickly as possible following the presentation of the word. No mention was made that their memory for the words would later be tested. Subjects in the control group made such judgments about 60 words, 20 involving a rhyme judgment, 20 involving a category judgment, and 20 involving a sentence judgment. Each rhyme judgment and each semantic judgment involved a different question. The procedure was the same for the experimental group, except that only two different semantic judgment questions of each type were used. For example, the *The girl dropped the* _____ *on the floor* question was used for 10 of the 20 words about which a sentence judgment was required.

On the unexpected memory test, subjects were presented with each judgment question previously encountered and were asked to recall the word (or words) that had followed the question. The results are shown in Figure 10–2. For the control group, Moscovitch and Craik found a large levels effect for the recall of words about which a ''yes'' response was made: approximately 85% recall for the semantically processed sentence judgment words versus about 34% recall for the phonemically processed words. However, the levels effect for words about which a ''yes'' response was made was greatly reduced for the experimental group: approximately 45% recall for the semantically processed sentence judgment words versus about 33% recall for the phonemically processed words.

Reducing the distinctiveness of the semantic encoding of the words by using the same sentence judgment question repeatedly reduced the facility with which the words were retrieved. Note, however, that memory for the semantically processed words still exceeded memory for the phonemically processed words for the experimental group. This suggests that even when the same semantic judgment question is used repeatedly, the distinctiveness of the resulting semantic encodings is still likely to be greater than the distinctiveness of the phonemic encodings produced by rhyming judgment questions. This is consistent with the suggestion that a semantic encoding of an item will in general be less likely to overlap other encodings in memory than will a phonemic encoding of an item. This is simply because the

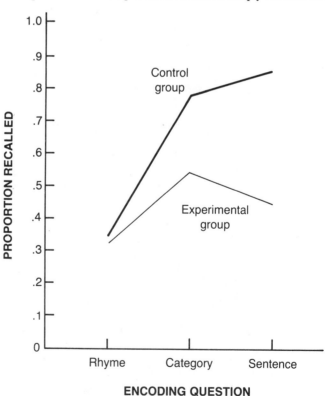

FIGURE 10–2 Proportion of words recalled as a function of type of encoding question answered about each word in the study by Moscovitch and Craik (1976). The results shown are only for words for which a ''yes'' response was made to the question. Control subjects experienced a unique question for each of the 20 words presented in each condition, whereas experimental subjects experienced only two different questions in each condition.

Source: Moscovitch, M., & Craik, F. I. M. (1976). Depth of processing, retrieval cues, and uniqueness of encoding as factors in recall. *Journal of Verbal Behavior, 15,* 451. Reprinted with permission of Academic Press.

number of features or dimensions along which semantic processing can vary is much greater than the number of features or dimensions along which phonemic processing can vary.

The importance of the distinctiveness of encodings is also evident in the results of a study by Eysenck (1979). In his study, he attempted to manipulate the distinctiveness of phonemic or acoustic encodings by using, as stimuli, words with irregular grapheme-phoneme correspondences, meaning that the words are not pronounced the way their appearance would suggest they should be. Examples of words used in Eysenck's study include *comb* and *glove*.

Eysenck compared retention of these words when processed either semantically or phonemically. In the phonemic processing condition, subjects were asked to pronounce the word either in the typical way or in an atypical, distinctive way. In the atypical, distinctive phonemic processing condition, for example, subjects were asked to pronounce *comb* to rhyme with *bomb* and *glove* to rhyme with *stove*. In the typical semantic processing condition, subjects were asked to produce a descriptor that typically modifies each noun, whereas in the atypical semantic processing condition, they were asked to generate a descriptor that only infrequently modifies each noun. The results from an unexpected recognition test are shown in Figure 10–3.

In the typical processing condition, the usual levels effect was found, with significantly more of the semantically processed words recognized (42% versus 34%). However, in the atypical processing condition, the levels effect was eliminated in that the number of semantically processed words recognized did not exceed significantly the number of phonemically processed words recognized (44% versus 43%). Thus even information processed at a nonsemantic level can be made more memorable if it is processed so as to make it distinctive.

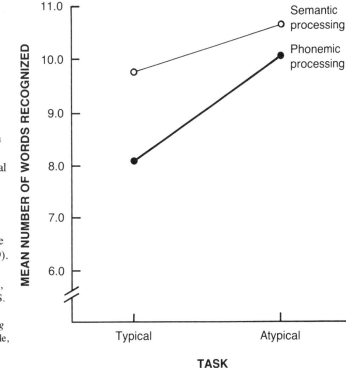

FIGURE 10–3   Mean number of words recognized, out of a total possible of 24, as a function of processing depth and processing typicality or distinctiveness, from the study by Eysenck (1979).

Source: Eysenck, M. W. (1979). Depth, elaboration, and distinctiveness. In L. S. Cermak & F. I. M. Craik (Eds.), *Levels of processing in human memory.* Hillsdale, NJ: Lawrence Erlbaum Associates.

It was pointed out in Chapter 6 that the levels/elaboration of processing view of memory is not a viable alternative to multistore models of memory and that there are serious problems with assessing depth or elaboration of processing independent of the level of retention of the information. However, it was also pointed out that this approach is not incompatible with multistore models, such as Broadbent's Maltese cross model.

In terms of the Maltese cross model, depth or elaboration of processing can be seen as operations of the processing system that promote the effective establishment of new long-term memory fragments containing the processed information. The notion of depth or elaboration of processing can also be seen as generally consistent with the cue-dependent retrieval failure view of forgetting (described in the preceding chapter). To the degree that deep elaborate processing of information produces distinctive memory traces, such processing produces memory traces for which effective cues will be available at the time of retrieval.

It should be noted here, however, that there are instances in which deep processing can result in a failure to distinguish recently acquired information from old information in memory. Recall from the preceding chapter the example of the ''Helen Keller'' subjects in the Sulin and Dooling (1974) study who tended to conclude incorrectly that the statement, *She was deaf, dumb, and blind,* was a part of a narrative they had read about Helen Keller. Such results show that subjects who succeed at integrating new episodic information with already existing schemas may subsequently have difficulty discriminating previously acquired information from that encountered in the most recent learning episode.

Thus the distinction between episodic and semantic memory is important with regard to the issue of distinctiveness. If the aim is to encourage the integration of new information with already existing schemas in semantic memory, then trying to make the encoding of the information distinctive may not be the best strategy to adopt. Distinctiveness of encoding may be most important when an individual is trying to establish an episodic memory representation for an event that will be readily retrievable on the basis of temporal/spatial cues (such as when and where the information was encoded) and easy to discriminate from other episodic memory representations.

✏️ *On what basis is it assumed that elaborate processing promotes the establishment of distinctive memory representations?*

IMAGERY MNEMONICS

Even in the preceding discussion of verbal mnemonics, there were hints of the degree to which special mnemonic techniques rely on or encourage the use of visual imagery to improve retention of information. In this section, consideration will be given to mnemonic techniques in which the focus is clearly on the use of visual imagery. The basic assumption underlying these techniques is that input referring to concrete entities is better recalled than input referring to abstract entities. The use of imagery in remembering concrete items obviously involves prior knowledge. In generating an image, a person relies on prior knowledge of what the object looks like.

Evidence for the Effectiveness of Imagery

In one study of the relationship between concreteness and memory, Bevan and Steger (1971) had children and adults study lists consisting of a mixture of actual objects, pictures of objects, and words that were names of objects. When subjects were asked to recall the names of the objects studied, the ordering of recall from best to worst was actual object, pictures, and words. Concreteness or imageability is positively related to memory for material even when consideration is limited to the study and recall of words. For example, in the preceding section, the study of Bower and Winzenz (1970) was described in which the memory of three groups of subjects was compared. One group was asked to rehearse a series of P-As, a second group was asked to form interacting images of the members of each pair, and the third group was asked to combine each pair of words into a sentence. The visual imagery instructions were found to be even more effective than the semantic elaboration instructions in promoting recall.

Additional evidence of the effectiveness of imagery encoding comes from a series of studies by Bower (1972). In one study, recall of a list of 20 P-As was compared for subjects asked to rehearse the pairs and for subjects asked to form interacting images. The performance of the imagery group exceeded that of the rehearsal group, with recall levels of 80% and 33%, respectively. Further evidence of the beneficial influence of imagery instructions comes from studies of memory for prose. For example, Anderson and Kulhavy (1972), Kulhavy and Swenson (1975), and Gambrell (1982) found that school-aged children instructed to image while reading recalled more of a story than did control subjects who were not so instructed.

In Chapter 8, the debate concerning whether the facilitative effects of imagery are due to the establishment of analog representations that are separate and distinct from underlying verbal propositional representations was reviewed. Recall that those who subscribe to the distinct analog representation position contend that at least part of the facilitative effect of imagery on memory retention derives from the multiple representations of information that are established when imagery is used in addition to the verbal processing of the information. Adherents of the view that long-term memory representations are always ultimately propositional representations argue that the generation of images has its effect by encouraging elaborate semantic processing of the underlying verbal information.

Ignoring for the moment the relative merits of these alternative interpretations, it is obvious that both are pointing to the contribution that imagery can play in encouraging the establishment of distinctive memory representations. Having analog as well as propositional representations of an event makes the memory record of the event more distinctive by increasing the number of potential cues that may successfully access the memory trace. Encouraging elaborate semantic processing of the information promotes the activation of features and between-item associations that also increase the potential pool of effective retrieval cues.

 What sorts of evidence suggests that instructions to generate mental images positively influences memory?

The Importance of Interactive Imagery Instructions

The importance of instructing subjects to form images that involve an interaction of the to-be-remembered items was also examined by Bower (1972). In a followup to the experiment described above, one group of subjects was told to form interacting images of the members of each P-A pair, whereas another group of subjects was told to form two separate images of the members of each pair. The interacting image group recalled 71% of the words, whereas the separate image group recalled 46% of the words. In an earlier study in 1970, Bower showed that a separate image group performed no better than a group given standard rehearsal instructions. Note, in the example given at the beginning of the chapter, Alan's use of interactive imagery as one component of the mnemonic technique being employed.

However, interactive imagery instructions are not universally effective in producing superior memory performance. Baker and Santa (1977) had subjects study a list of 28 concrete nouns presented aurally with a pause after every fourth word. One group of subjects heard the list with no special study instructions. Another group of subjects was told to form an interactive image linking the four words in each group. Half of the subjects in each group then experienced a free recall test on the words. The other half of the subjects were given a cued recall test that involved the presentation of strong associates of some of the words from the list.

For example, if the word *log* were part of the studied list, the word *tree* might be presented as a cue. Subjects were told to generate words based on their past experience that are associated with each cue word and to select from those generated any words actually studied as part of the to-be-remembered list for inclusion in their recall of the list. The results from the study are shown in Figure 10–4. On the free recall test, the typical facilitative effect of interactive imagery was observed. However, on the cued recall test, the subjects in the interactive imagery condition actually performed more poorly than those in the no-special-instructions group. Instructions to form interactive images may well result in the establishment of memory representations that are so specific that they may not include features that overlap those present in cues that are strong semantic associates of target items but were not present at the time of encoding.

These findings relate to Tulving's notion of **encoding specificity** and the **episodic ecphory model** of retrieval described in the preceding chapter. One of the keys to the effectiveness of the mnemonic techniques described in this chapter is the reliability with which they provide effective cues at the time of recall. However, one potential drawback to these techniques is they produce highly specific encodings of the to-be-remembered information. If, then, the situation at the time of retrieval is such that access to the mnemonic framework or cues is not readily accomplished, as in the cued recall test of the Baker and

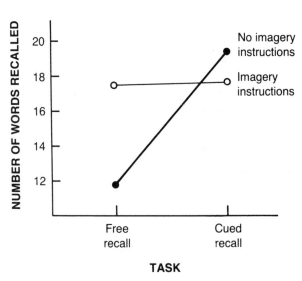

FIGURE 10–4 Effects of interactive imagery instructions as a function of type of recall task, from the study by Baker and Santa (1977).

Source: Glass, A. L., & Holyoak, K. J. (1986). *Cognition* (2nd ed.) New York: McGraw-Hill. Reproduced with permission of McGraw-Hill, Inc.

Santa study, the information may not be retrievable through other cues that have been associated with the target information in other contexts.

☑ *How can results from the study of interactive imagery instructions be interpreted within the context of encoding specificity?*

The Importance of Image Bizarreness

In addition to urging the use of interactive imagery, some professional mnemonists (e.g., Lorayne & Lucas, 1974) strongly advocate the importance of making the images formed as bizarre as possible. In the example given at the beginning of the chapter, note Alan's use of bizarre images as part of the overall mnemonic technique being employed. However, the research on the effects of image bizarreness has been far from consistent in demonstrating a positive influence of bizarreness on memory retention.

In one early study, Wollen, Weber, and Lowry (1972) examined the possibility that interaction and bizarreness make independent facilitative contributions to memory for information. Subjects were presented with a list of nine P-As to learn. To control the images used by subjects, the researchers used pictures such as those shown in Figure 10–5 to present the

NONINTERACTING—NONBIZARRE

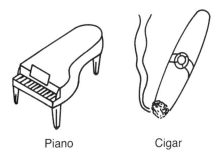

Piano   Cigar

NONINTERACTING—BIZARRE

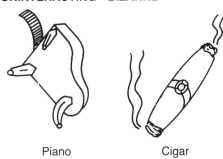

Piano   Cigar

INTERACTING—NONBIZARRE

Piano   Cigar

INTERACTING—BIZARRE

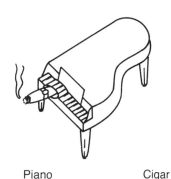

Piano   Cigar

FIGURE 10–5 Examples of the pictures used to present word pairs in the Wollen, Weber, and Lowry (1972) study of image bizarreness.

Source: Wollen, K. A., Weber, A., & Lowry, D. H. (1972). Bizarreness versus interaction of mental images as determinants of learning. *Cognitive Psychology, 3,* 520. Reprinted with permission of Academic Press.

to-be-remembered word pairs in the four possible combinations of bizarre/nonbizarre and interacting/noninteracting conditions. A control condition in which the word pairs were presented without accompanying pictures was also included.

At the time of test, subjects were given the stimulus word from each pair and were asked to recall the corresponding response word. The percentage of response words recalled in each of the four experimental conditions and in the control condition is shown in Table 10–1. For both interacting and noninteracting conditions, there was no significant difference as a function of the bizarreness of the images. However, there was a large effect of interaction, with recall in the interacting condition far exceeding recall in the noninteracting condition. Thus the study found further evidence of the facilitative effect of instructions to form interacting images but produced no support for the suggestion that generating bizarre images improves memory.

Conditions Contributing to the Bizarreness Effect

Although a number of other researchers have also reported no memory superiority for bizarre images (e.g., Collyer, Jonides, & Bevan, 1972; Cox & Wollen, 1981; Emmerich & Ackerman, 1979; Hauck, Walsh, & Kroll, 1976; Kroll, Schepeler, & Angin, 1986; Senter & Hoffman, 1976; Wollen & Cox, 1981a, 1981b; Wood, 1967), several studies have shown bizarre imagery to be beneficial (McDaniel & Einstein, 1986; Hirshman, Whelley, & Palij, 1989; Merry, 1980; Merry & Graham, 1978; Webber & Marshall, 1978; Wollen & Cox, 1981a, 1981b). In demonstrating a reliable positive bizarreness effect across a series of five experiments, McDaniel and Einstein (1986) used bizarre and common sentences in an incidental learning paradigm in which subjects were asked to form an interactive mental image of the sentence and to rate the vividness of the image generated on a 5-point scale. Examples of the sentences used include:

Bizarre: The dog rode the bicycle down the street.
Common: The fisherman pulled the lobster out of the barrel.

In demonstrating the bizarreness effect, McDaniel and Einstein (1986) identified one factor that they believe is largely responsible for the failure of other researchers to find the effect. This factor is the way in which bizarreness is manipulated within an experiment. In their Experiment 1, they found the bizarreness effect when imagery type was manipulated in a within-list design but not when imagery type was manipulated in a between-list design. That is, when subjects received some common sentences and some bizarre sentences in the same list (a within-list design), these subjects showed better memory for the bizarre sentences.

TABLE 10–1 Mean Percentage of Response Words Recalled in the Wollen, Weber, and Lowry (1972) Study

	Bizarreness		
Interaction	*Bizarre*	*Nonbizarre*	*Combined*
Interacting	74.1	73.3	73.7
Noninteracting	33.9	38.8	36.4
Combined	54.0	56.1	55.1
	Control condition	55.6	

However, when the memory of subjects who received only bizarre sentences was compared with the memory of subjects who received only common sentences (a between-list design), the two groups did not differ in their recall. McDaniel and Einstein note that the manipulation of bizarreness as a within-list variable is a feature of all of the cited studies in which bizarreness has been shown to be effective. They interpret this finding to be consistent with a distinctiveness explanation of the bizarreness effect. The distinctiveness of an event, they argue, is a function of its relation to other encoded events (Jacoby & Craik, 1979). Therefore, the encoding of a bizarre image will be relatively more distinctive in the context of other common images than in the context of a series of bizarre images.

📋 *According to McDaniel and Einstein, under what conditions are bizarre images likely to be better remembered than common images?*

Further Evidence for the Distinctiveness Interpretation

In order to establish that the actual formation of images is critical to the bizarreness effect found, McDaniel and Einstein, in a second experiment, also compared, using a within-list design, an imagery vividness rating condition (of the type described previously) with a semantic processing condition. In the semantic processing condition, subjects were asked to rate the degree to which the relationship described in the sentence was unusual. McDaniel and Einstein found the bizarreness effect in the imagery condition but not in the semantic processing conditioning. They conclude that instructions to rate imagery vividness result in a type of processing of the material that goes beyond semantic verbal processing.

In a final experiment, McDaniel and Einstein (1986) demonstrated that the bizarreness effect can also be found using a between-list design as long as subjects are exposed within the context of the experiment to contrasting material. In this experiment, subjects processed an initial target list of sentences under instructions to form images and rate their vividness. All of the sentences were either bizarre or common (a between-list design). Following the processing of this target list of sentences, subjects were asked to perform an intervening activity. The intervening activity involved either studying a list of common or bizarre sentences under intentional learning instructions that encouraged the use of imagery or performing simple math problems. Recall of the initial target list of sentences was analyzed as a function of type of intervening task performed. The results are shown in Table 10–2.

The bizarre sentences were recalled better than common sentences only when common sentences were encountered on the intervening task. McDaniel and Einstein argue that this finding is consistent with their distinctiveness interpretation of the bizarreness effect. A set of bizarre images will only be better recalled than a set of common images if they are encountered in the context of contrasting common images. Bizarre images are only distinctive to the extent that they are contrasted with more common images.

TABLE 10–2 Mean Proportion of Words Recalled from the Target List as a Function of Type of Intervening Task in the McDaniel and Einstein (1986) Experiment 5

	Type of Intervening Task		
Type of Target List	*Study Bizarre Sentences*	*Study Common Sentences*	*Perform Math Problems*
Bizarre	.13	.36	.45
Common	.16	.22	.41

Interestingly, McDaniel and Einstein (1986) found no difference in their Experiment 4 in subjects' ability to recognize words from the processed sentences as a function of imagery type. This finding is consistent with other studies suggesting that imagery bizarreness effects are likely to be limited to recall from memory. Therefore, it would appear that the beneficial effect of bizarre imagery is in making the encoded event more accessible or retrievable. This conclusion is consistent with findings that recall of the entire sentence given recall of a part of the sentence is sometimes higher for common sentences than for bizarre sentences (e.g., Pra Baldi, De Beni, Cornoldi, & Cavedon, 1985; Einstein, McDaniel, & Lackey, 1989, Experiment 3). Wollen and Margres (1987) interpret this pattern of findings as indicating that bizarre images are often more accessible than common images but that common images are better integrated than bizarre images.

☑ *What are the major findings presented by McDaniel and Einstein in arguing for a distinctiveness explanation of the bizarreness effect?*

The Possible Influence of Complexity

Although many of the published studies investigating imagery bizarreness appear to be consistent with McDaniel and Einstein's interpretation, the findings of a study by Kroll, Schepeler, and Angin (1986) are not. In this study, the researchers employed a within-list design in which subjects experienced both common and bizarre sentences. All of the bizarre sentences used suggested an image with high degree of interaction. On both immediate and delayed cued recall tests, nouns from bizarre sentences were no better recalled than nouns from common sentences. McDaniel and Einstein (1989) argue that this failure to find results consistent with those produced in the McDaniel and Einstein (1986) study using a within-list design may be a function of the more complex sentences used in the Kroll and colleagues' study.

Indeed, Hirshman, Whelley, and Palij (1989) found the bizarreness effect using the McDaniel and Einstein (1986) sentences but did not find the effect using the more complex sentences of Kroll and colleagues. McDaniel and Einstein (1989) suggest that complex sentences may make it more difficult for subjects to generate images. Thus, to the extent that the bizarreness effect is dependent on image generation, the bizarreness effect will be less likely to emerge with complex sentences as the stimulus materials.

☑ *What evidence suggests that sentence complexity may be important in determining whether the bizarreness effect is found using a within-list design?*

A Surprise Interpretation of the Bizarreness Effect

In proposing their distinctiveness interpretation of the bizarreness effect, McDaniel and Einstein (1986; Einstein & McDaniel, 1987) admitted that the specific mechanism by which distinctiveness produces better memory remains to be identified. In their study of the bizarreness effect, Hirshman, Whelley, and Palij (1989) argue that it is surprise, not distinctiveness, that is responsible for the effect. Bizarre images are better remembered than common images because they are more surprising. Hirshman and colleagues suggest that the more surprising an event is, the more likely the event is to be associated with general contextual cues that include the subject's internal representation of when and where the event is being experienced. Thus, to the extent that subsequent memory for the event is dependent on activation by these contextual cues, surprising events will be better remembered.

From this basic position, Hirshman and colleagues predicted that the bizarreness effect would decrease with an increase in the number of bizarre sentences in a list because bizarre sentences become less surprising as they become more numerous. This prediction was supported. When 4 of the 16 sentences in the list were bizarre, the bizarreness effect was found; but when 12 of the 16 sentences in the list were bizarre, the effect was not found. Similar results have been reported by Kroll and Tu (1988). Hirshman and colleagues contend that these findings are not easily explained by McDaniel and Einstein's distinctiveness hypothesis. Even when 12 of the 16 sentences in the list are bizarre, the presence of the four common sentences should provide the contrast necessary to make the bizarre images distinct and thus more memorable.

Hirshman and colleagues also predicted that the bizarreness effect would be more likely to emerge on a free recall test than on a cued recall test. This prediction was based on the following assumption: Performance on a free recall test is more dependent on general contextual cues whose association with the target information is assumed to be facilitated by the degree to which the target information is surprising. This prediction was also confirmed.

Hirshman and colleagues further evaluated the contention that contextual cues are more readily associated with surprising events than with nonsurprising events by investigating the influence of providing additional contextual cues on the memory for common and bizarre sentences. To the extent that bizarre images generated in the context of common images are surprising, they should be well-associated with contextual cues important to successful retrieval, and thus should be less likely than common images to benefit from additional contextual cues. The additional contextual cue provided in their Experiment 3 was a 10-second pause between blocks of bizarre and common sentences. That is, in this experiment, subjects saw a series of six sentences of one type followed by six sentences of the other type. In one condition there was a 10-second pause between the two groups of sentences, and subjects were advised of this pause before the sentences were presented. In the other condition, there was no such pause. The results from this experiment are shown in Table 10–3.

As predicted, the addition of the pause as a contextual cue selectively benefited the recall of the common sentences. In the no-pause condition, the recall of bizarre sentences significantly exceeded the recall of common sentences, but this bizarreness effect was reduced in the pause condition and was not statistically significant.

The general usefulness of this surprise interpretation of the bizarreness effect is yet to be determined, but such an interpretation is related to investigations of the relationship between imagery and affective or emotional responses to information. This relationship has been examined most extensively in studies of readers' responses to narrative stories (e.g., Sadoski, 1983, 1984, 1985; Sadoski & Goetz, 1985; Sadoski, Goetz, & Kangiser, 1988).

TABLE 10–3 Mean Proportion of Sentences Recalled as a Function of Whether There Was a Pause Between Blocks of Bizarre and Common Sentences in the Hirshman, Whelley, and Palij (1989) Experiment 3

	Pause Condition	
Type of Sentence	*No Pause*	*Pause*
Bizarre	.53	.47
Common	.32	.42

In these studies, readers were asked to rate paragraphs of a story they had read earlier as to either their tendency to arouse vivid imagery, their tendency to evoke an emotional response, or their importance to the plot and theme of the story.

The general pattern of findings has been that (1) reported imagery and reported affect are strongly correlated independent of the rated importance of the story segment, (2) the relationship between rated affect and rated importance is influenced somewhat by the imagery response to the story segment, and (3) the relationship between rated imagery and rated importance is strongly influenced by the affective response to the story segment.

In one study, Sadoski (1984) found evidence of a possible causal link between overall affect for a story, amount of text-related imagery for the story, and story recall. These results from the study of prose processing suggest that the affective responses to bizarre and common images may be another variable worth investigating in the continuing attempt to determine the conditions under which superior memory for bizarre images is most likely to be found. Perhaps the bizarreness effect is only found when bizarre images evoke a stronger affective response than do the common images. Some theorists, such as Zajonc (1980), argue that the possible mediating influence of affect on cognitive processes in general is an issue that warrants intensive investigation.

☑ *How do Hirshman and colleagues explain the bizarreness effect in terms of surprise?*

Specific Imagery Mnemonics

Peg-Word System

Although presented here as an imagery mnemonic, the **peg-word system** is actually a composite mnemonic in that it involves the use of rhymes and natural language mediators, in addition to imagery. The peg-word system is a serial order mnemonic designed to facilitate the retention of an association between an item and its serial position in a sequence. The first step in the use of the technique is to establish a series of pegs. The establishment of these pegs involves transforming the numbers representing the serial positions in the sequence into meaningful, highly imageable words through the aid of rhymes, as in the following scheme:

1 is a bun	6 is sticks
2 is a shoe	7 is heaven
3 is a tree	8 is a gate
4 is a door	9 is wine
5 is a hive	10 is a hen.

Following mastery of the number-to-peg transformations, other concepts can be associated with the pegs through the use of interactive imagery. For example, if the fifth item in the to-be-remembered sequence is *bear,* one might image a bear demolishing a hive. If the ninth item in the series is *coat,* one might image wine being poured on a coat. The preceding discussion of the influence of bizarreness is of course relevant here because one could attempt to generate images that are bizarre as well as interactive. Instead of imaging a bear demolishing a hive, one might image a bear bouncing a hive. Instead of imaging wine being poured on a coat, one might image a coat floating in a gigantic glass of wine.

As was mentioned earlier, this emphasis on bizarre imagery is one of the most common themes emphasized by professional mnemonists (e.g., Lorayne & Lucas, 1974). However, the research of McDaniel and Einstein (1986), Einstein and colleagues (1989), and Hirshman and colleagues (1989) suggests that the *consistent* use of bizarre images in the context of such a mnemonic technique may only be helpful to the extent that bizarre images contrast with more common images or to the extent that the bizarre images are made surprising by some other means.

At any rate, peg words, once they are firmly established in memory, facilitate formation of mediating images between a particular serial position and the to-be-remembered item. Through the associations formed, the system permits recall of items in order, recall of an item occupying a specific serial position in the series, and recall of a particular item's serial position. Experimental evidence of the system's usefulness was provided by Bugelski (1968). Control and experimental groups learned six lists of 10 P-As each, with each P-A consisting of a number paired with a concrete word. The experimental subjects were told to link the number and the word through imagery using pegs mastered previously. The control subjects did not learn the pegs and were not told to use imagery. Both immediate and delayed cued recall tests were given. The experimental group showed better performance on both tests, with the advantage more pronounced on the delayed test.

Lorayne and Lucas (1974) advocate the use of a more complex peg system than that described above. Their system is based on learning initially the phonetic alphabet for consonants. They argue that there are 10 *basic* consonant sounds in English and that these can be easily associated with the 10 digits 1–9, plus 0, through the use of memory aids. The following display shows the digit-consonant sound associations they recommend using, as well as a memory aid for mastering the association:

Digit/Consonant Pair	Memory Aid
1 = *t* or *d*	A typewritten small *t* has *one* downstroke.
2 = *n*	A typewritten small *n* has *two* downstrokes.
3 = *m*	A typewritten small *m* has *three* downstrokes.
4 = *r*	The word *four* ends with an *r*.
5 = *l*	The *five* fingers, thumb out, form a capital *L*.
6 = *j, sh, ch,* soft *g*	A *6* and a capital *J* are almost mirror images.
7 = *k,* hard *c,* hard *g*	You can make a capital *K* with two *7*'s.
8 = *f, v, ph*	An *8* and a handwritten *f* look similar.
9 = *p* or *b*	A *9* and a *p* are mirror images.
0 = *z, s,* soft *c*	The first sound in the word *zero* is *z*. (Lorayne & Lucas, 1974, p. 108)

Once these correspondences have been acquired, Lorayne and Lucas (1974) recommend learning a series of peg words based on these sounds of the phonetic alphabet for consonants. For example, since the number 1 is always represented by the sound *t* or *d*, the peg word for serial position 1 must contain that sound. Similarly, the peg word for serial position 2 must contain the sound *n*. Based on this scheme, Lorayne and Lucas suggest the following 10 peg words:

1. *t*ie   4. *r*ye
2. *N*oah   5. *l*aw
3. *M*a   6. *sh*oe

7. cow   9. bee

8. ivy   10. toes (since 10 contains a 1 and a 0, its peg word must contain the sound corresponding to 1 and the sound corresponding to 0). (Lorayne & Lucas, 1974, p. 119).

Once mastered, the peg words are used as described above to form an interactive image with the to-be-remembered word. Lorayne and Lucas's emphasis on the use of bizarre imagery can be seen in the following suggestion of an appropriate image:

> *You want to remember that number 3 will be scissors.* Associate scissors to your Peg Word for number 3, which is Ma. You might see yourself cutting your Ma in half with a gigantic pair of scissors. (That picture may make you shudder, but you won't forget it.) (Lorayne & Lucas, 1974, pp. 119–120)

Obviously, this peg system would require much more effort to master than would the *1 is a bun* system described previously, but Lorayne and Lucas present it as an extension of the use of the phonetic alphabet as a means of remembering numbers. They argue that numbers constitute the most difficult category of information to remember because they are so abstract. Thus numbers must be converted to words that can be imaged, and the digit-consonant correspondences given above are the basis for this conversion. Once these digit-consonant associations are mastered, additional rules have to be learned in order for the individual to be able to convert numbers to words and words to numbers with facility. These additional rules include: (1) vowels, *w,* and *y* are disregarded, as is *h,* except when it follows *s, c, p,* or *t;* (2) *th* is treated as *t;* (3) silent letters are disregarded, such that in converting *knee* to numbers, the result would be 2, not 72; (3) double letters are represented by only one digit, such that *letter* converts to 514, not 5114; and (4) the letter *x* converts to a number based on its sound in a particular word, such that in the word *fox, x* is pronounced *ks,* and the word thus converts to 870; whereas in the word *complexion, x* is pronounced *ksh,* and the word thus converts to 7395762.

Once the digit-consonant associations and the additional conversion rules are mastered, one is in a position to convert numbers to concrete words and to link the words by means of imagery. For example, if asked to remember the digit sequence 379205927153640, one might first group the digits as follows:

379   205   927   153   640

Then, one could proceed to convert each group of numbers into a word based on the digit-consonant associations presented earlier. Thus 379 might become *makeup.* The word *nozzle* is a phonetic conversion of 205. To link these two items, one might image makeup (perhaps a disgusting combination of lipstick, mascara, and face cream) oozing from a nozzle. The number 927 could be converted to the word *bank.* In turn, this word could be linked to the previous item in the sequence by imaging the nozzle protruding from the front door of a bank. And so on for the last two groups of numbers. (Go ahead—see if you can do it!)

Mastering this digit-consonant system, Lorayne and Lucas suggest, enables a person to develop a much more extensive peg-word system than the *1 is a bun* system. They point out that a person might well have to remember sequences longer than 10 items. In such a case, the person can use the previously mastered digit-consonant associations to generate as many additional pegs as are needed. For example, the peg for position 11 could be *tot* (where each of the 1s in 11 is represented by the sound *t*), and the peg for position 12 could be *tin*. Lorayne and Lucas argue that generating pegs on the basis of the learned conversion rules should make it relatively easy to learn a very large number of pegs.

What should be obvious by now is that the mastery of such a potentially flexible system requires a considerable effort. In fact, Lorayne and Lucas suggest the use of a game to help with the learning of the digit-consonant associations that involves trying to convert mentally any number encountered into sounds and words. Their argument is that, once mastered, such a system can be very useful. For example, the peg-word system could be used in conjunction with the substitute word technique mentioned earlier in the chapter to remember the 50 states in alphabetical order. First, using the method just described, one would generate 50 pegs. Then, taking the states in alphabetical order, one would use the substitute word technique in substituting a more meaningful word for each state name. Thus, the word *album* might be substituted for *Alabama,* the first state in an alphabetical listing. Then, one would proceed to create an image linking *album* and the first peg word *tie,* and so on through the list of 50 items.

⊿ *What are the basic steps involved in the use of a peg-word mnemonic system?*

Method of Loci

Related to the peg-word system is the method of loci, which dates back to the ancient Greeks (Yates, 1966). Greek orators taught the method as an aid to the memorization of lengthy passages. The method involves a person imagining himself or herself traveling along a very familiar path (e.g., through a well-known building, along a route often traveled, etc.) with distinctive locations or objects along it. These distinctive locations are the loci. As the person comes to each locus, he or she attaches, in order, the item to be remembered to the locus by means of visual imagery. Later, retrieval is made possible by again taking the walk and recalling the image associated with each locus as it is encountered. Alan's attempt, described at the beginning of the chapter, to remember his shopping list by using rooms of his house as the loci is an example of the method of loci.

Just as the peg-word system is limited by the number of peg-words mastered, the method of loci is limited by the number of loci mastered. However, the same loci can be used repeatedly by making each trip distinctive (e.g., a walk to campus on a rainy day, on a snowy morning, on a balmy summer evening, etc.). The essential feature of both the peg-word system and the method of loci is the provision of a distinctive, easily generated retrieval cue for each item to be produced. The cost of employing both systems is the time and effort involved in mastering the pegs or loci, and this investment of time and effort has to be weighed against the potential benefits of mastering such systems. Hunter (1977) and Herrmann (1988) note that the general usefulness of such systems is questionable in that the range of situations in which the primary objective is to remember a series of items in strict serial order is quite limited.

⊿ *What are the basic steps involved in the use of the method of loci?*

Keyword Method of Vocabulary Acquisition

The Basic Technique.   The **keyword method** of vocabulary acquisition, like the peg-word system, is a composite mnemonic in that it relies on both rhyme or sound, as well as imagery, as a means of making new vocabulary words more memorable. The procedure involves two steps (Atkinson, 1975). First, for each item to be acquired, the learner must establish an association between the item and a familiar English that sounds like a salient part of the to-be-learned item. This acoustically similar familiar word is the keyword. Then, the learner generates an interactive image linking the keyword and the definition of the to-be-learned item.

For example, in learning the Spanish word *lápiz,* one would first select a rhyming or sound-alike keyword, such as *trapeze.* Then, one would generate an image linking *trapeze* and the English definition of *lápiz,* which is pencil. One might image a pencil, dressed in a tutu, swinging on a trapeze. Then, at the time of test, when presented with *lápiz,* the sound of the item would help prompt the retrieval of *trapeze,* which in turn would access the image containing the definition. The keyword does not have to rhyme with the entire to-be-learned word. In trying to remember the Spanish word *pluma,* one might use the keyword *plume,* and then image a pen dangling from the end of a brightly colored plume. See Figure 10–6 for other examples of the use of the keyword method.

The usefulness of this technique was demonstrated by Atkinson and Raugh (1975) in a study of the acquisition of foreign language vocabulary. In Atkinson and Raugh's study, subjects attempted to learn the definitions of 120 Russian words. The control subjects were given no specific instructions as to strategy to use in learning the words. The experimental subjects were instructed to use the keyword method. On an immediate test, the keyword group recalled 72% of the meanings, whereas the control group recalled 46% of the meanings. On a delayed test six weeks later, the same pattern of results was obtained.

CABALLO—eye—HORSE

FIGURE 10–6 Illustrations used by Atkinson (1975) to demonstrate how mental images can be used to link keywords for Spanish vocabulary words to the English translations of the words. The middle word in each illustration is the keyword, and the word on the right is the English translation of the Spanish word.

Source: Atkinson, R. C. (1975). Mnemotechnics in second-language learning. *American Psychologist, 30,* 822. Copyright 1975 by the American Psychological Association. Reprinted by permission.

PATO—pot—DUCK

The superior performance evidenced with the keyword method can be seen to be a product of elaborative processing at both the phonemic and the semantic level. The elaborate phonemic processing involved in selecting and associating a familiar sound-alike keyword presumably helps in the retention of the pronunciation of the word, whereas the elaborate semantic processing involved in generating the interactive image presumably helps in the retention of the meaning of the word.

☑ *What steps are involved in the use of the keyword method, and how is the method related to the notion of elaboration of processing?*

The Keyword Method Applied to Vocabulary Acquisition in One's Own Language.

It should be noted that the use of the keyword method is not limited to the acquisition of foreign language vocabulary. Pressley and colleagues demonstrated the usefulness of the technique in the acquisition of English vocabulary words by native English-speaking children and adults (e.g., Levin, McCormick, Miller, Berry, & Pressley, 1982; Pressley, Levin, & Miller, 1982; Pressley, Levin, Kuiper, Bryant, & Michener, 1982; McDaniel & Pressley, 1989). For example, in learning the English word gemsbok, one might use the keyword *gem* to remember the meaning (antelope). In learning the English word *carlin,* one might use the keyword car to remember the meaning (old woman).

In the study by Pressley and colleagues (1982), the keyword method was compared with other methods designed to promote semantic processing of the studied meanings as well as with traditional control conditions. Such comparisons are important because in many of the early studies of the keyword method, performance in the keyword condition was compared only to performance in a control condition in which subjects were uninstructed as to strategy, as in the Atkinson and Raugh (1975) study, or were instructed to repeat the words and their definitions over and over to themselves.

In one of their studies (Experiment 1), Pressley and colleagues (1982) compared the traditional keyword-imagery method with a keyword-sentence condition, an imagery condition, a synonym condition, a read-and-copy condition, and the no-strategy control condition. The keyword-sentence condition required the selection of a keyword, as in the traditional keyword-imagery condition. However, instead of being told to create an interactive image linking the keyword and the definition of the to-be-remembered item, subjects were told to create meaningful sentences linking the keyword and the definition. Subjects in the imagery condition were told to image the definition of the word as a means of remembering it, and subjects in the synonym condition were told to think of a synonym for each vocabulary word presented. Subjects in the read-and-copy condition were asked to write down each vocabulary word and its meaning on a separate card. The results are shown in Table 10–4. Clearly, performance in the two keyword conditions exceeded that in the other conditions. Note, however, that these results suggest that specific instructions to use imagery may not be essential to the success of the keyword method.

McDaniel and Pressley (1989) have extended the research on the usefulness of the keyword method to examine its effect on the comprehension of text containing the vocabulary learned. In one study, English-speaking college students learned a series of English vocabulary words using either the keyword-imagery method, a semantic-context method, or the no-strategy control method. Subjects in the semantic-context condition saw each vocabulary word presented in the context of a three-sentence passage and were told to try to infer the meaning of the item from the context presented. The presentation of the meaning followed the subject's attempt at inferring the meaning from the context. Following vocab-

TABLE 10–4   Mean Percentage of Vocabulary Word Definitions Correctly Recalled in Experiment 1 of the Pressley, Levin, Kuiper, Bryant, and Michener (1982) Study

Condition	
Keyword-imagery	48.9
Keyword-sentence	55.0
Imagery	23.1
Synonym	20.9
Read-and-copy	24.1
No-strategy control	28.9

ulary learning, subjects in all conditions read two stories that contained some of the vocabulary words studied in the first part of the experiment. On a true-false comprehension test on the stories that specifically assessed comprehension of sentences containing vocabulary items, subjects in the keyword condition performed significantly better than subjects in the other two conditions.

☑ *What have Pressley and associates found with regard to the effectiveness of the keyword method in comparison to other techniques for learning vocabulary?*

Limitation on the Usefulness of the Keyword Method.   One important limitation on the usefulness of the keyword method may be the ease with which a keyword can be generated for the vocabulary items being studied (Desrochers & Begg, 1987). In most of the studies that have reported a beneficial effect of adopting the keyword strategy, the vocabulary words used were selected in part on the basis of the ease with which concrete keywords and concrete definitions could be generated for them.

Hall (1988) compared the keyword condition and the no-strategy-instruction control condition in the learning of two sets of English vocabulary words by English-speaking college students. One set of words (the easy keyword list) included only words for which concrete keywords and concrete definitions could be easily generated. The other set of words (the typical word list) included words that were selected without regard to whether a keyword was obvious and without regard to the concreteness of the definition. Examples of words from each list are shown in Table 10–5. Hall found that, with both brief and extensive training, performance in the keyword condition was slightly but nonsignificantly better than performance in the control condition on the easy keyword list. However, on the typical word list, performance was better in the control condition than in the keyword condition, particularly following extensive training in the use of the keyword method.

These results are important in illustrating that the usefulness of the keyword method is restricted by the ease with which keywords can be generated for the to-be-learned vocabulary items. The results also suggest that it may be important to stress to subjects during training on the keyword method that other strategies should be considered if the generation of keywords for particular vocabulary items proves difficult.

☑ *What factor does Hall's research suggest may limit the usefulness of the keyword method of vocabulary acquisition?*

Variant of the Keyword Method for Prose Learning.   Encouraging subjects to adopt strategies for learning from prose that are based on variants of the keyword method has begun to be investigated extensively (McCormick & Levin, 1987). An example of one of

TABLE 10–5 Examples of Easy Keyword Items and Their Definitions and Typical Keyword Items and Their Definitions from the Study by Hall (1988)

"Easy" Keyword Items		"Typical" Keyword Items	
Keyword	*Definition*	*Keyword*	*Definition*
RUGOSE	wrinkled	OBDURATE	hard-hearted
GRAMPUS	dolphin	MISCREANT	scoundrel
JAMBEAU	armor	CONCUPISCENCE	lust
LOGGIA	balcony	BOURN	brook
FACER	metal smoother	SALUBRIOUS	healthful
MATELOTE	stew	TRADUCE	to slander
DOLLOP	ice cream	FICTILE	malleable
GIRDLER	beetle	EFFLUGENCE	radiant splendor
CORNICH	road	NIGGARDLY	stingy
CLAYMORE	sword	FATUITY	foolishness
WINDLING	straw	TRAVAIL	painful exertion
COONCAN	card game	ASPERITY	sharpness of temper

Source: Hall, J. W. (1988). On the utility of keyword mnemonic for vocabulary learning. *Journal of Educational Psychology, 80,* 557. Copyright 1988 by the American Psychological Association. Reprinted by permission.

these variants comes from a study by Shriberg, Levin, McCormick, and Pressley (1982). In their study, eighth-grade children read a series of three-sentence passages describing the accomplishments of fictitious people. Subjects receiving instruction in a variant of the keyword method were encouraged to recode the fictitious person's name into a sound-alike familiar form. In remembering information about *Charlene McKune,* for example, subjects were encouraged to recode *McKune* as *raccoon.* Then, to remember that McKune was famous for possessing a cat that could count, subjects were encouraged to count raccoons as they jumped over a fence. To encourage the generation of such interactive images, subjects received mnemonic illustrations such as that shown in Figure 10–7.

The prediction was that engaging in such recoding and generating of interactive images would facilitate the recall of facts about the various persons described in the passages. The person's name would lead to retrieval of the familiar sound-alike word, which would in turn lead to retrieval of the image containing a fact about the person. Indeed, in three experiments, Shriberg and colleagues found that recall of facts in response to names was significantly greater for subjects receiving instruction in this mnemonic technique than for control subjects receiving no special mnemonic strategy instructions.

Results from this series of experiments also suggest that the use of the mnemonic illustrations may be very important in maximizing the facilitative effect of this variant of the keyword method in children's learning of prose. In one of their experiments, Shriberg and colleagues (1982) compared the mnemonic-instruction-plus-illustrations condition described above with a mnemonic-instruction condition in which subjects were simply encouraged to generate their own interactive images. Although subjects in both of these groups showed significantly greater recall of facts in response to names than did a no-strategy-instruction control group, the subjects in the mnemonic-instruction-plus-illustrations group recalled 40% more than the subjects in the mnemonic-instruction group that did not receive illustrations. This result is consistent with other studies showing a beneficial effect of

FIGURE 10–7 Example of a mnemonic illustration used by Shriberg, Levin, McCormick, and Pressley (1982) as part of an adaptation of the keyword method for prose learning.

Source: Shriberg, L. K., Levin, J. R., McCormick, C. B., & Pressley, M. (1982). Learning about "famous" people via the keyword method. *Journal of Educational Psychology, 74,* 241. Copyright 1982 by the American Psychological Association. Reprinted by permission.

mnemonic illustrations on children's memory for prose (e.g., Levin, Morrison, McGivern, Mastropieri, & Scruggs, 1986; Levin, Shriberg, & Berry, 1983; Shriberg, 1982).

In addition, it has been noted that, with children, the facilitative effect of the keyword method for vocabulary learning is more consistently found when experimenter-provided illustrations are used than when subjects are asked to generate their own images (Pressley, Levin, & Delaney, 1982). However, because of the practical problems inherent in producing mnemonic illustrations, McCormick and Levin (1987) suggest a "compromise" pictorial mnemonic that involves instructing subjects to generate their images in response to a scene described by the experimenter.

In the *McKune* example presented above, subjects would be asked to create an image of a cat counting raccoons jumping over a fence. This compromise imagery mnemonic has been shown to be effective in facilitating secondary school students' recall of prose (Mc-Cormick & Levin, 1984; McCormick, Levin, Cykowski, & Danilovics, 1984).

How can the keyword method be applied to the learning of prose, and what role does providing mnemonic illustrations appear to play in successful application of the keyword method to prose learning?

Name-Face Mnemonic

Lorayne and Lucas (1974) recommend a specific technique for remembering the association between names and faces that builds on their substitute word technique described earlier. The technique involves three basic steps. The first is to substitute a memorable sound-alike word or phrase for the to-be-remembered name. For example, *Alexander* might become *lick sander,* or *Pincus* might become *pin cushion.* The second step is to select a prominent, memorable feature from the to-be-remembered person's face. The possibilities here are numerous: bushy eyebrows, protruding buck teeth, arched nose, and so on. Finally, as the third step in the technique, Lorayne and Lucas recommend associating this prominent feature with the substitute word or phrase established in step two through the use of interactive imagery.

For example, if Alexander's prominent facial feature is bushy eyebrows, one might image those bushy eyebrows with a tongue protruding from them to lick a sander that is floating in front of Alexander's face. If Pincus's prominent facial feature is protruding buck teeth, one might image those teeth biting into a bright red pin cushion. Lorayne and Lucas contend that the technique is useful because it promotes elaborate processing of both the person's name and the person's face. Furthermore, it encourages the establishment of an association between the face and the name for which a cue (the prominent facial feature) will be present whenever the person is again encountered.

Morris, Jones, and Hampson (1978) have produced experimental evidence of the effectiveness of this technique. They found that a group trained in the use of the technique showed a 77% improvement in their ability to recall names in response to the faces over their performance on a set of names and faces learned prior to training. A control group of subjects who did not receive the training did not show improvement in performance on the second set of names and faces.

McCarty (1980) manipulated the three components of the face-name mnemonic by either specifying or not specifying for each face a prominent feature, a name transformation, and a visual image involving an interaction of the prominent feature and the name transformation. He found that only in the group in which all three components were provided did the ability to recall names in response to faces exceed significantly the performance of control subjects who were given none of the three components. In a second experiment, McCarty found that the effectiveness of a facial feature as a cue for recall of the name decreased with the frequency of its usage for different faces within the list and was very highly correlated with the rated distinctiveness of the feature.

Thus the results of McCarty's second experiment supported Lorayne and Lucas's (1974) contention that the identification and use of a distinctive facial feature is an important component of the name-face mnemonic. However, even though McCarty demonstrated clear empirical support for the name-face mnemonic advocated by Lorayne and Lucas, he noted that a limitation to the usefulness of the technique in a real-world situation is the difficulty that most people are likely to have in generating sound-alike words and phrases for the names. Indeed, Lorayne and Lucas admit that considerable practice may be necessary to become proficient at this task.

Other research on memory for faces has focused on the ability to recognize faces previously encountered rather than the memory for name-face associations (e.g., Smith & Winograd, 1978; Winograd, 1978, 1981). In one study, Smith and Winograd (1978) presented subjects with photographs of 50 faces. One group of subjects was simply told to study the faces so as to be able to remember them later. The other two groups of subjects were not told that their memory for the faces would later be tested. One of these groups was asked to judge whether each face had a large nose. The other group was asked to judge whether each face looked friendly. Smith and Winograd found that the group asked to rate the faces for friendliness were better able subsequently to discriminate those faces they had seen previously from others they had not seen than were the subjects in the other two groups, who did not differ from each other in their ability to discriminate old and new faces.

In a subsequent series of experiments, Winograd (1981) evaluated the hypothesis that judging traits such as friendliness enhances memory for faces by encouraging elaborate processing that involves the evaluation and encoding of a relatively large number of facial features. If this hypothesis is correct, then other orienting tasks that encourage an extensive scan of the face should be as good as a trait judgment task at promoting memory for faces. In two experiments, Winograd found that faces searched for their most distinctive physical feature were remembered as well as those evaluated on a general trait such as friendliness.

In subsequent experiments, Winograd (1981) evaluated the hypothesis that elaborate processing in the form of an extensive scan of the face is effective simply because the probability of encoding a highly distinctive feature increases as the number of features evaluated increases. This hypothesis was supported in one experiment in which it was found that simple judgments about features (e.g., *Does the person have thin lips?*) were as effective as trait judgments in promoting memory for faces as long as the features being judged were distinctive, based on ratings by an independent group of subjects.

In a final experiment, Winograd (1981) found that the superior memory for faces following trait judgments, as opposed to feature judgments of both nondistinctive and distinctive features, was more pronounced for faces rated high in distinctiveness. This result is also consistent with the assumption that trait judgments induce a scan of the face and that the effect of this scan on subsequent memory for the face is a function of whether the scan leads to the encoding of distinctive structural features. Thus, Winograd's research provides additional empirical support for Lorayne and Lucas's contention that identifying a distinctive facial feature is an important component of effective techniques for remembering faces.

📝 *How does the name-face mnemonic described by Lorayne and Lucas involve the selection of distinctive facial features, and how has Winograd shown distinctive features to be important to face recognition?*

CONCLUDING REMARKS: Themes of Associationism and Cognitivism

The discussion of mnemonic techniques illustrates again the themes of associationism and cognitivism that have been considered throughout the book. To the degree that associationism deals fundamentally with the establishment of linkages in memory, every mnemonic technique presented is an example of why associationism remains a dominant theme in learning and memory. However, traditional principles of associationism that emphasize the importance of factors such as frequency, recency, and contiguity are also clearly inadequate as a framework for explaining many of the phenomena considered in this chapter.

Particularly obvious in this account of mnemonics is the important role ascribed to imagery. As noted earlier in Chapter 8, any attempt to explain the effects of imagery inevitably leads to a consideration of cognitive states and operations that are beyond the scope of simple associationism. Even if one attempts to explain imagery effects in terms of underlying propositional representations, one has to resort to explanations in terms of elaboration of processing and distinctiveness of encoding that also go beyond simple principles of associationism. Therefore, a consideration of mnemonics, as with every other memory topic thus far considered, points to the usefulness of cognitive accounts of memory that incorporate basic notions of associationism and at the same time suggest the importance of processing operations that either underlie or arise from the formation of associations.

CHAPTER 11

Amnesia

APPLICATION: Beyond Normal Forgetting

Alan returns home from class one Thursday afternoon in late March feeling unwell. He has a headache that, over the course of the next two hours, becomes excruciatingly painful, even though he has taken several extra-strength aspirin tablets. In addition, he feels feverish and begins to experience chills. By the time his mother comes home from work, he is feeling so lousy that he has gone to bed. When his mother discovers that he has a temperature of 104°, she rushes him to the emergency room of a nearby hospital. By the time they reach the hospital, Alan has lapsed into a coma.

Medical tests eventually show that Alan is suffering from encephalitis. He remains in a coma for 10 days. Upon regaining consciousness, Alan initially appears to be cognitively unaffected by his ordeal. Testing by the hospital's neuropsychologist reveals that his I.Q. has not been affected, his memory span is normal, and his comprehension and use of language appear to be normal. However, it soon becomes evident that Alan's long-term memory has been affected by his illness. Systematic testing reveals that he has grossly impaired memory for events that occurred during the six-week period preceding his illness. For example, he cannot recall personally significant events such as the notice he had received just two weeks before his illness of his acceptance to Yale Law School. He also cannot recall generally significant events from the six-week period preceding his illness, such as the beginning of the U.S.-led war against Iraq.

In addition, it becomes increasingly obvious that Alan is not storing new long-term memories for events occurring after his return to consciousness. Even five weeks after regaining consciousness, Alan shows no memory for the three physicians who have been visiting him almost daily. He cannot remember the name of the rehabilitation hospital to which he has been transferred, even though members of his family have told him the name many times and even though he sees the name frequently on linen, on his daily menu choice card, and on the identification tags of all hospital staff members. Alan is clearly suffering from amnesia.

AMNESIA DEFINED

Amnesia refers to memory loss resulting from brain injury or trauma. The period over which the memory loss extends provides a basis for distinguishing between retrograde and anterograde amnesia.

Retrograde Amnesia

Retrograde amnesia refers to a loss of memory for events occurring prior to the brain trauma. Common causes of such memory loss include head trauma and ECS (electroconvulsive shock), which is used in the treatment of mental disorders such as depression. The memory loss associated with retrograde amnesia is temporally graded in that the closer an event is to the trauma, the more likely it is that memory for the event will be disrupted. Alan's loss of memory for events occurring during the six-week period preceding his illness is an example of retrograde amnesia.

☑ *What sort of memory loss characterizes retrograde amnesia?*

Anterograde Amnesia

Anterograde amnesia refers to the loss of memory for events occurring after the brain trauma. Thus this deficit involves loss of the ability to form new long-lasting memories. Alan's inability to remember information and events experienced after his illness is an example of anterograde amnesia. This memory loss is associated with damage to the medial temporal regions of the brain (Figure 11–1). Damage to this region of the brain is associated with Korsakoff's syndrome, which results from chronic alcoholism, certain types of encephalitis, and certain types of surgical procedures that were used in the past to treat severe cases of epilepsy. ECS has also been shown to be associated with anterograde amnesia (Squire & Slater, 1975; Squire & Fox, 1980).

Even though it is often useful to distinguish between these two types of amnesia, individuals suffering from a trauma-induced memory loss often exhibit both retrograde and anterograde amnesia. Squire (1987) suggests that this tendency to find both retrograde and anterograde amnesia in the same individual reflects the involvement of a common neural system in both types of amnesia. Specifically, Squire suggests that a disruption of the medial temporal region of the brain and its associated structures is the basis for both types of amnesia. This suggestion is based on the assumption that the **medial-temporal region,** including the hippocampus and the amygdala, is importantly involved in the establishment of long-term memory sites in the **neocortex** (i.e., the outer covering of the cerebrum).

☑ *What sort of memory deficit characterizes anterograde amnesia?*

Primary versus Secondary Amnesia

Baddeley (1982) argues that in assessing theoretical accounts of amnesia it is important to distinguish between primary and secondary amnesia. **Primary amnesia** refers to a profound deficit in long-term memory in the absence of deficits in other aspects of cognitive processing. **Secondary amnesia,** on the other hand, refers to memory difficulties arising as a result of deficits in other aspects of cognitive processing. For example, receptive aphasia (i.e., difficulty in comprehending language) and inattention could contribute to profound memory deficits. In drawing this distinction, Baddeley argues that much of the theoretical conflict

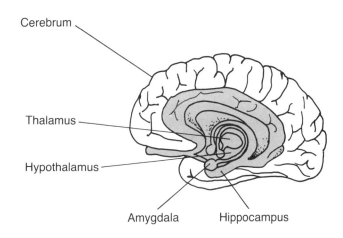

FIGURE 11–1 The human brain with the medial-temporal region in gray. This region includes structures of the limbic system such as the hippocampus and the amygdala. The surface of the cerebrum is known as the neocortex.

Cerebrum

Thalamus

Hypothalamus

Amygdala   Hippocampus

with regard to anterograde amnesia stems from the study of amnesic patients with secondary as well as primary amnesia. In particular, he notes that studies of Korsakoff patients often include patients with pronounced secondary deficits.

Squire (1987) notes that it is the selectivity of the deficits of those suffering from primary amnesia that underlies the interest of researchers in this disorder. Those suffering from primary amnesia typically show normal general intellectual ability and normal short-term memory, as reflected, for example, in measures of the memory span (Baddeley & Warrington, 1970; Drachman & Arbit, 1966; Talland, 1965). The deficits appear to be limited to the retrieval or encoding of long-term memories.

☑ *What is primary amnesia, and in what way is it a selective deficit?*

THEORETICAL ACCOUNTS OF AMNESIA

Consolidation Hypothesis

Squire (1986, 1987) suggests that both retrograde and anterograde amnesia can be explained as a disruption of the consolidation process in long-term memory. **Consolidation** refers to a process whereby storage in long-term memory becomes permanent only gradually, following establishment of the long-term memory trace. The assumption here is that information must reside undisturbed in long-term memory for a certain period of time in order to become a truly permanent part of the long-term store. However, consolidation is not seen by Squire to be a passive process. Instead, he argues that consolidation involves elaboration and reorganization of the stored information.

Squire suggests that the neural mechanism underlying this consolidation process is the operation of the medial temporal region of the brain, including the hippocampus and the amygdala, in establishing memory storage sites in the neocortex that can function independently to support the storage and retrieval of information. This neural system, it is argued, contributes to the storage of memories in the neocortex but is not itself a storage site. Brain trauma, then, can disrupt the continuing consolidation of information already residing in long-term memory, and thus result in retrograde amnesia, by damaging the neural system that contributes to the storage of memories in the neocortex.

Squire bases his arguments for such neural mechanisms on evidence from both humans and animals. In addition to relying on brain studies of humans suffering from amnesia, Squire also bases his description of the neural mechanisms involved in consolidation and amnesia on animal studies involving lesions, or surgical removal, of tissue in specific regions of the brain. He has noted that lesions in animals in the medial-temporal region, specifically in portions of the hippocampus and amygdala, produce amnesia that is very similar to that observed in humans.

To return to the example of Alan presented at the beginning of the chapter, Alan's failure to remember his acceptance to Yale Law School and the beginning of the U.S.-Iraq war would, on Squire's consolidation view, be attributed to the disruption of the neural system that was continuing to contribute to the consolidation of this information in long-term store at the time Alan became ill—even though this information would have been residing in long-term store in some form for several weeks at the time of the illness. In addition, trauma to this neural system in the brain, Squire contends, can also make future consolidation of new information impossible or unlikely and thus result in anterograde amnesia. For example, Alan's failure to remember from day to day the name of the hospital and the physicians who had been interacting with him for an extended period following his illness is explicable, in this view, in terms of a defect in the neural system that makes the consolidation of such newly encountered information possible.

One argument that has been leveled against the consolidation hypothesis as an explanation of retrograde amnesia focuses on the fact that lost memories are often recovered with the passage of time, with the older memories recovering first (Miller & Marlin, 1984). If the trauma disrupts the consolidation process, it is argued, then the affected memories should not become a permanent part of long-term store and should, therefore, not recover with the passage of time. Instead, these critics propose a retrieval explanation of retrograde amnesia that argues that trauma only makes information temporarily inaccessible, rather than permanently unavailable. Squire (1987) counters, however, by noting that recovery of memories following retrograde amnesia is not complete. Memories for events just prior to the trauma are permanently lost (Barbizet, 1970; Russell & Nathan, 1946; Squire, Slater, & Miller, 1981).

These findings are consistent with the assumption that the medial-temporal region of the hippocampus must interact in some way with sites in the neocortex for a certain period of time following initial encoding in order for the memory sites to be fully functional. A trauma disrupts this consolidation process and thus prevents the effective storage of memories for events closely preceding the trauma. Memories for more remote events may not be permanently lost because the consolidation process for these events may have proceeded sufficiently at the time of the trauma to establish their memory traces in the neocortex reasonably well. Even though they may not be accessible on the initial memory test following the trauma, these memories may be sufficiently consolidated to allow retrieval on a subsequent memory test, perhaps as a result of a slightly different ensemble of retrieval cues present at the time of the later test.

Another objection that has been raised to the consolidation hypothesis concerns the time period over which retrograde amnesia may extend. In one study of the effects of ECS on the memory performance of mice, Squire and Spanis (1984) exposed mice during a single training trial to "foot shock" upon their entering a dark compartment. Memory for the foot shock was tested after delays ranging from 15 to 84 days by measuring the amount time that passed when the mice were presented with the dark chamber before they entered the chamber (the step-through latency). For those mice receiving ECS, the memory test for the foot shock always occurred two weeks after the ECS. The results from the experiment are shown in Figure 11–2. Mice given ECS between 1 and 14 days following the learning trial exhibited retrograde amnesia in that they waited significantly less time before entering the darkened chamber than did control mice not actually given ECS, with the effect greater the shorter the delay between training and ECS. However, mice given ECS 21 to 70 days following training did not show retrograde amnesia. Thus, in mice, ECS-induced retrograde amnesia can extend over a period of at least two weeks.

In the case of humans, it would appear that retrograde amnesia can affect memory for events preceding the trauma by several years. For example, Squire, Slater, and Chace (1975) studied the memory for television programs of psychiatric patients undergoing ECS in 1974. The television programs used to test for memory were programs that had lasted only one year and had appeared sometime during the period from 1957 to 1972. The results are summarized in Figure 11–3.

The patients showed a selective memory deficit following ECS for the most recent shows, which had appeared on television two to three years earlier. Critics of the consolida-

FIGURE 11–2
Strength of memory for an avoidance response for mice subjected to ECS and for control mice not subjected to ECS, as a function of the time interval between the avoidance training and the receipt of ECS, from a study by Squire and Spanis (1984).

Source: Squire, L. R., & Spanis, C. W. (1984). Long gradient of retrograde amnesia in mice: Continuity with the findings in humans. *Behavioral Neuroscience, 98,* 347. In the public domain.

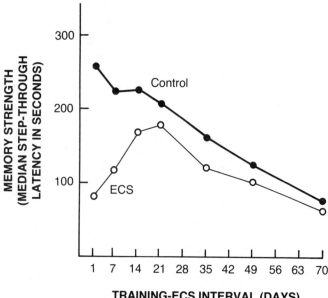

FIGURE 11–3 Performance of 16 depressed psychiatric patients on a multiple-choice test on television shows that appeared for one season during the period 1957–1972, from the study by Squire, Slater, and Chace (1975). ECS selectively impaired memory for the most recent shows, which had appeared two to three years earlier, as the study was conducted during 1974.

Source: Squire, L. R., Slater, P. C., & Chace, P. M. (1975). Retrograde amnesia: Temporal gradient in very long-term memory following electroconvulsive therapy. *Science, 187,* 78. Copyright 1975 by the American Association for the Advancement of Science.

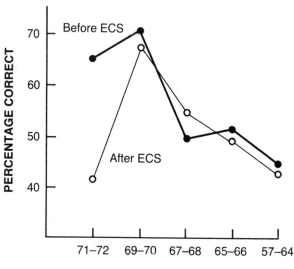

tion hypothesis suggest that it is unreasonable to assume that a consolidation process would continue for such long periods of time. Squire (1987), however, does not consider such findings problematical for his consolidation explanation, arguing that consolidation can continue for periods as long as several years. He observes that "consolidation is not an automatic process with a fixed duration. It is best regarded as a dynamic process that continues so long as information is being forgotten, and that results in the reorganization and stabilization of what remains" (Squire, 1987, p. 208).

Furthermore, Squire (1987) maintains that a retrieval explanation of amnesia is not a viable alternative to his consolidation explanation because it provides no basis for explaining why retrograde amnesia tends to be limited to memory for events preceding the trauma by no more than a few years. Amnesics' memory for events preceding the trauma by many years tends to be unimpaired. To be a serious contender to the consolidation hypothesis, Squire suggests, a retrieval explanation must explain why the trauma *selectively* makes the more recent memories inaccessible.

☑ *How does the consolidation hypothesis attempt to explain both anterograde and retrograde amnesia?*

Amnesia as a Defect of Episodic Long-Term Memory

In 1982, Baddeley proposed what he called a *minimal model* of amnesia. In this model, Baddeley suggested that amnesia represents a defect of episodic long-term memory. In so doing, Baddeley was invoking the distinction between episodic and semantic memory proposed by Tulving (1972, 1983, 1984) and discussed in Chapter 7. In support of this position, Baddeley cited evidence that semantic memory is intact in individuals with amnesia. He noted that amnesics' unimpaired ability to use language and general knowledge suggests that semantic memory is unimpaired.

Specifically, there is evidence that amnesics performance on vocabulary tests is unimpaired (Baddeley & Warrington, 1970; Baddeley & Wilson, 1983; Talland, 1965). There is also evidence that amnesics do not differ from subjects with normal memory in their ability to generate instances of semantic categories (e.g., *Name as many instances of animal as possible*) within a specified period of time (Baddeley & Warrington, 1970; Baddeley & Wilson, 1983). In addition, amnesics are unimpaired compared to normal controls in their ability to judge the truth and falsity of general knowledge statements such as *sharks have fins* under time constraints (Baddeley & Wilson, 1983).

In contrast, Baddeley argued, amnesics show gross deficits in the ability to remember specific events and information, such as what they had for breakfast and what activities they have engaged in on a particular day. Such deficits suggest a seriously impaired episodic memory. In characterizing the episodic long-term memory deficit of primary amnesics, Baddeley distinguished between conscious remembering and automatic memory procedures. This distinction is based on the notion that one can demonstrate evidence of learning without having conscious awareness that the necessary information is available in memory. Baddeley argued that primary amnesics are capable of new long-term learning, which will be evidenced if they are tested in a way that permits them to demonstrate their learning without requiring an awareness of when or how the information was acquired.

In support of this argument, there is evidence of classical conditioning of the eyeblink response in amnesics in the absence of memory for having previously been exposed to the testing apparatus (Weiskrantz & Warrington, 1979). Over the course of numerous conditioning trials, the subjects showed clear evidence of a conditioned reflex (i.e., blinking in response to the CS) and yet could not recall what the conditioning apparatus did.

There is also evidence that amnesics can learn as well as normals new motor skills such as performing a pursuit rotor task (Corkin, 1968), tracing a path through a maze (Starr & Phillips, 1970; Brooks & Baddeley, 1976), and performing a simple typing task (Baddeley, 1982). Amnesics also appear to be unimpaired in their ability to exhibit perceptual learning such as that involved in detecting an anomaly in a drawing faster and faster with repeated presentations of the drawing (Warrington & Weiskrantz, 1973), in assembling a jigsaw puzzle faster and faster with repeated presentations of the puzzle (Brooks & Baddeley, 1976), and in acquiring the skill of being able to read print reflected in a mirror (Cohen & Squire, 1980). Amnesics also show normal learning of cognitive tasks such as applying a numerical rule (Wood, Ebert, & Kinsbourne, 1982) and solving the Tower-of-Hanoi problem (Cohen, 1984), which is described in Figure 11–4.

The cognitive skill involved in improving the speed with which a passage is read was assessed for amnesics in a study by Musen, Shimamura, and Squire (1990). They found that the rate at which the reading speed of amnesic patients increased across three readings of the same passage was equal to that of normal subjects. The length of time over which prior exposure to the passage continued to facilitate the rereading of the passage was the same for amnesic subjects as for normal subjects, even though the amnesic subjects showed a pronounced impairment in their memory of what they had read. Squire, Cohen, and Zouzounis (1984) have also demonstrated that a skill acquired prior to the onset of amnesia is unaffected by the amnesic condition. Depressed psychiatric patients who acquired a mirror-reading skill prior to a series of ECS treatments showed no loss of the skill following the treatments.

Other examples of the unimpaired ability of amnesics to show new long-term learning include demonstrations of certain types of verbal learning. Warrington and Weiskrantz (1968, 1970) showed that amnesics can learn as well as normal subjects to recognize a word given a more and more fragmented version of it across trials (Figure 11–5).

Interestingly, the performance of amnesics on tasks in which the correct response is cued or primed in this way depends critically on how the task is described to subjects. Graf, Squire, and Mandler (1984) first presented normal and amnesic subjects with a list of words (e.g., *filly, cheese*). Then, the subjects were shown a list of word fragments (e.g., *fil-, che-*). When subjects were instructed to complete each fragment so as to form the first word that comes to mind, the amnesics produced just as many words from the initially presented list as did the normal subjects, even though each fragment could be expanded into at least 10 different words.

However, when the instructions indicated that subjects were to use the word fragments as cues for the recall of recently encountered words, normal subjects recalled more words

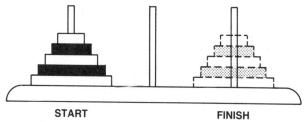

START   **FINISH**

FIGURE 11–4 The initial state for the five-disk Tower-of-Hanoi problem that was used by Cohen (1984) in his study of preserved memory abilities in amnesic patients. The problem required that five disks be moved from the peg on the left to the peg on the right, using the middle peg as needed. Only the top disk on a peg can be moved at one time, and no disk can be placed on top of a smaller disk.

Source: Cohen, N. J. (1984). Preserved learning capacity in amnesia: Evidence for multiple memory systems. In L. R. Squire & N. Butters (Eds.), *Neuropsychology of memory* (p. 89). New York: Guilford Press. Reprinted with permission.

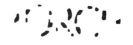

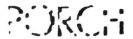

FIGURE 11–5   An example of fragmented versions of a word used by Warrington and Weiskrantz (1968, 1970).

Source: Reprinted by permission from *Nature,* Vol. 217, p. 972. Copyright 1968 Macmillan Magazines Limited.

PORCH

from the original list than did amnesics. Examination of the results showed that, whereas normal subjects recalled more of the original list items when told to use the fragments as cues for recall of list items than when told to use the fragments to form the first word that comes to mind, amnesics recalled about the same number of original list items under the two different instruction conditions.

Other priming effects are exhibited by amnesics in situations in which the priming is clearly of a semantic nature. When amnesic and normal subjects were initially presented with words such as *baby* and *chair,* both groups were twice as likely to produce these words later in response to the questions, ''What is the first word that comes to mind when you hear the word ''cry'' (or ''table'')?'' (Graf, Shimamura, & Squire, 1985). Similarly, presenting relatively rare words such as *raspberry, banker,* and *raccoon* increased dramatically and equally for amnesics and normal controls the probability of the words being produced subsequently as instances of the categories *fruits, professions,* and *animals* (Gardner, Boller, Moreines, & Butters, 1973). These priming effects in the amnesics were observed despite the fact that they could recall virtually none of the items initially presented.

In all of these examples, the amnesics showed either no awareness or greatly impaired awareness of the previous trials on which the skill was acquired. That is, the amnesics showed virtually no conscious awareness of prior learning episodes. Thus, in proposing his minimal model, Baddeley (1982) argued that certain automatic retrieval processes such as those involved in the types of learning tasks just summarized are spared in amnesics. What they lack is the ability to engage in conscious recollection. That is, they lack the ability to recognize whether information that comes into consciousness represents a true memory, presumably because the episodic information necessary for making such a decision (e.g., temporal, spatial, contextual information) is not a part of the amnesic's representation of the information.

What sorts of unimpaired long-term memory abilities exhibited by amnesics have been used to argue that amnesia is a defect of episodic long-term memory?

Amnesia as a Defect of Declarative Long-Term Memory

Baddeley (1984) subsequently argued that the pattern of findings summarized above is better interpreted in terms of the distinction between declarative and procedural knowledge that was described in Chapter 7 than it is in terms of the distinction between semantic and episodic memory. In doing so, Baddeley noted that certain implications of his original position that amnesia reflects a defective episodic memory system and an intact semantic memory system are not supported by the available evidence. For example, if the semantic system in amnesics is intact, then it is reasonable to expect that amnesics should show unimpaired ability to commit new information to semantic memory. Conversely, if the episodic system is impaired, amnesics should show impaired ability to recall personal episodes that occurred many years prior to the development of the amnesia.

Cermak and O'Connor (1983), however, found that an amnesic individual who was an expert on lasers prior to developing amnesia was unable to retain information on new developments in the field of lasers even though he demonstrated as he read the information that he was comprehending the material. Thus, amnesics do not appear to be able to update semantic memory, as Baddeley's original minimal model of amnesia would predict.

As Squire (1987) observes, the semantic memory of amnesics is impaired, just as in the case of episodic knowledge, when the semantic knowledge is tied to events occurring in the period just prior to the onset of the amnesia or in the period following the onset of the amnesia (Cohen & Squire, 1981; Shimamura & Squire, 1987). Furthermore, Zola-Morgan, Cohen, and Squire (1983) and Baddeley and Wilson (1983) have reported evidence of amnesics' unimpaired memory for personal episodes from the distant past. Thus just as they are not impaired in their ability to recall semantic information acquired well before the onset of the amnesia, amnesics do not appear to be impaired in their ability to recall episodic information acquired well before the onset of the amnesia, contrary to what Baddeley's original minimal model of amnesia would predict.

Therefore, Baddeley's (1984) reinterpretation of the evidence summarized above is that it more appropriately supports the view that amnesia reflects a defect in declarative memory, both episodic and semantic, for events and information experienced just prior to the onset of the amnesia and in the period following the onset of the amnesia. Baddeley's (1984) reinterpretation further suggests that procedural knowledge, based on what Baddeley (1982) originally called **automatic memory processes,** is typically unaffected in individuals exhibiting amnesia. This reinterpretation of the findings is based on the assumption that all of the examples of new or spared long-term learning cited above can reasonably be viewed as exemplars of procedural, as opposed to declarative, learning.

Squire (1987) strongly supports this reinterpretation:

> *Declarative memory is memory that is directly accessible to conscious recollection. It can be declared. It deals with the facts and data that are acquired through learning, and it is impaired in amnesia. In contrast, procedural memory is not accessible as specific facts, data, or time-and-place events. Procedural memory is memory that is contained within learned skills or modifiable cognitive operations. It is spared in amnesia. (p. 152)*

Given this widely accepted distinction between declarative and procedural knowledge, many of the examples given earlier of new long-term learning or spared long-term memory exhibited by amnesics are readily seen as involving procedural knowledge. The learning of motor skills (assembling a jigsaw puzzle), perception-based learning (mirror-reading), and cognitive skills (reading a passage more rapidly with repeated exposure to it) clearly appear to involve procedural learning.

The sort of simple classical conditioning demonstrated in amnesic patients by Weiskrantz and Warrington (1979) can also be viewed as procedural learning in that it can involve the expression of an acquired association in the absence of conscious recollection of the learning episode. Even the examples of verbal learning by amnesics involving cuing and priming can be seen as procedural learning. Learning to recognize a more and more fragmented version of a word, as in the Warrington and Weiskrantz (1973) study, involves that aspect of procedural learning that Squire (1987) describes as a ''modifiable cognitive operation'' that is not accessible to conscious recollection. Likewise, the spared semantic priming shown by amnesics in the studies by Graf and colleagues (1985) and Gardner and colleagues (1973) involves automatic memory procedures that can proceed in the absence of conscious recollection.

Squire and colleagues (e.g., Squire & Zola-Morgan, 1988; Musen et al., 1990) have suggested that, in place of the term **procedural learning**, the term **nondeclarative learning** be used to describe the type of learning that is spared in amnesics. It is the contention of Squire and colleagues that the term *nondeclarative* more clearly communicates that the type of learning that is intact in amnesics includes not only the procedures involved in the learning of motor skills but also the unconscious memory abilities tapped by tasks such as priming and classical conditioning.

Squire (1986, 1987) notes that amnesia produced by lesions in the medial-temporal region of monkeys and other animals is characterized by deficits and spared abilities that also correspond to the declarative/procedural (or nondeclarative) distinction. For example, as shown in Figure 11–6a, monkeys with lesions in the hippocampus and amygdala of the medial-temporal region showed grossly impaired recognition memory (Squire, 1986). The recognition memory task required that monkeys select on each trial the novel object of the two presented in order to receive a raisin as a reward. The familiar of the two objects had been presented alone 8 seconds to 10 minutes before the two objects were presented together. However, as shown in Figure 11–6b, these same monkeys showed unimpaired learning of a motor skill that involved maneuvering a Lifesaver candy along a metal rod and around a 90° bend in order to obtain it as a reward.

 On what basis does Baddeley argue that amnesia is best described as a selective defect of both episodic and semantic declarative memory, and how are findings of amnesics' unimpaired ability to demonstrate certain types of new long-term learning consistent with this view?

Consolidation Hypothesis Revisited

Squire's (1987) consolidation hypothesis described earlier was proposed with this characterization of amnesia in terms of declarative and procedural knowledge very much in mind. That is, Squire argues that damage to the medial-temporal region of the brain disrupts a neural system that is responsible specifically for the consolidation of declarative knowledge in long-term memory. Squire suggests that the declarative memory system may have evolved later than the procedural memory system, as natural selection operated to favor the emergence of a more generalized knowledge system that could make the output of various

---

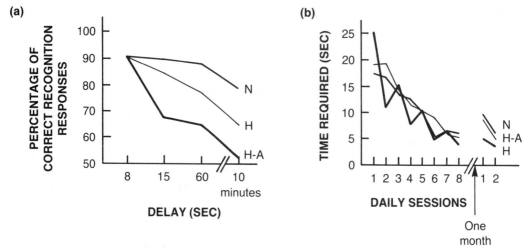

FIGURE 11–6 (a) Recognition memory performance by normal monkeys (N), monkeys with hippocampal lesions (H), and monkeys with lesions in both the hippocampus and amygdala (H-A). (b) Time required to complete a motor skill task across daily training sessions, before and after a one-month delay, for the same three groupings of monkeys (from Squire, 1986).

Source: Squire, L. R. (1986). Mechanisms of memory. *Science, 232*, 1616. Copyright 1986 by the American Association for the Advancement of Science.

specialized processing systems in the brain generally available to other specific processing systems.

The development of this generalized declarative memory system was dependent, Squire suggests, on the development of the medial-temporal region and its associated structures in the brain. Thus, damage to the medial-temporal region can result in profound deficits in declarative memory while leaving specialized procedural memory, which is not dependent on the medial temporal region, unaffected.

▣ *How is Squire's consolidation hypothesis compatible with the view that amnesia is characterized by defective declarative memory and intact procedural memory?*

CONCLUDING REMARKS: The Maltese Cross Model Revisited (Again)

*The suggestion that amnesia reflects intact procedural memory, combined with a defect in episodic and semantic declarative memory for events occurring just before, and in the entire period following, the onset of the condition, can be interpreted within in the context of Broadbent's Maltese cross model of memory that was described in Chapter 6. Recall that Broadbent (1984) stipulates that long-term memories for processing operations are stored in a component of memory he calls the **processing system** that is separate and distinct from the long-term associative store, which contains records of events and associations between events. This distinction in the Maltese cross model between the representation of processing operations and the representation of events provides a basis for explaining the selective deficits shown by amnesics.*

Within the framework of the Maltese cross model, it can be argued that individuals with anterograde amnesia have an intact processing system but have lost the ability to commit to long-term associative store new memory fragments containing associations between items. The assumption of an intact processing system is consistent with the types of procedural learning that amnesics exhibit. Procedural learning within the Maltese cross model would be represented within the processing system. The assumption of a deficit in the ability to form new long-term associative memory records is consistent with observations of deficits in both episodic and semantic memory for events and information experienced after the onset of the disorder.

Less easily interpreted within the Maltese cross model is the impaired memory of amnesic individuals for information acquired a relatively short time prior to the onset of the disorder. One could accommodate such findings by incorporating into the model some of Squire's (1987) assumptions about a long-lasting consolidation process within the long-term associative store, but Broadbent has not yet done so.

Regardless of whether the Maltese cross model ultimately proves to be a useful framework within which to interpret amnesia, the popularity of descriptions of amnesia that are based on the distinction between declarative and procedural knowledge and on the concept of consolidation is further evidence of the trend toward cognitive accounts of memory phenomena. Although the inability to form new associations is certainly a major component of the amnesic syndrome, current attempts to explain amnesia clearly go well beyond simple principles of associationism. In fact, the accounts of amnesia highlighted in this chapter show a trend toward explanations that blur the traditional distinctions between cognitive psychology and neuropsychology. That is, evidence from the study of the physiological functioning of the brain is influencing cognitive accounts of memory.

The cognitive psychologist's distinction between declarative and procedural knowledge is buttressed by the identification of damage within specific regions of the brain that is highly correlated with behavioral deficits that are consistent with the declarative/procedural distinction. Furthermore, the likelihood that the notion of consolidation will become a major part of cognitive accounts of amnesia and other memory phenomena will depend in part on the degree to which neuropsychologists and physiological psychologists succeed in demonstrating a physiological mechanism that corresponds to the hypothesized consolidation process.

REFERENCES

The numbers in **boldface** type that follow each entry indicate the pages on which the reference is cited in this book.

Abramson, L. Y., Seligman, M. E. P., & Teasdale, J. D. (1978). Learned helplessness in humans: Critique and reformulation. *Journal of Abnormal Psychology, 87,* 49–74. **102**

Ackrill, J. C. (1980). *Aristotle the philosopher.* Oxford: Oxford University Press. **2**

Adams, J. A. (1984). Learning of movement sequences. *Psychological Bulletin, 96,* 3–28. **81**

Adams, N., Castro, A. D., & Clark, D. L. (1974). State-dependent learning with a general anesthetic (Isoflurane) in man. *T.I.T. Journal of Life Sciences, 4,* 125–134. **241**

Allen, M. M. (1968). Rehearsal strategies and response cueing as determinants of organization in free recall. *Journal of Verbal Learning and Verbal Behavior, 7,* 58–63. **289**

Allison, J. (1983). *Behavioral economics.* New York: Praeger. **84**

Ameriks, K. (1982). *Kant's theory of mind.* Oxford: Clarendon Press of Oxford University Press. **3**

Amsel, A. (1962). Frustrative nonreward in partial reinforcement and discrimination learning: Some recent history and a theoretical extension. *Psychological Review, 69,* 306–328. **75**

Amsel, A., & Roussel, J. (1952). Motivational properties of frustration: Effect on a running response of the addition of frustration to the motivational complex. *Journal of Experimental Psychology, 43,* 363–368. **96**

Anderson, J. R. (1975). Item-specific and relation-specific interference in sentence memory. *Journal of Experimental Psychology: Human Learning and Memory, 1,* 249–260. **219**

Anderson, J. R. (1976). *Language, memory, and thought.* Hillsdale, NJ: Erlbaum. **220, 270**

Anderson, J. R. (1978). Arguments concerning representations for mental imagery. *Psychological Review, 85,* 249–277. **270**

Anderson, J. R. (1979). Further arguments concerning representations for mental imagery: A response to Hayes-Roth and Pylyshyn. *Psychological Review, 86,* 395–406. **270**

Anderson, J. R. (1983). *The architecture of cognition.* Cambridge, MA: Harvard University Press. **218, 220, 221, 223, 254, 255, 256, 257, 263, 270**

Anderson, J. R. (1984). Spreading activation. In J. R. Anderson & S. M. Kosslyn (Eds.), *Tutorials in learning and memory* (pp. 61–90). San Francisco: Freeman. **257**

Anderson, J. R. (1987). Skill acquisition: Compilation of weak-method problem solutions. *Psychological Review, 94,* 192–210. **218, 220, 224**

Anderson, J. R. (1989). Practice, working memory, and the ACT* theory of skill acquisition: A comment on Carlson, Sullivan, and Schneider (1989). *Journal of Experimental Psychology: Learning, Memory, and Cognition, 15,* 527–530. **218**

Anderson, J. R. (1990). *Cognitive psychology and its implications* (3rd ed.). New York: Freeman. **218, 220, 226, 254, 263**

Anderson, J. R., & Bower, G. H. (1972). Recognition and retrieval processes in free recall. *Psychological Review, 79,* 97–123. **291**

Anderson, J. R., & Bower, G. H. (1973). *Human associative memory.* New York: Winston. **218, 219, 254, 270, 295**

Anderson, J. R., & Bower, G. H. (1974). A propositional theory of recognition memory. *Memory & Cognition, 2,* 406–412. **291**

Anderson, R. C., & Kulhavy, R. W. (1972). Imagery and prose learning. *Journal of Educational Psychology, 63,* 242–243. **321**

Anderson, R. C., & Ortony, A. (1975). On putting apples into bottles—A problem of polysemy. *Cognitive Psychology, 7,* 167–180. **260**

Arabian, J. M., & Desiderato, O. (1975). Preference for signaled shock: A test of two hypotheses. *Animal Learning & Behavior, 3,* 191–195. **37, 103**

Atkinson, R. C. (1975). Mnemotechnics in second-language learning. *American Psychologist, 30,* 821–828. **331, 332**

Atkinson, R. C., & Raugh, M. R. (1975). An application of the mnemonic keyword method to the acquisition of a Russian vocabulary. *Journal of Experimental Psychology: Human Learning and Memory, 1,* 126–133. **332, 333**

Atkinson, R. C., & Shiffrin, R. M. (1968). Human memory: A proposed system and its control processes. In K. W. Spence & J. T. Spence (Eds.), *The psychology of learning and motivation* (Vol. 2, pp. 89–195). New York: Academic Press. **181, 184, 186**

Atkinson, R. C., & Shiffrin, R. M. (1971). The control of short-term memory. *Scientific American, 225,* 82–90. **181, 182, 185, 190, 191**

Ayllon, T. (1963). Intensive treatment of psychotic behavior by stimulus satiation and food reinforcement. *Behaviour Research and Therapy, 1,* 53–61. **79, 96**

Ayllon, T., & Azrin, N. H. (1968). *The token economy: A motivational system for therapy and rehabilitation.* New York: Appleton-Century-Crofts. **78**

Azrin, N. H. (1956). Some effects of two intermittent schedules of immediate and non-immediate punishment. *Journal of Psychology, 42,* 3–21. **95**

Baddeley, A. D. (1966a). The influence of acoustic and semantic similarity on long-term memory for word sequences. *Quarterly Journal of Experimental Psychology, 18,* 302–309. **188**

Baddeley, A. D. (1966b). Short-term memory for word sequences as a function of acoustic, semantic and formal similarity. *Quarterly Journal of Experimental Psychology, 18,* 362–365. **188, 201**

Baddeley, A. D. (1976). *The psychology of memory.* New York: Harper & Row. **188, 201**

Baddeley, A. D. (1978). The trouble with levels: A reexamination of Craik and Lockhart's framework for memory research. *Psychological Review, 85,* 139–152. **197, 201**

Baddeley, A. D. (1981). The concept of working memory: A view of its current state and probable future development. *Cognition, 10,* 17–23. **201, 204, 207**

Baddeley, A. D. (1982). Amnesia: A minimal model and an interpretation. In L. S. Cermak (Ed.), *Human memory and amnesia* (pp. 305–336). Hillsdale, NJ: Erlbaum. **341, 345, 347, 348**

Baddeley, A. D. (1983). Working memory. In D. E. Broadbent (Ed.), *Functional aspects of memory* (pp. 73–86). London: Royal Society. **201, 204, 205, 206, 207, 224**

Baddeley, A. D. (1984). Neuropsychological evidence and the semantic/episodic distinction. *Behavioral and Brain Sciences, 7,* 238–239. **237, 348**

Baddeley, A. D. (1988). Cognitive psychology and human memory. *Trends in Neurosciences, 11,* 176–181. **201**

Baddeley, A. D., Grant, S., Wight, E., & Thomson, N. (1975). Imagery and visual working memory. In P. M. A. Rabbitt & S. Dornic (Eds.), *Attention and performance V* (pp. 205–217). London: Academic Press. **204**

Baddeley, A. D., & Hitch, G. (1974). Working memory. In G. Bower (Ed.), *The psychology of learning and motivation: Advances in research and theory* (Vol. 8, pp. 47–89). New York: Academic Press. **201, 202, 207**

Baddeley, A. D., & Hitch, G. (1977). Recency reexamined. In S. Dornic (Ed.), *Attention and performance VI* (pp. 647–683). Hillsdale, NJ: Erlbaum. **201, 207**

Baddeley, A. D., & Lewis, V. J. (1981). Inner active processes in reading: The inner voice, the inner ear and the inner eye. In A. M. Lesgold & C. A. Perfetti (Eds.), *Interactive processes in reading* (pp. 107–129). Hillsdale, NJ: Erlbaum. **204**

Baddeley, A. D., & Lieberman, K. (1980). Spatial working memory. In R. S. Nickerson (Ed.), *Attention and performance VIII* (pp. 521–539). Hillsdale, NJ: Erlbaum. **204, 206**

Baddeley, A., Logie, R. Bressi, S., Della Sala, S., Spinnler, H. (1986). Dementia and working memory. *Quarterly Journal of Experimental Psychology: Section A, 38,* 603–618. **203**

Baddeley, A. D., Thomson, N., & Buchanan, M. (1975). Word length and the structure of short-term memory. *Journal of Verbal Learning and Verbal Behavior, 9,* 176–189. **202**

Baddeley, A. D., & Warrington, E. K. (1970). Amnesia and the distinction between long- and short-term memory. *Journal of Verbal Learning and Verbal Behavior, 9,* 176–189. **342, 345**

Baddeley, A. D., & Wilson, B. (1983). *Differences among amnesia and between amnesics: The role of single case methodology in theoretical analysis and practical treatment.* Paper presented at the Princeton Symposium on Amnesia, 1983. **345, 348**

Baddeley, A. D., & Wilson, B. (1988). Comprehension and working memory: A single case neuropsychological study. *Journal of Memory and Language, 27,* 479–498. **203**

Bahrick, H. P. (1984). Long-term memories: How durable, and how enduring? *Physiological Psychology, 12,* 53–58. **304**

Bain, A. (1855). *The senses and the intellect.* London: Parker. **6**

Bain, A. (1859). *The emotions and the will.* London: Parker. **6**

Baker, L., & Santa, J. L. (1977). Context, integration, and retrieval. *Memory & Cognition, 5,* 308–314. **322**

Balsam, P. D., & Gibbon, J. (1988). Formation of tone-US associations does not interfere with the formation of context-US associations in pigeons. *Journal of Experimental Psychology: Animal Behavior Processes, 14,* 401–412.

Bandura, A. (1986). *Social foundations of thought and action: A social cognitive theory.* Englewood Cliffs, NJ: Prentice-Hall. **104, 106**

Bandura, A., Blanchard, E. B., & Ritter, B. (1969). Relative efficacy of desensitization and modeling approaches for inducing behavioral, affective, and attitudinal changes. *Journal of Personality and Social Psychology, 13,* 173–199. **106**

Bandura, A., Grusec, J. E., & Menlove, F. L. (1966). Observational learning as a function of symbolization and incentive set. *Child Development, 37,* 499–506. **104**

Bandura, A., & Perloff, B. (1967). Relative efficacy of self-monitored and externally imposed reinforcement systems. *Journal of Personality and Social Psychology, 7,* 111–116. **75**

Bandura, A., Ross, D., & Ross, S. A. (1963). Imitation of film-mediated aggressive models. *Journal of Abnormal and Social Psychology, 66,* 3–11. **104**

Barbizet, J. (1970). *Human memory and its pathology.* San Francisco: Freeman. **343**

Barclay, J. R., Bransford, J. D., Franks, J. J., McCarrell, N. S., & Nitsch, K. (1974). Comprehension and semantic flexibility. *Journal of Verbal Learning and Verbal Behavior, 13,* 471–481. **259**

Barker, L. M., & Weaver, C. A. (1983). Rapid, permanent loss of memory for absolute intensity of taste and smell. *Bulletin of the Psychonomic Society, 21,* 281–284. **210**

Barnes, J. M., & Underwood, B. J. (1959). "Fate" of first-list associations in transfer theory. *Journal of Experimental Psychology, 58,* 97–105. **280**

Baron, A. (1965). Delayed punishment of a runway response. *Journal of Comparative and Physiological Psychology, 60,* 131–134.

Bartlett, F. C. (1932). *Remembering.* Cambridge: Cambridge University Press. **199, 226, 296, 297, 298**

Baum, M. (1970). Extinction of avoidance responding through response prevention (flooding). *Psychological Bulletin, 74,* 276–284. **99**

Beatty, W. W., & Shavalia, D. A. (1980). Rat spatial memory: Resistance to retroactive interference at long retention intervals. *Animal Learning & Behavior, 8,* 550–552. **135**

Beck, L. J. (1965). *The metaphysics of Descartes.* Oxford: Clarendon Press. **3**

Beecher, M. D. (1988). Some comments on the adaptationist approach to learning. In R. C. Bolles & M. D. Beecher (Eds.), *Evolution and learning* (pp. 239–248). Englewood Cliffs, NJ: Erlbaum. **167**

Belleza, F. S., Richards, D. L., & Geiselman, R. E. (1976). Semantic processing and organization in free recall. *Memory & Cognition, 4,* 415–421. **316**

Benedict, J. O., & Ayres, J. B. (1972). Factors affecting conditioning in the truly random control procedure in the rat. *Journal of Comparative and Physiological Psychology, 78,* 323–330. **51**

Berman, J. S., Miller, R. C., & Massman, R. J. (1985). Cognitive therapy versus systematic desensitization: Is one treatment superior? *Psychological Bulletin, 97,* 451–461. **41**

Bernstein, I. L., & Webster, M. M. (1980). Learned taste aversions in humans. *Physiology and Behavior, 25,* 363–366. **160**

Bevan, W., & Steger, J. A. (1971). Free recall and abstractness of stimuli. *Science, 172,* 597–599. **320**

Bhatt, R. S., Wasserman, E. A., Reynolds, W. F., Jr., & Knauss, K. S. (1988). Conceptual behavior in pigeons: Categorization of both familiar and novel examples from four classes of natural and artificial stimuli. *Journal of Experimental Psychology: Animal Behavior Processes, 14,* 219–234. **143**

Bitterman, M. E., Wodinsky J., & Candland, D. K. (1958). Some comparative psychology. *American Journal of Psychology, 71,* 94–110. **152**

Bjork, R. A., & Whitten, W. B. (1974). Recency-sensitive retrieval processes. *Cognitive Psychology, 6,* 173–189. **207**

Bloom, L., & Capatides, J. (1987). Sources of meaning in the acquisition of complex syntax: The sample case of causality. *Journal of Experimental Child Psychology, 43,* 112–128. **146**

Boakes, R. A., Halliday, M. S., & Poli, M. (1975). Response additivity: Effects of superimposed free reinforcement on a variable-interval baseline. *Journal of the Experimental Analysis of Behavior, 23,* 177–191. **112**

Bolles, R. C. (1970). Species-specific defense reactions and avoidance learning. *Psychological Review, 77,* 32–48. **162**

Bourne, L. E., Jr. (1970). Knowing and using concepts. *Psychological Review, 77,* 546–556. **139**

Bousfield, W. A. (1953). The occurrence of clustering in recall of randomly arranged associates. *Journal of General Psychology, 49,* 229–240.

Bousfield, W. A., & Wicklund, D. A. (1969). Rhyme as a determinant of clustering. *Psychonomic Science, 16,* 183–184. **314**

Bower, G. H. (1972). Mental imagery and associative learning. In L. W. Gregg (Ed.), *Cognition in learning and memory* (pp. 51–88). New York: Wiley. **321**

Bower, G. H. (1981). Mood and memory. *American Psychologist, 36,* 129–148. **241**

Bower, G. H., & Clark, M. C. (1969). Narrative stories as mediators for serial learning. *Psychonomic Science, 14,* 181–182. **188, 316**

Bower, G. H., Clark, M. C., Lesgold, A. M., & Winzenz, D. (1969). Hierarchical retrieval schemes in recall of categorized word lists. *Journal of Verbal Learning and Verbal Behavior, 8,* 323–343. **286, 287**

Bower, G. H., & Hilgard, E. R. (1981). *Theories of learning.* Englewood Cliffs, NJ: Prentice-Hall. **315**

Bower, G. H., & Winzenz, D. (1970). Comparison of associative learning strategies. *Psychonomic Science, 20,* 119–120. **315, 321**

Bransford, J. D., Barclay, J. R., & Franks, J. J. (1972). Sentence memory: A constructive versus interpretive approach. *Cognitive Psychology, 3,* 193–209. **199**

Bransford, J. D., & Johnson, M. K. (1972). Contextual prerequisites for understanding: Some investigations of comprehension and recall. *Journal of Verbal Learning and Verbal Behavior, 11,* 717–726. **227, 300**

Bransford, J. D., & Johnson, M. K. (1973). Considerations of some problems of comprehension. In W. G. Chase (Ed.), *Visual information processing* (pp. 383–438). New York: Academic Press. **300**

Bregman, E. O. (1934). An attempt to modify the emotional attitudes of infants by the conditioned response technique. *Journal of Genetic Psychology, 45,* 169–198. **161**

Breland, K., and Breland, M. (1961). The misbehavior of organisms. *American Psychologist, 16,* 681–684. **153, 156**

Brewer, W. F., & Treyens, J. C. (1981). Role of schemata in memory for places. *Cognitive Psychology, 13,* 207–230. **301**

Broadbent, D. E. (1958). *Perception and communication.* London: Pergamon. **14, 15, 177**

Broadbent, D. E. (1983). The functional approach to memory. In D. E. Broadbent (Ed.), *Functional aspects of memory* (pp. 1–11). London: Royal Society. **209, 211**

Broadbent, D. E. (1984). The Maltese cross: A new simplistic model for memory. *Behavioral and Brain Sciences, 7,* 55–94. **208, 350**

Broadbent, D. E., & Broadbent, M. H. P. (1981a). Articulatory suppression and the grouping of successive stimuli. *Psychological Research, 43,* 57–67. **212**

Broadbent, D. E., & Broadbent, M. H. P. (1981b). Recency effects in visual memory. *Quarterly Journal of Experimental Psychology, Section A, 33,* 1–15. **210**

Broadbent, D. E., Cooper, P. J., & Broadbent, M. H. P. (1978). A comparison of hierarchical and matrix retrieval schemes in recall. *Journal of Experimental Psychology: Human Learning and Memory, 4,* 486–497. **209, 287, 288**

Broadbent, D. E., Vines, R., & Broadbent, M. H. P. (1978). Recency effects in memory as a function of modality of intervening events. *Psychological Research, 40,* 5–13. **210**

Brogden, W. J., Lipman, E. A., & Culler, E. (1938). The role of incentive in conditioning and extinction. *American Journal of Psychology, 51,* 109–117. **97**

Brooks, C. I. (1969). Frustration to nonreward following limited reward experience. *Journal of Experimental Psychology, 81,* 403–405. **75**

Brooks, D. N., & Baddeley, A. D. (1976). What can amnesic patients learn? *Neuropsychologia, 14,* 111–122. **345, 346**

Brooks, L. R. (1967). The suppression of visualization in reading. *Quarterly Journal of Experimental Psychology, 19,* 289–299. **204, 205**

Brooks, L. R. (1968). Spatial and verbal components in the act of recall. *Canadian Journal of Psychology, 22,* 349–368. **265, 266, 269**

Brower, L. P. (1969). Ecological chemistry. *Scientific American, 220,* 22–29. **160**

Brown, J. (1958). Some tests of the decay theory of immediate memory. *Quarterly Journal of Experimental Psychology, 10,* 12–21. **179, 190**

Brown, P. L., & Jenkins, H. M. (1968). Auto-shaping of the pigeon's key-peck. *Journal of the Experimental Analysis of Behavior, 11,* 1–8. **35**

Brown, T. (1820). *Sketch of a system of philosophy of the human mind.* Edinburgh: Bell & Bradfute, Manners & Miller. **5**

Bruner, J. S., Goodnow, J. J., & Austin, G. A. (1956). *A study of thinking.* New York: Wiley. **139, 141**

Buchwald, A. M. (1967). Effects of immediate vs. delayed outcomes in associative learning. *Journal of Verbal Learning and Verbal Behavior, 6,* 317–320. **87**

Bugelski, B. R. (1968). Images as mediators in one-trial paired-associate learning. II: Self-timing in successive lists. *Journal of Experimental Psychology, 77,* 328–334. **329**

Bush, R. R., & Mosteller, F. (1955). *Stochastic models for learning.* New York: Wiley. **52**

Bustamante, J. A., Jordán, A., Vila, M., González, A., & Insua, A. (1970). State dependent learning in humans. *Physiology and Behavior, 5,* 793–796. **241**

Butler, R. A. (1954). Incentive conditions that influence visual exploration. *Journal of Experimental Psychology, 48,* 19–23. **83**

Calkins, M. W. (1896). Association: An essay analytic and experimental. *Psychological Review, Monograph Supplements, 1*(2). **277**

Callner, D. A. (1975). Behavioral treatment approaches to drug abuse: A critical review of the research. *Psychological Bulletin, 82,* 143–164. **40**

Capaldi, E. J. (1967). A sequential hypothesis of instrumental learning. In K. W. Spence & J. T. Spence (Eds.), *The psychology of learning and motivation* (Vol. 1, pp. 67–156). New York: Academic Press. **74**

Capaldi, E. J., Nawrocki, T. M., & Verry, D. R. (1982). Difficult serial anticipation learning in rats: Rule-encoding vs. memory. *Animal Learning & Memory, 10,* 167–170. **138**

Capaldi, E. J., & Verry, D. R. (1981). Serial order anticipation learning in rats: Memory for multiple hedonic events and their order. *Animal Learning & Behavior, 9,* 441–453. **137, 138**

Carr, T. H., & Brown, T. L. (1984). The Maltese cross: Simplistic yes, new no. *Behavioral and Brain Sciences, 7,* 69–71, 91–94. **214**

Ceraso, J., & Henderson, A. (1965). Unavailability and associative loss in RI and PI. *Journal of Experimental Psychology, 70,* 300–303. **284**

Cermak, L. S., & O'Connor, M. (1983). The anterograde and retrograde retrieval ability of a patient with amnesia due to encephalitis. *Neuropsychologia, 21,* 213–234. **348**

Chang, T. M. (1986). Semantic memory: Facts and models. *Psychological Bulletin, 99,* 199–220. **254, 262**

Cherfas, J. J. (1980). Signals for food: Reinforcers or informants? *Science, 209,* 1552–1553. **77, 85**

Cherry, E. C. (1953). Some experiments on the recognition of speech, with one and with two ears. *Journal of the Acoustical Society of America, 25,* 975–979. **14**

Chiesi, H. L., Spilich, G. J., & Voss, J. F. (1979). Acquisition of domain-related information in relation to high and low domain knowledge. *Journal of Verbal Learning and Verbal Behavior, 18,* 257–273. **227**

Chomsky, N. (1959). Review of Skinner's *Verbal Behavior. Language, 35,* 26–58. **172**

Chomsky, N. (1965). *Aspects of the theory of syntax.* Cambridge, MA: MIT Press. **68**

Cohen, G. (1977). *The psychology of cognition.* New York: Academic Press. **261**

Cohen, N. J. (1984). Preserved learning capacity in amnesia: Evidence for multiple memory systems. In L. R. Squire & N. Butters (Eds.), *Neu-*

ropsychology of memory (pp. 83–103). New York: Guilford Press. **236, 346**

Cohen, N. J., & Squire, L. R. (1980). Preserved learning and retention of pattern analyzing skill in amnesia: Dissociation of knowing how and knowing that. *Science, 210,* 207–209. **346**

Cohen, N. J., & Squire, L. R. (1981). Retrograde amnesia and remote memory impairment. *Neuropsychologia, 19,* 337–356. **348**

Cole, S., Hainsworth, F. R., Kamil, A. C., Mercier, T., & Wolf, L. L. (1982). Spatial learning as an adaptation in hummingbirds. *Science, 217,* 655–657. **165, 166**

Collier, G. H., Johnson, D. F., Hill, W. L., & Kaufman, L. W. (1986). The economics of the law of effect. *Journal of the Experimental Analysis of Behavior, 46,* 113–136. **84**

Collins, A. M., & Loftus, E. F. (1975). A spreading-activation theory of semantic processing. *Psychological Review, 82,* 407–428. **219, 250, 251, 252, 260, 261**

Collins, A. M., & Quillian, M. R. (1969). Retrieval time from semantic memory. *Journal of Verbal Learning and Verbal Behavior, 8,* 240–247. **219, 248, 249**

Collins, A. M., & Quillian, M. R. (1972). How to make a language user. In E. Tulving & W. Donaldson (Ed.), *Organization of memory* (pp. 309–351). New York: Academic Press. **248**

Collyer, S. C., Jonides, J., & Bevan, W. (1972). Images as memory aids: Is bizarreness helpful? *American Journal of Psychology, 85,* 31–38. **324**

Colombo, J. (1982). The critical period concept: Research, methodology, and theoretical issues. *Psychological Bulletin, 91,* 260–275. **170**

Coltheart, M. (1983). Iconic memory. In D. E. Broadbent (Ed.), *Functional aspects of memory* (pp. 45–56). London: Royal Society. **214**

Colwill, R. M., & Rescorla, R. A. (1988). The role of response-reinforcer associations increases throughout extended instrumental training. *Animal Learning & Behavior, 16,* 105–111. **66**

Conrad, C. (1972). Cognitive economy in semantic memory. *Journal of Experimental Psychology, 92,* 149–154. **250**

Conrad, R. (1964). Acoustic confusions in immediate memory. *British Journal of Psychology, 55,* 75–84. **188**

Cook, E. W., III, Hodes, R. L., & Lang, P. J. (1986). Preparedness and phobia: Effects of stimulus content on human visceral conditioning. *Journal of Abnormal Psychology, 95,* 195–207. **161**

Cook, M., & Mineka, S. (1990). Selective associations in the observational conditioning of fear in rhesus monkeys. *Journal of Experimental Psychology: Animal Behavior Processes, 16,* 372–389. **105**

Cook, M., Mineka, S., Wolkenstein, B., & Laitsch, K. (1985). Observational conditioning of snake fear in unrelated rhesus monkeys. *Journal of Abnormal Psychology, 94,* 591–610. **105**

Cooper, L. D., Aronson, L., Balsam, P. D., & Gibbon, J. (1990). Duration of signals for intertrial reinforcement and nonreinforcement in random control procedures. *Journal of Experimental Psychology: Animal Behavior Processes, 16,* 14–26. **103**

Corkin, S. (1968). Acquisition of motor skill after bilateral medial temporal excision. *Neuropsychologia, 6,* 255–265. **345**

Cox, S. D., & Wollen, K. A. (1981). Bizarreness and recall. *Bulletin of the Psychonomic Society, 18,* 244–245. **324**

Craik, F. I. M., & Lockhart, R. S. (1972). Levels of processing: A framework for memory research. *Journal of Verbal Learning and Verbal Behavior, 11,* 671–684. **197**

Craik, F. I. M., & Tulving, E. (1975). Depth of processing and the retention of words in episodic memory. *Journal of Experimental Psychology: General, 104,* 268–294. **194, 197, 198, 317**

Craik, F. I. M., & Watkins, M. J. (1973). The role of rehearsal in short-term memory. *Journal of Verbal Learning and Verbal Behavior, 12,* 599–607. **199**

Crawford, M., & Masterson, F. (1978). Components of the flight response can reinforce bar-press avoidance learning. *Journal of Experimental Psychology: Animal Behavior Processes, 4,* 144–151. **163**

Crespi, L. P. (1942). Quantitative variation of incentive and performance in the white rat. *American Journal of Psychology, 55,* 467–517. **113, 114**

Crowder, R. G. (1982). The demise of short-term memory. *Acta Psychologica, 50,* 291–323. **214**

Crowder, R. G. (1983). The purity of auditory memory. In D. E. Broadbent (Ed.), *Functional aspects of memory* (pp. 13–27). London: Royal Society. **214**

Crowder, R. G. (1984). Broadbent's Maltese cross memory model: Wisdom, but not especially unconventional. *Behavioral and Brain Sciences, 7,* 72, 91–94. **214**

Dalezman, J. J. (1974). *Free recall and short-term memory: A symbiotic relationship or?* Unpublished doctoral dissertation, Ohio State University. **207**

D'Amato, M. R., & Buckiewicz, J. (1980). Long-delay one-trial conditioned preference and retention in monkeys (*Cebus apella*). *Animal Learning & Behavior, 8,* 359–362. **160**

D'Amato, M. R., Fazzaro, J., & Etkin, M. (1968). Anticipatory responding and avoidance discrimination as factors in avoidance conditioning. *Journal of Experimental Psychology, 77,* 41–47. **100**

D'Amato, M. R., & Schiff, D. (1964). Long-term discriminated avoidance performance in the rat. *Journal of Comparative and Physiological Psychology, 57,* 123–126. **163**

Darley, C. F., & Glass, A. L. (1975). Effects of rehearsal and serial list position on recall. *Journal of Experimental Psychology: Human Learning and Memory, 1,* 453–458. **200**

Darwin, C. (1859). *The origin of species.* London: Murray. **8**

Darwin, C. (1871). *The expression of the emotions in man and animals.* London: Appleton. **8, 26**

Davis, M. (1970). Effects of interstimulus interval length and variability on startle-response habituation in the rat. *Journal of Comparative and Physiological Psychology, 72,* 177–192. **40**

Del Russo, J. E. (1975). Observational learning of discriminative avoidance in hooded rats. *Animal Learning & Behavior, 3,* 76–80. **105**

Demarest, J. (1983). The ideas of change, progress, and continuity in the comparative psychology of learning. In D. W. Rajecki (Ed.), *Comparing behavior: Studying man studying animals* (pp. 143–179). Hillsdale, NJ: Erlbaum. **167**

DeNike, L. D., & Spielberger, C. D. (1963). Induced mediating states in verbal conditioning. *Journal of Verbal Learning & Verbal Behavior, 1,* 339–345. **148**

Descartes, R. (1965). *Discourse on method, optics, geometry, and meteorology* (P. J. Olscamp, Trans.). Indianapolis: Bobbs-Merrill. (Original work published 1637) **172**

Descartes, R. (1988). Meditations on first philosophy. In J. Cottingham, R. Stoothoff, & D. Murdoch (Trans.), *Descartes: Selected philosophical writings* (pp. 73–122). Cambridge: Cambridge University Press. (Original work published 1641) **3**

Desrochers, A., & Begg, I. (1987). A theoretical account of encoding and retrieval processes in the use of imagery-based mnemonic techniques: The special case of the keyword method. In M. A. McDaniel & M. Pressley (Eds.), *Imagery and related mnemonic processes: Theories, individual differences, and applications* (pp. 56–77). New York: Springer- Verlag. **334**

DeVito, P. L., & Fowler, H. (1986). Effects of contingency violations on the extinction of a conditioned fear inhibitor and a conditioned fear excitor. *Journal of Experimental Psychology: Animal Behavior Processes, 12,* 99–115. **44**

Dewey, J. (1896). The reflex arc concept in psychology. *Psychological Review, 3,* 357–370.

Dewsbury, D. A. (1984). *Comparative psychology in the twentieth century.* Stroudsburg, PA: Hutchinson Ross. **152**

Dickinson, A., & Dearing, M. F. (1979). Appetitive-aversive interactions and inhibitory processes. In A. Dickinson & R. A. Boakes (Eds.), *Mechanisms of learning and motivation: A memorial volume to Jerzy Konorski* (pp. 203–228). Hillsdale, NJ: Erlbaum. **47**

Dobrzecka, C., Szwejkowska, G., & Konorski, J. (1966). Qualitative versus directional cues in two forms of differentiation. *Science, 153,* 87–89. **164**

Domjan, M. (1983). Biological constraints on instrumental and classical conditioning: Implications for general process theory. In G. H. Bower (Ed.), *Psychology of Learning and Motivation* (Vol. 17, pp. 215–277). New York: Academic Press. **164, 167**

Domjan, M., & Burkhard, B. (1982). *The principles of learning and behavior.* Monterey, CA: Brooks/Cole. **167**

Domjan, M., & Burkhard, B. (1986). *The principles of learning and behavior* (2nd ed.). Monterey, CA: Brooks/Cole. **138**

Drachman, D. A., & Arbit, J. (1966). Memory and the hippocampal complex. II. Is memory a multiple process? *Archives of Neurology, 15,* 52–61. **342**

Drugan, R. C., & Maier, S. F. (1982). The nature of the activity deficit produced by inescapable shock. *Animal Learning & Behavior, 10,* 401–406. **102**

Dufort, R. M., Guttman, N., & Kimble, G. A. (1954). One-trial discrimination reversal in the white rat. *Journal of Comparative and Physiological Psychology, 47,* 248–249. **125**

Durlach, P. J. (1983). Effect of signaling intertrial unconditioned stimuli in autoshaping. *Journal of Experimental Psychology: Animal Behavior Processes, 9,* 374–389. **103**

Dweck, C. S., & Repucci, N. D. (1973). Learned helplessness and reinforcement responsibility in children. *Journal of Personality and Social Psychology, 25,* 109–116. **102**

Dyal, J. A., & Systma, D. (1976). Relative persistence as a function of order of reinforcement schedules. *Journal of Experimental Psychology: Animal Behavior Processes, 2,* 370–375. **74**

Ebbinghaus, H. (1964). *Memory: A contribution to experimental psychology* (H. A. Ruger & C. E. Bussenius, Trans.). New York: Dover. (Original work published 1885) **190, 276**

Egeland, B. (1975). Effects of errorless training on teaching children to discriminate letters of the alphabet. *Journal of Applied Psychology, 60,* 533–536. **120**

Egger, M. D., & Miller, N. E. (1962). Secondary reinforcement in rats as a function of information value and reliability of the stimulus. *Journal of Experimental Psychology, 64,* 97–104. **49, 78**

Eich, E. (1985). Context, memory, and integrated item/context imagery. *Journal of Experimental Psychology: Learning, Memory, and Cognition, 11,* 764–770. **243**

Eich, E., & Birnbaum, I. M. (1982). Repetition, cuing, and state-dependent memory. *Memory & Cognition, 10,* 103–114. **242**

Eich, J. E. (1977). State-dependent retrieval of information in human episodic memory. In I. M. Birnbaum & E. S. Parker (Eds.), *Alcohol and human memory* (pp. 141–157). Hillsdale, NJ: Erlbaum. **241**

Eich, J. E. (1980). The cue-dependent nature of state-dependent retrieval. *Memory & Cognition, 8,* 157–173. **241**

Eich, J. E., Weingartner, H., Stillman, R. C., & Gillin, J. C. (1975). State-dependent accessibility of retrieval cues in the retention of a categorized list. *Journal of Verbal Learning and Verbal Behavior, 14,* 408–417. **241, 242**

Eikelboom, R., & Stewart, J. (1982). Conditioning of drug-induced physiological responses. *Psychological Review, 89,* 507–528. **36**

Einstein, G. O., & McDaniel, M. A. (1987). Distinctiveness and the mnemonic benefits of bizarre imagery. In M. A. McDaniel & M. Pressley (Eds.), *Imagery and related mnemonic processes: Theories, individual differences, and applications* (pp. 78–102). New York: Springer-Verlag. **244, 326**

Einstein, G. O., McDaniel, M. A., & Lackey, S. (1989). Bizarre imagery, interference, and distinctiveness. *Journal of Experimental Psychology: Learning, Memory, and Cognition, 15,* 137–146. **326, 329**

Eisenberger, R. (1972). Explanation of rewards that do not reduce tissue needs. *Psychological Bulletin, 77,* 319–339. **83**

Ekstrand, B. R. (1972). To sleep, perchance to dream (about why we forget). In C. P. Duncan, L. Sechrest, & A. W. Melton (Eds.), *Human memory: Festschrift in honor of Benton J. Underwood* (pp. 59–82). New York: Prentice-Hall. **277**

Emlen, S. T. (1975). The stellar-orientation system of a migratory bird. *Scientific American, 233,* 102–111. **168**

Emmerich, H., & Ackerman, B. (1979). A test of bizarre interaction as a factor in children's memory. *The Journal of Genetic Psychology, 134,* 225–232. **324**

Epstein, R., Kirshnit, C. E., Lanza, R. P., & Rubin, L. C. (1984). "Insight" in the pigeon: Antecedents and determinants of an intelligent performance. *Nature, 308,* 61–62. **91**

Ericsson, K. A., Chase, W. G., & Faloon, S. (1980). Acquisition of a memory skill. *Science, 208,* 1181–1182. **313**

Eron, L. (1982). Parent-child interaction, television violence, and aggression of children. *American Psychologist, 37,* 197–211. **105**

Estes, W. K. (1944). An experimental study of punishment. *Psychological Monographs, 57* (3, Whole No. 263). **95**

Estes, W. K., & Skinner, B. F. (1941). Some quantitative properties of anxiety. *Journal of Experimental Psychology, 29,* 390–400. **47**

Etscorn, F., & Stephens, R. (1973). Establishment of conditioned taste aversions with a 24-hour *CS-US* interval. *Physiological Psychology, 73,* 252–253. **160**

Eysenck, M. W. (1978). Levels of processing: A critique. *British Journal of Psychology, 69,* 157–169. **197, 215**

Eysenck, M. W. (1979). Depth, elaboration and distinctiveness. In L. S. Cermak & F. I. M. Craik (Eds.), *Levels of processing in human memory* (pp. 89–118). Hillsdale, NJ: Erlbaum. **319**

Fagan, J. F. (1969). Clustering of related but non-associated items in free recall. *Psychonomic Science, 16,* 92–93. **314**

Falk, J. L. (1971). The nature and determinants of adjunctive behavior. *Physiology and Behavior, 6,* 577–588. **81**

Fanselow, M. S., & Lester, L. S. (1988). A functional behavioristic approach to aversively motivated behavior: Predatory imminence as a determinant of the topography of defensive behavior. In R. C. Bolles & M. D. Beecher (Eds.), *Evolution and learning* (pp. 185–212). Englewood Cliffs, NJ: Erlbaum. **162**

Farley, J., Richards, W. G., Ling, L. J., Liman, E., & Alkon, D. L. (1983). Membrane changes in a single photoreceptor cause associative learning in *Hermissenda. Science, 221,* 1201–1203. **28**

Farmer, E. W., Berman, J. V. F., & Fletcher, Y. L. (1986). Evidence for a visuo-spatial scratch-pad in working memory. *Quarterly Journal of Experimental Psychology: Section A, 38,* 675–688. **204**

Farris, H. E. (1967). Classical conditioning of courting behavior in the Japanese quail, *Coturnix coturnix japonica. Journal of the Experimental Analysis of Behavior, 10,* 213–217. **28**

Fernald, D. (1984). *The Hans legacy.* Hillsdale, NJ: Erlbaum. **145**

Fernandez, A., & Glenberg, A. M. (1985). Changing environmental context does not reliably affect memory. *Memory & Cognition, 13,* 333–345. **243**

Fisher, R. P., & Craik, F. I. M. (1977). Interaction between encoding and retrieval operations in cued recall. *Journal of Experimental Psychology: Human Learning and Memory, 3,* 701–711. **199**

FitzGerald, P., & Broadbent, D. E. (1985). Order of report and the structure of temporary memory. *Journal of Experimental Psychology: Learning, Memory, and Cognition, 11,* 217–228. **215**

Flaherty, C. F. (1982). Incentive contrast: A review of behavioral changes following shifts in reward. *Animal Learning & Behavior, 10,* 409–440. **113**

Flexser, A. J., & Tulving, E. (1978). Retrieval independence in recognition and recall. *Psychological Review, 85,* 153–171. **293**

Fodor, J. A. (1975). *The language of thought.* New York: Thomas Y. Crowell. **172**

Forrester, W. E. (1970). Retroactive inhibition and spontaneous recovery in the A-B, D-C paradigm. *Journal of Verbal Learning and Verbal Behavior, 9,* 525–528. **281**

Fowler, H., & Miller, N. E. (1963). Facilitation and inhibition of runway performance by hind- and forepaw shock of various intensities. *Journal of Comparative and Physiological Psychology, 56,* 801–805. **95**

Fraenkel, F. D. (1975). The role of response-punishment contingency in the suppression of a positively-reinforced operant. *Learning and Motivation, 6,* 385–403. **95**

Franks, J. J., & Bransford, J. D. (1971). Abstraction of visual patterns. *Journal of Experimental Psychology, 90,* 65–74. **142, 143**

Gaioni, S. J., Hoffman, H. S., DePaulo, P., & Stratton, V. N. (1978). Imprinting in older ducklings: Some tests of a reinforcement model. *Animal Learning & Behavior, 6,* 19–26. **170**

Gallistel, C. R. (1990). Animal cognition: The representation of space, time, and number. *Annual Review of Psychology, 40,* 155–189. **93**

Galvani, P. F., Riddell, W. I., & Foster, K. M. (1975). Passive avoidance in rats and gerbils as a function of species-specific exploratory tendencies. *Behavioral Biology, 13,* 277–290. **163**

Gambrell, L. B. (1982). Induced mental imagery and text prediction performance of first and third graders. In J. A. Niles & L. A. Harris (Eds.), *New inquiries in reading research and instruction. Thirty-first yearbook of the National Reading Conference* (pp. 131–135). Rochester, NY: National Reading Conference. **321**

Gamzu, E., & Williams, D. R. (1971). Classical conditioning of a complex skeletal response. *Science, 171,* 923–925. **35**

Gamzu, E. R., & Williams, D. R. (1973). Associative factors underlying the pigeon's key pecking in autoshaping procedures. *Journal of the Experimental Analysis of Behavior, 19,* 225–232. **157**

Garcia, J., & Koelling, R. A. (1966). Relation of cue to consequence in avoidance learning. *Psychonomic Science, 4,* 123–124. **153**

Gardiner, J. M. (1974). Levels of processing in word recognition and subsequent free recall. *Journal of Experimental Psychology, 102,* 101–105. **198**

Gardiner, J. M. (1988). Recognition failures and free-recall failures: Implications for the relation between recall and recognition. *Memory & Cognition, 16*, 446–451. **292, 293**

Gardner, H., Boller, F., Moreines, J., & Butters, N. (1973). Retrieving information from Korsakoff patients: Effects of categorical cues and reference to the task. *Cortex, 9*, 165–175. **347, 349**

Gardner, R., & Gardner, B. (1969). Teaching sign language to a chimpanzee. *Science, 165*, 644–672. **144**

Gathercole, S. E., & Baddeley, A. D. (1989). Evaluation of the role of phonological STM in the development of vocabulary in children: A longitudinal study. *Journal of Memory and Language, 28*, 200–213. **203**

Gentry, G. V., Overall, J. E., & Brown, W. L. (1959). Transpositional responses of rhesus monkeys to stimulus objects of intermediate size. *American Journal of Psychology, 72*, 453–455. **123**

Gibbon, J., Baldock, M. D., Locurto, C., Gold, L., & Terrace, H. S. (1977). Trial and intertrial durations in autoshaping. *Journal of Experimental Psychology: Animal Behavior Processes, 3*, 264–284. **31**

Gibbon, J., & Balsam, P. (1981). Spreading association in time. In C. M. Locurto, H. S. Terrace, & J. Gibbon (Eds.), *Autoshaping and conditioning theory* (pp. 219–253). New York: Academic Press. **58**

Gibbon, J., Berryman, R., & Thompson, R. L. (1974). Contingency spaces and measures in classical and instrumental conditioning. *Journal of the Experimental Analysis of Behavior, 21*, 585–605. **51**

Gibson, J. J. (1966). *The senses considered as perceptual systems.* New York: Houghton Mifflin. **68**

Gillette, K., Martin, G. M., & Bellingham, W. P. (1980). Differential use of food and water cues in the formation of conditioned aversions by domestic chicks *(Gallus gallus). Journal of Experimental Psychology: Animal Behavior Processes, 6*, 99–111. **160**

Glanzer, M., & Cunitz, A. R. (1966). Two storage mechanisms in free recall. *Journal of Verbal Learning and Verbal Behavior, 5*, 351–360. **191, 192, 207**

Glass, A. L., & Holyoak, K. J. (1975). Alternative conceptions of semantic memory. *Cognition, 3*, 313–339. **252**

Glass, A. L., & Holyoak, K. J. (1986). *Cognition* (2nd ed.). New York: Random House. **142, 322**

Glaze, J. A. (1928). The association value of nonsense syllables. *Journal of Genetic Psychology, 35*, 255–267. **315**

Glenberg, A., & Adams, F. (1978). Type I rehearsal and recognition. *Journal of Verbal Learning and Verbal Behavior, 17*, 455–463. **200**

Glenberg, A. M., Bradley, M. M., Stevenson, J. A., Kraus, T. A., Tkachuk, M. J., Gretz, A. L., Fish, J. H., & Turpin, B. A. M. (1980). A two-process account of long-term serial position effects. *Journal of Experimental Psychology: Human Learning and Memory, 6*, 355–369. **207**

Godden, D. R., & Baddeley, A. D. (1975). Context-dependent memory in two natural environments: On land and underwater. *British Journal of Psychology, 66*, 325–331. **242**

Gonzalez, R. C., Gentry, G. V., & Bitterman, M. E. (1954). Relational discrimination of intermediate size in the chimpanzee. *Journal of Comparative and Physiological Psychology, 47*, 385–388. **123**

Goodwin, D. W., Powell, B., Bremer, D., Hoine, H., & Stern, J. (1969). Alcohol and recall: State dependent effects in man. *Science, 163*, 1358–1360. **241**

Gormezano, I., & Kehoe, E. J. (1975). Classical conditioning: Some methodological-conceptual issues. In W. K. Estes (Ed.), *Handbook of learning and cognitive processes* (Vol. 3, pp. 143–179). Hillsdale, NJ: Erlbaum. **58**

Gottlieb, G. (1973). Neglected developmental variables in the study of species identification in birds. *Psychological Bulletin, 79*, 362–372. **170**

Gould, J. L. (1975). Honey bee recruitment: The dance-language controversy. *Science, 189*, 685–693. **171**

Gould, J. L. (1985). How bees remember flower shapes. *Science, 227*, 1492–1494. **168**

Graf, P., & Schachter, D. L. (1985). Implicit and explicit memory for new associations in normal and amnesic subjects. *Journal of Experimental Psychology: Learning, Memory, and Cognition, 11*, 501–518. **225**

Graf, P., Shimamura, A. P., & Squire, L. R. (1985). Priming across modalities and across category levels: Extending the domain of preserved function in amnesia. *Journal of Experimental Psychology: Learning, Memory, and Cognition, 11,* 386–396. **347, 349**

Graf, P., Squire, L. R., & Mandler, G. (1984). The information that amnesic patients do not forget. *Journal of Experimental Psychology: Learning, Memory, and Cognition, 10,* 164–178. **346**

Grant, D. A. (1943). Sensitization and association in eyelid conditioning. *Journal of Experimental Psychology, 32,* 201–212. **32**

Grant, D. A., & Norris, E. B. (1947). Eyelid conditioning as influenced by the presence of sensitized beta-responses. *Journal of Experimental Psychology, 37,* 423–433. **32**

Grau, J. W., & Rescorla, R. A. (1984). Role of context in autoshaping. *Journal of Experimental Psychology: Animal Behavior Processes, 10,* 324–332. **58**

Gray, J. A. (1965). Stimulus intensity dynamism. *Psychological Bulletin, 63,* 180–196. **29**

Graziano, A. M., DeGiovanni, I. S., & Garcia, K. A. (1979). Behavioral treatment of children's fears: A review. *Psychological Bulletin, 86,* 804–830. **41**

Greene, D., Sternberg, B., & Lepper, M. R. (1976). Overjustification in a token economy. *Journal of Personality and Social Psychology, 34,* 1219–1234. **78**

Grolnick, W. S., & Ryan, R. M. (1987). Autonomy in children's learning: An experimental and individual difference investigation. *Journal of Personality and Social Psychology, 52,* 890–898. **86**

Grossen, N. E., & Kelley, M. J. (1972). Species-specific behavior and acquisition of avoidance behavior in rats. *Journal of Comparative and Physiological Psychology, 81,* 307–310. **163**

Grossen, N. E., Kostansek, D. J., & Bolles, R. C. (1969). Effects of appetitive discriminative stimuli on avoidance behavior. *Journal of Experimental Psychology, 81,* 340–343. **42**

Groves, P. M., & Thompson, R. F. (1970). Habituation: A dual-process theory. *Psychological Review, 77,* 419–450. **32, 40**

Gulley, N. (1962). *Plato's theory of knowledge.* London: Methuen. **2**

Gustavson, C. R., Kelly, D. J., Sweeney, M., & Garcia, J. (1976). Prey-lithium aversions: I. Coyotes and wolves. *Behavioral Biology, 17,* 61–72. **28**

Guthrie, E. R. (1935). *The psychology of learning.* New York: Harper. **36, 49, 66, 67**

Guthrie, E. R. (1952). *The psychology of learning* (Rev. ed.). New York: Harper & Row. **93, 106**

Guthrie, E. R., & Horton, G. P. (1946). *Cats in a puzzle box.* New York: Rinehart. **67**

Guttman, N., & Kalish, H. I. (1956). Discriminability and stimulus generalization. *Journal of Experimental Psychology, 51,* 79–88. **109**

Halgren, C. R. (1974). Latent inhibition in rats: Associative or nonassociative? *Journal of Comparative and Physiological Psychology, 86,* 74–78. **44**

Hall, J. W. (1988). On the utility of the keyword mnemonic for vocabulary learning. *Journal of Educational Psychology, 80,* 554–562. **334, 335**

Hamilton, E., & Cairns, H. (Eds.). (1961). *The collected dialogues of Plato.* New York: Pantheon, Bollingen Series LXXI. **2**

Hammond, L. J. (1966). Increased responding to CS– in differential CER. *Psychonomic Science, 5,* 337–338. **47, 48**

Hanson, H. M. (1959). Effects of discrimination training on stimulus generalization. *Journal of Experimental Psychology, 58,* 321–334. **115**

Harlow, H. F. (1949). The formation of learning sets. *Psychological Review, 56,* 51–65. **126**

Harlow, H. F. (1959). Learning set and error factor theory. In S. Koch (Ed.), *Psychology: A study of a science* (Vol. 2, pp. 492–537). New York: McGraw-Hill. **126**

Hartley, D. (1971). *Observations on man.* New York: Garland. (Original work published 1749) **5**

Hauck, P., Walsh, C., & Kroll, N. (1976). Visual imagery mnemonics: Common versus bizarre mental images. *Bulletin of the Psychonomic Society, 7,* 160–162. **324**

Hawkins, R. D., Abrams, T. W., Carew, T. J., & Kandel, E. R. (1983). A cellular mechanism of classical conditioning in Aplysia: Activity-dependent amplification of presynaptic facilitation. *Science, 219,* 400–405. **28**

Hayes, K. J., & Hayes, C. (1952). Imitation in a home-raised chimpanzee. *Journal of Comparative and Physiological Psychology, 45,* 450–459. **144**

Hayes, N. A., & Broadbent, D. E. (1988). Two modes of learning for interactive tasks. *Cognition, 28,* 249–276. **212**

Hayman, C. A. G., & Tulving, E. (1989). Is priming in fragment completion based on a "traceless" memory system? *Journal of Experimental Psy-*

chology: Learning, Memory, and Cognition, 15, 941–956. **238**

Hebb, D. O. (1955). Drives and the C.N.S. (conceptual nervous system). *Psychological Review, 62,* 243–254. **83**

Hefferline, R. F., & Perera, T. B. (1963). Proprioceptive discrimination of a covert operant without its observation by the subject. *Science, 139,* 834–835. **149**

Herman, L. M., Hovancik, J. R., Gory, J. D., & Bradshaw, G. L. (1989). Generalization of visual matching by a bottlenosed dolphin *(Tursiops truncatus)*: Evidence for invariance of cognitive performance with visual and auditory materials. *Journal of Experimental Psychology: Animal Behavior Processes, 15,* 124–136. **133**

Herrmann, D. J. (1988). *Memory improvement techniques.* New York: Ballantine. **331**

Herrnstein, R. J. (1958). Some factors influencing behavior in a two-response situation. *Transactions of the New York Academy of Sciences, 21,* 35–45. **127**

Herrnstein, R. J. (1961). Relative and absolute strength of response as a function of frequency of reinforcement. *Journal of the Experimental Analysis of Behavior, 4,* 267–272. **127**

Herrnstein, R. J. (1969). Method and theory in the study of avoidance. *Psychological Review, 76,* 49–69. **99**

Herrnstein, R. J. (1970). On the law of effect. *Journal of the Experimental Analysis of Behavior, 13,* 243–266. **127**

Herrnstein, R. J., & Loveland, D. H. (1964). Complex visual concepts in the pigeon. *Science, 146,* 549–551. **142**

Herrnstein, R. J., Loveland, D. H., & Cable, C. (1976). Natural concepts in pigeons. *Journal of Experimental Psychology: Animal Behavior Processes, 2,* 285–302. **143**

Hess, E. H. (1972). ''Imprinting'' in a natural laboratory. *Scientific American, 227,* 24–31. **170**

Hinson, J. M., & Staddon, J. E. R. (1978). Behavioral competition: A mechanism for schedule interactions. *Science, 202,* 432–434. **112**

Hinson, R. E., & Siegel, S. (1980). Trace conditioning as an inhibitory procedure. *Animal Learning & Behavior, 8,* 60–66. **45**

Hinson, R. E., & Siegel, S. (1986). Pavlovian inhibitory conditioning and tolerance to pentobarbital-induced hypothermia in rats. *Journal of*

Experimental Psychology: Animal Behavior Processes, 12, 363–370. **45**

Hintzman, D. L. (1978). *The psychology of learning and memory.* San Francisco: Freeman. **190**

Hintzman, D. L. (1984). Episodic versus semantic memory: A distinction whose time has come—and gone? *Behavioral and Brain Sciences, 7,* 240–241. **235, 236**

Hirshman, E., Whelley, M. M., & Palij, M. (1989). An investigation of paradoxical memory effects. *Journal of Memory and Language, 28,* 594–609. **244, 324, 326, 327, 329**

Hoffman, H. S., & Ratner, A. M. (1973). A reinforcement model of imprinting: Implications for socialization in monkeys and men. *Psychological Review, 80,* 527–544. **170**

Holland, P. C. (1977). Conditioned stimulus as a determinant of the form of the Pavlovian conditioned response. *Journal of Experimental Psychology: Animal Behavior Processes, 3,* 77–104. **36**

Holland, P. C. (1979). Differential effects of omission contingencies on various components of Pavlovian conditioned responding in rats. *Journal of Experimental Psychology: Animal Behavior Processes, 5,* 178–193. **37**

Holland, P. C. (1981). Acquisition of representation-mediated conditioned food aversions. *Learning and Motivation, 12,* 1–18. **38**

Holland, P. C. (1985). The nature of conditioned inhibition in serial and simultaneous feature negative discriminations. In R. Miller & N. Spear (Eds.), *Information processing in animals: Conditioned inhibition* (pp. 267–297). Hillsdale, NJ: Erlbaum. **58**

Holland, P. C., & Straub, J. J. (1979). Differential effect of two ways of devaluing the unconditioned stimulus after Pavlovian appetitive conditioning. *Journal of Experimental Psychology: Animal Behavior Processes, 5,* 65–78. **37**

Holyoak, K. J., & Glass, A. L. (1975). The role of contradictions and counterexamples in the rejection of false sentences. *Journal of Verbal Learning and Verbal Behavior, 14,* 215–239. **252, 253, 260, 261**

Homme, L. E., deBaca, P. C., Devine, J. V., Steinhorst, R., & Rickert, E. J. (1963). Use of the Premack principle in controlling the behavior of nursery school children. *Journal of the Experimental Analysis of Behavior, 6,* 544–545. **84**

Huber, S. J., Shulman, H. G., Paulson, G. W., & Shuttleworth, E. C. (1989). Dose-dependent memory impairment in Parkinson's disease. *Neurology, 39,* 438–440. **241**

Huesmann, L. R., Laperspetz, K., & Eron, L. D. (1984). Intervening variables in the TV violence-aggression relation: Evidence from two countries. *Developmental Psychology, 20,* 746–775. **104**

Hull, C. L. (1920). Quantitative aspects of the evolution of concepts. *Psychological Monographs, 28* (1, Whole No. 123). **139, 140**

Hull, C. L. (1943). *Principles of behavior.* New York: Appleton-Century-Crofts. **11, 37, 65, 82, 108, 110**

Hull, C. L. (1952). *A behavior system.* New Haven, CT: Yale University Press. **11, 89**

Hulme, C. (1979). The interaction of visual and motor memory for graphic forms following tracing. *Quarterly Journal of Experimental Psychology, 31,* 249–261. **211**

Hulme, C. (1981). *Reading retardation and multisensory teaching.* London: Routledge and Kegan Paul. **211**

Hulme, C., & Tordoff, V. (1989). Working memory development: The effects of speech rate, word length, and acoustic similarity on serial recall. *Journal of Experimental Child Psychology, 47,* 72–87. **202, 203**

Hulse, S. H. (1978). Cognitive structure and serial pattern learning by rats. In S. H. Hulse, H. Fowler, & W. K. Honig (Eds.), *Cognitive processes in animal behavior* (pp. 311–340). Hillsdale, NJ: Erlbaum. **138**

Hume, D. (1886). *A treatise on human nature.* London: Longmans. (Original work published 1739–1740) **4**

Hunter, I. M. L. (1977). Imagery, comprehension, and mnemonics. *Journal of Mental Imagery, 1,* 65–72. **331**

Hunter, W. S. (1913). The delayed reaction in animals and children. *Behavior Monographs, 2,* serial #6. **130, 134**

Hunter, W. S. (1920). The temporal maze and kinaesthetic sensory processes in the white rat. *Psychobiology, 2,* 1–18. **134, 135, 136**

Huttenlocher, J., & Kubieck, L. F. (1983). The source of relatedness effects on naming latency. *Journal of Experimental Psychology, 9,* 486–496. **253**

Hyde, T. S., & Jenkins, J. J. (1969). Differential effects of incidental tasks on the organization of recall of a list of highly associated words. *Journal of Experimental Psychology, 82,* 472–481. **195**

Hyde, T. S., & Jenkins, J. J. (1973). Recall for words as a function of semantic, graphic, and syntactic orienting tasks. *Journal of Verbal Learning and Verbal Behavior, 12,* 471–480. **197**

Isaacs, I. D., & Duncan, C. P. (1962). Reversal and nonreversal shifts within and between dimensions in concept formation. *Journal of Experimental Psychology, 64,* 580–585. **123**

Jackson, R. L., & Minor, T. R. (1988). Effects of signaling inescapable shock on subsequent escape learning: Implications for theories of coping and "learned helplessness." *Journal of Experimental Psychology: Animal Behavior Processes, 14,* 390–400. **103**

Jacobs, W. J., & LoLordo, V. M. (1977). The sensory basis of avoidance responding in the rat: Relative dominance of auditory or visual warning signals and safety signals. *Learning and Motivation, 8,* 448–466. **161, 163**

Jacobs, W. J., & LoLordo, V. M. (1980). Constraints on Pavlovian aversive conditioning: Implications for avoidance learning in the rat. *Learning and Motivation, 11,* 427–455.

Jacoby, L. L., & Craik, F. I. M. (1979). Effects of elaboration of processing at encoding and retrieval: Trace distinctiveness and recovery of initial context. In L. S. Cermak & F. I. M. Craik (Eds), *Levels of processing in human memory* (pp. 1–21). Hillsdale, NJ: Erlbaum. **325**

Jacoby, L. L., & Dallas, M. (1981). On the relationship between autobiographical memory and perceptual learning. *Journal of Experimental Psychology: General, 110,* 306–340. **233, 234, 236**

James, W. A. (1981). *The principles of psychology* (Vols. 1–2). Cambridge, MA: Harvard University Press. (Original work published 1890) **8, 176**

Jenkins, H. M., Barnes, R. A., & Barrera, F. J. (1981). Why autoshaping depends on trial spacing. In C. M. Locurto, H. S. Terrace, & J. Gibbon (Eds.), *Autoshaping and conditioning theory* (pp. 255–284). New York: Academic Press.

Jenkins, H. M., Barrera, F. J., Ireland, C., & Woodside, B. (1978). Signal-centered action patterns of dogs in appetitive classical conditioning. *Learning and Motivation, 9,* 272–296. **36**

Jenkins, H. M., & Moore, B. A. (1973). The form of the auto-shaped response with food or water reinforcers. *Journal of the Experimental Analysis of Behavior, 20,* 163–181. **35, 157**

Jenkins, J. G., & Dallenbach, K. M. (1924). Oblivescence during sleep and waking. *American Journal of Psychology, 35,* 605–612. **277, 278**

Jenkins, W. O., & Stanley, J. C. (1950). Partial reinforcement: A review and critique. *Psychological Bulletin, 47,* 193–234. **74**

Johnson, M. K., Bransford, J. D., & Solomon, S. (1973). Memory for tacit implications of sentences. *Journal of Experimental Psychology, 98,* 203–205. **230, 302**

Johnson, M. K., & Hasher, L. (1987). Human learning and memory. *Annual Review of Psychology, 38,* 631–668. **225**

Johnson-Laird, P. N., Herrmann, D. J., & Chaffin, R. (1984). Only connections: A critique of semantic networks. *Psychological Bulletin, 96,* 292–315. **254**

Jones, G. V. (1976). A fragmentation hypothesis of memory: Cued recall of pictures and of sequential position. *Journal of Experimental Psychology: General, 105,* 277–293. **209**

Jones, G. V. (1978). Tests of a structural theory of the memory trace. *British Journal of Psychology, 69,* 351–367. **209**

Jones, G. V. (1979). Multirate forgetting. *Journal of Experimental Psychology: Human Learning and Memory, 5,* 98–114. **209**

Jones, M. C. (1924). The elimination of children's fears. *Journal of Experimental Psychology, 7,* 383–390. **41**

Josephson, W. L. (1987). Television violence and children's aggression: Testing the priming, social script, and disinhibition predictions. *Journal of Personality and Social Psychology, 53,* 882–890. **104**

Kamin, L. J. (1969). Predictability, surprise, attention, and conditioning. In B. A. Campbell & R. M. Church (Eds.), *Punishment and aversive control* (pp. 279–296). New York: Appleton-Century-Crofts. **38, 51, 53, 119**

Kamin, L. J., Brimer, C. J., & Black, A. H. (1963). Conditioned suppression as a monitor of fear of the CS in the course of avoidance training. *Journal of Comparative and Physiological Psychology, 56,* 497–501. **100**

Kant, I. (1912). Prolegomena. In P. Carus (Ed. & Trans.), *Kant's Prolegomena.* Chicago: Open Court. (Original work published 1783) **3**

Kant, I. (1965). *Critique of pure reason* (N. K. Smith, Trans.). New York: St. Martin's Press. (Original work published 1781) **3**

Kantowitz, B. H., & Roediger, H. L., III. (1984). *Experimental psychology: Understanding psychological research.* St. Paul, MN: West. **20**

Kaplan, P. S. (1984). Importance of relative temporal parameters in trace autoshaping: From excitation to inhibition. *Journal of Experimental Psychology: Animal Behavior Processes, 10,* 113–126. **45**

Kellogg, R. T. (1982). When can we introspect accurately about mental processes? *Memory & Cognition, 10,* 141–144. **149**

Kendler, H. H., & D'Amato, M. F. (1955). A comparison of reversal shifts and nonreversal shifts in human concept formation behavior. *Journal of Experimental Psychology, 49,* 165–174. **123**

Kendler, T. S. (1950). An experimental investigation of transposition as a function of the difference between training and test stimuli. *Journal of Experimental Psychology, 40,* 552–562. **121**

Keppel, G. (1968). Retroactive and proactive inhibition. In T. R. Dixon & D. L. Horton (Eds.), *Verbal behavior and general behavior theory* (pp. 172–213). Englewood Cliffs, NJ: Prentice-Hall. **281**

Kihlstrom, J. F. (1980). Posthypnotic amnesia for recently learned material: Interactions with ''episodic'' and ''semantic'' memory. *Cognitive Psychology, 12,* 227–251. **234, 235**

Kihlstrom, J. F. (1984). A fact is a fact is a fact. *Behavioral and Brain Sciences, 7,* 243–244. **235, 236, 237**

Kintsch, W. (1974). *The representation of meaning in memory.* Hillsdale, NJ: Erlbaum. **261**

Kintsch, W. (1980). Semantic memory: A tutorial. In R. S. Nickerson (Ed.), *Attention and performance VIII* (pp. 595–620). Hillsdale, NJ: Erlbaum. **254, 262, 263**

Kish, G. B. (1955). Learning when the onset of illumination is used as reinforcing stimulus. *Journal of Comparative and Physiological Psychology, 48,* 261–264. **83**

Klatzky, R. L. (1984). Armchair theorists have more fun. *Behavioral and Brain Sciences, 7,* 244. **235, 236**

Kleiman, G. (1975). Speech recoding in reading. *Journal of Verbal Learning and Verbal Behavior, 14,* 323–339. **200**

Koffka, K. (1924). *The growth of the mind.* (R. M. Ogden, Trans.). London: Kegan Paul, Trench, Trubner. **90**

Köhler, W. (1925). *The mentality of apes* (E. Winter, Trans.). New York: Harcourt, Brace, & World. **90, 91, 92**

Kohn, B., & Dennis, M. (1972). Observation and discrimination learning in the rat. *Journal of Comparative and Physiological Psychology, 78,* 292–296. **105**

Kolers, P. A. (1976). Reading a year later. *Journal of Experimental Psychology: Human Learning and Memory, 2,* 554–565. **198**

Konorski, J. (1948). *Conditioned reflexes and neuronal organization* (S. Garry, Trans.). Cambridge: Cambridge University Press. **48**

Konorski, J. (1967). *Integrative activity of the brain.* Chicago: University of Chicago Press. **47**

Kornbrot, D. E. (1989). Organisation of keying skills: The effect of motor complexity and number of units. *Acta Psychologica, 70,* 19–41. **211**

Körner, S. (1955). *Kant.* Harmondsworth, England: Pelican. **3**

Kosslyn, S. M. (1975). Information representation in visual images. *Cognitive Psychology, 7,* 341–370. **267**

Kosslyn, S. M. (1980). *Image and mind.* Cambridge, MA: Harvard University Press. **268, 269**

Kosslyn, S. M. (1987). Seeing and imagining in the cerebral hemispheres: A computational approach. *Psychological Review, 94,* 148–175. **269**

Kosslyn, S. M., Ball, T. M., & Reiser, B. J. (1978). Visual images preserve metric spatial information: Evidence from studies of image scanning. *Journal of Experimental Psychology: Human Perception and Performance, 4,* 47–60. **265**

Kosslyn, S. M., Cave, C. B., Provost, D. A., & von Gierke, S. M. (1988). Sequential processes in image generation. *Cognitive Psychology, 20,* 319–343. **270**

Kosslyn, S. M., Holtzman, J. D., Farah, M. J., & Gazzaniga, M. S. (1985). A computational analysis of mental image generation: Evidence from functional dissociations in split-brain patients. *Journal of Experimental Psychology: General, 114,* 311–341. **269**

Kosslyn, S. M., Reiser, B. J., Farah, M. J., & Fliegel, S. L. (1983). Generating visual images: Units and relations. *Journal of Experimental Psychology: General, 112,* 278–303. **269**

Kozlowski, L. T., & Bryant, K. J. (1977). Sense of direction, spatial orientation, and cognitive maps. *Journal of Experimental Psychology: Human Perception and Performance, 3,* 590–598. **93**

Kremer, E. F. (1974). The truly random control procedure: Conditioning to static cues. *Journal of Comparative and Physiological Psychology, 86,* 700–707. **57**

Kroll, N. E. A., Schepeler, E. M., & Angin, K. T. (1986). Bizarre imagery: The misremembered mnemonic. *Journal of Experimental Psychology: Learning, Memory, and Cognition, 12,* 42–53. **324, 326**

Kroll, N. E. A., & Tu, S. (1988). The bizarre mnemonic. *Psychological Research, 50,* 28–37. **327**

Kuhn, T. S. (1970). *The structure of scientific revolutions* (2nd ed.). Chicago: University of Chicago Press. **18**

Kulhavy, R. W., & Swenson, I. (1975). Imagery instructions and the comprehension of text. *British Journal of Educational Psychology, 45,* 47–51. **321**

Lachman, R., & Naus, M. J. (1984). The episodic/semantic continuum in an evolved machine. *Behavioral and Brain Sciences, 7,* 244–246. **235**

Lakatos, I. (1970). Falsification and the methodology of scientific research programmes. In A. Musgrave & I. Lakatos (Eds.), *Criticism and the growth of knowledge* (pp. 91–195). New York: Cambridge University Press. **18**

Lamb, M. (1982). The bonding phenomenon: Misinterpretations and their implications. *Journal of Pediatrics, 101,* 555–557. **170**

Lashley, K. S. (1938). Conditional reactions in the rat. *Journal of Psychology, 6,* 311–324. **130**

Lashley, K. S. (1951). The problem of serial order in behavior. In L. A. Jeffress (Ed.), *Cerebral mechanisms in behavior* (pp. 112–136). New York: Wiley. **68**

Lashley, K. S. (1963). *Brain mechanisms and intelligence.* New York: Dover. **38**

Lashley, K. S., & Wade, M. (1946). The Pavlovian theory of generalization. *Psychological Review, 53,* 72–87. **110, 111**

Lawrence, D. H. (1952). The transfer of a discrimination along a continuum. *Journal of Comparative and Physiological Psychology, 45,* 511–516. **120**

Lawrence, D. H. (1963). The nature of a stimulus: Some relationships between learning and perception. In S. Koch (Ed.), *Psychology: A study of a science* (Vol. 4, pp. 179–212). New York: McGraw-Hill. **150**

Leahey, T. H. (1987). *A history of psychology: Main currents in psychological thought.* Englewood Cliffs, NJ: Prentice-Hall. **2, 4, 5, 8, 13**

Lenneberg, E. H. (1967). *Biological foundations of language.* New York: Wiley. **172**

Lepper, M. R., Greene, D., & Nisbett, R. E. (1973). Undermining children's intrinsic interest with extrinsic rewards. *Journal of Personality and Social Psychology, 28,* 129–137. **85, 86**

Lett, B. T. (1980). Taste potentiates color-sickness associations in pigeons and quail. *Animal Learning & Behavior, 8,* 193–198. **160**

Levin, J. R., McCormick, C.B., Miller, G. E., Berry, J. K., & Pressley, M. (1982). Mnemonic versus nonmnemonic vocabulary-learning strategies for children. *American Educational Research Journal, 19,* 121–136. **333**

Levin, J. R., Morrison, C. R., McGivern, J. E., Mastropieri, M. A., & Scruggs, T. E. (1986). Mnemonic facilitation of text-embedded science facts. *American Educational Research Journal, 23,* 489–506. **336**

Levin, J. R., Shriberg, L. K., & Berry, J. K. (1983). A concrete strategy for remembering abstract prose. *American Educational Research Journal, 20,* 277–290. **336**

Levin, R. B., & Gross, A. M. (1985). The role of relaxation in systematic desensitization. *Behaviour Research and Therapy, 23,* 187–196. **41**

Levine, M. (1966). Hypothesis behavior by humans during discrimination learning. *Journal of Experimental Psychology, 71,* 331–338. **139**

Levine, M. (1971). Hypothesis theory and nonlearning despite ideal S-R-reinforcement contingencies. *Psychological Review, 78,* 130–140. **149**

Lewis, R. S. (1986). Variation on a theme: Are the elements of episodic memory dissociable? *Behavioral and Brain Sciences, 9,* 567–568. **235**

Leyens, J. P., Camino, L., Parke, R. D., & Berkowitz, L. (1975). The effects of movie violence on aggression in a field setting as a function of group dominance and cohesion. *Journal of Personality and Social Psychology, 32,* 346–360. **104**

Lieberman, D. A., McIntosh, D. C., & Thomas, G. V. (1979). Learning when reward is delayed: A marking hypothesis. *Journal of Experimental Psychology: Animal Behavior Processes, 5,* 224–242. **163**

Lindberg, A. A. (1933). The formation of negative conditioned reflexes by coincidence in time with the process of differential inhibition. *Journal of General Psychology, 8,* 392–419. **48**

Lindblom, L. L., & Jenkins, H. M. (1981). Responses eliminated by noncontingent or negatively contingent reinforcement recover in extinction. *Journal of Experimental Psychology: Animal Behavior Processes, 7,* 175–190. **51**

Lindsay, P. H., & Norman, D. A. (1977). *Human information processing* (2nd ed.). New York: Academic Press. **254**

Lloyd, G. E. R. (Ed.). (1978). *Aristotle on mind and the senses.* Cambridge: Cambridge University Press. **2**

Locke, J. (1975). *An essay concerning human understanding* (P. Nidditch, Ed.). Oxford: Clarendon Press. (Original work published 1690) **4**

Loftus, E. F. (1975). Leading questions and the eyewitness report. *Cognitive Psychology, 7,* 560–572. **305**

Loftus, E. F. (1977). Shifting human color memory. *Memory & Cognition, 5,* 696–699. **304**

Loftus, E. F. (1979a). *Eyewitness testimony.* Cambridge: Harvard University Press. **304**

Loftus, E. F. (1979b). The malleability of memory. *American Scientist, 67,* 312–320. **304**

Loftus, E. F., & Greene, E. (1980). Warning: Even memory for faces may be contagious. *Law and Human Behavior, 4,* 323–334. **304**

Loftus, E. F., & Loftus, G. R. (1980). On the permanence of stored information in the brain. *American Psychologist, 35,* 409–420. **304**

Loftus, E. F., Loftus, G. R., & Hunt, E. B. (1984). Broadbent's Maltese cross memory model: Something old, something new, something borrowed, something missing. *Behavioral and Brain Sciences, 7,* 73–74, 91–94. **214**

Loftus, E. F., Miller, D. G., & Burns, H. J. (1978). Semantic integration of verbal information into a visual memory. *Journal of Experimental Psychology: Human Learning and Memory, 4,* 19–31. **305, 307**

Loftus, E. F., & Palmer, J. E. (1974). Reconstruction of automobile destruction: An example of the interaction between language and memory. *Journal of Verbal Learning and Verbal Behavior, 13,* 585–589.

Logie, R., Baddeley, A., Mané, A., Donchin, E., & Sheptak, R. (1989). Working memory in the acquisition of complex cognitive skills. *Acta Psychologica, 71,* 53–87. **206**

Lorayne, H., & Lucas, J. (1974). *The memory book.* New York: Stein and Day. **315, 323, 328, 329, 330, 336, 337**

Lorenz, K. Z. (1937). The companion in the bird's world. *Auk, 54,* 245–273. **154, 169**

Lorenz, K. Z. (1965). *Evolution and modification of behavior.* Chicago: University of Chicago Press. **152, 167**

Lorsbach, T. C., & Gray, J. W. (1986). Item identification speed and memory span performance in learning disabled children. *Contemporary Educational Psychology, 11,* 68–78. **202**

Lovaas, O. I. (1987). Behavioral treatment and normal educational and intellectual functioning in young autistic children. *Journal of Consulting and Clinical Psychology, 55,* 3–9. **75**

Lovaas, O. I., Berberich, J. P., Perdoff, B. F., & Schaeffer, B. (1966). Acquisition of imitative speech by schizophrenic children. *Science, 151,* 705–707. **79**

Lovaas, O. I., & Newsom, C. D. (1976). Behavior modification with psychotic children. In H. Leitenberg (Ed.), *Handbook of behavior modification and behavior therapy* (pp. 303–360). Englewood Cliffs, NJ: Prentice-Hall. **97**

Lubow, R. E. (1973). Latent inhibition. *Psychological Bulletin, 79,* 398–407. **44**

Lysle, T. T., & Fowler, H. (1985). Inhibition as a "slave" process: Deactivation of conditioned inhibition through extinction of conditioned excitation. *Journal of Experimental Psychology: Animal Behavior Processes, 11,* 71–94. **48**

Mackintosh, N. J. (1974). *The psychology of animal learning.* New York: Academic Press. **114, 127, 136**

Mackintosh, N. J. (1975). A theory of attention: Variations in the associability of stimuli with reinforcement. *Psychological Review, 82,* 276–298. **57**

Mackintosh, N. J., & Dickinson, A. (1979). Instrumental (type II) conditioning. In A. Dickinson & R. A. Boakes (Eds.), *Mechanisms of learning and motivation* (pp. 143–169). Hillsdale, NJ: Erlbaum. **66**

Mackintosh, N. J., & Honig, W. K. (1970). Blocking and attentional enhancement in pigeons. *Journal of Comparative and Physiological Psychology, 73,* 78–85. **119**

Macphail, E. M. (1968). Avoidance responding in pigeons. *Journal of the Experimental Analysis of Behavior, 11,* 629–632. **163**

Mandler, G., & Worden, P. E. (1973). Semantic processing without permanent storage. *Journal of Experimental Psychology, 100,* 277–283. **197**

Marler, P., & Peters, S. (1981). Sparrows learn adult song and more from memory. *Science, 213,* 780–782. **168**

Marsh, G. (1967). Relational learning in the pigeon. *Journal of Comparative and Physiological Psychology, 64,* 519–521. **122**

Marsh, G. (1969). An evaluation of three explanations for the transfer of discrimination effect. *Journal of Comparative and Physiological Psychology, 68,* 268–275. **120**

Marshall, P. H., Nau, K., & Chandler, C. K. (1980). A functional analysis of common and bizarre visual mediators. *Bulletin of the Psychonomic Society, 15,* 373–377.

Martin, M., & Jones, G. V. (1979). Modality dependence of loss of recency in free recall. *Psychological Research, 40,* 273–289. **210**

Marx, M. H., & Cronan-Hillix, W. A. (1987). *Systems and theories in psychology.* New York: McGraw-Hill. **5, 12**

Matthews, T. J., Bordi, F., & Depollo, D. (1990). Schedule-induced kinesic and taxic behavioral stereotypy in the pigeon. *Journal of Experimental Psychology: Animal Behavior Processes, 16,* 335–344. **81**

Mayhew, A. J. (1967). Interlist changes in subjective organization during free-recall learning. *Journal of Experimental Psychology, 74,* 425–430. **289**

Mazlish, B. (1975). *James and John Stuart Mill.* New York: Basic Books.

McArthur, L. Z., & Eisen, S. V. (1976). Achievements of male and female storybook characters as determinants of achievement behavior by boys and girls. *Journal of Personality and Social Psychology, 33,* 467–473. **105**

McCarty, D. L. (1980). Investigation of a visual imagery mnemonic device for acquiring face-name associations. *Journal of Experimental Psychology: Human Learning and Memory, 6,* 145–155. **337**

McCloskey, M. E., & Glucksberg, S. (1978). Natural categories: Well defined or fuzzy sets? *Memory & Cognition, 6,* 462–472. **260**

McCloskey, M., & Glucksberg, S. (1979). Decision processes in verifying category membership statements: Implications for models of semantic memory. *Cognitive Psychology, 11,* 1–37. **261, 262**

McCloskey, M., & Zaragoza, M. (1985a). Misleading postevent information and memory for events: Arguments and evidence against memory impairment hypotheses. *Journal of Experimental Psychology: General, 114,* 1–16. **306, 307, 308**

McCloskey, M., & Zaragoza, M. (1985b). Postevent information and memory: Reply to Loftus, Schooler, and Wagenaar. *Journal of Experimental Psychology: General, 114,* 381–387. **306**

McCormick, C. B., & Levin, J. R. (1984). A comparison of different prose-learning variations of the mnemonic keyword method. *American Educational Research Journal, 21,* 379–398. **336**

McCormick, C. B., & Levin, J. R. (1987). Mnemonic prose-learning strategies. In M. A. McDaniel & M. Pressley (Eds.), *Imagery and related mnemonic processes: Theories, individual differences, and applications* (pp. 392–406). New York: Springer-Verlag. **334, 336**

McCormick, C. B., Levin, J. R., Cykowski, F., & Danilovics, P. (1984). Mnemonic-strategy reduction of prose-learning interference. *Educational Communication and Technology Journal, 32,* 145–152. **336**

McDaniel, M. A., Anderson, D. C., Einstein, G. O., & O'Halloran, C. M. (1989). Modulation of environmental reinstatement effects through encoding strategies. *American Journal of Psychology, 102,* 523–548. **244**

McDaniel, M. A., & Einstein, G. O. (1986). Bizarre imagery as an effective memory aid: The importance of distinctiveness. *Journal of Experimental Psychology: Learning, Memory, and Cognition, 12,* 54–65. **324, 325, 326, 329**

McDaniel, M. A., & Einstein, G. O. (1989). Sentence complexity eliminates the mnemonic advantage of bizarre imagery. *Bulletin of the Psychonomic Society, 27,* 117–120. **326**

McDaniel, M. A., & Pressley, M. (1989). Keyword and context instruction of new vocabulary meanings: Effects on text comprehension and memory. *Journal of Educational Psychology, 81,* 204–213. **333**

McGeoch, J. A. (1932). Forgetting and the law of disuse. *Psychological Review, 39,* 352–370.

McGeoch, J. A. (1942). *The psychology of human learning.* New York: McKay. **279**

McKeon, R. (Ed.). (1941). *The basic works of Aristotle.* New York: Random House. **2**

McKoon, G., Ratcliff, R., & Dell, G. S. (1986). A critical evaluation of the semantic-episodic distinction. *Journal of Experimental Psychology: Learning, Memory, and Cognition, 12,* 295–306. **235, 236, 237, 238**

McNally, R. J. (1987). Preparedness and phobias: A review. *Psychological Bulletin, 101,* 283–303. **161**

Meichenbaum, D. H., & Goodman, J. (1971). Training impulsive children to talk to themselves: A means of developing self-control. *Journal of Abnormal Psychology, 77,* 115–126. **105**

Melton, A. W., & Irwin, J. M. (1940). The influence of degree of interpolated learning on retroactive inhibition and the overt transfer of specific responses. *American Journal of Psychology, 53,* 173–203. **280, 281**

Menzel, R. (1985). Learning in honey bees in an ecological and behavioral context. In B. Holldobler & H. Lindauer (Eds.), *Experimental behavioral ecology and sociobiology,* (pp. 55–74). Stuttgart: Fischer Verlag. **168**

Merry, R. (1980). Image bizarreness in incidental learning. *Psychological Reports, 46,* 427–430. **324**

Merry, R., & Graham, N. C. (1978). Imagery bizarreness in children's recall of sentences. *British Journal of Psychology, 69,* 315–321. **324**

Metcalfe, J. (1986). Premonitions of insight predict impending error. *Journal of Experimental Psychology: Learning, Memory, and Cognition, 12,* 623–634. **91**

Metcalfe, J., & Wiebe, D. (1987). Intuition in insight and noninsight problem solving. *Memory & Cognition, 15,* 238–246. **91, 92**

Meyer, D. E. (1970). On the representation and retrieval of stored semantic information. *Cognitive Psychology, 1,* 242–300. **258**

Meyer, D. E., & Schvaneveldt, R. W. (1971). Facilitation in recognizing pairs of words: Evidence of a dependence between retrieval operations. *Journal of Experimental Psychology, 90,* 227–234. **253**

Midlarsky, E., Bryan, J. H., & Brickman, P. (1973). Aversive approval: Interactive effects of modeling and reinforcement on altruistic behavior. *Child Development, 44,* 321–328. **105**

Miles, C. G., & Jenkins, H. M. (1973). Overshadowing in operant conditioning as a function of discriminability. *Learning and Motivation, 4,* 11–27. **117, 119**

Mill, J. (1829). *Analysis of the phenomena of the human mind.* London: Longmans and Dyer. **6**

Mill, J. S. (1884). *A system of logic.* London: Longmans, Green. (Original work published 1843) **6**

Miller, G. A. (1956). The magical number seven, plus or minus two: Some limits on our capacity for processing information. *Psychological Review, 63,* 81–97. **14, 313**

Miller, G. A., Galanter, E., & Pribram, K. H. (1960). *Plans and the structure of behavior.* New York: Holt, Rinehart, & Winston. **68**

Miller, N. E. (1948). Studies of fear as an acquirable drive. *Journal of Experimental Psychology, 38,* 89–101. **98**

Miller, R. R., Greco, C., Vigorito, M., & Marlin, N. A. (1983). Signaled tailshock is perceived as similar to a stronger unsignaled tailshock: Implications for a functional analysis of classical conditioning. *Journal of Experimental Psychology: Animal Behavior Processes, 9,* 105–131. **37, 103**

Miller, R. R., & Marlin, N. A. (1984). The physiology and semantics of consolidation. In G. C. Quarton, T. Melnechuk, & F. O. Schmitt (Eds.), *Memory consolidation* (pp. 85–110). Hillsdale, NJ: Erlbaum. **343**

Miller, R. R., & Schachtman, T. R. (1985). Conditioning context as an associative baseline: Implications for response generation and the nature of conditioned inhibition. In R. R. Miller & N. E. Spear (Eds.), *Information processing in animals: Conditioned inhibition* (pp. 51–88). Hillsdale, NJ: Erlbaum. **58**

Mineka, S. (1979). The role of fear in theories of avoidance learning, flooding, and extinction. *Psychological Bulletin, 86,* 985–1010. **99, 162**

Mitchell, D., Kirschbaum, E. H., & Perry, R. L. (1975). Effects of neophobia and habituation on the poison-induced avoidance of exteroceptive stimuli in the rat. *Journal of Experimental Psychology: Animal Behavior Processes, 1,* 47–55. **160**

Moltz, H. (1957). Latent extinction and the fractional anticipatory response mechanism. *Psychological Review, 64,* 229–241. **88**

Montague, W. E., Adams, J. A., & Kiess, H. O. (1966). Forgetting and natural language media-

tion. *Journal of Experimental Psychology, 72,* 829–833. **315**

Moore, B. R., & Stuttard, S. (1979). Dr. Guthrie and *Felis domesticus* or: Tripping over the cat. *Science, 205,* 1031–1033. **68**

Moore, J. W., & Stickney, K. J. (1985). Antiassociations: Conditioned inhibition in attentional-associative networks. In R. R. Miller & N. E. Spear (Eds.), *Information processing in animals: Conditioned inhibition* (pp. 209–232). Hillsdale, NJ: Erlbaum. **56**

Morgan, C. L. (1894). *An introduction to comparative psychology.* London: Scott. **61**

Morgan, R. L., & Underwood, B. J. (1950). Proactive inhibition as a function of response similarity. *Journal of Experimental Psychology, 40,* 592–603. **284**

Morris, C. C., Bransford, J. D., & Franks, J. J. (1977). Levels of processing versus transfer appropriate processing. *Journal of Verbal Learning and Verbal Behavior, 16,* 519–533. **240**

Morris, P. E., Jones, S., & Hampson, P. (1978). An imagery mnemonic for the learning of people's names. *British Journal of Psychology, 69,* 335–336. **337**

Morris, R. G., & Baddeley, A. D. (1988). Primary and working memory functioning in Alzheimer-type dementia. *Journal of Clinical and Experimental Neuropsychology, 10,* 279–296. **203**

Morris, R. G., Gick, M. L., & Craik, F. I. M. (1988). Processing resources and age differences in working memory. *Memory & Cognition, 16,* 362–366. **203**

Moscovitch, M., & Craik, F. I. M. (1976). Depth of processing, retrieval cues, and uniqueness of encoding as factors in recall. *Journal of Verbal Learning and Verbal Behavior, 15,* 447–458. **317, 318**

Müller, G. E., & Pilzecker, A. (1900). Experimentelle Beiträge zur Lehre vom Gedächtnis. *Zeitschrift für Psychologie,* Ergbd. 1. **277**

Murdock, B. B. (1962). The serial position effect of free recall. *Journal of Experimental Psychology, 64,* 482–488. **285**

Musen, G., Shimamura, A. P., & Squire, L. R. (1990). Intact text-specific reading skill in amnesia. *Journal of Experimental Psychology: Learning, Memory, and Cognition, 16,* 1068–1076. **346, 349**

Muter, P. (1984). Recognition and recall of words with a single meaning. *Journal of Experimental*

Psychology: Learning, Memory, and Cognition,
10, 198–202. **293**

Nadel, L., & Willner, J. (1980). Context and conditioning: A place for space. *Physiological Psychology, 8,* 218–228. **90**

Nadel, L., Willner, J., & Kurz, E. M. (1985). Cognitive maps and environmental context. In P. D. Balsam & A. Tomie (Eds.), *Context and learning* (pp. 385–406). Hillsdale, NJ: Erlbaum. **93**

Nairne, J. S., & Rescorla, R. A. (1981). Second-order conditioning with diffuse auditory reinforcers in the pigeon. *Learning and Motivation, 12,* 65–91. **38**

Neely, J. H. (1977). Semantic priming and retrieval from lexical memory: Role of inhibitionless spreading activation and limited capacity attention. *Journal of Experimental Psychology: General, 106,* 226–254. **253**

Neisser, U. (1984). Interpreting Harry Bahrick's discovery: What confers immunity against forgetting? *Journal of Experimental Psychology: General, 113,* 32–35. **304**

Nelson, T. O., Metzler, J., & Reed, D. A. (1974). Role of details in the long-term recognition of pictures and verbal descriptions. *Journal of Experimental Psychology, 102,* 184–186. **268**

Nicolaus, L. K., Cassel, J. F., Carlson, R. B., & Gustavson, C. R. (1983). Taste-aversion conditioning of crows to control predation on eggs. *Science, 220,* 212–214. **160**

Nilsson, L. G., Law, J., & Tulving, E. (1988). Recognition failure of recallable unique names: Evidence for an empirical law of memory and learning. *Journal of Experimental Psychology: Learning, Memory, and Cognition, 14,* 266–277. **293**

Nissen, M. J., & Bullemer, P. (1987). Attentional requirements of learning: Evidence from performance measures. *Cognitive Psychology, 19,* 1–32. **224**

O'Brien, E. J., & Wolford, C. R. (1982). Effect of delay in testing on retention of plausible versus bizarre mental images. *Journal of Experimental Psychology: Learning, Memory, and Cognition, 8,* 148–152.

Oden, D. L., Thompson, R. K. R., & Premack, D. (1988). Spontaneous transfer of matching by infant chimpanzees *(Pan troglodytes). Journal of Experimental Psychology: Animal Behavior Processes, 14,* 140–145. **133**

Ohman, A., Eriksson, A., & Olofsson, C. (1975). One-trial learning and superior resistance to extinction of autonomic responses conditioned to potentially phobic stimuli. *Journal of Comparative and Physiological Psychology, 88,* 619–627. **161**

Olton, D. S. (1978). Characteristics of spatial memory. In S. H. Hulse, H. Fowler, & W. K. Honig (Eds.), *Cognitive processes in animal behavior* (pp. 341–373). Hillsdale, NJ: Erlbaum. **135, 136**

Olton, D. S., & Samuelson, R. J. (1976). Remembrance of places passed: Spatial memory in rats. *Journal of Experimental Psychology: Animal Behavior Processes, 2,* 97–116. **135, 136**

Olton, D. S., & Schlosberg, P. (1978). Food-searching strategies in young rats: Win-shift predominates over win-stay. *Journal of Comparative and Physiological Psychology, 92,* 609–618. **166**

Paivio, A. (1971). *Imagery and verbal processes.* New York: Holt, Rinehart and Winston. **264**

Paivio, A. (1986). *Mental representations: A dual coding approach.* New York: Oxford University Press. **264**

Pate, J. L., & Rumbaugh, D. M. (1983). The language-like behavior of Lana chimpanzee: Is it merely discrimination and paired-associate learning? *Animal Learning & Behavior, 11,* 134–138. **147**

Patterson, F. G., & Linden, E. (1981). *The education of Koko.* New York: Holt, Rinehart and Winston. **147**

Pavlov, I. P. (1927). *Conditioned reflexes* (G. V. Anrep, Trans.). London: Oxford University Press. (Reprinted, New York: Dover, 1960) **26, 29, 39, 49, 51, 52, 152**

Pearce, J. M., & Hall, G. (1980). A model for Pavlovian learning: Variations in the effectiveness of conditioned but not of unconditioned stimuli *Psychological Review, 87,* 532–552. **47, 57**

Peden, B. F., Browne, M. P., & Hearst, E. (1977). Persistent approaches to a signal for food despite food omission for approaching. *Journal of Experimental Psychology: Animal Behavior Processes, 3,* 377–399. **37**

Pepperberg, I. M. (1987). Acquisition of the same/different concept by an African Grey parrot *(Psittacus erithacus)*: Learning with respect to categories of color, shape, and material. *Animal Learning & Behavior, 15,* 423–432. **148**

Perin, C. T. (1943). A quantitative investigation of the delay of reinforcement gradient. *Journal of Experimental Psychology, 32*, 37–51. **69, 86**

Perkins, C. C., Jr. (1968). An analysis of the concept of reinforcement. *Psychological Review, 75*, 155–172. **37**

Petersen, R. C. (1977). Retrieval failures in alcohol state-dependent learning. *Psychopharmacology, 55*, 141–146. **241**

Peterson, L. R., & Peterson, M. J. (1959). Short-term retention of individual verbal items. *Journal of Experimental Psychology, 58*, 193–198. **179, 184, 190**

Phillips, W. A. (1983). Short-term visual memory. In D. E. Broadbent (Ed.), *Functional aspects of memory* (pp. 57–71). London: Royal Society. **214**

Pichert, J. W., & Anderson, R. C. (1977). Taking different perspectives on a story. *Journal of Educational Psychology, 69*, 309–315.

Popper, K. R. (1963). *Conjectures and refutations: The growth of scientific knowledge*. New York: Basic Books. **18**

Posner, M. I., & Keele, S. W. (1968). On the genesis of abstract ideas. *Journal of Experimental Psychology, 77*, 353–363. **142**

Postman, L. (1969). Mechanisms of interference in forgetting. In G. A. Talland & N. C. Waugh (Eds.), *The pathology of memory* (pp. 195–210). New York: Academic Press. **282**

Postman, L. (1970). Effects of word frequency on acquisition and retention under conditions of free-recall learning. *Quarterly Journal of Experimental Psychology, 22*, 185–195. **289**

Postman, L., & Stark, K. (1969). Role of response availability in transfer and interference. *Journal of Experimental Psychology, 79*, 168–177. **282**

Postman, L., Stark, K., & Fraser, J. (1968). Temporal changes in interference. *Journal of Verbal Learning and Verbal Behavior, 7*, 672–694. **281, 282, 284**

Postman, L., & Underwood, B. J. (1973). Critical issues in interference theory. *Memory & Cognition, 1*, 19–40. **282**

Pra Baldi, A., De Beni, R., Cornoldi, C., & Cavedon, A. (1985). Some conditions for the occurrence of the bizarreness effect in free recall. *British Journal of Psychology, 76*, 427–436. **326**

Premack, D. (1959). Toward empirical behavior laws: I. Positive reinforcement. *Psychological Review, 66*, 219–233. **84**

Premack, D. (1962). Reversibility of the reinforcement relation. *Science, 136*, 255–257. **84, 85**

Premack, D. (1971). Language in chimpanzees? *Science, 172*, 808–822. **144, 147**

Premack, D. (1976). *Intelligence in ape and man*. Hillsdale, NJ: Erlbaum. **147**

Premack, D. (1983). The codes of man and beasts. *Behavioral & Brain Sciences, 6*, 125–167. **148**

Pressley, M., Levin, J. R., & Delaney, H. D. (1982). The mnemonic keyword method. *Review of Educational Research, 52*, 61–92. **336**

Pressley, M., Levin, J. R., Kuiper, N. A., Bryant, S. L., & Michener, S. (1982). Mnemonic versus nonmnemonic vocabulary-learning strategies: Additional comparisons. *Journal of Educational Psychology, 74*, 693–707. **333, 334**

Pressley, M., Levin, J. R., & Miller, G. E. (1982). The keyword method compared to alternative vocabulary-learning strategies. *Contemporary Educational Psychology, 7*, 50–60. **333**

Presson, C. C., DeLange, N., & Hazelrigg, M. D. (1989). Orientation specificity in spatial memory: What makes a path different from a map of the path? *Journal of Experimental Psychology: Learning, Memory, and Cognition, 15*, 887–897. **93**

Prokasy, W. F., & Whaley, F. L. (1963). Intertrial interval range shift in classical eyelid conditioning. *Psychological Reports, 12*, 55–58. **31**

Prytulak, L. S. (1971). Natural language mediation. *Cognitive Psychology, 2*, 1–56. **315**

Pylyshyn, Z. W. (1973). What the mind's eye tells the mind's brain: A critique of mental imagery. *Psychological Bulletin, 80*, 1–24. **267, 270**

Pylyshyn, Z. W. (1981). The imagery debate: Analogue media versus tacit knowledge. *Psychological Review, 88*, 16–45. **267**

Rachlin, H., & Green, L. (1972). Commitment, choice and self-control. *Journal of the Experimental Analysis of Behavior, 17*, 15–22. **128, 129**

Rajecki, D. (1973). Imprinting in precocial birds: Interpretation, evidence, and evaluation. *Psychological Review, 79*, 48–58. **170**

Rashotte, M. E., Griffin, R. W., & Sisk, C. L. (1977). Second-order conditioning of the pigeon's keypeck. *Animal Learning & Behavior, 5*, 25–38. **38**

Reder, L. M., Anderson, J. R., & Bjork, R. A. (1974). A semantic interpretation of encoding specificity. *Journal of Experimental Psychology, 102,* 648–656. **292**

Reisberg, D., Rappaport, I., & O'Shaughnessy, M. (1984). Limits of working memory: The digit digit-span. *Journal of Experimental Psychology: Learning, Memory, and Cognition, 10,* 203–221. **207**

Reiss, S., & Wagner, A. R. (1972). CS habituation produces a "latent inhibition effect" but no active "conditioned inhibition." *Learning and Motivation, 3,* 237–245. **44**

Reitman, J. S. (1971). Mechanisms of forgetting in short-term memory. *Cognitive Psychology, 2,* 185–195. **185**

Reitman, J. S. (1974). Without surreptitious rehearsal information in short-term memory decays. *Journal of Verbal Learning and Verbal Behavior, 13,* 365–377.

Rescorla, R. A. (1966). Predictability and number of pairings in Pavlovian fear conditioning. *Psychonomic Science, 4,* 383–384. **50**

Rescorla, R. A. (1967). Pavlovian conditioning and its proper control procedures. *Psychological Review, 74,* 71–80. **32, 45, 47, 49, 51**

Rescorla, R. A. (1968). Probability of shock in the presence and absence of CS in fear conditioning. *Journal of Comparative and Physiological Psychology, 66,* 1–5. **50**

Rescorla, R. A. (1969). Pavlovian conditioned inhibition. *Psychological Bulletin, 72,* 77–94. **40, 42**

Rescorla, R. A. (1970). Reduction in the effectiveness of reinforcement after prior excitatory conditioning. *Learning and Motivation, 1,* 372–381. **55**

Rescorla, R. A. (1971). Summation and retardation tests of latent inhibition. *Journal of Comparative and Physiological Psychology, 75,* 77–81. **44**

Rescorla, R. A. (1976). Second-order conditioning of Pavlovian conditioned inhibition. *Learning and Motivation, 7,* 161–172. **48**

Rescorla, R. A. (1979). Conditioned inhibition and extinction. In A. Dickinson & R. A. Boakes (Eds.), *Mechanisms of learning: A memorial volume to Jerzy Konorski* (pp. 83–110). Hillsdale, NJ: Erlbaum. **40**

Rescorla, R. A. (1982). Some consequences of associations between the excitor and the inhibitor in a conditioned inhibition paradigm. *Journal of Experimental Psychology: Animal Behavior Processes, 8,* 288–298. **44**

Rescorla, R. A. (1986). Extinction of facilitation. *Journal of Experimental Psychology: Animal Behavior Processes, 12,* 16–24. **58**

Rescorla, R. A. (1990). The role of information about the response-outcome relation in instrumental discrimination learning. *Journal of Experimental Psychology: Animal Behavior Processes, 16,* 262–270. **138**

Rescorla, R. A., Durlach, P. J., & Grau, J. W. (1985). Contextual learning in Pavlovian conditioning. In P. D. Balsam & A. Tomie (Eds.), *Context and learning* (pp. 23–56). Hillsdale, NJ: Erlbaum. **57**

Rescorla, R. A., & Holland, P. C. (1977). Associations in Pavlovian conditioned inhibition. *Learning and Motivation, 8,* 429–447. **48**

Rescorla, R. A., & Wagner, A. R. (1972). A theory of Pavlovian conditioning: Variations in the effectiveness of reinforcement and nonreinforcement. In A. H. Black & W. F. Prokasy (Eds.), *Classical conditioning II: Current research and theory* (pp. 64–99). New York: Appleton-Century-Crofts. **53, 56**

Restle, F. (1958). Toward a quantitative description of learning set data. *Psychological Review, 65,* 77–91. **127**

Reynolds, G. S. (1961). Attention in the pigeon. *Journal of the Experimental Analysis of Behavior, 4,* 203–208. **117**

Richardson-Klavehn, A., & Bjork, R. A. (1988). Measures of memory. *Annual Review of Psychology, 39,* 475–543. **225**

Riley, D. A., & Leuin, T. C. (1971). Stimulus-generalization gradients in chickens reared in monochromatic light and tested with single wavelength value. *Journal of Comparative and Physiological Psychology, 75,* 399–402. **111**

Rilling, M. (1977). Stimulus control and inhibitory processes. In W. K. Honig & J. E. R. Staddon (Eds.), *Handbook of operant behavior* (pp. 432–480). Englewood Cliffs, NJ. **117**

Rips, L. J., Shoben, E. J., & Smith, E. E. (1973). Semantic distance and the verification of semantic relations. *Journal of Verbal Learning and Verbal Behavior, 12,* 1–20. **250**

Rizley, R. C., & Rescorla, R. A. (1972). Associations in second-order conditioning and sensory preconditioning. *Journal of Comparative and Physiological Psychology, 81,* 1–11. **33, 38**

Rock, M. A. (1979). Keyboard symbols enable retarded children to "speak." *Smithsonian, 10,* 90–96. **148**

Roediger, H. L., III. (1984a). Does current evidence from dissociation experiments favor the episodic/semantic distinction? *Behavioral and Brain Sciences, 7,* 252–254. **235, 236**

Roediger, H. L., III. (1984b). The use of interference paradigms as a criterion for separating memory stores. *Behavioral and Brain Sciences, 7,* 78–79, 91–94. **214**

Rogers, T. B., Kuiper, N. A., & Kirker, W. S. (1977). Self-reference and the encoding of personal information. *Journal of Personality and Social Psychology, 35,* 677–688.

Roitblat, H. L. (1980). Codes and coding processes in pigeon short-term memory. *Animal Learning & Behavior, 8,* 341–351. **134**

Roitblat, H. L. (1982). The meaning of representation in animal memory. *Behavioral and Brain Sciences, 5,* 353–406. **133, 135**

Roitblat, H. L. (1986). *Introduction to comparative cognition.* San Francisco: Freeman.

Rosch, E. (1973). Natural categories. *Cognitive Psychology, 4,* 328–350. **142**

Rosch, E., & Mervis, C. B. (1975). Family resemblances: Studies in the internal structure of categories. *Cognitive Psychology, 7,* 573–605. **260**

Rosenfeld, H. M., & Baer, D. M. (1969). Unnoticed verbal conditioning of an aware experimenter by a more aware subject: The double-agent effect. *Psychological Review, 76,* 425–432. **149**

Rosenfeld, H. M., & Baer, D. M. (1970). Unbiased and unnoticed verbal conditioning: The double agent robot procedure. *Journal of the Experimental Analysis of Behavior, 14,* 99–105.

Ross, D. (1951). *Plato's theory of ideas.* Oxford: Oxford University Press. **2**

Ross, D. (1966). *Aristotle.* London: Methuen. **2**

Ross, R. T., & LoLordo, V. M. (1987). Evaluation of the relation between Pavlovian occasion-setting and instrumental discriminative stimuli: A blocking analysis. *Journal of Experimental Psychology: Animal Behavior Processes, 13,* 3–16. **150**

Roth, J. D., & Kosslyn, S. M. (1988). Construction of the third dimension in mental imagery. *Cognitive Psychology, 20,* 344–361. **270**

Rubin, D. C. (1977). Very long term memory for prose and verse. *Journal of Verbal Learning and Verbal Behavior, 16,* 611–621. **304**

Rumbaugh, D. M. (Ed.). (1977). *Language learning by a chimpanzee: The Lana project.* New York: Academic Press. **147**

Rumelhart, D. E. (1980). Schemata: The building blocks of cognition. In R. J. Spiro, B. C. Bruce, & W. F. Brewer (Eds.), *Theoretical issues in reading comprehension* (pp. 33–58). Hillsdale, NJ: Erlbaum. **231, 262**

Rumelhart, D. E., & Ortony, A. (1977). The representation of knowledge in memory. In R. C. Anderson & R. J. Spiro (Eds.), *Schooling and the acquisition of knowledge* (pp. 99–135). Hillsdale, NJ: Erlbaum. **228, 230, 262**

Rumelhart, D. E., & Siple, P. (1974). Process of recognizing tachistoscopically presented words. *Psychological Review, 81,* 99–118. **254**

Rundus, D. (1980). Maintenance rehearsal and long-term recency. *Memory & Cognition, 8,* 226–230. **200**

Rundus, D., & Atkinson, R. C. (1970). Rehearsal processes in free recall: A procedure for direct observation. *Journal of Verbal Learning and Verbal Behavior, 9,* 99–105. **192**

Russell, M., Dark, K. A., Cummins, R. W., Ellman, G., Callaway, E., & Peeke, H. V. S. (1984). Learned histamine release. *Science, 225,* 733–734. **28**

Russell, W. R., & Nathan, P. W. (1946). Traumatic amnesia. *Brain, 69,* 280–300. **343**

Sachs, J. S. (1967). Recognition memory for syntactic and semantic aspects of connected discourse. *Perception and Psychophysics, 2,* 437–442.

Sachs, L. B. (1969). Effects of stimulus comparison during discrimination training on subsequent transposition and generalization gradients. *Psychonomic Science, 14,* 247–248. **122**

Sadoski, M. (1983). An exploratory study of the relationships between reported imagery and the comprehension and recall of a story. *Reading Research Quarterly, 19,* 110–123. **327**

Sadoski, M. (1984). Text structure, imagery, and affect in the recall of a story by children. In J. A. Niles & L. A. Harris (Eds.), *Changing perspectives in research in reading/language process and instruction. Thirty-third yearbook of the National Reading Conference* (pp. 48–53). Rochester, NY: National Reading Conference. **327, 328**

Sadoski, M. (1985). The natural use of imagery in story comprehension and recall: Replication and extension. *Reading Research Quarterly, 20,* 658–667. **327**

Sadoski, M., & Goetz, E. T. (1985). Relationships between affect, imagery, and importance ratings for segments of a story. In J. A. Niles & R. Lalik (Eds.), *Issues in literacy: A research perspective. Thirty-fourth yearbook of the National Reading Conference* (pp. 180–185). Rochester, N.Y.: National Reading Conference. **327**

Sadoski, M., Goetz, E. T., & Kangiser, S. (1988). Imagination in story response: Relationships between imagery, affect, and structural importance. *Reading Research Quarterly, 23,* 320–336. **327**

Safarjan, W. R., & D'Amato, M. R. (1981). One-trial, long-delay conditioned preference in rats. *Psychological Record, 31,* 413–426. **160**

Salame, P., & Baddeley, A. (1987). Noise, unattended speech and short-term memory. *Ergonomics, 30,* 1185–1194. **203**

Santa, J. L., Ruskin, A. B., Snuttjer, D., & Baker, L. (1975). Retrieval in cued recall. *Memory & Cognition, 3,* 341–348. **287**

Santi, A., & Roberts, W. A. (1985). Prospective representation: The effects of varied mapping of sample stimuli to comparison stimuli and differential trial outcomes on pigeons' working memory. *Animal Learning & Behavior, 13,* 103–108. **134**

Saufley, W. H., Jr., Otaka, S. R., & Bavaresco, J. L. (1985). Context effects: Classroom tests and context independence. *Memory & Cognition, 13,* 522–528. **243, 244**

Schacter, D. L. (1987). Implicit memory: History and current status. *Journal of Experimental Psychology: Learning, Memory, and Cognition, 13,* 501–518. **225**

Schneiderman, N., Fuentes, I., & Gormezano, I. (1962). Acquisition and extinction of the classically conditioned eyelid response in the albino rabbit. *Science, 136,* 650–652. **28**

Schneirla, T. C. (1933). Motivation and efficiency in ant learning. *Journal of Comparative Psychology, 15,* 243–266. **152**

Schull, J. (1979). A conditioned opponent theory of Pavlovian conditioning and habituation. In G. H. Bower (Ed.), *Psychology of learning and motivation* (Vol. 13, pp. 57–90). New York: Academic. **47**

Schwartz, B. (1973). Maintenance of keypecking in pigeons by a food avoidance but not a shock avoidance contingency. *Animal Learning & Behavior, 1,* 164–166. **163**

Schwartz, B. (1974). On going back to nature: A review of Seligman and Hager's *Biological boundaries of learning. Journal of the Experimental Analysis of Behavior, 21,* 183–198. **159**

Schwartz, B. (1975). Discriminative stimulus location as a determinant of positive and negative behavioral contrast in the pigeon. *Journal of the Experimental Analysis of Behavior, 23,* 167–176. **112**

Schwartz, B., & Williams, D. A. (1972). The role of the response-reinforcer contingency in negative automaintenance. *Journal of the Experimental Analysis of Behavior, 17,* 351–357. **157**

Seligman, M. E. P. (1968). Chronic fear produced by unpredictable shock. *Journal of Comparative and Physiological Psychology, 66,* 402–411. **103**

Seligman, M. E. P. (1970). On the generality of the laws of learning. *Psychological Review, 77,* 406–418. **155, 157**

Seligman, M. E. P. (1971). Phobias and preparedness. *Behavior Therapy, 2,* 307–320. **40**

Seligman, M. E. P. (1975). *Helplessness: On depression, development, and death.* San Francisco: Freeman. **102**

Seligman, M. E. P., & Johnston, J. C. (1973). A cognitive theory of avoidance learning. In F. J. McGuigan & D. B. Lumsden (Eds.), *Contemporary approaches to conditioning and learning* (pp. 98–111). Washington, DC: Winston. **100, 101, 106**

Seligman, M. E. P., & Maier, S. F. (1967). Failure to escape traumatic shock. *Journal of Experimental Psychology, 74,* 1–9. **101, 102**

Senter, R. J., & Hoffman, R. R. (1976). Bizarreness as a nonessential variable in mnemonic imagery: A confirmation. *Bulletin of the Psychonomic Society, 7,* 163–164. **324**

Shapiro, K. L., Jacobs, W. J., & LoLordo, V. M. (1980). Stimulus-reinforcer interactions in Pavlovian conditioning of pigeons: Implications for selective associations. *Animal Learning & Behavior, 8,* 586–594. **161**

Shapiro, S. I., & Bell, J. A. (1970). Subjective organization and free recall: Performance of high, moderate, and low organizers. *Psychonomic Science, 21,* 71–72. **289**

Sheffield, F. D. (1965). Relation between classical conditioning and instrumental learning. In W. F. Prokasy (Ed.), *Classical conditioning: A sympo-*

sium (pp. 302–322). New York: Appleton-Century-Crofts. **37**

Sheffield, F. D., & Roby, T. B. (1950). Reward value of a nonnutritive sweet taste. *Journal of Comparative and Physiological Psychology, 43,* 471–481. **83**

Shepard, R. N., & Chipman, S. (1970). Second-order isomorphism of internal representations: Shapes of states. *Cognitive Psychology, 1,* 1–17. **265**

Shepard, R. N., & Metzler, J. (1971). Mental rotation of three-dimensional objects. *Science, 171,* 701–703. **266, 267, 270**

Shettleworth, S. J. (1975). Reinforcement and the organization of behavior in golden hamsters: Hunger, environment, and food reinforcement. *Journal of Experimental Psychology: Animal Behavior Processes, 104,* 56–87. **163**

Shettleworth, S. J. (1978). Reinforcement and the organization of behavior in golden hamsters: Sunflower seed and nest paper reinforcers. *Animal Learning & Behavior, 6,* 352–362. **163**

Shiffrin, R. M., & Cook, J. R. (1978). Short-term forgetting of item and order information. *Journal of Verbal Learning and Verbal Behavior, 17,* 189–218. **185**

Shimamura, A. P., & Squire, L. R. (1987). A neuropsychological study of fact memory and source amnesia. *Journal of Experimental Psychology: Learning, Memory, and Cognition, 13,* 464–473. **348**

Shriberg, L. (1982). *Comparison of two mnemonic encoding strategies on children's recognition and recall of abstract prose information.* Unpublished doctoral dissertation, University of Wisconsin, Madison, WI. **336**

Shriberg, L. K., Levin, J. R., McCormick, C. B., & Pressley, M. (1982). Learning about "famous" people via the keyword method. *Journal of Educational Psychology, 74,* 238–247. **335, 336**

Shulman, H. G., & Martin, E. (1970). Effects of response set similarity on unlearning and spontaneous recovery. *Journal of Experimental Psychology, 86,* 230–235. **281**

Shurtleff, D., & Ayres, J. J. B. (1981). One-trial backward excitatory fear conditioning in rats: Acquisition, retention, extinction, and spontaneous recovery. *Animal Learning & Behavior, 9,* 65–74. **47**

Sidman, M. (1953). Avoidance conditioning with brief shock and no exteroceptive warning signal. *Science, 118,* 157–158. **99**

Sidman, M., Rauzin, R., Lazar, R., Cunningham, S., Tailby, W., & Carrigan, P. (1982). A search for symmetry in the conditional discriminations of rhesus monkeys, baboons, and children. *Journal of the Experimental Analysis of Behavior, 37,* 23–44. **133**

Sidman, M., & Tailby, W. (1982). Conditional discrimination vs. matching to sample: An expansion of the testing paradigm. *Journal of the Experimental Analysis of Behavior, 37,* 5–22. **133**

Siegel, S. (1975). Conditioning insulin effects. *Journal of Comparative and Physiological Psychology, 89,* 189–199. **36**

Siegel, S. (1976). Morphine analgesic tolerance: Its situation specificity supports a Pavlovian conditioning model. *Science, 193,* 323–325. **36**

Siegel, S., & Domjan, M. (1971). Backward conditioning as an inhibitory procedure. *Learning and Motivation, 2,* 1–11. **45**

Skinner, B. F. (1938). *The behavior of organisms.* New York: Appleton-Century-Crofts. **65, 69, 95, 108**

Skinner, B. F. (1948). Superstition in the pigeon. *Journal of Experimental Psychology, 38,* 168–172. **80**

Skinner, B. F. (1950). Are theories of learning necessary? *Psychological Review, 57,* 193–216. **17**

Skinner, B. F. (1953). *Science and human behavior.* New York: Macmillan. **71**

Skinner, B. F. (1956). A case history in scientific method. *American Psychologist, 11,* 221–233. **152**

Skinner, B. F. (1957). *Verbal behavior.* New York: Appleton. **172**

Slobin, D. I. (1979). *Psycholinguistics.* Glenview, IL: Scott, Foresman. **172**

Smith, A. D., & Winograd, E. (1978). Adult age differences in remembering faces. *Developmental Psychology, 14,* 443–444. **337**

Smith, E. E. (1978). Theories of semantic memory. In W. K. Estes (Ed.), *Handbook of learning and cognitive processes* (Vol. 6, pp. 1–56). Hillsdale, NJ: Erlbaum. **257, 258, 259, 260**

Smith, E. E., Shoben, E. J., & Rips, L. J. (1974). Structure and process in semantic memory: A featural model for semantic decisions. *Psychological Review, 81,* 214–241. **258, 259**

Smith, J. C., & Roll, D. L. (1967). Trace conditioning with X-rays as an aversive stimulus. *Psychonomic Science, 9,* 11–12. **31**

Smith, N. K. (1949). *The philosophy of David Hume*. London: Macmillan. **5**

Smith, S. M. (1979). Remembering in and out of context. *Journal of Experimental Psychology: Human Learning and Memory, 5,* 460–471. **242, 243**

Smith, S. M. (1982). Enhancement of recall using multiple environmental contexts during learning. *Memory & Cognition, 10,* 405–412. **242**

Smith, S. M. (1984). A comparison of two techniques for reducing context-dependent forgetting. *Memory & Cognition, 12,* 477–482. **242**

Smith, S. M. (1985). Background music and context-dependent memory. *American Journal of Psychology, 98,* 591–603. **242**

Smith, S. M. (1986). Environmental context-dependent recognition memory using a short-term memory task for input. *Memory & Cognition, 14,* 347–354. **242**

Smith, S. M., Glenberg, A., & Bjork, R. A. (1978). Environmental context and human memory. *Memory & Cognition, 6,* 342–353. **242**

Snow, C. E., and Hoefnagel-Hoehle, M. (1978). The critical period for learning acquisition: Evidence from second-language learning. *Child Development, 49,* 1114–1128. **172**

Snyder, M., & Uranowitz, S. W. (1978). Reconstructing the past: Some cognitive consequences of person perception. *Journal of Personality and Social Psychology, 36,* 941–950. **302**

Solomon, R. L., & Corbit, J. D. (1974). An opponent process theory of motivation: I. Temporal dynamics of affect. *Psychological Review, 81,* 119–145. **45, 46**

Solomon, R. L., Kamin, L. J., & Wynne, L. C. (1953). Traumatic avoidance learning: The outcomes of several extinction procedures with dogs. *Journal of Abnormal and Social Psychology, 48,* 291–302. **99**

Soltysik, S. S. (1985). Protection from extinction: New data and a hypothesis of several varieties of conditioned inhibition. In R. R. Miller & N. E. Spear (Eds.), *Information processing in animals: Conditioned inhibition* (pp. 369–394). Hillsdale, NJ: Erlbaum. **41**

Spear, N. E. (1978). *The processing of memories: Forgetting and retention*. Hillsdale, NJ: Erlbaum. **29**

Spear, N. E., Miller, J. S., & Jagielo, J. A. (1990). Animal memory and learning. *Annual Review of Psychology, 41,* 169–211. **133, 136**

Spence, K. W. (1937). The differential response in animals to stimuli varying within a single dimension. *Psychological Review, 44,* 430–444. **115, 116, 117, 121, 122**

Spence, K. W. (1956). *Behavior theory and conditioning*. New Haven: Yale University. **89**

Sperling, G. (1960). The information available in brief visual presentation. *Psychological Monographs, 74* (Whole No. 498). **182, 183, 210**

Sperling, G. (1963). A model for visual memory tasks. *Human Factors, 5,* 19–31. **182**

Spinnler, H., Della Sala, S., Bandera, R., & Baddeley, A. D. (1988). Dementia, aging, and the structure of human memory. *Cognitive Neuropsychology, 5,* 193–211. **203**

Spiro, R. J. (1977). Remembering information from text: The "state of schema" approach. In R. C. Anderson, R. J. Spiro, & W. E. Montague (Eds.), *Schooling and the acquisition of knowledge* (pp. 137–165). Hillsdale, NJ: Erlbaum. **303**

Spiro, R. J. (1980a). Accommodative reconstruction in prose recall. *Journal of Verbal Learning and Verbal Behavior, 19,* 84–95. **303**

Spiro, R. J. (1980b). Constructive processes in prose comprehension and recall. In R. J. Spiro, B. C. Bruce, & W. F. Brewer (Eds.), *Theoretical issues in reading comprehension: Perspectives from cognitive psychology, linguistics, artificial intelligence, and education* (pp. 245–278). Hillsdale, NJ: Erlbaum. **303**

Squire, L. R. (1986). Mechanisms of memory. *Science, 232,* 1612–1619. **342, 349, 350**

Squire, L. R. (1987). *Memory and brain*. New York: Oxford University Press. **341, 342, 343, 344, 345, 348, 349, 351**

Squire, L. R., Cohen, N. J., & Zouzounis, J. A. (1984). Preserved memory in retrograde amnesia: Sparing of a recently acquired skill. *Neuropsychologia, 22,* 145–152. **346**

Squire, L. R., & Fox, M. M. (1980). Assessment of remote memory: Validation of the television test by repeated testing during a seven-day period. *Behavioral Research Methods and Instrumentation, 12,* 583–586. **341**

Squire, L. R., & Slater, P. C. (1975). Forgetting in very long-term memory as assessed by an improved questionnaire technique. *Journal of Experimental Psychology: Human Learning and Memory, 1,* 50–54. **341**

Squire, L. R., Slater, P. C., & Chace, P. M. (1975). Retrograde amnesia: Temporal gradient in very long-term memory following electroconvulsive therapy. *Science, 187,* 77–79. **343, 344**

Squire, L. R., Slater, P. C., & Miller, P. L. (1981). Retrograde amnesia following ECT: Long-term follow-up studies. *Archives of General Psychiatry, 38,* 89–95. **343**

Squire, L. R., & Spanis, C. W. (1984). Long gradient of retrograde amnesia in mice: Continuity with the findings in humans. *Behavioral Neuroscience, 98,* 345–348. **343, 344**

Squire, L. R., & Zola-Morgan, S. (1988). Memory: Brain systems and behavior. *Trends in Neuroscience, 11,* 125–127. **349**

Staats, A. W. (1968). *Learning, language, & cognition: Theory, research, and method for the study of human behavior and its development.* New York: Holt, Rinehart and Winston. **172**

Staddon, J. E. R., & Simmelhag, V. (1971). The "superstition" experiment: A re-examination of its implications for the principles of adaptive behavior. *Psychological Review, 78,* 3–43. **81, 85**

Stadler, M. A. (1989). On learning complex procedural knowledge. *Journal of Experimental Psychology: Learning, Memory, and Cognition, 15,* 1061–1069. **149**

Starr, A., & Phillips, L. (1970). Verbal and motor memory in the amnesic syndrome. *Neuropsychologia, 8,* 75–88. **345**

Stern, L. (1985). The structures and strategies of human memory. Homewood, IL: Dorsey Press. **285**

Stewart, D. (1792). *Elements of the philosophy of the human mind.* London: A. Straham & T. Caddell. **5**

Straub, R. O., Seidenberg, M. S., Bever, T. G., & Terrace, H. S. (1979). Serial learning in the pigeon. *Journal of the Experimental Analysis of Behavior, 32,* 137–148. **137**

Straub, R. O., & Terrace, H. S. (1981). Generalization of serial learning in the pigeon. *Animal Learning & Behavior, 9,* 454–468. **137**

Sulin, R. A., & Dooling, D. J. (1974). Intrusions of a thematic idea in retention of prose. *Journal of Experimental Psychology, 103,* 255–262. **302, 320**

Switalski, R. W., Lyons, J., & Thomas, D. R. (1966). Effects of interdimensional training on stimulus generalization. *Journal of Experimental Psychology, 72,* 661–666. **111**

Talland, G. A. (1965). *Deranged memory.* New York: Academic Press. **342, 345**

Tarpy, R. M., & Sawabini, F. L. (1974). Reinforcement delay: A selective review of the last decade. *Psychological Bulletin, 81,* 984–997. **86**

Taub, E., Bacon, R. C., & Berman, A. J. (1965). Acquisition of a trace-conditioned avoidance response after deafferentation of the responding limb. *Journal of Comparative and Physiological Psychology, 59,* 275–279. **100**

Terrace, H. S. (1963). Errorless transfer of a discrimination across two continua. *Journal of the Experimental Analysis of Behavior, 6,* 223–232. **119**

Terrace, H. S. (1979). *Nim.* New York: Knopf. **147**

Terrace, H. S. (1987). Chunking by a pigeon in a serial learning task. *Nature, 325,* 149–151. **137**

Terrace, H. S., Petitto, L. A., Sanders, R. J., & Bever, T. G. (1979). Can an ape create a sentence? *Science, 206,* 891–206. **147**

Thistlethwaite, D. (1951). A critical review of latent learning and related experiments. *Psychological Bulletin, 48,* 97–129. **88**

Thompson, R. F., & Spencer, W. A. (1966). Habituation: A model phenomenon for the study of neuronal substrates of behavior. *Psychological Review, 73,* 16–43. **40**

Thomson, D. M., & Tulving, E. (1970). Associative encoding and retrieval: Weak and strong cues. *Journal of Experimental Psychology, 86,* 255–262. **238, 239, 240**

Thorndike, E. L. (1898). Animal intelligence: An experimental study of the associative processes in animals. *Psychological Review Monograph Supplement, 2,* 1–109. **9**

Thorndike, E. L. (1905). *The elements of psychology.* New York: A. G. Seiler. **9**

Thorndike, E. L. (1911). *Animal intelligence: Experimental studies.* New York: Macmillan. **64, 90, 94, 108**

Thorndike, E. L. (1932). *Fundamentals of learning.* New York: Teachers College, Columbia University. **9, 64, 159**

Thorndike, E. L. (1935). *The psychology of wants, interests, and attitudes.* New York: Appleton-Century-Crofts. **158**

Thorndike, E. L. (1965). *Animal intelligence.* New York: Hafner. (Original work published 1911) **9**

Thorpe, W. H. (1956). The language of birds. *Scientific American, 195*(4), 128–138. **168**

Tighe, T. J. (1973). Subproblem analysis of discrimination learning. In J. T. Spence (Ed.), *The psy-*

chology of learning and motivation (Vol. 7, pp. 183–226). New York: Academic Press. **125**

Tighe, T. J. (1982). *Modern learning theory: Foundations and fundamental issues.* New York: Oxford University Press. **90**

Tighe, T. J., Glick, J., & Cole, M. (1971). Subproblem analysis of discrimination-shift learning. *Psychonomic Science, 24,* 159–160. **125**

Timberlake, W. (1984). Behavioral regulation and learned performance: Some misapprehensions and disagreements. *Journal of the Experimental Analysis of Behavior, 41,* 355–375. **84**

Timberlake, W., & Allison, J. (1974). Response deprivation: An empirical approach to instrumental performance. *Psychological Review, 81,* 146–164. **84**

Timberlake, W., & Grant, D. L. (1975). Auto-shaping in rats to the presentation of another rat predicting food. *Science, 190,* 690–692. **36**

Tinbergen, N. (1969). *The study of instinct.* Oxford University Press. (Original work published in 1951) **168**

Tinklepaugh, O. L. (1928). An experimental study of representative factors in monkeys. *Journal of Comparative and Physiological Psychology, 8,* 197–236. **66**

Tolman, E. C. (1932). *Purposive behavior in animals and men.* New York: Appleton. **12, 38, 66, 86, 100**

Tolman, E. C. (1938). The determiners of behavior at a choice point. *Psychological Review, 45,* 1–51. **152**

Tolman, E. C. (1948). Cognitive maps in rats and men. *Psychological Review, 55,* 189–208. **88, 90, 93**

Tolman, E. C. (1959). Principles of purposive behavior. In S. Koch (Ed.), *Psychology: A study of a science* (Vol. 2, pp. 92–157). New York: McGraw-Hill. **12**

Tolman, E. C., & Honzik, C. H. (1930a). "Insight" in rats. *University of California Publications in Psychology, 4,* 215–232. **12**

Tolman, E. C., & Honzik, C. H. (1930b). Introduction and removal of reward, and maze performance in rats. *University of California Publications in Psychology, 4,* 257–275. **89**

Tolman, E. C., Ritchie, B. F., & Kalish, D. (1946). Studies in spatial learning: II. Place learning versus response learning. *Journal of Experimental Psychology, 36,* 221–229. **90, 91**

Tomie, A. (1976). Interference with autoshaping by prior context conditioning. *Journal of Experimental Psychology: Animal Behavior Processes, 2,* 323–334. **57**

Tulving, E. (1962). Subjective organization in free recall of "unrelated" words. *Psychological Review, 69,* 344–354. **287, 289**

Tulving, E. (1964). Intratrial and intertrial retention: Notes towards a theory of free-recall verbal learning. *Psychological Review, 71,* 219–237. **287**

Tulving, E. (1966). Subjective organization and effects of repetition in multitrial free-recall learning. *Journal of Verbal Learning and Verbal Behavior, 5,* 193–198. **290**

Tulving, E. (1972). Episodic and semantic memory. In E. Tulving & W. Donaldson (Eds.), *Organization of memory* (pp. 381–403). New York: Academic Press. **231, 232, 292, 345**

Tulving, E. (1974). Cue-dependent forgetting. *American Scientist, 62,* 74–82. **283**

Tulving, E. (1976). Ecphoric processes in recall and recognition. In J. Brown (Ed.), *Recall and recognition* (pp. 37–74). New York: Wiley. **283**

Tulving, E. (1983). *Elements of episodic memory.* Oxford: Clarendon Press/Oxford University Press. **231, 232, 234, 235, 240, 292, 294, 304, 305**

Tulving, E. (1984). Précis of *Elements of episodic memory. Behavioral and Brain Sciences, 7,* 223–268. **231, 232, 235, 238, 240, 283, 292, 294, 304, 345**

Tulving, E. (1985). How many memory systems are there? *American Psychologist, 40,* 385–398. **238, 292, 304**

Tulving, E. (1986a). Episodic and semantic memory: Where should we go from here? *Behavioral and Brain Sciences, 9,* 573–577. **238**

Tulving, E. (1986b). What kind of a hypothesis is the distinction between episodic and semantic memory? *Journal of Experimental Psychology: Learning, Memory, and Cognition, 12,* 307–311. **238**

Tulving, E., & Osler, S. (1967). Transfer effects in whole-part free-recall learning. *Canadian Journal of Psychology, 21,* 253–262. **291**

Tulving, E., & Psotka, J. (1971). Retroactive inhibition in free recall: Inaccessibility of information available in the memory store. *Journal of Experimental Psychology, 87,* 1–8. **282, 283**

Tulving, E., Schacter, D. L., McLachlan, D. R., & Moscovitch, M. (1988). Priming of semantic autobiographical knowledge: A case study of retrograde amnesia. *Brain and Cognition, 8,* 3–20. **235**

Tulving, E., & Thomson, D. M. (1971). Retrieval processes in recognition memory: Effects of associative context. *Journal of Experimental Psychology, 87,* 116–124. **240**

Tulving, E., & Thomson, D. M. (1973). Encoding specificity and retrieval processes in episodic memory. *Psychological Review, 80,* 352–373. **240, 292**

Tulving, E., & Watkins, O. C. (1977). Recognition failure of words with a single meaning. *Memory & Cognition, 5,* 513–522. **293**

Turkkan, J. S. (1989). Classical conditioning: The new hegemony. *Behavioral and Brain Sciences, 12,* 121–179. **24**

Turner, M. (1967). *Philosophy and the science of behavior.* New York: Appleton-Century-Crofts. **5**

Twitmyer, E. B. (1974). A study of the knee jerk. *Journal of Experimental Psychology, 103,* 1047–1066. **28, 58**

Tzeng, O. J. L. (1973). Positive recency effect in delayed free recall. *Journal of Verbal Learning and Verbal Behavior, 12,* 436–439. **207**

Ucros, C. G. (1989). Mood state-dependent memory: A meta-analysis. *Cognition and Emotion, 3,* 139–169. **242**

Underwood, B. J. (1957). Interference and forgetting. *Psychological Review, 64,* 48–60.

Underwood, B. J. (1969). Attributes of memory. *Psychological Review, 76,* 559–573. **284**

Underwood, B. J. (1983). *Attributes of memory.* Glenview, IL: Scott, Foresman. **279**

Underwood, B. J., & Ekstrand, B. R. (1966). An analysis of some shortcomings in the interference theory of forgetting. *Psychological Review, 73,* 540–549. **284**

Underwood, B. J., & Freund, J. S. (1968). Effect of temporal separation of two tasks on proactive inhibition. *Journal of Experimental Psychology, 78,* 50–54. **284**

Urcuoli, P. J., & Zentall, T. R. (1986). Retrospective coding in pigeons' delayed matching-to-sample. *Journal of Experimental Psychology: Animal Behavior Processes, 12,* 69–77. **134**

Vallar, G., & Baddeley, A. D. (1984). Fractionation of working memory: Neuropsychological evidence for a phonological short-term store. *Journal of Verbal Learning and Verbal Behavior, 23,* 151–161. **203**

Vallar, G., & Baddeley, A. (1987). Phonological short-term store and sentence processing. *Cognitive Neuropsychology, 4,* 417–438. **203**

VanDercar, D. H., & Schneiderman, N. (1967). Interstimulus interval functions in different response systems during classical discrimination conditioning of rabbits. *Psychonomic Science, 9,* 9–10. **31**

Vaughan, W., Jr. (1988). Formation of equivalence sets in pigeons. *Journal of Experimental Psychology: Animal Behavior Processes, 14,* 36–42. **144**

von Frisch, K. (1964). *Biology: The science of life.* New York: HarperCollins. **171**

von Frisch, K. (1967). Honeybees: Do they use direction and distance information provided by their dances? *Science, 158,* 1072–1076. **170**

Voss, J. F. (1984). On learning and learning from text. In H. Handl, N. L. Stein, & T. Trabasso (Eds.), *Learning and comprehension of text* (pp. 193–212). Hillsdale, NJ: Erlbaum. **228**

Wagner, A. R. (1981). SOP: A model of automatic memory processing in animal behavior. In N. E. Spear and R. R. Miller (Eds.), *Information processing in animals: Memory mechanisms* (pp. 5–47). Hillsdale, NJ: Erlbaum.

Wagner, A. R., & Larew, M. B. (1985). Opponent processes and Pavlovian inhibition. In R. R. Miller and N. E. Spear (Eds.), *Information processing in animals: Conditioned inhibition* (pp. 233–265). Hillsdale, NJ: Erlbaum. **45**

Warren, J. M. (1966). Reversal learning and the formation of learning sets by cats and rhesus monkeys. *Journal of Comparative and Physiological Psychology, 61,* 421–428. **127**

Warrington, E. K., & Weiskrantz, L. (1968). New method of testing long-term retention with special reference to amnesic patients. *Nature, 217,* 972–974. **346, 347**

Warrington, E. K., & Weiskrantz, L. (1970). Amnesic syndrome: Consolidation or retrieval? *Nature, 228,* 628–630. **346, 347**

Warrington, E. K., & Weiskrantz, L. (1973). An analysis of short-term and long-term memory deficits in man. In J. A. Deutsch (Ed.), *The physiological basis of memory* (pp. 365–395). New York: Academic Press. **224, 346, 349**

Warrington, E. K., & Weiskrantz, L. (1974). The effect of prior learning on subsequent retention of amnesic patients. *Neuropsychologia, 12,* 419–428. **209, 235, 237**

Wasserman, E. A. (1973). Pavlovian conditioning with heat reinforcement produces stimulus-directed pecking in chicks. *Science, 181,* 875–877. **36**

Wasserman, E. A. (1981). Response evocation in autoshaping: Contributions of cognitive and comparative-evolutionary analyses to an understanding of directed action. In C. M. Locurto, H. S. Terrace, & J. Gibbon (Eds.), *Autoshaping and conditioning theory* (pp. 21–54). New York: Academic Press. **38, 93**

Wasserman, E. A., Franklin, S. R., & Hearst, E. (1974). Pavlovian appetitive contingencies and approach versus withdrawal to conditioned stimuli in pigeons. *Journal of Comparative and Physiological Psychology, 86,* 616–627. **47, 48**

Wasserman, E. A., Hunter, N. B., Gutowski, K. A., & Bader, S. A. (1975). Autoshaping chicks with heat reinforcement: The role of stimulus-reinforcer and response-reinforcer relations. *Journal of Experimental Psychology: Animal Behavior Processes, 1,* 158–169. **36**

Watkins, M. J. (1984). Models as toothbrushes. *Behavioral and Brain Sciences, 7,* 86, 91–94. **214**

Watkins, M. J., & Tulving, E. (1975). Episodic memory: When recognition fails. *Journal of Experimental Psychology: General, 104,* 5–29. **292**

Watkins, O. C., & Watkins, M. J. (1975). Buildup of proactive inhibition as a cue-overload effect. *Journal of Experimental Psychology: Human Learning and Memory, 1,* 442–452. **243, 285**

Watson, J. B. (1913). Psychology as the behaviorist views it. *Psychological Review, 20,* 158–177. **10**

Watson, J. B. (1914). *Behavior: An introduction to comparative psychology.* New York: Holt. **10**

Watson, J. B. (1919). *Psychology from the standpoint of a behaviorist.* Philadelphia: Lippincott. **10**

Watson, J. B. (1930). *Behaviorism* (rev. ed.). New York: Norton. **10**

Watson, J. B., & Rayner, R. (1920). Conditioned emotional reactions. *Journal of Experimental Psychology, 3,* 1–14. **28, 29, 40, 97, 161**

Waugh, N. C., & Norman, D. A. (1965). Primary memory. *Psychological Review, 72,* 89–104. **180**

Webber, S. M., & Marshall, P. H. (1978). Bizarreness effects in imagery as a function of processing level and delay. *Journal of Mental Imagery, 2,* 291–300. **324**

Weingartner, H., Eich, J. E., & Allen, R. (1976). Alcohol state dependent associative processes. *Proceedings of the American Psychological Association, 8,* 1009–1010. **241**

Weise, P., & Bitterman, M. E. (1951). Response selection in discrimination learning. *Psychological Review, 58,* 185–195. **130, 131**

Weiskrantz, L., & Warrington, E. K. (1979). Conditioning in amnesic patients. *Neuropsychologia, 17,* 187–194. **345, 349**

Weisman, R. G., & Litner, J. S. (1969). Positive conditioned reinforcement of Sidman avoidance behavior in rats. *Journal of Comparative and Physiological Psychology, 68,* 597–603. **42**

Wessells, M. G. (1982). *Cognitive psychology.* New York: Harper & Row. **198, 286**

Wickens, D. D. (1987). The dual meanings of context: Implications for research, theory, and applications. In D. S. Gorfein & R. R. Hoffmann (Eds.), *Memory and learning: The Ebbinghaus centennial conference* (pp. 135–152). Hillsdale, NJ: Erlbaum. **244**

Widom, C. S. (1989). Does violence beget violence? A critical examination of the literature. *Psychological Bulletin, 106,* 3–28. **105**

Wilcoxon, H. C., Dragoin, W. B., & Kral, P. A. (1971). Illness-induced aversions in rat and quail: Relative salience of visual and gustatory cues. *Science, 171,* 826–828. **160**

Wilhite, S. C. (1981). Word-frequency cuing effects: Recognition and encoding interference factors. *American Journal of Psychology, 94,* 323–339. **209**

Wilhite, S. C. (1982). Sentence coding: Tests of the address-contents model and the fragmentation-conceptual focus hypothesis. *Quarterly Journal of Experimental Psychology, Section A, 34,* 259–274. **209**

Wilhite, S. C. (1988). Reading for a multiple-choice test: Headings as schema activators. *Journal of Reading Behavior, 20,* 215–228. **228**

Wilhite, S. C. (1989). Headings as memory facilitators: The importance of prior knowledge. *Journal of Educational Psychology, 81,* 115–117. **228**

Wilhite, S. C. (1991). Evidence of a negative environmental reinstatement effect. *British Journal of Psychology, 82,* 325–342. **243**

Wilkins, A. T. (1971). Conjoint frequency, category size, and categorization time. *Journal of Verbal Learning and Verbal Behavior, 10,* 382–385. **250**

Williams, B. (1978). *Descartes: The project of pure inquiry.* Harmondsworth, England: Pelican. **3**

Willingham, D. B., Nissen, M. J., & Bullemer, P. (1989). On the development of procedural knowledge. *Journal of Experimental Psychology: Learning, Memory, and Cognition, 15,* 1047–1060. **224, 225, 226**

Wilson, G. T., & Davison, G. C. (1971). Processes of fear reduction in systematic desensitization. *Psychological Bulletin, 76,* 1–14. **41**

Winograd, E. (1978). Encoding operations which facilitate memory for faces across the life span. In M. M. Gruneberg, P. E. Morris, & R. N. Sykes (Eds), *Practical aspects of memory* (pp. 255–262). New York: Academic Press. **337**

Winograd, E. (1981). Elaboration and distinctiveness in memory for faces. *Journal of Experimental Psychology: Human Learning and Memory, 7,* 181–190. **337, 338**

Witcher, E. S., & Ayres, J. J. B. (1984). A test of two methods for extinguishing Pavlovian conditioned inhibition. *Animal Learning & Behavior, 12,* 149–156. **44**

Wollen, K. A., & Cox, S. (1981a). The bizarreness effect in a multitrial intentional learning task. *Bulletin of the Psychonomic Society, 18,* 296–298. **324**

Wollen, K. A., & Cox, S. (1981b). Sentence cuing and the effectiveness of bizarre imagery. *Journal of Experimental Psychology: Human Learning and Memory, 7,* 386–392. **324**

Wollen, K. A., & Margres, M. G. (1987). Bizarreness and the imagery multiprocess model. In M. A. McDaniel and M. Pressley (Eds.), *Imagery and related mnemonic processes: Theories, individual differences, and applications* (pp. 103–128). New York: Springer-Verlag. **326**

Wollen, K. A., Weber, A., & Lowry, D. H. (1972). Bizarreness versus interaction of mental images as determinants of learning. *Cognitive Psychology, 3,* 518–523. **323, 324**

Wolpe, J. (1958). *Psychotherapy by reciprocal inhibition.* Stanford, CA: Stanford University Press. **40, 47**

Wolters, G. (1984). Memory: Two systems or one system with many subsystems? *Behavioral and Brain Sciences, 7,* 256–257. **236**

Wood, F., Ebert, V., & Kinsbourne, M. (1982). The episodic-semantic memory distinction in memory and amnesia: Clinical and experimental observations. In L. S. Cermak (Ed.), *Human*

memory and amnesia (pp. 167–193). Hillsdale, NJ: Erlbaum. **346**

Wood, G. (1967). Mnemonic systems in recall. *Journal of Educational Psychology Monographs, 58* (6, Whole No. 645). **324**

Wood, G. (1972). Organizational processes and free recall. In E. Tulving & W. Donaldson (Eds.), *Organization of memory* (pp. 49–91). New York: Academic Press. **289**

Worsham, R. W. (1975). Temporal discrimination factors in the delayed matching-to-sample task in monkeys. *Animal Learning & Behavior, 3,* 93–97. **134**

Wright, J. P. (1980). *The skeptical realism of David Hume.* Manchester, England: Manchester University Press. **4**

Yates, F. A. (1966). *The art of memory.* Chicago: University of Chicago Press. **312, 331**

Yolton, J. (1970). *Locke and the compass of human understanding.* Cambridge: Cambridge University Press. **4**

Zafiropoulou, M., & McPherson, F. M. (1986). ''Preparedness'' and the severity and outcome of clinical phobias. *Behaviour Research and Therapy, 24,* 221–222. **161**

Zajonc, R. B. (1980). Feeling and thinking: Preferences need no inferences. *American Psychologist, 35,* 151–175. **328**

Zaragoza, M. S., & Koshmider, J. W., III. (1989). Misled subjects may know more than their performance implies. *Journal of Experimental Psychology: Learning, Memory, and Cognition, 15,* 246–255. **306, 308**

Zaragoza, M. S., McCloskey, M., & Jamis, M. (1987). Misleading postevent information and recall of the original event: Further evidence against the memory impairment hypothesis. *Journal of Experimental Psychology: Learning, Memory, and Cognition, 13,* 36–44. **306, 308**

Zentall, T. R., & Hogan, D. E. (1975). Key pecking in pigeons produced by pairing keylight with inaccessible grain. *Journal of the Experimental Analysis of Behavior, 23,* 199–206. **105**

Zimmer-Hart, C. L., & Rescorla, R. A. (1974). Extinction of Pavlovian conditioned inhibition. *Journal of Comparative and Physiological Psychology, 86,* 837–845. **44, 48, 56**

Zola-Morgan, S., Cohen, N. J., & Squire, L. R. (1983). Recall of remote episodic memory in amnesia. *Neuropsychologia, 21,* 487–500. **236, 348**

INDEX ━━━━━━━━━━━━━━

A

Abstract modeling, 105
Abstract working memory,
   211–213
Acquired distinctiveness, 119–120
ACT. *See* Adaptive Control of
   Thought
Adaptationist approach, 166–167
Adaptive Control of Thought
   (ACT):
   imagery and, 270
   procedural and declarative
      knowledge and, 218–226
   semantic memory and,
      254–258
Additivity hypothesis, 112–113
Amnesia:
   anterograde, 223–224, 341
   consolidation hypothesis of,
      342–345, 349–350
   as a defect of declarative
      long-term memory, 348–349
   as a defect of episodic
      long-term memory,
      345–347
   definition of, 340
   primary versus secondary,
      341–342
   retrograde, 340
   semantic versus episodic
      knowledge and, 235, 237
   types of, 340–342
Analogous similarities, 166–167
Analog properties, imagery and,
   265–267
Animal(s):
   concept learning in, 138–144
   intelligence, 61
   language learning in,
      144–148, 170–172

Animal memory:
   delayed matching to sample
      and, 133–134
   fixed-action patterns, 168–169
   radial arm maze and, 135–136
   reinforcement sequences,
      137–138
Anterograde amnesia, 223–224,
   341
Anxiety hierarchy, 40–41
Aristotle, 2
Arousal, optimal level of, 83
Articulatory rehearsal loop,
   201–204
Associationism:
   amnesia and, 351
   British, 5–6, 25
   mnemonic techniques and, 338
   multistore models and, 214–216
   representation in long-term
      memory and, 226, 245,
      270–271
   Rescorla-Wagner model, 53
   retrieval from long-term
      memory and, 274, 291,
      309
   theme of, 16
   versus cognitivism, 76–78,
      85–93, 110–111,
      121–123, 137–138, 158
   See also Stimulus-response;
      Stimulus-stimulus
Associations:
   assumption of causation, 5
   belongingness, 159
   Pavlov and, 26
   remote, 275
Associations, formation of:
   contiguity and, 5, 25
   creativity and, 6
   frequency and, 25

law of resemblance and, 5
recency and, 25, 29
reinforcement and, 6
summation and, 6
Associative blocking, 52–53,
   117, 119
Associative continuity
   assumption, 240
Associative frequency effects,
   250
Associative inhibition, 67–68
Associative value, 53
Atkinson-Shiffrin modal model
   of memory, 181
   capacity differences, 187–188
   coding differences, 188–189
   forgetting rates, 190
   free recall serial position
      effect, 190–192
   long-term store, 186–187
   sensory registers, 182–183
   short-term store, 183–186
Automatic memory processes,
   348
Autoshaping, 35, 157–158
Aversion therapy, 40
Avoidance:
   cognitive theory of, 100–101
   cued, 97–99
   free operant, 99
   safety hypothesis of, 99–100
   signals and, 102–104
   two-factor theory of cued,
      97–99
Awareness in learning, 148–149

B

Backward-conditioned
   inhibition, 45–47
Backward pairings procedure, 30

Sensitization, 32
Sensory preconditioning, 34
Sensory registers/memory,
    182–183
Sensory store, 209–210
Sequential hypothesis, 74
Serial position effect, 190–192
Serial reversal shift, 125
Shape-encoding processing
    subsystem, 270
Shaping by successive
    approximations, 79
Short-term store, 183–186
Sign stimuli, 168
Simultaneous discrimination,
    120–130
Simultaneous pairings
    procedure, 29–30
Simultaneous task procedure,
    201
Skinner, B. F., 17, 18, 65, 69,
    70–71, 80–81, 95, 108, 152
Skinner box, 70
Spatial suppression task, 204–205
Species-specific defense
    reactions (SSDRs),
    162–163
Species-specific food-getting
    responses, 163–164
Species-typical behaviors, 152
Speeded verification task, 248
Spontaneous recovery, 39
Spreading activation model,
    251–254
State-dependent memory,
    241–242
Stimulus-as-coded, 150
Stimulus control, 109
Stimulus differentiation, 44–45
Stimulus generalization:
    classical conditioning and, 29
    concept learning, 138–144
    decrement, 43
    measuring, 109
    theories of, 110–111
Stimulus generalization,
    conditional discrimination
    and:
    definition of, 130–131
    delayed matching to sample,
    133–134

matching to sample, 131–133
sequential responding,
    134–138
Stimulus generalization,
    simultaneous
    discrimination, and:
concurrent schedules of
    reinforcement, 127–130
shifts in discrimination,
    123–127
transposition of choices,
    120–123
Stimulus generalization,
    successive discrimination,
    and, 111
acquired distinctiveness and
    fading, 119–120
behavioral contrast, 112–114
interdimensional
    discrimination, 116–117
intradimensional
    discrimination, 114–116
overshadowing and blocking,
    117, 119
Stimulus-response (S-R):
    Guthrie and, 36, 66–68
    Hull and, 11–12
    rewards and theory of, 66–68
    theories, 36–38
    Thorndike and, 9–10, 61–65
    Watson and, 10
Stimulus-stimulus (S-S) theory,
    12–14
    cognitive, 38–39
    purposive behaviorism,
    12–14
    traditional, 35–36, 66–68
Subjective organization, 287,
    289–291
Successive discrimination,
    111–120
Sufficiency/transparency
    tradeoff, 257
Summation, principle of, 6
Summation test, 42–43
Superstition, 80–81
Symbolic modeling, 105
Synergistic ecphory model of
    retrieval, 294–295
Systematic desensitization,
    40–41

T

Tabula rasa, 4, 25
Task analysis, 79–80
Taste aversions, conditioned,
    31, 153–154, 160–161
Taxis, 168
Temporal conditioning, 31
Terminal responses, 81
Theories:
    characteristics of, 17–18
    paradigms and, 18–19
    reasons for developing, 17
Thorndike, Edward L., 9–10,
    61–65, 90, 94, 108,
    158–159
Time-out from positive
    reinforcement, 96
Timing:
    in classical conditioning,
    29–32
    in instrumental learning, 87,
    128–130
Token economy, 78
Tolman, Edward, 12–14, 86,
    88, 90, 91, 93, 152
Trace pairings procedure, 30
Transformation of detail, 299
Transposition, stimulus
    generalization and,
    120–23
Trial-and-error learning, 9,
    62–64, 90
Truly random control, 32
Two-factor theory:
    of cued avoidance, 97–99
    of forgetting, 280
Two-stage theory of recall,
    291–292
Type I versus Type II
    processing, 193–194

U

Unconditioned response (UR),
    28
Unconditioned stimulus (US), 28
    contingency of conditioned
    stimulus (CS) and, 51
    explicitly unpaired, 45
    predictability of, 50